## PRENTICE HALL
# LITERATURE

**GRADE 8 • VOLUME TWO**

## COMMON CORE EDITION ©

Upper Saddle River, New Jersey

Boston, Massachusetts

Chandler, Arizona

Glenview, Illinois

ALWAYS LEARNING

PEARSON

Acknowledgments appear on page R59, which constitutes an extension of this copyright page.

ISBN-13: 978-0-13-320874-0
ISBN-10:    0-13-320874-5
3 4 5 6 7 8 9 10 VO63  15 14 13 12

# Master Teacher Board

**Heather Barnes**
Language Arts Instructor
Central Crossing High School
Grove City, Ohio

**Lee Bromberger**
English Department Chairperson
Mukwonago High School
Mukwonago, Wisconsin

**Cathy Cassy**
Communication Arts Curriculum Supervisor 6-12
St. Louis Public Schools
St. Louis, Missouri

**Judy Castrogiavanni**
English Teacher
Abington Heights School
Clarks Summit, Pennsylvania

**Ann Catrillo**
Sr. English & AP Teacher; Department Chairperson
East Stroudsburg High School South
East Stroudsburg, Pennsylvania

**Susan Cisna**
Instructor Middle School Education
Eastern Illinois University
Charleston, Illinois

**Linda Fund**
Reading Specialist
Ezra L. Nolan Middle School #40
Jersey City, New Jersey

**Gail Hacker**
Adjunct Professor
Springfield College School of Human Services
North Charleston, South Carolina

**Patricia Matysik**
English Department Chairperson
Belleville West Middle School
Belleville, Illinois

**Gail Phelps**
Literacy Intervention Coach
Oak Grove High School
Little Rock, Arkansas

**Julie Rucker**
Literacy Coach/English Teacher
Tift County High School
Tifton, Georgia

**Kathy Ryan**
Curriculum Coordinator
Rockwood Schools
St. Louis, Missouri

**Matthew Scanlon**
Vice Principal
Kinnelon High School
Kinnelon, New Jersey

**Renee Trotier**
Freshman Principal
Lafayette High School
Wildwood, Missouri

**Carolyn Waters**
Language Arts Supervisor
Cobb County Schools
Marietta, Georgia

**Martha Wildman**
Social Studies Teacher
Las Cruces Public Schools
Las Cruces, New Mexico

**Melissa Williams**
District Supervisor
Delsea Regional Schools
Franklinville, New Jersey

**Charles Youngs**
English Language Arts Facilitator
Bethel Park High School
Bethel Park, Pennsylvania

# Contributing Authors

*The contributing authors guided the direction and philosophy of Pearson Prentice Hall Literature. Working with the development team, they helped to build the pedagogical integrity of the program and to ensure its relevance for today's teachers and students.*

 **Grant Wiggins, Ed.D.,** is the President of Authentic Education in Hopewell, New Jersey. He earned his Ed.D. from Harvard University and his B.A. from St. John's College in Annapolis. Grant consults with schools, districts, and state education departments on a variety of reform matters; organizes conferences and workshops; and develops print materials and Web resources on curricular change. He is the coauthor, with Jay McTighe, of *Understanding by Design* and *The Understanding by Design Handbook*, the award-winning and highly successful materials on curriculum published by ASCD. His work has been supported by the Pew Charitable Trusts, the Geraldine R. Dodge Foundation, and the National Science Foundation. *The Association for Supervision of Curriculum Development (ASCD), publisher of the "Understanding by Design Handbook" co-authored by Grant Wiggins and registered owner of the trademark "Understanding by Design," has not authorized, approved, or sponsored this work and is in no way affiliated with Pearson or its products.*

**Jeff Anderson** has worked with  struggling writers and readers for almost 20 years. Anderson's specialty is the integration of grammar and editing instruction into the processes of reading and writing. He has published two books, *Mechanically Inclined: Building Grammar, Usage, and Style into Writer's Workshop* and *Everyday Editing: Inviting Students to Develop Skill and Craft in Writer's Workshop,* as well as a DVD, *The Craft of Grammar.* Anderson's work has appeared in *English Journal.* Anderson won the NCTE Paul and Kate Farmer Award for his *English Journal* article on teaching grammar in context.

**Arnetha F. Ball, Ph.D.,** is a  Professor at Stanford University. Her areas of expertise include language and literacy studies of diverse student populations, research on writing instruction, and teacher preparation for working with diverse populations. She is the author of *African American Literacies Unleashed* with Dr. Ted Lardner, and *Multicultural Strategies for Education and Social Change.*

**Sheridan Blau** is Professor of  Education and English at the University of California, Santa Barbara, where he directs the South Coast Writing Project and the Literature Institute for Teachers. He has served in senior advisory roles for such groups as the National Board for Professional Teaching Standards, the College Board, and the American Board for Teacher Education. Blau served for twenty years on the National Writing Project Advisory Board and Task Force, and is a former president of NCTE. Blau is the author of *The Literature Workshop: Teaching Texts and Their Readers,* which was named by the Conference on English Education as the 2004 Richard Meade Award winner for outstanding research in English education.

**William G. Brozo, Ph.D.,** is  a Professor of Literacy at George Mason University in Fairfax, Virginia. He has taught reading and language arts in junior and senior high school and is the author of numerous texts on literacy development. Dr. Brozo's work focuses on building capacity among teacher leaders, enriching the literate culture of schools, enhancing the literate lives of boys, and making teaching more responsive to the needs of all students. His recent publications include *Bright Beginnings for Boys: Engaging Young Boys in Active Literacy* and the *Adolescent Literacy Inventory.*

**Doug Buehl** is a teacher, author, and  national literacy consultant. He is the author of *Classroom Strategies for Interactive Learning* and coauthor of *Reading and the High School Student: Strategies to Enhance Literacy;* and *Strategies to Enhance Literacy and Learning in Middle School Content Area Classrooms.*

**Jim Cummins, Ph.D,** is a profes-  sor in the Modern Language Centre at the University of Toronto. He is the author of numerous publications, including *Negotiating Identities: Education for Empowerment in a Diverse Society.* Cummins coined the acronyms BICS and CAPT to help differentiate the type of language ability students need for success.

**Harvey Daniels, Ph.D.,** has been  a classroom teacher, writing project director, author, and university professor. "Smokey" serves as an international consultant to schools, districts, and educational agencies. He is known for his work on student-led book clubs, as recounted in *Literature Circles: Voice and Choice in Book Clubs & Reading Groups* and *Mini Lessons for Literature Circles.* Recent works include *Subjects Matter: Every Teacher's Guide to Content-Area Reading* and *Content Area Writing: Every Teacher's Guide.*

**Jane Feber** taught language arts in  Jacksonville, Florida, for 36 years. Her innovative approach to instruction has earned her several awards, including the NMSA Distinguished Educator Award, the NCTE Edwin A. Hoey Award, the Gladys Prior Award for Teaching Excellence, and the Florida Council of Teachers of English Teacher of the Year Award. She is a National Board Certified Teacher, past president of the Florida Council of Teachers of English and is the author of *Creative Book Reports* and *Active Word Play*.

**Danling Fu, Ph.D.**, is Professor  of Language and Culture in the College of Education at the University of Florida. She researches and provides inservice to public schools nationally, focusing on literacy instruction for new immigrant students. Fu's books include *My Trouble is My English* and *An Island of English* addressing English language learners in the secondary schools. She has authored chapters in the *Handbook of Adolescent Literacy Research* and in *Adolescent Literacy: Turning Promise to Practice*.

**Kelly Gallagher** is a full-time English  teacher at Magnolia High School in Anaheim, California. He is the former co-director of the South Basin Writing Project at California State University, Long Beach. Gallagher wrote *Reading Reasons: Motivational Mini-Lessons for the Middle and High School, Deeper Reading: Comprehending Challenging Texts 4-12,* and *Teaching Adolescent Writers.* Gallagher won the Secondary Award of Classroom Excellence from the California Association of Teachers of English—the state's top English teacher honor.

**Sharroky Hollie, Ph.D.**, is an  assistant professor at California State University, Dominguez Hills, and an urban literacy visiting professor at Webster University, St. Louis. Hollie's work focuses on professional development, African American education, and second language methodology. He is a contributing author in two texts on culturally and linguistically responsive teaching. He is the Executive Director of the Center for Culturally Responsive Teaching and Learning and the co-founding director of the Culture and Language Academy of Success, an independent charter school in Los Angeles.

**Dr. Donald J. Leu, Ph.D.**, teaches  at the University of Connecticut and holds a joint appointment in Curriculum and Instruction and in Educational Psychology. He directs the New Literacies Research Lab and is a member of the Board of Directors of the International Reading Association. Leu studies the skills required to read, write, and learn with Internet technologies. His research has been funded by groups including the U.S. Department of Education, the National Science Foundation, and the Bill & Melinda Gates Foundation.

**Jon Scieszka** founded GUYS READ,  a nonprofit literacy initiative for boys, to call attention to the problem of getting boys connected with reading. In 2008, he was named the first U.S. National Ambassador for Young People's Literature by the Library of Congress. Scieszka taught from first grade to eighth grade for ten years in New York City, drawing inspiration from his students to write *The True Story of the 3 Little Pigs!, The Stinky Cheese Man*, the *Time Warp Trio* series of chapter books, and the *Trucktown* series of books for beginning readers.

**Sharon Vaughn, Ph.D.**, teaches  at the University of Texas at Austin. She is the previous Editor-in-Chief of the *Journal of Learning Disabilities* and the co-editor of *Learning Disabilities Research and Practice*. She is the recipient of the American Education Research Association SIG Award for Outstanding Researcher. Vaughn's work focuses on effective practices for enhancing reading outcomes for students with reading difficulties. She is the author of more than 100 articles and numerous books designed to improve research-based practices in the classroom.

**Karen K. Wixson** is Dean of the  School of Education at the University of North Carolina, Greensboro. She has published widely in the areas of literacy curriculum, instruction, and assessment. Wixson has been an advisor to the National Research Council and helped develop the National Assessment of Educational Progress (NAEP) reading tests. She is a past member of the IRA Board of Directors and co-chair of the IRA Commission on RTI. Recently, Wixson served on the English Language Arts Work Team that was part of the Common Core State Standards Initiative.

*Each unit addresses a BIG Question to enrich exploration of literary concepts and reading strategies.*

Is *truth* the same for everyone?

INFORMATIONAL TEXT HIGHLIGHTED

Comparing Characters
of Different Eras

# Skills at a Glance

This page provides a quick look at the skills you will learn and practice in Unit 1.

## Reading Skills

Make Predictions
- Make and Support Predictions
- Read Ahead to Confirm or Modify Predictions

Author's Purpose
- Recognize Details Indicating Author's Purpose
- Evaluate Whether the Author Achieves His or Her Purpose

## Reading for Information

Use Information to Solve a Problem

Identify Central Idea and Details

## Literary Analysis

Theme

Central Idea

Plot

Conflict and Resolution

Comparing Narrative Structure

Mood

Author's Style

Comparing Characters of Different Eras

## Vocabulary

Big Question Vocabulary

Roots: *-scope-, -trib-, -limin-, -judex-, -lum-, -duc-, -sol-, -equi-*

Using a Dictionary and Thesaurus

## Conventions

Common and Proper Nouns

Plural Nouns

Using Concrete, Abstract, and Possessive Nouns

Personal Pronouns

Reflexive Pronouns

Revising for Pronoun-Antecedent Agreement

## Writing

Writing About the Big Question

New Ending

Letter

Personal Narrative

Observation Journal

Timed Writing

Writing Workshop: Explanatory Text: Description of a Person

Writing Workshop: Narrative Text: Autobiographical Essay

## Speaking and Listening

Radio Broadcast

Role Play

Effective Listening and Note-Taking

## Research and Technology

Research Report

Brochure

 **Common Core State Standards Addressed in This Unit**

**Reading Literature** RL.8.1, RL.8.2, RL.8.3, RL.8.4, RL.8.5, RL.8.10

**Reading Informational Text** RI.8.2, RI.8.3, RI.8.4, RI.8.5, RI.8.10

**Writing** W.8.2, W.8.2.c, W.8.2.d, W.8.2.f, W.8.3, W.8.3.a, W.8.3.b, W.8.3.c, W.8.3.d, W.8.3.e, W.8.5, W.8.6, W.8.7, W.8.8

**Speaking and Listening** SL.8.1, SL.8.1.d, SL.8.2, SL.8.3, SL.8.6

**Language** L.8.1, L.8.2, L.8.3, L.8.4, L.8.4.b, L.8.4.c, L.8.4.d, L.8.6

[For the full wording of the standards, see the standards chart in the front of your textbook.]

# Can all *conflicts* be resolved?

INFORMATIONAL TEXT HIGHLIGHTED

**PHLit Online!**
www.PHLitOnline.com
Interactive resources provide
personalized instruction and
activities online.

# Skills at a Glance

This page provides a quick look at the skills you will learn and practice in Unit 2.

## Reading Skills

Compare and Contrast
  Ask Questions to Compare and Contrast
  Compare Characters' Perspectives
Make Inferences
  Use Details to Make Inferences
  Identify Connections to Make Inferences

## Reading for Information

Compare Summaries to an Original Text
Evaluate Persuasive Appeals

## Literary Analysis

Character and Plot
Theme
Setting
Character Traits
Comparing Types of Narratives
Point of View
Theme
Comparing Symbols

## Vocabulary

Big Question Vocabulary
Prefixes: *de-, mis-, per-*
Suffixes: *-ee, -ity*
Roots: *-nounc-* or *-nunc-, -spec-*
Word Origins

## Conventions

Action and Linking Verbs
Principal Parts of Regular Verbs
Revising Verb Phrases for Mood
Simple Tenses of Verbs
Tense and Mood of Verbs
Revising for Subject-Verb Agreement

## Writing

Writing About the Big Question
Description
Character Profile
Dialogue
Personal Essay
Timed Writing
Writing Workshop: Argument: Critical Review
Writing Workshop: Narrative Text: Short Story

## Speaking and Listening

Oral Response
Panel Discussion
Conducting Interviews

## Research and Technology

Oral Report
Summary of an Article

---

 **Common Core State Standards Addressed in This Unit**

**Reading Literature** RL.8.1, RL.8.2, RL.8.3, RL.8.4, RL.8.6, RL.8.10
**Reading Informational Text** RI.8.1, RI.8.2, RI.8.10
**Writing** W.8.1.a, W.8.1.b, W.8.2, W.8.2.b, W.8.3, W.8.3.a, W.8.3.b, W.8.3.d, W.8.4, W.8.5, W.8.9
**Speaking and Listening** SL.8.1, SL.8.1.a, SL.8.1.b, SL.8.1.c, SL.8.1.d, SL.8.4, SL.8.6
**Language** L.8.1, L.8.1.b, L.8.1.c, L.8.2.c, L.8.3.a, L.8.4, L.8.4.a, L.8.4.b, L.8.4.c, L.8.5, L.8.6
[For the full wording of the standards, see the standards chart in the front of your textbook.]

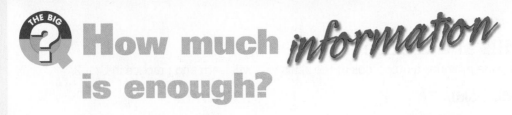

**How much _information_ is enough?**

INFORMATIONAL TEXT HIGHLIGHTED

# Skills at a Glance

This page provides a quick look at the skills you will learn and practice in Unit 3.

## Reading Skills

Main Idea
Identify the Implied Main Idea
Make Connections

Fact and Opinion
Use Clue Words to Distinguish
Fact From Opinion
Ask Questions to Evaluate Support

## Reading for Information

Analyze Treatment, Scope, and
Organization of Ideas

Analyze Proposition and Support

## Literary Analysis

Point of View and Purpose

Organizational Structure

Word Choice and Tone

Narrative Essay

Biography and Autobiography

Comparing Types of Organization

Persuasive Techniques

Word Choice

Comparing Tone

## Vocabulary

Big Question Vocabulary

Suffixes: -ance, -ly

Roots: -nym-, -val-, -vad-, -bellum-,
-pass-, -tract-

Words With Multiple Meanings

## Conventions

Adjectives and Articles

Adverbs

Revising to Correct Comparative
and Superlative Forms

Conjunctions

Prepositions

Revising Sentences by Combining
With Conjunctions

## Writing

Writing About the Big Question

Biographical Sketch

Reflective Essay

Evaluation of Persuasive Argument

Response

Timed Writing

Writing Workshop: Informative Text:
How-to Essay

Writing Workshop: Argument: Editorial

## Speaking and Listening

Skit

Speech

Evaluating an Oral Presentation

## Research and Technology

Multimedia Presentation

Snapshot of Arguments

---

**© Common Core State Standards Addressed in This Unit**

**Reading Literature** RL.8.10
**Reading Informational Text** RI.8.2, RI.8.3, RI.8.4, RI.8.5, RI.8.8, RI.8.9, RI.8.10
**Writing** W.8.1, W.8.1.a, W.8.1.b, W.8.1.c, W.8.1.d, W.8.1.e, W.8.2, W.8.2.b, W.8.2.c, W.8.6, W.8.7, W.8.9, W.8.9.b
**Speaking and Listening** SL.8.1, SL.8.2, SL.8.3, SL.8.4, SL.8.5, SL.8.6
**Language** L.8.1, L.8.4, L.8.4.a, L.8.4.b, L.8.4.c., L.8.5.c, L.8.6
[For the full wording of the standards, see the standards chart in the front of your textbook.]

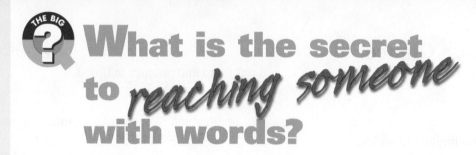

**What is the secret to _reaching someone_ with words?**

Figurative and Connotative Language
Meaning and Tone

Using Context
Sound Devices

Context Clues
Figurative Language

INFORMATIONAL TEXT HIGHLIGHTED

Contents   **xxi**

# Skills at a Glance

This page provides a quick look at the skills you will learn and practice in Unit 4.

## Reading Skills

Context Clues
  Preview to Identify Unfamiliar Words
  Reread and Read Ahead to Confirm Meaning
Paraphrase
  Reread to Clarify Meaning
  Read Aloud Fluently According to Punctuation

## Reading for Information

Compare and Contrast Features
  of Consumer Materials
Analyze Technical Directions

## Literary Analysis

Connotative Meanings
Simile; Metaphor
Allusion
Sound Devices
Figurative Language
Comparing Poetry and Prose
Forms of Poetry
Imagery
Comparing Types of Description

## Vocabulary

Big Question Vocabulary
Prefixes: *im-, in-, trans-*
Suffixes: *-ous, -ive*
Roots: *-cede-, -ceed-, -vert-*
Idioms

## Conventions

Subject Complements
Direct and Indirect Objects
Choosing Between Active and Passive Voice
Prepositional Phrases

Infinitive Phrases
Revising to Vary Sentence Patterns

## Writing

Writing About the Big Question
Poem
Study for a Poem
Writing Workshop: Argument:
  Problem-and-Solution Essay
Lyric or Narrative Poem
Review
Timed Writing
Writing Workshop: Informative Text:
  Comparison-and-Contrast Essay

## Speaking and Listening

Poetry Recitation
Evaluation Form
Evaluating Media Messages

## Research and Technology

Mini-Anthology
Poet's Profile

---

**Ⓒ  Common Core State Standards
  Addressed in This Unit**

**Reading Literature** RL.8.1, RL.8.2, RL.8.4, RL.8.5,
RL.8.10

**Reading Informational Text** RI.8.4, RI.8.5, RI.8.7,
RI.8.10

**Writing** W.8.1, W.8.2, W.8.2.a, W.8.2.b, W.8.3, W.8.4,
W.8.8, W.8.9

**Speaking and Listening** SL.8.1, SL.8.2, L.8.5.b,
SL.8.6

**Language** L.8.1, L.8.2.c, L.8.4.a, L.8.4.b, L.8.5, L.8.5.a,
L.8.5.b, L.8.6

[For the full wording of the standards, see the standards
chart in the front of your textbook.]

## Is it our *differences* or our *similarities* that matter most?

Character
Conflict

Draw Conclusions
Setting and Character

Compare and Contrast
Features and Elements

# Skills at a Glance

This page provides a quick look at the skills you will learn and practice in Unit 5.

## Reading Skill

Draw Conclusions
  Make Connections

Cause and Effect
  Use Background Information to
  Link Historical Causes With Effects
  Ask Questions to Analyze
  Cause-and-Effect Relationships

## Reading for Information

Compare and Contrast Features
  and Elements

Evaluate Unity and Coherence

## Literary Analysis

Character

Conflict

Elements of Drama

Setting and Character

Comparing Adaptations to Originals

Dialogue

Character's Motivation

Comparing Sources With
  a Dramatization

## Vocabulary

Amazing Words:
  Big Question Vocabulary

Prefixes: *in-*

Suffixes: *-ory, -ist*

Borrowed and Foreign Words

## Conventions

Participial Phrases

Revising to Combine Sentences
  Using Gerunds and Participles

Dangling and Misplaced Modifiers

Clauses

Revising to Combine Sentences
  Using Clauses

## Writing

Writing About the Big Question

Public Service Announcement

Writing Workshop: Informative Text:
  Business Letter

Diary Entries

Film Review

Timed Writing

Writing Workshop: Informative Text:
  Research Report

## Speaking and Listening

Debate

Guided Tour

Delivering a Narrative
  Presentation

## Research and Technology

Bulletin Board Display

---

 **Common Core State Standards
Addressed in This Unit**

**Reading Literature** RL.8.1, RL.8.3, RL.8.4, RL.8.5, RL.8.6, RL.8.7, RL.8.9, RL.8.10

**Reading Informational Text** RI.8.5, RI.8.6, RI.8.10

**Writing** W.8.1, W.8.2, W.8.2.a, W.8.3, W.8.4, W.8.7, W.8.8, W.8.9, W.8.10

**Speaking and Listening** SL.8.1, SL.8.4, SL.8.6

**Language** L.8.1, L.8.1.a, L.8.2.b, L.8.4.b, L.8.6

[For the full wording of the standards, see the standards chart in the front of your textbook.]

# Are yesterday's *heroes* important today?

# Skills at a Glance

This page provides a quick look at the skills you will learn and practice in Unit 6.

## Reading Skill

Summarize
  Reread to Identify Main Events or Ideas
  Use Graphics to Organize Main Events
Purpose for Reading
  Ask Questions to Set a Purpose for Reading
  Adjust Your Reading Rate According to Purpose

## Reading for Information

Evaluate Structural Patterns
Evaluate the Treatment, Scope, and Organization of Ideas

## Literary Analysis

Social and Cultural Context
Theme
Mythology
Oral Tradition
Comparing Heroic Characters
Cultural Context
Author's Influences
Comparing Works on a Similar Theme

## Vocabulary

Big Question Vocabulary
Roots: *-sacr-, -grat-, -nat-, -her-, -aud-*
Dialect
Suffixes: *-ful, -eer*
Figurative Language

## Conventions

Sentence Structure
Commas
Using Language to Maintain Interest
Semicolons and Colons
Capitalization
Revising Run-on Sentences and Sentence Fragments

## Writing

Writing About the Big Question
Myth
Critical Analysis
Writing Workshop: Informative Text: Multimedia Report
Research Proposal
Persuasive Speech
Timed Writing
Writing Workshop: Explanatory Text: Cause-and-Effect Essay

## Speaking and Listening

Oral Presentation
Storytelling Workshop
Delivering a Persuasive Speech Using Multimedia

## Research and Technology

Letter
Newspaper Article

 **Common Core State Standards Addressed in This Unit**

**Reading Literature** RL.8.2, RL.8.3, RL.8.4, RL.8.5, RL.8.7, RL.8.9, RL.8.10
**Reading Informational Text** RI.8.3, RI.8.7, RI.8.10
**Writing** W.8.1, W.8.2, W.8.3, W.8.3.b, W.8.3.e, W.8.5, W.8.7, W.8.10
**Speaking and Listening** SL.8.1, SL.8.5, SL.8.6
**Language** L.8.1, L.8.2, L.8.4.b, L.8.5, L.8.6
[For the full wording of the standards, see the standards chart in the front of your textbook.]

# Literature

## ▶ Poetry

# Informational Text—Literary Nonfiction

▶ **Functional Text**

▶ **Literature in Context—Reading in the Content Areas**

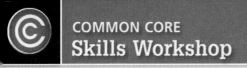

## ▶ Writing Workshops

## ▶ Vocabulary Workshops

## ▶ Communications Workshops

**The Common Core State Standards** will prepare you to succeed in college and your future career. They are separated into four sections—Reading (Literature and Informational Text), Writing, Speaking and Listening, and Language. Beginning each section, the College and Career Readiness Anchor Standards define what you need to achieve by the end of high school. The grade-specific standards that follow define what you need to know by the end of your current grade level.

# Ⓒ Common Core Reading Standards

## College and Career Readiness Anchor Standards

### Key Ideas and Details

1. Read closely to determine what the text says explicitly and to make logical inferences from it; cite specific textual evidence when writing or speaking to support conclusions drawn from the text.

2. Determine central ideas or themes of a text and analyze their development; summarize the key supporting details and ideas.

3. Analyze how and why individuals, events, and ideas develop and interact over the course of a text.

### Craft and Structure

4. Interpret words and phrases as they are used in a text, including determining technical, connotative, and figurative meanings, and analyze how specific word choices shape meaning or tone.

5. Analyze the structure of texts, including how specific sentences, paragraphs, and larger portions of the text (e.g., a section, chapter, scene, or stanza) relate to each other and the whole.

6. Assess how point of view or purpose shapes the content and style of a text.

### Integration of Knowledge and Ideas

7. Integrate and evaluate content presented in diverse formats and media, including visually and quantitatively, as well as in words.

8. Delineate and evaluate the argument and specific claims in a text, including the validity of the reasoning as well as the relevance and sufficiency of the evidence.

9. Analyze how two or more texts address similar themes or topics in order to build knowledge or to compare the approaches the authors take.

### Range of Reading and Level of Text Complexity

10. Read and comprehend complex literary and informational texts independently and proficiently.

## Grade 8 Reading Standards for Literature

### Key Ideas and Details

1. Cite the textual evidence that most strongly supports an analysis of what the text says explicitly as well as inferences drawn from the text.

2. Determine a theme or central idea of a text and analyze its development over the course of the text, including its relationship to the characters, setting, and plot; provide an objective summary of the text.

3. Analyze how particular lines of dialogue or incidents in a story or drama propel the action, reveal aspects of a character, or provoke a decision.

### Craft and Structure

4. Determine the meaning of words and phrases as they are used in a text, including figurative and connotative meanings; analyze the impact of specific word choices on meaning and tone, including analogies or allusions to other texts.

5. Compare and contrast the structure of two or more texts and analyze how the differing structure of each text contributes to its meaning and style.

6. Analyze how differences in the points of view of the characters and the audience or reader (e.g., created through the use of dramatic irony) create such effects as suspense or humor.

### Integration of Knowledge and Ideas

7. Analyze the extent to which a filmed or live production of a story or drama stays faithful to or departs from the text or script, evaluating the choices made by the director or actors.

8. (Not applicable to literature)

9. Analyze how a modern work of fiction draws on themes, patterns of events, or character types from myths, traditional stories, or religious works such as the Bible, including describing how the material is rendered new.

### Range of Reading and Level of Text Complexity

10. By the end of the year, read and comprehend literature, including stories, dramas, and poems, at the high end of grades 6–8 text complexity band independently and proficiently.

## Grade 8 Reading Standards for Informational Text

### Key Ideas and Details

1. Cite the textual evidence that most strongly supports an analysis of what the text says explicitly as well as inferences drawn from the text.

2. Determine a central idea of a text and analyze its development over the course of the text, including its relationship to supporting ideas; provide an objective summary of the text.

3. Analyze how a text makes connections among and distinctions between individuals, ideas, or events (e.g., through comparisons, analogies, or categories).

### Craft and Structure

4. Determine the meaning of words and phrases as they are used in a text, including figurative, connotative, and technical meanings; analyze the impact of specific word choices on meaning and tone, including analogies or allusions to other texts.

5. Analyze in detail the structure of a specific paragraph in a text, including the role of particular sentences in developing and refining a key concept.

6. Determine an author's point of view or purpose in a text and analyze how the author acknowledges and responds to conflicting evidence or viewpoints.

### Integration of Knowledge and Ideas

7. Evaluate the advantages and disadvantages of using different mediums (e.g., print or digital text, video, multimedia) to present a particular topic or idea.

8. Delineate and evaluate the argument and specific claims in a text, assessing whether the reasoning is sound and the evidence is relevant and sufficient; recognize when irrelevant evidence is introduced.

9. Analyze a case in which two or more texts provide conflicting information on the same topic and identify where the texts disagree on matters of fact or interpretation.

### Range of Reading and Level of Text Complexity

10. By the end of the year, read and comprehend literary nonfiction at the high end of the grades 6–8 text complexity band independently and proficiently.

# Ⓒ Common Core Writing Standards

## College and Career Readiness Anchor Standards

### Text Types and Purposes

1. Write arguments to support claims in an analysis of substantive topics or texts, using valid reasoning and relevant and sufficient evidence.

2. Write informative/explanatory texts to examine and convey complex ideas and information clearly and accurately through the effective selection, organization, and analysis of content.

3. Write narratives to develop real or imagined experiences or events using effective technique, well-chosen details, and well-structured event sequences.

### Production and Distribution of Writing

4. Produce clear and coherent writing in which the development, organization, and style are appropriate to task, purpose, and audience.

5. Develop and strengthen writing as needed by planning, revising, editing, rewriting, or trying a new approach.

6. Use technology, including the Internet, to produce and publish writing and to interact and collaborate with others.

### Research to Build and Present Knowledge

7. Conduct short as well as more sustained research projects based on focused questions, demonstrating understanding of the subject under investigation.

8. Gather relevant information from multiple print and digital sources, assess the credibility and accuracy of each source, and integrate the information while avoiding plagiarism.

9. Draw evidence from literary or informational texts to support analysis, reflection, and research.

### Range of Writing

10. Write routinely over extended time frames (time for research, reflection, and revision) and shorter time frames (a single sitting or a day or two) for a range of tasks, purposes, and audiences.

## Grade 8 Writing Standards

### Text Types and Purposes

1. Write arguments to support claims with clear reasons and relevant evidence.

   a. Introduce claim(s), acknowledge and distinguish the claim(s) from alternate or opposing claims, and organize the reasons and evidence logically.

   b. Support claim(s) with logical reasoning and relevant evidence, using accurate, credible sources and demonstrating an understanding of the topic or text.

   c. Use words, phrases, and clauses to create cohesion and clarify the relationships among claim(s), counterclaims, reasons, and evidence.

   d. Establish and maintain a formal style.

   e. Provide a concluding statement or section that follows from and supports the argument presented.

2. Write informative/explanatory texts to examine a topic and convey ideas, concepts, and information through the selection, organization, and analysis of relevant content.

   a. Introduce a topic clearly, previewing what is to follow; organize ideas, concepts, and information into broader categories; include formatting (e.g., headings), graphics (e.g., charts, tables), and multimedia when useful to aiding comprehension.

   b. Develop the topic with relevant, well-chosen facts, definitions, concrete details, quotations, or other information and examples.

   c. Use appropriate and varied transitions to create cohesion and clarify the relationships among ideas and concepts.

   d. Use precise language and domain-specific vocabulary to inform about or explain the topic.

   e. Establish and maintain a formal style.

   f. Provide a concluding statement or section that follows from and supports the information or explanation presented.

3. Write narratives to develop real or imagined experiences or events using effective technique, relevant descriptive details, and well-structured event sequences.

   a. Engage and orient the reader by establishing a context and point of view and introducing a narrator and/or characters; organize an event sequence that unfolds naturally and logically.

   b. Use narrative techniques, such as dialogue, pacing, description, and reflection, to develop experiences, events, and/or characters.

   c. Use a variety of transition words, phrases, and clauses to convey sequence, signal shifts from one time frame or setting to another, and show the relationships among experiences and events.

   d. Use precise words and phrases, relevant descriptive details, and sensory language to capture the action and convey experiences and events.

   e. Provide a conclusion that follows from and reflects on the narrated experiences or events.

## Production and Distribution of Writing

**4.** Produce clear and coherent writing in which the development, organization, and style are appropriate to task, purpose, and audience.

**5.** With some guidance and support from peers and adults, develop and strengthen writing as needed by planning, revising, editing, rewriting, or trying a new approach, focusing on how well purpose and audience have been addressed.

**6.** Use technology, including the Internet, to produce and publish writing and present the relationships between information and ideas efficiently as well as to interact and collaborate with others.

## Research to Build and Present Knowledge

**7.** Conduct short research projects to answer a question (including a self-generated question), drawing on several sources and generating additional related, focused questions that allow for multiple avenues of exploration.

**8.** Gather relevant information from multiple print and digital sources, using search terms effectively; assess the credibility and accuracy of each source; and quote or paraphrase the data and conclusions of others while avoiding plagiarism and following a standard format for citation.

**9.** Draw evidence from literary or informational texts to support analysis, reflection, and research.

   a. Apply *grade 8 Reading standards* to literature (e.g., "Analyze how a modern work of fiction draws on themes, patterns of events, or character types from myths, traditional stories, or religious works such as the Bible, including describing how the material is rendered new").

   b. Apply *grade 8 Reading standards* to literary nonfiction (e.g., "Delineate and evaluate the argument and specific claims in a text, assessing whether the reasoning is sound and the evidence is relevant and sufficient; recognize when irrelevant evidence is introduced").

## Range of Writing

**10.** Write routinely over extended time frames (time for research, reflection, and revision) and shorter time frames (a single sitting or a day or two) for a range of discipline-specific tasks, purposes, and audiences.

# ⒸCommon Core
## Speaking and Listening Standards

### College and Career Readiness Anchor Standards

#### Comprehension and Collaboration

**1.** Prepare for and participate effectively in a range of conversations and collaborations with diverse partners, building on others' ideas and expressing their own clearly and persuasively.

**2.** Integrate and evaluate information presented in diverse media and formats, including visually, quantitatively, and orally.

**3.** Evaluate a speaker's point of view, reasoning, and use of evidence and rhetoric.

#### Presentation of Knowledge and Ideas

**4.** Present information, findings, and supporting evidence such that listeners can follow the line of reasoning and the organization, development, and style are appropriate to task, purpose, and audience.

**5.** Make strategic use of digital media and visual displays of data to express information and enhance understanding of presentations.

**6.** Adapt speech to a variety of contexts and communicative tasks, demonstrating command of formal English when indicated or appropriate.

# Grade 8 Speaking and Listening Standards

## Comprehension and Collaboration

1. Engage effectively in a range of collaborative discussions (one-on-one, in groups, and teacher-led) with diverse partners on *grade 8 topics, texts, and issues,* building on others' ideas and expressing their own clearly.

    a. Come to discussions prepared, having read or researched material under study; explicitly draw on that preparation by referring to evidence on the topic, text, or issue to probe and reflect on ideas under discussion.

    b. Follow rules for collegial discussions and decision-making, track progress toward specific goals and deadlines, and define individual roles as needed.

    c. Pose questions that connect the ideas of several speakers and respond to others' questions and comments with relevant evidence, observations, and ideas.

    d. Acknowledge new information expressed by others, and, when warranted, qualify or justify their own views in light of the evidence presented.

2. Analyze the purpose of information presented in diverse media and formats (e.g., visually, quantitatively, orally) and evaluate the motives (e.g., social, commercial, political) behind its presentation.

3. Delineate a speaker's argument and specific claims, evaluating the soundness of the reasoning and relevance and sufficiency of the evidence and identifying when irrelevant evidence is introduced.

## Presentation of Knowledge and Ideas

4. Present claims and findings, emphasizing salient points in a focused, coherent manner with relevant evidence, sound valid reasoning, and well-chosen details; use appropriate eye contact, adequate volume, and clear pronunciation.

5. Integrate multimedia and visual displays into presentations to clarify information, strengthen claims and evidence, and add interest.

6. Adapt speech to a variety of contexts and tasks, demonstrating command of formal English when indicated or appropriate. (See grade 8 Language standards 1 and 3 for specific expectations.)

# Common Core Language Standards

## College and Career Readiness Anchor Standards

### Conventions of Standard English

1. Demonstrate command of the conventions of standard English grammar and usage when writing or speaking.

2. Demonstrate command of the conventions of standard English capitalization, punctuation, and spelling when writing.

### Knowledge of Language

3. Apply knowledge of language to understand how language functions in different contexts, to make effective choices for meaning or style, and to comprehend more fully when reading or listening.

### Vocabulary Acquisition and Use

4. Determine or clarify the meaning of unknown and multiple-meaning words and phrases by using context clues, analyzing meaningful word parts, and consulting general and specialized reference materials, as appropriate.

5. Demonstrate understanding of figurative language, word relationships, and nuances in word meanings.

6. Acquire and use accurately a range of general academic and domain-specific words and phrases sufficient for reading, writing, speaking, and listening at the college and career readiness level; demonstrate independence in gathering vocabulary knowledge when considering a word or phrase important to comprehension or expression.

## Grade 8 Language Standards

### Conventions of Standard English

1. Demonstrate command of the conventions of standard English grammar and usage when writing or speaking.

   a. Explain the function of verbals (gerunds, participles, infinitives) in general and their function in particular sentences.

   b. Form and use verbs in the active and passive voice.

   c. Form and use verbs in the indicative, imperative, interrogative, conditional, and subjunctive mood.

   d. Recognize and correct inappropriate shifts in verb voice and mood.

**2.** Demonstrate command of the conventions of standard English capitalization, punctuation, and spelling when writing.

    a. Use punctuation (comma, ellipsis, dash) to indicate a pause or break.

    b. Use an ellipsis to indicate an omission.

    c. Spell correctly.

## Knowledge of Language

**3.** Use knowledge of language and its conventions when writing, speaking, reading, or listening.

    a. Use verbs in the active and passive voice and in the conditional and sub-junctive mood to achieve particular effects (e.g., emphasizing the actor or the action; expressing uncertainty or describing a state contrary to fact).

## Vocabulary Acquisition and Use

**4.** Determine or clarify the meaning of unknown and multiple-meaning words and phrases based on *grade 8 reading and content*, choosing flexibly from a range of strategies.

    a. Use context (e.g., the overall meaning of a sentence or paragraph; a word's position or function in a sentence) as a clue to the meaning of a word or phrase.

    b. Use common, grade-appropriate Greek or Latin affixes and roots as clues to the meaning of a word (e.g., *precede, recede, secede*).

    c. Consult general and specialized reference materials (e.g., dictionaries, glossaries, thesauruses), both print and digital, to find the pronunciation of a word or determine or clarify its precise meaning or its part of speech.

    d. Verify the preliminary determination of the meaning of a word or phrase (e.g., by checking the inferred meaning in context or in a dictionary).

**5.** Demonstrate understanding of figurative language, word relationships, and nuances in word meanings.

    a. Interpret figures of speech (e.g. verbal irony, puns) in context.

    b. Use the relationship between particular words to better understand each of the words.

    c. Distinguish among the connotations (associations) of words with similar denotations (definitions) (e.g., *bullheaded, willful, firm, persistent, resolute*).

**6.** Acquire and use accurately grade-appropriate general academic and domain-specific words and phrases; gather vocabulary knowledge when considering a word or phrase important to comprehension or expression.

# PRENTICE HALL
# LITERATURE

GRADE 8 • VOLUME TWO

COMMON CORE EDITION ©

Upper Saddle River, New Jersey

Boston, Massachusetts

Chandler, Arizona

Glenview, Illinois

ALWAYS LEARNING

PEARSON

**THE BIG ?**

# What is the secret to *reaching someone* with words?

## Poetry

**Online!**

**www.PHLitOnline.com**

### *Hear It!*
- Selection summary audio
- Selection audio
- BQ Tunes

### *See It!*
- Author videos
- Big Question video
- Get Connected videos
- Background videos
- More about the authors
- Illustrated vocabulary words
- Vocabulary flashcards

### *Do It!*
- Interactive journals
- Interactive graphic organizers
- Grammar tutorials
- Interactive vocabulary games
- Test practice

# What is the secret to reaching someone with words?

Think of how limited our lives would be without words. Words, written or spoken, are the building blocks that make meaningful communication possible. When two people connect, it is often the result of verbal communication—whether it is between child and parent, friend and friend, or writer and reader. This communication takes different forms, such as agreement or disagreement, satisfaction in gaining knowledge, or the experience that occurs when someone reads a powerful, meaningful text.

Writers use different techniques to express ideas. All writers share one common starting point, however. Whether their goal is to inform, persuade, or entertain, writers know that in order to create something with significance they must first reach a reader with words.

## Exploring the Big Question

Ⓒ **Collaboration: One-on-One Discussion** Start thinking about the Big Question by describing a specific example of each of the following situations.

- A news story in the media about a recent historical event
- A situation that allowed you to express your individuality
- An experience that you found difficult to put into words
- A conversation that inspired you to try a new activity or approach
- A text message, e-mail, or blog entry that made you laugh
- A story, poem, or article that changed your perspective

Discuss with a partner how each situation reveals a different aspect of the human desire to communicate. Use the Big Question vocabulary in your discussion.

**Connecting to the Literature** Each reading in this unit will give you additional insight into the Big Question.

**PHLit**
**Online!**
www.PHLitOnline.com

- Big Question video
- Illustrated vocabulary words
- Interactive vocabulary games
- BQ Tunes

# Learning Big Question Vocabulary

**Common Core State Standards**

**Speaking and Listening**
**1.** Engage effectively in a range of collaborative discussions with diverse partners on *grade 8 topics, texts, and issues,* building on others' ideas and expressing their own clearly.

**Language**
**6.** Acquire and use accurately grade-appropriate general academic and domain-specific words and phrases; gather vocabulary knowledge when considering a word or phrase important to comprehension or expression.

**Acquire and Use Academic Vocabulary** Academic vocabulary is the language you encounter in textbooks and on standardized tests. Review the definitions of these academic vocabulary words.

---

**benefit** (ben′ ə fit) *n.* advantage; positive result

**connection** (kə nek′ shən) *n.* link; tie; relationship

**cultural** (kul′ chər əl) *adj.* relating to the customs and beliefs of a group

**individuality** (in′ də vij′ o͞o al′ə tē) *n.* characteristics that set a person or thing apart from others

**inform** (in fôrm′) *v.* tell; give information or knowledge

**relevant** (rel′ ə vənt) *adj.* connected to the topic being discussed

**significance** (sig nif′ ə kəns) *n.* importance

**valid** (val′ id) *adj.* true; backed by evidence

---

Use these words as you complete Big Question activities in this unit that involve reading, writing, speaking, and listening.

**Gather Vocabulary Knowledge** Additional Big Question words are listed below. Categorize the words by deciding whether you know each one well, know it a little bit, or do not know it at all.

---

| experience | meaningful | misunderstood |
| express | media | sensory |
| feedback | | |

---

Then, do the following:

1. Write the definitions of the words you know.

2. Using a print or online dictionary, look up the meaning of each word you do not know. Then, write the meaning.

3. Confirm the meaning and pronunciation of each word you think you know. Revise your definition if necessary.

4. Use as many words as possible in a paragraph about the obstacles and difficulties you might encounter when trying to reach someone with words.

# Elements of Poetry

## Poetry is the most musical of literary forms.

The **structure** of a poem is the way the words, lines, and groups of lines are arranged.

**Lines** Most poetry is arranged in **lines,** or groupings of words. A line may not be a complete sentence. A poet may *break*, or end, a line to emphasize a word or an idea, or to create a pattern of rhythm or rhyme.

**Stanzas** Lines may be grouped in **stanzas**—logical sections of ideas, like paragraphs in an essay. A two-line stanza is a **couplet,** three lines is a **tercet,** four lines is a **quatrain.**

**Rhyme** The **rhyme scheme** is the pattern of rhymes at the ends of lines. Each new rhyme is assigned a letter of the alphabet, as shown below.

| | |
|---|---|
| The path of least resistance, | **a** |
| Is short, but it's boring. | **b** |
| Choose the tougher distance | **a** |
| For soaring. | **b** |

**Meter** The pattern of stressed and unstressed syllables in a poem is the **meter.** Each unit of stressed and unstressed syllables in a poem is called a **foot.**

The example below shows how poetry can be marked to show the meter. An accent (´) marks each stressed syllable. A horseshoe symbol (˘) marks each unstressed syllable. Vertical lines (|) divide each line into feet.

| |
|---|
| Sómebŏdў, \| Nóbŏdў— |
| Ă fáce \| iš sŏ neár |

The chart below shows a fuller analysis of the meter and other structural elements of a poem.

### from "The Village Blacksmith," Henry Wadsworth Longfellow

| | |
|---|---|
| His hair \| is crisp, \| and black, \| and long, | This stanza has six lines. The poet begins each line with a capital letter. |
| His face \| is like \| the tan; | The regular beat is like the rhythmic pounding of a hammer. |
| His brow \| is wet \| with hon \| est sweat, | The second, fourth, and sixth lines rhyme. This *abcbdb* rhyme scheme reinforces the sense of pounding and emphasizes the word *man* at the end of the stanza. |
| He earns \| whate'er \| he can, | |
| And looks \| the whole \| world in \| the face, | Internal rhyme calls attention to the vivid image. |
| For he owes \| not an \| y man. | The change in meter at the end of the stanza slows readers down so that they think about the last line. |

**Poetic Forms** A poem's form is usually defined by its purpose and characteristics. **Formal verse** follows fixed, traditional patterns that may include a specific rhyme scheme, meter, line length, or stanza structure. **Free verse** uses poetic language, but does not follow a fixed pattern. Three main categories of poetry are lyric, narrative, and dramatic. Within these categories are forms of poetry that have specific structures and features.

**Lyric poetry** expresses the thoughts and feelings of a single speaker, often in very musical verse. The chart below describes some forms of lyric poetry.

**Narrative poetry** tells a story. Most narrative poetry, including **ballads** and **epic poetry,** follows a formal structure with set stanzas, strong rhythms, and a regular rhyme scheme.

**Dramatic poetry** presents a drama in verse. The action is told through the words the characters speak.

**Speaker** The **speaker** is the person or character who communicates the words of the poem. Do not assume that the voice in the poem is the poet's, even when the poem is written in the first person. The poet creates the character of the speaker, just as a songwriter may invent a character to express his or her feelings and ideas in a song.

**Imagery** Poets create word pictures for readers by using **imagery,** or vivid language that appeals to the five senses. Imagery can enhance the meaning of a poem by providing a context or setting a scene. Imagery also helps create a poem's emotional impact.

## In This Section

**Elements of Poetry**

**Analyzing Poetic Language**

**Close Read: Analyzing the Impact of Word Choice**
- Model Text
- Practice Text

**After You Read**

 Common Core State Standards

RL.8.4, RL.8.5
[For the full wording of the standards, see the standards chart in the front of your textbook.]

**Forms of Lyric Poetry**

| Sonnet "Harriet Beecher Stowe," p. 735 | A sonnet is a fourteen-line poem of praise with a specific rhyme scheme. A **Petrarchan sonnet** follows a rhyme scheme of abba/abba/cde/cde. A **Shakespearean sonnet** has a rhyme scheme of abab/cdcd/efef/gg. |
|---|---|
| Ode "Ode to Enchanted Light," p. 685 | An ode is a formal poem of honor or celebration. Odes often have a regular meter and end rhyme, but the number and length of their lines and stanzas can vary. |
| Elegy "O Captain, My Captain," p. 777 | An elegy is a formal poem reflecting on death or another serious theme. The structure, meter, and rhyme scheme of elegies can vary considerably. |
| Haiku | A haiku is a short, unrhymed poem, often about nature. It has one three-line stanza that follows a 5-7-5 syllabic pattern. |

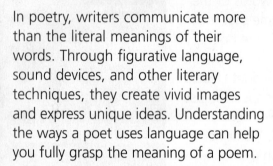
# Analyzing Poetic Language

## Poets create **meaning** through their imaginative use of **language**.

**Common Core State Standards**

**Reading Literature 4.** Determine the meaning of words and phrases as they are used in a text, including figurative and connotative meanings; analyze the impact of specific word choices on meaning and tone, including analogies or allusions to other texts.

In poetry, writers communicate more than the literal meanings of their words. Through figurative language, sound devices, and other literary techniques, they create vivid images and express unique ideas. Understanding the ways a poet uses language can help you fully grasp the meaning of a poem.

**Figurative Language** Words and phrases have **literal** meanings—the meanings you find in a dictionary. **Figurative language** describes and compares things in ways that are not meant to be taken literally. By using the following types of figurative language, a poet can put intense focus on a particular quality and present it in a rich and unique way.

**Similes and metaphors** highlight a shared quality of two things that are otherwise different.

- A **simile** uses the word *like* or *as* to compare two things: *The icy water hurt like a thousand bee stings.*
- A **metaphor** compares by describing one thing as if it were another: *The icy water was a thousand stinging bees.*
- An **extended metaphor** carries a metaphor throughout part or all of a poem.

**Personification** assigns human qualities to a non-human subject. In the example below, the clarinets and drums are personified.

> **Example:**
> The clarinets sang merrily,
> While the drums grumbled and complained.

An **analogy** explains, clarifies, or illustrates by drawing comparisons.

In the example below, the poet uses the analogy of deleted computer files to clarify the idea that memories exist someplace but are inaccessible.

> Age betrayed her daily now.
> Memories gone, but where?
> Somewhere inaccessible,
> The way a computer file
> Deleted accidentally,
> Is there
> But not there.

**Allusions** are direct or implied references to people, places, events, literary works, or artworks, as in the following example:

> In desperate times be brave and bold
> Your Cinderella story is not yet told.

## Sound Devices

The sounds of words contribute to the musical quality of a poem. Sounds can also strengthen meaning by emphasizing significant words and by connecting ideas. Look for these sound devices as you read poetry.

**Alliteration** is the repetition of initial consonant sounds:

- *He climbs the <u>h</u>ill and <u>h</u>uffs and <u>h</u>eaves.*

The repeated *h* sound strengthens the impression of labored breathing.

**Consonance** is the repetition of consonant sounds in stressed syllables with different vowel sounds:

- *Gulls gracefully pa<u>ss</u> acro<u>ss</u> the sky.*

The repeated *s* sound creates a sense of graceful movement from word to word.

**Assonance** is the repetition of vowel sounds in stressed syllables that do not rhyme:

- *C<u>a</u>lling and squ<u>aw</u>king like crows, they f<u>ou</u>ght.*

The repetition of the *aw* sound reinforces the sense of the simile.

**Repetition** is the repeated use of a word or phrase:

- *<u>Time</u> and <u>time</u> again I lose track of <u>time</u>.*

The repetition emphasizes a key idea.

**Onomatopoeia** is the use of words that imitate sounds:

- *The wind <u>whooshed</u> in and slammed the door with a <u>bang</u>.*

The words *whooshed* and *bang* appeal to the sense of sound.

## Connotations and Tone

A word's **connotations** are the ideas associated with that word beyond its **denotation,** or literal definition. Connotations can be positive or negative. The chart below shows how the word *diva* can have both negative and positive connotations.

| The actress is a *diva.* | |
|---|---|
| **Denotation:** successful female performer | |
| **Negative** | **Positive** |
| arrogance, ego, bossiness | power, confidence, talent |
| **Context:** the actress has a temper tantrum | **Context:** the actress gives a great performance |

**Tone** is the attitude the writer projects in a poem. Word choice and other poetic elements work together to convey the tone of a poem.

| Combination of Elements | Tone Created |
|---|---|
| **Word choices:** *exquisite, rare, inspire* <br> **Connotations:** positive <br> **Meter:** musical | • respectful <br> • admiring |
| **Word choices:** *isolated, loneliness* <br> **Connotations:** negative <br> **Meter:** slow beat | • sorrowful <br> • pitying |
| **Word choices:** *helter-skelter, whiz* <br> **Connotations:** positive/amusing <br> **Meter:** bouncy beat | • carefree <br> • playful |

# Close Read: Analyzing the Impact of Word Choice

## To understand the meaning of a poem, consider the impact of the author's choice of words and phrases.

Word choice affects every element of a poem. For example, a poet following a formal structure might choose a particular word not only because it has the intended denotation and connotation, but also because it has the right number of syllables. Poets also select words for their sounds. They choose vocabulary that reveals the personality of the speaker in a poem and use figurative language to enhance meaning. All the word choices work together to build the overall effect the poet wants to achieve.

Use the questions in the following chart to guide you as you analyze the overall impact of word choice on the meaning of a poem.

| Clues to Word Choice Analysis | | |
|---|---|---|
| **Structure** <br> • How does the poem look on the page? <br> • Are the lines divided into stanzas? <br> • Is there a rhyme scheme? <br> • Is there a regular metrical rhythm? <br> • Is it formal or free verse? | **Poetic Language** <br> • How does imagery appeal to the five senses? <br> • Does the poem contain figurative language, such as similes, metaphors, and personification? <br> • Are there any allusions to other texts or ideas? | **Sound Devices** <br> • What sounds stand out when you read the poem aloud? <br> • Where does the poet use rhyme? Is each rhyme exact or near? <br> • How does meter affect the sound of the poem? <br> • Are there examples of alliteration, assonance, consonance, repetition, or onomatopoeia? |
| **Speaker** <br> • Who is the speaker? <br> • What do the word choices and imagery tell you about the speaker's thoughts and feelings? | **Connotation** <br> • What are the connotations of key words? <br> • Are there any words that have strong positive or negative connotations? | **Tone** <br> • What adjective would you use to describe the tone of the poem? <br> • Which elements help create that tone? |

# Model

**About the Text** Nikki Giovanni is an African American poet with a life-long commitment to equality and civil rights. Like the speaker in the poem below, Giovanni spent summers at her grandparents' home in Tennessee. Growing up in the 1950s, Giovanni experienced firsthand the kind of discrimination described in the poem.

---

### "A Poem for My Librarian, Mrs. Long"

(You never know what troubled little girl needs a book.)
### by Nikki Giovanni

At a time when there was no tv before 3:00 P.M.
And on Sunday none until 5:00
We sat on front porches watching
The jfg sign go on and off greeting
5 The neighbors, discussing the political
Situation congratulating the preacher
On his sermon

There was always radio which brought us
Song from wlac in nashville and what we would now call
10 Easy listening or smooth jazz but when I listened
Late at night with my portable (that I was so proud of)
Tucked under my pillow
I heard nat king cole and matt dennis, june christy and ella fitzgerald
And sometimes sarah vaughan sing black coffee
15 Which I now drink
It was just called music

There was a bookstore uptown on gay street
Which I visited and inhaled that wonderful odor
Of new books
20 Even today I read hardcover as a preference paperback only
As a last resort

And up the hill on vine street
(The main black corridor) sat our carnegie library
Mrs. Long always glad to see you
25 The stereoscope always ready to show you faraway

---

**Structure** This lyric poem is written in free verse. It has no consistent or formal structural elements.

**Poetic Language** The speaker refers to black and white recording artists. This allusion stresses her assumption of equality.

**Poetic Language** The imagery in these lines emphasizes the speaker's passion for books.

**Speaker** The "black corridor" refers to the segregation of the time. This reality contrasts with the earlier "integrated" allusions to singers.

© EXEMPLAR TEXT

## Model continued

**Structure** A line break separates the word *southern* from *Whites*, subtly suggesting that the desire to humiliate was not limited to southern whites.

**Sound Devices** In these lines, alliteration (*but, brought, books, back; held, heart, happily, house*) and assonance (*held, them, chest*) create a musicality that reflects the speaker's enthusiastic appreciation of books.

**Tone** The poem recognizes harsh realities, such as discrimination, but the overall tone is optimistic and hopeful. Spring suggests renewal and the possibility of a better future.

Places to dream about

Mrs. Long asking what are you looking for today
When I wanted *Leaves of Grass* or alfred north whitehead
She would go to the big library uptown and I now know
30 Hat in hand to ask to borrow so that I might borrow
Probably they said something humiliating since southern
Whites like to humiliate southern blacks

But she nonetheless brought the books
Back and I held them to my chest
35 Close to my heart
And happily skipped back to grandmother's house
Where I would sit on the front porch
In a gray glider and dream of the world
Far away

40 I love the world where I was
I was safe and warm and grandmother gave me neck kisses
When I was on my way to bed

But there was a world
Somewhere
45 Out there
And Mrs. Long opened that wardrobe
But no lions or witches scared me
I went through
Knowing there would be
Spring

# Independent Practice

**About the Texts** Jacqueline Woodson is an African American poet and novelist whose works reflect her interest in writing for and about young people. Although she takes on many different points of view in her writing, she says her writing is always "emotionally autobiographical."

The speaker of both poems is Lonnie Collins Motion, who lives in Brooklyn, New York, with his foster mother, Miss Edna.

---

### "Describe Somebody" by Jacqueline Woodson

Today in class Ms. Marcus said
*Take out your poetry notebooks and describe somebody.*
*Think carefully,* Ms. Marcus said.
*You're gonna read it to the class.*
5 I wrote, Ms. Marcus is tall and a little bit skinny.
Then I put my pen in my mouth and stared down
at the words.
Then I crossed them out and wrote
Ms. Marcus's hair is long and brown.
10 Shiny.
When she smiles it makes you feel all good inside.
I stopped writing and looked around the room.
Angel was staring out the window.
Eric and Lamont were having a pen fight.
15 They don't care about poetry.
*Stupid words,* Eric says.
*Lots and lots of stupid words.*
Eric is tall and a little bit mean.
Lamont's just regular.
20 Angel's kinda chubby. He's got light brown hair.
Sometimes we all hang out,
play a little ball or something. Angel's real good
at science stuff. Once he made a volcano
for science fair and the stuff that came out of it
25 looked like real lava. Lamont can
draw superheroes real good. Eric—nobody
at school really knows this but
he can sing. Once, Miss Edna took me
to a different church than the one

---

**Speaker** What details in the opening lines help you decide who the speaker is?

**Connotation** What are other words the speaker could have used to convey a more positive impression?

**Structure** Describe the structure of this poem.

**Sound Devices** How does alliteration enhance the image in this line?

**Practice continued**

30 we usually go to on Sunday.
I was surprised to see Eric up there
with a choir robe on. He gave me a mean look
like I'd better not
say nothing about him and his dark green robe with
35 gold around the neck.
After the preacher preached
Eric sang a song with nobody else in the choir singing.
Miss Edna started dabbing at her eyes
whispering *Yes, Lord.*
40 Eric's voice was like something
that didn't seem like it should belong
to Eric.
Seemed like it should be coming out of an angel.

Now I gotta write a whole new poem
45 'cause Eric would be real mad if I told the class
about his angel voice.

**Poetic Language**
What type of comparison does the speaker make here? What is the effect of this comparison?

**Tone** How would you describe the speaker's tone in the poem's final lines?

## "Almost Summer Sky" by Jacqueline Woodson

*It was the trees first,* Rodney[1] tells me.
It's raining out. But the rain is light and warm.
And the sky's not all close to us like it gets
sometimes. It's way up there with
5 some blue showing through.
*Late spring sky,* Ms. Marcus says. *Almost summer sky.*
And when she said that, I said
*Hey Ms. Marcus, that's a good title*
*for a poem, right?*
10 *You have a poet's heart, Lonnie.*
That's what Ms. Marcus said to me.
I have a poet's heart.
That's good. A good thing to have.
And I'm the one who has it.

15 Now Rodney puts his arm around my shoulder
We keep walking. There's a park
eight blocks from Miss Edna's house
That's where we're going.
Me and Rodney to the park.
20 Rain coming down warm
Rodney with his arm around my shoulder
Makes me think of Todd and his pigeons
how big his smile gets when they fly.

*The trees upstate ain't like other trees you seen, Lonnie*
25 Rodney squints up at the sky, shakes his head
smiles.
*No, upstate they got maple and catalpa and scotch pine,*[2]
*all kinds of trees just standing.*
*Hundred-year-old trees big as three men.*

30 *When you go home this weekend,* Ms. Marcus said.
*Write about a perfect moment.*

---

**Poetic Language** How does the imagery in the opening lines of the poem establish a contrast?

**Sound Devices** Why might the speaker think these words would be a good title for a poem?

**Speaker** Why do you think Lonnie thinks a poet's heart is a good thing to have?

**Speaker** How does Rodney's point of view compare and contrast with Lonnie's point of view?

**Poetic Language** What type of comparison is used in line 29? What is the effect of this comparison?

---

1. **Rodney** one of Miss Edna's sons.
2. **catalpa** (kə tal' pə) tree with heart-shaped leaves; **scotch pine** tree with yellow wood, grown for timber.

**Practice continued**

*Yeah, Little Brother,* Rodney says.
*You don't know about shade till you lived upstate.*
*Everybody should do it—even if it's just for a little while.*

35 Way off, I can see the park—blue-gray sky
touching the tops of trees.

*I had to live there awhile,* Rodney said.
*Just to be with all that green, you know?*
I nod, even though I don't.
40 I can't even imagine moving away from here,
from Rodney's arm around my shoulder,
from Miss Edna's Sunday cooking,
from Lily[3] in her pretty dresses and great
big smile when she sees me.

45 Can't imagine moving away

From
Home.

*You know what I love about trees,* Rodney says.
*It's like . . . It's like their leaves are hands*
*reaching*
50 *out to you. Saying Come on over here, Brother.*
*Let me just . . . Let me just . . .*
Rodney looks down at me and grins.
*Let me just give you some shade for a while.*

**Connotation** What are the connotations of the word *green* in this stanza?

**Structure** What idea does the poet convey by breaking these lines in this way?

**Poetic Language** What is the effect of the figurative language in the closing lines of the poem?

---

**3. Lily** Lonnie's sister, who lives in a different foster home.

*from* **Describe Somebody •**
**Almost Summer Sky**

**1. Key Ideas and Details (a)** What does the speaker know about Eric that others do not? **(b) Infer:** Why would Eric be mad if the class knew this information?

**2. Key Ideas and Details**
**(a) Speculate:** In "Almost Summer Sky," what is Rodney's perfect moment? **(b)** What do you think Lonnie's perfect moment might be? **(c) Draw Conclusions:** How are both boys observant in the way that poets are?

**3. Craft and Structure (a)** What tells you these poems are written in **free verse? (b)** How is the free-verse structure well suited to convey the **speaker** of these poems?

**4. Craft and Structure (a)** Use a chart like the one shown to analyze the figurative language in the poems.

| | Ideas Compared | Ideas Conveyed |
|---|---|---|
| "Describe Somebody," lines 40–43 | | |
| "Almost Summer Sky," lines 49–53 | | |

**(b) Collaborate:** In a group, use the chart to guide a discussion about the use of poetic language in these poems.

**5. Integration of Knowledge and Ideas Compare and Contrast:** Are the tones of the two poems more similar or more different? Why?

**6. Integration of Knowledge and Ideas** Read the following poem. Notice that it tells the same story as "Describe Somebody." Compare and contrast the two poems. Consider the structure, speaker, word choice, and tone of each poem.

**Poem to Describe**
I look around and start to write
About the guys: their hair, their height
Describing them I start to see
They're not so bad. They're just like me
There's something they each care about
Like me, they each have fears and doubts
And passions they don't want to share.
They don't let on how much they care.
Eric wouldn't let me tell
A poem that says he sings so well.
The guys have never heard him sing.
Too bad—it's an angelic thing.

## © Leveled Texts

Build your skills and improve your comprehension of poetry with texts of increasing complexity.

Read **Poetry Collection 1** to discover how poets use their imaginations to create vivid descriptions.

Read **Poetry Collection 2** to see how writers use poetry to express their views of the world.

## © Common Core State Standards

Meet these standards with either **Poetry Collection 1** (p. 654) or **Poetry Collection 2** (p. 663).

**Reading Literature**
**4.** Determine the meaning of words and phrases as they are used in a text, including figurative and connotative meanings; analyze the impact of specific word choices on meaning and tone, including analogies or allusions to other texts. *(Literary Analysis: Spiral Review)*

**Writing**
**4.** Produce clear and coherent writing in which the development, organization, and style are appropriate to task, purpose, and audience. *(Writing: Poem)*

**Speaking and Listening**
**6.** Adapt speech to a variety of contexts and tasks, demonstrating command of formal English when indicated or appropriate. *(Speaking and Listening: Poetry Recitation)*

**Language**
**4.a.** Use context (e.g., the overall meaning of a sentence or paragraph; a word's position or function in a sentence) as a clue to the meaning of a word or phrase. *(Reading Skill: Using Context)*

**4.b.** Use common, grade-appropriate Greek or Latin affixes and roots as clues to the meaning of a word (e.g., *precede, recede, secede*). *(Vocabulary: Word Study)*

**5.b.** Use the relationship between particular words to better understand each of the words. *(Reading Skill: Using Context)*

# Reading Skill: Using Context

The **context** of a word is the information in the words that surround it. Before you read poetry, **preview the lines to identify unfamiliar words.** As you read, look for these types of context clues to help determine a meaning for words you do not know.

- **synonym/definition/restatement:** words that mean the same as the unfamiliar word
- **antonym/contrast:** words that are opposite in meaning
- **comparison:** words that show a connection or relationship
- **explanation/example:** words that give more information
- **sentence role:** words that show how the word functions

## Using the Strategy: Context Clues Chart

Use this **context clues chart** to help you determine a word's meaning.

| With her hair all *disheveled* / Looking like she had just awoken | |
|---|---|
| Explanation | Looking like she had just awoken |
| Sentence Role | describes hair |

**Meaning:** Disheveled probably means *messy*, like hair looks after sleeping

# Literary Analysis: Sound Devices

**Sound devices** create musical effects that appeal to the ear. Poets use these techniques to achieve specific purposes and to convey the mood, tone, and meaning of a poem. Common sound devices include the following:

- **alliteration:** repetition of initial consonant sounds—*we won*
- **onomatopoeia:** words that imitate sounds—*buzz* or *hiss*
- **rhyme:** repetition of sounds at ends of words—*spring fling.* Rhymes occurring at the ends of two or more lines are called *external rhyme* or *end rhyme. Internal rhyme* occurs within a single line, as in "The rain in Spain stays mainly in the plain."
- **Rhyme scheme:** the pattern of end rhyme in a poem, described by assigning each rhyme a letter (*a, b, c, d,* etc.)
- **meter:** a poem's rhythm—the strong and weak stresses, as well as pauses, that we give words and syllables when we read

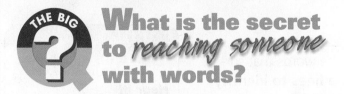

**W**hat is the secret to *reaching someone* with words?

## Writing About the Big Question

In the poems in Collection 1, poets go beyond relying only on the meaning of words to communicate. They choose words for their sound quality and for the moods the words inspire. Use these sentence starters to develop your ideas about the Big Question.

I (notice/do not notice) the **sensory** effect of words like swoosh, *smush, scrunch, crunch, munch,* and *splash.* Some words I like for their sounds are _____ and _____ because _____.

**While You Read** Look for specific words that grab your attention and help build a connection between you and the poem.

## Vocabulary

Read each word and its definition. Decide whether you know the word well, know it a little bit, or do not know it at all. After you read, see how your knowledge of each word has increased.

- **flatterer** (flat´ ər ər) *n.* one who praises insincerely to win approval (p. 655) *I do not take Liz's compliments seriously because she is a <u>flatterer</u>.* flatter *v.* flattery *n.* flatteringly *adv.*

- **scampering** (skam´ pər iŋ) *v.* running quickly (p. 657) *The scared rabbit went <u>scampering</u> away.* scamper *v.*

- **reeds** (rēdz) *n.* tall slender grasses that grow in wetland areas (p. 657) *A duck hid in a clump of marsh <u>reeds</u>.* reedy *adj.*

- **immensity** (i men´ sə tē) *n.* vastness; hugeness (p. 658) *The <u>immensity</u> of the universe makes me feel small and insignificant.* immense *adj.* immensely *adv.*

- **rapture** (rap´ chər) *n.* ecstasy (p. 658) *Athletes dream of Olympic gold with <u>rapture</u>.* rapturous *adj.* rapturously *adv.*

### Word Study

The **Latin prefix** *im-* means "not." Combined with the root *mensus* meaning "measured," **immensity** describes something you cannot measure.

# Eleanor Farjeon

**(1881–1965)**

**"Cat!"** (page 654)

Eleanor Farjeon spent much of her childhood reading fantasy stories in the attic of her family's house in London, England. She also enjoyed playing games of make-believe with her little brother. When she grew up, she drew on memories of her childhood to inspire dozens of books of poetry and stories for children and young adults. Farjeon's 1931 poem "Morning Has Broken" became a huge hit when it was set to music by pop singer Cat Stevens forty years later.

# Walter de la Mare

**(1873–1956)**

**"Silver"** (page 657)

The British poet and novelist Walter de la Mare loved the magical world of imagination. Yet, for eighteen years, he worked at an ordinary job as a bookkeeper for an oil company. He wrote during his lunch hour. Every night at bedtime, he read one of his new poems to his four children. In 1908, the British government gave him a grant that allowed him to retire at age thirty-five and write full-time for the rest of his life.

# Georgia Douglas Johnson

**(1886–1966)**

**"Your World"** (page 658)

Georgia Douglas Johnson was born in Atlanta, Georgia, and lived in Washington, D.C., as an adult. She used her love of music and words to create poems, stories, and plays, and also had a career as a newspaper columnist. One of the first well-known African American women writers, Johnson became part of the Harlem Renaissance. She hosted weekly conversations among African American writers at her home in Washington.

# CAT!

*Eleanor Farjeon*

▲ **Critical Viewing** Which of these two drawings most resembles the cat described in the poem? Explain your choice. **[Connect]**

*Cat!*
Scat!
After her, after her,
Sleeky flatterer,

5   Spitfire chatterer,
Scatter her, scatter her
        Off her mat!
        *Wuff!*
        *Wuff!*

10      Treat her rough!
Git her, git her,
Whiskery spitter!
Catch her, catch her,
Green-eyed scratcher!

15      Slathery
        Slithery
        Hisser,
        Don't miss her!
Run till you're dithery,[1]

20      Hithery
        Thithery[2]
        *Pftts! pftts!*
        How she spits!
        *Spitch! Spatch!*

25      Can't she scratch!
Scritching the bark
Of the sycamore tree,
She's reached her ark
And's hissing at me

30      *Pftts! pftts!*
        *Wuff! wuff!*
            Scat,
            Cat!
            That's
35          *That!*

**Vocabulary**
**flatterer** (flat´ ər ər) *n.*
one who praises
insincerely to win
approval

**Context**
Which words in lines
10–14 provide a syn-
onym that helps you
determine the meaning
of *git*?

**Sound Devices**
Find two made-up
words that imitate cat
sounds. How do they
help you imagine the
poem's action?

---

1. **dithery** (di*th*´ rē) *adj.* nervous and confused; in a dither.
2. **Hithery/Thithery** made-up words based on *hither* and *thither*, which mean "here"
and "there."

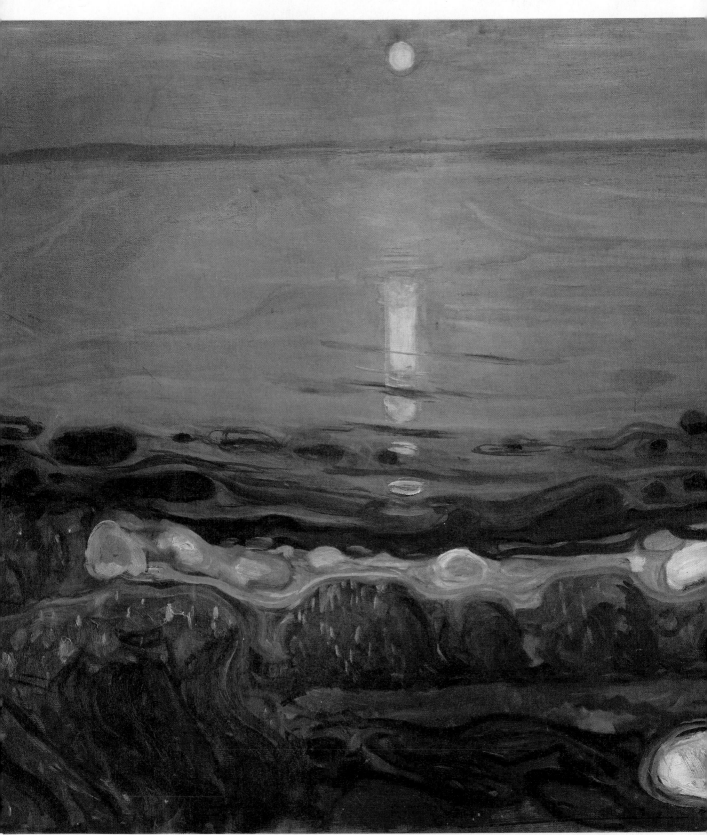

***A Summer Night on the Beach,*** Edvard Munch, ©2003 The Munch Museum/The Munch-Ellingsen Group/
Artists Rights Society (ARS), New York/ADAGP, Paris.

# Silver

## Walter de la Mare

Slowly, silently, now the moon
Walks the night in her silver shoon;[1]
This way, and that, she peers, and sees
Silver fruit upon silver trees;
5    One by one the casements[2] catch
Her beams beneath the silvery thatch;[3]
Couched in his kennel, like a log,
With paws of silver sleeps the dog;
From their shadowy coat the white breasts peep
10   Of doves in a silver-feathered sleep;
A harvest mouse goes scampering by,
With silver claws, and silver eye;
And moveless fish in the water gleam,
By silver reeds in a silver stream.

---

1. **shoon** (sho͞on) *n.* old-fashioned word for "shoes."
2. **casements** (kās′ mənts) *n.* windows that open out like doors.
3. **thatch** (thach) *n.* roof made of straw or other plant material.

◀ **Critical Viewing**
How does this painting capture the mood
and images of the poem? **[Connect]**

**Sound Devices**
Identify examples of
alliteration in lines 1–5.

**Vocabulary**
**scampering** (skam′ pər
iŋ) *v.* running quickly

**reeds** (rēdz) *n.* tall
slender grasses that
grow in wetland areas

Spiral Review
**Connotation** Iden-
tify the connotations
of the word "peep"
in line 9. How do the
word's connotations
contribute to the
poem's mood?

# Your World

## GEORGIA DOUGLAS JOHNSON

Your world is as big as you make it.
I know, for I used to abide
In the narrowest nest in a corner,
My wings pressing close to my side.

5  But I sighted the distant horizon
Where the sky line encircled the sea
And I throbbed with a burning desire
To travel this immensity.

I battered the cordons[1] around me
10  And cradled my wings on the breeze
Then soared to the uttermost reaches
With rapture, with power, with ease!

---

1. **cordons** (kôr´ dənz) *n.* lines or cords that restrict free movement.

**Vocabulary**
**immensity** (i men´ sə tē)
*n.* vastness; hugeness
**rapture** (rap´ chər)
*n.* ecstasy

## Critical Thinking

Cite textual evidence to support your responses.

© **1. Key Ideas and Details (a) Interpret:** Why is the cat running in "Cat!"? **(b) Infer:** How does the poem's speaker feel about the cat?

© **2. Key Ideas and Details (a)** What "walks the night" in "Silver"? **(b) Analyze Causes and Effects:** What effects does this "walk" have on everyday objects? **(c) Generalize:** What mood does the poet create as he describes these effects?

© **3. Key Ideas and Details (a)** Where does the speaker of "Your World" say that she used to live? **(b) Restate:** What was her "burning desire"? **(c) Interpret:** How did she reach her goal?

© **4. Integration of Knowledge and Ideas (a)** What sounds Fly and rhythms do these poets use to connect with readers? **(b)** How do these devices contribute to the overall effect of the poems? *[Connect to the Big Question: What is the secret to reaching someone with words?]*

## Reading Skill: Context

1. Explain how **context** helps you determine the meaning of *scritching* (line 26) in "Cat!"

2. What kind of context clues help you clarify the meaning of *abide* (line 2) in "Your World"? Explain.

## Literary Analysis: Sound Devices

3. **Craft and Structure** Complete the chart with examples of **sound devices.** Not all sound devices are used in each poem.

|  | Cat! | Silver | Your World |
|---|---|---|---|
| **alliteration** |  |  |  |
| **onomatopoeia** |  |  |  |
| **rhyme** (internal/external) |  |  |  |
| **meter** (rhythmic patterns) |  |  |  |

4. **Craft and Structure** Explain how at least one of the sound devices listed above contributes to the mood, tone, and meaning of a poem.

## Vocabulary

**Acquisition and Use** In each group, identify the word that does not belong. Explain how its meaning differs from those of the other words.

1. flatterer, praiser, complainer
2. sleeping, dozing, scampering
3. silence, immensity, hugeness
4. rapture, misery, unhappiness
5. landscape, horizon, scenery
6. grasses, roses, reeds

**Word Study** Use the context of the sentences and what you know about the **Latin prefix im-** to explain each answer.

1. Would you believe someone who told an *improbable* story?
2. Is it safe to use medicines that are *impure*?

### Word Study

The **Latin prefix im-** means "not."

**Apply It** Explain how the prefix *im-* contributes to the meanings of these words. Consult a dictionary if necessary.

immoderate
impossible
immaterial

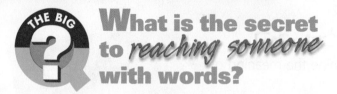

**What is the secret to *reaching someone* with words?**

## Writing About the Big Question

The writers in Collection 2 take advantage of the musical quality of poetry to communicate with readers. They use strong rhythms to convey feelings about their world. Use this sentence starter to develop your ideas about the Big Question.

> Words set to a beat, whether poetry or song lyrics, can create a memorable **experience** for a listener because _____.

**While You Read** Look for lines in the poetry in which the sounds and rhythms help communicate the poets' ideas.

## Vocabulary

Read each word and its definition. Decide whether you know the word well, know it a little bit, or do not know it at all. After you read, see how your knowledge of each word has increased.

- **resounding** (rē zound´ iŋ) *adj.* sounding loudly (p. 663) *His voice echoed, resounding in the empty hall.* resound *v.* resoundingly *adv.* sound *n.*

- **strife** (strīf) *n.* conflict (p. 665) *Strife between the two groups led to war.* strive *v.*

- **modes** (mōdz) *n.* ways of doing or behaving (p. 665) *In a big city, you can choose from many different modes of transportation.* modal *adj.* modality *n.*

- **spite** (spīt) *n.* nastiness (p. 665) *His angry, hateful words were spoken out of spite.* spiteful *adj.* spitefulness *n.* spitefully *adv.*

- **singularity** (siŋ´ gyə ler´ ə tē) *n.* unique or unusual quality (p. 666) *The cricket's chirp has an unmistakable singularity.* singular *adj.* singularly *adv.* single *adj.*

- **imprint** (im´ print) *v.* make a lasting mark (p. 666) *The star will imprint his hands in the wet cement.* print *n.* or *v.*

### Word Study

The **Latin prefix im-** means "in" or "into."

In "Thumbprint," the poet wants to leave her **imprint**, or create a lasting impression, in the minds of her readers.

# Nikki Giovanni

**(b. 1943)**

**"The Drum (for Martin Luther King, Jr.)"** (p. 663)

As a college student in the 1960s, Nikki Giovanni became involved in the civil rights movement. In the 1970s, she began writing poetry that expressed her pride in her African American heritage. Her poems are known for their musical rhythms, and she has recorded several of her works set to gospel music.

# Alfred, Lord Tennyson

**(1809–1892)**

**"Ring Out, Wild Bells"** (p. 664)

Alfred, Lord Tennyson's faith in life was shattered in his twenties when his close friend Arthur Henry Hallam died suddenly while on a trip. Tennyson wrote the long poem "In Memoriam A.H.H." as a tribute to his friend. It helped make Tennyson one of the most popular English poets of his time. "Ring Out, Wild Bells" is part of this famous poem.

# Eve Merriam

**(1916–1992)**

**"Thumbprint"** (p. 666)

Eve Merriam fell in love with words at an early age. As a child, she enjoyed playing with rhythms, rhymes, and puns. As an adult, she never lost her feeling that words could be fun. She once said, "I find it difficult to sit still when I hear poetry or read it out loud. . . . It's like a shot of adrenaline or oxygen when I hear rhymes and word play."

# The Drum

**(for Martin Luther King, Jr.)**

## Nikki Giovanni

The drums . . . Pa-Rum . . . the rat-tat-tat . . . of drums . . .
The Pied Piper[1] . . . after leading the rats . . . to death . . .
took the children . . . to dreams . . . Pa-Rum Pa-Rum . . .

The big bass drums . . . the kettles roar . . . the sound of
animal flesh . . . resounding against the wood . . . Pa-Rum
Pa-Rum . . .

Kunta Kinte[2] was making a drum . . . when he was captured . . .
Pa-Rum . . .
Thoreau[3] listened . . . to a different drum . . . rat-tat-tat-Pa-
Rum . . .
King said just say . . . I was a Drum Major . . . for peace . . . Pa-
Rum Pa-Rum . . . rat-tat-tat Pa-rum . . .

Drums of triumph . . . Drums of pain . . . Drums of life . . .
Funeral drums . . . Marching drums . . . Drums that call . . .
Pa-Rum
Pa-Rum . . . the Drums that call . . . rat-tat-tat-tat . . . the
Drums are calling . . . Pa-Rum Pa-Rum . . . rat-tat-tat Pa-
Rum . . .

---

1. **Pied Piper** musician in folklore who led away a town's children after he rid the town of rats.
2. **Kunta Kinte** (ko͞on´ tə kin´ tā) ancestor of *Roots* author Alex Haley.
3. **Thoreau** (thə rō´) (1817–1862) Henry David, American writer who wrote, "If a man does not keep pace with his companions, perhaps it is because he hears a different drummer."

**Vocabulary**
**resounding** (ri zound´ iŋ) *adj.* sounding loudly

**Sound Devices**
What words in the poem imitate the sounds that drums make?

◀ **Critical Viewing**
What can make the sound of a poem similar to the sound of a drum? **[Compare]**

# Ring Out,

Alfred, Lord Tennyson

# Wild Bells

Ring out, wild bells, to the wild sky,
    The flying cloud, the frosty light:
    The year is dying in the night;
Ring out, wild bells, and let him die.

5   Ring out the old, ring in the new,
    Ring, happy bells, across the snow:
    The year is going, let him go;
Ring out the false, ring in the true.

Ring out the grief that saps the mind,
10    For those that here we see no more;
    Ring out the feud of rich and poor,
Ring in redress to all mankind.

Ring out a slowly dying cause,
    And ancient forms of party strife;
15    Ring in the nobler modes of life,
With sweeter manners, purer laws.

Ring out the want, the care, the sin,
    The faithless coldness of the times;
    Ring out, ring out thy mournful rhymes,
20 But ring the fuller minstrel[1] in.

Ring out false pride in place and blood,
    The civic[2] slander and the spite;
    Ring in the love of truth and right,
Ring in the common love of good.

25   Ring out old shapes of foul disease;
    Ring out the narrowing lust of gold;
    Ring out the thousand wars of old,
Ring in the thousand years of peace.

---

1. **fuller minstrel** (min′ strəl) *n.* singer of the highest rank.
2. **civic** (siv′ ik) *adj.* relating to cities or citizens.

**Sound Devices**
How many beats do you hear in each line?

**Context**
How can the pattern of things "rung out" and "rung in" help you determine the meaning of *saps* in line 9?

**Vocabulary**
**strife** (strīf) *n.* conflict
**modes** (mōdz) *n.* ways of doing or behaving
**spite** (spīt) *n.* nastiness

# Thumbprint

**Eve Merriam**

On the pad of my thumb
are whorls,[1] whirls, wheels
in a unique design:
mine alone.
5  What a treasure to own!
My own flesh, my own feelings.
No other, however grand or base,
can ever contain the same.
My signature,
10  thumbing the pages of my time.
My universe key,
my singularity.

Impress, implant,
I am myself,
15  of all my atom parts I am the sum.
And out of my blood and my brain
I make my own interior weather,
my own sun and rain.
Imprint my mark upon the world,
20  whatever I shall become.

---

1. **whorls** (hwôrlz) *n.* circular ridges that form the pattern of fingerprints.

**Sound Devices**
Which repeated consonant sounds create alliteration in lines 1–6?

**Vocabulary**
**singularity** (sin´ gyə ler´ ə tē) *n.* unique or unusual quality
**imprint** (im´ print) *v.* make a lasting mark

## Critical Thinking

© 1. **Key Ideas and Details (a)** What kinds of people and drums are mentioned in "The Drum"? **(b) Interpret:** Why is a drummer a good symbol for a leader like Martin Luther King, Jr.?

© 2. **Key Ideas and Details (a)** Name four things the speaker in "Ring Out, Wild Bells" wants to "ring out" and "ring in." **(b) Interpret:** How will the future that the speaker envisions differ from the past?

© 3. **Key Ideas and Details (a) Interpret:** In "Thumbprint," explain lines 14 and 15. **(b) Infer:** What do these lines reveal is important to the speaker?

© 4. **Integration of Knowledge and Ideas** How do the sounds and rhythms of "The Drum" help the poet communicate her ideas? *[Connect to the Big Question: What is the secret to reaching someone with words?]*

*Cite textual evidence to support your responses.*

## Reading Skill: Context

1. What **context clues** help you clarify the meaning of *feud* (line 11) in "Ring Out, Wild Bells"?

2. Explain how context helps you figure out the meaning of *base* (line 7) in "Thumbprint."

## Literary Analysis: Sound Devices

3. **Craft and Structure** Complete the chart with examples of **sound devices.** Not all sound devices are used in each poem.

| | The Drum | Ring Out, Wild Bells | Thumbprint |
|---|---|---|---|
| **alliteration** | | | |
| **onomatopoeia** | | | |
| **rhyme** (internal/external) | | | |
| **meter** (rhythmic patterns) | | | |

4. **Craft and Structure** Explain how at least one of the sound devices listed above contributes to the mood, tone, and meaning of a poem.

## Vocabulary

**Acquisition and Use** In each group, identify the word that does not belong. Explain how its meaning differs from those of the other words.

1. imprint, forget, mark

2. malice, spite, kindness

3. ordinariness, uniqueness, singularity

4. peace, goodwill, strife

5. modes, moods, fashions

6. echoing, resounding, whispering

**Word Study** Use the context of the sentences and what you know about the **Latin prefix im-** to explain each answer.

1. What happens to someone who is *imprisoned*?

2. Are *imports* shipped into or out of a country?

### Word Study

The **Latin prefix im-** means "in" or "into."

**Apply It** Explain how the prefix *im-* contributes to the meanings of these words. Consult a dictionary if necessary.

immersion
immigrant
impress

# Integrated Language Skills

## Poetry Collections 1 and 2

**Poetry Collection 1**

### Conventions: Subject Complements

A **subject complement** is a noun, pronoun, or adjective that follows a linking verb and completes the thought by telling something about the subject.

Three types of subject complements are *predicate nouns, predicate pronouns,* and *predicate adjectives.*

- A **predicate noun** or **predicate pronoun** follows a linking verb and *identifies,* or renames, the subject of the sentence.

- A **predicate adjective** follows a linking verb and *describes* the subject of the sentence.

**Poetry Collection 2**

| Predicate Noun | Predicate Pronoun | Predicate Adjective |
|---|---|---|
| Ronnie will be the <u>captain</u> of the team. | The two winners are <u>they</u>. | The flight to Houston was <u>swift</u>. |
| *Captain* renames the subject, *Ronnie.* | *They* identifies the subject, *winners.* | *Swift* describes the subject, *flight.* |

**Practice A** Identify the subject and subject complement in each sentence. A sentence may have more than one subject and complement.

1. The cat is a green-eyed scratcher.
2. The reeds and stream were silver in the moonlight.
3. The speaker in "Your World" is she.
4. The mood of "Silver" is quiet and gentle.

ⓒ **Reading Application** In the poems in Collection 1, find one sentence that has a subject complement.

**Practice B** In each sentence, identify the subject, linking verb, and subject complement(s), noting the type of complement.

1. The speaker's thumbprint is a unique pattern.
2. The drums sound loud and triumphant.
3. The sky and the bells seemed wild.
4. The end of the year was a symbol for Tennyson.

ⓒ **Writing Application** Rewrite the following sentence with a predicate noun. Then, rewrite it with a predicate adjective. *Tennyson was one whom the English admired.*

# Writing

 **Common Core State Standards**

**W.8.4; SL.8.6**
[For the full wording of the standards, see page 650.]

 **Poetry** Write a **poem that uses rhythm and sound devices.** If you wish, use one of the poems in Poetry Collection 1 or 2 as a model.

- Before you start, prewrite to choose a main idea to develop. Then, review the literature to see how the poets use sound devices like rhyme, rhythm, and repetition in their poems.

- Select a poetic form with regular rhyme and meter, or use free verse. Whatever you choose, maintain consistency in style throughout.

- Decide what mood you want to convey, whether serious, aggressive, exciting, or quiet. Plan rhythms and sound devices that will best convey these moods and emotions.

- As you draft, carefully consider the words you choose. Read them aloud for their sound as well as for their meaning.

**Grammar Application** Consider adding unusual subject complements to your poem.

**Writing Workshop:** *Work in Progress*

**Prewriting for Exposition** Problem-and-solution essays describe a problem and suggest one or more possible solutions. To prepare for an essay you may write, list some issues that matter to you, along with a problem associated with each. Save this Problem-and-Solution List in your writing portfolio.

Use this prewriting activity to prepare for the **Writing Workshop** on page 708.

# Listening and Speaking

Choose a poem to present in a **poetry recitation.** Memorize a poem that uses sound devices effectively. You may choose a poem from these collections or a favorite poem or song.

- To prepare, notice how sound devices contribute to the overall mood and meaning. Keep these in mind as you practice.

- While rehearsing, aim for appropriate enunciation, emphasis, volume, and tone of voice. Speak clearly and naturally, not too fast or too slow. Modulate, or vary, your voice to express the tone of the poem. Add gestures if they enhance your presentation. Maintain eye contact with your audience.

- Practice reciting your poem with a natural rhythm. Monitor your reading for effect and for errors in pronunciation.

- When you are ready, recite the poem for your class.

**PHLit Online!**
www.PHLitOnline.com

- Interactive graphic organizers
- Grammar tutorial
- Interactive journals

## Leveled Texts

Build your skills and improve your comprehension of poetry with texts of increasing complexity.

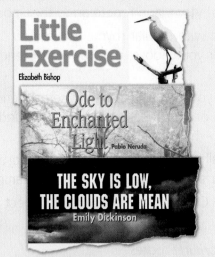

**Poetry Collection 3** looks at life in the big city from a variety of angles.

**Poetry Collection 4** examines nature and its many moods.

## Common Core State Standards

Meet these standards with either **Poetry Collection 3** (p. 675) or **Poetry Collection 4** (p. 683).

**Reading Literature**
**4.** Determine the meaning of words and phrases as they are used in a text, including figurative and connotative meanings; analyze the impact of specific word choices on meaning and tone, including analogies or allusions to other texts. *(Literary Analysis: Figurative Language)*

**Writing**
**1.** Write arguments to support claims with clear reasons and relevant evidence. *(Research and Technology: Mini-Anthology)*

**4.** Produce clear and coherent writing in which the development, organization, and style are appropriate to task, purpose, and audience. *(Writing: Study for a Poem)*

**9.** Draw evidence from literary or informational texts to support analysis, reflection, and research. *(Research and Technology: Mini-Anthology)*

**Language**
**1.** Demonstrate command of the conventions of standard English grammar and usage when writing or speaking. *(Conventions: Direct and Indirect Objects)*

**4.a.** Use context as a clue to the meaning of a word or phrase. **4.d.** Verify the preliminary determination of the meaning of a word or phrase. *(Reading Skill: Context Clues)*

**5.b.** Use the relationship between particular words to better understand each of the words. *(Reading Skill: Context Clues)*

## Reading Skill: Context Clues

**Context,** the words and phrases surrounding a word, can help you understand new words. When you are confused by an unfamiliar word, **reread and read ahead** for context clues.

Once you have figured out a possible meaning, *verify* the meaning by inserting it in place of the unfamiliar word. Reread the sentence. If it makes sense, the meaning you chose is probably correct. If the sentence does not make sense, read ahead to look for additional context clues, or consult a dictionary.

### Using the Strategy: Context Clues Chart

This **context clues chart** shows types of context clues. Use it to help you identify context clues surrounding an unfamiliar word.

| Comparison/ Contrast | Restatement | Definition | Example |
|---|---|---|---|
| I *never shop* anymore, but last year I was a shopping <u>enthusiast</u>. | Do not <u>veto</u> our request. Your *rejection* can hurt many people. | The <u>tare</u> of the truck, *its weight when empty*, was ten tons. | She <u>agonized</u>, *biting her nails*, *sleeping poorly*, and *crying*. |

## Literary Analysis: Figurative Language

**Figurative language** is writing or speech that is not meant to be taken literally. The use of figurative language can help poets set a mood, convey a tone, and create imagery. Figurative language includes these *figures of speech*:

- A **simile** compares two apparently unlike things using the words *like* or *as*: *His eyes were as black as coal.*

- A **metaphor** compares two apparently unlike things by saying that one thing *is* the other: *The world is my oyster.*

- **Personification** is a comparison in which a nonhuman subject is given human characteristics: *The trees toss in their sleep.*

As you read, notice the way figurative language allows writers to present ideas in fresh, unusual ways.

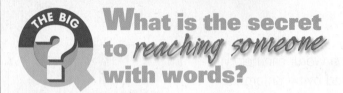

**THE BIG ?**

# What is the secret to *reaching someone* with words?

## Writing About the Big Question

In Collection 3, three poets carefully craft their words to help us experience life in the big city. Use this sentence starter to develop your ideas about the Big Question.

Even if you have never been to a place, a talented poet can help you **experience** how it might feel to be there by _____.

**While You Read** Notice how the poets reach out to readers by using their skill with words.

## Vocabulary

Read each word and its definition. Decide whether you know the word well, know it a little bit, or do not know it at all. After you read, see how your knowledge of each word has increased.

- **ponderous** (pän´ dər əs) *adj.* very heavy (p. 675) *We heard his ponderous footsteps echoing in the stairwell.* ponderously *adv.* ponder *v.*

- **bellow** (bel´ ō) *v.* make a deep, loud sound like a bull (p. 675) *Listen to him bellow like an injured animal when the doctor injects the needle.* bellowing *adj.*

- **urban** (ʉr´ bən) *adj.* related to the city or city life (p. 675) *Skyscrapers lined the urban landscape.* suburban *adj.* urbanite *n.* urbane *adj.*

- **roam** (rōm) *v.* go aimlessly; wander (p. 677) *We keep our cat inside so she will not roam.* roamer *n.*

- **dew** (do͞o) *n.* tiny drops of moisture that condense on cooled objects at night (p. 677) *We sat down on a grassy slope, damp with dew, to gaze at the stars.* dewy *adj.* dewpoint *n.*

### Word Study

The **Latin suffix -ous** means "full of" or "characterized by."

In the poem "Concrete Mixers," the poet describes the vehicles as **ponderous**, very heavy or full of weight, like elephants.

# Patricia Hubbell

**(b. 1928)**

**"Concrete Mixers"** (page 675)

Patricia Hubbell began writing poetry when she was ten years old. She liked to sit in a tree and look down on her family's farm, where she often saw things she would capture later in verse. Hubbell, who has been writing poetry and children's books for more than forty years, explains "Poem ideas are everywhere; you have to listen and watch for them."

# Langston Hughes

**(1902–1967)**

**"Harlem Night Song"** (page 677)

One of Langston Hughes's most famous poems, "The Negro Speaks of Rivers," was written while traveling on a train to visit his father in Mexico. Fresh out of high school, Hughes was making the trip to convince his father to pay for a writing program at Columbia University. His father agreed, and Hughes's writing career was launched. Though he remained at Columbia for only a year, Hughes developed a lifelong love for the New York neighborhood of Harlem, the setting of many of his stories, poems, and plays.

# Richard García

**(b. 1941)**

**"The City Is So Big"** (page 678)

Richard García has been writing poetry since the 1950s. He published his first poetry collection in 1973, but then stopped writing for six years. An encouraging letter from Nobel Prize winner Octavio Paz inspired him to write again. In addition to writing, García was the Poet-in-Residence for years at the Children's Hospital in Los Angeles, where he led poetry and art workshops for hospitalized children.

# Concrete Mixers

## Patricia Hubbell

The drivers are washing the concrete mixers;
Like elephant tenders they hose them down.
Tough gray-skinned monsters standing ponderous,
Elephant-bellied and elephant-nosed,
5  Standing in muck up to their wheel-caps,
Like rows of elephants, tail to trunk.
Their drivers perch on their backs like mahouts,[1]
Sending the sprays of water up.
They rid the trunk-like trough of concrete,
10  Direct the spray to the bulging sides,
Turn and start the monsters moving.
      Concrete mixers
      Move like elephants
      Bellow like elephants
15        Spray like elephants
    Concrete mixers are urban elephants,
    Their trunks are raising a city.

---

1. **mahouts** (mə houts´) *n.* in India and the East Indies, an elephant driver or keeper.

◀ **Critical Viewing**
What details in this picture of cement mixers
support the comparison in the poem? **[Connect]**

**Context Clues**
Reread lines 1–8. What context clues help reveal the meaning of *muck*? Explain.

**Spiral Review**
**Tone** In line 4, the concrete mixers are referred to as "elephant-bellied" and "elephant-nosed." What tone does this metaphor suggest?

**Vocabulary**
**ponderous** (pän´ dər əs) *adj.* very heavy

**bellow** (bel´ ō) *v.* make a deep, loud sound like a bull

**urban** (ʉr´ bən) *adj.* related to the city or city life

# HARLEM *Night Song*

## Langston Hughes

Come,
Let us **roam** the night together
Singing.

I love you.

5   Across
The Harlem roof-tops
Moon is shining.
Night sky is blue.
Stars are great drops
10  Of golden **dew**.

Down the street
A band is playing.

I love you.

Come,
15  Let us roam the night together
Singing.

# The City Is So Big

## Richard García

**Context Clues**
Which words help you confirm that *quake* means "tremble"?

The city is so big
Its bridges quake with fear
I know, I have seen at night

The lights sliding from house to house
5　And trains pass with windows shining
Like a smile full of teeth

I have seen machines eating houses
And stairways walk all by themselves
And elevator doors opening and closing
10　And people disappear.

## Critical Thinking

Cite textual evidence to support your responses.

1. **Key Ideas and Details (a)** In "Concrete Mixers," where are the drivers as they wash the mixers? **(b) Interpret:** How does the poet show the mixers' size?

2. **Key Ideas and Details (a)** In "Harlem Night Song," which phrases are repeated? **(b) Analyze:** How does the repetition emphasize the joyful mood of the poem?

3. **Key Ideas and Details (a)** In "The City Is So Big," what three unusual events does the speaker say he has seen? **(b) Interpret:** In your own words, explain what the speaker has actually seen.

4. **Integration of Knowledge and Ideas** How does each poet use language to communicate the sights, sounds, and experiences of a city? *[Connect to the Big Question: What is the secret to reaching someone with words?]*

## Reading Skill: Context Clues

**1.** Using the **context** surrounding the word *trough* in line 9 of "Concrete Mixers," explain what a trough looks like and what it does on a concrete mixer.

**2.** Read the text before and after the term *elephant tenders* in line 2 of "Concrete Mixers." **(a)** What do you think this term means? **(b)** Explain your reasoning.

## Literary Analysis: Figurative Language

**3. Craft and Structure** Use a chart like the one shown to analyze examples of **figurative language** in each poem.

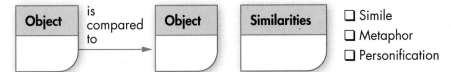

☐ Simile
☐ Metaphor
☐ Personification

**4. Craft and Structure** In a small group, review your charts. Discuss how the poets' use of figurative language appeals to the readers' senses and emotions. Then, evaluate which poem makes the most effective use of figurative language.

## Vocabulary

**Acquisition and Use** Based on your knowledge of the italicized words, answer the following questions. Explain your responses.

**1.** If you wanted to *roam,* where might you go?

**2.** What emotion might a *ponderous* sigh reveal?

**3.** Why might someone choose to live in an *urban* location?

**4.** In what types of situations might it be impolite to *bellow*?

**5.** Where are you most likely to find *dew*?

**Word Study** Use the context and what you know about the **Latin suffix -ous** to explain your answer to each question.

**1.** Which is more *nutritious,* a carrot or a marshmallow?

**2.** Do good athletes follow a *rigorous* training schedule?

### Word Study

The **Latin suffix -ous** means "full of" or "characterized by."

**Apply It** Explain how the suffix *-ous* contributes to the meanings of these words. Consult a dictionary if necessary.

**glorious**
**omnivorous**
**outrageous**

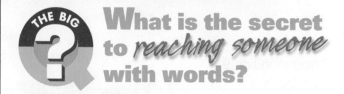

**THE BIG ?**

## What is the secret to *reaching someone* with words?

## Writing About the Big Question

In Collection 4, three poets reach out to readers as they share their ideas about nature. Use these sentence starters to develop your ideas about the Big Question.

Written works about nature that get the most positive **feedback** from me are ones that _____. This is because those writers **express** _____.

**While You Read** Look for ways the poets use words to convey their unique thoughts and ideas to readers.

## Vocabulary

Read each word and its definition. Decide whether you know the word well, know it a little bit, or do not know it at all. After you read, see how your knowledge of each word has increased.

- **uneasily** (un ēz´ ə lē) *adv.* restlessly (p. 683) *Awake, she tossed uneasily all night.* uneasy *adj.*

- **unresponsive** (un ri spän´ siv) *adj.* not reacting (p. 683) *Her illness was unresponsive to treatment.* unresponsively *adv.* unresponsiveness *n.* respond *v.*

- **boulevard** (bool´ ə värd´) *n.* wide road (p. 683) *We walked along the boulevard, in the shade of huge oak trees.*

- **cicada** (si cā´ də) *n.* large, flying insect; the male makes a loud, high-pitched noise (p. 685) *Like grasshoppers and crickets, a cicada makes noise by rubbing parts of its body together.*

- **rut** (rut) *n.* a groove in the ground (p. 686) *I fell off my bike when I hit a rut in the road.* rutted *adj.*

- **debates** (dē bāts´) *v.* tries to decide (p. 686) *Tim debates whether to go out or stay in.* debate *n.* debatable *adj.*

### Word Study

The **Latin suffix -ive** indicates a tendency toward something.

In the poem "Little Exercise," the poet describes the islands of mangrove trees as **unresponsive**, because they do not tend to respond to the power of the storm.

# Elizabeth Bishop

**(1911–1979)**

**"Little Exercise"** (page 683)

Although she was born in Massachusetts, Elizabeth Bishop was raised by her grandparents in Nova Scotia, Canada. During her life, she lived and taught at various times in Europe, Brazil, New York City, and Boston. In thirty-five years, she published five volumes of poetry and won nearly every major American poetry award, including the National Book Award.

# Pablo Neruda

**(1904–1973)**

**"Ode to Enchanted Light"** (page 685)

Chile's most acclaimed poet, Pablo Neruda won the Nobel Prize for Literature in 1971. Many of his poems are meditations on nature or on love. The son of a teacher and a railway worker, Neruda was a larger-than-life figure who inspired the Italian movie *Il Postino (The Postman)*, in which a shy postal worker seeks the famous poet's romantic advice.

# Emily Dickinson

**(1830–1886)**

**"The Sky Is Low, the Clouds Are Mean"** (page 686)

Emily Dickinson considered books her "strongest friend." Withdrawn and shy, she spent most of her time at home in Amherst, Massachusetts, reading and writing. Most of her 1,775 poems were discovered after her death, including one that begins "I'm nobody! Who are you?" She may have considered herself a "nobody" during her lifetime, but she is now considered one of the most important American poets.

# Little Exercise

## Elizabeth Bishop

Think of the storm roaming the sky uneasily
like a dog looking for a place to sleep in,
listen to it growling.

Think how they must look now, the mangrove keys[1]
5   lying out there unresponsive to the lightning
in dark, coarse-fibered[2] families,

where occasionally a heron may undo his head,
shake up his feathers, make an uncertain comment
when the surrounding water shines.

10   Think of the boulevard and the little palm trees
all stuck in rows, suddenly revealed
as fistfuls of limp fish-skeletons.

It is raining there. The boulevard
and its broken sidewalks with weeds in every crack,
15   are relieved to be wet, the sea to be freshened.

Now the storm goes away again in a series
of small, badly lit battle-scenes,
each in "Another part of the field."[3]

Think of someone sleeping in the bottom of a row-boat
20   tied to a mangrove root or the pile of a bridge;
think of him as uninjured, barely disturbed.

---

1. **mangrove keys** little islands where mangrove trees grow. Mangrove trees (shown in the photo at left) have large tangled roots that provide shelter for many types of animals.
2. **coarse-fibered** having a structure of rough-textured strands.
3. **"Another part of the field"** Stage directions in plays, such as Shakespeare's *Macbeth*, often use this phrase to switch the action to a different location in a big battle.

**Vocabulary**
**uneasily** (un ēz´ ə lē) *adv.* restlessly

**unresponsive** (un´ ri spän´ siv) *adj.* not reacting

**Context Clues**
Read ahead from the word *heron* in line 7. Which words help you confirm what type of animal a heron is?

**Vocabulary**
**boulevard** (bool´ ə värd´) *n.* wide road

# Ode to Enchanted Light

## Pablo Neruda

Under the trees light
has dropped from the top of the sky,
light
like a green
5   latticework of branches,
shining
on every leaf,
drifting down like clean
white sand.

10   A cicada sends
its sawing song
high into the empty air.

The world is
a glass overflowing
15   with water.

**Figurative Language**
What figure of speech
is used in lines 3–5?
Explain.

**Vocabulary**
**cicada** (si cā´ də) *n.*
large, flying insect; the
male makes a loud,
high-pitched noise

# THE SKY IS LOW, THE CLOUDS ARE MEAN

## Emily Dickinson

**Vocabulary**
**rut** (rut) *n.* a groove in the ground
**debates** (dē bāts´) *v.* tries to decide

The sky is low, the clouds are mean,
A travelling flake of snow
Across a barn or through a rut
Debates if it will go.

5   A narrow wind complains all day
How some one treated him;
Nature, like us, is sometimes caught
Without her diadem.[1]

---

**1. diadem** (dī´ ə dem´) *n.* crown.

## Critical Thinking

Cite textual evidence to support your responses.

**1. Key Ideas and Details (a)** Who is the one person included in "Little Exercise"? **(b) Compare and Contrast:** How do that person's surroundings contrast with his behavior? **(c) Speculate:** Why is it unimportant whether he is "tied to a mangrove root or the pile of a bridge"?

**2. Key Ideas and Details Infer:** What could "Little Exercise" be considered a "little exercise" in?

**3. Key Ideas and Details (a) Forms of Poetry:** Review page 639. What makes Neruda's poem an ode? **(b) Analyze:** What is his purpose when he describes the world as "a glass overflowing with water"?

**4. Key Ideas and Details Interpret:** In "The Sky Is Low, the Clouds Are Mean," what mood do the words *rut, complain,* and *mean* convey?

**5. Integration of Knowledge and Ideas** In each poem, how does the poet appeal to the reader's mind, emotions, or both? Explain. *[Connect to the Big Question: What is the secret to reaching someone with words?]*

# After You Read
## Poetry Collection 4

**Little Exercise •
Ode to Enchanted Light •
The Sky Is Low, the Clouds
Are Mean**

## Reading Skill: Context Clues

1. The word *pile* (line 20) of "Little Exercise" is used in an unusual way. **(a)** Use **context clues** to determine a possible meaning. **(b)** Explain your reasoning.

2. Read the text before and after *latticework* (line 5) in "Ode to Enchanted Light." **(a)** What might this term mean? **(b)** Explain your reasoning, and then confirm your definition using a dictionary.

## Literary Analysis: Figurative Language

© **3. Craft and Structure** Use a chart to analyze the **figurative language** in each poem.

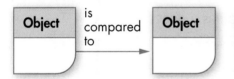 

☐ Simile
☐ Metaphor
☐ Personification

© **4. Craft and Structure** In a small group, review your charts. Discuss how the poets' use of figurative language appeals to the readers' senses and emotions. Then, evaluate which poem makes the most effective use of figurative language.

## Vocabulary

© **Acquisition and Use** Based on your knowledge of the italicized words, answer the following questions.

1. What should a customer do if a salesperson is *unresponsive*?
2. What kind of road surfaces get very few *ruts*?
3. How is a *boulevard* different from an alley or a lane?
4. What decision on a trip might cause a family to *debate*?
5. What situation might cause someone to wait *uneasily*?

**Word Study** Use context and what you know about the **Latin suffix *-ive*** to explain your answer to each question.

1. Does an *active* person keep busy or just sit around?
2. Is taking the *initiative* a sign of leadership?

### Word Study

The **Latin suffix *-ive*** shows a tendency toward something.

**Apply It** Explain how the suffix *-ive* contributes to the meanings of these words. Consult a dictionary if necessary.

**argumentative
disruptive
massive**

# Integrated Language Skills

## Poetry Collections 3 and 4

**Poetry Collection 3**

### Conventions: Direct and Indirect Objects

A **direct object** is a noun or pronoun that receives the action of a verb and answers the question *Whom?* or *What?*

An **indirect object** is a noun or pronoun that comes after an action verb and answers the question *To whom?*, *For whom?*, *To what?*, or *For what?*

**Poetry Collection 4**

| Direct Object | Indirect Object |
|---|---|
|       S    V         DO |       S    V   IO      DO |
| **Sentence:** Bill baked some cookies. | **Sentence:** Bill baked Marissa some cookies. |
| **Baked what?**      cookies | **Baked for whom?**    Marissa |

A sentence cannot have an indirect object unless it also has a direct object. To find the indirect object, first find the direct object. Then, ask one of the four indirect object questions above.

**Practice A** In each sentence, identify the subject (S), verb (V), direct object (DO), and indirect object (IO). Some sentences do not include indirect objects.

1. Patricia Hubbell gives her readers a colorful impression of concrete mixers.
2. The "trunks" of the concrete mixers build the city.
3. Langston Hughes writes a love poem.
4. The elevated trains add light to the city.

© **Reading Application** Find two lines of poetry in Collection 3 that have direct objects. Identify the verb and the direct object in each.

**Practice B** In each sentence, identify the subject (S), verb (V), direct object (DO), and indirect object (IO), if there is one. Then rewrite each sentence with a different direct object.

1. Neruda's poem gives us beautiful images.
2. The storm showed the poet a new view of the islands.
3. Emily Dickinson watched the snowflakes.
4. Elizabeth Bishop offers her readers a "Little Exercise."

© **Writing Application** Write two sentences, each with a direct object and an indirect object, about one of the poems you read.

**PH** **WRITING COACH** Further instruction and practice are available in *Prentice Hall Writing Coach.*

# Writing

**Poem** Write a **study for a poem** about one of two settings—a busy city or the countryside. Your study should plan for the figurative language that will work best in your poem. If you wish, use one of the poems in Poetry Collection 3 or 4 as a model.

- List the objects, sights, and sounds that come to mind when you think about a bustling city scene or a natural landscape.
- Review the poems and the figurative language the poets use. To think of fresh ways to describe the items in your list, use this sentence starter: _____ *is like* _____ *because* _____ .
- Jot down several ideas. Then, choose one or two you like best.
- In a few sentences, explain your plan. Include details about the comparisons and figurative language your poem will present.

**Grammar Application** Use punctuation, such as commas and periods, for effect in your poem.

**Writing Workshop:** *Work in Progress*

**Prewriting for Argumentative Texts** Review your Problem-and-Solution List. Choose one problem and set of solutions that you would like to explore further. Research this problem and its possible solutions, and write a quick summary of your findings. Then, save this Research Summary in your writing portfolio.

# Research and Technology

 **Build and Present Knowledge** Different poems speak to different people. Follow your own personal interests to help you create a **mini-anthology**, a collection of three poems on a similar topic or theme. Follow these steps:

- First, choose a topic or theme that speaks to you, such as the beauty of the natural world or the thrill of sports.
- Next, visit your library or browse the Internet to research poems on this subject or theme.
- After you have selected three poems you like, write an introduction defending why you chose each one and how it affected you. Include your own interpretation of the poets' use of literary devices, such as figurative language.
- To complete the anthology, design a cover with drawings or use appropriate software to create graphics that are inspired by your response to one of the poems.

 **Common Core State Standards**

**L.8.1; W.8.1, W.8.4, W.8.9**
[For the full wording of the standards, see page 670.]

Use this prewriting activity to prepare for the **Writing Workshop** on page 708.

**PHLit Online!**
www.PHLitOnline.com
- Interactive graphic organizers
- Grammar tutorial
- Interactive journals

# Test Practice: Reading

## Context Clues

### Fiction Selection

**Directions:** *Read the selection. Then, answer the questions.*

In the early days, Cat walked upright on two legs and swam as naturally as any ocean creature. But Cat was boastful, with far too much *pride* for his own good. "Ha!" he said to Dog, "You must *lumber* clumsily on four legs. I stride *elegantly* on two. You are inferior to me." To Turtle, he said, "Ha! I glide sleekly through the crests and curls of waves like a true *aquatic* creature. You struggle through the water. A wave easily flips you over—and then you *flounder* with your legs in the air!"

"Enough!" boomed the Great Mother. "Cat, your bragging has gone too far. You will no longer walk on two legs or be a graceful swimmer." The Great Mother's *reprimand* didn't tame the Cat's *arrogance* completely. Although today Cat walks on four legs and fears the water, he still remains quite pleased with himself!

1. The word *lumber* most nearly means—
   A. to stand upright.
   B. to swim with grace and speed.
   C. to walk or move in a clumsy way.
   D. to quickly climb to the top of a tree.

2. Which of the following is the closest **antonym** of *elegantly*?
   A. awkwardly
   B. fearfully
   C. swiftly
   D. gracefully

3. Which of the following context clues *best* helps you determine the meaning of *aquatic*?
   A. creature
   B. crests and curls of waves
   C. struggle through
   D. easily flips

4. What type of context clue in the passage helps you determine that *flounder* means "thrash about wildly"?
   A. contrast
   B. explanation/example
   C. sentence role
   D. comparison

### Writing for Assessment

Interpret the meaning of either *reprimand* or *arrogance*, based on context. In a one-paragraph response, explain how context clues in the selection help you understand the word you chose.

## Nonfiction Selection

**Directions:** *Read the selection. Then, answer the questions.*

(1) When it comes to eating, cats are *carnivorous*. (2) Unlike animals that eat only plants, or animals that eat a little of everything, cats eat only meat. (3) They are also *predators*, animals that hunt prey. (4) Members of the cat family include lions, tigers, cheetahs, leopards, and jaguars. (5) Although most kinds of wild cats are *nocturnal*, a few are more active during the day. (6) Most cats are *solitary* hunters, traveling alone. (7) Some, such as lions, live in groups. (8) A lion *pride* may include up to twenty individuals.

**1.** Which phrase from sentence 2 helps you most in determining the meaning of *carnivorous* in sentence 1?
   **A.** unlike animals
   **B.** eat only plants
   **C.** eat a little of everything
   **D.** eat only meat

**2.** What type of context clue is represented by the phrase that immediately follows the word *predators*?
   **A.** definition
   **B.** contrast
   **C.** comparison
   **D.** example

**3.** Which of the following context clues helps you determine the meaning of *nocturnal*?
   **A.** traveling alone
   **B.** members of the cat family
   **C.** animals that hunt prey
   **D.** more active during the day

**4.** The word *solitary* most nearly means—
   **A.** alone
   **B.** in a group
   **C.** together
   **D.** linked

## Writing for Assessment

**Connecting Across Texts**
In a two-paragraph explanation, describe how you can use context clues to help determine the meaning of *pride* in each selection. Be sure to provide specific examples of context clues in your writing.

www.PHLitOnline.com
- Online practice
- Instant feedback

# Reading for Information

## Analyzing Functional Texts

| Recipe | Product Information | Menu |
|--------|---------------------|------|
| 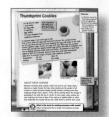 |  |  |

**Common Core State Standards**

**Reading Informational Text**
**5.** Analyze in detail the structure of a specific paragraph in a text, including the role of particular sentences in developing and refining a key concept.

**Writing**
**2.b.** Develop the topic with relevant, well-chosen facts, definitions, concrete details, quotations, or other information and examples. *(Timed Writing)*

**Language**
**6.** Acquire and use accurately grade-appropriate general academic and domain-specific words and phrases; gather vocabulary knowledge when considering a word or phrase important to comprehension or expression.

## Reading Skill: Compare and Contrast Features of Consumer Materials

Different types of documents offer different types of information. For example, a cookie recipe tells you how to make cookies, but it might not provide nutritional content. When you read **consumer materials,** note the **features and elements** and the types of information offered. As you read, use a chart like the one shown to note information that the texts have in common and information that is particular to each.

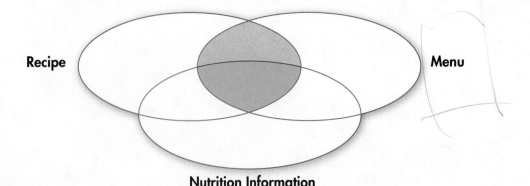

Recipe      Menu

**Nutrition Information**

## Content-Area Vocabulary

These words appear in the selections that follow. You may also encounter them in other content-area texts.

- **calories** (kal´ ər ēz) *n.* units of the energy supplied by food

- **nutrients** (nü´ trē ənts) *n.* any substances that a living thing needs to eat for energy, growth, and repair of tissues

- **cholesterol** (kə les´ tə rol´) *n.* white fatty substance found in the blood and in some foods

# Thumbprint Cookies

½ cup brown sugar
1 cup butter
2–3 egg yolks
2 cups flour
egg whites
1½ cups chopped nuts
raspberry preserves

A list of ingredients tells readers what goes into the food they will be making.

To separate eggs, crack each egg in half. Over a bowl, pour the egg back and forth between the cracked halves. Let the egg white fall into the bowl, keeping the egg yolk intact in the shell. Cream together sugar, butter, and egg yolks. Beat flour into this mixture. Form balls and dip into slightly beaten egg whites. Roll balls in chopped nuts. Put on lightly greased cookie sheet and make a thumbprint on each ball. Bake at 350° for 8 minutes. Remove from oven and reset thumbprint. Bake 8 to 10 minutes longer. Fill print with raspberry preserves.

| | | |
|---|---|---|
| Preparation: | 25 min. | Yield: 30 |
| Baking: | 18 min. | Can freeze |

Separating an egg      Using a teaspoon

Photographs and captions help to clarify the written instructions.

## ABOUT DROP COOKIES

Whoever invented drop cookies, which we used to call "drop cakes," deserves a medal. Except for bars, drop cookies are the easiest of all cookies to make, because shaping usually involves nothing more than dropping dough from a spoon. A few call for patting down the dough or spreading it out with the tip of a knife. In most cases, drop cookies are very forgiving: No harm is done if the mixture is slightly stiffer or softer than expected; the results will just be a little flatter or puffier than usual.

**Features:**

- information provided for the benefit of consumers
- numerical data
- guidelines, warnings, or recommendations regarding the use of a product
- text written for a general audience

# USE THE NUTRITION FACTS LABEL TO EAT HEALTHIER

*U.S. Food and Drug Administration*

## Nutrition Facts

Serving Size 1 cup (228g)
Servings Per Container 2

**Amount Per Serving**

**Calories** 250      Calories from Fat 110

| | **% Daily Value\*** |
|---|---|
| **Total Fat** 12g | 18% |
| Saturated Fat 3g | 15% |
| *Trans* Fat 3g | |
| **Cholesterol** 30mg | 10% |
| **Sodium** 470mg | 20% |
| **Potassium** 700mg | 20% |
| **Total Carbohydrates** 31g | 10% |
| Dietary Fiber 0g | 0% |
| Sugars 5g | |
| **Protein** 5g | |
| Vitamin A | 4% |
| Vitamin C | 2% |
| Calcium | 20% |
| Iron | 4% |

\* Percent Daily Values are based on a 2,000 calorie diet. Your Daily Values may be higher or lower depending on your calorie needs.

| | | Calories: | 2,000 | 2,500 |
|---|---|---|---|---|
| Total fat | Less than | | 65g | 80g |
| Sat fat | Less than | | 20g | 25g |
| Cholesterol | Less than | | 300mg | 300mg |
| Sodium | Less than | | 2,400mg | 2,400mg |
| Total Carbohydrate | | | 300g | 375g |
| Dietary Fiber | | | 25g | 30g |

### Check the serving size and number of servings.

- The Nutrition Facts Label information is based on ONE serving, but many packages contain more. Look at the serving size and how many servings you are actually consuming. If you double the servings you eat, you double the calories and nutrients, including the Percent Daily Values.

- When you compare calories and nutrients between brands, check to see if the serving size is the same.

The label provides information about specific nutrients found in foods.

### For protein, choose foods that are lower in fat.

- Most Americans get plenty of protein, but not always from the healthiest sources.

- When choosing a food for its protein content, such as meat, poultry, dry beans, milk and milk products, make choices that are lean, low-fat, or fat free.

### Look for foods that are rich in these nutrients.

- Use the label not only to limit fat and sodium, but also to increase nutrients that promote good health and may protect you from disease.

- Some Americans don't get enough vitamins A and C, potassium, calcium, and iron, so choose the brand with the higher Percent Daily Value for these nutrients.

- Get the most nutrition for your calories—compare the calories to the nutrients you would be getting to make a healthier food choice.

## Calories count, so pay attention to the amount.

- This is where you'll find the number of calories per serving and the calories from fat in each serving.

- Fat-free doesn't mean calorie-free. Lower fat items may have as many calories as full-fat versions.

- If the label lists that 1 serving equals 3 cookies and 100 calories, and you eat 6 cookies, you've eaten 2 servings, or twice the number of calories and fat.

> Call-out boxes help consumers understand and use the information provided.

## Know your fats and reduce sodium for your health.

- To help reduce your risk of heart disease, use the label to select foods that are lowest in saturated fat, *trans* fat and cholesterol.

- *Trans* fat doesn't have a Percent Daily Value, but consume as little as possible, because it increases your risk of heart disease.

- The Percent Daily Value for total fat includes all different kinds of fats.

- To help lower blood cholesterol, replace saturated and *trans* fats with monounsaturated and polyunsaturated fats found in fish, nuts, and liquid vegetable oils.

- Limit sodium to help reduce your risk of high blood pressure.

## Reach for healthy, wholesome carbohydrates.

- Fiber and sugars are types of carbohydrates. Healthy sources, like fruits, vegetables, beans, and whole grains, can reduce the risk of heart disease and improve digestive functioning.

- Whole grain foods can't always be identified by color or name, such as multi-grain or wheat. Look for the "whole" grain listed first in the ingredient list, such as whole wheat, brown rice, or whole oats.

- There isn't a Percent Daily Value for sugar, but you can compare the sugar content in grams among products.

- Limit foods with added sugars (sucrose, glucose, fructose, corn or maple syrup), which add calories but not other nutrients, such as vitamins and minerals. Make sure that added sugars are not one of the first few items in the ingredients list.

**Features:**
- a list of available foods
- information about foods being offered
- text written for a specific audience

# Sarasota County Schools

# Lunch Menu
## May 1, 2007

| **Tuesday** |
| --- |
| Hamburger w/ Pickles |
| Hot Dog |
| Cottage Cheese & Fruit Plate |
| Oven Fries/Baked Beans |
| Peaches/Shiny Red Apple |
| |
| Frozen Fruit Stick |

The list of available foods gives consumers several choices.

This menu includes a nutritional analysis so that consumers can make informed decisions about the foods they eat.

# Nutritional Analysis

| Menu Item | Portion | Calories | Protein | Fat | Sodium | Carbohydrates | Vitamin C |
| --- | --- | --- | --- | --- | --- | --- | --- |
| Hamburger w/ Pickles | 1 Each | 281 | 20.17g | 11.55g | 942mg | 29.98g | 0mg |
| Hot Dog | 1 Each | 280 | 10g | 16g | 800mg | 24g | 0mg |
| Cottage Cheese & Fruit Plate | 1 Each | 136 | 13.68g | 1.6g | 498mg | 18.83g | 20.64mg |
| Oven Fries | ½ cup | 78 | 1.3g | 2.61g | 16mg | 13.04g | 7.82mg |
| Baked Beans | ½ cup | 110 | 2.95g | .13g | 491mg | 25.92g | 5.81mg |
| Peaches | ½ cup | 66 | 0g | 0g | 6mg | 18g | 2mg |
| Apples | 1 Each | 81 | 0g | .5g | 0mg | 21g | 7mg |
| Frozen Fruit Stick | 1 Stick | 43 | .32g | .11g | 5mg | 10.3g | 11.78mg |

## Comparing Functional Texts

**© 1. Key Ideas and Details (a)** When you **compare and contrast the features** of the **consumer materials** you have read, what similarities do you find between the recipe and the school lunch menu? **(b)** What does the school lunch menu tell you that the recipe does not? **(c)** What does the recipe tell you that the menu does not?

## Content-Area Vocabulary

**2. (a)** Review the definitions of the words *nutrients*, *calories*, and *cholesterol*, and determine how the words are related. **(b)** Use each of the words in a brief letter to your school's principal in which you propose healthful foods for your school's cafeteria menu.

## 🕐 Timed Writing

### Informative Text: Essay

**Format**
The prompt directs you to write a brief essay. Therefore, you will need to express your ideas in three to five paragraphs.

Compare the Nutrition Facts label to the nutritional analysis in the school lunch menu. Evaluate both texts to determine which one you find more useful. Explain the results of your evaluation in a brief essay.
(30 minutes)

**Academic Vocabulary**
When you *evaluate* something, you make a judgment about its value based on examination and analysis.

### 5-Minute Planner

Complete these steps before you begin to write:

**1.** Read the prompt carefully, noting the key highlighted words.

**2.** Review the Nutrition Facts label and the nutritional analysis chart. Compare and contrast their features and elements.

**3.** Make notes about the strengths and weaknesses of each document. Consider which document is easier to use and which format is easier to read.

**4.** Based on your notes, decide which document you find more useful. Use details from your notes and from the texts as support as you draft your essay.

## Comparing Poetry and Prose

Poetry and prose are two major classifications of literature.

- **Prose** is the common form of written language. It includes both fiction and nonfiction. Stories, articles, and novels are all prose.

- **Poetry** is distinguished from prose by its use of precise words, deliberate line lengths, and sound devices such as rhythm, rhyme, and alliteration. Poems are often more indirect—hinting at meaning rather than directly stating it. This results in writing that relies more heavily on figurative language than prose and is more open to interpretation.

Although poets and prose writers use different techniques, both try to convey **mood** and meaning to the reader. Also, in both forms, vivid descriptions and details create a picture of a physical **setting**—the look of the land, or the feel of a certain time and place.

As you read these two selections, you will see that both are set in the Georgia landscape. Both have a similar **theme**—how the natural world can surprise. But their topics, moods, and styles are very different.

Analyze and compare the elements of both works using a chart like the one shown. Consider how the genre of each text—prose or poetry—helps to define its style and convey its message.

|  | Setting | Mood | Style | Theme |
|---|---|---|---|---|
| Snake on the Etowah |  |  |  |  |
| Vanishing Species |  |  |  |  |

## Common Core State Standards

**Reading Literature**

**2.** Determine a theme or central idea of a text and analyze its development over the course of the text, including its relationship to the characters, setting, and plot.

**5.** Compare and contrast the structure of two or more texts and analyze how the differing structure of each text contributes to its meaning and style.

**Writing**

**1.** Write arguments to support claims with clear reasons and relevant evidence. *(Timed Writing)*

**www.PHLitOnline.com**

- Vocabulary flashcards
- Interactive journals
- More about the authors

- Selection audio
- Interactive graphic organizers

# What is the secret to *reaching someone* with words?

## Writing About the Big Question

Both of these writers make us see how the world of nature can bring surprises, beauty, and sometimes fear or humor. Use this sentence starter to develop your ideas.

A writer can make "small" events **meaningful** by _____.

# Meet the Authors

## David Bottoms (b. 1949)

### Author of "Snake on the Etowah"

David Bottoms was born in Canton, Georgia. He grew up hiking in the southern woods and fishing in rivers like the Etowah. Those memories of rural and small-town life appear throughout his poetry. Images of water and animals such as snakes and turtles show the beauty of nature along with its dangers.

**A Distinguished Career** In 1979, when Bottoms was twenty-nine, his first full-length book, *Shooting Rats at the Bibb County Dump,* won him the Walt Whitman Award. Since then, his poems have appeared frequently. He teaches writing at Georgia State and was named Georgia's poet laureate in 2000.

## Bailey White (b. 1950)

### Author of "Vanishing Species"

Bailey White still lives in the house where she grew up, in the longleaf pine woods of Thomasville, Georgia. Local settings and characters, along with gentle humor, color her writing.

**An Old-Fashioned Storyteller** Bailey White taught grade school in south Georgia for many years but became known to thousands of people nationwide after she began reading her writing on National Public Radio. Though White travels, she likes to come home to a place "full of people whose lives I know so well that I can tell the story of every missing finger and call every old lady's cat by name."

# Snake
## on the Etowah
### David Bottoms

Kicking through woods and fields, I'd spooked several
and once stepped on a coachwhip among gravestones,
at least one garter curled like a bow
under ivy in my yard.
5  Once I even woke on the hazy bank of a lake,
wiped dew from my eyes and found
on my ankle
a cottonmouth draped like a bootlace.

I thought I knew how beauty could poison
10  a moment with fear,
but wading that low river, feet wide on rocks—
my rod hung on the backswing, my jitterbug
snagged on the sun—
I felt something brush my thigh.
15  The bronze spoon of a copperhead drifted
between my legs.

Out came the little tongue reaching
in two directions,
the head following upriver,
20  following down, then a wide undulation[1] of tail,
a buff and copper swish. The river eased
around it in a quivering V,
while inside my shudder
it slipped out—
25  spiny, cool, just below
the surface, sidling against the current.

---

**1. undulation** (un´jə lā´ shən) *n.* curvy, wavy form.

**Spiral Review**
**Imagery** How does the imagery in lines 12 and 13 create an effect of stillness?

**Vocabulary**
**sidling** (sīd´ liŋ) *v.* moving sideways in a sly manner

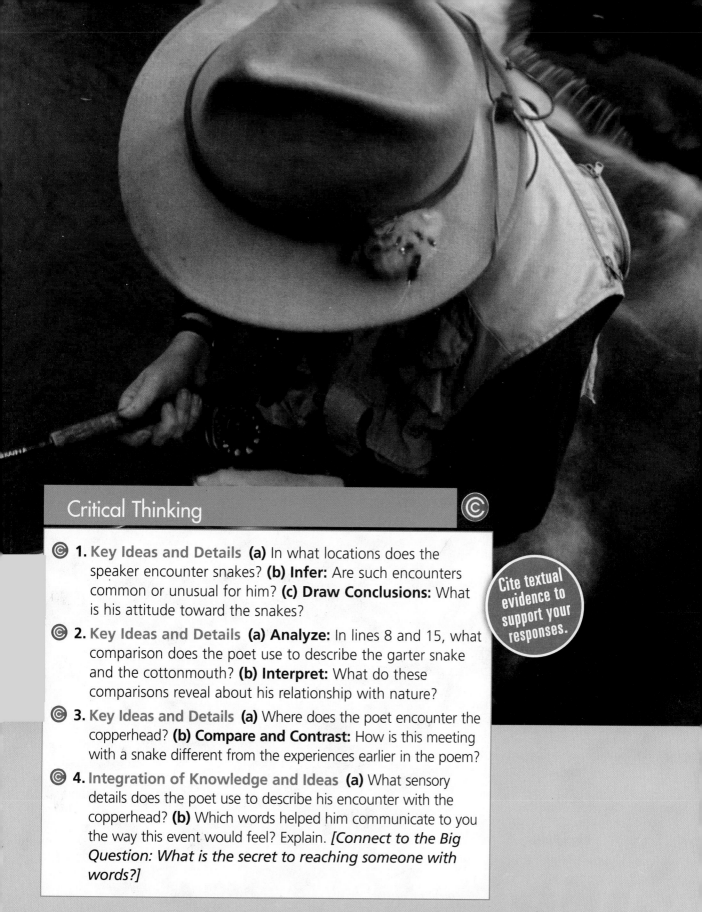

## Critical Thinking

© 1. **Key Ideas and Details (a)** In what locations does the speaker encounter snakes? **(b) Infer:** Are such encounters common or unusual for him? **(c) Draw Conclusions:** What is his attitude toward the snakes?

© 2. **Key Ideas and Details (a) Analyze:** In lines 8 and 15, what comparison does the poet use to describe the garter snake and the cottonmouth? **(b) Interpret:** What do these comparisons reveal about his relationship with nature?

© 3. **Key Ideas and Details (a)** Where does the poet encounter the copperhead? **(b) Compare and Contrast:** How is this meeting with a snake different from the experiences earlier in the poem?

© 4. **Integration of Knowledge and Ideas (a)** What sensory details does the poet use to describe his encounter with the copperhead? **(b)** Which words helped him communicate to you the way this event would feel? Explain. *[Connect to the Big Question: What is the secret to reaching someone with words?]*

Cite textual evidence to support your responses.

# Vanishing Species

## Bailey White

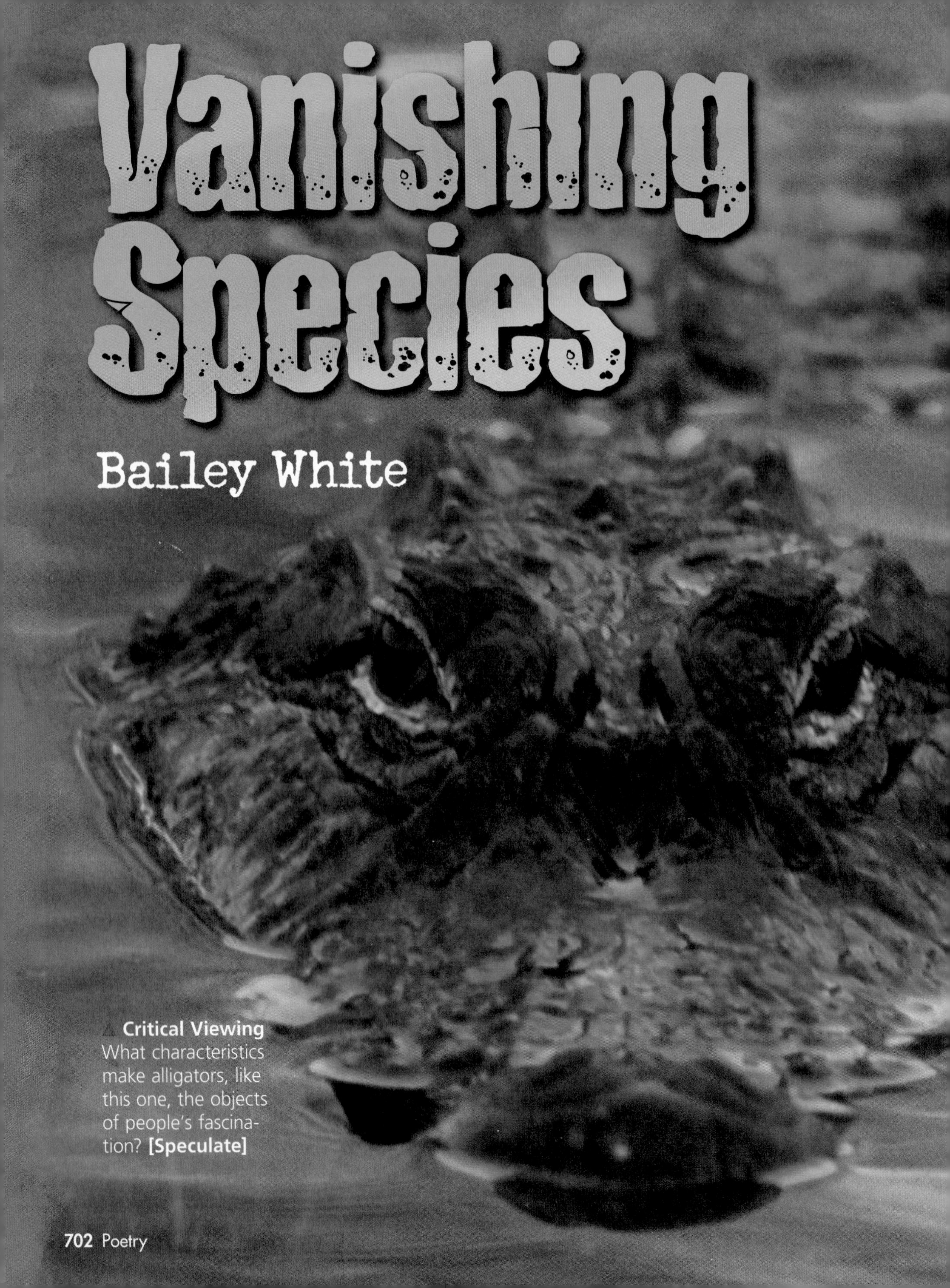

▲ **Critical Viewing**
What characteristics
make alligators, like
this one, the objects
of people's fascina-
tion? **[Speculate]**

Many years ago a man came down here with a whole station wagon full of recording equipment. He was on a quest to acquire and preserve amazing and unusual natural sounds from all over the world. He had just been in the South Seas recording Tasmanian devils, and somewhere he had heard about my aunt Belle's alligator, the one she had trained to bellow on command.

This was back in the days when alligators had been hunted to the brink of extinction,[1] and people believed that their bellow, one of the most truly majestic of all animal sounds, might soon be lost forever.

My aunt loaded Mr. Linley and all his recording equipment into her pickup truck and backed him down to the edge of the pond where the alligator lived. Then she revved up the engine a couple of times, and pretty soon here came the alligator.

**Vocabulary**
**acquire** (ə kwīr´)
*v.* get; obtain

**Reading Check**
What was unique about "aunt Belle's alligator"?

---

1. **extinction** (ek stiŋk´ shən) *n.* dying out of a species.

**The alligator**

slumped down

in the middle,

we saw the

water begin

to quiver

around his

jowls, and the

**bellowing**

began.

We hadn't been too impressed with Mr. Linley at first. He just seemed like a quiet, pale little man with quick-moving hands and a nervous flicker in his eyes. But when that alligator came crawling up out of the mud, Mr. Linley slung his tape recorder over his shoulder, plugged in a bunch of black cables, pressed RECORD, then vaulted out of the truck and went crawling down the bank to meet him. We'd never seen anyone do that before. My aunt's alligator ate things that came out of the back of that truck. He ate everything that came out of the back of that truck. But we didn't want to be recorded, so we didn't say anything.

Aunt Belle revved the engine a few more times then shut it off. A quail bird whistled. The hot engine ticked. Then we saw the alligator swell up. Mr. Linley stuck out a microphone as long as his arm, right up to those ragged jaws. The alligator slumped down in the middle, we saw the water begin to quiver around his jowls, and the bellowing began. It went on for a full two minutes. Mr. Linley didn't flinch. He held that microphone steady with all his heart.

When it ended, Mr. Linley and the alligator moved at the same time. Mr. Linley made it into the back of the truck in two leaps, but it seemed like that alligator almost took flight. He crashed into the tailgate just as Mr. Linley crashed into the back of the cab. The alligator left a big dent in the tailgate, with teeth marks scraped through the paint, and Mr. Linley left a shiny smear down the back of the cab where he rubbed the dust off as he slumped down.

We were impressed. Now we understood that nervous flicker in Mr. Linley's eyes and those quivering hands.

And now that it was all over, Mr. Linley became quite garrulous. He sat down on our porch and eagerly showed us how his equipment worked. He played back the alligator bellowing. It was amazing. It was better than the real thing. You could hear drops of water fall from the alligator's top teeth into the muddy puddle that swirled around his bottom jaw. You could hear that little pink flap of skin at the back of

his throat open up. You could hear time and distance. You could hear silence.

Then Mr. Linley played some of his other recordings for us. He played star-nosed moles snuffling on a moonlight night. He played an almost extinct worm crawling through dead leaves. He played whales, he played sharks, he played icebergs groaning.

But when he started playing his recording of Viennese cats, our dog began to howl. He was an old bird dog, tied up to his doghouse in the backyard, and he really began to do some fancy howling. It was almost like a yodel. Mr. Linley got excited.

"I've never heard a dog do that," he said.

And quick as a flash he whipped out his unidirectional microphone. The dog howled, the little needle jumped up into the red, and Mr. Linley did his work. •

After a few minutes the dog shut up. Mr. Linley began dismantling his equipment. He unplugged the cables, shoved all the levers over to the far left, and rewound the tape. Then he stopped. His hands stopped trembling. His eyes grew steady. He didn't breathe. Something was wrong. He had erased his alligator recording. He had taped the howling dog right over it.

So back we went to the edge of the pond; back Mr. Linley crawled into the mud. My aunt revved and revved the engine. But the alligator just lay there, eye to eye with Mr. Linley. He didn't raise up his tail. He didn't raise up his head. He didn't slump down in the middle. Water didn't quiver around his jowls. He just lay silent in the mud and glared at Mr. Linley.

Finally we drove back home. Mr. Linley packed up his equipment, bid us a desultory good-bye, and went off to record the courtship **rituals** of the Komodo dragon. We never heard from him again.

**Poetry and Prose**
How does White's description of the alligator recording show that it was "better than the real thing"?

**Vocabulary**
**rituals** (rich´ o͞o əlz) *n.* practices done at regular times

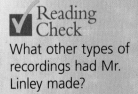
**Reading Check**
What other types of recordings had Mr. Linley made?

**Vocabulary**
**resurgence** (ri sur´ jəns)
*n.* reappearance; revival

Since then, laws protecting alligators have resulted in a resurgence in their population. They have been removed from the endangered species list. And almost any summer night in any southern swamp or river or pond you can hear alligators bellowing. We're not worried about them anymore. But I sometimes wonder whatever happened to that little Mr. Linley.

## Critical Thinking

*Cite textual evidence to support your responses.*

1. **Key Ideas and Details** **(a)** Why does Mr. Linley come to visit the narrator's aunt? **(b) Infer:** What first impression does he give? **(c) Compare and Contrast:** How does his behavior with the alligator contradict this impression?

2. **Key Ideas and Details** **(a)** Once the recording is successful, what does Mr. Linley do? **(b) Infer:** How do the narrator and her aunt react? **(c) Connect:** Why does the dog start to howl?

3. **Key Ideas and Details** **(a)** What happens to the alligator recording? **(b) Interpret:** What do Mr. Linley's reactions show about him? **(c) Speculate:** What do you think happens to Mr. Linley after this incident?

4. **Integration of Knowledge and Ideas** **(a)** How does the narrator's conversational style and descriptive language help make this story funny for readers? **(b)** What words or details helped the writer communicate the way this episode took place? Explain. *[Connect to the Big Question: What is the secret to reaching someone with words?]*

## Comparing Poetry and Prose

**©** **1. Craft and Structure** Although "Snake on the Etowah" does not have regular meter or rhyme, what characteristics of poetry does it have?

**©** **2. Craft and Structure (a)** Identify examples of figurative language such as simile and metaphor in the poem. **(b)** How do these figures of speech contribute to the mood?

**©** **3. Key Ideas and Details** In what ways does the humor in "Vanishing Species" depend on **(a)** characterization and **(b)** memorable images?

**©** **4. Key Ideas and Details** Complete Venn diagrams to compare these selections. Develop separate diagrams, like the one shown, for setting and theme.

**Snake on the Etowah**

**Differences:**
river

**Similarities:**
• Georgia
• Bodies of water

**Differences:**
pond

**Vanishing Species**

## ⏱ Timed Writing

### Argument: Analytical Essay

Write an essay supporting a claim about the relationship between genre and theme. To arrive at a claim, analyze how Bottoms and White, working in different genres, express similar themes. Compare and contrast elements such as setting, mood, and style. Then, draw conclusions about how much the genre—poetry or prose—accounts for the differences in the way the theme is presented. State this claim and support it with evidence from both texts. **(40 minutes)**

### 5-Minute Planner

**1.** Read the prompt carefully and completely.

**2.** Gather your ideas by answering these questions:
- How similar are the themes of the two works?
- How do the different writers look at and portray nature?
- What element of each work expresses the theme most clearly?

**3.** Determine your claim, which will become the basis of your essay.

**4.** Reread the prompt, and then draft your essay.

# Writing Workshop

Common Core
State Standards

**Writing**
**1.** Write arguments to support claims with clear reasons and relevant evidence.
**1.d.** Establish and maintain a formal style.

## Write an Argument

### Argument: Problem-and-Solution Essay

**Defining the Form** In a **problem-and-solution essay,** a writer identifies a problem and then offers a way to solve it. You might use elements of this type of writing in letters, editorials, and speeches.

**Assignment** Write an essay in which you identify a problem your school, community, or country faces. Then, propose an appealing solution to the problem you describe. Include these elements:

✔ a well-defined *statement of the problem and proposed solution*

✔ *evidence, examples, and reasoning that support your arguments*

✔ *support that answers readers' concerns*

✔ a structure that includes an *introduction, body, and conclusion*

✔ a *clear and formal style* with which to present your ideas

To preview the criteria on which your essay may be judged, see the rubric on page 713.

 **Writing Workshop:** *Work in Progress*

Review the work you did on pages 669 and 689.

## Prewriting/Planning Strategy

**Use a sentence starter.** Complete one of these four sentence starters to help you brainstorm for possible topics:

- Our community should fix _____.
- School would be better if____.
- I wish people would _____.
- I get annoyed when _____.

Write your endings in a cluster diagram like this one, and then choose one of the issues you have raised as your topic.

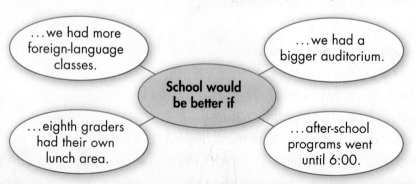

...we had more foreign-language classes.

...we had a bigger auditorium.

School would be better if

...eighth graders had their own lunch area.

...after-school programs went until 6:00.

## Generating Ideas

**Ideas** are the building blocks of all good writing. Before you begin writing, it is important to develop ideas you have about your topic. To generate ideas, try one or more of these methods:

**Accessing Prior Knowledge** Ask, "What do I already know about this problem and its possible solutions?" Jot down any relevant personal experiences, as well as ideas that you've gotten from reading.

**Brainstorming With Others** Get together with classmates and have a brainstorming session to discuss the problem and your ideas for solutions. As you brainstorm, try to be accepting of all ideas—no matter how unusual. The purpose of the brainstorming session is to list as many ideas as you can. Later, when you review your list, you can decide how many of the ideas could actually work.

**Researching** Identify and use various resources to find solutions to your problem. These resources may be books, Web pages, articles, individuals with expert knowledge, government agencies, or organizations. Focus on information related to defining your problem as well as finding solutions. For example, someone researching solutions to a water shortage in the Southeast might look at the actions of communities in the West that have faced the same problem.

**Drawing Analogies** Think about whether your problem may have similarities to another situation. By drawing analogies, or making comparisons, you can add ideas to your list. The chart shows one example in which drawing analogies helped inspire a solution.

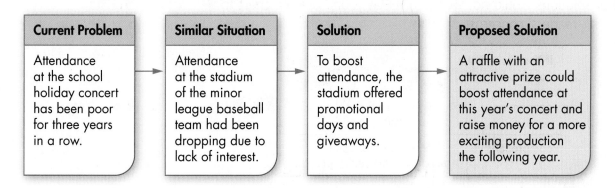

| Current Problem | Similar Situation | Solution | Proposed Solution |
|---|---|---|---|
| Attendance at the school holiday concert has been poor for three years in a row. | Attendance at the stadium of the minor league baseball team had been dropping due to lack of interest. | To boost attendance, the stadium offered promotional days and giveaways. | A raffle with an attractive prize could boost attendance at this year's concert and raise money for a more exciting production the following year. |

# Drafting Strategies

Choose the most promising ideas that come out of your prewriting and develop them into an essay using the following steps:

**Use an appropriate structure.** Set up your argument with an introduction that defines and explains the problem. Follow that up with a thesis statement that provides an outline of your proposed solution.

**Promote your solution.** Use the body of your essay to explain and "sell" your solution to readers. Present reasons for your solution and support these reasons with evidence. Some common reasons are listed in this chart.

| If a Solution Is... | It Means | Example | Support |
|---|---|---|---|
| **Economical** | It is affordable. | Fluorescent bulbs cost less money. | Statistics (cost comparison) |
| **Comprehensive** | It will solve the entire problem. | Good nutrition, exercise, and less stress help with heart problems. | Statistics and expert opinions |
| **Practical** | It can be easily carried out. | Community policing helps prevent crime. | Examples, statistics, and expert opinions |

**Offer support.** Include examples, analogies, statistics, and expert opinions as evidence that your solution makes the most sense. Be sure to indicate the weaknesses of other solutions. Finally, write a conclusion in which you restate why your solution would be effective.

# Revising Strategies

**Revise to anticipate reader concerns.** Be sure to indicate why other solutions would not work as well as yours. Use the chart to address readers' concerns.

| If You Claim Your Solution Is... | Revising Question |
|---|---|
| economical | Why are other solutions more expensive? |
| comprehensive | Why do other solutions not address the entire problem? |
| practical | Why are other solutions harder to carry out? |

**Common Core State Standards**

**Writing**
**1.a.** Introduce claim(s), acknowledge and distinguish the claim(s) from alternate or opposing claims, and organize the reasons and evidence logically.
**1.b.** Support claim(s) with logical reasoning and relevant evidence, using accurate, credible sources and demonstrating an understanding of the topic or text.
**1.c.** Use words, phrases, and clauses to create cohesion and clarify the relationships among claim(s), counterclaims, reasons, and evidence.
**1.e.** Provide a concluding statement or section that follows from and supports the argument presented.
**Language**
**1.b.** Form and use verbs in the active and passive voice.
**3.a.** Use verbs in the active and passive voice to achieve particular effects (e.g., emphasizing the actor or the action).

## Choosing Between Active and Passive Voice

In grammar, **voice** describes the verb form that shows whether the subject of a sentence is performing the action or receiving it. Your writing can be stronger when you write most sentences in the active voice.

**Identifying Active and Passive Voice** A verb is in the **active voice** when the subject performs the action. A verb is in the **passive voice** when its subject does not perform the action.

| Active Voice | Passive Voice |
|---|---|
| Lightning **struck** the barn. | The barn **was struck** by lightning. |
| My family **is painting** the house. | The house **is being painted** by my family. |

While most writing advisors prefer the active voice, the passive voice can be used to stress the action, not the performer. It can also be used when the performer is unknown.

**To show unknown performer:** *The office was closed.*
**To stress action:** *The goal was exceeded.*

**Revising for Voice** To assess your use of voice, follow these steps:

1. Locate the subject and verb in each sentence. Determine whether the subject performs the action.

2. If the subject performs the action, consider using the active voice.

   **Subject:** We            **Verb:** declare
   **Active Voice:** *We declared the experiment a success.*

3. If the performer of the action is unknown or unimportant, you might want to use the passive voice. A passive verb is a verb phrase made from a form of *be* with a past participle.

   **Subject:** unknown        **Verb:** declare
   **Passive Voice:** *The building was declared unsafe.*

### Grammar in Your Writing
Choose two paragraphs in your draft. Underline every verb and identify it as active or passive. Analyze your choices. When appropriate, rewrite sentences in the active voice.

**PH | WRITING COACH**

Further instruction and practice are available in *Prentice Hall Writing Coach.*

# Student Model: Amnesti Terrell, Memphis, TN

 Common Core
State Standards

**Language**
**2.c.** Spell correctly.

## My Neighborhood

As I look out my bedroom window, I see the whole neighborhood. I see a lot of things, both good and bad. I see children playing outside on the weekends and after school. I see parades marching through the street during the holidays. I see watchful neighbors keeping an eye on the neighborhood. All of these are great sights, but they get overlooked because of all of the problems in the neighborhood. My neighborhood used to be nice and quiet, but lately it has become worse. Fights are breaking out for no good reason, trash is littering the streets, and kids have nothing to do but hang out on the streets. Something needs to change before it is too late.

The first thing that I would like to change to improve my neighborhood is to make it safer. I want to be able to walk inside a store and not have to wait until a fight is over so I can leave. People have to stop trying to impress others by picking fights with everyone they see. I could feel safer if people were more respectful toward each other.

I also want to change the appearance of my neighborhood. There is trash everywhere. I hate having to clean up after someone else just because they do not know how to put trash into a trash can. I would also like to add some things. People in the neighborhood need a place to play and think. A playground would be a safe place for small children to play. This would be a place where the children would not have to worry about careless drivers or street fights. I would also like to build a community center for teens to have fun, play sports, and be themselves. The center would be a place that helps teens figure out that they can do anything if they put their minds to it. It could be called The Hope Center.

Finally, I would like to change the attitude toward the schools in my neighborhood. Walker Elementary and Ford Road Elementary have math and spelling bees every year, but they do not grab the headlines. Neither school gets positive recognition in the media. Positive attention would help everyone feel better about schools and the work teachers and students do.

My neighborhood is not bad. It just needs a few adjustments like any other neighborhood. So as I look out of my bedroom window, I see what it once was, what it has become, and what it has the potential to be. By committing to local safety and community spaces, we could take important steps toward improvements that can help everyone. I will do everything I can to help improve my neighborhood.

In the introduction, Amnesti clearly defines the problem in a way that conveys a sense of urgency.

She addresses possible solutions in paragraphs 2–4 by explaining three ideas to improve the quality of life in her neighborhood.

The essay uses the proper conventions of grammar, usage, and mechanics.

Amnesti organizes her essay with a conclusion that summarizes her solution.

# Editing and Proofreading

Proofread to correct errors in grammar, spelling, and punctuation.

**Focus on spelling homophones.** A **homophone** is a word that sounds the same as another word but is spelled differently. People often choose the wrong homophone if they are writing quickly and not paying close attention to spelling. If you use a computer program to write your essay, you should run a spell-check. Be extra careful with homophones, however. The spell-check will miss mistakes that occur when words like *there*, *their*, and *they're* are spelled correctly but used incorrectly.

# Publishing and Presenting

Consider one of the following ways to share your writing:

**Post your ideas.** Post your essay online or on a bulletin board, along with the essays written by other class members.

**Implement the solution.** If it is possible, carry out the solution you propose in your essay. Then, evaluate how well it worked. Write a summary of the results and post it with your essay.

# Reflecting on Your Writing

**Writer's Journal** Jot down your answer to this question:

*What did you learn about the difficulties in solving problems?*

# Rubric for Self-Assessment

Find evidence in your writing to address each category. Then, use the rating scale to grade your work.

**Spiral Review**

Earlier in the unit, you learned about **subject complements** (p. 668) and **direct and indirect objects** (p. 688). Review your essay to be sure you have used subject complements and direct and indirect objects correctly.

| Criteria | Rating Scale |
| --- | --- |
| | not very                          very |
| **Focus:** How clearly do you define the problem and proposed solution(s)? | 1  2  3  4  5 |
| **Organization:** How well do you employ an appropriate structure that includes an introduction, body, and conclusion? | 1  2  3  4  5 |
| **Support/Elaboration:** How effectively do you support your arguments with evidence, examples, and reasoning? | 1  2  3  4  5 |
| **Support/Elaboration:** How well do you anticipate reader concerns by offering counterarguments? | 1  2  3  4  5 |
| **Conventions:** How effective is your use of active and passive voice? | 1  2  3  4  5 |

## Leveled Texts

Build your skills and improve your comprehension of poetry with
texts of increasing complexity.

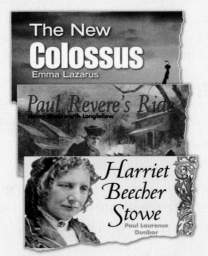

**Poetry Collection 5** explores
different emotions—
thankfulness, desperation, and
thoughtlessness.

**Poetry Collection 6** celebrates
figures and events in American
history in verse.

## Common Core State Standards

Meet these standards with either **Poetry Collection 5** (p. 718) or **Poetry Collection 6** (p. 728).

**Reading Literature**

**5.** Compare and contrast the structure of two or more
texts and analyze how the differing structure of each text
contributes to its meaning and style. (*Literary Analysis:
Forms of Poetry*)

**Spiral Review RL.8.4**

**Writing**

**3.** Write narratives to develop real or imagined experiences
or events using effective technique, relevant descriptive
details, and well-structured event sequences. (*Writing:
Lyric or Narrative Poem*)

**Speaking and Listening**

**1.** Engage effectively in a range of collaborative
discussions with diverse partners, building on others'

ideas and expressing their own clearly. (*Speaking and
Listening: Evaluation Form*)

**Language**

**1.** Demonstrate command of the conventions of standard
English grammar and usage when writing or speaking.
(*Conventions: Prepositional Phrases*)

**2.a.** Use punctuation (comma, ellipsis, dash) to indicate a
pause or break. (*Writing: Lyric or Narrative Poem*)

**4.b.** Use common, grade-appropriate Greek or Latin
affixes and roots as clues to the meaning of a word (e.g,
*precede, recede, secede*). (*Vocabulary: Word Study*)

# Reading Skill: Paraphrase

**Paraphrasing** is restating a text in your own words. When you paraphrase, you look for specific details in the text that help explain the writer's main idea or message. Then you use simpler language to express that meaning.

Paraphrasing helps you check your understanding. Before you paraphrase, **reread to clarify** meaning. Then, follow these steps:

- Identify the most basic information in each sentence.
- Restate details simply, using synonyms for the writer's words.
- Look up unfamiliar words. Replace unusual words and sentence structures with language that is more like everyday speech.

## Using the Strategy: Paraphrase Chart

Use a **paraphrase chart** to help you rephrase a writer's ideas.

| Poem | |
|------|------|
| Line from poem | |
| Basic information | |
| Paraphrase | |

# Literary Analysis: Forms of Poetry

Two major forms of poetry are lyric poetry and narrative poetry.

- A **lyric poem** uses "musical" verse to express the thoughts and feelings of a single **speaker**—the person "saying" the poem. Its purpose is to create a vivid impression in readers' minds.

- A **narrative poem** tells a story in verse and includes the elements of a short story—characters, setting, conflict, and plot.

As you read, compare and contrast the structure of each form of poetry. Poets often tap readers' prior knowledge and emotions by including **allusions**—references to people, places, or things from other artistic works.

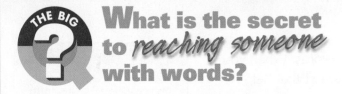

## What is the secret to *reaching someone* with words?

### Writing About the Big Question

The poems in Poetry Collection 5 were written at widely different times. Yet, they all share the characteristic of reaching readers through the emotions they convey. Use these sentence starters to develop your ideas about the Big Question.

I can find poems written in the past **relevant** as long as they _____. I do not find them relevant if they _____.

**While You Read** Look for words and phrases that trigger emotions in you.

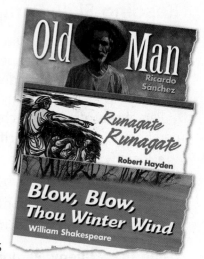

## Vocabulary

Read each word and its definition. Decide whether you know the word well, know it a little bit, or do not know it at all. After you read, see how your knowledge of each word has increased.

- **legacy** (leg´ ə sē) *n.* something physical or spiritual handed down from an ancestor (p. 718) *Norman's legacy will be the number of lives he touched.*

- **aromas** (ə rō´ məz) *n.* smells (p. 719) *Some aromas, like the smell of freshly cut grass and warm cinnamon bread, remind me of home.* *aromatic adj.*

- **supple** (sup´ əl) *adj.* yielding; soft (p. 719) *The baby's skin was soft and supple.* *suppleness n.*

- **beckoning** (bek´ ə niŋ) *adj.* calling; summoning (p. 720) *I could not resist Hawaii's beckoning breezes.* *beckon v.*

- **shackles** (shak´ əlz) *n.* metal bonds used to restrain prisoners (p. 721) *The defendant's ankles were bound together by shackles.* *shackled adj. shackle v.*

- **ingratitude** (in grat´ i tōōd) *n.* lack of thankfulness or appreciation (p. 723) *Your ingratitude makes me want to take back my gift.* *ungrateful adj. ingrate n.*

### Word Study

The **Latin prefix** *in-* means "not" or "lacking."

In "Blow, Blow, Thou Winter Wind," the speaker refers to man's **ingratitude**, or lack of thankfulness, for the gift of friendship.

## Ricardo Sánchez

**(1941–1995)**

**"Old Man"** (page 718)

Ricardo Sánchez was born in El Paso, Texas. His family had roots in Spanish, Mexican, and Native American cultures. Most of Sánchez's work explores and celebrates his rich cultural heritage. In the poem "Old Man," Sánchez offers a portrait of a grandfather he remembers with love.

## Robert Hayden

**(1913–1980)**

**"Runagate Runagate"** (page 720)

Raised in a poor Detroit neighborhood, Robert Hayden was the first African American poet appointed as Consultant of Poetry to the Library of Congress. His poetry covers a wide range of subjects—from personal remembrances to celebrations of the history and achievements of African Americans.

## William Shakespeare

**(1564–1616)**

**"Blow, Blow, Thou Winter Wind"** (page 723)

William Shakespeare is regarded by some as the greatest writer in the English language. Born in Stratford-on-Avon, a small town in England, he moved to London as a young man and spent most of his adult life there. Shakespeare was an actor, a producer, and a director. However, he is most famous for his plays and poems.

# Old Man

## Ricardo Sánchez

*El Pan Nuestro (Our Daily Bread)*, ©1905, Ramon Frade, Instituto de Cultura. Puertorriqueña, San Juan

remembrance
*(smiles/hurts sweetly)*
October 8, 1972

**▲ Critical Viewing**
What aspects of this man's appearance might help him earn the respect of others? **[Analyze]**

old man
with brown skin
talking of past
    when being shepherd
5      in utah, nevada, colorado and
        new mexico
was life lived freely;

old man,
    grandfather,
10 wise with time
running rivulets on face,
deep, rich furrows,[1]
    each one a legacy,
deep, rich memories of life . . .

**Vocabulary**
**legacy** (leg´ ə sē) *n.* something physical or spiritual handed down from an ancestor

---

**1. rivulets . . . furrows** here, the wrinkles on the old man's face.

15 "you are indio,[2]
          among other things,"
    he would tell me
          during nights spent
    so long ago
20        amidst familial gatherings
    in albuquerque . . .

    old man, loved and respected,
    he would speak sometimes
    of pueblos,[3]
25        san juan, santa clara,
          and even santo domingo,
    and his family, he would say,
          came from there:
          some of our blood was here,
30        he would say,
          before the coming of coronado,[4]
    other of our blood
          came with los españoles,[5]
    and the mixture
35  was rich,
          though often painful . . .
    old man,
    who knew earth
          by its awesome aromas
40  and who felt
    the heated sweetness
          of chile verde[6]
    by his supple touch,
    gone into dust is your body
45        with its stoic[7] look and resolution,
    but your reality, old man, lives on
    in a mindsoul touched by you . . .

    Old Man . . .

---

2. **indio** (in′ dē ō) *n.* Indian; Native American.
3. **pueblos** (pweb′ lōz) *n.* here, Native American towns in central and northern New Mexico.
4. **coronado** (kôr′ ə nä′ dō) The sixteenth-century Spanish explorer Francisco Vásquez de Coronado journeyed through what is today the American Southwest.
5. **los españoles** (lôs es pä′ nyō lās) *n.* Spaniards.
6. **chile verde** (chil′ lē ver′ dā) *n.* green pepper.
7. **stoic** (stō′ ik) *adj.* calm in the face of suffering.

# Runagate Runagate

## Robert Hayden

> **Background** The term *runagate* refers to the runaway slaves who escaped to the North from slave states via the Underground Railroad. "Conductors," or guides, led the slaves by night to appointed "stations," where they received food, shelter, and clothing.

▲ **Critical Viewing**
In this illustration, who are the *runagates* and "conductors" to which the Background refers? How can you tell? **[Apply]**

**Vocabulary**
**beckoning** (bek´ ə niŋ)
*adj.* calling; summoning

### I.

Runs falls rises stumbles on from darkness into darkness
and the darkness thicketed with shapes of terror
and the hunters pursuing and the hounds pursuing
and the night cold and the night long and the river
5  to cross and the jack-muh-lanterns[1] **beckoning** beckoning
and blackness ahead and when shall I reach that somewhere
morning and keep on going and never turn back and keep
   on going
          Runagate
             Runagate
10                Runagate

Many thousands rise and go
many thousands crossing over
          O mythic North
          O star-shaped yonder Bible city

---

**1. jack-muh-lanterns** (jak´ mə lan´ tərnz) *n.* jack-o'-lanterns, shifting lights seen over a marsh at night.

15 Some go weeping and some rejoicing
   some in coffins and some in carriages
   some in silks and some in shackles

                  Rise and go or fare you well

No more auction block for me
20 no more driver's lash for me

         If you see my Pompey, 30 yrs of age,
         new breeches, plain stockings, negro shoes;
         if you see my Anna, likely young mulatto
         branded E on the right cheek, R on the left,
25       catch them if you can and notify subscriber.²
         Catch them if you can, but it won't be easy.
         They'll dart underground when you try to catch them,
         plunge into quicksand, whirlpools, mazes,
         turn into scorpions when you try to catch them.

30 And before I'll be a slave
   I'll be buried in my grave

         North star and bonanza gold
         I'm bound for the freedom, freedom-bound
         and oh Susyanna don't you cry for me

35               Runagate

                 Runagate

      II.
   Rises from their anguish and their power,

                 Harriet Tubman,

                 woman of earth, whipscarred,
40               a summoning, a shining

                 Mean to be free

   And this was the way of it, brethren brethren,
   way we journeyed from Can't to Can.

---

2. **subscriber** (səb skrīb´ ər) *n.* here, the person from whom the slave Pompey ran away.

**Vocabulary**
**shackles** (shak´ əlz) *n.*
metal bonds used to
restrain prisoners

**Forms of Poetry**
How does the perspective of the first-person point of view change between lines 19–20 and lines 21–29?

**Forms of Poetry**
In what way is this poem an example of both lyric and narrative forms?

Reading
Check
What challenges do the runaway slaves face?

**Paraphrase**
Paraphrase lines 45–53
by describing in your
own words what is
happening.

45　Moon so bright and no place to hide,
　　the cry up and the patterollers[3] riding,
　　hound dogs belling in bladed air.
　　And fear starts a-murbling, Never make it,
　　we'll never make it. *Hush that now,*
50　and she's turned upon us, leveled pistol
　　glinting in the moonlight:
　　Dead folks can't jaybird-talk, she says;
　　You keep on going now or die, she says.

　　Wanted　　Harriet Tubman　　alias The General
55　alias Moses　　Stealer of Slaves
　　In league with Garrison　　Alcott　　Emerson
　　Garrett　　Douglass　　Thoreau　　John Brown[4]

　　Armed and known to be Dangerous

　　Wanted　Reward　Dead or Alive

60　Tell me, Ezekiel, oh tell me do you see
　　mailed Jehovah[5] coming to deliver me?

　　Hoot-owl calling in the ghosted air,
　　five times calling to the hants[6] in the air.
　　Shadow of a face in the scary leaves,
65　shadow of a voice in the talking leaves:

　　Come ride-a my train

**Paraphrase**
Paraphrase lines 67–73
by explaining what
the "train" is, where it
comes from, and where
it is going.

　　*Oh that train, ghost-story train*
　　*through swamp and savanna movering movering,*
　　*over trestles of dew, through caves of the wish,*
70　*Midnight Special on a sabre track movering movering,*
　　*first stop Mercy and the last Hallelujah.*

　　Come ride-a my train

　　　　Mean mean mean to be free.

---

**3. patterollers** (pa´ tər ôl ərz) *n.* dialect for *patrollers,* people who hunt for runaways.
**4. Garrison . . . John Brown** various abolitionists, people who were against slavery.
**5. Ezekiel** (i zē´ kē əl) **. . . Jehovah** (ji hō və) Ezekiel was a Hebrew prophet of the sixth century B.C.; *Jehovah* is another word for "God."
**6. hants** (hants) *n.* dialect term for *ghosts.*

# Blow, Blow, Thou Winter Wind

## William Shakespeare

Blow, blow, thou winter wind.
Thou art not so unkind
   As man's ingratitude.
Thy tooth is not so keen,
5  Because thou art not seen,
   Although thy breath be rude.
Heigh-ho! Sing, heigh-ho! unto the green holly.
Most friendship is feigning, most loving mere folly.[1]
   Then, heigh-ho, the holly!
10     This life is most jolly.

---

**1. feigning . . . folly** Most friendship is fake, most loving is foolish.

**Vocabulary**
**ingratitude** (in grat´ i to͞od) *n.* lack of thankfulness or appreciation

**Spiral Review**
**Analogy** What two things does Shakespeare compare in the first stanza? How are they alike?

Forms of Poetry
To what does the speaker compare the winter's chill in this lyric poem?

Freeze, freeze, thou bitter sky,
That dost not bite so nigh
    As benefits forgot.
Though thou the waters warp,[2]
15    Thy sting is not so sharp
    As friend remembered not.
Heigh-ho! Sing, heigh-ho! unto the green holly.
Most friendship is feigning, most loving mere folly.
    Then, heigh-ho, the holly!
20    This life is most jolly.

---

2. **warp** v. freeze.

## Critical Thinking

Cite textual evidence to support your responses.

1. **Key Ideas and Details (a) Interpret:** Interpret the meaning and significance of the following lines: "Old Man" (lines 8–14); "Runagate Runagate" (lines 1–2); "Blow, Blow . . ." (line 8). **(b) Discuss:** In a small group, discuss your responses. Then, share your ideas with the class.

2. **Integration of Knowledge and Ideas (a)** Compare word choice and language patterns in the contemporary poem "Old Man" with those in Shakespeare's "Blow, Blow, Thou Winter Wind." **(b)** Does the fact that the poems reflect different times influence your response to them? Why or why not? *[Connect to the Big Question: What is the secret to reaching someone with words?]*

## Reading Skill: Paraphrase

1. **(a)** What synonyms could be used for the following words and phrases in lines 44–47 of "Old Man": *gone into dust, resolution,* and *mindsoul.* **(b) Paraphrase** these lines.
2. Reread the first stanza of "Runagate . . ." **(a)** Write the lines in sentences. **(b)** Paraphrase each sentence.

## Literary Analysis: Forms of Poetry

©️ 3. **Craft and Structure** Use a chart like this one to compare and contrast the purposes and characteristics of the **lyric** and **narrative poems** in this collection.

|  | Form: lyric or narrative? | What characteristics make it lyric or narrative? | How does the form help the poet achieve his purpose? |
| --- | --- | --- | --- |
| Old Man | | | |
| Runagate… | | | |
| Blow, Blow… | | | |

©️ 4. **Craft and Structure (a)** What overall impression does "Old Man" convey? **(b)** How do the lines "remembrance / (smiles / hurts sweetly)" connect with this impression?

©️ 5. **Craft and Structure (a)** List two **allusions** in "Runagate . . ." **(b)** How might these allusions tap into emotional connections with the past?

## Vocabulary

©️ **Acquisition and Use** For each item, write a sentence that correctly uses both of the words provided.

1. prisoner; shackles
2. supple; aging
3. tantrum; ingratitude
4. aromas; cooking
5. home; beckoning
6. legacy; ancestor

**Word Study** Use context and what you know about the **Latin prefix in-** to explain your answer to each question.

1. Why would an employer fire an *incompetent* worker?
2. Should jury members focus on *insignificant* details in a trial?

## Word Study

The **Latin prefix *in-*** means "not" or "lacking."

**Apply It** Explain how the prefix *in-* contributes to the meanings of these words. Consult a dictionary if necessary.

inability
incurable
inconclusive

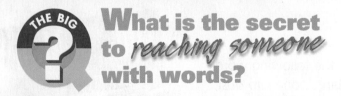

**What is the secret to *reaching someone* with words?**

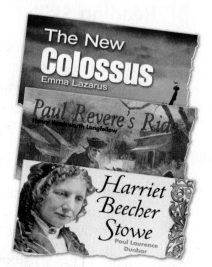

## Writing About the Big Question

The poets in Poetry Collection 6 reach out to readers by highlighting important figures and events in American history. Use this sentence starter to develop your ideas about the Big Question.

The description of an event from history needs to _____ in order to have **significance** for me.

**While You Read** Look for details that help explain why we remember and celebrate our history.

## Vocabulary

Read each word and its definition. Decide whether you know the word well, know it a little bit, or do not know it at all. After you read, see how your knowledge of each word has increased.

- **exiles** (ek´ sīlz) *n.* people who are forced to live in another country (p. 729) *During the French Revolution, exiles from France settled in the Caribbean.* exile *v.*

- **yearning** (yʉr´ nin) *v.* feeling longing; painfully wanting something (p. 729) *They watched the clock, yearning for lunchtime.* yearning *n.* yearn *v.*

- **somber** (säm´ bər) *adj.* dark; gloomy (p. 732) *It is hard to joke when you are in a somber mood.* somberly *adv.*

- **defiance** (dē fī´ əns) *n.* refusal to obey authority (p. 734) *In defiance of a court's order to return to their jobs, the workers refused to do so.* defiant *adj.* defy *v.*

- **peril** (per´ əl) *n.* danger (p. 734) *Her reckless actions put her health and safety in peril.* perilous *adj.* perilously *adv.*

- **transfigured** (trans fig´ yərd) *adj.* changed; transformed in a glorious way (p. 736) *She was glowing, transfigured by the experience of becoming a new mother.* transfiguration *n.*

### Word Study

The **Latin prefix *trans-*** means "change."

In "Harriet Beecher Stowe," the speaker suggests that both black and white Americans were **transfigured**, or changed, by the anti-slavery movement.

# Emma Lazarus

**(1849–1887)**

**"The New Colossus"** (page 728)

Emma Lazarus wrote "The New Colossus" to inspire others to donate money for the Statue of Liberty's pedestal. The final lines of the poem were so inspirational that they were permanently inscribed on the pedestal itself. Raised in New York City, where she studied languages, Lazarus published a book of poems and translations at seventeen. Later, drawing on her Jewish heritage, she wrote several works celebrating America as a place of refuge for people persecuted in Europe.

# Henry Wadsworth Longfellow

**(1807–1882)**

**"Paul Revere's Ride"** (page 731)

Henry Wadsworth Longfellow started college at age fifteen and was asked to be the first professor of modern languages at Bowdoin College at the age of nineteen. He was one of the "fireside poets," a group of writers whose popular poems were read aloud by nineteenth-century families as they gathered around a fireplace. He wrote several long poems on topics in American history.

# Paul Laurence Dunbar

**(1872–1906)**

**"Harriet Beecher Stowe"** (page 735)

Paul Laurence Dunbar was the son of former slaves. Encouraged by his mother, he began writing poetry at an early age. Dunbar was inspired by Harriet Beecher Stowe's novel *Uncle Tom's Cabin,* and in his own work he honored people who fought for the rights of African Americans.

# The New Colossus

## Emma Lazarus

**Background** The title and first two lines of Lazarus's poem refer to the Colossus of Rhodes, one of the Seven Wonders of the Ancient World. A huge statue of the sun god Helios, it was built around 280 B.C. and stood at the entrance to the harbor of the Greek island of Rhodes. At 100 feet tall, it was around three-fifths the size of our Statue of Liberty. It commemorated a great military victory but only stood for 54 years before an earthquake toppled it.

Not like the brazen giant of Greek fame,
With conquering limbs astride from land to land;
Here at our sea-washed, sunset gates shall stand
A mighty woman with a torch, whose flame
5   Is the imprisoned lightning, and her name
Mother of Exiles. From her beacon-hand
Glows world-wide welcome; her mild eyes command
The air-bridged harbor that twin cities frame.
"Keep, ancient lands, your storied pomp!"[1] cries she
10  With silent lips. "Give me your tired, your poor,
Your huddled masses yearning to breathe free,
The wretched refuse of your teeming[2] shore.
Send these, the homeless, tempest-tost[3] to me,
I lift my lamp beside the golden door!"

---

1. **pomp** (pämp) *n.* stately or brilliant display; splendor.
2. **teeming** (tēm´ iŋ) *adj.* swarming with people.
3. **tempest-tost** (tem´ pist tôst) *adj.* here, having suffered a stormy ocean journey.

Vocabulary
**exiles** (ek´ sīlz) *n.* people who are forced to live in another country

**yearning** (yʉr´ niŋ) *v.* feeling longing for; painfully wanting something

# Paul Revere's Ride

## Henry Wadsworth Longfellow

Listen, my children, and you shall hear
Of the midnight ride of Paul Revere,
On the eighteenth of April, in Seventy-five;
Hardly a man is now alive
5  Who remembers that famous day and year.

He said to his friend, "If the British march
By land or sea from the town to-night,
Hang a lantern aloft in the belfry arch
Of the North Church tower as a signal light,—
10  One, if by land, and two, if by sea;
And I on the opposite shore will be,
Ready to ride and spread the alarm
Through every Middlesex village and farm,
For the country folk to be up and to arm."

15  Then he said, "Good night!" and with muffled oar
Silently rowed to the Charlestown shore,
Just as the moon rose over the bay,
Where swinging wide at her moorings lay
The *Somerset*, British man-of-war;[1]
20  A phantom ship, with each mast and spar
Across the moon like a prison bar,
And a huge black hulk, that was magnified
By its own reflection in the tide.

Meanwhile, his friend, through alley and street,
25  Wanders and watches with eager ears,

---

**1. man-of-war** (man´ əv wôr´) *n.* armed naval vessel; warship.

◀ **Critical Viewing**
Based on this painting, what do you think the mood of this poem will be? **[Predict]**

**Forms of Poetry**
What is the conflict in this poem?

**Spiral Review**
**Figurative Language**
What does the metaphor in lines 20–21 suggest about the speaker's feelings toward the British?

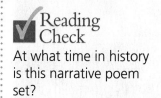

Reading Check
At what time in history is this narrative poem set?

Till in the silence around him he hears
The muster[2] of men at the barrack door,
The sound of arms, and the tramp of feet,
And the measured tread of the grenadiers,[3]
30  Marching down to their boats on the shore.

Then he climbed the tower of the Old North Church,
By the wooden stairs, with stealthy tread,
To the belfry-chamber overhead,
And startled the pigeons from their perch
35  On the somber rafters, that round him made
Masses and moving shapes of shade,—
By the trembling ladder, steep and tall,
To the highest window in the wall,
Where he paused to listen and look down
40  A moment on the roofs of the town,
And the moonlight flowing over all.

Beneath, in the churchyard, lay the dead,
In their night-encampment on the hill,
Wrapped in silence so deep and still
45  That he could hear, like a sentinel's tread,[4]
The watchful night-wind, as it went
Creeping along from tent to tent,
And seeming to whisper, "All is well!"
A moment only he feels the spell
50  Of the place and the hour, and the secret dread
Of the lonely belfry and the dead;
For suddenly all his thoughts are bent
On a shadowy something far away,
Where the river widens to meet the bay,—
55  A line of black that bends and floats
On the rising tide, like a bridge of boats.

Meanwhile, impatient to mount and ride,
Booted and spurred, with a heavy stride
On the opposite shore walked Paul Revere.
60  Now he patted his horse's side,
Now gazed at the landscape far and near,
Then, impetuous,[5] stamped the earth,

**Vocabulary**
**somber** (säm´ bər)
*adj.* dark; gloomy

▼ **Critical Viewing**
What would make the Old North Church, shown here, a good place from which to signal Revere? **[Speculate]**

---

2. **muster** (mus´ tər) *n.* assembly of troops summoned for inspection, roll call, or service.
3. **grenadiers** (gren´ ə dirz´) *n.* members of a special regiment or corps.
4. **sentinel's** (sent´ 'n əlz) **tread** (tred) footsteps of a guard.
5. **impetuous** (im pech´ ōō əs) *adj.* done suddenly with little thought.

And turned and tightened his saddle-girth;[6]
But mostly he watched with eager search
65 The belfry-tower of the Old North Church,
As it rose above the graves on the hill,
Lonely and spectral and somber and still.
And lo! as he looks, on the belfry's height
A glimmer, and then a gleam of light!
70 He springs to the saddle, the bridle he turns,
But lingers and gazes, till full on his sight
A second lamp in the belfry burns!

A hurry of hoofs in a village street,
A shape in the moonlight, a bulk in the dark,
75 And beneath, from the pebbles, in passing, a spark
Struck out by a steed flying fearless and fleet:
That was all! And yet, through the gloom and the light,
The fate of a nation was riding that night;
And the spark struck out by that steed in his flight,
80 Kindled the land into flame with its heat.

He has left the village and mounted the steep,
And beneath him, tranquil and broad and deep,
Is the Mystic,[7] meeting the ocean tides;
And under the alders that skirt its edge,
85 Now soft on the sand, now loud on the ledge,
Is heard the tramp of his steed as he rides.

It was twelve by the village clock,
When he crossed the bridge into Medford town.
He heard the crowing of the cock,
90 And the barking of the farmer's dog,
And felt the damp of the river fog,
That rises after the sun goes down.

It was one by the village clock,
When he galloped into Lexington.
95 He saw the gilded weathercock
Swim in the moonlight as he passed,
And the meeting-house windows, blank and bare,
Gaze at him with a spectral glare,
As if they already stood aghast
100 At the bloody work they would look upon.

---

6. **saddle-girth** (gᵊrth) *n.* band put around the belly of a horse for holding a saddle.
7. **Mystic** (mis´ tik) river in Massachusetts.

**Paraphrase**
Paraphrase this stanza by identifying what is happening and who is participating in the action.

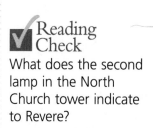
**Reading Check**
What does the second lamp in the North Church tower indicate to Revere?

It was two by the village clock,
When he came to the bridge in Concord town.
He heard the bleating of the flock,
And the twitter of birds among the trees,
105 And felt the breath of the morning breeze
Blowing over the meadows brown.
And one was safe and asleep in his bed
Who at the bridge would be first to fall,
Who that day would be lying dead,
110 Pierced by a British musket-ball.

**Paraphrase**
Paraphrase this stanza by explaining who was fighting and what the result of the fight was.

You know the rest. In the books you have read,
How the British Regulars fired and fled,—
How the farmers gave them ball for ball,
From behind each fence and farm-yard wall,
115 Chasing the red-coats down the lane,
Then crossing the fields to emerge again
Under the trees at the turn of the road,
And only pausing to fire and load.

**Vocabulary**
**defiance** (dē fī′ əns) *n.* refusal to obey authority
**peril** (per′ əl) *n.* danger

So through the night rode Paul Revere;
120 And so through the night went his cry of alarm
To every Middlesex village and farm,—
A cry of defiance and not of fear,
A voice in the darkness, a knock at the door,
And a word that shall echo forevermore!
125 For, borne on the night-wind of the Past,
Through all our history, to the last,
In the hour of darkness and peril and need,
The people will waken and listen to hear
The hurrying hoof-beats of that steed,
130 And the midnight message of Paul Revere.

**Forms of Poetry**
What is the resolution of the conflict in this poem?

# Harriet Beecher Stowe

**Paul Laurence Dunbar**

**Background** Harriet Beecher Stowe is the author of *Uncle Tom's Cabin,* a classic antislavery novel. Her work, written before the Civil War, brought the horror of slavery into the public eye. When Abraham Lincoln met Stowe, he said, "So you're the little woman who wrote the book that made this great war!"

She told the story, and the whole world wept
    At wrongs and cruelties it had not known
    But for this fearless woman's voice alone.
    She spoke to the consciences that long had slept:

**Vocabulary**
**transfigured** (trans figʹ yərd) *adj.* changed; transformed in a glorious way

5   Her message, Freedom's clear reveille,[1] swept
     From heedless hovel[2] to complacent throne.
     Command and prophecy were in the tone
     And from its sheath the sword of justice leapt.
   Around two peoples swelled the fiery wave,
10     But both came forth transfigured from the flame
  Blest be the hand that dared be strong to save,
     And blest be she who in our weakness came—
     Prophet and priestess! At one stroke she gave
     A race to freedom and herself to fame.

---

1. **reveille** (revʹ ə lē) *n.* early morning bugle or drum signal to waken soldiers.
2. **heedless hovel** (hēdʹ lis huvʹ əl) small, miserable, poorly kept dwelling place.

## Critical Thinking

**Cite textual evidence to support your responses.**

1. **Key Ideas and Details (a) Interpret:** Interpret the meaning and significance of the following lines: "The New Colossus" (line 9); "Paul Revere's Ride" (lines 78–80); "Harriet Beecher Stowe" (lines 9–10). **(b) Discuss:** In a small group, discuss your responses. Then, share your ideas with the class.

2. **Integration of Knowledge and Ideas** All three of these poems were written in the nineteenth century. Review a more modern poem from earlier in this unit, such as "Describe Somebody" (p. 645) or "The Drum" (p. 663). **(a) Analyze:** How do the language patterns and word choice in these three poems compare with those found in a more contemporary poem? **(b) Evaluate:** Does the fact that the poems reflect different time periods influence your response to them? Why or why not?

3. **Integration of Knowledge and Ideas (a)** Which of these historical poems do you find the most exciting or inspiring? **(b)** Which details and elements provoke your response? *[Connect to the Big Question: What is the secret to reaching someone with words?]*

# After You Read
## Poetry Collection 6

The New Colossus •
Paul Revere's Ride •
Harriet Beecher Stowe

## Reading Skill: Paraphrase

1. **(a)** Which words in lines 3–6 from "The New Colossus" answer the questions *Whom?* or *What?* **(b) Paraphrase** the lines using a structure that is more like everyday speech.

2. Reread the second stanza of "Paul Revere's Ride." **(a)** Write the lines in sentences. **(b)** Paraphrase each sentence.

## Literary Analysis: Forms of Poetry

3. **Craft and Structure** Use a chart to compare and contrast the **lyric** and **narrative poems** in this collection.

| | Form: lyric or narrative? | What characteristics make it lyric or narrative? | How does the form help the poet achieve his or her purpose? |
|---|---|---|---|
| Colossus | | | |
| Revere's Ride | | | |
| Stowe | | | |

4. **Craft and Structure (a)** What overall impression does "The New Colossus" convey? **(b)** How does the **allusion** at the beginning connect to this impression?

5. **Craft and Structure** Review the definition of a **sonnet** on page 639. What elements of "Harriet Beecher Stowe" fit the form of a sonnet?

## Vocabulary

**Acquisition and Use** For each item, write a sentence that correctly uses both of the words or phrases provided.

1. exiles; persecution
2. homesick; yearning
3. memorial service; somber
4. defiance; authority
5. carelessly; peril
6. birth; transfigured

**Word Study** Use context and what you know about the **Latin prefix *trans-*** to explain your answer to each question.

1. How might you try to *transform* a classroom bully?
2. What might cause someone to undergo a *transition*?

### Word Study

The **Latin prefix *trans-*** means "change."

**Apply It** Explain how the prefix *trans-* contributes to the meanings of these words. Consult a dictionary if necessary.

transplant
transcribe
translation

# Integrated Language Skills

## Poetry Collections 5 and 6

### Conventions: Prepositional Phrases

**Poetry Collection 5**

A **preposition** shows the relationship between two words or phrases. A **prepositional phrase** begins with a preposition and ends with the noun, noun phrase, or pronoun that follows it. As a unit, a prepositional phrase acts like an adjective or an adverb.

| Prepositional Phrase | Explanation |
|---|---|
| The cup *of milk* tipped over. | The prepositional phrase *of milk* acts like an adjective and tells which cup. |
| The milk spilled *onto the floor*. | The prepositional phrase *onto the floor* acts like an adverb and tells where the milk spilled. |

**Poetry Collection 6**

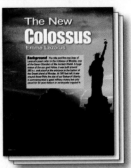

Avoid ending a sentence with a preposition in formal writing, such as reports, essays, and business letters. In some cases, the preposition is grammatically incorrect and should be omitted:

**Incorrect:** *They didn't know where he was at.*

**Correct:** *They didn't know where he was.*

In other instances, the sentence should be reworded:

**Incorrect:** *Which country did he emigrate from?*

**Correct:** *From which country did he emigrate?*

**Practice A** Identify the prepositional phrase or phrases in each sentence. Tell if the prepositional phrase acts like an adjective or adverb.

1. Harriet Tubman led many slaves to safety.
2. Many runaways escaped at night and traveled on foot.
3. The speaker has doubts about friendship.
4. He honors the memory of his grandfather.

**ⓒ Reading Application** In Poetry Collection 5, find two prepositional phrases that act as adjectives and two prepositional phrases that act as adverbs.

**Practice B** Rewrite the following sentences, adding prepositional phrases to tell more about the italicized words.

1. The Statue of Liberty is *located* ____.
2. Revere *rode* ____, warning the *citizens* ___.
3. His *ride* ____ was an important *event* ___.
4. Abolitionists like Stowe were *involved* ___.

**ⓒ Writing Application** Locate a copy of the Pledge of Allegiance and identify eight prepositional phrases it contains. For each, decide whether the phrase functions as an adjective or adverb.

**PH WRITING COACH** | Further instruction and practice are available in *Prentice Hall Writing Coach*.

# Writing

**Narrative Text** Write a **lyric or narrative poem** about an admirable person from history or from your own life.

- If you are writing a lyric poem, brainstorm for details about the person's qualities.

- If you are writing a narrative poem, list the events, characters, and details of setting you will include in the poem.

Use your notes to draft and revise the lines of your poem.

- To revise word choice in a lyric poem, look for places to add words that have a musical quality and convey strong emotions.

- To revise word choice in a narrative poem, replace dull description with dynamic language to further plot or characterization.

Punctuate based on how you want your poem to be read. For a pause or break, use a comma, an ellipsis (. . .), or a dash (—); for a full stop, use a period.

**Grammar Application** If your poem contains incomplete sentences that have only subordinate clauses, add main clauses to complete them.

### Writing Workshop: *Work-in-Progress*

**Prewriting for Exposition** For a comparison-and-contrast essay, create a chart with categories such as *literary characters, scientific processes,* or *historical events*. List several items under each heading. Think about ways the items in each list are alike and different. Circle two items to use as a focus. Save this Topic Ideas Chart.

# Speaking and Listening

**Comprehension and Collaboration** Prepare an oral presentation of one of the poems in these collections. In a group, develop an **evaluation form** for the presentations. Follow these steps:

- Identify the different qualities of an effective delivery, such as varying tone of voice, using pauses for dramatic effect, reading clearly, and adjusting reading rates.

- List categories to evaluate the poems themselves, such as choice of language and effect on the listener.

- Decide on a rating scale and a layout for your form.

- Share the form with classmates to help them prepare to read poetry aloud. Then, use it to evaluate the oral presentations.

**Common Core State Standards**

**L.8.1, L.2.a; W.8.3; SL.8.1**
[For the full wording of the standards, see page 714.]

Use this prewriting activity to prepare for the **Writing Workshop** on page 780.

**PHLit Online!**
www.PHLitOnline.com
- Interactive graphic organizers
- Grammar tutorial
- Interactive journals

##  Leveled Texts

Build your skills and improve your comprehension of poetry with texts of increasing complexity.

**Poetry Collection 7** shows how places and people can inspire joy in others.

**Poetry Collection 8** uses sensory details to bring experiences to life.

##  Common Core State Standards

Meet these standards with either **Poetry Collection 7** (p. 744) or **Poetry Collection 8** (p. 757).

**Reading Literature**
**1.** Cite textual evidence that most strongly supports an analysis of what the text says explicitly as well as inferences drawn from the text. *(Reading Skill: Paraphrase)*

**Spiral Review RL.8.4**

**Writing**
**1.** Write arguments to support claims with clear reasons and relevant evidence. *(Writing: Review)*

**8.** Gather relevant information from multiple print and digital sources, using search terms effectively; assess the credibility and accuracy of each source; and quote or paraphrase the data and conclusions of others while avoiding plagiarism and following a standard format for citation. *(Research and Technology: Profile)*

**9.** Draw evidence from literary or informational texts to support analysis, reflection, and research. *(Writing: Review)*

**Language**
**1.a.** Explain the function of verbals in general and their function in particular sentences. *(Conventions: Infinitive Phrases)*

**6.** Acquire and use accurately grade-appropriate general academic and domain-specific words and phrases; gather vocabulary knowledge when considering a word or phrase important to comprehension or expression. *(Vocabulary: Word Study)*

# Reading Skill: Paraphrase

Poetry often expresses ideas in language that does not sound like everyday speech. **Paraphrasing** is restating something in your own words. Stopping occasionally to paraphrase a line or a group of lines can clarify the meanings of words and phrases that contribute to the main ideas and improve your understanding.

- First, **read aloud fluently according to punctuation.** Pause briefly at commas, dashes, and semicolons and longer after end marks like periods to help you find units of meaning.

- Next, restate the meaning of each complete thought in your own words. Rephrase unusual or complicated expressions into simpler language, using synonyms for the writer's words.

# Literary Analysis: Imagery

A *writer's style* is his or her unique use of language. One key component of style is the use of imagery to convey ideas. **Imagery** is language that appeals to the senses. Poets use imagery to help readers imagine sights, sounds, textures, tastes, and smells.

- **With imagery:** The train thundered past, roaring, screaming.
- **Without imagery:** The train went by.

For each poem, use a chart like the one shown to note imagery.

## Using the Strategy: Sensory Web

Record details beneath each heading on a **sensory web** like this one.

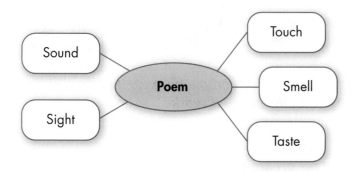

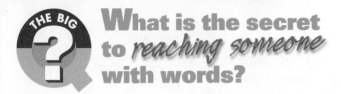

## What is the secret to *reaching someone* with words?

## Writing About the Big Question

The poets in Poetry Collection 7 carefully chose words to convey a speakers' ideas about specific people and places. Use this sentence starter to develop your ideas about the Big Question.

If someone who did not know me asked me to describe my hometown or my family, I would choose **sensory** images such as _____ and _____.

**While You Read** Notice the way the speakers of the poems connect their emotions with the sensory images that they describe.

## Vocabulary

Read each word and its definition. Decide whether you know the word well, know it a little bit, or do not know it at all. After you read, see how your knowledge of each word has increased.

- **pollen** (päl′ ən) *n.* powdery grains on seed plants that aid in reproduction (p. 746) *Insects and wind carry pollen from flower to flower.* pollinate *v.* pollination *n.*

- 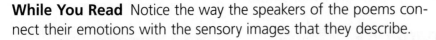 **recede** (ri sēd′) *v.* move away (p. 747) *As the clouds began to recede, the sky brightened.* receded *adj.* recession *n.*

- **inexpressible** (in′ eks pres′ ə bəl) *adj.* not able to be described (p. 751) *Words were not enough to capture his feelings of inexpressible joy.* inexpressive *adj.* expressive *adj.*

- **remote** (ri mōt′) *adj.* aloof; cold; distant (p. 752) *He was once warm and friendly, but lately he has grown remote.* remotely *adv.* remoteness *n.*

- **wearisome** (wir′ i səm) *adj.* tiresome (p. 752) *His complaining had grown wearisome and we eventually stopped working with him.* weary *adj.*

- **extinguished** (ek stiŋ′ gwisht) *v.* put out; ended (p. 752) *When he injured his knee, he saw his dream of a football career extinguished.* extinguishable *adj.*

### Word Study

The **Latin roots -cede-** and **-ceed-** mean "go" or "yield."

In the poem "New World," the speaker describes meadows that seem to **recede**, or go away, as day turns to dusk.

## John Updike

**(1932–2009)**

**"January"** (page 744)

Although he is best known as a Pulitzer Prize-winning novelist, John Updike also wrote poetry, essays, short stories, and literary criticism. As a child growing up on a farm in Pennsylvania, Updike enjoyed reading so much that his mother encouraged him to write. In 2003, Updike received the National Medal for the Humanities. He had previously won the National Medal of Art. Only a handful of writers have been honored with both prizes.

## N. Scott Momaday

**(b. 1934)**

**"New World"** (page 746)

A Kiowa Indian, N. Scott Momaday is known for his poetry, plays, art, and essays. As a writer, Momaday strives to pass on Kiowa oral traditions. His father, a great teller of Kiowa stories, inspired Momaday to write: ". . . it was only after I became an adult that I understood how fragile [the stories] are, because they exist only by word of mouth, always just one generation away from extinction."

## Alice Walker

**(b. 1944)**

**"For My Sister Molly Who in the Fifties"** (page 749)

Alice Walker, the youngest of eight children, grew up in Georgia, where her parents were farmers. She is one of the best-known and best-loved African American writers. Walker's poems frequently deal with the preservation of her culture and heritage. Her novel *The Color Purple,* was made into a movie in 1985, directed by Steven Spielberg and starred Whoopi Goldberg and Oprah Winfrey. *The Color Purple* has also been produced as a Broadway show.

# January

## John Updike

**Paraphrase**
Read lines 1–4 according to punctuation. Then, put this stanza into your own words.

The days are short,
   The sun a spark
Hung thin between
   The dark and dark.

5  Fat snowy footsteps
   Track the floor,
And parkas pile up
   Near the door.

The river is
10    A frozen place
Held still beneath
    The trees' black lace.

The sky is low.
    The wind is gray.
15 The radiator
    Purrs all day.

▲ **Critical Viewing**
Compare and contrast the artist's concept of winter with Updike's. **[Compare and Contrast]**

# NEW WORLD
## N. Scott Momaday

▲ **Critical Viewing**
What aspects of this painting convey the idea of a "new world"? **[Analyze]**

**Vocabulary**
**pollen** (päl´ ən) *n.* powdery grains on seed plants that aid in reproduction

**1.**

First Man,
behold:
the earth
glitters
5   with leaves;
the sky
glistens
with rain.
Pollen
10   is borne
on winds
that low
and lean
upon
15   mountains.
Cedars
blacken
the slopes—
and pines.

**2.**

20   At dawn
eagles
hie and
hover[1]
above
25   the plain
where light
gathers
in pools.
Grasses
30   shimmer
and shine.
Shadows
withdraw
and lie
35   away
like smoke.

---

**1. hie and hover** fly swiftly and then hang as if suspended in the air.

*Wallowa Lake, Harley,* Abby Aldrich Rockefeller Folk Art Center, Williamsburg, VA.

**3.**

   At noon
   turtles
   enter
40  slowly
   into
   the warm
   dark loam.[2]
   Bees hold
45  the swarm.
   Meadows
   recede
   through planes
   of heat
50  and pure
   distance.

**4.**

   At dusk
   the gray
   foxes
55  stiffen
   in cold;
   blackbirds
   are fixed
   in the
60  branches.
   Rivers
   follow
   the moon,
   the long
65  white track
   of the
   full moon.

**Spiral Review**
**Tone** Which words and phrases in the poem support the author's tone of wonder and majesty? Explain.

**Vocabulary**
**recede** (ri sēd´) *v.* move away

**Imagery**
What images convey a sense of the temperature in the final stanza?

2. **loam** (lōm) rich, dark soil.

# For My Sister Molly Who In The Fifties

## Alice Walker

◀ **Critical Viewing**
How would you describe the relationship between the girls in this painting? **[Infer]**

Once made a fairy rooster from
Mashed potatoes
Whose eyes I forget
But green onions were his tail

5 And his two legs were carrot sticks
A tomato slice his crown.
Who came home on vacation
When the sun was hot
and cooked

10 and cleaned
And minded least of all
The children's questions
A million or more
Pouring in on her

15 Who had been to school
And knew (and told us too) that certain
Words were no longer good
And taught me not to say us for we
No matter what "Sonny said" up the

20 road.

FOR MY SISTER MOLLY WHO IN THE FIFTIES
Knew Hamlet[1] well and read into the night
And coached me in my songs of Africa
A continent I never knew

25 But learned to love
Because "they" she said could carry
A tune
And spoke in accents never heard
In Eatonton.

**Imagery**
What do the images in the first stanza tell you about Molly?

**Reading Check**
What are two things the speaker appreciates about her sister?

---

1. **Hamlet** play by William Shakespeare.

30 Who read from *Prose and Poetry*
And loved to read "Sam McGee from Tennessee"[2]
On nights the fire was burning low
And Christmas wrapped in angel hair[3]
And I for one prayed for snow.

**Paraphrase**
Restate lines 35–42 in
your own words.

35 WHO IN THE FIFTIES
Knew all the written things that made
Us laugh and stories by
The hour          Waking up the story buds
Like fruit. Who walked among the flowers
40 And brought them inside the house
And smelled as good as they
And looked as bright.
Who made dresses, braided
Hair. Moved chairs about
45 Hung things from walls
Ordered baths
Frowned on wasp bites
And seemed to know the endings
Of all the tales
50 I had forgot.

**Paraphrase**
In your own words,
explain the growing
distance between Molly
and her siblings.

WHO OFF INTO THE UNIVERSITY
Went exploring     To London and
To Rotterdam
Prague and to Liberia
55 Bringing back the news to us
Who knew none of it
But followed
crops and weather
funerals and
60 Methodist Homecoming;
easter speeches,
*groaning* church.

---

2. **"Sam McGee from Tennessee"** reference to the title character in the Robert Service
poem, "The Cremation of Sam McGee."
3. **angel hair** fine, white, filmy Christmas tree decoration.

WHO FOUND ANOTHER WORLD
Another life        With gentlefolk
65  Far less trusting
And moved and moved and changed
Her name
And sounded precise
When she spoke        And frowned away
70  Our sloppishness.

WHO SAW US SILENT
Cursed with fear    A love burning
Inexpressible
And sent me money not for me
75  But for "College."
Who saw me grow through letters
The words misspelled        But not
The longing        Stretching
Growth
80  The tied and twisting
Tongue
Feet no longer bare
Skin no longer burnt against
The cotton.

85  WHO BECAME SOMEONE OVERHEAD
A light        A thousand watts
Bright and also blinding
And saw my brothers cloddish

**Vocabulary**
**inexpressible** (in´ eks pres´ ə bəl) *adj.* not able to be described

**Imagery**
What images describe the sensations of growing up?

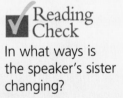Reading Check
In what ways is the speaker's sister changing?

## Vocabulary

**remote** (ri mōt´) *adj.*
aloof; cold; distant

**wearisome** (wir´ i
səm) *adj.* tiresome

**extinguished**
(ek stiŋ´ gwisht) *v.*
put out; ended

And me destined to be
90 Wayward[4]
My mother remote     My father
A wearisome farmer
With heartbreaking
Nails.

95 FOR MY SISTER MOLLY WHO IN THE FIFTIES
Found much
Unbearable
Who walked where few had
Understood     And sensed our
100 Groping after light
And saw some extinguished
And no doubt mourned.

FOR MY SISTER MOLLY WHO IN THE FIFTIES
Left us.

---

4. **wayward** (wā´ wərd) *adj.* headstrong; disobedient.

## Critical Thinking

**Cite textual evidence to support your responses.**

© 1. **Key Ideas and Details (a)** In "January," what are three things the speaker associates with January? **(b)** How does he describe these things? **(c) Draw Conclusions:** Based on these descriptions, what kind of attitude does he have toward winter? Explain.

© 2. **Key Ideas and Details (a)** In "New World," what three times of day are identified? **(b) Infer:** Why does the poet describe these times? **(c) Interpret:** What might these times represent?

© 3. **Key Ideas and Details (a)** In "For My Sister Molly Who in the Fifties," what are three things the speaker learns from Molly? **(b) Analyze:** What is the significance of these three things? **(c) Evaluate:** Why are these lessons important to her?

© 4. **Integration of Knowledge and Ideas (a)** List five images that the speaker uses to describe Molly in "For My Sister . . ." **(b)** How do these images help us understand Molly? **(c)** How do the poet's words help us appreciate the speaker's changing relationship with Molly? *[Connect to the Big Question: What is the secret to reaching someone with words?]*

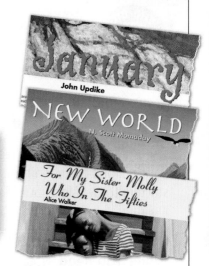

## Reading Skill: Paraphrase

**1.** Use the punctuation in lines 21–29 of "For My Sister . . ." to identify two complete thoughts. **Paraphrase** the lines.

**2.** Fill in a chart like the one shown with your paraphrases.

| Original Lines | Paraphrase |
|---|---|
| *January*: (lines 13–16) | |
| *New World*: (lines 37–45) | |
| *For My Sister Molly…*: (lines 15–17) | |

## Literary Analysis: Imagery

© **3. Craft and Structure (a)** What **imagery** does Updike use in "January" to describe winter days? **(b)** How does Updike's word choice and overall style affect the poem's meaning?

© **4. Craft and Structure (a)** What moods, or feelings, does the imagery in "For My Sister . . ." create? **(b)** How well does the free verse structure work with the images to create mood and meaning? Explain.

## Vocabulary

© **Acquisition and Use** Use a vocabulary word from page 742 to change each sentence so that it makes sense. Explain your answers.

**1.** When the rain stops, the water level will rise.

**2.** Friends grow closer if they do not see each other for years.

**3.** Bees gather petals from flowers to make honey.

**4.** When sunlight filled the room, the candles were lit.

**5.** She was so nervous, her thoughts were easy to share.

**6.** He was energized after years of backbreaking work.

**Word Study** Use context to answer each question.

**1.** Would a war's victor be likely to *cede* territory to the loser?

**2.** Would a negative review *exceed* an author's expectations?

### Word Study

The **Latin roots -*cede*-** and **-*ceed*-** mean "go" or "yield."

**Apply It** Explain how the roots -*cede*- and -*ceed*- contribute to the meanings of these words. Consult a dictionary, if necessary.

succeed
secede
intercede

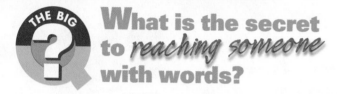

**What is the secret to *reaching someone* with words?**

## Writing About the Big Question

The poems in Poetry Collection 8 explore how words make connections between people and the world. Use these sentence starters to develop your ideas about the Big Question.

I feel a **connection** to other people when I _____.

I feel a **connection** with the natural world when I _____.

**While You Read** Note how the poets use words and images to establish connections.

## Vocabulary

Read each word and its definition. Decide whether you know the word well, know it a little bit, or do not know it at all. After you read, see how your knowledge of each word has increased.

- **jostling** (jäs´ liŋ) *n.* the act of knocking into, often on purpose (p. 757) *With all the jostling taking place in the crowd, I was elbowed several times. jostle v.*

- **impertinently** (im pʉrt´ 'n ənt lē) *adv.* disrespectfully (p. 757) *"You are older, not wiser," he said impertinently to his mother. impertinent adj. pertinent adj.*

- **exquisite** (eks´ kwiz it) *adj.* very beautiful (p. 757) *This exquisite vase was hand-painted by an artist known for her unique, lovely designs. exquisitely adv. exquisiteness n.*

- **vertical** (vʉr´ ti kəl) *adj.* straight up and down; upright (p. 758) *A pine tree's trunk is tall and vertical. vertically adv.*

- **burrow** (bʉr´ ō) *n.* passage or hole for shelter (p. 758) *The gopher dove into its burrow. burrow v.*

- **tongue** (tuŋ) *n.* language (p. 760) *Our guide spoke to the village chief in his native tongue.*

### Word Study

The **Latin word root -vert-** means "turn."

In the poem "Drum Song," the speaker figuratively describes a tree trunk as "**vertical** earth." The speaker is describing earth, which is normally horizontal, and turning it upright.

# E. E. Cummings

**(1894–1962)**

**"your little voice / Over the wires came leaping"** (page 757)

During World War I, Edward Estlin Cummings joined a volunteer ambulance corps in France. The unusual writing style of his letters back home convinced French censors he was a spy, and he was imprisoned for three months. In his poetry, Cummings is known for his experimental, playful style, unusual punctuation, and unconventional arrangement of words.

# Wendy Rose

**(b. 1948)**

**"Drum Song"** (page 758)

Wendy Rose believes that "For everything in this universe there is a song to accompany its existence; writing is another way of singing these songs." One of the foremost Native American poets, Rose also illustrates many of her poems with pen and ink drawings and watercolors.

# Amy Ling

**(1939–1999)**

**"Grandma Ling"** (page 759)

Amy Ling was born in China and lived there with her family for six years before moving to the United States. In addition to writing poetry, Ling worked as an editor of American literature anthologies. She was instrumental in bringing the work of Asian American writers to a wider audience. In the 1960s, Ling visited her grandmother in Taiwan and wrote about their first meeting in "Grandma Ling."

# your little voice
## Over the wires came leaping

# E. E. Cummings

your little voice
                Over the wires came leaping
and i felt suddenly
dizzy
5        With the jostling and shouting of merry flowers
wee skipping high-heeled flames
courtesied[1] before my eyes
                or twinkling over to my side
Looked up
10  with impertinently exquisite faces
floating hands were laid upon me
I was whirled and tossed into delicious dancing
up
Up
15  with the pale important
                stars and the Humorous
                    moon

dear girl
How i was crazy how i cried when i heard
20                over time
and tide and death
leaping
Sweetly
        your voice

---

1. **courtesied** (kʉrt´ sēd) v. bowed with bended knees; curtsied.

## Vocabulary

**jostling** (jäs´ liŋ) n. the act of knocking into, often on purpose

**impertinently** (im pʉrt´ 'n ənt lē) adv. disrespectfully

**exquisite** (eks´ kwiz it) adj. very beautiful

◀ Critical Viewing
What details in this artwork illustrate the poem's ideas about communication? **[Analyze]**

# Drum Song

## Wendy Rose

**Spiral Review**
**Tone** What tone does the author create by repeating the word *Listen*? Explain.

Listen. Turtle
    your flat round feet
    of four claws each
    go slow, go steady,
5    from rock to water
    to land to rock to
water.

Listen. Woodpecker
    you lift your red head
10    on wind, perch
    on vertical earth
    of tree bark and
branch.

**Vocabulary**
**vertical** (vʉr´ ti kəl) *adj.* straight up and down; upright
**burrow** (bʉr´ ō) *n.* passage or hole for shelter

Listen. Snowhare[1]
15    your belly drags,
    your whiskers dance
    bush to burrow
    your eyes turn up
    to where owls
20  hunt.

Listen. Women
    your tongues melt,
    your seeds are planted
    mesa[2] to mesa a shake
25    of gourds,[3]
    a line of mountains
    with blankets
    on their
hips.

**Imagery**
To what senses does the imagery in the last stanza appeal?

1. **Snowhare** (snō´ har´) *n.* snowshoe hare; a large rabbit whose color changes from brown to white in winter and whose broad feet resemble snowshoes.
2. **mesa** (mā´ sə) *n.* small, high plateau with steep sides.
3. **gourds** (gôrdz) *n.* dried, hollowed-out shells of fruits such as melons and pumpkins.

# Grandma Ling

## Amy Ling

*Woman with White Kerchief (Uygur),* Lunda Hoyle Gill

If you dig that hole deep enough
you'll reach China, they used to tell me,
a child in a backyard in Pennsylvania.
Not strong enough to dig that hole,

▲ **Critical Viewing**
What thoughts might
go through your head
if you were meeting a
foreign relative for the
first time? **[Connect]**

5  I waited twenty years,
   then sailed back, half way around the world.

In Taiwan I first met Grandma.
Before she came to view, I heard
her slippered feet softly measure
10 the tatami[1] floor with even step;
the aqua paper-covered door slid open
and there I faced
my five foot height, sturdy legs and feet,
square forehead, high cheeks, and wide-set eyes;
15 my image stood before me,
acted on by fifty years.

She smiled, stretched her arms
to take to heart the eldest daughter
of her youngest son a quarter century away.
20 She spoke a tongue I knew no word of,
and I was sad I could not understand,
but I could hug her.

1. **tatami** (tə tä´ mē) *adj.* woven of rice straw.

## Critical Thinking

**1. Key Ideas and Details (a)** In "your little voice . . . ," what effect does the little voice have on the speaker? **(b) Infer:** Why does the speaker react this way?

**2. Key Ideas and Details (a)** What is each of the animals doing in "Drum Song"? **(b) Analyze:** How do the animals and the women interact with their environments?

**3. Key Ideas and Details (a)** In "Grandma Ling," what prevents the grandmother and granddaughter from communicating in their first meeting? **(b) Speculate:** What might they want to tell or ask each other? **(c) Analyze:** How do they finally communicate, and what are they saying?

**4. Integration of Knowledge and Ideas** How do each of the poems show us the types of connections that are possible in the world? *[Connect to the Big Question: What is the secret to reaching someone with words?]*

Cite textual evidence to support your responses.

your little voice
Over the wires came leaping
E.E. Cummings

Drum Song
**Wendy Rose**
Listen. Turtle
your flat round feet

Grandma
Ling
**Amy Ling**

## Reading Skill: Paraphrase

**1.** Use the punctuation in lines 17–19 of "Grandma Ling" to identify two complete thoughts. **Paraphrase** these lines.

**2.** Paraphrase the original lines in a chart like the one shown.

| Original Lines | Paraphrase |
|---|---|
| *your little voice*…: (lines 1–4) | |
| *Drum Song*: (lines 8–13) | |
| *Grandma Ling*: (lines 15–16) | |

## Literary Analysis: Imagery

© **3. Craft and Structure (a)** List three images from "your little voice . . . " **(b)** What mood, or feeling, does this **imagery** create? **(c)** How well does the unusual structure of the poem combine with the imagery to create this mood? Explain.

© **4. Craft and Structure (a)** In "Grandma Ling," what imagery is used in the first stanza? **(b)** How does the *author's style* and use of images affect the poem's meaning?

## Vocabulary

© **Acquisition and Use** Use a vocabulary word from page 754 to change each sentence so that it makes sense. Explain your answers.

**1.** The rude child spoke respectfully.

**2.** We looked up at the horizontal towers of the skyscrapers.

**3.** The chipmunk ran to hide in the open air.

**4.** My friend has terrible taste in clothes and always looks good.

**5.** We'll need a translator who is familiar with their native food.

**6.** In the crowded store, people had no trouble moving through the aisles.

**Word Study** Use context to explain each answer.

**1.** What would happen if a glass of water were suddenly *inverted*?

**2.** If something *diverts* your attention, does it help you focus?

### Word Study

The **Latin root -vert-** means "turn."

**Apply It** Explain how the root -*vert*- contributes to the meanings of these words. Consult a dictionary if necessary.

avert
evert
revert

# Integrated Language Skills

## Poetry Collections 7 and 8

**Poetry Collection 7**

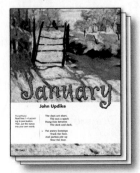

### Conventions: Infinitive Phrases

An **infinitive** is a form of verb that comes after the word *to* and acts as a noun, an adjective, or an adverb. An **infinitive phrase** is an infinitive with a modifier or a complement, all acting together as a single part of speech.

Do not confuse prepositional phrases that begin with the preposition *to* with infinitive phrases. An infinitive phrase always contains a verb; a prepositional phrase never contains a verb.

**Prepositional Phrase:** I went *to the tennis court.*
**Infinitive Phrase:** I went *to play tennis at school.*

**Poetry Collection 8**

| Infinitive | Infinitive Phrase |
|---|---|
| to ski | *To ski in New Mexico,* you must travel into the mountains. |
| to give | I need *to give you my new cell phone number.* |

**Practice A** Identify the infinitive phrase in each sentence.

1. To capture January's bleakness, Updike uses words like *dark, black,* and *gray.*
2. Momaday wants readers to focus on nature's beauty.
3. Molly taught her sister to use correct grammar.
4. She left home to explore the world.

© **Reading Application** In "For My Sister Molly Who in the Fifties," find at least two examples of infinitive phrases. Explain the connecting role the infinitive phrase plays in each sentence.

**Practice B** Identify the infinitive in each sentence. Then use that infinitive to write a sentence of your own.

1. Because of its unusual structure, it is easy to recognize E. E. Cummings's poetry.
2. Just to hear her voice made him dizzy.
3. The speaker asks Turtle to listen.
4. The child knew it was not possible to dig a hole to China.

© **Writing Application** Using Item 1 as a model, write three more sentences using infinitive phrases. Follow this sentence starter: Because of_____, it is easy to_____.

**PH** **WRITING COACH** | Further instruction and practice are available in *Prentice Hall Writing Coach.*

# Writing

**Argumentative Text** A review of a literary work is an evaluation of its strengths and weaknesses. Write a **review** of the three poems in Poetry Collection 7 or 8. Evaluate each poem based on sound, word choice, and imagery.

- To evaluate the sound of a poem, read it aloud and decide how well its sound and rhythm match its subject.
- To evaluate word choice and imagery, determine whether the poets use vivid and appropriate words and images.
- As you draft, support your claims with references to lines from the poems. Finally, offer your overall opinion of each poem.

**Grammar Application** Check your review to be sure you have used infinitive phrases correctly.

**Writing Workshop:** *Work in Progress*

**Prewriting for Exposition** Review the items that you circled on the Topic Ideas Chart in your portfolio. List all the ways that the two items are alike. Then, list all the ways that the two items are different. Finally, put this Categories Map in your portfolio.

# Research and Technology

**Build and Present Knowledge** Write a **profile** of one of the poets featured in Poetry Collection 7 or 8. Follow these steps:

- Use search terms to gather information from several print or online sources about the poet's life, writings, and influences. Reliable sources should be accurate and recent. Choose websites that end with *.edu* or *.org.* When researching, paraphrase—do not copy—your sources, unless you are using a direct quotation. If you include a quotation, note the source, using the appropriate citation style (see pp. R34–R35).
- As you draft, explain how the poet's work reflects his or her heritage, traditions, attitudes, and beliefs.
- Provide specific details about when and where the poet lived and how this influenced the characterization and settings in the poet's major works.
- While drafting, be sure to develop an effective balance between research information and original ideas. Be careful to credit ideas that are not your own.

**Common Core State Standards**

**L.8.1.a; W.8.1, W.8.8, W.8.9**
[For the full wording of the standards, see page 740.]

Use this prewriting activity to prepare for the **Writing Workshop** on page 780.

**PHLit Online!**
www.PHLitOnline.com

- Interactive graphic organizers
- Grammar tutorial
- Interactive journals

# Test Practice: Reading

## Paraphrase

### Fiction Selection

**Directions:** *Read the selection. Then, answer the questions.*

1    Once upon a midnight dreary, while I pondered, weak and
       weary,
2    Over many a quaint and curious volume of forgotten lore,
3    While I nodded, nearly napping, suddenly there came a tapping,
4    As of someone gently rapping, rapping at my chamber door.
5    "Tis some visitor," I muttered, "tapping at my chamber door—
6        Only this, and nothing more."

            —from "The Raven" by Edgar Allan Poe

**1.** According to punctuation, when should
the reader come to a complete stop?
   **A.** after lines 1 and 3
   **B.** after lines 2 and 5
   **C.** after lines 4 and 6
   **D.** at the end of every line

**2.** Which is the *best* paraphrase of "quaint
and curious volume of forgotten lore"
(line 2)?
   **A.** interesting book of myths
   **B.** old and interesting book of old stories
   **C.** antique and difficult book of old tales
   **D.** question and answer books

**3.** According to punctuation, when should
the reader pause in line 3?
   **A.** after each comma
   **B.** after the final comma
   **C.** after the 1st and 3rd commas
   **D.** after the 2nd and 3rd commas

**4.** Which paraphrase of lines 3 and 4 is the
*most* accurate?
   **A.** While I began to fall asleep, someone
softly tapped on the door to my room.
   **B.** As the speaker enjoys his book, he
hears a tapping sound on his door.
   **C.** While I was sleeping, I heard a knock.
   **D.** As I nodded off to sleep, someone
rapped, rapped, rapped, at my bedroom door.

### Writing for Assessment

Write a one-paragraph response in which
you paraphrase the verse to explain what
happened. Be sure to restate the events in
your own words.

## Nonfiction Selection

**Directions:** *Read the selection. Then, answer the questions.*

**(1)** Edgar Allan Poe's poems and stories have chilled readers for over 150 years. **(2)** While his work spans many genres, he is best known for his psychological thrillers. **(3)** "The Raven," possibly his most famous poem, is a haunting tale of a man's growing anguish as he mourns the death of his beloved. **(4)** The dark mood of the poem is enhanced by Poe's skillful use of repetition, rhyme, and word choice.

**(5)** It is no wonder that much of Poe's writing was so dark. **(6)** Both his parents died when he was a toddler. **(7)** His wealthy foster family disowned him when he accumulated massive debts. **(8)** After his young wife died, he struggled with depression. **(9)** The exact nature of Poe's early death at age forty remains a mystery to this day. **(10)** Many people feel his mysterious death is appropriate, given the nature of his writing.

1. Which of the following is the *best* paraphrase of "chilled readers," in sentence 1?
   A. cold and tired readers
   B. excited and pleased readers
   C. thrilled and scared readers
   D. dismayed and annoyed readers

2. Why might paraphrasing sentence 3 be helpful to readers?
   A. The sentence is poorly written.
   B. The sentence references Poe's other works.
   C. The vocabulary in the sentence is challenging.
   D. The tone of the sentence is complex.

3. Which is the *best* paraphrase of "he accumulated massive debts," in sentence 7?
   A. he borrowed a lot of money
   B. he accounted for all his debts
   C. he loaned out lots of money
   D. he became bankrupt

4. What main idea does a paraphrase of the second paragraph help to clarify?
   A. Poe spent his childhood as an orphan.
   B. Poe's life was tragic.
   C. Poe died young.
   D. Poe's writing is admired.

## Writing for Assessment

### Connecting Across Texts

In a brief essay, paraphrase ideas and details from each selection to explain how Poe achieves a dark mood of discontent in his poem "The Raven."

www.PHLitOnline.com
- Online practice
- Instant feedback

# Reading for Information

## Analyzing Functional Texts

### Technical Directions

### Consumer Document

**Common Core
State Standards**

**Reading Informational Text**
**4.** Determine the meaning of words and phrases as they are used in a text, including figurative, connotative, and technical meanings.

**Language**
**6.** Acquire and use accurately grade-appropriate general academic and domain-specific words and phrases; gather vocabulary knowledge when considering a word or phrase important to comprehension or expression.

## Reading Skill: Analyze Technical Directions

**Technical directions** offer step-by-step instruction on how to assemble, operate, or repair a mechanical device. A warranty gives directions on what to do if the device does not function properly. When you encounter any set of directions, first **analyze** the directions to be sure you understand all of the steps. *Text features* can help you clarify key points. Use a checklist like the one shown to be sure you follow the directions correctly.

### Checklist for Following Technical Directions

- ☐ Read all the directions completely before starting to follow them.
- ☐ Look for clues such as bold type or capital letters that point out specific sections or important information.
- ☐ Use diagrams to locate and name the parts of the product.
- ☐ Follow each step in the exact order given.
- ☐ Do not skip any steps.

## Content-Area Vocabulary

These words appear in the selections that follow. You may also encounter them in other content-area texts.

- **defects** (dē´fekts) *n.* shortcomings or failings in someone or something; faults in mechanics or design
- **modification** (mod´ə fə kā´shən) *n.* change; adjustment
- **exclusion** (ek sklü´zhən) *n.* barring someone or something from participation or consideration

# Using Your Answering Machine

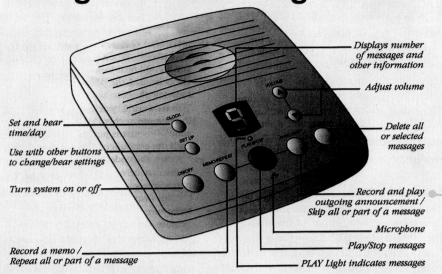

Displays number of messages and other information

Adjust volume

Delete all or selected messages

Set and hear time/day

Use with other buttons to change/hear settings

Turn system on or off

Record and play outgoing announcement / Skip all or part of a message

Microphone

Play/Stop messages

PLAY Light indicates messages

Record a memo / Repeat all or part of a message

## Setting the Clock

You'll need to set the clock so that it can announce the day and time that each message is received. Press PLAY/STOP to exit Setting the Clock at any time.

1 Press and hold CLOCK until the Message Window displays CLOCK, and the default day is announced.

2 To change the day setting, hold down MEMO/REPEAT or until the correct day is announced. Then release the button.

3 Press and release CLOCK. The current hour setting is announced.

4 To change the hour setting, hold down MEMO/REPEAT or ANNC/SKIP until the correct hour is announced. Then release the button.

5 Press and release CLOCK. The current minutes setting is announced.

6 To change the minutes setting, hold down MEMO/REPEAT or ANNC/SKIP until the correct minutes setting is announced. Then release the button.

7 Press and release CLOCK. The new day and time are announced.

**To check the clock,** press and release CLOCK.

**NOTE:** In the event of a power failure, see the instructions on the bottom of the unit to reset the clock.

## Recording Your Announcement

Before using this answering system, you should record the announcement (up to one minute long) that callers will hear when the system answers a call. If you choose not to record an announcement, the system answers with a prerecorded announcement: *"Hello. Please leave a message after the tone."*

1 Press and hold ANNC/SKIP. The system beeps. Speak toward the microphone normally, from about nine inches away. While you are recording, the Message Window displays—.

2 To stop recording, release ANNC/SKIP. The system automatically plays back your announcement.

**To review your announcement,** *press and release* ANNC/SKIP.

## Turning the System On/Off

Use ON/OFF to turn the system on and off. When the system is off, the Message Window is blank.

## Volume Control

Use volume buttons (▲ and ▼) to adjust the volume of the system's speaker. Press the top button (▲) to increase volume. Press the bottom button (▼) to decrease volume. The system beeps three times when you reach the maximum or minimum volume setting.

## Announcement Monitor

You can choose whether to hear the announcement when your system answers a call, or have it silent (off) on your end (your caller will still hear an announcement).

1 Press and hold SET UP. After the Ring Select setting is announced, continue to press and release SET UP until the system announces "Monitor is on (or off)."

2 Press and release ANNC/SKIP or MEMO/REPEAT until the system announces your selection.

3 Press and release PLAY/STOP or SET UP to exit.

## Listening to Your Messages

As the system plays back messages, the Message Window displays the number of the message playing. Before playing each message, the system announces the day and time the message was received. After playing the last message, the system announces "End of messages."

**Play all messages**—Press and release PLAY/STOP. If you have no messages, the system announces "No messages."

**Play new messages only**—Hold down PLAY/STOP for about two seconds, until the system begins playing. If you have no new messages, the system announces "No new messages."

**Repeat entire messages**—Press and release MEMO/REPEAT.

**Repeat part of message**—Hold down MEMO/REPEAT until you hear a beep, then release to resume playing. The more beeps you hear, the farther back in the message you will be when you release the button.

**Repeat previous message**—Press MEMO/REPEAT twice, continue this process to hear other previous messages.

**Skip to next message**—Press and release ANNC/SKIP.

**Skip part of a message**—Hold down ANNC/SKIP until you hear a beep, then release to resume playing. The more beeps you hear, the farther into the message you will be when you release the button.

**Stop message playback**—Press and release PLAY/STOP.

The boxed words are visual cues that tell the reader to hold down or release a button on the answering machine.

## Saving Messages

The system automatically saves your messages if you do not delete them. The system can save about 12 minutes of messages, including your announcement, for a total of up to 59 messages. When memory is full, you must delete some or all messages before new messages can be recorded.

## Deleting Messages

**Delete all messages**—Hold down DELETE. The system announces "Messages deleted" and permanently deletes messages. The Message Window displays **0**. If you haven't listened to all of the messages, the system beeps five times, and does not delete messages.

**Delete selected messages**—Press and release DELETE while the message you want to delete is being played. The system beeps once, and continues with the next message. If you want to check a message before you delete it, you can press MEMO/REPEAT to replay the message before deleting it.

When the system reaches the end of the last message, the messages not deleted are renumbered, and the Message Window displays the total number of messages remaining in memory.

## Recording a Memo

You can record a memo to be stored as an incoming message. The memo can be up to three minutes long, and will be played back with other messages.

1 Press and hold MEMO/REPEAT. After the beep, speak toward the microphone.

2 To stop recording, release MEMO/REPEAT.

3 To play the memo, press PLAY/STOP.

## When Memory is Full

The system can record approximately 12 minutes of messages, including your announcement, for a total of up to 59 messages. When memory is full, or 59 messages have been recorded, the Message Window flashes **F**. Delete messages to make room for new ones.

When memory is full, the system answers calls after 10 rings, and sounds two beeps instead of your announcement.

# Limited Warranty for Answering Machine

**Features:**
- information regarding the buyer's rights when a product does not function properly
- instructions for returning a defective product to the manufacturer for repair or replacement
- legal language that specifies the manufacturer's responsibilities

## Our Warranty

The company warrants, for one year, to the original owner, this product to be free from defects in design, materials, and workmanship, according to the terms and conditions set forth below.

## Warranty Duration

This warranty to the original owner shall terminate one (1) year after the date of its original purchase.

> Bold subheadings tell the reader what aspect of the warranty is discussed in each section.

## Statement of Remedy

If, during the warranty period, this product fails to operate under normal use, due to defects in design, materials, or workmanship, the warrantor will either, at its option, repair or replace the defective unit and return it to you without charge.

## Conditions

This limited warranty does not cover
- Product that has been subjected to misuse, neglect, or physical damage
- Product that has been damaged due to repair, alteration, or modification by anyone other than one of the warrantor's authorized service representatives
- Product that has been improperly installed
- Product purchased or serviced outside the United States
- Product whose serial number has been removed
- Product without valid proof of purchase

## Obtaining Warranty Service

To obtain warranty service in the United States, please follow these instructions:
1. Check the owner's manual to be sure you are operating the answering machine correctly.
2. Once you have determined that your answering machine is defective, contact Customer Service using the company's toll-free phone number. You will receive instructions regarding where to return the product.

> This section of the warranty gives specific directions for returning a defective product to the manufacturer.

3. Pack the answering machine in a padded cardboard box. Be sure to include the following:

- all parts and accessories that were included in the original package
- a copy of the sales receipt
- a detailed description of the problem
- your daytime phone number
- your return shipping address

4. Ship the product to the company's repair facility using the address provided. You will be responsible for the cost of shipping the answering machine to the repair facility. The company will cover the cost of return shipment. The repair or replacement process should take approximately 30 days.

## Limitations of Warranty

The warranty set forth above is the sole and entire warranty for this product. It supersedes all other communications related to this product. There are no other express warranties, whether written or oral, other than this printed limited warranty.

This warranty does not cover or provide for indirect, special, incidental, consequential, or similar damages (including, but not limited to lost profits or revenue, inability to use the product, the cost of substitute equipment, and claims by third parties) resulting from the use of this product.

Some states do not allow the exclusion or limitation of incidental or consequential damages, so the above limitation or exclusion may not apply to you.

This section includes important information regarding directions that appear earlier in the document.

## Comparing Functional Texts

 **1. Integration of Knowledge and Ideas (a)** In what ways do both the technical directions and the warranty help readers to make better use of a **complex mechanical device? (b)** In what ways are these two documents different? Explain your response.

## Content-Area Vocabulary

**2.** Use all three vocabulary words from page 766 in a brief paragraph that explains why warranties cover only *defects,* while singling out for *exclusion* any consumer *modification* of the item.

## ⏱ Timed Writing

### Expository Text: Explanation

> **Format and Details**
> The prompt directs you to explain a process. Therefore, you will need to use sequence words, such as *first, next,* and *finally.*

> Choose an answering machine function from the technical directions you have read. For example, you might choose "Recording Your Announcement." Then, write a few paragraphs explaining how to use that function. Refer to the source document for the steps, but use your own words. (30 minutes)

> **Academic Vocabulary**
> A *source* document is the text from which you received information.

### 5-Minute Planner

Complete these steps before you begin to write:

**1.** Read the prompt carefully. Look for key words like the ones highlighted in color to help you understand the assignment.

**2.** Reread the source document and choose an answering machine function to use as the basis for your explanation.

**3. Analyze the technical directions** to identify the steps involved in using the function you choose. Note any parts of the instructions that are unclear or confusing, and jot down ideas about how you can explain them more clearly.

**4.** Use your notes and the source document to prepare an outline. Then, use it to help you organize your explanation.

# Comparing Literary Works

**The Road Not Taken • O Captain! My Captain!**

## Comparing Types of Description

**Descriptive writing** paints pictures with words. A variety of descriptions can be used in poetry to present **levels of meaning.**

- **Literal meaning** is the actual, everyday meaning of words.

- In contrast, **figurative meaning** is based on the symbolic nature of language, using imaginative, innovative ways to express ideas.

An **analogy** is a figurative description that compares two or more things that are similar in some ways, but otherwise unalike. In literature, analogies may extend over the course of a work. For example, a poem that literally describes the ocean also can be read as an analogy: It may compare the ocean to life because both are vast, deep, and ever-changing. The poem, therefore, has two levels of meaning—one literal and one figurative or symbolic.

When you think a poem may have levels of meaning, think about whether the poet is using an analogy or other type of figurative description to emphasize an idea. Follow these steps as you read the poems by Frost and Whitman:

- Record your ideas about what the descriptions might symbolize, or represent.

- List some of the words and images that give you clues about the figurative meaning in a chart like the one shown.

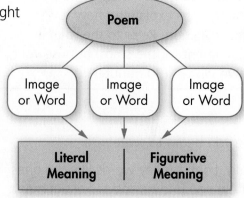

- Determine whether or not the figurative meaning develops over the course of the poem.

- Finally, compare the analogies in the two poems.

**Common Core State Standards**

**Reading Literature**

**1.** Cite the textual evidence that most strongly supports an analysis of what the text says explicitly as well as inferences drawn from the text.

**4.** Determine the meaning of words and phrases as they are used in a text, including figurative and connotative meanings; analyze the impact of specific word choices on meaning and tone, including analogies or allusions to other texts.

**Writing**

**9.** Draw evidence from literary or informational texts to support analysis, reflection, and research. *(Timed Writing)*

**www.PHLitOnline.com**

- Vocabulary flashcards
- Interactive journals
- More about the authors
- Selection audio
- Interactive graphic organizers

# What is the secret to reaching someone with words?

## Writing About the Big Question

These poets use different approaches to language in their writing—one uses simple, direct language and structure, and the other writes in a more flowery style. Use this sentence starter to develop your ideas.

For a poem to be **meaningful** to me, it should _____.

# Meet the Authors

## Robert Frost (1874–1963)

### Author of "The Road Not Taken"

One of the best-known and best-loved American poets, Robert Frost was a four-time winner of the Pulitzer Prize. Though he was born in San Francisco, Frost spent most of his life in New England—the subject of many of his poems.

**"The Gift Outright"** Frost's reading of his poem "The Gift Outright" at the inauguration of John F. Kennedy in 1961 was a memorable moment for poetry in the twentieth century.

## Walt Whitman (1819–1892)

### Author of "O Captain! My Captain!"

Although he is now considered one of the greatest American poets, Walt Whitman could not find a commercial publisher and was forced to pay for the publication of his masterpiece *Leaves of Grass* in 1855. This collection of poems about the United States has continued to influence poetry ever since.

**The Poet and the War** During the Civil War, Whitman worked in military hospitals in Washington, D.C., where he saw his beloved President Lincoln from afar. Lincoln's assassination less than a week after the Union victory deeply moved Whitman. He wrote "O Captain! My Captain!" in tribute to the fallen leader.

# The Road Not Taken

## Robert Frost

Two roads diverged in a yellow wood,
And sorry I could not travel both
And be one traveler, long I stood
And looked down one as far as I could
5  To where it bent in the undergrowth;

Then took the other, as just as fair,
And having perhaps the better claim,
Because it was grassy and wanted wear;
Though as for that, the passing there
10  Had worn them really about the same,

And both that morning equally lay
In leaves no step had trodden black.
Oh, I kept the first for another day!
Yet knowing how way leads on to way,
15  I doubted if I should ever come back.

I shall be telling this with a sigh
Somewhere ages and ages hence:
Two roads diverged in a wood, and I—
I took the one less traveled by,
20  And that has made all the difference.

**Vocabulary**
**diverged** (dì vʉrj´ d)
v. branched off

**Description**
What is the literal subject of this poem?

**Description**
What clue in the final stanza hints that the poem is about more than a hike in the woods?

## Critical Thinking

1. **Key Ideas and Details (a)** In the first five lines, where does the speaker remember being? **(b) Infer:** Based on these lines, what can you tell about the speaker's character and attitude toward life?

2. **Key Ideas and Details (a)** Which road does the speaker finally choose? **(b) Deduce:** Why does the speaker choose one road over the other? **(c) Analyze:** Find two statements suggesting that the speaker believes he has made a significant choice.

3. **Key Ideas and Details (a) Speculate:** Why does the speaker predict that he will remember this decision? **(b) Generalize:** What message does the poem communicate about decisions in general?

4. **Integration of Knowledge and Ideas (a)** How does the language Frost uses let him reach a wide readership with his message? **(b)** How might Frost answer this Big Question? *[Connect to the Big Question: What is the secret to reaching someone with words?]*

Cite textual evidence to support your responses.

▲ **Critical Viewing** What details in this photograph of Lincoln's funeral procession reflect the importance of Lincoln's death to Americans like Whitman? **[Analyze]**

# O Captain! My Captain!

## Walt Whitman

O Captain! my Captain! our fearful trip is done,
The ship has weather'd every rack,[1] the prize we
    sought is won,
The port is near, the bells I hear, the people all
    exulting,
While follow eyes the steady keel,[2] the vessel grim
    and daring;
5      But O heart! heart! heart!
        O the bleeding drops of red,
          Where on the deck my Captain lies,
          Fallen cold and dead.

    O Captain! my Captain! rise up and hear the bells;
10  Rise up—for you the flag is flung—for you the
    bugle trills,
For you bouquets and ribbon'd wreaths—for you
    the shores a-crowding,
For you they call, the swaying mass, their eager
    faces turning;
    Here Captain! dear father!

**Vocabulary**
**exulting** (eg zult´ iŋ)
*v.* rejoicing

**Description**
In this stanza, what does the speaker describe literally?

---

**1. rack** (rak) *n.* destruction or ruin.
**2. keel** (kēl) *n.* main beam that extends along the bottom of a ship and supports the frame.

                        This arm beneath your head!
15                          It is some dream that on the deck,
                            You've fallen cold and dead.

    My Captain does not answer, his lips are pale
        and still,
    My father does not feel my arm, he has no pulse
        nor will,
    The ship is anchor'd safe and sound, its voyage
        closed and done,
20  From fearful trip the victor ship comes in with
        object won;
            Exult O shores, and ring O bells!
                But I with mournful tread,
                    Walk the deck my Captain lies,
                        Fallen cold and dead.

**Description**
What is the symbolic meaning of the safely anchored ship?

## Critical Thinking

**1. Key Ideas and Details (a)** What has happened to the Captain? **(b) Infer:** Why does the timing of this event make it doubly unfortunate? **(c) Interpret:** How does the mood or feeling of the poem reflect what has happened?

**2. Key Ideas and Details (a)** What words in the poem relate to the sea and sailing? **(b) Compare:** In what ways does Lincoln's leadership resemble a captain's role on a ship? **(c) Draw Conclusions:** What kind of leader does the speaker consider Lincoln?

**3. Craft and Structure Forms of Poetry:** Review page 639. How does the tone and purpose of Whitman's poem fit the form of an *elegy*?

**4. Integration of Knowledge and Ideas** Is it more powerful to hear about someone's life and death described in symbolic language, as in Whitman's poem? Or is direct description more powerful, as in a speech given at a funeral? Explain your reasoning. *[Connect to the Big Question: What is the secret to reaching someone with words?]*

*Cite textual evidence to support your responses.*

## After You Read

# The Road Not Taken •
# O Captain! My Captain!

## Comparing Types of Description

**1. Craft and Structure (a)** In "The Road Not Taken," what descriptive language shows that the two roads are alike and different? **(b)** What kind of choice might these two roads represent? Explain.

**2. Key Ideas and Details (a)** In "O Captain! My Captain!" what is the ship's destination? **(b)** What is the "fearful trip" that the ship has "weathered"? **(c)** How does this trip and the rest of the poem reveal the poet's response to a historic event?

**3. Craft and Structure** Use this chart to analyze the ideas and emotions that each poem conveys through the use of analogy.

| Literal Meaning | Analogy | Ideas and Emotions |
|---|---|---|
| Two roads separate | | |
| A ship's captain dies | | |

 ## Timed Writing

### Explanatory Text: Essay

The insights of both Frost's and Whitman's poems are expressed through figurative description. In an essay, explain whether these descriptions remain relevant and help convey ideas important to readers today. **(40 minutes)**

### 5-Minute Planner

**1.** Read the prompt carefully and completely.

**2.** Gather your ideas by jotting down answers to these questions:
  - How common are the experiences that each poem describes?
  - Which poet better expresses emotions through description?
  - How does each poet's use of analogies help readers understand the importance of the event described?
  - Which message is easier for you to interpret? Why?

**3.** Make sure that you address the prompt and support your response with relevant details from the poems.

**4.** Use the charts on page 772 and this page to help draft your essay.

# Writing Workshop

## Write an Informative Text

### Exposition: Comparison-and-Contrast Essay

In a comparison-and-contrast essay, a writer examines the similarities and differences between two or more subjects. You might use elements of this type of writing in comparisons of literary works, product comparisons, and news analyses.

**Assignment** Write a comparison-and-contrast essay to analyze the similarities and differences between two or more subjects. Your essay should feature the following elements:

✔ a *topic involving two or more subjects* that are different in some ways and similar in other ways

✔ an introduction that presents the *thesis,* or main point; a body that shows similarities and differences; and a conclusion that restates and reinforces the thesis

✔ a *parallel structure* that emphasizes comparisons and contrasts

✔ error-free writing, including *correct use of parallelism in grammatical forms*

To preview the criteria on which your comparison-and-contrast essay may be judged, see the rubric on page 787.

 **Writing Workshop:** *Work in Progress*

Review the work you did on pages 739 and 763.

**WRITE GUY**
*Jeff Anderson, M.Ed.*

### What Do You Notice?

**Structure and Style**

Read these sentences from Mary C. Curtis's essay. "The Season's Curmudgeon Sees the Light."

*Spring has never done much for me. I was always an autumn kind of gal: My birthday is in September. When red and gold creep into the leaves, I see beauty, not death. A slight chill in the air feels just right.*

*I planned an October wedding. When I raised my face to kiss the groom, I didn't want any beads of sweat ruining the moment.*

With a partner, discuss the structure, style, and tone of the writing. Think of ways you might use similar elements in your writing.

 **Common Core State Standards**

**Writing**
**2** Write informative/explanatory texts to examine a topic and convey ideas, concepts, and information through the selection, organization, and analysis of relevant content.
**2.a.** Introduce a topic clearly, previewing what is to follow; organize ideas, concepts, and information into broader categories; include formatting, graphics, and multimedia when useful to aiding comprehension.
**2.b.** Develop the topic with relevant, well-chosen facts, definitions, concrete details, quotations, or other information and examples.

**Reading-Writing Connection**

To get the feel for comparison-and-contrast essays, read "The Season's Curmudgeon Sees the Light," by Mary C. Curtis, on page 545.

# Prewriting/Planning Strategies

**Create a personal-experience timeline.** Every time you outgrow your clothes, you can see how you are changing. In addition to physical change, you undergo changes in attitude and perspective. Use a timeline like the one shown to chart ways you have changed over time. Next, choose two entries as one possible topic for your comparison-and-contrast essay.

| Preschool | Kindergarten | Grade 2 | Grade 4 | Grade 6 | Grade 8 |
|---|---|---|---|---|---|
| Enjoyed playing alone in sandbox | Liked dressing as a superhero, finger painting | Wanted to do everything perfectly | Understood it was OK to make mistakes | Joined the swimming team | Helped team win swim meet |

**Narrow your topic.** Before you finalize your topic, examine it to be sure you can discuss it fully. A topic such as "The Best Vacation Spots," for example, is much too broad in scope to be addressed adequately in a short essay. You might narrow it to "Atlanta vs. San Francisco—Which Is More Family-Friendly?" Review your topic to divide it into separate parts, aspects, or subtopics. Choose one of these subtopics as your new, narrowed topic.

**Use a Venn diagram.** To gather details, organize information about the ideas you will compare by using a Venn diagram, as shown here. Jot down as many similarities as you can in the center section, and note several differences in the outer sections of each circle. When you have finished, circle the items that most vividly show comparisons and contrasts. Then, include these details in your essay. When you write your essay, plan to *juxtapose* these details—set them side-by-side—to emphasize their differences and similarities. Look at this example:

**Buses**
- above ground
- comfortable
- see where you are going
- get caught in traffic

- faster than walking
- cheap
- do not have to park

**Subways**
- underground
- claustrophobic
- cannot see where you are going
- avoid traffic

# Drafting Strategies

**Common Core State Standards**

**Writing**
**2.b.** Develop the topic with relevant, well-chosen facts, definitions, concrete details, quotations, or other information and examples.

**Select the best organizational format.** There are two common ways to organize a comparison-and-contrast essay. Review these options and use a structure that is appropriate to your topic and audience.

- **Block method** Present all the details about one aspect first, and then present all the details about the next aspect. The block method works well if you are writing about more than two aspects of a topic, or if your topic is complex.

- **Point-by-point organization** Discuss each aspect of your subjects in turn. For example, if you are comparing buses and subways, you might first discuss the cost of each form of transportation, then the convenience, and so on.

| Block |
| --- |
| I. Buses |
| a. cheaper |
| b. more routes |
| c. better views |
| II. Trains |
| a. better seats |
| b. faster |
| c. quieter |

**Use parallel structure.** No matter which overall organizational method you choose, be sure to keep the paragraphs in the body *parallel*, or consistent, in structure and style. This makes it easier for your reader to follow and understand your points. For example, for the first aspect you compare, you might choose the SEE method (shown in the chart below) to develop the comparison in your supporting paragraphs. Then you would use the same method to develop support for the second aspect. Study the example in the chart.

- State the topic of the paragraph.

- Extend the idea by restating it in a new way, applying it to a particular case, or contrasting it with another point.

- Elaborate with specific examples, facts, or explanations.

| Point-by-Point |
| --- |
| I. Introduction |
| II. Cost of each |
| III. Accessibility of each |
| IV. View from each |
| V. Disadvantages of each |

| Statement | Extension | Elaboration |
| --- | --- | --- |
| Buses and trains are two forms of public transportation that offer advantages and disadvantages in the area of convenience. | A bus can often drop you off very close to your final destination, but trains are limited to designated stations along the railroad line. | If people's origins and destinations are near train stations, trains are usually more convenient. Trains do not get caught in traffic and are generally faster than buses. |

# Writers on Writing

## Jacqueline Woodson On Including Details

> Jacqueline Woodson is the author of "Describe Somebody" (p. 645) and "Almost Summer Sky" (p. 647).

In this passage from my novel *Hush,* Toswiah, the narrator, tells of her family's transition from their Boulder, Colorado, home. They were forced to leave after her father witnessed a murder, and as a result, are now part of a Witness Protection Program that has moved them to a tiny apartment in a big city. Toswiah and her family have left everything they loved behind them—even their old names.

*"I write because I love creating new worlds."*
—Jacqueline Woodson

**Professional Model:**

### from *Hush*

Some mornings, waking up in this new place, I don't know where I am. The apartment is tiny. The kitchen is not even a whole room away from the living room, just a few steps and a wide doorway with no door separating it. Not even one fireplace. Daddy sits by the window staring out, hardly ever saying anything. Maybe he thinks if he looks long and hard enough, Denver will reappear, . . . Maybe he thinks the tall gray buildings all smashed against each other will separate and squat down, that the Rocky Mountains will rise up behind them. . . .

When Daddy looks over to where me and my sister, Anna, sit watching TV, he looks surprised, like he's wondering why we aren't downstairs in the den. No den here, though. No dining room. No extra bathrooms down the hall and at the top of the stairs. Just five rooms with narrow doorways here.

 Here, I spent a lot of time imagining what it would be like to leave the place I loved. I wanted to really focus on small details.

 Toswiah's father is very depressed about the current situation. I put him by the window to show his sadness and to also show what he was seeing.

 The family has gone from a grand house to a small apartment. I spent time trying to give details about each to show the difference.

# Revising Strategies

**Check overall balance.** Reread your draft. Use one color to highlight details about one aspect of your comparison. Use additional colors to mark details about other aspects. If your draft has more of one color, add details on an aspect that is less developed.

**Check organization and structure.** If your rereading reveals a confusing overall organization, consider rearranging sections to fit the block method or point-by-point organization. If your review indicates an inconsistent paragraph structure, revise your work to develop your arguments in a parallel way.

**Common Core State Standards**

**Writing**

**2.b.** Develop the topic with relevant, well-chosen facts, definitions, concrete details, quotations, or other information and examples.

**2.d.** Use precise language and domain-specific vocabulary to inform about or explain the topic.

| Original Version | Revised to Include Parallelism |
|---|---|
| Bus routes crisscross the city, traveling down every major street and into every neighborhood. I took the train once, and it dropped me off on the outskirts of town. | *Bus routes crisscross the city,* traveling down every major street and into every neighborhood. *The train, on the other hand, skirts the city,* traveling down tracks far from many common destinations. |

**Delete unnecessary details.** Copy your thesis onto an index card. Run the card down your draft as you read through the introduction, body, and conclusion, one line at a time. Identify any details that do not directly support your thesis. Delete the details or rewrite them to develop your main idea. In the example shown, the deleted detail did not develop the main argument comparing buses and trains.

> Buses cost 85¢ a ride. ~~Of course, you can walk for free or take a cab that costs $1.00 for each quarter mile.~~ Trains cost $1.25.

## Peer Review

Invite a classmate to read your draft to evaluate its organization, balance, and use of parallel structure. Ask your reader:

- if the overall organization you chose for your comparison is clear
- if your essay is missing support for an aspect of your comparison
- if you are consistent in the way you develop your arguments

Revise your draft, based on this feedback.

## Revising to Vary Sentence Patterns

To keep your writing lively, avoid writing sentences that follow a dull pattern. Many sentences begin with nouns, as in *The <u>waiter</u> took our order.*

**Using a Variety of Sentence Beginnings** To avoid beginning every sentence with a noun, consider these options:

**Adjective:** <u>Surprised</u>, the waiter rushed over.

**Adverb:** <u>Running quickly</u>, he arrived at our table.

**Prepositional Phrase:** <u>After a delay</u>, the food arrived.

**Using Appositives and Appositive Phrases** To pack information into your sentences, use appositives, noun phrases that define or explain other words in the sentence.

**Appositive:** The cat, <u>a tabby</u>, prowled the yard.

**Appositive Phrase:** The dog, <u>my mother's longtime pet</u>, was happy to see us.

**Fixing Repetitive Sentence Patterns** To fix a series of sentences that start the same way, follow these steps:

1. **Identify the existing pattern of sentence beginnings.**
   - Draw a triangle around each noun that starts a sentence.
   - Draw a box around each adjective that starts a sentence.
   - Draw a circle around each prepositional phrase that starts a sentence.

2. **Review your results.** Count the number of triangles, boxes, and circles. If you have too many of one shape, rewrite the sentence beginnings to build greater variety.

3. **Consider using appositives to include more information.** Identify a key noun in a sentence and write a brief noun phrase to define the word. Use commas to set the appositive or the appositive phrase off from the rest of the sentence.

> **PH | WRITING COACH**
>
> Further instruction and practice are available in *Prentice Hall Writing Coach*.

### Grammar in Your Writing

Choose three paragraphs in your draft. Review the sentence beginnings. If you have not used enough variety, revise by beginning some sentences according to the rules presented here.

## Comparing Struggles for Equality

The civil rights movement of the 1950s and 1960s had a lot in common with the women's suffrage movement that began with the Seneca Falls Convention in 1848. Both movements involved a group of people who were denied rights and who fought to obtain those rights.

Although in most ways the two struggles were similar, the specific rights each group fought for were different. Women wanted the right to vote in elections, the right to own property in their own names, and the right to keep their own wages. African Americans fought for the end to segregation. Like the women, they wanted to be treated with equal rights. However, the civil rights movement was about fairness in schools, jobs, and public places like buses and restaurants.

Both movements protested in nonviolent ways. They held marches, boycotts, and demonstrations to raise the public's consciousness and get the laws changed. In 1917, Alice Paul and other women picketed at the White House. In 1963, more than 200,000 Americans, led by Dr. Martin Luther King, Jr., marched on Washington, D.C. They wanted Congress to pass laws to end discrimination.

Both movements were about equality. The Declaration of Independence, an important document in the struggle for equality, states: "We hold these truths to be self-evident, that all men are created equal; that they are endowed by their Creator with certain unalienable rights; that among these are life, liberty, and the pursuit of happiness."

Protesters in both the civil rights movement and the women's suffrage movement felt that they were being denied rights that were given to them by this statement from the Declaration of Independence. Both groups were able to change the laws so that they could have their rights. Women were given the right to vote in 1920 by Amendment 19 to the Constitution. Similarly, the Civil Rights Act of 1964 outlawed discrimination in hiring and ended segregation in public places.

In conclusion, the civil rights movement of the 1950s and 1960s and the women's suffrage movement were both about equality under the law. They are both good examples of how much work and determination it takes to change the laws. It is good to know, however, that the laws can be changed.

Carolyn begins her essay with a thesis statement that introduces the subjects of her comparison. She indicates that she will focus more on similarities.

The writer focuses first on the differences in the specific rights being sought.

Carolyn uses point-by-point organization to compare the movements.

The writer provides a quotation to support an idea.

The conclusion restates the introduction, driving home the point.

# Editing and Proofreading

Proofread to correct errors in spelling, grammar, and punctuation.

**Focus on items in a series.** Use commas to separate words, phrases, or clauses in a series. To avoid confusion, use semicolons when some items already contain commas. Use colons to introduce lists.

**Commas:** Recyling is cheaper, easier, and cleaner than dumping.

**Semicolons:** We visited Moab, Utah; Lima, Ohio; and Bath, Maine.

**Colons:** I will compare the following: beets, carrots, and celery.

# Publishing and Presenting

Consider one of the following ways to share your writing:

**Publish a column.** If you compared subjects of local interest, such as two restaurants or several stores, submit your essay to your local newspaper or post it on a community blog or Web site.

**Start a family tradition.** If you have compared two subjects of interest to your family—two uncles, two birthdays, two vacations—read your essay at a family gathering.

# Reflecting on Your Writing

**Writer's Journal** Jot down your answer to this question:

*If you could write your essay again, what would you do differently?*

## Rubric for Self-Assessment

Find evidence in your writing to address each category. Then, use the rating scale to grade your work.

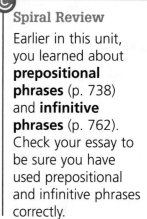

**Spiral Review**

Earlier in this unit, you learned about **prepositional phrases** (p. 738) and **infinitive phrases** (p. 762). Check your essay to be sure you have used prepositional and infinitive phrases correctly.

| Criteria | Rating Scale |
|---|---|
| | *not very*                   *very* |
| **Focus:** How clearly do you introduce and develop your thesis? | 1  2  3  4  5 |
| **Organization:** How effectively do you highlight the points of comparison? | 1  2  3  4  5 |
| **Support/Elaboration:** How well do you use parallel structure to emphasize key comparisons and contrasts? | 1  2  3  4  5 |
| **Conventions:** How correct is your grammar, especially your use of parallelism in grammatical forms? | 1  2  3  4  5 |

# Vocabulary Workshop

## Idioms

An **idiom** is a figurative expression that has a very different meaning than the literal meanings of the words it contains. For example, people use the expression *shooting the breeze* to mean "having a casual conversation." The chart shows examples of common English idioms based on farming, weather, and sailing terms.

| Idiom | Source | Meaning |
|---|---|---|
| a needle in a haystack | farming | something extremely difficult to find |
| a tempest in a teapot | weather | a problem that seems serious but is actually insignificant |
| rock the boat | sailing | disturb the balance of a group or situation |

**Common Core State Standards**

**Language**
**5.a.** Interpret figures of speech in context.

**Practice A** Identify the idiom that is part of each sentence.

1. Ian, a budding musician, has sung since the age of five.
2. Jasey ran slowly for most of the race, but then the tide turned.
3. The neighbors started a grassroots campaign to keep their streets free of litter.
4. I thought he would blow a gasket when he lost his keys.
5. What's the holdup with this project?

**Practice B** Find the idiom in each sentence. Then, explain the meaning of the idiom.

1. After she won the tennis match, Janine was on cloud nine.
2. I disagreed with my friend's opinion, but I didn't want to make waves.
3. Out of left field, Ms. Sampson announced that we would have a quiz tomorrow.
4. Since I spent a week in Mexico, my progress in speaking Spanish has been smooth sailing.
5. After I learned the secret, it was difficult to keep it under my hat.
6. We are trying not to go overboard, but we are ordering plenty of food for the class picnic.

- Illustrated vocabulary words
- Interactive vocabulary games
- Vocabulary flashcards

**Activity** Copy each idiom onto a separate note card like the one shown. Identify the source of the idiom (such as sports, music, or weather). Then, define the idiom and use it in a sentence. Refer to printed or online dictionaries of idioms.

**count your chickens before they've hatched**

**come out of one's shell**

**fit as a fiddle**

**throw in the towel**

**step up to the plate**

**skim the surface**

Idiom:

Source:

Meaning:

Example sentence:

## Comprehension and Collaboration

With a partner, make a list of ten idioms that you use. You can list idioms that appear in your textbook, idioms you know, or idioms you find online by doing a Web search with the keyword "idioms." Together, write a funny short story using these idioms.

# Communications Workshop

## Evaluating Media Messages

Messages sent via television, radio, and the Internet are meant to make you think or act a certain way. Practice being an active and critical listener and viewer by following these suggestions.

### Learn the Skills

Use these strategies to complete the activity on page 791.

**Look critically at images.** The media flash images at us at amazing speeds and levels of complexity. Some are graphic; others are realistic; still others are digitally created. All are intended to catch the attention of and influence an audience. Be aware of how certain images are designed to affect your impressions and opinions.

**Listen critically to words and sounds.** The creator of a message can create a mood that influences an audience by using "buzz words" (words that trigger specific associations), music, or sound effects that play on emotions.

**Be aware of persuasive appeals and rhetorical techniques.** Some messages suggest that you jump on a bandwagon. Others use celebrity spokespeople. Still others use statistics and facts to impress an audience. Being aware of these persuasive strategies will help you to assess media messages. In addition, being alert for **rhetorical techniques** such as repetition, loaded terms, and leading questions will help you understand how the message may be swaying you. Recognizing media techniques will make you a smarter viewer.

**Look for hidden agendas.** It is essential to distinguish fact from opinion, especially when looking for information or point of view. Sometimes, messages are hidden. Look beyond the surface of a media message by paraphrasing it. Ask yourself: Which facts, values, and ideas are being presented?

**Identify slant or bias.** Often, complex subjects are presented from only one point of view. In its most extreme form, this becomes **propaganda** that unfairly boosts one point of view while misrepresenting another. For example, political ads often address only one side of a controversial issue. As a viewer, distinguish between messages that inform and propaganda that is meant to mislead.

**Common Core State Standards**

**Reading Informational Text**
**7.** Evaluate the advantages and disadvantages of using different mediums to present a particular topic or idea.

**Speaking and Listening**
**2.** Analyze the purpose of information presented in diverse media and formats and evaluate the motives behind its presentation.
**3.** Delineate a speaker's argument and specific claims, evaluating the soundness of the reasoning and relevance and sufficiency of the evidence and identifying when irrelevant evidence is introduced.

## Practice the Skills

© **Presentation of Knowledge and Ideas** Use what you've learned in this workshop to perform the following task.

---

### ACTIVITY: Evaluate Media Messages

Watch several television commercials. Then, follow the steps below.

- Summarize each commercial.
- Identify the purpose and point of view of each message.
- Identify techniques, such as buzz words, loaded terms, and leading questions, used to deliver the message.
- Explain the effect each commercial had on you.
- Use the Evaluation Guide to interpret the commercials.

---

Use an Evaluation Guide like the one below to evaluate the content of each commercial.

---

### Evaluation Guide

**Visual and Sound Techniques**
Identify which of the following techniques are used and how they influence the message.

- ☐ Flashy graphics
- ☐ Digital effects
- ☐ Sound effects
- ☐ Lighting
- ☐ Appealing use of color
- ☐ Music

**The role of media**
- How did each message focus your attention?
- How did each message affect, change, or shape your opinion?

**Effect of the message**
Interpret how the use of the following techniques creates a point of view and impacts, or affects, you as a viewer. Then, comment on the evidence that supports each commercial's claims.

- ☐ Rhetorical devices
- ☐ Hidden agendas
- ☐ Fact vs. opinion
- ☐ Bias or slant

How persuasive was the evidence? **Comments:**

**Credibility**
How would you rate the credibility of this message? Explain.

_____ Excellent _____ Good _____ Fair _____ Poor

---

© **Comprehension and Collaboration** Discuss your findings with a classmate. Discuss how critical viewing and listening helps to uncover motives behind the messages. Compare the insights you gained from listening for rhetorical devices and persuasive appeals.

# Cumulative Review

## I. Reading Literature

**Directions:** *Read the poem. Then, answer each question that follows.*

Common Core
State Standards

RL.8.4; L.8.4.a; W.8.2.b
[For the full wording of the standards, see the standards chart in the front of your textbook.]

### A Pinch of Salt
by Robert Graves

WHEN a dream is born in you
  With a sudden clamorous pain,
When you know the dream is true
  And lovely, with no flaw nor stain,
5  O then, be careful, or with sudden clutch
You'll hurt the delicate thing you prize so much.

Dreams are like a bird that mocks,
  Flirting the feathers of his tail.
When you seize at the salt-box,
10  Over the hedge you'll see him sail.
Old birds are neither caught with salt nor chaff:
They watch you from the apple bough and laugh.

Poet, never chase the dream.
  Laugh yourself, and turn away.
15  <u>Mask</u> your hunger; let it seem
  Small matter if he come or stay;
But when he nestles in your hand at last,
Close up your fingers tight and hold him fast.

1. Which of the following is a **simile** found in the poem?

   A. *When a dream is born in you*
   B. *O then, be careful, or with sudden clutch*
   C. *Poet, never chase the dream*
   D. *Dreams are like a bird that mocks*

2. Which pattern best describes the **rhyme scheme** of stanza 1?

   A. *abcabc*
   B. *ababcc*
   C. *abcdef*
   D. *ababaa*

3. What **sound device** is used in the phrase *flirting the feathers of his tail*?

   A. onomatopoeia
   B. internal rhyme
   C. alliteration
   D. repetition

4. Which statement *best* explains the use of **personification** in the first stanza?

   A. A dream is said to be truthful, although it can cause pain.
   B. A dream, like a child, can be hurt if treated too roughly.
   C. A dream is like a delicate bird.
   D. A dream is like a prize that can be won in a contest.

5. To whom or what might the "he" refer in line 17 of the poem?

   A. the poet
   B. the bird
   C. the dream
   D. memories

6. Which of the following *best* **paraphrases** the lines "… let it seem / small matter if he go or stay" in lines 15–16?

   A. Make him feel small so he will leave.
   B. Do not make it obvious that you see him.
   C. Let him feel so small that you will not notice when he leaves.
   D. Let it seem unimportant to you if he comes or goes.

7. Which **form of poetry** best describes this poem?

   A. lyric
   B. elegy
   C. narrative
   D. free verse

8. **Vocabulary** Which word or phrase is closest in meaning to the underlined word <u>mask</u>?

   A. a covering
   B. feed
   C. a face
   D. hide

 Timed Writing

9. In an essay, explain the **speaker's attitude** toward "dreams" and decide whether you agree with him. Use specific examples from the poem to support your ideas.

 GO ON

## II. Reading Informational Text

**Directions:** *Read the passages. Then, answer each question that follows.*

**Common Core State Standards**

**RI.8.2; L.8.1.b; W.8.4**
[For the full wording of the standards, see the standards chart in the front of your textbook.]

### "You-Till"

**Product Description:** This 4-horsepower, gas-engine rotary tiller is equipped with spinning blades to loosen soil. It is perfect for preparing soil for planting vegetables or flowers.

**Cost: $49.95**

**Easy-to-Use Instructions:**

1. Fill the 1-gal. tank with diesel gasoline. Replace gas cap tightly.
2. Press and hold the start button.
3. Adjust lever on right handle to adjust motor speed.
4. Release start button to turn off.

**Caution!** Always clear the soil of rocks and debris before using tiller!

### "Hoe for Health"

This specially designed hoe is perfectly engineered to <u>eliminate</u> unnecessary back strain. The rubber-coated handle is angled for optimum balance and strength.

**Yours for the low cost of $14.99**

**How to Care for Your "Hoe for Health":**

- Store in a shed or covered area.
- Clean your hoe of dirt, and dry before storing.

1. According to the product description, what is the purpose of a rotary tiller?
   A. It breaks up the soil.
   B. It keeps the soil from forming crusts.
   C. It helps you to spread seeds.
   D. It helps you spread the mulch layer.

2. What features do the documents have in common?
   A. Both contain directions.
   B. Both provide a product description.
   C. Both contain caution notes.
   D. Both list manufacturer information.

3. Why is "You-Till" more suitable for the needs of a professional gardener?
   A. It uses gasoline.
   B. It can till soil more quickly than a hoe.
   C. It costs more and will last longer.
   D. It is a safer machine.

4. According to the text, what is the biggest difference between the two products?
   A. The till has an engine; the hoe does not.
   B. The hoe needs to be stored inside.
   C. The hoe has a rubber handle.
   D. The hoe is washable.

# III. Writing and Language Conventions

**Directions:** *Read the passage. Then, answer each question.*

(1) Many people have problems writing thank-you cards. (2) You might *want* to thank people for their kindness and generosity but you never get around to it. (3) Here is how to solve your problem. (4) Buy a set of blank cards and envelopes. (5) Stamps should be bought, too. (6) Send an e-mail to your friends and relatives, asking them to send you their mailing addresses. (7) Put those addresses in an address book. (8) When someone does a nice deed for you, you can start writing: the envelopes, addresses, and stamps are at your fingertips!

1. Which of the following provides the *best* support for the idea stated in sentence 1?
   A. How many times have you meant to send a card but didn't?
   B. Thank-you cards are an obligation we all have.
   C. People also dislike writing letters of recommendation.
   D. Writing thank-you notes is a centuries-old tradition.

2. Which is the *most* effective way to combine sentences 4 and 5?
   A. Buy stamps, and a set of blank cards and envelopes, too.
   B. Buy a set of blank cards, envelopes, and stamps.
   C. Purchase stamps, and also blank cards and envelopes.
   D. Blank cards, stamps, and envelopes should be bought at the store.

3. Which sentence in the passage uses the **passive voice** and should be fixed?
   A. sentence 1
   B. sentence 3
   C. sentence 5
   D. sentence 7

4. Which possible revision to sentence 3 contains an **indirect object?**
   A. I will tell you how to solve your problem.
   B. I will solve your problem for you.
   C. Solving problems is easy.
   D. The solution is clear, and here it is.

5. Which revision to sentence 7 shows the strongest cause-and-effect relationship?
   A. Put those addresses in an address book so that you be able to find them later.
   B. Put those addresses in a book in which you keep addresses.
   C. After you buy an address book, put the addresses you get into it.
   D. Put the addresses in an address book, where they belong.

6. Which of the possible revisions to sentence 5 includes a **subject complement?**
   A. Stamps should be bought in advance.
   B. Stamps are useful items to have on hand.
   C. You should buy stamps, too.
   D. Do not forget stamps.

# Performance Tasks

**Directions:** *Follow the instructions to complete the tasks below as required by your teacher.*

*As you work on each task, incorporate both general academic vocabulary and literary terms you learned in this unit.*

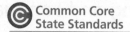
**Common Core State Standards**

RL.8.1, RL.8.4, RL.8.5; W.8.2, W.8.9; SL.8.1, SL.8.6; L.8.1, L.8.3, L.8.4, L.8.5, L.8.6

[For the full wording of the standards, see the standards chart in the front of your textbook.]

## Writing

### Task 1: Literature [RL.8.4; W.8.9]

**Analyze the Effect of Word Choice on a Poem's Meaning and Tone**

*Write an essay in which you analyze a poet's word choices and their impact on meaning and tone.*

- Identify a poem from this unit whose meaning and tone seem clear to you.

- State your interpretation of the poem's overall meaning in a few sentences. Then, characterize the poem's tone by using adjectives that describe the main attitude of the poem's speaker.

- Support your interpretation of the poem's meaning by showing how specific words, phrases, and figurative language help to communicate an aspect of the meaning you identified.

- Support your characterization of tone by indicating how the connotations of particular words and phrases help produce the tone you identified.

- Check your writing to identify and correct any misplaced or dangling modifiers.

### Task 2: Literature [RL.8.5; W.8.4]

**Contrast the Structure of Two Poems**

*Write an essay in which you contrast the structures of two poems and explain how their different structures affect style and meaning.*

- Choose two poems from this unit that have notable differences in structure. For example, you might choose a sonnet and a free verse poem.

- Explain how the poems differ by contrasting such characteristics as rhyme scheme, line length, number of lines in stanzas, and pattern of stressed syllables (meter).

- Describe how these differences in structure combine to affect the formality or informality of each poem's style.

- Finally, explain how the differences in structure contribute to the overall meaning and effect of the poem.

### Task 3: Literature [RL.8.4; W.8.2; L.8.3]

**Analyze the Sound Devices in a Poem**

*Write an essay in which you analyze the effect of sound devices in a poem from this unit.*

- Select a poem that uses sound devices—such as rhyme, rhythm, or alliteration—in a powerful way.

- Identify specific word or phrase choices and explain which sound device each example represents.

- Describe the effect of these sound devices on the poem's tone. For example, explain whether they make the poem seem musical, exciting, or mournful.

- Check your writing to make sure that you consistently use active voice and that you vary sentence patterns.

# Speaking and Listening

© **Task 4: Literature** [RL.8.4; L.8.5]

## Analyze Word Choice by Doing a Close Reading

*Read aloud a poem from this unit. Then, discuss the meaning of specific words and phrases in that poem.*

- Select a poem in which the author has made several interesting word choices with literal, figurative, and connotative meanings.
- Read the poem aloud to a group. Then, review the poem, line by line.
- As you review, identify examples of simile, metaphor, and personification and analyze their meanings.
- For other types of word choices, distinguish between the literal meanings and connotations of particular words.
- Then, analyze how the connotations affect the meaning of the stanzas in which they appear and the overall poem.

© **Task 5: Literature** [RL.8.5; SL.8.1]

## Read Two Poems Aloud to Compare Their Structures

*Read two poems aloud. Then, discuss how their structures affect the poems' meaning and style.*

- Choose two poems from this unit that have distinct structures.
- As a group, identify the characteristics of each poem's structure, including meter, rhyme scheme, line length, number of lines, and regular or irregular stanzas.
- Have two group members read the poems aloud, emphasizing structural elements, such as stressed syllables, rhymed words, and stanza breaks.
- Based on the readings, compare and contrast the two poems' structures. In your discussion, analyze the way that each structure contributes to the poem's style and reinforces its overall meaning.

© **Task 6: Literature** [RL.8.2; SL.8.1]

## Hold a Panel Discussion About Three Poems

*Choose three poems from this unit that address a similar topic and explain how each poet brings a different perspective to that topic.*

- Identify three poems in this unit that have the same general topic, such as nature or a historical event.
- Ask panel members to characterize the poet's attitude toward the topic and to identify one or more themes in each of the poems.
- To support their claims, panel members should identify specific lines or sections of the poem that best reflect the theme and poet's attitude.
- Each panel member should ask additional questions and make comments that connect to and build on the comments of other panel members.

---

### What is the secret to reaching someone with words?

At the beginning of Unit 4, you participated in a discussion about the Big Question. Now that you have finished the unit, write a response to the question. Discuss how your views have developed since you discussed the question. Give specific examples from the poems, as well as from other subjects and your personal experiences, to support your ideas. Use Big Question vocabulary words (see p. 637) in your response.

# Featured Titles

In this unit, you have read a wide variety of poems by many different poets. Continue to read on your own. Select works that you enjoy, but challenge yourself to explore new poets and works of increasing depth and complexity. The titles suggested below will help you get started.

## Literature

### Black Hair

by Gary Soto  EXEMPLAR TEXT

In this wide-ranging collection of **poetry,** Gary Soto reaches back to his roots—growing up poor in a Fresno neighborhood. In works like "Oranges," a poem about wanting to impress a girl but having very little to impress her with, Soto looks back with fondness, humor, and insight on his earlier years.

### The Heart of a Chief

by Joseph Bruchac

A bright, courageous eleven-year-old Native American boy fights injustice and prejudice in this **novel** by author Bruchac, whose own mother was Abenaki. Through a mixture of humor and seriousness, sprinkled with lots of realistic dialogue, this first-person story provides readers with a unique perspective from which to view the world.

### Classic Poems to Read Aloud

edited by James Berry  EXEMPLAR TEXT

**Poetry** by poets from all over the world is included in this collection, organized by subject. Read such classic poems as Lewis Carroll's "Jabberwocky" and W. H. Auden's "Funeral Blues" alongside contemporary gems like Shel Silverstein's "It's Dark in Here."

### Locomotion

by Jacqueline Woodson

In this gripping story, told through a series of **poems,** a boy named Lonnie discovers the power of self-expression. At first, Lonnie is not sure what to write when he gets a poetry assignment. However, eventually, through poetry, he is able to explore his grief over his parents' deaths and celebrate the enjoyment he gets from close relationships with his friends and foster family.

## Informational Texts

### A Street Through Time

by Anne Millard

Have you ever wondered how your neighborhood would look one hundred, five hundred, or even several thousand years ago? This fascinating book follows an English port city through time, from the Stone Age to the present day. Discover how nature and human activities can shape a landscape in dramatic ways.

### Discoveries: Lines of Communication

Advances in technology have transformed the way we communicate. Read this collection of **essays** to learn more about these topics: "Samuel Morse's Dream," "Astronauts Take Off in Russian," "Welcome to the Blogosphere," and "Misleading Statistics."

# Preparing to Read Complex Texts

**Attentive Reading** As you read on your own, ask yourself questions about the text. The questions shown below and others that you ask as you read will help you learn and enjoy literature even more.

**Common Core
State Standards**

**Reading Literature/Informational Text 10.** By the end of the year, read and comprehend literature, including stories, dramas, and poems, and literary nonfiction at the high end of grades 6–8 text complexity band independently and proficiently.

## When reading poetry, ask yourself...

- Who is the speaker of the poem? What kind of person does the speaker seem to be? How do I know?

- What is the poem about?

- If the poem is telling a story, who are the characters and what happens to them?

- Does any one line or section state the poem's theme, or meaning, directly? If so, what is that line or section?

- If there is no direct statement of a theme, what details help me to see the poem's deeper meaning?

© **Key Ideas and Details**

- How does the poem look on the page? Is it long and rambling or short and concise? Does it have long or short lines?

- Does the poem have a formal structure or is it free verse?

- How does the form affect how I read the poem?

- How many stanzas form this poem? What does each stanza tell me?

- Do I notice repetition, rhyme, or meter? Do I notice other sound devices? How do these elements affect how I read the poem?

- Even if I do not understand every word, do I like the way the poem sounds? Why or why not?

- Do any of the poet's word choices seem especially interesting or unusual? Why?

- What images do I notice? Do they create clear word-pictures in my mind? Why or why not?

- Would I like to read this poem aloud? Why or why not?

© **Craft and Structure**

- Has the poem helped me understand its subject in a new way? If so, how?

- Does the poem remind me of others I have read? If so, how?

- In what ways is the poem different from others I have read?

- What information, ideas, or insights have I gained from reading this poem?

- Do I find the poem moving, funny, or mysterious? How does the poem make me feel?

- Would I like to read more poems by this poet? Why or why not?

© **Integration of Ideas**

# Is it our differences or our similarities that matter most?

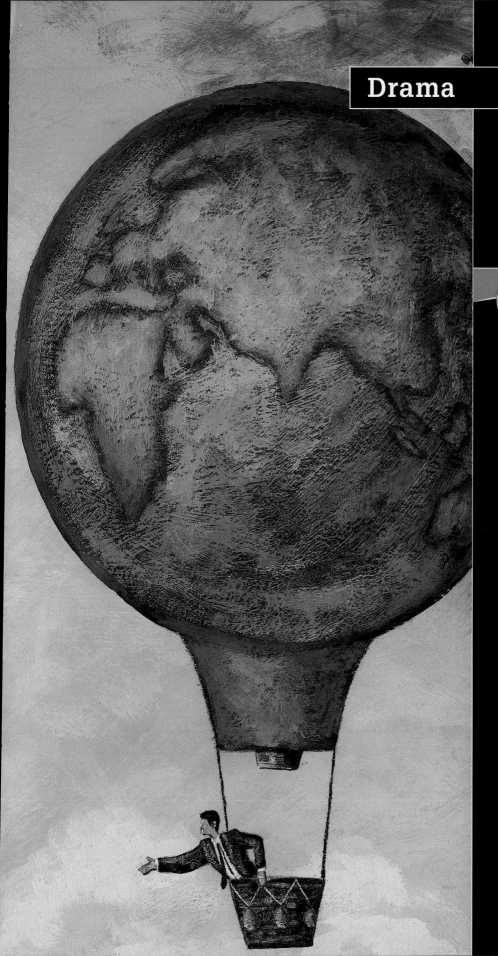

## PHLit Online!
### www.PHLitOnline.com

**Hear It!**
- Selection summary audio
- Selection audio
- BQ Tunes

**See It!**
- Author videos
- Big Question video
- Get Connected videos
- Background videos
- More about the authors
- Illustrated vocabulary words
- Vocabulary flashcards

**Do It!**
- Interactive journals
- Interactive graphic organizers
- Grammar tutorials
- Interactive vocabulary games
- Test practice

# Is it our *differences* or our *similarities* that matter most?

There are many ways for people to distinguish themselves from one another. People often choose to identify themselves—or to classify others—based on race, religion, national origin, or economic class. Or they might choose a different category, such as academic or athletic achievement. At the same time, as human beings with similar needs and desires, we have much in common.

The health of a society depends on how we handle differences and similarities. We debate about whether to find value in differences, or whether we should focus on similarities. We ask whether many standards we use to judge one another are only superficial realities, or whether they represent deep qualities such as character or beliefs. However we answer these questions, it is important to explore the ways in which we balance our differences and our similarities.

## Exploring the Big Question

© **Collaboration: One-on-One Discussion** Start thinking about the Big Question by making a list of various ways in which similarities and differences among people influence behavior. Describe one specific example of each of these situations in which similarities and differences matter.

- A well-off employer considering how much to pay a worker
- A group of people trying to escape religious discrimination
- An event at school that brings different social groups together
- A visit to a family from a different ethnic background

Share your examples with a partner. Discuss how people in these situations might act if they based their actions on differences alone, similarities alone, or taking both factors into consideration.

**Connecting to the Literature** Each reading in this unit will give you additional insight into the Big Question.

**PHLit**
**Online!**
**www.PHLitOnline.com**
- Big Question video
- Illustrated vocabulary words
- Interactive vocabulary games
- BQ Tunes

# Learning Big Question Vocabulary

**Acquire and Use Academic Vocabulary** Academic vocabulary is the language you encounter in textbooks and on standardized tests. Review the definitions of these academic vocabulary words.

**class** (klas) *n.* a group of people or objects

**discriminate** (di skrim´ i nāt´) *v.* see the difference between; tell apart; also, treat one group unfairly

**distinguish** (di stiŋ´ gwish) *v.* see the difference between; tell apart

**divide** (də vīd´) *v.* separate

**identify** (i den´ tə fī´) *v.* recognize as being

**judge** (juj) *v.* form an opinion about; evaluate

**represent** (rep´ ri zent´) *v.* stand for; speak for

Use these words as you complete Big Question activities in this unit that involve reading, writing, speaking, and listening.

**Gather Vocabulary Knowledge** Additional Big Question words are listed below. Categorize the words by deciding whether you know each one well, know it a little bit, or do not know it at all.

| | | |
|---|---|---|
| assumption | separate | tolerance |
| common | superficial | unify |
| generalization | sympathy | |

Then, do the following:

1. Write the definitions of the words you know.
2. Consult a dictionary to confirm the definitions of the words you know. Revise your definitions if necessary.
3. Using a print or an online dictionary, look up the meanings of the words you do not know. Then, write the meanings.
4. Use all of the words in a brief paragraph about a specific conflict in which either a crucial difference or a key similarity among individuals or groups of people affected the outcome.

# Elements of Drama

In drama, dialogue and action work together to develop characters and tell a story.

**Drama** is a genre of literature that is meant to be performed. **Plays,** or dramatic performances, have entertained audiences for thousands of years. In drama, the dialogue and action tell the story.

The **playwright,** or dramatist, is the author of the **script,** the written version of a play. The script contains **dialogue,** the words spoken by the characters, and **stage directions** that provide instructions on how the play should be performed.

A play takes place at a particular time and location, called the **setting.** As a play develops, we learn about the **characters** and the struggle, or **conflict,** they face.

Events in the **plot** move forward, and the action builds until it reaches a **climax,** the point when the conflict reaches its peak. As the play comes to a close, the conflict is usually settled. This part of the play is called the **resolution.**

A successful play is one in which the playwright provides the reader or audience with believable, **well-rounded characters.** Such characters remind us of people we know in real life. Playwrights portray well-rounded characters through the careful development of dialogue that reveals not only *what* the characters say but *how* and *why* they say it.

### Elements of Drama

| Element | Function |
|---|---|
| Dialogue | • reveals the nature of characters<br>• advances the plot<br>• establishes theme, the work's central message about life or human nature |
| Characters | • show qualities, or traits, and motivations<br>• face one or more conflicts<br>• develop theme through their words and actions |
| Plot | • develops suspense<br>• focuses on a conflict, or struggle between opposing forces<br>• builds to a climax, or turning point, the point of maximum interest<br>• shows relationships between characters' actions and events<br>• expresses theme |
| Stage Directions | • describe scenery, lighting, and sound effects<br>• tell how characters should behave |
| Setting | • describes the time and place in which the action occurs<br>• creates mood |

## Types of Drama

Two general categories of drama are comedy and tragedy.

A **comedy** usually deals with a light subject or handles a dark subject in an upbeat way. Comedies often present everyday characters in amusing situations. They are humorous in tone and end happily.

In a **tragedy,** events lead to the downfall or death of the main character. This character can be an average person but is often a heroic figure who displays a **tragic flaw,** a human trait such as pride or greed, that brings about his or her destruction. A tragedy may teach a powerful lesson about human nature.

A playwright may combine elements of both comedy and tragedy in a single work. For example, some comedies use humor to express a serious message about life or human nature. Likewise, a tragedy might include **comic relief**—a scene or an incident that provides a break from the otherwise serious events of the play.

## The Changing World of Drama

For centuries, plays were intended to be viewed by a live audience or read in script form. Today, technology has changed the ways in which we experience plays. We can still watch a play with live actors onstage, but we can also watch a performance onscreen in a movie theater or at home in front of our televisions or computers.

### In This Section

**Elements of Drama**

**Analyzing Dramatic Elements**

**Close Read: Character, Action, and Theme**
- Model Text
- Practice Text

**After You Read**

 Common Core
State Standards

RL.8.3, RL.8.6
[For the full wording of the standards, see the standards chart in the front of your textbook.]

## Types of Drama Today

| Live Theater | Film/Movies | Television Drama | Radio Drama |
|---|---|---|---|
| • performed live for an audience<br>• follows a written script<br>• divides into acts and scenes<br>• uses dialogue to tell the audience what is happening<br>• uses scenery and lighting for visual effects | • recorded on film or digital medium and shown in theaters or streamed online<br>• follows a script called a screenplay<br>• is often made up of many short scenes<br>• uses a camera to direct audience's attention to certain details | • recorded or performed live<br>• follows a script called a teleplay<br>• uses long and short scenes<br>• like film, uses a camera to direct audience's attention<br>• may be streamed online over the Internet | • recorded or performed live<br>• follows a script called a radio play<br>• uses long and short scenes<br>• uses dialogue and sound effects to tell the audience what is happening |

# Analyzing Dramatic Elements

In drama, conflict, dialogue, and stage directions make the characters and their actions come alive.

**Common Core State Standards**

**Reading Literature 3.** Analyze how particular lines of dialogue or incidents in a story or drama propel the action, reveal aspects of a character, or provoke a decision.

**Reading Literature 6.** Analyze how differences in the points of view of the characters and the audience or reader create such effects as suspense or humor.

Drama has the power to reveal important truths about life and human nature. Whether you are reading or watching a play, realistic characters can remind you of yourself or people you know. Even if just for a moment, you may feel as strongly about their situations as you do about real life. It is through the play's action, conflict, and dialogue that this magic takes place.

**Action and Conflict** In most plays, characters face a **conflict,** or struggle between opposing forces, that drives the **action.**

- An **external conflict** involves a character confronting an outside force, such as a physical obstacle, an enemy, nature, or society.
- An **internal conflict** is a struggle that occurs within a character. It often involves the character's feelings, beliefs, and values.

**Dialogue and Character Development** In drama, most of what you learn about characters comes from dialogue. Playwrights use dialogue in the following ways:

- to show a character's personality;
- to express a character's thoughts and feelings about events and other characters.

**Character Motivation** When a playwright writes a play, he or she must decide who the characters are and what their personalities are like. The playwright must also determine how each character will respond to events in the plot. For example, will the character explain through dialogue how he or she feels, or will events force the character to make a decision that moves the plot in a new direction? The playwright answers such questions by developing each character's motivation.

**Character motivation** refers to the reasons why a character feels or behaves a certain way. The following chart demonstrates how character motivation works.

| Character Motivation | Resulting Action |
|---|---|
| Anna likes Max, a new boy at school, and wants to meet him. | Anna's friend Jenna is having a party. At Anna's request, Jenna invites both Anna and Max to the party. |
| A man must get on the last train out of his war-torn country. | The man sleeps at the station the night before to guarantee his spot on the train. |

Character motivation typically sets up a **cause-and-effect relationship** between events in a play. In the first example, Anna's desire to get to know the new boy causes her to ask Jenna to invite them both to a party. The resulting action is the effect.

**Complex Characters** To create plays that audiences care about, playwrights strive to develop **complex characters.** These characters display strengths and weaknesses and exhibit a full range of emotions. Sometimes, complex characters have multiple motivations.

**Characters in Written Drama** In a live performance, the actors use their facial expressions, body language, and tones of voice to help the audience understand the characters. When you read a play, however, you must gather clues to fully understand the characters and their motivations and conflicts. Here are some questions to ask yourself:

- Do the stage directions call for certain movements, facial expressions, or vocal intonations? (Example: *She nods in agreement.*)
- Do punctuation marks in a speech express a character's mood or feeling? (Example: That's amazing! I had no idea!)
- Do the characters use certain words that reveal their relationships? (Example: Honey, why didn't you call me?)

**Dramatic Irony** Sometimes the audience or readers of a play know more than the characters know. Such situations are examples of **dramatic irony,** a technique that can create humor or build suspense. The chart shows an example of dramatic irony and two possible ways that the situation might be revealed to the audience but hidden from the other characters.

| |
|---|
| **Situation:** The audience knows a character's true identity, while the other characters believe she is someone she is not. |
| **Possibility 1:** The character puts on a disguise during a scene in which other characters are not present. |
| **Possibility 2:** The character reveals she is in disguise by delivering a speech called an **aside.** An aside can be heard by the audience but not by other characters. |

When a playwright uses dramatic irony, the point of view of the audience is very different from the points of view of the characters. Therefore, the words and actions of the characters have a different meaning for the audience than they do for the play's characters.

**Theme in Drama** The unique combination of elements in a play helps express its theme. As characters face conflicts and undergo growth and change, their actions and attitudes deliver important messages about life and human nature. To determine the theme of a dramatic work, ask yourself these questions:

- How have events caused the characters to change?
- Do events in the play remind me of my own experiences? If so, what did those experiences teach me?
- What might have been the playwright's purpose for writing the play?

# Close Read: Character, Action, and Theme

## In drama, characters propel the action and develop the theme.

In drama, playwrights develop characters who come alive through dialogue and stage directions. As the action of the play advances, powerful messages about life and human nature reveal themselves. The following questions can help you get the most out of reading a play.

### Clues to Analyzing Character, Plot, and Theme

**Dialogue**
- What do the characters say?
- How do they say it?
- How do they react to comments made by other characters?
- How does the dialogue help to develop the plot?

**Stage Directions**
- What do you learn from the physical descriptions of the characters?
- How do the characters behave onstage?
- How does background and information about the setting influence the plot?
- What mental image do the stage directions help create?

**Character**
- What personality traits do the characters show?
- What problems or conflicts do they face?
- How do they attempt to resolve the conflicts?
- What decisions do they make?

**Character Motivations**
- What do characters want? Why do they behave as they do?
- How does their behavior affect the plot?
- How are the characters' goals or desires theatened?

**Action/Plot**
- What actions do the characters carry out?
- How do the characters react to events?
- How is tension built and then released?
- What is the climax, and how are the conflicts resolved?

**Theme**
- What ideas do the main characters' goals or desires reveal?
- Do any events or feelings expressed by the characters remind you of your own experiences in life?
- What message does the play's outcome suggest about life or human nature?

# Model

**About the Text** *Kindertransport* takes place in Germany in 1938, during the violent rule of Adolf Hitler's Nazi party. In the play, the Nazis are waging a brutal campaign against Jews. Great Britain has responded with Kindertransport ("Children's Transport"), a program that offers Jewish children safe passage to Britain. In this scene, nine-year-old Eva is on a train heading out of Germany.

---

### from *Kindertransport* by Diane Samuels

*(Enter a Nazi border OFFICER. He approaches EVA . . .)*

**OFFICER:** No councillor in here?

**EVA:** She's in the next carriage.

**OFFICER** *(picking up EVA'S case)*: Whose case is this?

**EVA:** Mine.

**OFFICER:** Stand up straight.

*(EVA stands.)*

Turn your label around then. It's gone the wrong way. Can't see your number.

**EVA** *(turning the label round. Quietly)*: Sorry.

**OFFICER:** Speak up.

**EVA:** Sorry.

**OFFICER:** Sir! Sorry, Sir.

**EVA:** Sorry, Sir.

**OFFICER:** No one will know what to do with you if they can't see your number.

*(Silence)*

Will they?

**EVA:** No, Sir.

**OFFICER:** Might have to remove you from the train.

*(Silence.)*

Mightn't we?

**EVA:** Yes, Sir.

---

**Action/Plot** The officer's severe words and threatening behavior create tension.

**Dialogue** From this dialogue, we learn that the officer is not just strict but may even be capable of cruelty toward Eva.

**Stage Directions** The stage directions indicating Eva's silence help capture the terror she feels as the officer questions her.

# Independent Practice

**About the Selection** This excerpt, from Cherie Bennett's play, *Anne Frank & Me,* begins after Nicole, a typical suburban American teenager, bumps her head in an accident. She then wakes up in another time and place—Paris in 1942. Nicole's new family is Jewish. Soon after the Nazis arrest the family, they are put on a train to Auschwitz. This is where Nicole meets Anne Frank, the real writer of *The Diary of a Young Girl.*

**Stage Directions**
This stage direction describes the action during Nicole's monologue. What does the word *shove* tell you about the experience of being put on the train?

**Action/Plot** What major event in the plot occurs at this point?

**Character** What relationship between the girls does this dialogue establish?

---

### from *Anne Frank & Me* by Cherie Bennett

**At Rise:** *During the following monologue,* Nazis *shove more people into the cattle car.*

**Nicole** *(pre-recorded)*: Right now we are in Westerbork, in Holland. Earlier today they opened the door and shoved more people into our car. They speak Dutch. I can't understand them at all. I try to keep track of the dates as best I can. I think it is the 3rd of September, 1944. Surely the war will be over soon.

*(Train sounds. **Nicole** makes her way to the bucket in the corner which is used as a toilet. A **Girl** sits in front of the bucket, asleep, her back is to us.)*

**Nicole:** *(tapping the **Girl** on the shoulder).* I'm sorry to disturb you, but I need to use the—

*(The girl turns around. It is **Anne Frank**, thin, huge eyes. Their eyes meet. Some memory is instantly triggered in **Nicole**. She knows this girl, knows things about her. But how?)*

**Anne:** *Spreekn U Nederlander?* [Sprek´ ən oo ned´ ər land  ər?] *(**Nicole** just stares.)* So you speak French, then? Is this better?

**Nicole:** I . . . I need to use the—

**Anne:** It's all right. I'll hold my coat for you to give you some privacy. *(**Nicole** goes to the bucket, **Anne** holds her coat open to shield her.)*

**Nicole:** Thank you.

**Anne:** Just please do the same for me when the time comes. Have you been in here a long time? *(**Nicole** finishes, fixes her dress.)*

**NICOLE:** Seventeen days, starting just outside Paris.

**ANNE:** It smells like it.

**NICOLE:** Does it? I can't even tell anymore.

**ANNE:** It's all right. It's not important.

**NICOLE:** Look, I know this sounds crazy, but . . . I know you.

**ANNE:** Have you been to Amsterdam?

**NICOLE:** No, never.

**ANNE:** Well, I've never been to Paris. Although I will go some day, I can assure you of that.

**NICOLE:** I do know you. Your name is . . . Anne Frank.

**ANNE:** *(shocked).* That's right! Who are you?

**NICOLE:** Nicole Bernhardt. I know so much about you . . . you were in hiding for a long time, in a place you called . . . the Secret Annex[1]—

**ANNE:** How could you know that?

**NICOLE:** *(her memory is flooded).* You were with your parents, and your older sister . . . Margot! And . . . some other people . . .

**ANNE:** Mr. Pfeffer and the Van Pels, they're all back there asleep—

**NICOLE:** Van Daans!

**ANNE:** *(shocked).* I only called them that in my diary. How could you know that?

**NICOLE:** And Peter! Your boyfriend's name was Peter!

**ANNE:** How could you know that?

**NICOLE:** You thought your parents would disapprove that you were kissing him—

**ANNE:** How is this possible?

**NICOLE:** You kept a diary. I read it.

**ANNE:** But . . . I left my diary in the Annex when the Gestapo came. You couldn't have read it.

**NICOLE:** But I did.

**Dialogue** What is Anne's reaction to Nicole's words? Why?

**Character** What does the punctuation in these lines help reveal about both characters?

---

1. **Secret Annex** name given to the space in an Amsterdam office building, where in 1942, thirteen-year-old Anne Frank and her family went into hiding.

**Practice continued**

ANNE: How?

NICOLE: I don't know.

ANNE: *(skeptical).* This is a very, very strange conversation.

NICOLE: I feel like it was . . . I know this sounds crazy . . . but I feel like it was in the future.

ANNE: This is a joke, right? Peter put you up to this.

NICOLE: No—

ANNE: Daddy, then, to take my mind off—

NICOLE: No.

ANNE: *(cynical).* Maybe you're a mind reader! *(She closes her eyes.)* What number am I thinking of right now?

NICOLE: I have no idea. Do you believe in time travel?

ANNE: I'm to believe that you're from the future? Really, I'm much more intelligent than I look.

NICOLE: I don't know how I know all this. I just do.

ANNE: Maybe you're an angel.

NICOLE: That would certainly be news to me.

**Stage Directions**
What do these stage directions tell you about Anne's emotions?

## After You Read  *from* **Anne Frank & Me**

**1. Key Ideas and Details (a) Identify:** In what city does the train journey begin? **(b) Generalize:** What are the conditions on the train? **(c) Speculate:** Why are the people treated this way?

**2. Key Ideas and Details (a) Make a Judgment:** Read the short biography of Anne Frank on page 969 and the excerpts from her diary on pages 970–974. Does Cherie Bennett's Anne Frank seem like the real Anne Frank? Explain. **(b) Discuss:** Compare your answers with a partner's.

**3. Key Ideas and Details Analyze:** Anne Frank and her family were actually on the transport that left Holland for Auschwitz on September 3, 1944. These details become the setting for Cherie Bennett's play. Why is it important for the play to be historically accurate?

**4. Craft and Structure (a) Analyze:** Explain how this scene presents an example of dramatic irony. What does the reader understand about the situation that the characters themselves do not know? **(b) Make Connections:** How does the dramatic irony affect your involvement with the story?

**5. Craft and Structure Interpret:** Based on the scene you just read and on your prior knowledge, is this play best characterized as a comedy or tragedy? Explain.

**6. Integration of Knowledge and Ideas (a)** Analyze the stage directions and dialogue in this scene to identify details that make Anne and Nicole believable characters. How do these elements help you understand the characters of both the protagonist, Nicole, and Anne? Record your ideas in a chart like the one below.

| Character Description | |
|---|---|
| **Anne** huge eyes | **Nicole** anxious, confused |

**(b) Collaborate:** Compare charts with a partner. What additional information might you write on your chart?

## Drama

Build your skills and improve your comprehension of drama.

Read **The Governess** to find out what motivates a woman to play a cruel joke on her employee.

## Common Core State Standards

Meet these standards with **The Governess** (p. 818).

### Reading Literature

**1.** Cite the textual evidence that most strongly supports an analysis of what the text says explicitly as well as inferences drawn from the text. *(Reading Skill: Draw Conclusions)*

**3.** Analyze how particular lines of dialogue or incidents in a story or drama propel the action, reveal aspects of a character, or provoke a decision. *(Literary Analysis: Setting and Character)*

### Writing

**1.** Write arguments to support claims with clear reasons and relevant evidence. *(Writing: Public Service Announcement)*

### Speaking and Listening

**4.** Present claims and findings, emphasizing salient points in a focused, coherent manner with relevant evidence; sound, valid reasoning; and well-chosen details. *(Speaking and Listening: Debate)*

### Language

**1.a.** Explain the function of verbals (gerunds, participles, infinitives) in general and their function in particular sentences. *(Conventions: Participial Phrases)*

**4.b.** Use common, grade-appropriate Greek or Latin affixes and roots as clues to the meaning of a word. *(Vocabulary: Word Study)*

**6.** Acquire and use accurately grade-appropriate general academic and domain-specific words and phrases; gather vocabulary knowledge when considering a word or phrase important to comprehension or expression. *(Vocabulary: Word Study)*

# Reading Skill: Draw Conclusions

**Drawing conclusions** means reaching decisions or forming opinions after considering details in a text. An author may state information directly or even have a character tell the reader something important. However, meaning in literature is usually suggested through details. To draw conclusions from a play, notice what the characters say and do.

- Look for statements that reveal underlying ideas and attitudes.
- Analyze interactions that show how characters treat each other.
- Notice actions that create a clear pattern of behavior.

**Make connections** among these items to decide what that pattern tells you about the character.

## Using the Strategy: Conclusions Flow Chart

Use a **conclusions flow chart** chart like the one shown to record your observations about characters and draw conclusions from them.

# Literary Analysis: Setting and Character

Most characterization in plays is accomplished through dialogue. Setting is largely established through the way the characters react to the onstage world that the playwright has created.

**Stage directions**, or notes that tell how a play should be performed, also give readers insight into the characters, setting, and action. They describe the scenery, costumes, lighting, and sound and may tell how the characters feel, move, and speak. Stage directions are usually printed in italics and set in brackets.

[*It is late evening. The stage is dark, except for the glow of a small lamp beside the bed.*]

When you read a play, notice key lines of dialogue that help you understand a character, the setting, and the situation. Use the stage directions to develop a mental image of how a stage production would look and sound.

# Is it our *differences* or our *similarities* that matter most?

## Writing About the Big Question

The characters in *The Governess* come from different levels of society, which affects the way they treat each other. Use this sentence starter to develop your ideas about the Big Question.

An employer might **discriminate** against an employee, or treat her unfairly because _____.

**While You Read** Think about which differences influence the way the Mistress treats the governess.

## Vocabulary

Read each word and its definition. Decide whether you know the word well, know it a little bit, or do not know it at all. After you read, see how your knowledge of each word has increased.

- **inferior** (in fir´ ē ər) *adj.* lower in status or rank (p. 819) *The nobility thought that peasants were inferior.* inferiority *n.*

- **discrepancies** (di skrep´ ən sēz) *n.* differences; inconsistencies (p. 819) *There were discrepancies between the witnesses' stories of what took place the night of the accident.*

- **discharged** (dis chärjd´) *v.* fired; released (p. 821) *Because she was always late, the manager discharged her.* charge *n.*

- **satisfactory** (sat´ is fak´ tə rē) *adj.* adequate; sufficient to meet a requirement (p. 822) *The group's final statement was satisfactory to all committee members.* satisfaction *n.* satisfactorily *adv.* satisfy *v.*

- **lax** (laks) *adj.* not strict or exact (p. 822) *Patients who are lax about taking medications risk becoming sicker.* laxity *n.*

- **guileless** (gīl´ lis) *adj.* not trying to hide anything or trick people; innocent (p. 824) *Jessica was so guileless that people always took advantage of her.* guile *n.* guilelessness *n.* beguiling *adj.*

### Word Study

The **Latin suffix -ory** means "of," "relating to," or "characterized by."

In this play, the Mistress thinks Julia's answer to a question is not **satisfactory.** She means that the answer was not satisfying, or that it was not good enough.

# Meet
# Neil Simon
## (b. 1927)

## Author of
## *The*
## GOVERNESS

Neil Simon has been called the best-loved playwright of the twentieth century. Millions of people have enjoyed his plays and films. He is best known for his comedies—plays that poke gentle fun at people's behavior.

**Life in New York**  Simon grew up in the Washington Heights neighborhood of New York City. He began as a writer for radio and television then moved on to write comedies for the stage. New York is the setting for many of his most popular plays, including *The Odd Couple, Plaza Suite,* and *Barefoot in the Park.* In the 1980s, Simon drew on his own life for three bittersweet plays that made critics view his work more seriously: *Brighton Beach Memoirs, Biloxi Blues,* and *Broadway Bound.*

## DID YOU KNOW?

Simon once had four hit plays running on Broadway at the same time. His 1991 play *Lost in Yonkers* won the Pulitzer Prize.

## BACKGROUND FOR THE PLAY

### A Governess's Life

In the nineteenth century, when *The Governess* is set, upper-class families in Europe and the United States hired governesses to teach and look after their children. Governesses were often educated single women for whom there were few other ways to make a living. The life of a govern-ess was often lonely because she belonged to neither the ser-vant class nor the upper class.

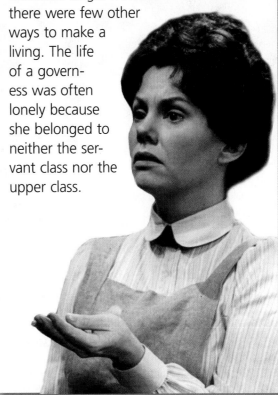

# The Governess
## Neil Simon

▲ **Critical Viewing**
Which person in this scene is playing the part of the governess? How can you tell? **[Analyze]**

**Draw Conclusions**
What conclusion can you draw about the relationship between Julia and the Mistress?

**MISTRESS.** Julia! [*Calls again*] Julia!

[*A young governess, JULIA, comes rushing in. She stops before the desk and curtsies.*]

**JULIA.** [*Head down*] Yes, madame?

**MISTRESS.** Look at me, child. Pick your head up. I like to see your eyes when I speak to you.

**JULIA.** [*Lifts her head up*] Yes, madame. [*But her head has a habit of slowly drifting down again*]

**MISTRESS.** And how are the children coming along with their French lessons?

**JULIA.** They're very bright children, madame.

**MISTRESS.** Eyes up . . . They're bright, you say. Well, why not? And mathematics? They're doing well in mathematics, I assume?

**JULIA.** Yes, madame. Especially Vanya.

**MISTRESS.** Certainly. I knew it. I excelled in mathematics. He gets that from his mother, wouldn't you say?

**JULIA.** Yes, madame.

**MISTRESS.** Head up . . . [*She lifts head up*] That's it. Don't be afraid to look people in the eyes, my dear. If you think of yourself as inferior, that's exactly how people will treat you.

**JULIA.** Yes, ma'am.

**MISTRESS.** A quiet girl, aren't you? . . . Now then, let's settle our accounts. I imagine you must need money, although you never ask me for it yourself. Let's see now, we agreed on thirty rubles[1] a month, did we not?

**JULIA.** [*Surprised*] Forty, ma'am.

**MISTRESS.** No, no, thirty. I made a note of it. [*Points to the book*] I always pay my governess thirty . . . Who told you forty?

**JULIA.** You did, ma'am. I spoke to no one else concerning money . . .

**MISTRESS.** Impossible. Maybe you *thought* you heard forty when I said thirty. If you kept your head up, that would never happen. Look at me again and I'll say it clearly. *Thirty rubles a month.*

**JULIA.** If you say so, ma'am.

**MISTRESS.** Settled. Thirty a month it is . . . Now then, you've been here two months exactly.

**JULIA.** Two months and five days.

**MISTRESS.** No, no. Exactly two months. I made a note of it. You should keep books the way I do so there wouldn't be these discrepancies. So—we have two months at thirty rubles a month . . . comes to sixty rubles. Correct?

---

**1. rubles** (roo´ bəlz) *n.* Russian currency; similar to U.S. dollars.

**Vocabulary**
**inferior** (in fir´ ē ər) *adj.* lower in status or rank

**Setting and Character**
What actions and expressions do the stage directions help you to picture?

**Vocabulary**
**discrepancies** (di skrep´ ən sēz) *n.* differences; inconsistencies

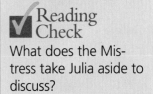
Reading Check
What does the Mistress take Julia aside to discuss?

**Setting and Character**
Which stage directions help you understand the way the characters speak the dialogue?

▼ **Critical Viewing**
If you were Julia, why would you feel intimidated by the Mistress, shown in the picture? Explain. **[Connect]**

**JULIA.** [*Curtsies*] Yes, ma'am. Thank you, ma'am.

**MISTRESS.** Subtract nine Sundays . . . We did agree to subtract Sundays, didn't we?

**JULIA.** No, ma'am.

**MISTRESS.** Eyes! Eyes! . . . Certainly we did. I've always subtracted Sundays. I didn't bother making a note of it because I always do it. Don't you recall when I said we will subtract Sundays?

**JULIA.** No, ma'am.

**MISTRESS.** Think.

**JULIA.** [*Thinks*] No, ma'am.

**MISTRESS.** You weren't thinking. Your eyes were wandering. Look straight at my face and look hard . . . Do you remember now?

**JULIA.** [*Softly*] Yes, ma'am.

**MISTRESS.** I didn't hear you, Julia.

**JULIA.** [*Louder*] Yes, ma'am.

**MISTRESS.** Good. I was sure you'd remember . . . Plus three holidays. Correct?

**JULIA.** Two, ma'am. Christmas and New Year's.

**MISTRESS.** And your birthday. That's three.

**JULIA.** I worked on my birthday, ma'am.

**MISTRESS.** You did? There was no need to. My governesses never worked on their birthdays . . .

**JULIA.** But I did work, ma'am.

**MISTRESS.** But that's not the question, Julia. We're discussing financial matters now. I will, however, only count two holidays if you insist . . . Do you insist?

**JULIA.** I did work, ma'am.

**MISTRESS.** Then you *do* insist.

**JULIA.** No, ma'am.

**MISTRESS.** Very well. That's three holidays, therefore we take off twelve rubles. Now then, four days little Kolya was sick, and there were no lessons.

**JULIA.** But I gave lessons to Vanya.

**MISTRESS.** True. But I engaged you to teach two children, not one. Shall I pay you in full for doing only half the work?

**JULIA.** No, ma'am.

**MISTRESS.** So we'll deduct it . . . Now, three days you had a toothache and my husband gave you permission not to work after lunch. Correct?

**JULIA.** After four. I worked until four.

**MISTRESS.** [*Looks in the book*] I have here: "Did not work after lunch." We have lunch at one and are finished at two, not at four, correct?

**JULIA.** Yes, ma'am. But I—

**MISTRESS.** That's another seven rubles . . . Seven and twelve is nineteen . . . Subtract . . . that leaves . . . forty-one rubles . . . Correct?

**JULIA.** Yes, ma'am. Thank you, ma'am.

**MISTRESS.** Now then, on January fourth you broke a teacup and saucer, is that true?

**JULIA.** Just the saucer, ma'am.

**MISTRESS.** What good is a teacup without a saucer, eh? . . . That's two rubles. The saucer was an heirloom.[2] It cost much more, but let it go. I'm used to taking losses.

**JULIA.** Thank you, ma'am.

**MISTRESS.** Now then, January ninth, Kolya climbed a tree and tore his jacket.

**JULIA.** I forbid him to do so, ma'am.

**MISTRESS.** But he didn't listen, did he? . . . Ten rubles . . . January fourteenth, Vanya's shoes were stolen . . .

**JULIA.** But the maid, ma'am. You discharged her yourself.

---

2. **heirloom** (er′ lōōm′) *n.* treasured possession passed down from generation to generation.

**Spiral Review**
**Conflict** How does the difference between the social classes of Julia and the Mistress help create the play's conflict?

**Vocabulary**
**discharged** (dis chärjd′) *v.* fired; released

**Reading Check**
How does the Mistress punish Julia for the actions of Kolya?

## History Connection

### What Is Women's Work?

Throughout the nineteenth century, jobs for women were scarce. Most professions were unavailable to anyone except men. Low-wage factory jobs, such as making clothing, were available to working-class women and girls. A majority of uneducated women, however, were domestic servants.

A middle-class woman with some education could become a teacher or a governess. An unmarried woman who needed to support herself had few other options.

Like domestic workers and factory workers, governesses earned very little. They were viewed as servants.

## Connect to the Literature

Would Julia behave differently if she were paid better or if she could pursue other career options? Explain.

### Vocabulary

**satisfactory** (sat´ is fak´ tə rē) *adj.* adequate; sufficient to meet a requirement

**lax** (laks) *adj.* not strict or exact

**MISTRESS.** But you get paid good money to watch everything. I explained that in our first meeting. Perhaps you weren't listening. Were you listening that day, Julia, or was your head in the clouds?

**JULIA.** Yes, ma'am.

**MISTRESS.** Yes, your head was in the clouds?

**JULIA.** No, ma'am. I was listening.

**MISTRESS.** Good girl. So that means another five rubles off [*Looks in the book*] . . . Ah, yes . . . The sixteenth of January I gave you ten rubles.

**JULIA.** You didn't.

**MISTRESS.** But I made a note of it. Why would I make a note of it if I didn't give it to you?

**JULIA.** I don't know, ma'am.

**MISTRESS.** That's not a satisfactory answer, Julia . . . Why would I make a note of giving you ten rubles if I did not in fact give it to you, eh? . . . No answer? . . . Then I must have given it to you, mustn't I?

**JULIA.** Yes, ma'am. If you say so, ma'am.

**MISTRESS.** Well, certainly I say so. That's the point of this little talk. To clear these matters up. Take twenty-seven from forty-one, that leaves . . . fourteen, correct?

**JULIA.** Yes, ma'am. [*She turns away, softly crying*]

**MISTRESS.** What's this? Tears? Are you crying? Has something made you unhappy, Julia? Please tell me. It pains me to see you like this. I'm so sensitive to tears. What is it?

**JULIA.** Only once since I've been here have I ever been given any money and that was by your husband. On my birthday he gave me three rubles.

**MISTRESS.** Really? There's no note of it in my book. I'll put it down now. [*She writes in the book.*] Three rubles. Thank you for telling me. Sometimes I'm a little lax with my accounts . . . Always shortchanging myself. So then, we take three more from fourteen . . . leaves eleven . . . Do you wish to check my figures?

**JULIA.** There's no need to, ma'am.

**MISTRESS.** Then we're all settled. Here's your salary for two months, dear. Eleven rubles. [*She puts the pile of coins on the desk.*] Count it.

**JULIA.** It's not necessary, ma'am.

**MISTRESS.** Come, come. Let's keep the records straight. Count it.

**JULIA.** [*Reluctantly counts it*] One, two, three, four, five, six, seven, eight, nine, ten . . . ? There's only ten, ma'am.

**MISTRESS.** Are you sure? Possibly you dropped one . . . Look on the floor, see if there's a coin there.

**JULIA.** I didn't drop any, ma'am. I'm quite sure.

**MISTRESS.** Well, it's not here on my desk, and I *know* I gave you eleven rubles. Look on the floor.

**JULIA.** It's all right, ma'am. Ten rubles will be fine.

**MISTRESS.** Well, keep the ten for now. And if we don't find it on the floor later, we'll discuss it again next month.

**JULIA.** Yes, ma'am. Thank you, ma'am. You're very kind, ma'am.

[*She curtsies and then starts to leave.*]

**MISTRESS.** Julia!

[JULIA *stops, turns.*]

Come back here.

[*She goes back to the desk and curtsies again.*]

Why did you thank me?

**JULIA.** For the money, ma'am.

**MISTRESS.** For the money? . . . But don't you realize what I've done? I've cheated you . . . *Robbed* you! I have no such notes in my book. I made up whatever came into my mind. Instead of the eighty rubles which I owe you, I gave you only ten. I have actually stolen from you and you still thank me . . . Why?

**JULIA.** In the other places that I've worked, they didn't give me anything at all.

▼ **Critical Viewing**
Does this photograph accurately capture Julia's personality? Why or why not?
**[Make a Judgment]**

**MISTRESS.** Then they cheated you even worse than I did . . . I was playing a little joke on you. A cruel lesson just to teach you. You're much too trusting, and in this world that's very dangerous . . . I'm going to give you the entire eighty rubles. [*Hands her an envelope*] It's all ready for you. The rest is in this envelope. Here, take it.

**JULIA.** As you wish, ma'am. [*She curtsies and starts to go again.*]

**MISTRESS.** Julia! [JULIA *stops.*] Is it possible to be so spineless? Why don't you protest? Why don't you speak up? Why don't you cry out against this cruel and unjust treatment? Is it really possible to be so guileless, so innocent, such a—pardon me for being so blunt—such a simpleton?

**JULIA.** [*The faintest trace of a smile on her lips*] Yes, ma'am . . . it's possible.

[*She curtsies again and runs off. The* MISTRESS *looks after her a moment, a look of complete bafflement on her face. The lights fade.*]

## Critical Thinking

1. **Key Ideas and Details** **(a)** What does the Mistress want to discuss with Julia? **(b) Connect:** Why does Julia's position make this discussion difficult for her?

2. **Key Ideas and Details** **(a)** What are the reasons the Mistress gives for cutting Julia's pay? **(b) Infer:** Why does Julia respond the way she does?

3. **Key Ideas and Details** **(a)** What final action does the Mistress take to try to make Julia fight back? **(b) Analyze:** Is the mistress being kind, cruel, or both? Explain. **(c) Speculate:** Do you think Julia will behave differently in the future? Why or why not?

4. **Integration of Knowledge and Ideas** **(a)** Beyond class, what differences between the Mistress and Julia help to explain their behavior? **(b)** If Julia had been from the same social class, would the Mistress have acted differently? Explain. *[Connect to the Big Question: Is it our differences or our similarities that matter most?]*

Cite textual evidence to support your responses.

## Reading Skill: Draw Conclusions

1. Identify three of the Mistress's lines that demonstrate a particular attitude or behavior. **(a)** Based on these lines, what **conclusions** can you draw about the reasons for the Mistress's behavior? **(b)** Does your opinion of the Mistress change between the middle and the end of the play? Explain.

2. Based on Julia's responses, what can you conclude about the general treatment of governesses at the time of this play?

## Literary Analysis: Setting and Character

ⓒ **3. Craft and Structure** **(a)** List one example of dialogue and two examples of **stage directions** from *The Governess* in a chart like the one shown. **(b)** How does each example help you understand the characters, situation, and setting?

| Describing an Action | Showing How a Character Feels |
|---|---|
|  |  |
|  |  |

## Vocabulary

ⓒ **Acquisition and Use** Use a vocabulary word from page 816 to rewrite each of the following sentences so that it has the opposite meaning.

1. The testimony of the two witnesses was in total agreement.
2. Josie was so clever that no one could play a trick on her.
3. Because he forgot to study, Cy got a poor mark on the test.
4. The debaters treated each other as equals.
5. Ben's work was so outstanding that he was given a raise.
6. No one took a long lunch because the boss watched the clock.

**Word Study** Use context and what you know about the **Latin suffix -ory** to explain your answer to each question.

1. Why might someone undergo *exploratory* surgery?
2. If Bill acts in a *supervisory* manner, is he showing leadership?

### Word Study

The **Latin suffix -ory** means "of," "relating to," or "characterized by."

**Apply It** Explain how the suffix -ory contributes to the meanings of these words. Consult a dictionary, if necessary.

**migratory**
**circulatory**
**mandatory**

# Integrated Language Skills

## The Governess

### Conventions: Participial Phrases

A **participle** is a verb form that is used as an adjective. A **participial phrase** is made up of a participle with its modifiers and complements, such as adverbs or objects.

Participles commonly end in *-ing* (present participle) or *-ed* (past participle). The entire participial phrase is used as an adjective.

| Participial Phrases and the Words They Modify |
| --- |
| Traveling quickly, we got to the game on time. (The participial phrase modifies the subject, *we*.) |
| The tourist, confused by the signs, got lost. (The participial phrase modifies the subject, *tourist*.) |
| The hallways are clogged with students going to class. (The participial phrase modifies the object, *students*.) |

**Practice A** Identify the participial phrase in each sentence below. Then identify the noun that it modifies.

1. Julia, feeling anxious and afraid, knocked on the mistress's door.

2. The mistress's accounts, settled once a month, were always accurate.

3. The children, celebrating the holiday, did not have their lessons today.

4. There are envelopes containing our pay.

Ⓒ **Writing Application** Write one sentence about a servant and one about an employer. Use a participial phrase in each sentence.

**Practice B** Use a participial phrase to combine the two sentences into one sentence.

1. Julia carried her suitcase. Julia boarded the carriage.

2. The mistress frowned slightly. The mistress told Julia to count her money carefully.

3. The children ran to their rooms. The children feared the thunder and lightning.

Ⓒ **Writing Application** Write three sentences, using each of these participial phrases: *walking the dog, amused by the joke, containing good nutrients.* Place one phrase at the start, one in the middle, and one at the end of its sentence.

**PH | WRITING COACH**    Further instruction and practice are available in *Prentice Hall Writing Coach.*

# Writing

 **Argumentative Text** Write a **public service announcement (PSA)** that persuades listeners to support the fair treatment of workers. Follow these steps:

- Choose a figure from politics, business, or entertainment as your spokesperson. Write your script with this person in mind.
- Summarize the claims you will use to persuade your audience.
- Make a list of specific words, phrases, images, sound effects, or symbols that will help you support your claims.
- Using elements from your notes, write a script for radio or television to be delivered by your celebrity spokesperson.

**Grammar Application** Make sure your PSA makes use of a variety of phrases and clauses, including adverbial and adjectival forms.

### Writing Workshop: *Work in Progress*

**Prewriting for Workplace Writing** Jot down five careers that interest you. Choose one career and then list the reasons it appeals to you. Save this Career List in your portfolio.

# Speaking and Listening

 **Presentation of Knowledge and Ideas** Form two teams to **debate** this proposal: "The minimum working age should be lowered to thirteen for jobs in retail stores."

Choose a moderator to keep time and to see that the debaters follow the rules. Follow these steps to prepare:

- Conduct research to identify evidence and examples that support your position. Differentiate facts from opinions so that you can establish a factual basis for your arguments.
- Jot down thoughts and reasons that will help bolster your argument. Craft a thesis, or statement of your position, from your notes. Present this thesis during your opening statement.
- Prepare for your opponents' arguments by thinking about the topic from their perspective. For example, you might anticipate the argument that working will take time away from schoolwork by countering that it will develop responsibility.
- During the debate, each participant should build on or respond to the arguments presented by the previous speaker. All debaters should use a respectful tone, particularly when pointing out flaws or weaknesses in opponents' arguments.

 **Common Core State Standards**

**L.8.4.b, L.8.6, L.8.1.a; W.8.1; SL.8.4**
[For the full wording of the standards, see page 814.]

Use this prewriting activity to prepare for the **Writing Workshop** on page 842.

**PHLit Online!**
www.PHLitOnline.com

- Interactive graphic organizers
- Grammar tutorial
- Interactive journals

# Test Practice: Reading

## Draw Conclusions

### Fiction Selection

**Directions:** *Read the selection. Then, answer the questions.*

As I came into town, I could see that much had changed over the years. The huge trees that had once shaded the streets were gone. The houses looked smaller to my adult eyes. Many stores along High Street were empty, with "For Rent" signs in the windows. There was no workday bustle—nobody going to lunch or rushing to meetings. At the end of the street was a brand-new shopping mall, but its parking lot was only half-full. Feeling hopeless, I wondered what I would do here. I considered turning around and heading straight back to Los Angeles, yet as I neared my parents' street, I remembered the mere six dollars in my bank account.

1. What evidence points to the conclusion that the town is no longer prosperous?
   A. There are "For Rent" signs and empty stores.
   B. There is storm damage and the trees are gone.
   C. There is a new shopping mall and the trees are gone.
   D. People are going to lunch and to meetings.

2. Which conclusion is *most* logical?
   A. The narrator is excited.
   B. The narrator has never visited the town before.
   C. The narrator lived in the town years ago.
   D. The narrator is starting a business.

3. The excerpt "The houses looked smaller to my adult eyes" suggests that—
   A. the narrator has a child
   B. the narrator is thinking about buying a house in the town.
   C. the narrator thinks the houses are big.
   D. the narrator was a child the last time he or she was in the town.

4. You can conclude from the passage that the narrator—
   A. is only passing through town.
   B. is visiting old friends.
   C. has financial trouble.
   D. doesn't drive a car.

### Writing for Assessment

Write a few sentences in which you describe the narrator. Use details from the passage to help you draw your conclusions about him or her.

## Nonfiction Selection

**Directions:** *Read the selection. Then, answer the questions.*

In a growing trend often referred to as the "boomerang" effect, young adults are graduating from college and moving back home. Graduation used to signal independence. Now, following the traditional post-college path is not that easy. Jobs are scarce, salaries are low, and rent and other expenses are high. The appeal of traveling the world has also led some recent graduates to live at home and save money until they have enough to travel. More and more older adult children are moving back in with their parents, too. Their reasons range from career changes to the same type of financial concerns that recent college graduates face. Since the 1970s, the number of "boomerangs" has risen from less than 10% of all 20- to 34-year olds to 35%. Some reports even say the number may be as high as 50%!

1. Which conclusion is *most* logical?
   A. Parents hope to support their children.
   B. It costs less to live at home with parents than to live on one's own.
   C. Living at home provides better job opportunities.
   D. Adults look forward to moving home.

2. According to the selection, which *best* describes the "traditional post-college path"?
   A. Students graduate, get jobs, and support themselves.
   B. Students graduate and move home.
   C. Students graduate and buy a house.
   D. Students graduate, get married, and have children.

3. Which conclusion about new college graduates is *most* accurate?
   A. Many of them are too lazy to work.
   B. Many cannot support themselves yet.
   C. Many change jobs often.
   D. Many buy new houses right away.

4. Which detail helps you conclude that some young adults are waiting to start a career?
   A. Young adults want to spend more time with their parents.
   B. Young adults are taking more time to finish school.
   C. Young adults want to start a career, but jobs are scarce.
   D. Young adults want to travel before settling into a job.

## Writing for Assessment

**Connecting Across Texts**

Write a short essay in which you conclude why the narrator of the first selection is moving home. Use information from the second selection to support your ideas.

www.PHLitOnline.com
- Online practice
- Instant feedback

# Reading for Information

## Analyzing Functional Texts

| Public Document | Contract | Job Application |
|---|---|---|
|  |  |  |

**Common Core State Standards**

**Reading Informational Text**
**1.** Cite the textual evidence that most strongly supports an analysis of what the text says explicitly as well as inferences drawn from the text.

**Language**
**6.** Acquire and use accurately grade-appropriate general academic and domain-specific words and phrases; gather vocabulary knowledge when considering a word or phrase important to comprehension or expression.

## Reading Skill: Compare and Contrast Features and Elements

Functional texts often use a variety of elements and features, such as headings, lists, and type treatments, to convey information clearly and obviously. **Comparing and contrasting these features and elements** will help you better understand the information provided in functional texts. Once you understand the information, you can make generalizations. When you *make generalizations,* you combine specific facts and information stated in the text to draw general conclusions, as in this example.

| Information | | Information | | Generalization |
|---|---|---|---|---|
| The U.S. Department of Labor permits youth ages 14–15 to work fewer hours on school days than on non-school days. | **+** | The contract for the work-study program includes academic requirements. | **=** | Employers and the U.S. Department of Labor do not want young people's jobs to interfere with their schoolwork. |

## Content-Area Vocabulary

These words appear in the selections that follow. You may also encounter them in other content-area texts.

- **administering** (ad min´ is tər iŋ) *v.* managing the affairs of
- **termination** (tər´ mə nā´ shən) *n.* the end of something
- **breach** (brēch) *n.* act of breaking or neglect of a law, trust, or duty

# Wage and Hour Division
## Basic Information

**U.S. Department of Labor
Employment Standards Administration**

**The U.S. Department of Labor's Wage and Hour Division (WHD) is responsible for administering and enforcing laws that establish minimally acceptable standards for wages and working conditions in this country, regardless of immigration status.**

### Youth Employment

The Fair Labor Standards Act (FLSA) regulates the employment of youth.

### Jobs Youth Can Do:

- 13 or younger: baby-sit, deliver newspapers, or work as an actor or performer
- Ages 14–15: office work, grocery store, retail store, restaurant, movie theater, or amusement park
- Ages 16–17: any job not declared hazardous
- Age 18: no restrictions

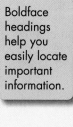

Boldface headings help you easily locate important information.

Bulleted lists make it easy to compare the jobs that different age groups are permitted to hold.

### Hours Youth Ages 14 and 15 Can Work:

- After 7 a.m. and until 7 p.m. (Hours are extended to 9 p.m. June 1–Labor Day)
- Up to 3 hours on a school day
- Up to 18 hours in a school week
- Up to 8 hours on a non-school day
- Up to 40 hours in a non-school week

*Note: Different rules apply to youth employed in agriculture. States also regulate the hours that youth under age 18 may work.*

**Features:**

- items for applicant to complete
- specified area for each party to sign
- text written for a specific audience

# 2006-2007 Work Study Contract

**New College of Florida** Office of Admissions and Financial Aid

_____ is approved to work for _____ in _____.
**Student's Name** · · · · · · · · · · · · · · · · · · · · **Supervisor's Name** · · · · · · · · · **Department Name**

He/She has been awarded $_____ in Work Study for the _____ year.
· · · · · · · · · · · · · · · · **Amount** · · · · · · · · · · · · · · · · · · · · · · · · · · · · · · · · · **Academic Year**

### I, the student, understand that I have the right:

✔ To be treated fairly and courteously.
✔ NOT to be discriminated against based on race, color, religion, sex, marital status, age, national origin, handicapped condition or status as a disabled or Vietnam era veteran.
✔ NOT to have to perform duties beyond the usual responsibilities of a student worker.

✔ To be informed of changes or activities that may affect how and when I perform my job.
✔ To be warned of actions that may cause dismissal.
✔ To be informed of reasons for **termination**.

### I, the student, understand that I have the responsibility:

✔ To keep any and all information seen or heard in the performance of my duties confidential. I may not copy, remove, or allow unauthorized access to institutional documents, files, or mailing lists and that a **breach** of this responsibility can result in immediate dismissal.
✔ To maintain satisfactory academic progress as stated in the Financial Aid policy which can be viewed online.
✔ To dress in an appropriate manner for my position.

✔ To be on time for every shift and stay until the shift is complete.
✔ To call my supervisor if I am sick or will be late.
✔ To perform my duties in an efficient, professional manner.
✔ To ask for assistance or clarification on any job assignment that is unclear to me.
✔ To notify my supervisor if I intend to quit my job.

> Rights and responsibilities are grouped under boldface headings.

### I, the supervisor, understand that I have the right:

✔ To interview and hire an efficient and courteous Work Study student.
✔ To choose the student who appears to best fit my needs.

✔ To terminate my Work Study student after following the procedure prescribed in the New College Work Study Employer Guide if he/she is not performing satisfactorily.

### I, the supervisor, understand that I have the responsibility:

✔ To provide reasonable assignments for the Work Study student that I hire.
✔ To teach the student how to perform the duties assigned to him/her.

✔ To turn in time sheets for the student to the Financial Aid Office on the assigned days if the time sheets are complete.

_____ _____ _____
**Student's Signature** · · · · · · · · · · · · **Date**

_____ _____ _____
**Supervisor's Signature** · · · · · · · · · **Date**

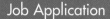

**Features:**

- descriptions of available positions
- space to fill in contact information, education, and experience
- text written for a specific audience

# Tampa Museum of Art

The job title, a key term, is underlined to get the reader's attention.

## Be a Museum Volunteer!

### Teens

<u>Junior Docents</u>

The text includes a clear description of the duties of a junior docent.

Meet new friends while learning about art and culture. Participate in the Tampa Museum of Art's Junior Docent Program! The Junior Docent program at the Tampa Museum of Art is an exciting experience for teenagers to explore history and culture through art. As a Junior Docent, you will learn about the Museum's collection and assist with family programming including our *Art Spot* classes, Family Day activities, and student and family tours.

A Junior Docent's major responsibilities are to explain art processes and objects to the general public during Saturday afternoon student and family tours, and to assist the art teachers and museum educators with the weekly *Art Spot* classes. Being a Junior Docent requires the ability and desire to engage in on-going learning about the Tampa Museum of Art's collections and exhibitions.

Junior Docent Meetings are held two Wednesday afternoons a month from 3:30 p.m. to 5:30 p.m. In addition to the meetings, Junior Docents will work one Saturday a month from 10:00 to 2:00 p.m. The Junior Docent team will also have an opportunity to attend one off-site event each month to learn more about the art community in Tampa and enjoy some fun!

Refreshments are provided.

# Tampa Museum of Art
## VOLUNTEER APPLICATION

**FOR:**

Docent _____ Intern _____ Junior Docent _____ Other _____

Date of Application: _____ Social Security # _____

Name: _____ Home Phone: _____

Address: _____ Zip: _____

Current Employer: _____ Business Phone: _____

Driver's License Number: _____ E-mail address: _____

**EDUCATION:**

College: _____ Major: _____

Degree: _____ Year: _____ Do you have any art history background? _____

**WORK AND VOLUNTEER EXPERIENCE:**
List professional and/or volunteer work. Indicate hours of current commitments.

_____

_____

Have you ever worked with the following groups?

Children (ages 3+) _____ Teenagers _____ Senior Citizens _____ Handicapped _____ Disadvantaged? _____

Have you ever been a museum docent? _____ Where? _____

Other (please specify)? _____ Where? _____

Please indicate any other relevant experience or interests (i.e., teaching experience, travel, etc.)

_____

_____

**AVAILABILITY:**

If you are interested in becoming a docent, are you able to make a one-year commitment (10 hours per week) to the program? _____

Do you prefer to volunteer weekdays? _____ Weekends? _____ Thursday evenings? _____

How did you hear about the program? _____

**PLEASE INCLUDE THE FOLLOWING INFORMATION:**

In case of emergency please notify: NAME _____

Telephone # _____ Relationship? _____

_____ _____
Date                     Volunteer Signature

---

Features such as write-on lines and boxes allow applicants to provide requested information.

## Comparing Functional Texts

**1. Craft and Structure (a) Compare and contrast the features and elements** of the public document with those of the contract. **(b)** How does each text help the reader understand the information presented? **(c)** What **generalizations** can you make about the types of information included in each document? Explain.

## Content-Area Vocabulary

**2. (a)** The words *administering* and *administration* are each formed by adding a suffix to *administer.* In each case, explain how the suffix alters the meaning and part of speech of the base word. **(b)** Use each word in a sentence that shows its meaning.

## 🕐 Timed Writing

### Explanatory Text: Essay

> **Format and Audience**
> The prompt gives specific directions about your audience and the type of information to include in your answer.

What should you consider when deciding whether or not to volunteer at the Tampa Museum of Art? Using the information given in the job application, write an essay for a school newspaper. Explain how a student should go about making a decision. (30 minutes)

> **Academic Vocabulary**
> When you *explain* something, you make it clear using descriptions, details, and facts.

### 5-Minute Planner

Complete these steps before you begin to write:

**1.** Read the prompt carefully and completely. Look for key words like the ones highlighted in color to help you understand the assignment.

**2.** Reread the volunteer application. As you read, consider what details in the text are most important.

**3.** Think about your audience—the students reading the school newspaper. Consider the questions they would need to answer before they could decide whether or not to volunteer.

**4.** Plan the order in which you will place your information.

**5.** Refer to your notes as you write your essay.

## Comparing Adaptations to Originals

A literary **adaptation** is a work that has been changed or adjusted to fit a different form or genre. For example, a novel may be adapted into a play or a movie. When adapting a literary work, an author may change or delete parts of the original to suit the new form and purpose. For instance, since a play depends almost entirely on dialogue to entertain an audience, the narration or description that is included in a story has to be cut or conveyed in a new way.

To compare an adaptation to the original work, remember the differences in the two literary forms. Keep those differences in mind as you analyze the two works.

- First, look for the elements that the writer has kept from the original as well as those he has left out.

- Next, look for new elements the writer has introduced.

- Finally, compare the purposes and styles of the two authors. Determine if one style results in a lighter, more humorous treatment or whether the styles are mostly the same.

"The Ninny" and *The Governess* both borrow plot patterns from traditional fairy tales. In many fairy tales, such as "Cinderella," the main character is a humble young servant who works for a cruel master or mistress. The servant undergoes a series of tests and trials and is eventually rewarded for his or her loyalty and humility. As you read "The Ninny," analyze how Chekhov updates this plot pattern to develop the central idea of the story.

As you read Chekhov's short story "The Ninny," use a Venn diagram like the one shown to analyze the similarities and differences between this work and Neil Simon's dramatic adaptation, *The Governess* (p. 818).

**Common Core State Standards**

**Reading Literature**

**5.** Compare and contrast the structure of two or more texts and analyze how the differing structure of each text contributes to its meaning and style.

**9.** Analyze how a modern work of fiction draws on themes, patterns of events, or character types from myths, traditional stories, or religious works such as the Bible, including describing how the material is rendered new.

**Writing**

**4.** Produce clear and coherent writing in which the development, organization, and style are appropriate to task, purpose, and audience. *(Timed Writing)*

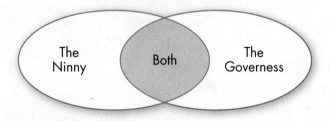

www.PHLitOnline.com

- Vocabulary flashcards
- Interactive journals
- More about the authors
- Selection audio
- Interactive graphic organizers

# Is it our *differences* or our *similarities* that matter most?

## Writing About the Big Question

In "The Ninny" and *The Governess,* two people from very different backgrounds have a disagreement. Use these sentence starters to develop your ideas about the Big Question.

> When two people come from different social **classes**, conflicts can arise over issues such as _____ and _____. This is because _____.

# Meet the Author

## Anton Chekhov (1860–1904)

### Author of "The Ninny"

Anton Pavlovich Chekhov originally planned to be a doctor, and studied medicine in Moscow. To pay for medical school and support his family, he began to write humorous articles and stories for journals.

**A Master of the Short Story** Chekhov wrote more than two hundred short stories. Some are comic, while others show the small tragedies of ordinary life. All show sympathy and understanding for their characters. The stories also paint a realistic and detailed picture of Russian life in both cities and peasant villages.

Despite his success as a writer, Chekhov was surprisingly modest about the writer's role. He wrote: "It is time for writers to admit that nothing in this world makes sense. Only fools . . . think they know and understand everything."

Chekhov was also an accomplished writer of plays. *The Seagull* (1896), *Three Sisters* (1901), and *The Cherry Orchard* (1903) are among his plays that are performed regularly throughout the world. Chekhov died of the lung disease tuberculosis at age forty-four at a health spa in Germany.

*Woman in a Chair*, John Collier, Courtesy of the artist

▶ **Critical Viewing**
What character traits does the woman in this painting seem to possess? **[Analyze]**

# The Ninny
## Anton Chekhov
**Translated by Robert Payne**

**Vocabulary**
**account** (ə kount´) *n.* a bill for work done

**Adaptations**
How do the opening situation and characters compare with those in Simon's play (p. 818)?

Just a few days ago I invited Yulia Vassilyevna, the governess of my children, to come to my study. I wanted to settle my account with her.

"Sit down, Yulia Vassilyevna," I said to her. "Let's get our accounts settled. I'm sure you need some money, but you keep standing on ceremony and never ask for it. Let me see. We agreed to give you thirty rubles a month, didn't we?"

"Forty."

"No, thirty. I made a note of it. I always pay the governess thirty. Now, let me see. You have been with us for two months?"

"Two months and five days."

"Two months exactly. I made a note of it. So you have sixty rubles coming to you. Subtract nine Sundays. You know you don't tutor Kolya on Sundays, you just go out for a walk. And then the three holidays . . ."

Yulia Vassilyevna blushed and picked at the trimmings of her dress, but said not a word.

"Three holidays. So we take off twelve rubles. Kolya was sick for four days—those days you didn't look after him. You looked after Vanya, only Vanya. Then there were the three days you had a toothache, when my wife gave you permission to stay away from the children after dinner. Twelve and seven makes nineteen. Subtract. . . . That leaves . . . hm . . . forty-one rubles. Correct?"

Yulia Vassilyevna's left eye reddened and filled with tears. Her chin trembled. She began to cough nervously, blew her nose, and said nothing.

"Then around New Year's Day you broke a cup and saucer. Subtract two rubles. The cup cost more than that—it was an heirloom, but we won't bother about that. We're the ones who pay. Another matter. Due to your carelessness Kolya climbed a tree and tore his coat. Subtract ten. Also, due to your carelessness the chambermaid[1] ran off with Vanya's boots. You ought to have kept your eyes open. You get a good salary. So we dock off five more. . . . On the tenth of January you took ten rubles from me."

"I didn't," Yulia Vassilyevna whispered.

"But I made a note of it."

"Well, yes—perhaps . . ."

"From forty-one we take twenty-seven. That leaves fourteen."

Her eyes filled with tears, and her thin, pretty little nose was shining with perspiration. Poor little child!

"I only took money once," she said in a trembling voice. "I took three rubles from your wife . . . never anything more."

"Did you now? You see, I never made a note of it. Take three from fourteen. That leaves eleven. Here's your money, my dear. Three, three, three . . . one and one. Take it, my dear."

I gave her the eleven rubles. With trembling fingers she took them and slipped them into her pocket.

---

1. **chambermaid** female household servant whose main job is to clean and care for bedrooms.

**Vocabulary**
**carelessness** (kār´ ləs nəs) *n.* lack of responsibility

**Spiral Review**
**Characterization**
Why does Yulia agree so quickly with her employer's assertion that she took ten rubles, when she first insisted she did not?

Reading Check
Why is Yulia crying?

"*Merci*,"[2] she whispered.

I jumped up, and began pacing up and down the room. I was in a furious temper.

"Why did you say '*merci*'?" I asked.

"For the money."

". . . Don't you realize I've been cheating you? I steal your money, and all you can say is '*merci*'!"

"In my other places they gave me nothing."

"They gave you nothing! Well, no wonder! I was playing a trick on you—a dirty trick . . . I'll give you your eighty rubles, they are all here in an envelope made out for you. Is it possible for anyone to be such a nitwit? Why didn't you protest? Why did you keep your mouth shut? Is it possible that there is anyone in this world who is so spineless? Why are you such a ninny?"

She gave me a bitter little smile. On her face I read the words: "Yes, it is possible."

I apologized for having played this cruel trick on her, and to her great surprise gave her the eighty rubles. And then she said "*merci*" again several times, always timidly, and went out. I gazed after her, thinking how very easy it is in this world to be strong.

2. *merci* (mer sē´) French for "thank you." In the nineteenth century, many upper-class Russians spoke French.

**Vocabulary**
**spineless** (spīn´ ləs)
*adj.* lacking in courage

**timidly** (tim´ id lē)
*adv.* in a shy or fearful manner

## Critical Thinking

*Cite textual evidence to support your responses.*

© **1. Key Ideas and Details** **(a)** Who tells the story of "The Ninny"? **(b) Connect:** What is this person's relationship with Yulia?

© **2. Key Ideas and Details** **(a) Evaluate:** Are any of the reasons the narrator gives for cutting Yulia's pay justifiable? **(b) Infer:** What do Yulia's responses suggest about her personality?

© **3. Key Ideas and Details** **Make a Judgment:** Does the narrator regret or take pleasure in the effect of his "cruel trick" on Yulia? Explain.

© **4. Integration of Knowledge and Ideas** **(a)** What differences separate these characters? **(b)** At the story's conclusion, have they grown more different or more alike? Explain. *[Connect to the Big Question: Is it our differences or our similarities that matter most?]*

# The Governess • The Ninny

## Comparing Adaptations to Originals

**1. (a)** How does Chekhov change the plot pattern of a traditional fairy tale in "The Ninny"? **(b)** What central idea is revealed by this change?

**2.** Use a chart like the one shown to find similarities and differences between "The Ninny" and *The Governess*.

| | Relationships | Events | Endings | Style/Tone |
|---|---|---|---|---|
| **"The Ninny"** | | | | |
| ***The Governess*** | | | | |

## ⏱ Timed Writing

### Explanatory Text: Essay

In an essay, compare and contrast the characterization, events, style, endings, and tone of Neil Simon's adaptation with the original short story. Use textual evidence to support your ideas. (40 minutes)

### 5-Minute Planner

**1.** Read the prompt carefully and completely.

**2.** Gather your ideas by jotting down answers to these questions:

- Why do you think Chekhov chose to write about Yulia and her employer in a first-person story form rather than as a play?

- What is the biggest change that Simon made?

- What purpose is served by Simon's adaptation as a play? Which message is easier for you to interpret? Why?

- How much do the different elements of drama and short story account for the differences between these specifi c works?

- Which version—the story or the play—is more effective? Why?

**3.** To organize your essay, use one of your answers to the questions above as your main thesis. Then, draft the body of your essay by using each of the elements listed in the writing prompt as a point of comparison.

**4.** Reread the prompt, and then draft your essay.

# Writing Workshop

 **Common Core State Standards**

**Writing**
**2.** Write informative/explanatory texts to examine a topic and convey ideas, concepts, and information through the selection, organization, and analysis of relevant content.
**2.a.** Introduce a topic clearly, previewing what is to follow; organize ideas, concepts, and information into broader categories; include formatting, graphics, and multimedia when useful to aiding comprehension.
**2.d.** Use precise language and domain-specific vocabulary to inform about or explain the topic.
**2.e.** Establish and maintain a formal style.

## Write an Informative Text

### Workplace Writing: Business Letter

**Defining the Form** A **business letter** is a document written with a formal tone and with a specific purpose in mind. You might use elements of a business letter when you write a letter of complaint, a letter to an editor, or a cover letter for a job application.

**Assignment** Write a business letter related to career development with the goal of applying for a job. Include these elements:

✔ *conventional business letter format*, including date, proper salutation, body, closing, and signature
✔ a *clearly stated purpose* for the letter that is connected to the position for which you are applying
✔ content that is clear, concise, and focused
✔ points supported by *facts and details*
✔ a *voice* and style appropriate to your *audience* and *purpose*
✔ error-free grammar, including the use of *gerunds and participles*

To preview the criteria on which your business letter may be judged, see the rubric on page 847.

 **Writing Workshop:** *Work in Progress*

Review the work you did on page 827.

## Prewriting/Planning Strategy

**Plan your support.** Choose a job for which you think you are qualified. Identify three personal qualities that make you a good candidate for that job. To support your purpose, list examples of past accomplishments that demonstrate these qualities.

| Job: Newspaper Delivery | |
|---|---|
| **Qualities** | **Accomplishments** |
| Dependability | Never missed a day of soccer practice |
| Punctuality | Always on time for school |
| Honesty | Found a lost wallet and turned it in to the police |

## Use Appropriate Voice

**Voice** is the unique tool a writer uses to communicate ideas. Just as a singer adjusts his or her voice to match the material (using a gentle voice for a lullaby and a strong voice for an opera), a writer adjusts his or her voice to match the situation. Since writers cannot adjust their volume, they rely instead on tools such as word choice, tone, and attitude to achieve a purpose. To help ensure that you use an appropriate voice for business purposes, try these methods:

**Determining Your Attitude** Ask yourself, "What is my attitude toward my audience?" In a business situation, that attitude should include respect for the person you are addressing.

**Using a Professional Tone** In business correspondence, use a professional tone. This is different from the tone you use when talking to friends and family. It is important that you avoid the following:

- slang or rude comments
- details from your personal life

Instead, use precise language, telling your reader what he or she needs to know and closing in a respectful way.

**Adjusting Your Voice** All business letters should have a polite, formal tone. However, your voice can vary, depending on your purpose. Consult the chart and these examples for more details:

- When **writing a cover letter** to accompany a job application, your language should convey the impression that you are sincerely interested, qualified, and available for an interview.

- When **writing a letter of complaint,** you should use firm language to express your disappointment and the idea that you expect the reader to take action to correct the situation.

> **PH** **WRITING COACH**
>
> Further instruction and practice are available in *Prentice Hall Writing Coach.*

|  | **Nonprofessional Tone** | **Professional Tone** |
|---|---|---|
| **Cover Letter** | I think your company is awesome and I would love to work there! | You will notice on my résumé that my education and experience have prepared me well for this job. |
| **Letter of Complaint** | Your CD player is a rip-off! It broke and wrecked my party! | This product does not work properly. |

# Drafting Strategies

**Follow the format.** A business letter must follow an appropriate format to give your letter a professional look. Include each part of a business letter noted in the chart. (For more on letter formats, see pages R26–R27.)

**Make your point.** In the first paragraph, state your purpose for writing. In the paragraphs that follow, present a more detailed explanation. Include important supporting information that will help the recipient to fully consider your request. Make sure you address the expectations of your intended audience. For example, if you are writing a cover letter for a job application, communicate how your skills, personality traits, and experience will prove valuable to your employer if you are hired.

# Revising Strategies

**Revise for businesslike language.** Review your draft carefully. Casual language that you might use in a note or a text message to a friend does not belong in a business letter. Circle any instances of language that assume too familiar a tone. Replace items you have circled with serious, polite language that communicates respect and that will reflect positively on you. If you are expecting the recipient to take action or consider you for a job, you want him or her to take you seriously.

**Revise for conciseness.** Business letters should be brief. Review your letter for wordiness. Condense any passages that are too long, as has been done in the example in the following chart.

 **Common Core State Standards**

**Writing**
**2.b.** Develop the topic with relevant, well-chosen facts, definitions, concrete details, quotations, or other information and examples.
**2.e.** Establish and maintain a formal style.

**Language**
**1.a.** Explain the function of verbals (gerunds, participles, infinitives) in general and their function in particular sentences.

---

**Parts of a Business Letter**

**Heading:** the writer's address and the date

**Inside address:** the name and address of the recipient

**Salutation:** The salutation, or greeting to the recipient, is followed by a colon.
*Examples:* Dear Mr. Davies:
Dear Sir or Madam:
To Whom It May Concern:

**Body:** The main part of the letter presents the writer's purpose and the information that supports it.

**Closing:** The closing begins with a capital letter and ends with a comma.
*Examples:* Yours truly,
With best regards,
Sincerely,

**Signature:** The writer's name is typed below the closing. Between the closing and the typed name, the writer adds a handwritten signature.

---

| Original | Revised |
|---|---|
| If you agree that my educational background and experience are qualifications that match your requirements, please call to arrange an interview at your convenience. | If you agree that I am qualified for this job, please call to arrange an interview. |

## Revising to Combine Sentences Using Gerunds and Participles

Gerunds and participles are **verbals**, or verb forms that are used as different parts of speech.

**Identifying Gerunds** A **gerund** is a verb form ending in *-ing* that is used as a noun.

> **As subject:** *Baking* cookies is Heather's hobby.
>
> **As direct object:** Lucille enjoys *swimming.*
>
> **As predicate noun:** David's greatest talent is *playing* the piano.
>
> **As object of a preposition:** Randall never gets tired of *surfing.*

**Identifying Participles** A **participle** is a verb form that is used as an adjective. There are two kinds of participles: present participles and past participles. The present participle resembles a gerund in that it ends in *-ing.*

> **Present participle:** The *chirping* canary sang sweetly.
>
> **Past participle:** We hiked off the *beaten* path.

**PH WRITING COACH**

Further instruction and practice are available in *Prentice Hall Writing Coach.*

**Revising Sentences** To combine choppy or short sentences using gerunds and participles, follow these steps:

**1.** Identify pairs of sentences that sound choppy.

**2.** Determine whether you can tighten the sentences by revising to include a gerund or a participle.

**3.** Identify the main idea and insert the less important idea into a gerund or participial phrase.

| Choppy Sentences | |
| --- | --- |
| The sisters like to draw and paint. They like to play together. | |
| **Combined with Gerunds:** | **Combined with Participle:** |
| The sisters like *drawing* and *painting* together. | *Playing together,* the sisters like to draw and paint. |

### Grammar in Your Writing

Choose three paragraphs in your draft. Find pairs of sentences that deal with the same subject. If they are too choppy or repetitive, combine them using gerunds or participles.

This letter of complaint follows appropriate business writing style.

**Common Core State Standards**

**Language**
**2.c.** Spell correctly.

555 Somestrange Place
Fernandina Beach, FL 32034
September 21, 2010

> Business letters use two-letter abbreviations for states. Those for Florida and California are shown here.

Customer Service
Ace Software Company
1234 Citrus Parkway #514
Los Angeles, CA 33333

Dear Customer Service Manager:

> Brad uses a gender-neutral salutation since he does not know if the recipient will be a man or a woman.

I recently purchased software from my local Office Supply Superstore. A brightly colored sticker on your box stated that I would receive a free software title if I completed your rebate procedure correctly. Eagerly looking forward to receiving my new computer software, I find myself seriously disappointed with your service instead.

> Brad describes his purpose for writing in the opening paragraph.

I sent in everything just as you asked, but you sent me a postcard saying the UPC code was invalid. Please explain how this can be true. I am sure that is not true because I carefully cut the code off the box myself. What is even worse is that you cashed the check I sent to pay for shipping without shipping a thing.

I truly would like to receive the software I was promised. At the very least, I would like a refund for the $2.95 check I sent. I am including a copy of each of the following: the completed rebate form, the UPC code from the box, and my receipt.

Mistakes can happen. I am sure this is just a simple error. I hope you will work to resolve this quickly because I would like to continue purchasing your products.

> Brad indicates, politely but firmly, how and why the company should resolve his problem.

Sincerely,

*Brad Bean*

Brad Bean

Encl:  Copy of completed rebate form
       Copy of UPC code
       Copy of receipt

> Two common business letter abbreviations are "Attn:" for Attention and "encl." for *enclosures*.

# Editing and Proofreading

Read through your draft, and correct errors in punctuation, spelling, and grammar.

**Focus on spelling plurals.** Most plural forms of nouns follow basic rules, such as these:

- Add -*s* to most nouns: *effect/effects*.
- Add -*es* to nouns that end in *s, ss, sh, ch,* and *x*: *dress/dresses*.

# Publishing and Presenting

Consider one of the following ways to share your writing.

**Share your letter.** Read your letter to a partner. Ask how he or she would respond to receiving it.

**Send your letter.** Mail an error-free copy of your letter to the person or group to whom you wrote. Or, find the e-mail address and send your letter electronically. Develop a plan of action or agenda for a written or verbal follow-up after sending your letter.

# Reflecting on Your Writing

**Writer's Journal** Jot down your answers to this question:

*Were you confident that your letter made the impression you were trying to make? Why or why not?*

# Rubric for Self-Assessment

Find evidence in your writing to address each category. Then, use the rating scale to grade your work.

**Spiral Review**
Earlier in the unit, you learned about **participial phrases** (p. 826). Review your letter to be sure that you have used participial phrases correctly.

| Criteria | Rating Scale |
|---|---|
| | not very      very |
| **Focus:** How clearly do you state the purpose of the letter? | 1  2  3  4  5 |
| **Organization:** How effectively is your business-letter format organized? | 1  2  3  4  5 |
| **Support/Elaboration:** How well is each point supported by facts and details? | 1  2  3  4  5 |
| **Style and Voice:** How well have you used language that is appropriate for your audience and purpose? | 1  2  3  4  5 |
| **Conventions:** How correct is your grammar, especially your use of gerunds and participles? | 1  2  3  4  5 |

## © Drama

Build your skills and improve your comprehension of drama.

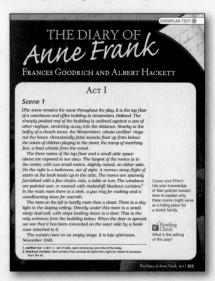

Read **The Diary of Anne Frank, Act I**
to find out how eight people survive in an attic,
under constant threat of discovery by the Nazis.

## © Common Core State Standards

Meet these standards with **The Diary of Anne Frank, Act I** (p. 854).

**Reading Literature**

**3.** Analyze how particular lines of dialogue or incidents in a story or drama propel the action, reveal aspects of a character, or provoke a decision. (*Literary Analysis: Dialogue*)

**4.** Analyze the impact of specific word choices on meaning and tone, including analogies or allusions to other texts. (*Literary Analysis: Dialogue*)

**6.** Analyze how differences in the points of view of the characters and the audience or reader (e.g., created through the use of dramatic irony) create such effects as suspense or humor. (*Literary Analysis: Dialogue*)

**Writing**

**3.** Write narratives to develop real or imagined experiences or events using effective technique, relevant descriptive details, and well-structured event sequences. (*Writing: Diary Entries*)

**Speaking and Listening**

**6.** Adapt speech to a variety of contexts and tasks, demonstrating command of formal English when indicated or appropriate. (*Speaking and Listening: Guided Tour*)

**Language**

**1.** Demonstrate command of the conventions of standard English grammar and usage when writing or speaking. (*Conventions: Dangling and Misplaced Modifiers*)

**4.b.** Use common, grade-appropriate Greek or Latin affixes and roots as clues to the meaning of a word. (*Vocabulary: Word Study*)

**6.** Acquire and use accurately grade-appropriate general academic and domain-specific words and phrases; gather vocabulary knowledge when considering a word or phrase important to comprehension or expression. (*Vocabulary: Word Study*)

# Reading Skill: Cause and Effect

A **cause** is an event, action, or feeling that produces a result, or **effect.** When you read a work that is set in a particular time and place, you can **use background information to link historical causes with effects.** Background information may include the introduction to a literary work, information provided in footnotes, facts you learned in other classes, and information you already know. Read the background information that accompanies this play to help you consider how events in the play are linked to history.

## Using the Strategy: Connections Chart

Keep track of your analysis in a **connections chart** like this one.

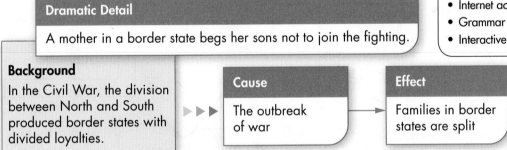

| Dramatic Detail |
| --- |
| A mother in a border state begs her sons not to join the fighting. |

**Background**
In the Civil War, the division between North and South produced border states with divided loyalties.

▶ ▶ ▶

**Cause**
The outbreak of war

**Effect**
Families in border states are split

# Literary Analysis: Dialogue

**Dialogue** is a conversation between or among characters. Through dialogue, we listen in on character's conversations, learning about their unique qualities as well as their hopes and dreams. Playwrights also set the tone of a scene and convey its significance by carefully choosing the words that characters say.

Dialogue serves another key function: to develop a story's **plot** and subplots. Conflicts come to life as characters confide in friends, argue with enemies, and plan their next actions. As you read *The Diary of Anne Frank,* notice how the dialogue develops characters, establishes tone and meaning, and propels the plot. Also, pay attention to what characters and the audience know. Sometimes, that difference in perspective, revealed through dialogue, can result in *dramatic irony,* a situation in which the audience knows more than the characters about events.

# Frank Family and World War II Timelines

Shown on these pages is a brief timeline of events in the lives of a single Jewish family, the Frank family. The Franks—Otto and Edith, and their daughters, Anne and Margot—lived in Europe during a period of Nazi terror in which Jews were forced to flee their homes or go into hiding—or face persecution. This period of anti-Jewish violence and mass murder is known as the Holocaust. The major events of the period are shown on the bottom half of the timeline.

## Timeline of the Frank Family

**1929** Anne Frank is born in Frankfurt, Germany.

**Summer 1933** Alarmed by Nazi actions in Germany, Otto Frank begins the process of moving his family to safety in the Netherlands.

**1934** Anne starts kindergarten at the Montessori school in Amsterdam.

**1941** Growing Nazi restrictions on the daily lives of Dutch Jews force the Frank girls to attend an all-Jewish school.

**June 12, 1942** Otto gives Anne a diary for her thirteenth birthday.

**July 6, 1942** The Franks go into hiding after receiving an order for Margot to report to a forced labor camp. They hide in the attic rooms above Mr. Frank's workplace with the help of close friends. Another family, the Van Pels (called the "Van Daans" in her diary), joins them, followed by Fritz Pfeffer ("Dussel"), months later.

**1925**   **1930**   **1935**   **1940**

## Timeline of World Events

**January 1933** Adolf Hitler comes to power in Germany. Over the next few months, all political parties, except the Nazi Party, are banned. Jews are dismissed from medical, legal, government, and teaching positions.

**1935** The Nuremberg Laws are passed in Germany, stripping Jews of their rights as German citizens. Laws passed over the next several years further isolate Jews, including the requirement to wear a yellow Star of David.

**September 1, 1939** Germany invades Poland, triggering the beginning of World War II.

**May 1940** The Nazis invade the Netherlands. Once in control, they set up a brutal police force, the Gestapo, to administer laws to isolate Dutch Jews from the rest of the Dutch population.

**August 4, 1944**
The hiding place of the Franks is discovered and the families are arrested.

**September 3, 1944**
All eight of those who hid in the attic are deported from the Netherlands to the Auschwitz death camp.

**March 1945\***
Anne and Margot die of the disease typhus in the Bergen-Belsen concentration camp.

**1947** Anne's diary is published in Dutch. Over the next few years it is translated and published in France, Germany, the United States, Japan, and Great Britain.

**1960** The hiding place of the Franks is converted into a permanent museum that tells the story of Anne and those who hid with her.

| 1945 | 1950 | 1955 | 1960 |
|------|------|------|------|

**May 1945** The Allies win as the war in Europe ends.

**June 1944** The Allies carry out a successful invasion of France. Their success gives many who live under Nazi occupation hope that the end of the war is near.

**January 1943** The Battle of Stalingrad marks the turning of the tide against the Nazis.

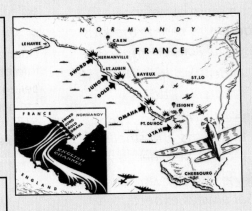

**May 1960** Adolf Eichmann, one of the last major Nazi figures to be tried, is captured and put on trial in Israel. He is convicted and executed for his role in arranging the transport of Jews to concentration camps and ghettoes, where an estimated six million Jews died.

\*Estimate. Exact date unknown.

**Is it our *differences* or our *similarities* that matter most?**

## Writing About the Big Question

In this drama, five adults and three teenagers struggle with their differences but face a common danger. To develop your ideas about the Big Question, choose the word in this sentence starter that best matches your opinion. Complete the sentence to support your idea.

Danger tends to **(unify/divide)** people because _____.

**While You Read** Notice how the characters respond to the multiple stresses of their situation.

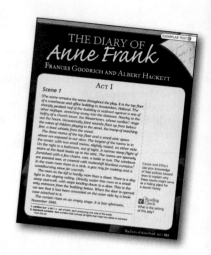

## Vocabulary

Read each word and its definition. Decide whether you know the word well, know it a little bit, or do not know it at all. After you read, see how your knowledge of each word has increased.

- **conspicuous** (kən spik´ yōō əs) *adj.* noticeable (p. 859) *The black stain on the white sofa was conspicuous.* conspicuously *adv.* conspicuousness *n.*

- **tension** (ten´ shən) *n.* a nervous, worried, or excited state that makes relaxation impossible (p. 863) *After the gas main explosion, there was tension in the neighborhood.* tense *adj.*

- **resent** (ri zent´) *v.* feel angry out of a sense of unfairness (p. 872) *With a report due, she began to resent the kids playing outside.* resentment *n.* resentful *adj.* resentfully *adv.*

- **insufferable** (in suf´ ər ə bəl) *adj.* unbearable (p. 874) *Cam's rude behavior was insufferable.* insufferably *adv.*

- **bewildered** (bē wil´ dərd) *adj.* hopelessly confused (p. 886) *The dog seemed bewildered by the sights and smells of the new neighborhood.* bewilderment *n.* bewilderingly *adv.*

- **fatalist** (fā´ təl ist) *n.* one who believes that all events are determined by fate (p. 898) *A fatalist, Sal always expects the worst.* fatalism *n.* fatalistically *adv.* fatalistic *adj.*

### Word Study

The **Greek suffix -ist** indicates a noun that means "one who does, makes, practices, is skilled in, or believes in."

In this play, a character claims to be a **fatalist**—someone who believes that our lives are guided by fate and not by our own actions.

Author of

# THE DIARY OF
# *Anne Frank*

Frances Goodrich (1890–1984) and Albert Hackett (1900–1995) spent two years writing a play based on the world-renowned book *Anne Frank: The Diary of a Young Girl*. As part of their research for the play, they visited with Anne's father, Otto. The play won a Pulitzer Prize, the Drama Critics Circle award, and a Tony Award.

**A Successful Partnership** Goodrich and Hackett began working together in 1927 and were married in 1931. The couple's writing career included screenplays for such classic films as *The Thin Man* (1934), *It's a Wonderful Life* (1946), and *Father of the Bride* (1950).

## BACKGROUND FOR THE PLAY

**Nazi Occupation**
On September 1, 1939, Nazi Germany launched a sudden attack on Poland that triggered World War II. Over the next several years, the armies of Nazi Germany swept across Europe, conquering and occupying many countries. In each country the Nazis occupied, the Jews were rounded up and sent by train to forced labor camps and death camps. The Nazi occupation of the Netherlands is the background for **The Diary of Anne Frank,** a play based on the actual diary of a young German-Jewish girl whose family chose to hide from the Nazis.

### Did You Know?
**Before they began writing together, Goodrich and Hackett were actors.**

## CHARACTERS

| | |
|---|---|
| Anne Frank | Peter Van Daan |
| Otto Frank | Mr. Kraler |
| Edith Frank | Mrs. Van Daan |
| Margot Frank | Mr. Van Daan |
| Miep Gies | Mr. Dussel |

# THE DIARY OF Anne Frank

## FRANCES GOODRICH AND ALBERT HACKETT

# ACT I

## Scene 1

[*The scene remains the same throughout the play. It is the top floor of a warehouse and office building in Amsterdam, Holland. The sharply peaked roof of the building is outlined against a sea of other rooftops, stretching away into the distance. Nearby is the belfry of a church tower, the Westertoren, whose carillon[1] rings out the hours. Occasionally faint sounds float up from below: the voices of children playing in the street, the tramp of marching feet, a boat whistle from the canal.*

*The three rooms of the top floor and a small attic space above are exposed to our view. The largest of the rooms is in the center, with two small rooms, slightly raised, on either side. On the right is a bathroom, out of sight. A narrow steep flight of stairs at the back leads up to the attic. The rooms are sparsely furnished with a few chairs, cots, a table or two. The windows are painted over, or covered with makeshift blackout curtains.[2] In the main room there is a sink, a gas ring for cooking and a woodburning stove for warmth.*

*The room on the left is hardly more than a closet. There is a sky-light in the sloping ceiling. Directly under this room is a small steep stairwell, with steps leading down to a door. This is the only entrance from the building below. When the door is opened we see that it has been concealed on the outer side by a book-case attached to it.*

*The curtain rises on an empty stage. It is late afternoon, November 1945.*

---

**1. carillon** (kar´ ə län´) *n.* set of bells, each producing one note of the scale.
**2. blackout curtains** dark curtains that conceal all lights that might be visible to bombers from the air.

**Cause and Effect**
Use your knowledge of Nazi policies toward Jews to explain why these rooms might serve as a hiding place for a Jewish family.

**Reading Check**
What is the setting of this play?

▲ During the war, the Allies bombed industrial areas that had been taken over by the Germans.

*The rooms are dusty, the curtains in rags. Chairs and tables are overturned.*

*The door at the foot of the small stairwell swings open.* MR. FRANK *comes up the steps into view. He is a gentle, cultured European in his middle years. There is still a trace of a German accent in his speech.*

*He stands looking slowly around, making a supreme effort at self-control. He is weak, ill. His clothes are threadbare.*

*After a second he drops his rucksack on the couch and moves slowly about. He opens the door to one of the smaller rooms, and then abruptly closes it again, turning away. He goes to the window at the back, looking off at the Westertoren as its carillon strikes the hour of six, then he moves restlessly on.*

*From the street below we hear the sound of a barrel organ³ and children's voices at play. There is a many-colored scarf hanging from a nail.* MR. FRANK *takes it, putting it around his*

---

3. **barrel organ** *n.* mechanical musical instrument often played by street musicians in past decades.

*neck. As he starts back for his rucksack, his eye is caught by something lying on the floor. It is a woman's white glove. He holds it in his hand and suddenly all of his self-control is gone. He breaks down, crying.*

*We hear footsteps on the stairs.* MIEP GIES *comes up, looking for* MR. FRANK. MIEP *is a Dutch girl of about twenty-two. She wears a coat and hat, ready to go home. She is pregnant. Her attitude toward* MR. FRANK *is protective, compassionate.*]

**MIEP.** Are you all right, Mr. Frank?

**MR. FRANK.** [*Quickly controlling himself*] Yes, Miep, yes.

**MIEP.** Everyone in the office has gone home . . . It's after six. [*Then pleading*] Don't stay up here, Mr. Frank. What's the use of torturing yourself like this?

**MR. FRANK.** I've come to say good-bye . . . I'm leaving here, Miep.

**MIEP.** What do you mean? Where are you going? Where?

**MR. FRANK.** I don't know yet. I haven't decided.

**MIEP.** Mr. Frank, you can't leave here! This is your home! Amsterdam is your home. Your business is here, waiting for you . . . You're needed here . . . Now that the war is over, there are things that . . .

**MR. FRANK.** I can't stay in Amsterdam, Miep. It has too many memories for me. Everywhere there's something . . . the house we lived in . . . the school . . . that street organ playing out there . . . I'm not the person you used to know, Miep. I'm a bitter old man. [*Breaking off*] Forgive me. I shouldn't speak to you like this . . . after all that you did for us . . . the suffering . . .

**MIEP.** No. No. It wasn't suffering. You can't say we suffered. [*As she speaks, she straightens a chair which is overturned.*]

**MR. FRANK.** I know what you went through, you and Mr. Kraler. I'll remember it as long as I live. [*He gives one last look around.*] Come, Miep. [*He starts for the steps, then remembers his rucksack, going back to get it.*]

**MIEP.** [*Hurrying up to a cupboard*] Mr. Frank, did you see? There are some of your papers here. [*She brings a bundle of papers to him.*] We found them in a heap of rubbish on the floor after . . . after you left.

**Cause and Effect**
The war in Europe ended in May 1945, but many who survived the camps did not return until the fall. What effect has the war had on Mr. Frank?

**Dialogue**
What do Mr. Frank's words and the hesitation in his speech tell you about his feelings?

**Cause and Effect**
What events might make it harder for Mr. Frank to think of Amsterdam as home? Explain.

**Reading Check**
Why does Miep want Mr. Frank to stay?

**MR. FRANK.** Burn them. [*He opens his rucksack to put the glove in it.*]

**MIEP.** But, Mr. Frank, there are letters, notes . . .

**MR. FRANK.** Burn them. All of them.

**MIEP.** Burn this? [*She hands him a paper-bound notebook.*]

**MR. FRANK.** [*quietly*] Anne's diary. [*He opens the diary and begins to read.*] "Monday, the sixth of July, nineteen forty-two." [*To* MIEP] Nineteen forty-two. Is it possible, Miep? . . . Only three years ago. [*As he continues his reading, he sits down on the couch.*] "Dear Diary, since you and I are going to be great friends, I will start by telling you about myself. My name is Anne Frank. I am thirteen years old. I was born in Germany the twelfth of June, nineteen twenty-nine. As my family is Jewish, we emigrated to Holland when Hitler came to power."

[*As* MR. FRANK *reads on, another voice joins his, as if coming from the air. It is* ANNE'S VOICE.]

**MR. FRANK AND ANNE.** "My father started a business, importing spice and herbs. Things went well for us until nineteen forty. Then the war came, and the Dutch capitulation,[4] followed by the arrival of the Germans. Then things got very bad for the Jews."

[MR. FRANK'S VOICE *dies out.* ANNE'S VOICE *continues alone. The lights dim slowly to darkness. The curtain falls on the scene.*]

**ANNE'S VOICE.** You could not do this and you could not do that. They forced Father out of his business. We had to wear yellow stars.[5] I had to turn in my bike. I couldn't go to a Dutch school any more. I couldn't go to the movies, or ride in an automobile, or even on a streetcar, and a million other things. But somehow we children still managed to have fun. Yesterday Father told me we were going into hiding. Where, he wouldn't say. At five o'clock this morning Mother woke me and told me to hurry and get dressed. I was to put on as many clothes as I could. It would look too suspicious if we walked along carrying suitcases. It wasn't until we were on our way that I learned where we were going. Our hiding place was to be upstairs in the building where

---

**Cause and Effect**
Anne is referring to Adolf Hitler, the German dictator who persecuted Jews throughout Europe. What other historical causes and effects do you learn here?

**Dialogue**
In the play, Anne's lines are often spoken to her diary, as if the diary were another character. What significant plot event is revealed in this speech?

---

4. **capitulation** (kə pich´ ə lā´ shən) *n.* surrender.
5. **yellow stars** Stars of David, the six-pointed stars that are symbols of Judaism. The Nazis ordered all Jews to wear them on their clothing.

Father used to have his business. Three other people were coming in with us . . . the Van Daans and their son Peter . . . Father knew the Van Daans but we had never met them . . .

[*During the last lines the curtain rises on the scene. The lights dim on.* ANNE'S VOICE *fades out.*]

## Scene 2

[*It is early morning, July 1942. The rooms are bare, as before, but they are now clean and orderly.*

MR. VAN DAAN, *a tall, portly[6] man in his late forties, is in the main room, pacing up and down, nervously smoking a cigarette. His clothes and overcoat are expensive and well cut.*

MRS. VAN DAAN *sits on the couch, clutching her possessions, a hatbox, bags, etc. She is a pretty woman in her early forties. She wears a fur coat over her other clothes.*

PETER VAN DAAN *is standing at the window of the room on the right, looking down at the street below. He is a shy, awkward boy of sixteen. He wears a cap, a raincoat, and long Dutch trousers, like "plus fours."[7] At his feet is a black case, a carrier for his cat.*

*The yellow Star of David is* conspicuous *on all of their clothes.*]

---

**6. portly** (pôrt´ lē) *adj.* large and heavy.
**7. plus fours** *n.* loose knickers (short pants) worn for active sports.

▼ **Critical Viewing**
This photograph shows the Frank family with some friends before their years in hiding. How would you describe their mood, judging from their expressions? **[Connect]**

**Vocabulary**
**conspicuous** (kən spik´ yoo əs) *adj.* noticeable

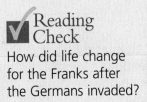
Reading Check

How did life change for the Franks after the Germans invaded?

**MRS. VAN DAAN.** [*Rising, nervous, excited*] Something's happened to them! I know it!

**MR. VAN DAAN.** Now, Kerli!

**MRS. VAN DAAN.** Mr. Frank said they'd be here at seven o'clock. He said . . .

**MR. VAN DAAN.** They have two miles to walk. You can't expect . . .

**MRS. VAN DAAN.** They've been picked up. That's what's happened. They've been taken . . .

[MR. VAN DAAN *indicates that he hears someone coming.*]

**MR. VAN DAAN.** You see?

[PETER *takes up his carrier and his schoolbag, etc., and goes into the main room as* MR. FRANK *comes up the stairwell from below.* MR. FRANK *looks much younger now. His movements are brisk, his manner confident. He wears an overcoat and carries his hat and a small cardboard box. He crosses to the* VAN DAANS, *shaking hands with each of them.*]

**MR. FRANK.** Mrs. Van Daan, Mr. Van Daan, Peter. [*Then, in explanation of their lateness*] There were too many of the Green Police[8] on the streets . . . we had to take the long way around.

[*Up the steps come* MARGOT FRANK, MRS. FRANK, MIEP *(not pregnant now) and* MR. KRALER. *All of them carry bags, packages, and so forth. The Star of David is conspicuous on all of the* FRANKS' *clothing.* MARGOT *is eighteen, beautiful, quiet, shy.* MRS. FRANK *is a young mother, gently bred, reserved. She, like* MR. FRANK, *has a slight German accent.* MR. KRALER *is a Dutchman, dependable, kindly.*

*As* MR. KRALER *and* MIEP *go upstage to put down their parcels,* MRS. FRANK *turns back to call* ANNE.]

**MRS. FRANK.** Anne?

[ANNE *comes running up the stairs. She is thirteen, quick in her movements, interested in everything, mercurial[9] in her emotions. She wears a cape, long wool socks and carries a schoolbag.*]

**Dialogue**
How do the authors convey a mood of anxiety through the Van Daans' dialogue?

**Cause and Effect**
Read the footnote on the "Green Police." Why do the Franks fear this force?

---

8. **Green Police** the Dutch Gestapo, or Nazi police, who wore green uniforms and were known for their brutality. Those in danger of being arrested or deported feared the Gestapo, especially because of their practice of raiding houses to round up victims in the middle of the night—when people are most confused and vulnerable.

9. **mercurial** (mər kyoor′ ē əl) *adj.* quick or changeable in behavior.

**MR. FRANK.** [*Introducing them*] My wife, Edith. Mr. and Mrs. Van Daan . . . their son, Peter . . . my daughters, Margot and Anne.

[MRS. FRANK *hurries over, shaking hands with them.*]

[ANNE *gives a polite little curtsy as she shakes* MR. VAN DAAN'S *hand. Then she immediately starts off on a tour of investigation of her new home, going upstairs to the attic room.*

MIEP *and* MR. KRALER *are putting the various things they have brought on the shelves.*]

**MR. KRALER.** I'm sorry there is still so much confusion.

**MR. FRANK.** Please. Don't think of it. After all, we'll have plenty of leisure to arrange everything ourselves.

**MIEP.** [*To* MRS. FRANK] We put the stores of food you sent in here. Your drugs are here . . . soap, linen here.

**MRS. FRANK.** Thank you, Miep.

**MIEP.** I made up the beds . . . the way Mr. Frank and Mr. Kraler said. [*She starts out.*] Forgive me. I have to hurry. I've got to go to the other side of town to get some ration books[10] for you.

**MRS. VAN DAAN.** Ration books? If they see our names on ration books, they'll know we're here.

**MR. KRALER.** There isn't anything . . .

**MIEP.** Don't worry. Your names won't be on them. [*As she hurries out*] I'll be up later.

**MR. FRANK.** Thank you, Miep.

**MRS. FRANK.** [*To* MR. KRALER] It's illegal, then, the ration books? We've never done anything illegal.

**MR. FRANK.** We won't be living here exactly according to regulations.

[*As* MR. KRALER *reassures* MRS. FRANK, *he takes various small things, such as matches, soap, etc., from his pockets, handing them to her.*]

**MR. KRALER.** This isn't the black market,[11] Mrs. Frank. This is

---

10. **ration** (rash´ ən) **books** *n.* books of stamps given to ensure the equal distribution of scarce items, such as meat or gasoline, in times of shortage.
11. **black market** illegal way of buying scarce items without ration stamps.

▲ **Critical Viewing**
What will having ration books, like the one above, allow the Franks to do? **[Connect]**

**Cause and Effect**
Why might Mrs. Frank be afraid of doing something illegal? Why is her fear illogical?

**Reading Check**
How are Miep and Mr. Kraler helping the Franks and Van Daans?

what we call the white market . . . helping all of the hundreds and hundreds who are hiding out in Amsterdam.

[*The carillon is heard playing the quarter-hour before eight.* MR. KRALER *looks at his watch.* ANNE *stops at the window as she comes down the stairs.*]

**ANNE.** It's the Westertoren!

**MR. KRALER.** I must go. I must be out of here and downstairs in the office before the workmen get here. [*He starts for the stairs leading out.*] Miep or I, or both of us, will be up each day to bring you food and news and find out what your needs are. Tomorrow I'll get you a better bolt for the door at the foot of the stairs. It needs a bolt that you can throw yourself and open only at our signal. [*To* MR. FRANK] Oh . . . You'll tell them about the noise?

**MR. FRANK.** I'll tell them.

**MR. KRALER.** Good-bye then for the moment. I'll come up again, after the workmen leave.

**MR. FRANK.** Good-bye, Mr. Kraler.

**MRS. FRANK.** [*Shaking his hand*] How can we thank you?

[*The others murmur their good-byes.*]

**MR. KRALER.** I never thought I'd live to see the day when a man like Mr. Frank would have to go into hiding. When you think—

[*He breaks off, going out.* MR. FRANK *follows him down the steps, bolting the door after him. In the interval before he returns,* PETER *goes over to* MARGOT, *shaking hands with her. As* MR. FRANK *comes back up the steps,* MRS. FRANK *questions him anxiously.*]

**MRS. FRANK.** What did he mean, about the noise?

**MR. FRANK.** First let us take off some of these clothes.

[*They all start to take off garment after garment. On each of their coats, sweaters, blouses, suits, dresses, is another yellow Star of David.* MR. *and* MRS. FRANK *are underdressed quite simply. The others wear several things, sweaters, extra dresses, bathrobes, aprons, nightgowns, etc.*]

**MR. VAN DAAN.** It's a wonder we weren't arrested, walking along the streets . . . Petronella with a fur coat in July . . . and that cat of Peter's crying all the way.

**Cause and Effect**
What does the description of the characters' clothing indicate about how long they expect to be in hiding?

**ANNE.** [*As she is removing a pair of panties*] A cat?

**MRS. FRANK.** [*Shocked*] Anne, please!

**ANNE.** It's alright. I've got on three more.

[*She pulls off two more. Finally, as they have all removed their surplus clothes, they look to* MR. FRANK, *waiting for him to speak.*]

**MR. FRANK.** Now. About the noise. While the men are in the building below, we must have complete quiet. Every sound can be heard down there, not only in the workrooms, but in the offices too. The men come at about eight-thirty, and leave at about five-thirty. So, to be perfectly safe, from eight in the morning until six in the evening we must move only when it is necessary, and then in stockinged feet. We must not speak above a whisper. We must not run any water. We cannot use the sink, or even, forgive me, the w.c.[12] The pipes go down through the workrooms. It would be heard. No trash . . .

[MR. FRANK *stops abruptly as he hears the sound of marching feet from the street below. Everyone is motionless, paralyzed with fear.* MR. FRANK *goes quietly into the room on the right to look down out of the window.* ANNE *runs after him, peering out with him. The tramping feet pass without stopping. The* tension *is relieved.* MR. FRANK, *followed by* ANNE, *returns to the main room and resumes his instructions to the group.*] . . . No trash must ever be thrown out which might reveal that someone is living up here . . . not even a potato paring. We must burn everything in the stove at night. This is the way we must live until it is over, if we are to survive.

[*There is silence for a second.*]

**MRS. FRANK.** Until it is over.

**MR. FRANK.** [*Reassuringly*] After six we can move about . . . we can talk and laugh and have our supper and read and play games . . . just as we would at home. [*He looks at his watch.*] And now I think it would be wise if we all went to our rooms, and were settled before eight o'clock. Mrs. Van Daan, you and your husband will be upstairs. I regret that there's no place up there for Peter. But he will be here, near us. This will be our common room, where we'll meet to talk and eat and read, like one family.

---

12. **w.c.** water closet; bathroom.

**Vocabulary**
**tension** (ten´ shən) *n.* a nervous, worried, or excited state that makes relaxation impossible

**Cause and Effect**
Why is the sound of marching feet alarming to the families?

**Cause and Effect**
Why must the families maintain different schedules for day and night?

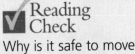
Reading Check
Why is it safe to move around after 6 P.M.?

**MR. VAN DAAN.** And where do you and Mrs. Frank sleep?

**MR. FRANK.** This room is also our bedroom.

[*Together*] { **MRS. VAN DAAN.** That isn't right. We'll sleep here and you take the room upstairs.

**MR. VAN DAAN.** It's your place.

**MR. FRANK.** Please. I've thought this out for weeks. It's the best arrangement. The only arrangement.

**MRS. VAN DAAN.** [*To* MR. FRANK] Never, never can we thank you. [*Then to* MRS. FRANK] I don't know what would have happened to us, if it hadn't been for Mr. Frank.

**MR. FRANK.** You don't know how your husband helped me when I came to this country . . . knowing no one . . . not able to speak the language. I can never repay him for that. [*Going to* VAN DAAN] May I help you with your things?

**MR. VAN DAAN.** No. No. [*To* MRS. VAN DAAN] Come along, *liefje.*[13]

**MRS. VAN DAAN.** You'll be all right, Peter? You're not afraid?

**PETER.** [*Embarrassed*] Please, Mother.

[*They start up the stairs to the attic room above.* MR. FRANK *turns to* MRS. FRANK.]

**MR. FRANK.** You too must have some rest, Edith. You didn't close your eyes last night. Nor you, Margot.

**ANNE.** I slept, Father. Wasn't that funny? I knew it was the last night in my own bed, and yet I slept soundly.

**MR. FRANK.** I'm glad, Anne. Now you'll be able to help me straighten things in here. [*To* MRS. FRANK *and* MARGOT] Come with me . . . You and Margot rest in this room for the time being.

[*He picks up their clothes, starting for the room on the right.*]

**MRS. FRANK.** You're sure . . .? I could help . . . And Anne hasn't had her milk . . .

**MR. FRANK.** I'll give it to her. [*To* ANNE *and* PETER] Anne, Peter . . . it's best that you take off your shoes now, before you forget.

[*He leads the way to the room, followed by* MARGOT.]

**MRS. FRANK.** You're sure you're not tired, Anne?

---

**Dialogue**
What does this dialogue reveal about the relationship between Anne and her parents?

---

13. *liefje* (lēf´ hyə) Dutch for "little love."

**ANNE.** I feel fine. I'm going to help Father.

**MRS. FRANK.** Peter, I'm glad you are to be with us.

**PETER.** Yes, Mrs. Frank.

[MRS. FRANK *goes to join* MR. FRANK *and* MARGOT.]
[*During the following scene* MR. FRANK *helps*
MARGOT *and* MRS. FRANK *to hang up their*
*clothes. Then he persuades them both to lie down and rest. The*
VAN DAANS *in their room above settle themselves. In the main*
*room* ANNE *and* PETER *remove their shoes.* PETER *takes his cat*
*out of the carrier.*]

**ANNE.** What's your cat's name?

**PETER.** Mouschi.

**ANNE.** Mouschi! Mouschi! Mouschi! [*She picks up the cat,*
*walking away with it. To* PETER] I love cats. I have one . . .
a darling little cat. But they made me leave her behind. I
left some food and a note for the neighbors to take care of
her . . . I'm going
to miss her terribly. What is yours? A him or a her?

**PETER.** He's a tom. He doesn't like strangers. [*He takes the*
*cat from her, putting it back in its carrier.*]

**ANNE.** [*Unabashed*] Then I'll have to stop being a stranger,
won't I? Is he fixed?

**PETER.** [*Startled*] Huh?

**ANNE.** Did you have him fixed?

**PETER.** No.

**ANNE.** Oh, you ought to have him fixed—to keep him from—
you know, fighting. Where did you go to school?

**PETER.** Jewish Secondary.

**ANNE.** But that's where Margot and I go! I never saw you around.

**PETER.** I used to see you . . . sometimes . . .

**ANNE.** You did?

**PETER.** . . . In the school yard. You were always in the middle
of a bunch of kids. [*He takes a penknife from his pocket.*]

**ANNE.** Why didn't you ever come over?

**Dialogue**
In what way does this
dialogue between Peter
and Anne highlight the
differences between
their personalities?

**Reading
Check**
Where did Peter see
Anne before they
went into hiding?

**PETER.** I'm sort of a lone wolf. [*He starts to rip off his Star of David.*]

**ANNE.** What are you doing?

**PETER.** Taking it off.

**ANNE.** But you can't do that. They'll arrest you if you go out without your star.

[*He tosses his knife on the table.*]

**PETER.** Who's going out?

**ANNE.** Why, of course! You're right! Of course we don't need them any more. [*She picks up his knife and starts to take her star off.*] I wonder what our friends will think when we don't show up today?

**PETER.** I didn't have any dates with anyone.

**ANNE.** Oh, I did. I had a date with Jopie to go and play ping-pong at her house. Do you know Jopie de Waal?

**PETER.** No.

**ANNE.** Jopie's my best friend. I wonder what she'll think when she telephones and there's no answer? . . . Probably she'll go over to the house . . . I wonder what she'll think . . . we left everything as if we'd suddenly been called away . . . breakfast dishes in the sink . . . beds not made . . . [*As she pulls off her star, the cloth underneath shows clearly the color and form of the star.*] Look! It's still there! [PETER *goes over to the stove with his star.*] What're you going to do with yours?

**PETER.** Burn it.

**ANNE.** [*She starts to throw hers in, and cannot.*] It's funny, I can't throw mine away. I don't know why.

**PETER.** You can't throw . . .? Something they branded you with . . .? That they made you wear so they could spit on you?

**ANNE.** I know. I know. But after all, it is the Star of David, isn't it?

[*In the bedroom, right,* MARGOT *and* MRS. FRANK *are lying down.* MR. FRANK *starts quietly out.*]

**Cause and Effect**
Think about what the yellow star represents in the historical context of World War II. Why is it important to Peter to remove the star?

▼ **Critical Viewing**
Why do you think the Nazis forced Jews to wear yellow stars like this one, bearing the Dutch word for "Jew"? **[Infer]**

**PETER.** Maybe it's different for a girl.

[MR. FRANK *comes into the main room.*]

**MR. FRANK.** Forgive me, Peter. Now let me see. We must find a bed for your cat. [*He goes to a cupboard.*] I'm glad you brought your cat. Anne was feeling so badly about hers. [*Getting a used small washtub*] Here we are. Will it be comfortable in that?

**PETER.** [*Gathering up his things*] Thanks.

**MR. FRANK.** [*Opening the door of the room on the left*] And here is your room. But I warn you, Peter, you can't grow any more. Not an inch, or you'll have to sleep with your feet out of the skylight. Are you hungry?

**PETER.** No.

**MR. FRANK.** We have some bread and butter.

**PETER.** No, thank you.

**MR. FRANK.** You can have it for luncheon then. And tonight we will have a real supper . . . our first supper together.

**PETER.** Thanks. Thanks. [*He goes into his room. During the following scene he arranges his possessions in his new room.*]

**MR. FRANK.** That's a nice boy, Peter.

**ANNE.** He's awfully shy, isn't he?

**MR. FRANK.** You'll like him, I know.

**ANNE.** I certainly hope so, since he's the only boy I'm likely to see for months and months.

[MR. FRANK *sits down, taking off his shoes.*]

**MR. FRANK.** Annele,[14] there's a box there. Will you open it?

[*He indicates a carton on the couch.* ANNE *brings it to the center table. In the street below there is the sound of children playing.*]

**ANNE.** [*As she opens the carton*] You know the way I'm going to think of it here? I'm going to think of it as a boarding house. A very peculiar summer boarding house, like the one that we—[*She breaks off as she pulls out some photographs.*] Father! My movie stars! I was wondering where they were! I was looking for them this morning . . . and Queen Wilhelmina![15] How wonderful!

**Dialogue**
What does this dialogue tell you about Mr. Frank as a person?

Reading Check
Why had the Franks left their house in a messy state?

---

14. **Annele** (än′ ə lə) nickname for "Anne."
15. **Queen Wilhelmina** (vil′ hel mē′ nä) Queen of the Netherlands from 1890 to 1948.

**MR. FRANK.** There's something more. Go on. Look further. [*He goes over to the sink, pouring a glass of milk from a thermos bottle.*]

**ANNE.** [*Pulling out a pasteboard-bound book*] A diary! [*She throws her arms around her father.*] I've never had a diary. And I've always longed for one. [*She looks around the room.*] Pencil, pencil, pencil, pencil. [*She starts down the stairs.*] I'm going down to the office to get a pencil.

**MR. FRANK.** Anne! No! [*He goes after her, catching her by the arm and pulling her back.*]

**ANNE.** [*Startled*] But there's no one in the building now.

**MR. FRANK.** It doesn't matter. I don't want you ever to go beyond that door.

**ANNE.** [*Sobered*] Never . . .? Not even at nighttime, when everyone is gone? Or on Sundays? Can't I go down to listen to the radio?

**MR. FRANK.** Never. I am sorry, Anneke.[16] It isn't safe. No, you must never go beyond that door.

[*For the first time* ANNE *realizes what "going into hiding" means.*]

**ANNE.** I see.

**Cause and Effect**
Why is Anne forbidden to go downstairs?

**MR. FRANK.** It'll be hard, I know. But always remember this, Anneke. There are no walls, there are no bolts, no locks that anyone can put on your mind. Miep will bring us books. We will read history, poetry, mythology. [*He gives her the glass of milk.*] Here's your milk. [*With his arm about her, they go over to the couch, sitting down side by side.*] As a matter of fact, between us, Anne, being here has certain advantages for you. For instance, you remember the battle you had with your mother the other day on the subject of overshoes? You said you'd rather die than wear overshoes? But in the end you had to wear them? Well now, you see, for as long as we are here you will never have to wear overshoes! Isn't that good? And the coat that you inherited from Margot, you won't have to wear that any more. And the piano! You won't have to practice on the piano. I tell you, this is going to be a fine life for you!

---

**16. Anneke** (än´ ə kə) nickname for "Anne."

[ANNE'S *panic is gone.* PETER *appears in the doorway of his room, with a saucer in his hand. He is carrying his cat.*]

**PETER.** I . . . I . . . I thought I'd better get some water for Mouschi before . . .

**MR. FRANK.** Of course.

[*As he starts toward the sink the carillon begins to chime the hour of eight. He tiptoes to the window at the back and looks down at the street below. He turns to* PETER, *indicating in pantomime that it is too late.* PETER *starts back for his room. He steps on a creaking board. The three of them are frozen for a minute in fear. As* PETER *starts away again,* ANNE *tiptoes over to him and pours some of the milk from her glass into the saucer for the cat.* PETER *squats on the floor, putting the milk before the cat.* MR. FRANK *gives* ANNE *his fountain pen, and then goes into the room at the right. For a second* ANNE *watches the cat, then she goes over to the center table, and opens her diary.*

In the room at the right, MRS. FRANK *has sat up quickly at the sound of the carillon.* MR. FRANK *comes in and sits down beside her on the settee, his arm comfortingly around her.*

Upstairs, in the attic room, MR. *and* MRS. VAN DAAN *have hung their clothes in the closet and are now seated on the iron bed.* MRS. VAN DAAN *leans back exhausted.* MR. VAN DAAN *fans her with a newspaper.*

ANNE *starts to write in her diary. The lights dim out, the curtain falls.*]

**Cause and Effect**
How does the fear of discovery affect the behavior of the two families?

**Reading Check**
What positive aspects about living in hiding does Mr. Frank point out to comfort Anne?

◀ The radio was a crucial link to news of the war—especially through non-German stations such as the BBC (British Broadcasting Corporation).

*In the darkness* ANNE'S VOICE *comes to us again, faintly at first, and then with growing strength.*]

**ANNE'S VOICE.** I expect I should be describing what it feels like to go into hiding. But I really don't know yet myself. I only know it's funny never to be able to go outdoors . . . never to breathe fresh air . . . never to run and shout and jump. It's the silence in the nights that frightens me most. Every time I hear a creak in the house, or a step on the street outside, I'm sure they're coming for us. The days aren't so bad. At least we know that Miep and Mr. Kraler are down there below us in the office. Our protectors, we call them. I asked Father what would happen to them if the Nazis found out they were hiding us. Pim said that they would suffer the same fate that we would . . . Imagine! They know this, and yet when they come up here, they're always cheerful and gay as if there were nothing in the world to bother them . . . Friday, the twenty-first of August, nineteen forty-two. Today I'm going to tell you our general news. Mother is unbearable. She insists on treating me like a baby, which I loathe. Otherwise things are going better. The weather is . . .

[*As* ANNE'S VOICE *is fading out, the curtain rises on the scene.*]

# Scene 3

[*It is a little after six o'clock in the evening, two months later.*
     MARGOT *is in the bedroom at the right, studying.* MR. VAN DAAN *is lying down in the attic room above.*
     *The rest of the "family" is in the main room.* ANNE *and* PETER *sit opposite each other at the center table, where they have been doing their lessons.* MRS. FRANK *is on the couch.* MRS. VAN DAAN *is seated with her fur coat, on which she has been sewing, in her lap. None of them are wearing their shoes.*
     *Their eyes are on* MR. FRANK, *waiting for him to give them the signal which will release them from their day-long quiet.* MR. FRANK, *his shoes in his hand, stands looking down out of the window at the back, watching to be sure that all of the workmen have left the building below.*
     *After a few seconds of motionless silence,* MR. FRANK *turns from the window.*]

**MR. FRANK.** [*Quietly, to the group*] It's safe now. The last workman has left.

[*There is an immediate stir of relief.*]

**ANNE.** [*Her pent-up energy explodes.*] WHEE!

**MR. FRANK.** [*Startled, amused*] Anne!

**MRS. VAN DAAN.** I'm first for the w.c.

[*She hurries off to the bathroom.* MRS. FRANK *puts on her shoes and starts up to the sink to prepare supper.* ANNE *sneaks* PETER'S *shoes from under the table and hides them behind her back.* MR. FRANK *goes in to* MARGOT'S *room.*]

**MR. FRANK.** [*To* MARGOT] Six o'clock. School's over.

[MARGOT *gets up, stretching.* MR. FRANK *sits down to put on his shoes. In the main room* PETER *tries to find his.*]

**PETER.** [*To* ANNE] Have you seen my shoes?

**ANNE.** [*Innocently*] Your shoes?

**PETER.** You've taken them, haven't you?

**ANNE.** I don't know what you're talking about.

**PETER.** You're going to be sorry!

**ANNE.** Am I?

[PETER *goes after her.* ANNE, *with his shoes in her hand, runs from him, dodging behind her mother.*]

**MRS. FRANK.** [*Protesting*] Anne, dear!

**PETER.** Wait till I get you!

**ANNE.** I'm waiting!
[PETER *makes a lunge for her. They both fall to the floor.* PETER *pins her down, wrestling with her to get the shoes.*]

Don't! Don't! Peter, stop it. Ouch!

**MRS. FRANK.** Anne! . . . Peter!

[*Suddenly* PETER *becomes self-conscious. He grabs his shoes roughly and starts for his room.*]

**ANNE.** [*Following him*] Peter, where are you going? Come dance with me.

**PETER.** I tell you I don't know how.

✔ Reading Check

Why does Anne take Peter's shoes?

**ANNE.** I'll teach you.

**PETER.** I'm going to give Mouschi his dinner.

**ANNE.** Can I watch?

**PETER.** He doesn't like people around while he eats.

**ANNE.** Peter, please.

**PETER.** No! [*He goes into his room.* ANNE *slams his door after him.*]

**MRS. FRANK.** Anne, dear, I think you shouldn't play like that with Peter. It's not dignified.

**ANNE.** Who cares if it's dignified? I don't want to be dignified.

[MR. FRANK *and* MARGOT *come from the room on the right.* MARGOT *goes to help her mother.* MR. FRANK *starts for the center table to correct* MARGOT'S *school papers.*]

**MRS. FRANK.** [*To* ANNE] You complain that I don't treat you like a grownup. But when I do, you resent it.

**ANNE.** I only want some fun . . . someone to laugh and clown with . . . After you've sat still all day and hardly moved, you've got to have some fun. I don't know what's the matter with that boy.

**MR. FRANK.** He isn't used to girls. Give him a little time.

**ANNE.** Time? Isn't two months time? I could cry. [*Catching hold of* MARGOT] Come on, Margot . . . dance with me. Come on, please.

**MARGOT.** I have to help with supper.

**ANNE.** You know we're going to forget how to dance . . . When we get out we won't remember a thing.

[*She starts to sing and dance by herself.* MR. FRANK *takes her in his arms, waltzing with her.* MRS. VAN DAAN *comes in from the bathroom.*]

**MRS. VAN DAAN.** Next? [*She looks around as she starts putting on her shoes.*] Where's Peter?

**ANNE.** [*As they are dancing*] Where would he be!

**MRS. VAN DAAN.** He hasn't finished his lessons, has he? His father'll kill him if he catches him in there with that cat and his work not done. [MR. FRANK *and* ANNE *finish their dance. They bow to each other with extravagant formality.*]

---

**Cause and Effect**
What is the effect of Mrs. Frank's upbringing on the way she expects Anne to act?

**Vocabulary**
**resent** (ri zent´) *v.* feel angry out of a sense of unfairness

**Dialogue**
What subplot does this dialogue develop?

Anne, get him out of there, will you?

**ANNE.** [*At* PETER'S *door*] Peter? Peter?

**PETER.** [*Opening the door a crack*] What is it?

**ANNE.** Your mother says to come out.

**PETER.** I'm giving Mouschi his dinner.

**MRS. VAN DAAN.** You know what your father says. [*She sits on the couch, sewing on the lining of her fur coat.*]

**PETER.** For heaven's sake, I haven't even looked at him since lunch.

**MRS. VAN DAAN.** I'm just telling you, that's all.

**ANNE.** I'll feed him.

**PETER.** I don't want you in there.

**MRS. VAN DAAN.** Peter!

**PETER.** [*To* ANNE] Then give him his dinner and come right out, you hear?

[*He comes back to the table.* ANNE *shuts the door of* PETER'S *room after her and disappears behind the curtain covering his closet.*]

**MRS. VAN DAAN.** [*To* PETER] Now is that any way to talk to your little girl friend?

**PETER.** Mother . . . for heaven's sake . . . will you please stop saying that?

**MRS. VAN DAAN.** Look at him blush! Look at him!

**PETER.** Please! I'm not . . . anyway . . . let me alone, will you?

**MRS. VAN DAAN.** He acts like it was something to be ashamed of. It's nothing to be ashamed of, to have a little girl friend.

**PETER.** You're crazy. She's only thirteen.

**MRS. VAN DAAN.** So what? And you're sixteen. Just perfect. Your father's ten years older than I am. [*To* MR. FRANK I warn you, Mr. Frank, if this war lasts much longer, we're going to be related and then . . .

**MR. FRANK.** *Mazeltov!*[17]

**Dialogue**
Based on this dialogue, how does Mrs. Van Daan feel about the growing friendship between Anne and Peter?

**Reading Check**
Why does Peter react negatively in response to his mother's hints about Anne?

---

**17.** *Mazeltov* (mä´ zəl tōv´) "good luck" in Hebrew and Yiddish.

**MRS. FRANK.** [*Deliberately changing the conversation*] I wonder where Miep is. She's usually so prompt.

[*Suddenly everything else is forgotten as they hear the sound of an automobile coming to a screeching stop in the street below. They are tense, motionless in their terror. The car starts away. A wave of relief sweeps over them. They pick up their occupations again.* ANNE *flings open the door of* PETER'S *room, making a dramatic entrance. She is dressed in* PETER'S *clothes.* PETER *looks at her in fury. The others are amused.*]

**ANNE.** Good evening, everyone. Forgive me if I don't stay. [*She jumps up on a chair.*] I have a friend waiting for me in there. My friend Tom. Tom Cat. Some people say that we look alike. But Tom has the most beautiful whiskers, and I have only a little fuzz. I am hoping . . . in time . . .

**PETER.** All right, Mrs. Quack Quack!

**ANNE.** [*Outraged—jumping down*] Peter!

**PETER.** I heard about you . . . How you talked so much in class they called you Mrs. Quack Quack. How Mr. Smitter made you write a composition . . . " 'Quack, Quack,' said Mrs. Quack Quack."

**ANNE.** Well, go on. Tell them the rest. How it was so good he read it out loud to the class and then read it to all his other classes!

**PETER.** Quack! Quack! Quack . . . Quack . . . Quack . . .

[ANNE *pulls off the coat and trousers.*]

**ANNE.** You are the most intolerable, insufferable boy I've ever met!

[*She throws the clothes down the stairwell.* PETER *goes down after them.*]

**PETER.** Quack, Quack, Quack!

**MRS. VAN DAAN.** [*To* ANNE] That's right, Anneke! Give it to him!

**ANNE.** With all the boys in the world . . . Why I had to get locked up with one like you! . . .

**PETER.** Quack, Quack, Quack, and from now on stay out of my room!

[*As* PETER *passes her,* ANNE *puts out her foot, tripping him. He picks himself up, and goes on into his room.*]

**Vocabulary**
**insufferable**
(in suf´ ə rə bəl) *adj.*
unbearable

**MRS. FRANK.** [*Quietly*] Anne, dear . . . your hair. [*She feels* ANNE'S *forehead.*] You're warm. Are you feeling all right?

**ANNE.** Please, Mother. [*She goes over to the center table, slipping into her shoes.*]

**MRS. FRANK.** [*Following her*] You haven't a fever, have you?

**ANNE.** [*Pulling away*] No. No.

**MRS. FRANK.** You know we can't call a doctor here, ever. There's only one thing to do . . . watch carefully. Prevent an illness before it comes. Let me see your tongue.

**ANNE.** Mother, this is perfectly absurd.

**MRS. FRANK.** Anne, dear, don't be such a baby. Let me see your tongue. [*As* ANNE *refuses,* MRS. FRANK *appeals to* MR. FRANK] Otto . . .?

**MR. FRANK.** You hear your mother, Anne.

[ANNE *flicks out her tongue for a second, then turns away.*]

**MRS. FRANK.** Come on—open up! [*As* ANNE *opens her mouth very wide*] You seem all right . . . but perhaps an aspirin . . .

**MRS. VAN DAAN.** For heaven's sake, don't give that child any pills. I waited for fifteen minutes this morning for her to come out of the w.c.

**ANNE.** I was washing my hair!

**MR. FRANK.** I think there's nothing the matter with our Anne that a ride on her bike, or a visit with her friend Jopie de Waal wouldn't cure. Isn't that so, Anne?

[MR. VAN DAAN *comes down into the room. From outside we hear faint sounds of bombers going over and a burst of ack-ack.*][18]

**MR. VAN DAAN.** Miep not come yet?

**MRS. VAN DAAN.** The workmen just left, a little while ago.

---

18. **ack-ack** (ak´ ak´) *n.* slang for an anti-aircraft gun's fire.

## LITERATURE IN CONTEXT

### History Connection

### Air Raids

When the families hear bombers and anti-aircraft guns overhead, they are hearing familiar sounds of the time. World War II was the first major war that involved the massive aerial bombing of cities.

Often, the first sound to alert people to an attack was the ghostly wailing of an air raid siren. This meant "Take cover!" Then, the drone of bomber engines and the crackle and burst of anti-aircraft fire would take over—the sounds that Anne hears. Finally, there would be the whistling of bombs dropping, the whine of a falling plane, or the sound of explosions. These were sounds heard by many families throughout Europe. This was the soundtrack of war.

### Connect to the Literature

Why might the sound of bombers, like this American B-17, cause mixed feelings of anxiety and anticipation for those in hiding?

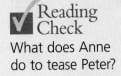

**Reading Check**
What does Anne do to tease Peter?

**MR. VAN DAAN.** What's for dinner tonight?

**MRS. VAN DAAN.** Beans.

**MR. VAN DAAN.** Not again!

**MRS. VAN DAAN.** Poor Putti! I know. But what can we do? That's all that Miep brought us.

[MR. VAN DAAN *starts to pace, his hands behind his back.* ANNE *follows behind him, imitating him.*]

**ANNE.** We are now in what is known as the "bean cycle." Beans boiled, beans en casserole, beans with strings, beans without strings . . .

[PETER *has come out of his room. He slides into his place at the table, becoming immediately absorbed in his studies.*]

**MR. VAN DAAN.** [*To* PETER] I saw you . . . in there, playing with your cat.

**MRS. VAN DAAN.** He just went in for a second, putting his coat away. He's been out here all the time, doing his lessons.

**MR. FRANK.** [*Looking up from the papers*] Anne, you got an excellent in your history paper today . . . and very good in Latin.

**ANNE.** [*Sitting beside him*] How about algebra?

**MR. FRANK.** I'll have to make a confession. Up until now I've managed to stay ahead of you in algebra. Today you caught up with me. We'll leave it to Margot to correct.

**ANNE.** Isn't algebra *vile*, Pim!

**MR. FRANK.** Vile!

**MARGOT.** [*To* MR. FRANK] How did I do?

**ANNE.** [*Getting up*] Excellent, excellent, excellent, excellent!

**MR. FRANK.** [*To* MARGOT] You should have used the subjunctive[19] here . . .

**MARGOT.** Should I? . . . I thought . . . look here . . . I didn't use it here . . .

[*The two become absorbed in the papers.*]

**ANNE.** Mrs. Van Daan, may I try on your coat?

---

19. **subjunctive** (səb juŋk′ tiv) *n.* form of a verb that is used to express doubt or uncertainty.

**Dialogue**
Based on this dialogue, what is Mr. Frank's attitude toward education?

**MRS. FRANK.** No, Anne.

**MRS. VAN DAAN.** [*Giving it to* ANNE] It's all right . . . but careful with it. [ANNE *puts it on and struts with it.*] My father gave me that the year before he died. He always bought the best that money could buy.

**ANNE.** Mrs. Van Daan, did you have a lot of boy friends before you were married?

**MRS. FRANK.** Anne, that's a personal question. It's not courteous to ask personal questions.

**MRS. VAN DAAN.** Oh I don't mind. [*To* ANNE] Our house was always swarming with boys. When I was a girl we had . . .

**MR. VAN DAAN.** Oh, God. Not again!

**MRS. VAN DAAN.** [*Good-humored*] Shut up! [*Without a pause, to* ANNE, MR. VAN DAAN *mimics* MRS. VAN DAAN, *speaking the first few words in unison with her.*] One summer we had a big house in Hilversum. The boys came buzzing round like bees around a jam pot. And when I was sixteen! . . . We were wearing our skirts very short those days and I had good-looking legs. [*She pulls up her skirt, going to* MR. FRANK.] I still have 'em. I may not be as pretty as I used to be, but I still have my legs. How about it, Mr. Frank?

**MR. VAN DAAN.** All right. All right. We see them.

**MRS. VAN DAAN.** I'm not asking you. I'm asking Mr. Frank.

**PETER.** Mother, for heaven's sake.

**MRS. VAN DAAN.** Oh, I embarrass you, do I? Well, I just hope the girl you marry has as good. [*Then to* ANNE] My father used to worry about me, with so many boys hanging round. He told me, if any of them gets fresh, you say to him . . . "Remember, Mr. So-and-So, remember I'm a lady."

**ANNE.** "Remember, Mr. So-and-So, remember I'm a lady." [*She gives* MRS. VAN DAAN *her coat.*]

**MR. VAN DAAN.** Look at you, talking that way in front of her! Don't you know she puts it all down in that diary?

**MRS. VAN DAAN.** So, if she does? I'm only telling the truth!

[ANNE *stretches out, putting her ear to the floor, listening to what*

**Dialogue**
What does Mrs. Van Daan's comment about her father reveal about her values?

**Dialogue**
What do Mrs. Van Daan's words and actions reveal about her personality?

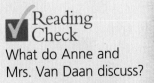

**Reading Check**
What do Anne and Mrs. Van Daan discuss?

*is going on below. The sound of the bombers fades away.]*

**MRS. FRANK.** [*Setting the table*] Would you mind, Peter, if I moved you over to the couch?

**ANNE.** [*Listening*] Miep must have the radio on.

[PETER *picks up his papers, going over to the couch beside* MRS. VAN DAAN.]

**MR. VAN DAAN.** [*Accusingly, to* PETER] Haven't you finished yet?

**PETER.** No.

**MR. VAN DAAN.** You ought to be ashamed of yourself.

**PETER.** All right. All right. I'm a dunce. I'm a hopeless case. Why do I go on?

**MRS. VAN DAAN.** You're not hopeless. Don't talk that way. It's just that you haven't anyone to help you, like the girls have. [*To* MR. FRANK] Maybe you could help him, Mr. Frank?

**MR. FRANK.** I'm sure that his father . . .?

**MR. VAN DAAN.** Not me. I can't do anything with him. He won't listen to me. You go ahead . . . if you want.

**MR. FRANK.** [*Going to* PETER] What about it, Peter? Shall we make our school coeducational?

**MRS. VAN DAAN.** [*Kissing* MR. FRANK] You're an angel, Mr. Frank. An angel. I don't know why I didn't meet you before I met that one there. Here, sit down, Mr. Frank . . . [*She forces him down on the couch beside* PETER.] Now, Peter, you listen to Mr. Frank.

**MR. FRANK.** It might be better for us to go into Peter's room.

[PETER *jumps up eagerly, leading the way.*]

**MRS. VAN DAAN.** That's right. You go in there, Peter. You listen to Mr. Frank. Mr. Frank is a highly educated man.

[*As* MR. FRANK *is about to follow* PETER *into his room,* MRS. FRANK *stops him and wipes the lipstick from his lips. Then she closes the door after them.*]

**ANNE.** [*On the floor, listening*] Shh! I can hear a man's voice talking.

**MR. VAN DAAN.** [*To* ANNE] Isn't it bad enough here without your sprawling all over the place?

[ANNE *sits up*.]

**MRS. VAN DAAN.** [*To* MR. VAN DAAN] If you didn't smoke so much, you wouldn't be so bad-tempered.

**MR. VAN DAAN.** Am I smoking? Do you see me smoking?

**MRS. VAN DAAN.** Don't tell me you've used up all those cigarettes.

**MR. VAN DAAN.** One package. Miep only brought me one package.

**MRS. VAN DAAN.** It's a filthy habit anyway. It's a good time to break yourself.

**MR. VAN DAAN.** Oh, stop it, please.

**MRS. VAN DAAN.** You're smoking up all our money. You know that, don't you?

**MR. VAN DAAN.** Will you shut up?
[*During this,* MRS. FRANK *and* MARGOT *have studiously kept their eyes down. But* ANNE, *seated on the floor, has been following the discussion interestedly.* MR. VAN DAAN *turns to see her staring up at him.*] And what are you staring at?

**ANNE.** I never heard grownups quarrel before. I thought only children quarreled.

**MR. VAN DAAN.** This isn't a quarrel! It's a discussion. And I never heard children so rude before.

**ANNE.** [*Rising, indignantly*] I, rude!

**MR. VAN DAAN.** Yes!

**MRS. FRANK.** [*Quickly*] Anne, will you get me my knitting? [ANNE *goes to get it.*] I must remember, when Miep comes, to ask her to bring me some more wool.

**MARGOT.** [*Going to her room*] I need some hairpins and some soap. I made a list. [*She goes into her bedroom to get the list.*]

**MRS. FRANK.** [*To* ANNE] Have you some library books for Miep when she comes?

**ANNE.** It's a wonder that Miep has a life of her own, the way we make her run errands for us. Please, Miep, get me some starch. Please take my hair out and have it cut. Tell me all the latest news, Miep. [*She goes over, kneeling on the couch beside* MRS. VAN DAAN] Did you know she was engaged?

**Dialogue**
What plot conflict do the lines of dialogue here develop?

> I never heard grownups quarrel before. I thought only children quarreled.

Reading Check
In what way does Mr. Frank offer to help Peter?

His name is Dirk, and Miep's afraid the Nazis will ship him off to Germany to work in one of their war plants. That's what they're doing with some of the young Dutchmen . . . they pick them up off the streets—

**MR. VAN DAAN.** [*Interrupting*] Don't you ever get tired of talking? Suppose you try keeping still for five minutes. Just five minutes.

[*He starts to pace again. Again* ANNE *follows him, mimicking him.* MRS. FRANK *jumps up and takes her by the arm up to the sink, and gives her a glass of milk.*]

**MRS. FRANK.** Come here, Anne. It's time for your glass of milk.

**MR. VAN DAAN.** Talk, talk, talk. I never heard such a child. Where is my . . .? Every evening it's the same talk, talk, talk. [*He looks around.*] Where is my . . .?

**MRS. VAN DAAN.** What're you looking for?

**MR. VAN DAAN.** My pipe. Have you seen my pipe?

**MRS. VAN DAAN.** What good's a pipe? You haven't got any tobacco.

**MR. VAN DAAN.** At least I'll have something to hold in my mouth! [*Opening* MARGOT'S *bedroom door*] Margot, have you seen my pipe?

**MARGOT.** It was on the table last night.

[ANNE *puts her glass of milk on the table and picks up his pipe, hiding it behind her back.*]

**MR. VAN DAAN.** I know. I know. Anne, did you see my pipe? . . . Anne!

**MRS. FRANK.** Anne, Mr. Van Daan is speaking to you.

**ANNE.** Am I allowed to talk now?

**MR. VAN DAAN.** You're the most aggravating . . . The trouble with you is, you've been spoiled. What you need is a good old-fashioned spanking.

**ANNE.** [*Mimicking* MRS. VAN DAAN] "Remember, Mr. So-and-So, remember I'm a lady." [*She thrusts the pipe into his mouth, then picks up her glass of milk.*]

**MR. VAN DAAN.** [*Restraining himself with difficulty*] Why aren't you nice and quiet like your sister Margot? Why do you have to show off all the time? Let me give you a little

**Dialogue**
What cultural attitudes does Mr. Van Daan show in this dialogue?

advice, young lady. Men don't like that kind of thing in a girl. You know that? A man likes a girl who'll listen to him once in a while . . . a domestic girl, who'll keep her house shining for her husband . . . who loves to cook and sew and . . .

**ANNE.** I'd cut my throat first! I'd open my veins! I'm going to be remarkable! I'm going to Paris . . .

**MR. VAN DAAN.** [*Scoffingly*] Paris!

**ANNE.** . . . to study music and art.

**MR. VAN DAAN.** Yeah! Yeah!

**ANNE.** I'm going to be a famous dancer or singer . . . or something wonderful.

[*She makes a wide gesture, spilling the glass of milk on the fur coat in* MRS. VAN DAAN'S *lap.* MARGOT *rushes quickly over with a towel.* ANNE *tries to brush the milk off with her skirt.*]

▼ **Critical Viewing**
Why might the designers of this stamp have chosen such a happy photograph of Anne? **[Speculate]**

**MRS. VAN DAAN.** Now look what you've done . . . you clumsy little fool! My beautiful fur coat my father gave me . . .

**ANNE.** I'm so sorry.

**MRS. VAN DAAN.** What do you care? It isn't yours . . . So go on, ruin it! Do you know what that coat cost? Do you? And now look at it! Look at it!

**ANNE.** I'm very, very sorry.

**MRS. VAN DAAN.** I could kill you for this. I could just kill you!

[MRS. VAN DAAN *goes up the stairs, clutching the coat.* MR. VAN DAAN *starts after her.*]

**MR. VAN DAAN.** Petronella . . . *Liefje! Liefje!* . . . Come back . . . the supper . . . come back!

**MRS. FRANK.** Anne, you must not behave in that way.

**ANNE.** It was an accident. Anyone can have an accident.

**MRS. FRANK.** I don't mean that. I mean the answering back. You must not answer back. They are our guests. We must always show the greatest courtesy to them. We're all living under terrible tension. [*She stops as* MARGOT *indicates that* VAN DAAN *can hear. When he is gone, she continues.*]

**Cause and Effect**
How is the characters' situation affecting them?

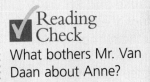 Reading Check
What bothers Mr. Van Daan about Anne?

The Diary of Anne Frank, Act I **881**

That's why we must control ourselves . . . You don't hear Margot getting into arguments with them, do you? Watch Margot. She's always courteous with them. Never familiar. She keeps her distance. And they respect her for it. Try to be like Margot.

**ANNE.** And have them walk all over me, the way they do her? No, thanks!

**MRS. FRANK.** I'm not afraid that anyone is going to walk all over you, Anne. I'm afraid for other people, that you'll walk on them. I don't know what happens to you, Anne. You are wild, self-willed. If I had ever talked to my mother as you talk to me . . .

**ANNE.** Things have changed. People aren't like that any more. "Yes, Mother." "No, Mother." "Anything you say, Mother." I've got to fight things out for myself! Make something of myself!

**MRS. FRANK.** It isn't necessary to fight to do it. Margot doesn't fight, and isn't she . . .?

**ANNE.** [*Violently rebellious*] Margot! Margot! Margot! That's all I hear from everyone . . . how wonderful Margot is . . . "Why aren't you like Margot?"

**MARGOT.** [*Protesting*] Oh, come on, Anne, don't be so . . .

**ANNE.** [*Paying no attention*] Everything she does is right, and everything I do is wrong! I'm the goat around here! . . . You're all against me! . . . And you worst of all!

[*She rushes off into her room and throws herself down on the settee, stifling her sobs.* MRS. FRANK *sighs and starts toward the stove.*]

**MRS. FRANK.** [*To* MARGOT] Let's put the soup on the stove . . . if there's anyone who cares to eat. Margot, will you take the bread out? [MARGOT *gets the bread from the cupboard.*] I don't know how we can go on living this way . . . I can't say a word to Anne . . . she flies at me . . .

**MARGOT.** You know Anne. In half an hour she'll be out here, laughing and joking.

**MRS. FRANK.** And . . . [*She makes a motion upwards, indicating the* VAN DAANS.] . . . I told your father it wouldn't work . . . but no . . . no . . . he had to ask them, he said . . . he owed it to him, he said. Well, he knows now that I was right!

These quarrels! . . . This bickering!

**MARGOT.** [*With a warning look*] Shush. Shush.

[*The buzzer for the door sounds.* MRS. FRANK *gasps, startled.*]

**MRS. FRANK.** Every time I hear that sound, my heart stops!

**MARGOT.** [*Starting for* PETER'S *door*] It's Miep. [*She knocks at the door.*] Father?

[MR. FRANK *comes quickly from* PETER'S *room.*]

**MR. FRANK.** Thank you, Margot. [*As he goes down the steps to open the outer door*] Has everyone his list?

**MARGOT.** I'll get my books. [*Giving her mother a list*] Here's your list.
[MARGOT *goes into her and* ANNE'S *bedroom on the right.* ANNE *sits up, hiding her tears, as* MARGOT *comes in.*]
Miep's here.
[MARGOT *picks up her books and goes back.* ANNE *hurries over to the mirror, smoothing her hair.*]

**MR. VAN DAAN.** [*Coming down the stairs*] Is it Miep?

**MARGOT.** Yes. Father's gone down to let her in.

**MR. VAN DAAN.** At last I'll have some cigarettes!

**MRS. FRANK.** [*To* MR. VAN DAAN] I can't tell you how unhappy I am about Mrs. Van Daan's coat. Anne should never have touched it.

**MR. VAN DAAN.** She'll be all right.

**MRS. FRANK.** Is there anything I can do?

**MR. VAN DAAN.** Don't worry.

[*He turns to meet* MIEP. *But it is not* MIEP *who comes up the steps. It is* MR. KRALER, *followed by* MR. FRANK. *Their faces are grave.* ANNE *comes from the bedroom.* PETER *comes from his room.*]

**MRS. FRANK.** Mr. Kraler!

**MR. VAN DAAN.** How are you, Mr. Kraler?

**MARGOT.** This is a surprise.

**MRS. FRANK.** When Mr. Kraler comes, the sun begins to shine.

**MR. VAN DAAN.** Miep is coming?

**MR. KRALER.** Not tonight.

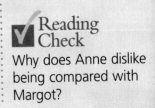

Reading Check

Why does Anne dislike being compared with Margot?

**Cause and Effect**
Why would a visit from an outside friend be especially welcome to those in hiding?

▼ **Critical Viewing**
This photograph shows the front of the Secret Annex. What are some pros and cons of this hiding place? **[Assess]**

[KRALER *goes to* MARGOT *and* MRS. FRANK *and* ANNE, *shaking hands with them.*]

**MRS. FRANK.** Wouldn't you like a cup of coffee? . . . Or, better still, will you have supper with us?

**MR. FRANK.** Mr. Kraler has something to talk over with us. Something has happened, he says, which demands an immediate decision.

**MRS. FRANK.** [*Fearful*] What is it?

[MR. KRALER *sits down on the couch. As he talks he takes bread, cabbages, milk, etc., from his briefcase, giving them to* MARGOT *and* ANNE *to put away.*]

**MR. KRALER.** Usually, when I come up here, I try to bring you some bit of good news. What's the use of telling you the bad news when there's nothing that you can do about it? But today something has happened . . . Dirk . . . Miep's Dirk, you know, came to me just now. He tells me that he has a Jewish friend living near him. A dentist. He says he's in trouble. He begged me, could I do anything for this man? Could I find him a hiding place? . . . So I've come to you . . . I know it's a terrible thing to ask of you, living as you are, but would you take him in with you?

**MR. FRANK.** Of course we will.

**MR. KRALER.** [*Rising*] It'll be just for a night or two . . . until I find some other place. This happened so suddenly that I didn't know where to turn.

**MR. FRANK.** Where is he?

**MR. KRALER.** Downstairs in the office.

**MR. FRANK.** Good. Bring him up.

**MR. KRALER.** His name is Dussel . . . Jan Dussel.

**MR. FRANK.** Dussel . . . I think I know him.

**MR. KRALER.** I'll get him.

[*He goes quickly down the steps and out.* MR. FRANK *suddenly becomes conscious of the others.*]

**MR. FRANK.** Forgive me. I spoke without consulting you. But I knew you'd feel as I do.

**MR. VAN DAAN.** There's no reason for you to consult

anyone. This is your place. You have a right to do exactly as you please. The only thing I feel . . . there's so little food as it is . . . and to take in another person . . .

[PETER *turns away, ashamed of his father.*]

**MR. FRANK.** We can stretch the food a little. It's only for a few days.

**MR. VAN DAAN.** You want to make a bet?

**MRS. FRANK.** I think it's fine to have him. But, Otto, where are you going to put him? Where?

**PETER.** He can have my bed. I can sleep on the floor. I wouldn't mind.

**MR. FRANK.** That's good of you, Peter. But your room's too small . . . even for *you.*

**ANNE.** I have a much better idea. I'll come in here with you and Mother, and Margot can take Peter's room and Peter can go in our room with Mr. Dussel.

**MARGOT.** That's right. We could do that.

**MR. FRANK.** No, Margot. You mustn't sleep in that room . . . neither you nor Anne. Mouschi has caught some rats in there. Peter's brave. He doesn't mind.

**ANNE.** Then how about *this?* I'll come in here with you and Mother, and Mr. Dussel can have my bed.

**MRS. FRANK.** *No. No. No!* Margot will come in here with us and he can have her bed. It's the only way. Margot, bring your things in here. Help her, Anne.

[MARGOT *hurries into her room to get her things.*]

**ANNE.** [*To her mother*] Why Margot? Why can't I come in here?

**MRS. FRANK.** Because it wouldn't be proper for Margot to sleep with a . . . Please, Anne. Don't argue. Please.

[ANNE *starts slowly away.*]

**MR. FRANK.** [*To* ANNE] You don't mind sharing your room with Mr. Dussel, do you, Anne?

**ANNE.** No. No, of course not.

**MR. FRANK.** Good. [ANNE *goes off into her bedroom, helping* MARGOT. MR. FRANK *starts to search in the cupboards.*]

**Cause and Effect**
What possible effects will Dussel's arrival have on the families' living situation?

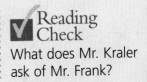

**Reading Check**
What does Mr. Kraler ask of Mr. Frank?

Where's the cognac?

**MRS. FRANK.** It's there. But, Otto, I was saving it in case of illness.

**MR. FRANK.** I think we couldn't find a better time to use it. Peter, will you get five glasses for me?

[PETER *goes for the glasses.* MARGOT *comes out of her bedroom, carrying her possessions, which she hangs behind a curtain in the main room.* MR. FRANK *finds the cognac and pours it into the five glasses that* PETER *brings him.* MR. VAN DAAN *stands looking on sourly.* MRS. VAN DAAN *comes downstairs and looks around at all the bustle.*]

**MRS. VAN DAAN.** What's happening? What's going on?

**MR. VAN DAAN.** Someone's moving in with us.

**MRS. VAN DAAN.** In here? You're joking.

**MARGOT.** It's only for a night or two . . . until Mr. Kraler finds him another place.

**MR. VAN DAAN.** Yeah! Yeah!

[MR. FRANK *hurries over as* MR. KRALER *and* DUSSEL *come up.* DUSSEL *is a man in his late fifties, meticulous, finicky . . . bewildered now. He wears a raincoat. He carries a briefcase, stuffed full, and a small medicine case.*]

**Vocabulary**
**bewildered**
(bē wil´ dərd) *adj.*
hopelessly confused

**MR. FRANK.** Come in, Mr. Dussel.

**MR. KRALER.** This is Mr. Frank.

**DUSSEL.** Mr. Otto Frank?

**MR. FRANK.** Yes. Let me take your things. [*He takes the hat and briefcase, but* DUSSEL *clings to his medicine case.*] This is my wife Edith . . . Mr. and Mrs. Van Daan . . . their son, Peter . . . and my daughters, Margot and Anne.

[DUSSEL *shakes hands with everyone.*]

**MR. KRALER.** Thank you, Mr. Frank. Thank you all. Mr. Dussel, I leave you in good hands. Oh . . . Dirk's coat.

[DUSSEL *hurriedly takes off the raincoat, giving it to* MR. KRALER. *Underneath is his white dentist's jacket, with a yellow Star of David on it.*]

**DUSSEL.** [*To* MR. KRALER] What can I say to thank you . . .?

**MRS. FRANK.** [*To* DUSSEL] Mr. Kraler and Miep . . . They're our life line. Without them we couldn't live.

**MR. KRALER.** Please. Please. You make us seem very heroic. It isn't that at all. We simply don't like the Nazis. [*To* MR. FRANK, *who offers him a drink*] No, thanks. [*Then going on*] We don't like their methods. We don't like . . .

**MR. FRANK.** [*Smiling*] I know. I know. "No one's going to tell us Dutchmen what to do with our damn Jews!"

**MR. KRALER.** [*To* DUSSEL] Pay no attention to Mr. Frank. I'll be up tomorrow to see that they're treating you right. [*To* MR. FRANK] Don't trouble to come down again. Peter will bolt the door after me, won't you, Peter?

**PETER.** Yes, sir.

**MR. FRANK.** Thank you, Peter. I'll do it.

**Dialogue**
Does Mr. Frank accept Mr. Kraler's explanation of why he is helping the families? Explain.

◀ **Critical Viewing**
How does the layout in this diagram help you to imagine what life might have been like for the residents of the Secret Annex? **[Infer]**

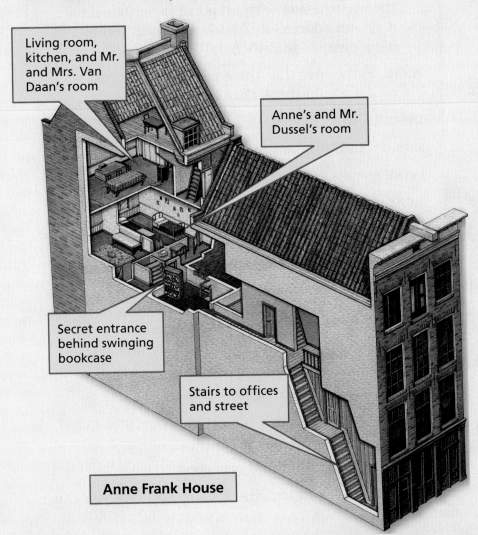

Living room, kitchen, and Mr. and Mrs. Van Daan's room

Anne's and Mr. Dussel's room

Secret entrance behind swinging bookcase

Stairs to offices and street

**Anne Frank House**

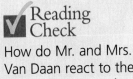
✓ Reading Check
How do Mr. and Mrs. Van Daan react to the news of Mr. Dussel moving in?

**MR. KRALER.** Good night. Good night.

**GROUP.** Good night, Mr. Kraler. We'll see you tomorrow, etc., etc.

[MR. KRALER *goes out with* MR. FRANK, MRS. FRANK *gives each one of the "grownups" a glass of cognac.*]

**MRS. FRANK.** Please, Mr. Dussel, sit down.

[MR. DUSSEL *sinks into a chair.* MRS. FRANK *gives him a glass of cognac.*]

**DUSSEL.** I'm dreaming. I know it. I can't believe my eyes. Mr. Otto Frank here! [*To* MRS. FRANK] You're not in Switzerland then? A woman told me . . . She said she'd gone to your house . . . the door was open, everything was in disorder, dishes in the sink. She said she found a piece of paper in the wastebasket with an address scribbled on it . . . an address in Zurich. She said you must have escaped to Zurich.

**ANNE.** Father put that there purposely . . . just so people would think that very thing!

**DUSSEL.** And you've been *here* all the time?

**MRS. FRANK.** All the time . . . ever since July.

[ANNE *speaks to her father as he comes back.*]

**ANNE.** It worked, Pim . . . the address you left! Mr. Dussel says that people believe we escaped to Switzerland.

**MR. FRANK.** I'm glad. . . . And now let's have a little drink to welcome Mr. Dussel.
[*Before they can drink,* MR. DUSSEL *bolts his drink.* MR. FRANK *smiles and raises his glass.*]
To Mr. Dussel. Welcome. We're very honored to have you with us.

**MRS. FRANK.** To Mr. Dussel, welcome.

[*The* VAN DAANS *murmur a welcome. The "grownups" drink.*]

**MRS. VAN DAAN.** Um. That was good.

**MR. VAN DAAN.** Did Mr. Kraler warn you that you won't

get much to eat here? You can imagine . . . three ration books among the seven of us . . . and now you make eight.

[PETER *walks away, humiliated. Outside a street organ is heard dimly.*]

**DUSSEL.** [*Rising*] Mr. Van Daan, you don't realize what is happening outside that you should warn me of a thing like that. You don't realize what's going on . . .

[as MR. VAN DAAN *starts his characteristic pacing,* DUSSEL *turns to speak to the others.*]
Right here in Amsterdam every day hundreds of Jews disappear . . . They surround a block and search house by house. Children come home from school to find their parents gone. Hundreds are being deported . . . people that you and I know . . . the Hallensteins . . . the Wessels . . .

**MRS. FRANK.** [*In tears*] Oh, no. No!

**DUSSEL.** They get their call-up notice . . . come to the Jewish theater on such and such a day and hour . . . bring only what you can carry in a rucksack. And if you refuse the call-up notice, then they come and drag you from your home and ship you off to Mauthausen.[20] The death camp!

**MRS. FRANK.** We didn't know that things had got so much worse.

**DUSSEL.** Forgive me for speaking so.

**ANNE.** [*Coming to* DUSSEL] Do you know the de Waals? . . . What's become of them? Their daughter Jopie and I are in the same class. Jopie's my best friend.

**DUSSEL.** They are gone.

**ANNE.** Gone?

**DUSSEL.** With all the others.

**ANNE.** Oh, no. Not Jopie!

[*She turns away, in tears.* MRS. FRANK *motions to* MARGOT *to comfort her.* MARGOT *goes to* ANNE, *putting her arms comfortingly around her.*]

**MRS. VAN DAAN.** There were some people called Wagner. They lived near us . . .?

**Cause and Effect**
How does Dussel's news affect Anne?

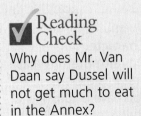
Reading Check
Why does Mr. Van Daan say Dussel will not get much to eat in the Annex?

---

**20. Mauthausen** (mou′ tou′ zən) village in Austria that was the site of a Nazi concentration camp.

**MR. FRANK.** [*Interrupting, with a glance at* ANNE] I think we should put this off until later. We all have many questions we want to ask . . . But I'm sure that Mr. Dussel would like to get settled before supper.

**DUSSEL.** Thank you. I would. I brought very little with me.

**MR. FRANK.** [*Giving him his hat and briefcase*] I'm sorry we can't give you a room alone. But I hope you won't be too uncomfortable. We've had to make strict rules here . . . a schedule of hours . . . We'll tell you after supper. Anne, would you like to take Mr. Dussel to his room?

**ANNE.** [*Controlling her tears*] If you'll come with me, Mr. Dussel? [*She starts for her room.*]

**DUSSEL.** [*Shaking hands with each in turn*] Forgive me if I haven't really expressed my gratitude to all of you. This has been such a shock to me. I'd always thought of myself as Dutch. I was born in Holland. My father was born in Holland, and my grandfather. And now . . . after all these years . . . [*He breaks off.*] If you'll excuse me.

[DUSSEL *gives a little bow and hurries off after* ANNE. MR. FRANK *and the others are subdued.*]

**ANNE.** [*Turning on the light*] Well, here we are.

[DUSSEL *looks around the room. In the main room* MARGOT *speaks to her mother.*]

**MARGOT.** The news sounds pretty bad, doesn't it? It's so different from what Mr. Kraler tells us. Mr. Kraler says things are improving.

**MR. VAN DAAN.** I like it better the way Kraler tells it.

[*They resume their occupations, quietly.* PETER *goes off into his room. In* ANNE'S *room,* ANNE *turns to* DUSSEL.]

**ANNE.** You're going to share the room with me.

**DUSSEL.** I'm a man who's always lived alone. I haven't had to adjust myself to others. I hope you'll bear with me until I learn.

**ANNE.** Let me help you. [*She takes his briefcase.*] Do you always live all alone? Have you no family at all?

**DUSSEL.** No one. [*He opens his medicine case and spreads his bottles on the dressing table.*]

**ANNE.** How dreadful. You must be terribly lonely.

© **Spiral Review**
**Character Development** What first impressions do you have of Dussel's character from his dialogue up to this point in the play?

**DUSSEL.** I'm used to it.

**ANNE.** I don't think I could ever get used to it. Didn't you even have a pet? A cat, or a dog?

**DUSSEL.** I have an allergy for fur-bearing animals. They give me asthma.

**ANNE.** Oh, dear. Peter has a cat.

**DUSSEL.** Here? He has it here?

**ANNE.** Yes. But we hardly ever see it. He keeps it in his room all the time. I'm sure it will be all right.

**DUSSEL.** Let us hope so. [*He takes some pills to fortify himself.*]

**ANNE.** That's Margot's bed, where you're going to sleep. I sleep on the sofa there. [*Indicating the clothes hooks on the wall*] We cleared these off for your things. [*She goes over to the window.*] The best part about this room . . . you can look down and see a bit of the street and the canal. There's a

### Reading Check

Why did Dussel believe he was safe from persecution as a Jew?

houseboat . . . you can see the end of it . . . a bargeman lives there with his family . . . They have a baby and he's just beginning to walk and I'm so afraid he's going to fall into the canal some day. I watch him. . . .

**DUSSEL.** [*Interrupting*] Your father spoke of a schedule.

**ANNE.** [*Coming away from the window*] Oh, yes. It's mostly about the times we have to be quiet. And times for the w.c. You can use it now if you like.

**DUSSEL.** [*Stiffly*] No, thank you.

**ANNE.** I suppose you think it's awful, my talking about a thing like that. But you don't know how important it can get to be, especially when you're frightened . . . About this room, the way Margot and I did . . . she had it to herself in the afternoons for studying, reading . . . lessons, you know . . . and I took the mornings. Would that be all right with you?

**DUSSEL.** I'm not at my best in the morning.

**ANNE.** You stay here in the mornings then. I'll take the room in the afternoons.

**DUSSEL.** Tell me, when you're in here, what happens to me? Where am I spending my time? In there, with all the people?

**ANNE.** Yes.

**DUSSEL.** I see. I see.

**ANNE.** We have supper at half past six.

**DUSSEL.** [*Going over to the sofa*] Then, if you don't mind . . . I like to lie down quietly for ten minutes before eating. I find it helps the digestion.

**ANNE.** Of course. I hope I'm not going to be too much of a bother to you. I seem to be able to get everyone's back up.

[DUSSEL *lies down on the sofa, curled up, his back to her.*]

**DUSSEL.** I always get along very well with children. My patients all bring their children to me, because they know I get on well with them. So don't you worry about that.

[ANNE *leans over him, taking his hand and shaking it gratefully.*]

**ANNE.** Thank you. Thank you, Mr. Dussel.

**Dialogue**
Based on this dialogue, how well do you think Anne and Dussel will get along as the plot develops?

[*The lights dim to darkness. The curtain falls on the scene.* ANNE'S VOICE *comes to us faintly at first, and then with increasing power.*]

**ANNE'S VOICE.** . . . And yesterday I finished Cissy Van Marxvelt's latest book. I think she is a first-class writer. I shall definitely let my children read her. Monday the twenty-first of September, nineteen forty-two. Mr. Dussel and I had another battle yesterday. Yes, Mr. Dussel! According to him, nothing, I repeat . . . nothing, is right about me . . . my appearance, my character, my manners. While he was going on at me I thought . . . sometime I'll give you such a smack that you'll fly right up to the ceiling! Why is it that every grownup thinks he knows the way to bring up children? Particularly the grownups that never had any. I keep wishing that Peter was a girl instead of a boy. Then I would have someone to talk to. Margot's a darling, but she takes everything too seriously. To pause for a moment on the subject of Mrs. Van Daan. I must tell you that her attempts to flirt with father are getting her nowhere. Pim, thank goodness, won't play.

[*As she is saying the last lines, the curtain rises on the darkened scene.* ANNE'S VOICE *fades out.*]

**Cause and Effect**
Are Anne's reactions here a result of her circumstances, or would they occur in any time period? Explain.

> Mr. Dussel and I had another battle yesterday.

## Scene 4

[*It is the middle of the night, several months later. The stage is dark except for a little light which comes through the skylight in* PETER'S *room.*

*Everyone is in bed.* MR. *and* MRS. FRANK *lie on the couch in the main room, which has been pulled out to serve as a makeshift double bed.*

MARGOT *is sleeping on a mattress on the floor in the main room, behind a curtain stretched across for privacy. The others are all in their accustomed rooms.*

*From outside we hear two drunken soldiers singing "Lili Marlene." A girl's high giggle is heard. The sound of running feet is heard coming closer and then fading in the distance. Throughout the scene there is the distant sound of airplanes passing overhead.*

*A match suddenly flares up in the attic. We dimly see* MR. VAN DAAN. *He is getting his bearings. He comes quickly down the stairs, and goes to the cupboard where the food is stored. Again the match flares up, and is as quickly blown out.*]

Reading Check
What does Anne explain to Dussel?

*The dim figure is seen to steal back up the stairs.*

*There is quiet for a second or two, broken only by the sound of airplanes, and running feet on the street below.*

*Suddenly, out of the silence and the dark, we hear* ANNE *scream.]*

**ANNE.** [*Screaming*] No! No! Don't . . . don't take me!

[*She moans, tossing and crying in her sleep. The other people wake, terrified.* DUSSEL *sits up in bed, furious.*]

**DUSSEL.** Shush! Anne! Anne, for God's sake, shush!

**ANNE.** [*Still in her nightmare*] Save me! Save me!

[*She screams and screams.* DUSSEL *gets out of bed, going over to her, trying to wake her.*]

**DUSSEL.** For God's sake! Quiet! Quiet! You want someone to hear?

[*In the main room* MRS. FRANK *grabs a shawl and pulls it around her. She rushes in to* ANNE, *taking her in her arms.* MR. FRANK *hurriedly gets up, putting on his overcoat.* MARGOT *sits up, terrified.* PETER'S *light goes on in his room.*]

**MRS. FRANK.** [*To* ANNE, *in her room*] Hush, darling, hush. It's all right. It's all right. [*Over her shoulder to* DUSSEL] Will you be kind enough to turn on the light, Mr. Dussel? [*Back to* ANNE] It's nothing, my darling. It was just a dream.

[DUSSEL *turns on the light in the bedroom.* MRS. FRANK *holds* ANNE *in her arms. Gradually* ANNE *comes out of her nightmare still trembling with horror.* MR. FRANK *comes into the room, and goes quickly to the window, looking out to be sure that no one outside has heard* ANNE'S *screams.* MRS. FRANK *holds* ANNE, *talking softly to her. In the main room* MARGOT *stands on a chair, turning on the center hanging lamp. A light goes on in the* VAN DAANS' *room overhead.* PETER *puts his robe on, coming out of his room.*]

**DUSSEL.** [*To* MRS. FRANK, *blowing his nose*] Something must be done about that child, Mrs. Frank. Yelling like that! Who knows but there's somebody on the streets? She's endangering all our lives.

**MRS. FRANK.** Anne, darling.

**DUSSEL.** Every night she twists and turns. I don't sleep. I spend half my night shushing her. And now it's nightmares!

[MARGOT *comes to the door of* ANNE'S *room, followed by* PETER. MR. FRANK *goes to them, indicating that everything is all right.* PETER *takes* MARGOT *back.*]

**MRS. FRANK.** [*To* ANNE] You're here, safe, you see? Nothing has happened. [*To* DUSSEL] Please, Mr. Dussel, go back to bed. She'll be herself in a minute or two. Won't you, Anne?

**DUSSEL.** [*Picking up a book and a pillow*] Thank you, but I'm going to the w.c. The one place where there's peace!

[*He stalks out.* MR. VAN DAAN, *in underwear and trousers, comes down the stairs.*]

**MR. VAN DAAN.** [*To* DUSSEL] What is it? What happened?

**DUSSEL.** A nightmare. She was having a nightmare!

**MR. VAN DAAN.** I thought someone was murdering her.

**DUSSEL.** Unfortunately, no.

[*He goes into the bathroom.* MR. VAN DAAN *goes back up the stairs.* MR. FRANK, *in the main room, sends* PETER *back to his own bedroom.*]

**MR. FRANK.** Thank you, Peter. Go back to bed.

[PETER *goes back to his room.* MR. FRANK *follows him, turning out the light and looking out the window. Then he goes back to*

**Dialogue**
How do the lines delivered by Dussel and Mrs. Frank reveal important differences between them?

**Reading Check**
Why does Anne scream in the middle of the night?

*the main room, and gets up on a chair, turning out the center hanging lamp.*]

**MRS. FRANK.** [*To* ANNE] Would you like some water? [ANNE *shakes her head.*] Was it a very bad dream? Perhaps if you told me . . . ?

**ANNE.** I'd rather not talk about it.

**MRS. FRANK.** Poor darling. Try to sleep then. I'll sit right here beside you until you fall asleep. [*She brings a stool over, sitting there.*]

**ANNE.** You don't have to.

**MRS. FRANK.** But I'd like to stay with you . . . very much. Really.

**ANNE.** I'd rather you didn't.

**MRS. FRANK.** Good night, then. [*She leans down to kiss* ANNE. ANNE *throws her arm up over her face, turning away.* MRS. FRANK, *hiding her hurt, kisses* ANNE'S *arm.*] You'll be all right? There's nothing that you want?

**ANNE.** Will you please ask Father to come.

**MRS. FRANK.** [*After a second*] Of course, Anne dear. [*She hurries out into the other room.* MR. FRANK *comes to her as she comes in.*] *Sie verlangt nach Dir!*[21]

**MR. FRANK.** [*Sensing her hurt*] Edith, *Liebe, schau . . .*[22]

**MRS. FRANK.** *Es macht nichts! Ich danke dem lieben Herrgott, dass sie sich wenigstens an Dich wendet, wenn sie Trost braucht! Geh hinein, Otto, sie ist ganz hysterisch vor Angst.*[23] [*As* MR. FRANK *hesitates*] *Geh zu ihr.*[24]
[*He looks at her for a second and then goes to get a cup of water for* ANNE. MRS. FRANK *sinks down on the bed, her face in her hands, trying to keep from sobbing aloud.* MARGOT *comes over to her, putting her arms around her.*] She wants nothing of me. She pulled away when I leaned down to kiss her.

**MARGOT.** It's a phase . . . You heard Father . . . Most girls go through it . . . they turn to their fathers at this age . . . they give all their love to their fathers.

---

**21.** *Sie verlangt nach Dir* (sē fer´ laŋt´ nä´ dir´) German for "She is asking for you."
**22.** *Liebe, schau* (lē´ bə shou´) German for "Dear, look."
**23.** *Es macht . . . vor Angst* German for "It's all right. I thank dear God that at least she turns to you when she needs comfort. Go in, Otto, she is hysterical because of fear."
**24.** *Geh zu ihr* (gē´ tsoo´ ēr´) German for "Go to her."

**MRS. FRANK.** You weren't like this. You didn't shut me out.

**MARGOT.** She'll get over it . . .

[*She smooths the bed for* MRS. FRANK *and sits beside her a moment as* MRS. FRANK *lies down. In* ANNE'S *room* MR. FRANK *comes in, sitting down by* ANNE. ANNE *flings her arms around him, clinging to him. In the distance we hear the sound of ack-ack.*]

**ANNE.** Oh, Pim. I dreamed that they came to get us! The Green Police! They broke down the door and grabbed me and started to drag me out the way they did Jopie.

**MR. FRANK.** I want you to take this pill.

**ANNE.** What is it?

**MR. FRANK.** Something to quiet you.

[*She takes it and drinks the water. In the main room* MARGOT *turns out the light and goes back to her bed.*]

**MR. FRANK.** [*To* ANNE] Do you want me to read to you for a while?

**ANNE.** No. Just sit with me for a minute. Was I awful? Did I yell terribly loud? Do you think anyone outside could have heard?

**MR. FRANK.** No. No. Lie quietly now. Try to sleep.

**ANNE.** I'm a terrible coward. I'm so disappointed in myself. I think I've conquered my fear . . . I think I'm really grown-up . . . and then something happens . . . and I run to you like a baby . . . I love you, Father. I don't love anyone but you.

**MR. FRANK.** [*Reproachfully*] Annele!

**ANNE.** It's true. I've been thinking about it for a long time. You're the only one I love.

**MR. FRANK.** It's fine to hear you tell me that you love me. But I'd be happier if you said you loved your mother as well . . . She needs your help so much . . . your love . . .

**ANNE.** We have nothing in common. She doesn't understand me. Whenever I try to explain my views on life to her she asks me if I'm constipated.

**MR. FRANK.** You hurt her very much just now. She's crying. She's in there crying.

**ANNE.** I can't help it. I only told the truth. I didn't want her

Reading
Check
What happens in
Anne's nightmare?

**Dialogue**
What insights does Anne have about herself, as revealed in this dialogue?

here . . . [*Then, with sudden change*] Oh, Pim, I was horrible, wasn't I? And the worst of it is, I can stand off and look at myself doing it and know it's cruel and yet I can't stop doing it. What's the matter with me? Tell me. Don't say it's just a phase! Help me.

**MR. FRANK.** There is so little that we parents can do to help our children. We can only try to set a good example . . . point the way. The rest you must do yourself. You must build your own character.

**ANNE.** I'm trying. Really I am. Every night I think back over all of the things I did that day that were wrong . . . like putting the wet mop in Mr. Dussel's bed . . . and this thing now with Mother. I say to myself, that was wrong. I make up my mind, I'm never going to do that again. Never! Of course I may do something worse . . . but at least I'll never do that again! . . . I have a nicer side, Father . . . a sweeter, nicer side. But I'm scared to show it. I'm afraid that people are going to laugh at me if I'm serious. So the mean Anne comes to the outside and the good Anne stays on the inside, and I keep on trying to switch them around and have the good Anne outside and the bad Anne inside and be what I'd like to be . . . and might be . . . if only . . . only . . .

[*She is asleep.* MR. FRANK *watches her for a moment and then turns off the light, and starts out. The lights dim out. The curtain falls on the scene.* ANNE'S VOICE *is heard dimly at first, and then with growing strength.*]

**Vocabulary**
**fatalist** (fā′ təl ist) *n.* one who believes that all events are determined by fate

**ANNE'S VOICE.** . . . The air raids are getting worse. They come over day and night. The noise is terrifying. Pim says it should be music to our ears. The more planes, the sooner will come the end of the war. Mrs. Van Daan pretends to be a fatalist. What will be, will be. But when the planes come over, who is the most frightened? No one else but Petronella! . . . Monday, the ninth of November, nineteen forty-two. Wonderful news! The Allies have landed in Africa. Pim says that we can look for an early finish to the war. Just for fun he asked each of us what was the first thing we wanted to do when we got out of here. Mrs. Van Daan longs to be home with her own things, her needlepoint chairs, the Beckstein piano her father gave her . . . the best that money could buy. Peter would like to go to a movie. Mr. Dussel wants to get back to his dentist's drill.

**Dialogue**
What does Anne's narration tell the audience about the war? How does this information add to the movement of the plot?

He's afraid he is losing his touch. For myself, there are so many things . . . to ride a bike again . . . to laugh till my belly aches . . . to have new clothes from the skin out . . . to have a hot tub filled to overflowing and wallow in it for hours . . . to be back in school with my friends . . .

[*As the last lines are being said, the curtain rises on the scene. The lights dim on as* ANNE'S VOICE *fades away.*]

## Scene 5

[*It is the first night of the Hanukkah*[25] *celebration.* MR. FRANK *is standing at the head of the table on which is the Menorah.*[26] *He lights the Shamos,*[27] *or servant candle, and holds it as he says the blessing. Seated listening is all of the "family," dressed in their best. The men wear hats,* PETER *wears his cap.*]

**MR. FRANK.** [*Reading from a prayer book*] "Praised be Thou, oh Lord our God, Ruler of the universe, who has sanctified us with Thy commandments and bidden us kindle the Hanukkah lights. Praised be Thou, oh Lord our God, Ruler of the universe, who has wrought wondrous deliverances for our fathers in days of old. Praised be Thou, oh Lord our God, Ruler of the universe, that Thou has given us life and sustenance and brought us to this happy season." [MR. FRANK *lights the one candle of the Menorah as he continues.*] "We kindle this Hanukkah light to celebrate the great and wonderful deeds wrought through the zeal with which God filled the hearts of the heroic Maccabees, two thousand years ago. They fought against indifference, against tyranny and oppression, and they restored our Temple to us. May these lights remind us that we should ever look to God, whence cometh our help." Amen.

**ALL.** Amen.

[MR. FRANK *hands* MRS. FRANK *the prayer book.*]

**MRS. FRANK.** [*Reading*] "I lift up mine eyes unto the mountains, from whence cometh my help. My help cometh from the Lord who made heaven and earth. He will not suffer thy foot to be moved. He that keepeth thee will not slumber. He that keepeth Israel doth neither slumber nor sleep. The Lord is

---

**Cause and Effect**
Why might the story of Hanukkah have special meaning for the families in hiding?

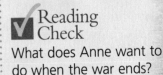

**Reading Check**
What does Anne want to do when the war ends?

---

25. **Hanukkah** (khä´ nŏŏ kä´) *n.* Jewish celebration that lasts eight days.
26. **Menorah** (mə nō´ rə) *n.* candle holder with nine candles, used during Hanukkah.
27. ***Shamos*** (shä´ məs) *n.* candle used to light the others in a menorah.

▲ **Critical Viewing**
This photo is from
a production of this
play. How well does it
capture the mood of
this scene? **[Assess]**

thy keeper. The Lord is thy shade upon thy right hand. The sun shall not smite thee by day, nor the moon by night. The Lord shall keep thee from all evil. He shall keep thy soul. The Lord shall guard thy going out and thy coming in, from this time forth and forevermore." Amen.

**ALL.** Amen.

[MRS. FRANK *puts down the prayer book and goes to get the food and wine.* MARGOT *helps her.* MR. FRANK *takes the men's hats and puts them aside.*]

**DUSSEL.** [*Rising*] That was very moving.

**ANNE.** [*Pulling him back*] It isn't over yet!

**MRS. VAN DAAN.** Sit down! Sit down!

**ANNE.** There's a lot more, songs and presents.

**DUSSEL.** Presents?

**MRS. FRANK.** Not this year, unfortunately.

**MRS. VAN DAAN.** But always on Hanukkah everyone gives presents . . . everyone!

**DUSSEL.** Like our St. Nicholas' Day.[28]

[*There is a chorus of "no's" from the group.*]

**MRS. VAN DAAN.** No! Not like St. Nicholas! What kind of a Jew are you that you don't know Hanukkah?

**MRS. FRANK.** [*As she brings the food*] I remember particularly the candles . . . First one, as we have tonight. Then the second night you light two candles, the next night three . . . and so on until you have eight candles burning. When there are eight candles it is truly beautiful.

**MRS. VAN DAAN.** And the potato pancakes.

**MR. VAN DAAN.** Don't talk about them!

**MRS. VAN DAAN.** I make the best *latkes* you ever tasted!

**MRS. FRANK.** Invite us all next year . . . in your own home.

**MR. FRANK.** God willing!

**MRS. VAN DAAN.** God willing.

---

28. **St. Nicholas' Day** December 6, the day Christian children in the Netherlands receive gifts.

**Dialogue**
What do Dussel's lines reveal about his familiarity with Hanukkah?

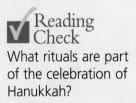

**Reading Check**
What rituals are part of the celebration of Hanukkah?

**Cause and Effect**
How do world events make this Hanukkah different from others that the families have celebrated?

**MARGOT.** What I remember best is the presents we used to get when we were little . . . eight days of presents . . . and each day they got better and better.

**MRS. FRANK.** [*Sitting down*] We are all here, alive. That is present enough.

**ANNE.** No, it isn't. I've got something . . . [*She rushes into her room, hurriedly puts on a little hat improvised from the lamp shade, grabs a satchel bulging with parcels and comes running back.*]

**MRS. FRANK.** What is it?

**ANNE.** Presents!

**MRS. VAN DAAN.** Presents!

**DUSSEL.** Look!

**MR. VAN DAAN.** What's she got on her head?

**PETER.** A lamp shade!

**ANNE.** [*She picks out one at random.*] This is for Margot. [*She hands it to* MARGOT, *pulling her to her feet.*] Read it out loud.

**MARGOT.** [*Reading*]
"You have never lost your temper.
You never will, I fear,
You are so good.
But if you should,
Put all your cross words here."
[*She tears open the package.*] A new crossword puzzle book! Where did you get it?

**Cause and Effect**
How do Anne's gifts reflect the reality of the families' situation?

**ANNE.** It isn't new. It's one that you've done. But I rubbed it all out, and if you wait a little and forget, you can do it all over again.

**MARGOT.** [*Sitting*] It's wonderful, Anne. Thank you. You'd never know it wasn't new.

[*From outside we hear the sound of a streetcar passing.*]

**ANNE.** [*With another gift*] Mrs. Van Daan.

**MRS. VAN DAAN.** [*Taking it*] This is awful . . . I haven't anything for anyone . . . I never thought . . .

**MR. FRANK.** This is all Anne's idea.

**MRS. VAN DAAN.** [*Holding up a bottle*] What is it?

**ANNE.** It's hair shampoo. I took all the odds and ends of soap and mixed them with the last of my toilet water.

**MRS. VAN DAAN.** Oh, Anneke!

**ANNE.** I wanted to write a poem for all of them, but I didn't have time. [*Offering a large box to* MR. VAN DAAN] Yours, Mr. Van Daan, is really something . . . something you want more than anything. [*As she waits for him to open it*] Look! Cigarettes!

**MR. VAN DAAN.** Cigarettes!

**ANNE.** Two of them! Pim found some old pipe tobacco in the pocket lining of his coat . . . and we made them . . . or rather, Pim did.

**MRS. VAN DAAN.** Let me see . . . Well, look at that! Light it, Putti! Light it.

[MR. VAN DAAN *hesitates.*]

**ANNE.** It's tobacco, really it is! There's a little fluff in it, but not much.

[*Everyone watches intently as* MR. VAN DAAN *cautiously lights it. The cigarette flares up. Everyone laughs.*]

**PETER.** It works!

**MRS. VAN DAAN.** Look at him.

**MR. VAN DAAN.** [*Spluttering*] Thank you, Anne. Thank you.

[ANNE *rushes back to her satchel for another present.*]

**ANNE.** [*Handing her mother a piece of paper*] For Mother, Hanukkah greeting.

[*She pulls her mother to her feet.*]

**MRS. FRANK.** [*She reads*] "Here's an I.O.U. that I promise to pay. Ten hours of doing whatever you say. Signed, Anne Frank." [MRS. FRANK, *touched, takes* ANNE *in her arms, holding her close.*]

**DUSSEL.** [*To* ANNE] Ten hours of doing what you're told? Anything you're told?

**ANNE.** That's right.

**DUSSEL.** You wouldn't want to sell that, Mrs. Frank?

**MRS. FRANK.** Never! This is the most precious gift I've ever had!

[*She sits, showing her present to the others.* ANNE *hurries back*

**Cause and Effect**
What effect do Anne's gifts have on the group's spirits?

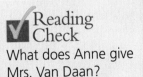

Reading Check
What does Anne give Mrs. Van Daan?

The Diary of Anne Frank, Act I **903**

*to the satchel and pulls out a scarf, the scarf that* MR. FRANK *found in the first scene.*]

**ANNE.** [*Offering it to her father*] For Pim.

**MR. FRANK.** Anneke . . . I wasn't supposed to have a present!

[*He takes it, unfolding it and showing it to the others.*]

**ANNE.** It's a muffler . . . to put round your neck . . . like an ascot, you know. I made it myself out of odds and ends . . . I knitted it in the dark each night, after I'd gone to bed. I'm afraid it looks better in the dark!

**MR. FRANK.** [*Putting it on*] It's fine. It fits me perfectly. Thank you, Annele.

[ANNE *hands* PETER *a ball of paper with a string attached to it.*]

**ANNE.** That's for Mouschi.

**PETER.** [*Rising to bow*] On behalf of Mouschi, I thank you.

**ANNE.** [*Hesitant, handing him a gift*] And . . . this is yours . . . from Mrs. Quack Quack. [*As he holds it gingerly in his hands*] Well . . . open it . . . Aren't you going to open it?

**PETER.** I'm scared to. I know something's going to jump out and hit me.

**ANNE.** No. It's nothing like that, really.

**MRS. VAN DAAN.** [*As he is opening it*] What is it, Peter? Go on. Show it.

**ANNE.** [*Excitedly*] It's a safety razor!

**DUSSEL.** A what?

**ANNE.** A razor!

**MRS. VAN DAAN.** [*Looking at it*] You didn't make that out of odds and ends.

**ANNE.** [*To* PETER] Miep got it for me. It's not new. It's second-hand. But you really do need a razor now.

**DUSSEL.** For what?

**ANNE.** Look on his upper lip . . . you can see the beginning of a mustache.

**DUSSEL.** He wants to get rid of that? Put a little milk on it and let the cat lick it off.

**PETER.** [*Starting for his room*] Think you're funny, don't you.

**DUSSEL.** Look! He can't wait! He's going in to try it!

**PETER.** I'm going to give Mouschi his present!

[*He goes into his room, slamming the door behind him.*]

**MR. VAN DAAN.** [*Disgustedly*] Mouschi, Mouschi, Mouschi.

[*In the distance we hear a dog persistently barking.* ANNE *brings a gift to* DUSSEL.]

**ANNE.** And last but never least, my roommate, Mr. Dussel.

**DUSSEL.** For me? You have something for me?

[*He opens the small box she gives him.*]

**ANNE.** I made them myself.

**DUSSEL.** [*Puzzled*] Capsules! Two capsules!

**ANNE.** They're ear-plugs!

**DUSSEL.** Ear-plugs?

**ANNE.** To put in your ears so you won't hear me when I thrash around at night. I saw them advertised in a magazine. They're not real ones . . . I made them out of cotton and candle wax. Try them . . . See if they don't work . . . see if you can hear me talk . . .

**DUSSEL.** [*Putting them in his ears*] Wait now until I get them in . . . so.

**ANNE.** Are you ready?

**DUSSEL.** Huh?

**ANNE.** Are you ready?

**DUSSEL.** Good God! They've gone inside! I can't get them out! [*They laugh as* MR. DUSSEL *jumps about, trying to shake the plugs out of his ears. Finally he gets them out. Putting them away*] Thank you, Anne! Thank you!

[*Together*]
- **MR. VAN DAAN.** A real Hanukkah!
- **MRS. VAN DAAN.** Wasn't it cute of her?
- **MRS. FRANK.** I don't know when she did it.
- **MARGOT.** I love my present.

**ANNE.** [*Sitting at the table*] And now let's have the song, Father . . . please . . . [*To* DUSSEL] Have you heard the Hanukkah song, Mr. Dussel? The song is the whole thing!

> I knitted it in the dark each night, after I'd gone to bed. I'm afraid it looks better in the dark!

**Dialogue**
What subplot does this dialogue develop?

✓ Reading Check

How does Mr. Dussel anger Peter?

[*She sings.*] "Oh, Hanukkah! Oh, Hanukkah! The sweet celebration . . ."

**MR. FRANK.** [*Quieting her*] I'm afraid, Anne, we shouldn't sing that song tonight. [*To* DUSSEL] It's a song of jubilation, of rejoicing. One is apt to become too enthusiastic.

**ANNE.** Oh, please, please. Let's sing the song. I promise not to shout!

**MR. FRANK.** Very well. But quietly now . . . I'll keep an eye on you and when . . .

[*As* ANNE *starts to sing, she is interrupted by* DUSSEL, *who is snorting and wheezing.*]

**DUSSEL.** [*Pointing to* PETER] You . . . You! [PETER *is coming from his bedroom, ostentatiously holding a bulge in his coat as if he were holding his cat, and dangling* ANNE'S *present before it.*] How many times . . . I told you . . . Out! Out!

**MR. VAN DAAN.** [*Going to* PETER] What's the matter with you? Haven't you any sense? Get that cat out of here.

**PETER.** [*Innocently*] Cat?

**MR. VAN DAAN.** You heard me. Get it out of here!

**PETER.** I have no cat. [*Delighted with his joke, he opens his coat and pulls out a bath towel. The group at the table laugh, enjoying the joke.*]

**DUSSEL.** [*Still wheezing*] It doesn't need to be the cat . . . his clothes are enough . . . when he comes out of that room . . .

**MR. VAN DAAN.** Don't worry. You won't be bothered any more. We're getting rid of it.

**DUSSEL.** At last you listen to me. [*He goes off into his bedroom.*]

**MR. VAN DAAN.** [*Calling after him*] I'm not doing it for you. That's all in your mind . . . all of it! [*He starts back to his place at the table.*] I'm doing it because I'm sick of seeing that cat eat all our food.

**PETER.** That's not true! I only give him bones . . . scraps . . .

**MR. VAN DAAN.** Don't tell me! He gets fatter every day! Damn cat looks better than any of us. Out he goes tonight!

**PETER.** No! No!

**Dialogue**
What does the dialogue between Peter and Mr. Dussel reveal about both their personalities?

**ANNE.** Mr. Van Daan, you can't do that! That's Peter's cat. Peter loves that cat.

**MRS. FRANK.** [*Quietly*] Anne.

**PETER.** [*To* MR. VAN DAAN] If he goes, I go.

**MR. VAN DAAN.** Go! Go!

**MRS. VAN DAAN.** You're not going and the cat's not going! Now please . . . this is Hanukkah . . . Hanukkah . . . this is the time to celebrate . . . What's the matter with all of you? Come on, Anne. Let's have the song.

**ANNE.** [*Singing*]
"Oh, Hanukkah! Oh, Hanukkah! The sweet celebration."

**Cause and Effect**
How do the families' circumstances influence Mr. Van Daan's opinion about keeping a cat?

✓ Reading Check
Who triggers the argument over the cat?

**MR. FRANK.** [*Rising*] I think we should first blow out the candle . . . then we'll have something for tomorrow night.

**MARGOT.** But, Father, you're supposed to let it burn itself out.

**MR. FRANK.** I'm sure that God understands shortages. [*Before blowing it out*] "Praised be Thou, oh Lord our God, who hast sustained us and permitted us to celebrate this joyous festival."

[*He is about to blow out the candle when suddenly there is a crash of something falling below. They all freeze in horror, motionless. For a few seconds there is complete silence.* MR. FRANK *slips off his shoes. The others noiselessly follow his example.* MR. FRANK *turns out a light near him. He motions to* PETER *to turn off the center lamp.* PETER *tries to reach it, realizes he cannot and gets up on a chair. Just as he is touching the lamp he loses his balance. The chair goes out from under him. He falls. The iron lamp shade crashes to the floor. There is a sound of feet below, running down the stairs.*]

**MR. VAN DAAN.** [*Under his breath*] God Almighty! [*The only light left comes from the Hanukkah candle.* DUSSEL *comes from his room.* MR. FRANK *creeps over to the stairwell and stands listening. The dog is heard barking excitedly.*] Do you hear anything?

**MR. FRANK.** [*In a whisper*] No. I think they've gone.

**MRS. VAN DAAN.** It's the Green Police. They've found us.

**MR. FRANK.** If they had, they wouldn't have left. They'd be up here by now.

**MRS. VAN DAAN.** I know it's the Green Police. They've gone to get help. That's all. They'll be back!

**MR. VAN DAAN.** Or it may have been the Gestapo,[29] looking for papers . . .

**MR. FRANK.** [*Interrupting*] Or a thief, looking for money.

**MRS. VAN DAAN.** We've got to do something . . . Quick! Quick! Before they come back.

**MR. VAN DAAN.** There isn't anything to do. Just wait.

[MR. FRANK *holds up his hand for them to be quiet. He is listening intently. There is complete silence as they all strain to hear any sound from below. Suddenly* ANNE *begins to sway. With a low*

**Cause and Effect**
Why is everyone reacting fearfully?

---

**29. Gestapo** (gə stä′ pō) *n.* secret police force of the German Nazi state, known for its terror tactics and brutality.

*cry she falls to the floor in a faint.* MRS. FRANK *goes to her quickly, sitting beside her on the floor and taking her in her arms.*]

**MRS. FRANK.** Get some water, please! Get some water!

[MARGOT *starts for the sink.*]

**MR. VAN DAAN.** [*Grabbing* MARGOT] No! No! No one's going to run water!

**MR. FRANK.** If they've found us, they've found us. Get the water. [MARGOT *starts again for the sink.* MR. FRANK, *getting a flashlight*] I'm going down.

[MARGOT *rushes to him, clinging to him.* ANNE *struggles to consciousness.*]

**MARGOT.** No, Father, no! There may be someone there, waiting . . . It may be a trap!

**MR. FRANK.** This is Saturday. There is no way for us to know what has happened until Miep or Mr. Kraler comes on Monday morning. We cannot live with this uncertainty.

**MARGOT.** Don't go, Father!

**MRS. FRANK.** Hush, darling, hush. [MR. FRANK *slips quietly out, down the steps and out through the door below.*] Margot! Stay close to me. [MARGOT *goes to her mother.*]

**MR. VAN DAAN.** Shush! Shush!

[MRS. FRANK *whispers to* MARGOT *to get the water.* MARGOT *goes for it.*]

**MRS. VAN DAAN.** Putti, where's our money? Get our money. I hear you can buy the Green Police off, so much a head. Go upstairs quick! Get the money!

**MR. VAN DAAN.** Keep still!

**MRS. VAN DAAN.** [*Kneeling before him, pleading*] Do you want to be dragged off to a concentration camp? Are you going to stand there and wait for them to come up and get you? Do something, I tell you!

**MR. VAN DAAN.** [*Pushing her aside*] Will you keep still!

[*He goes over to the stairwell to listen.* PETER *goes to his mother, helping her up onto the sofa. There is a second of silence, then* ANNE *can stand it no longer.*]

**ANNE.** Someone go after Father! Make Father come back!

> It's the Green Police. They've found us.

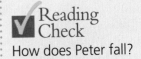

**Reading Check**

How does Peter fall?

**PETER.** [*Starting for the door*] I'll go.

**MR. VAN DAAN.** Haven't you done enough?

[*He pushes* PETER *roughly away. In his anger against his father* PETER *grabs a chair as if to hit him with it, then puts it down, burying his face in his hands.* MRS. FRANK *begins to pray softly.*]

**ANNE.** Please, please, Mr. Van Daan. Get Father.

**MR. VAN DAAN.** Quiet! Quiet!

[ANNE *is shocked into silence.* MRS. FRANK *pulls her closer, holding her protectively in her arms.*]

**MRS. FRANK.** [*Softly, praying*] "I lift up mine eyes unto the mountains, from whence cometh my help. My help cometh from the Lord who made heaven and earth. He will not suffer thy foot to be moved . . . He that keepeth thee will not slumber . . ."

[*She stops as she hears someone coming. They all watch the door tensely.* MR. FRANK *comes quietly in.* ANNE *rushes to him, holding him tight.*]

**MR. FRANK.** It was a thief. That noise must have scared him away.

**MRS. VAN DAAN.** Thank God.

**MR. FRANK.** He took the cash box. And the radio. He ran away in such a hurry that he didn't stop to shut the street door. It was swinging wide open. [*A breath of relief sweeps over them.*] I think it would be good to have some light.

**MARGOT.** Are you sure it's all right?

**MR. FRANK.** The danger has passed. [MARGOT *goes to light the small lamp.*] Don't be so terrified, Anne. We're safe.

**DUSSEL.** Who says the danger has passed? Don't you realize we are in greater danger than ever?

**MR. FRANK.** Mr. Dussel, will you be still!

[MR. FRANK *takes* ANNE *back to the table, making her sit down with him, trying to calm her.*]

**DUSSEL.** [*Pointing to* PETER] Thanks to this clumsy fool, there's someone now who knows we're up here! Someone now knows we're up here, hiding!

**MRS. VAN DAAN.** [*Going to* DUSSEL] Someone knows we're here, yes. But who is the someone? A thief! A thief! You think a

---

**Dialogue**
What plot line does this exchange between Peter and his father develop?

thief is going to go to the Green Police and say . . . I was robbing a place the other night and I heard a noise up over my head? You think a thief is going to do that?

**DUSSEL.** Yes. I think he will.

**MRS. VAN DAAN.** [*Hysterically*] You're crazy!

[*She stumbles back to her seat at the table.* PETER *follows protectively, pushing* DUSSEL *aside.*]

**DUSSEL.** I think some day he'll be caught and then he'll make a bargain with the Green Police . . . if they'll let him off, he'll tell them where some Jews are hiding!

[*He goes off into the bedroom. There is a second of appalled silence.*]

**MR. VAN DAAN.** He's right.

**ANNE.** Father, let's get out of here! We can't stay here now . . . Let's go . . .

**MR. VAN DAAN.** Go! Where?

**MRS. FRANK.** [*Sinking into her chair at the table*] Yes. Where?

**MR. FRANK.** [*Rising, to them all*] Have we lost all faith? All courage? A moment ago we thought that they'd come for us. We were sure it was the end. But it wasn't the end. We're alive, safe. [MR. VAN DAAN *goes to the table and sits.* MR. FRANK *prays.*]
"We thank Thee, oh Lord our God, that in Thy infinite mercy Thou hast again seen fit to spare us." [*He blows out the candle, then turns to* ANNE.] Come on, Anne. The song! Let's have the song!
[*He starts to sing.* ANNE *finally starts falteringly to sing, as* MR. FRANK *urges her on. Her voice is hardly audible at first.*]

**ANNE.** [*Singing*]
"Oh, Hanukkah! Oh, Hanukkah! The sweet . . . celebration . . ."

[*As she goes on singing, the others gradually join in, their voices still shaking with fear.* MRS. VAN DAAN *sobs as she sings.*]

**GROUP.** Around the feast . . . we . . . gather
In complete . . . jubilation . . .
Happiest of sea . . . sons
Now is here.
Many are the reasons for good cheer.

**Cause and Effect**
What do Mr. Dussel's lines about the Green Police suggest about their methods for finding Jews?

Reading Check
What is Dussel afraid the thief will do?

[DUSSEL *comes from the bedroom. He comes over to the table, standing beside* MARGOT, *listening to them as they sing.*]

"Together/We'll weather/Whatever tomorrow may bring."

[*As they sing on with growing courage, the lights start to dim.*]

"So hear us rejoicing/And merrily voicing/The Hanukkah song that we sing./Hoy!"

[*The lights are out. The curtain starts slowly to fall.*]

"Hear us rejoicing/And merrily voicing/The Hanukkah song that we sing."

[*They are still singing, as the curtain falls.*]

**Dialogue**
What is the effect of this song as a finale to the act?

## Critical Thinking

**Cite textual evidence to support your responses.**

© **1. Key Ideas and Details  (a)** In Scene 1, what objects does Mr. Frank find in the secret rooms? **(b) Connect:** How are these objects connected with the rest of the act?

© **2. Key Ideas and Details  (a)** What special meaning does Hanukkah have for the families? **(b) Deduce:** What do Anne's presents show about her? **(c) Interpret:** Why do the others react with enthusiasm to their presents?

© **3. Key Ideas and Details  (a) Evaluate:** With a partner, discuss Mr. Frank's statement, "There are . . . no locks that anyone can put on your mind." How does Anne prove that this is true? **(b) Discuss:** Share your answer with a partner and then with the class.

© **4. Integration of Knowledge and Ideas  (a)** What does Mr. Frank's reaction to the crisis involving the thief reveal about his personality, as compared with Mr. Van Daan's? **(b)** In general, what do the stresses faced by the families tend to bring out more—their differences or their similarities? Support your answer with specific examples. *[Connect to the Big Question: Is it our differences or our similarities that matter most?]*

## Reading Skill: Cause and Effect

1. **(a)** What is the historical **cause** that forces the Franks into hiding? **(b)** What **effects** does it have on their daily lives?
2. Anne and Peter discuss the Stars of David. **(a)** What effects do the Nazis intend the stars to have? **(b)** What background information helps you understand the intended effect?

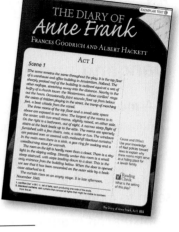

## Literary Analysis: Dialogue

**3. Craft and Structure** Complete an organizer like the one shown with examples of **dialogue** that achieve each purpose.

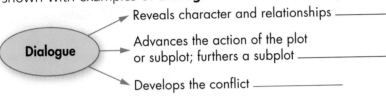

- Reveals character and relationships ——————
- Advances the action of the plot or subplot; furthers a subplot ——————
- Develops the conflict ——————

**4. Craft and Structure (a)** After Mr. Kraler asks if Dussel can join the group, what does the dialogue among the characters reveal about their personalities? **(b)** How does Dussel's dialogue on his arrival affect the scene's tone?

**5. Craft and Structure** Consider what you know about Anne's eventual fate. How does this knowledge add dramatic irony to the dialogue at the end of the act?

## Vocabulary

**Acquisition and Use** Use a vocabulary word from page 852 to rewrite each sentence to convey the same basic meaning.

1. The summer sun in the desert is difficult to tolerate.
2. The hole in Bryan's sweater is in a noticeable place.
3. Kevin believes that success in life is out of his hands.
4. Jasmine and Carly feel that Alberto gets too much attention.
5. Hostility between the cats has created a stressful situation.
6. Sam was confused by all the buttons on his new camera.

**Word Study** Use context and what you know about the **Greek suffix -ist** to explain your answer to each question.

1. Is a *violinist* someone who sells violins?
2. If you were a *humorist*, what might you do for a living?

### Word Study

The **Greek suffix -ist** means "one who does, makes, practices, is skilled in, or believes in."

**Apply It** Explain how the suffix -ist contributes to the meanings of these words. Consult a dictionary, if necessary.

bicyclist
moralist
artist

# Integrated Language Skills

## The Diary of Anne Frank, Act I

### Conventions:
### Dangling and Misplaced Modifiers

A **modifier** is a word, phrase, or clause that clarifies the meaning of a word or group of words in a sentence.

A phrase or clause that acts as a modifier should be placed as close as possible to the word it modifies. If it is placed far away, it might seem to modify the wrong word or no word at all.

A **misplaced modifier** seems to modify the wrong word.

| Confusing | Clear |
|---|---|
| We returned the toy to the store that was broken. | We returned the toy that was broken to the store. |

A **dangling modifier** is one that cannot sensibly modify any word in the sentence.

| Confusing | Clear |
|---|---|
| Staring at the ceiling, the idea became clear. | As I was staring at the ceiling, the idea became clear. |

**Practice A** In each sentence, identify the misplaced modifier and the word(s) it modifies.

1. Anne gave gifts to people that were made from recycled items.

2. Writing in her diary things she felt made Anne happy.

3. When she was thirteen years old, Anne's elderly grandmother died.

4. Anne's family joined the Van Daans with a cat.

© **Reading Application** Identify three modifiers in Act I and explain whether each is correctly placed.

**Practice B** Identify the dangling modifier in each sentence, and indicate the word it seems to modify.

1. Living in the attic rooms, it was lonely.

2. To survive, steady nerves help.

3. When young, adults can seem arbitrary and strange.

4. Getting angrier and angrier, time seemed to stand still.

© **Writing Application** Rewrite each sentence in Practice B so that it makes sense by adding a word for the dangling modifier to modify.

 **WRITING COACH** Further instruction and practice are available in *Prentice Hall Writing Coach*.

# Writing

 **Common Core
State Standards**

**L.8.1; W.8.3; SL.8.6**
[For the full wording of the
standards, see page 848.]

ⓒ **Narrative Text** To explore the perspectives of two characters other
than Anne, write two **diary entries** about an event from the play.
Follow these steps:

- Choose an event that affects at least two characters. Make a
  two-column chart to take notes that show how each person
  might have viewed the event. This chart will help you compare
  and contrast their perspectives.

- Consider how a single event takes on a different importance
  depending on the character viewing it.

- Write each diary entry from each character's point of view. Include
  a description of the event, using carefully chosen details such as
  remembered dialogue. Show each character's feelings and add
  details to describe how people looked and acted during the event.

**Grammar Application** Check your writing. Be sure you have used a
variety of complete sentences that include properly placed modifiers.

**Writing Workshop:** *Work in Progress*

**Prewriting for Exposition** For a research report that you may
write, think of something that you have always wanted to investigate further, such as how World War II ended. Generate a list of
questions that could spark your research. Save this Questions List.

Use this prewriting
activity to prepare for
the **Writing Workshop**
on page 982.

# Speaking and Listening

Use the photos, descriptions, and major events of the play, along
with original research, to present a **guided tour** of daily life in the
"Secret Annex." Follow these steps:

- Review the play for details about the layout of the rooms, the
  food the family ate, and the stresses of life in a cramped attic.

- Keep in mind that the play is a dramatization. The basic facts
  are true, but some elements have been fictionalized. Check
  the validity of major events and details in the play by consulting Anne's real diary (a primary source) and reliable secondary
  sources, such as the Web site of the Anne Frank House.

- For extra impact, include a dramatic soliloquy (solo speech)
  from the play. Whatever material you choose to present, vary
  your voice and use dynamic gestures and an appropriate tone
  to achieve the purpose of conveying the atmosphere of the
  "Secret Annex" to your audience.

www.PHLitOnline.com

- Interactive graphic organizers
- Grammar tutorial
- Interactive journals

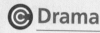 **Drama**

Build your skills and improve your comprehension of drama.

Read **The Diary of Anne Frank, Act II** to learn what happens as conditions worsen and tension mounts in the cramped attic rooms.

 **Common Core State Standards**

Meet these standards with **The Diary of Anne Frank, Act II** (p. 919).

**Reading Literature**

**3.** Analyze how particular lines of dialogue or incidents in a story or drama propel the action, reveal aspects of a character, or provoke a decision. (*Literary Analysis: Character's Motivation*)

**7.** Analyze the extent to which a filmed or live production of a story or drama stays faithful to or departs from the text or script, evaluating the choices made by the director or actors. (*Writing: Film Review*)

**Writing**

**2.** Write informative/explanatory texts to examine a topic and convey ideas, concepts, and information through the selection, organization, and analysis of relevant content. (*Writing: Film Review; Research and Technology: Bulletin Board Display*)

**4.** Produce clear and coherent writing in which the development, organization, and style are appropriate to task, purpose, and audience. (*Research and Technology: Bulletin Board Display*)

**7.** Conduct short research projects to answer a question, drawing on several sources and generating additional related, focused questions that allow for multiple avenues of exploration. (*Research and Technology: Bulletin Board Display*)

**Speaking and Listening**

**1.** Engage effectively in a range of collaborative discussions with diverse partners, building on others' ideas and expressing their own clearly. (*Research and Technology: Bulletin Board Display*)

**Language**

**1.** Demonstrate command of the conventions of standard English grammar and usage when writing or speaking. (*Conventions: Clauses*)

**4.b.** Use common, grade-appropriate Greek or Latin affixes and roots as clues to the meaning of a word (e.g., *precede, recede, secede*). (*Vocabulary: Word Study*)

# Reading Skill: Cause and Effect

**Cause-and-effect** relationships explain the connections between events, but they do not always follow the simple pattern of a single cause producing a single effect.

To help you discover these patterns in a literary work, **ask questions to analyze cause-and-effect relationships,** such as:

- What other causes might have triggered this event?
- What are all the possible effects—or chains of effects—that might result from this cause?
- Are these events really related? Just because two events occur in order does not mean they have a cause-and-effect relationship. They may be coincidental or random events.

## Using the Strategy: Cause-and-Effect Charts

Three relationships are shown in these **cause-and-effect charts**.

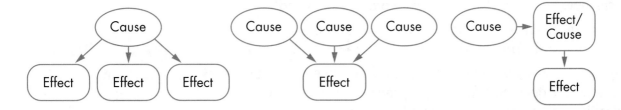

# Literary Analysis: Character's Motivation

A **character's motivation** is the reason he or she takes a particular action. This reason may be internal, external, or a mix of both. *Internal motivations* are based on emotions, such as loneliness or jealousy. *External motivations* are sparked by settings, events, or situations, like a war or poverty.

Characters are often affected by their environment. In this play two main **settings** have a major impact on the characters' actions: the raging war being fought across Europe and the confines of the attic in which the characters are forced to hide.

As you read, consider each character's possible motivations for each action he or she takes.

**Is it our *differences* or our *similarities* that matter most?**

## Writing About the Big Question

As the war drags on, conditions worsen in the "Secret Annex" and differences among the residents lead to conflict. Use these sentence starters to develop your ideas about the Big Question.

> **Superficial** differences between people can become magnified when _____. It is difficult to preserve **sympathy** and **tolerance** for others when you are facing _____.

**While You Read** Look for ways in which the families are or are not able to preserve their human dignity amid their suffering.

## Vocabulary

Read each word and its definition. Decide whether you know the word well, know it a little bit, or do not know it at all. After you read, see how your knowledge of each word has increased.

- **inarticulate** (in´ är tik´ yōō lit) *adj.* unable to express oneself (p. 923) *Confusion made him inarticulate. inarticulately adv.*

- **apprehension** (ap´ rē hen´ shən) *n.* a fearful feeling about what will happen next (p. 926) *I squeezed into the cave, despite my apprehension. apprehensive adj.*

- **blackmail** (blak´ māl´) *n.* the practice of making someone do what you want by threatening to reveal his or her secrets (p. 926) *Her fear that her criminal past might be exposed made her vulnerable to blackmail. blackmail v.*

- **forlorn** (fôr lôrn´) *adj.* sad and lonely (p. 931) *The child was forlorn when he was the last to be picked up. forlornly adv.*

- **intuition** (in´ tōō ish´ ən) *n.* ability to sense immediately, without reasoning (p. 934) *Pat's intuition told her that something was wrong. intuitive adj. intuitively adv.*

- **ineffectually** (in´ e fek´ chōō ə lē) *adv.* without producing the desired results (p. 950) *The fan spun ineffectually in the overheated room. ineffectual adj. effect n.*

### Word Study

The **Latin prefix *in-*** can mean "into" or "within."

In this play, a character claims to have **intuition**, a feeling within herself that she knows what is going to happen, without having a logical explanation for it.

# THE DIARY OF
## Anne Frank

Character's
Why do yo
writes a
ings t
in h

**Review and Anticipate** In Act I, Anne Frank's father visits the attic where his family and four others hid from the Nazis during World War II. As he holds Anne's diary, the offstage voice of Anne draws him into the past as the families begin their new life hiding from the Nazis. As months drag on, fear and lack of privacy in the attic rooms contribute to increasing tension between the family members. Act I ends on the first night of Hanukkah. The group's celebration is interrupted by the sounds of a thief below, who may have heard them. Read Act II to learn whether the hiding place has been discovered.

## ACT II

### Scene 1

[*In the darkness we hear* ANNE'S VOICE, *again reading from the diary.*]

**ANNE'S VOICE.** Saturday, the first of January, nineteen forty-four. Another new year has begun and we find ourselves still in our hiding place. We have been here now for one year, five months and twenty-five days. It seems that our life is at a standstill.

[*The curtain rises on the scene. It is late afternoon. Everyone is bundled up against the cold. In the main room* MRS. FRANK *is taking down the laundry which is hung across the back.* MR. FRANK *sits in the chair down left, reading.* MARGOT *is lying on the couch with a blanket over her and the many-colored knitted scarf around her throat.* ANNE *is seated at the center table, writing in her diary.* PETER, MR. *and* MRS. VAN DAAN *and* DUSSEL *are all in their own rooms, reading or lying down.*
 *As the lights dim on,* ANNE'S *voice continues, without a break.*]

**Reading Check**
How much time has passed since the Franks first went into hiding?

Motivation
ou think Anne
bout her feel-
ward her mother
er diary?

**ANNE'S VOICE.** We are all a little thinner. The Van Daans' "discussions" are as violent as ever. Mother still does not understand me. But then I don't understand her either. There is one great change, however. A change in myself. I read somewhere that girls of my age don't feel quite certain of themselves. That they become quiet within and begin to think of the miracle that is taking place in their bodies. I think that what is happening to me is so wonderful . . . not only what can be seen, but what is taking place inside. Each time it has happened I have a feeling that I have a sweet secret.

[*We hear the chimes and then a hymn being played on the carillon outside. The buzzer of the door below suddenly sounds. Everyone is startled. MR. FRANK tiptoes cautiously to the top of the steps and listens. Again the buzzer sounds, in MIEP's V-for-Victory signal.*][1]

**MR. FRANK.** It's Miep!

[*He goes quickly down the steps to unbolt the door. MRS. FRANK calls upstairs to the VAN DAANS and then to PETER.*]

**MRS. FRANK.** Wake up, everyone! Miep is here!

[ANNE *quickly puts her diary away.* MARGOT *sits up, pulling the blanket around her shoulders.* MR. DUSSEL *sits on the edge of his bed, listening, disgruntled.* MIEP *comes up the steps, followed by* MR. KRALER. *They bring flowers, books, newspapers, etc.* ANNE *rushes to* MIEP, *throwing her arms affectionately around her.*] Miep . . . and Mr. Kraler . . . What a delightful surprise!

**MR. KRALER.** We came to bring you New Year's greetings.

**MRS. FRANK.** You shouldn't . . . you should have at least one day to yourselves. [*She goes quickly to the stove and brings down teacups and tea for all of them.*]

**ANNE.** Don't say that, it's so wonderful to see them! [*Sniffing at* MIEP's *coat*] I can smell the wind and the cold on your clothes.

▼ **Critical Viewing**
Behind this bookcase are stairs leading to the hiding place. How does this photograph help you understand the tension in the play? **[Assess]**

---

1. **V-for-Victory signal** three short rings and one long one (the letter *V* in Morse code).

**MIEP.** [*Giving her the flowers*] There you are. [*Then to* MARGOT, *feeling her forehead*] How are you, Margot? . . . Feeling any better?

**MARGOT.** I'm all right.

**ANNE.** We filled her full of every kind of pill so she won't cough and make a noise. [*She runs into her room to put the flowers in water.* MR. *and* MRS. VAN DAAN *come from upstairs. Outside there is the sound of a band playing.*]

**MRS. VAN DAAN.** Well, hello, Miep. Mr. Kraler.

**MR. KRALER.** [*Giving a bouquet of flowers to* MRS. VAN DAAN] With my hope for peace in the New Year.

**PETER.** [*Anxiously*] Miep, have you seen Mouschi? Have you seen him anywhere around?

**MIEP.** I'm sorry, Peter. I asked everyone in the neighborhood had they seen a gray cat. But they said no.

[MRS. FRANK *gives* MIEP *a cup of tea.* MR. FRANK *comes up the steps, carrying a small cake on a plate.*]

**MR. FRANK.** Look what Miep's brought for us!

**MRS. FRANK.** [*Taking it*] A cake!

**MR. VAN DAAN.** A cake! [*He pinches* MIEP'S *cheeks gaily and hurries up to the cupboard.*] I'll get some plates.

[DUSSEL, *in his room, hastily puts a coat on and starts out to join the others.*]

**MRS. FRANK.** Thank you, Miepia. You shouldn't have done it. You must have used all of your sugar ration for weeks. [*Giving it to* MRS. VAN DAAN] It's beautiful, isn't it?

**MRS. VAN DAAN.** It's been ages since I even saw a cake. Not since you brought us one last year. [*Without looking at the cake, to* MIEP] Remember? Don't you remember, you gave us one on New Year's Day? Just this time last year? I'll never forget it because you had "Peace in nineteen forty-three" on it. [*She looks at the cake and reads*] "Peace in nineteen forty-four!"

**MIEP.** Well, it has to come sometime, you know. [*As* DUSSEL *comes from his room*] Hello, Mr. Dussel.

**Cause and Effect**
What does the dialogue about the cake reveal about life under German occupation?

Reading Check
What occasion are the families celebrating?

The Diary of Anne Frank, Act II **921**

**MR. KRALER.** How are you?

**MR. VAN DAAN.** [*Bringing plates and a knife*] Here's the knife, *liefje*. Now, how many of us are there?

**MIEP.** None for me, thank you.

**MR. FRANK.** Oh, please. You must.

**MIEP.** I couldn't.

**MR. VAN DAAN.** Good! That leaves one . . . two . . . three . . . seven of us.

**DUSSEL.** Eight! Eight! It's the same number as it always is!

**MR. VAN DAAN.** I left Margot out. I take it for granted Margot won't eat any.

**ANNE.** Why wouldn't she!

**MRS. FRANK.** I think it won't harm her.

**MR. VAN DAAN.** All right! All right! I just didn't want her to start coughing again, that's all.

**DUSSEL.** And please, Mrs. Frank should cut the cake.

[*Together*] {
  **MR. VAN DAAN.** What's the difference?

  **MRS. VAN DAAN.** It's not Mrs. Frank's cake, is it, Miep? It's for all of us.
}

**DUSSEL.** Mrs. Frank divides things better.

[*Together*] {
  **MRS. VAN DAAN.** [*Going to* DUSSEL] What are you trying to say?

  **MR. VAN DAAN.** Oh, come on! Stop wasting time!
}

**MRS. VAN DAAN.** [*To* DUSSEL] Don't I always give everybody exactly the same? Don't I?

**MR. VAN DAAN.** Forget it, Kerli.

**MRS. VAN DAAN.** No. I want an answer! Don't I?

**DUSSEL.** Yes. Yes. Everybody gets exactly the same . . . except Mr. Van Daan always gets a little bit more.

[VAN DAAN *advances on* DUSSEL, *the knife still in his hand.*]

**MR. VAN DAAN.** That's a lie!

[DUSSEL *retreats before the onslaught of the* VAN DAANS.]

**MR. FRANK.** Please, please! [*Then to* MIEP] You see what a little sugar cake does to us? It goes right to our heads!

---

**Character's Motivation**
Beyond the excuse he gives, what is another possible reason that Mr. Van Daan leaves out Margot?

**Character's Motivation**
How do the pressures of life in hiding affect the relationship between Dussel and the Van Daans?

**MR. VAN DAAN.** [*Handing* MRS. FRANK *the knife*] Here you are, Mrs. Frank.

**MRS. FRANK.** Thank you. [*Then to* MIEP *as she goes to the table to cut the cake*] Are you sure you won't have some?

**MIEP.** [*Drinking her tea*] No, really, I have to go in a minute.

[*The sound of the band fades out in the distance.*]

**PETER.** [*To* MIEP] Maybe Mouschi went back to our house . . . they say that cats . . . Do you ever get over there . . . ? I mean . . . do you suppose you could . . . ?

**MIEP.** I'll try, Peter. The first minute I get I'll try. But I'm afraid, with him gone a week . . .

**DUSSEL.** Make up your mind, already someone has had a nice big dinner from that cat!

[PETER *is furious,* inarticulate. *He starts toward* DUSSEL *as if to hit him.* MR. FRANK *stops him.* MRS. FRANK *speaks quickly to ease the situation.*]

**MRS. FRANK.** [*To* MIEP] This is delicious, Miep!

**MRS. VAN DAAN.** [*Eating hers*] Delicious!

**MR. VAN DAAN.** [*Finishing it in one gulp*] Dirk's in luck to get a girl who can bake like this!

**Vocabulary**
**inarticulate**
(in´ är tik´ yo͞o lit)
*adj.* unable to express oneself

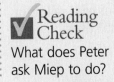
Reading Check
What does Peter ask Miep to do?

**MIEP.** [*Putting down her empty teacup*] I have to run. Dirk's taking me to a party tonight.

**ANNE.** How heavenly! Remember now what everyone is wearing, and what you have to eat and everything, so you can tell us tomorrow.

**MIEP.** I'll give you a full report! Good-bye, everyone!

**MR. VAN DAAN.** [*To* MIEP] Just a minute. There's something I'd like you to do for me.

[*He hurries off up the stairs to his room.*]

**MRS. VAN DAAN.** [*Sharply*] Putti, where are you going? [*She rushes up the stairs after him, calling hysterically.*] What do you want? Putti, what are you going to do?

**MIEP.** [*To* PETER] What's wrong?

**PETER.** [*His sympathy is with his mother.*] Father says he's going to sell her fur coat. She's crazy about that old fur coat.

**DUSSEL.** Is it possible? Is it possible that anyone is so silly as to worry about a fur coat in times like this?

**PETER.** It's none of your darn business . . . and if you say one more thing . . . I'll, I'll take you and I'll . . . I mean it . . . I'll . . .

[*There is a piercing scream from* MRS. VAN DAAN *above. She grabs at the fur coat as* MR. VAN DAAN *is starting downstairs with it.*]

**MRS. VAN DAAN.** No! No! No! Don't you dare take that! You hear? It's mine! [*Downstairs* PETER *turns away, embarrassed, miserable.*] My father gave me that! You didn't give it to me. You have no right. Let go of it . . . you hear?

[MR. VAN DAAN *pulls the coat from her hands and hurries downstairs.* MRS. VAN DAAN *sinks to the floor, sobbing. As* MR. VAN DAAN *comes into the main room the others look away, embarrassed for him.*]

**Character's Motivation**
Are Mr. Van Daan's reasons for selling his wife's fur coat selfish or unselfish? Explain.

**MR. VAN DAAN.** [*To* MR. KRALER] Just a little—discussion over the advisability of selling this coat. As I have often reminded Mrs. Van Daan, it's very selfish of her to keep it when people outside are in such desperate need of clothing . . . [*He gives the coat to* MIEP.] So if you will please to sell it for us? It should fetch a good price. And by the way, will you get me cigarettes. I don't care what kind they are . . . get all you can.

**MIEP.** It's terribly difficult to get them, Mr. Van Daan. But I'll try. Good-bye.

[*She goes. MR. FRANK follows her down the steps to bolt the door after her. MRS. FRANK gives MR. KRALER a cup of tea.*]

**MRS. FRANK.** Are you sure you won't have some cake, Mr. Kraler?

**MR. KRALER.** I'd better not.

**MR. VAN DAAN.** You're still feeling badly? What does your doctor say?

**MR. KRALER.** I haven't been to him.

**MRS. FRANK.** Now, Mr. Kraler! . . .

**MR. KRALER.** [*Sitting at the table*] Oh, I tried. But you can't get near a doctor these days . . . they're so busy. After weeks I finally managed to get one on the telephone. I told him I'd like an appointment . . . I wasn't feeling very well. You know what he answers . . . over the telephone . . . Stick out your tongue! [*They laugh. He turns to MR. FRANK as MR. FRANK comes back.*] I have some contracts here . . . I wonder if you'd look over them with me . . .

**MR. FRANK.** [*Putting out his hand*] Of course.

**MR. KRALER.** [*He rises*] If we could go downstairs . . . [*MR. FRANK starts ahead; MR. KRALER speaks to the others.*] Will you forgive us? I won't keep him but a minute. [*He starts to follow MR. FRANK down the steps.*]

**MARGOT.** [*With sudden foreboding*] What's happened? Something's happened! Hasn't it, Mr. Kraler?

[*MR. KRALER stops and comes back, trying to reassure MARGOT with a pretense of casualness.*]

**MR. KRALER.** No, really. I want your father's advice . . .

**MARGOT.** Something's gone wrong! I know it!

**MR. FRANK.** [*Coming back, to MR. KRALER*] If it's something that concerns us here, it's better that we all hear it.

**MR. KRALER.** [*Turning to him, quietly*] But . . . the children . . . ?

**MR. FRANK.** What they'd imagine would be worse than any reality.

Is it possible that anyone is so silly as to worry about a fur coat in times like this?

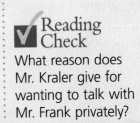

**Reading Check**

What reason does Mr. Kraler give for wanting to talk with Mr. Frank privately?

Vocabulary
**apprehension**
(ap´ rē hen´ shən) *n.*
a fearful feeling about
what will happen next

[*As* MR. KRALER *speaks, they all listen with intense*
*apprehension.* MRS. VAN DAAN *comes down the stairs*
*and sits on the bottom step.*]

**MR. KRALER.** It's a man in the storeroom . . . I don't know
whether or not you remember him . . . Carl, about fifty,
heavy-set, nearsighted . . . He came with us just before
you left.

**MR. FRANK.** He was from Utrecht?

**MR. KRALER.** That's the man. A couple of weeks ago, when I
was in the storeroom, he closed the door and asked me . . .
how's Mr. Frank? What do you hear from Mr. Frank? I told
him I only knew there was a rumor that you were in Switzerland. He said he'd heard that rumor too, but he thought
I might know something more. I didn't pay any attention
to it . . . but then a thing happened yesterday . . . He'd
brought some invoices to the office for me to sign. As I was
going through them, I looked up. He was standing staring
at the bookcase . . . your bookcase. He said he thought he
remembered a door there . . . Wasn't there a door there that
used to go up to the loft? Then he told me he wanted more
money. Twenty guilders[2] more a week.

**MR. VAN DAAN.** Blackmail!

**MR. FRANK.** Twenty guilders? Very modest blackmail.

**MR. VAN DAAN.** That's just the beginning.

**DUSSEL.** [*Coming to* MR. FRANK] You know what I think? He
was the thief who was down there that night. That's how
he knows we're here.

**MR. FRANK.** [*To* MR. KRALER] How was it left? What did you
tell him?

**MR. KRALER.** I said I had to think about it. What shall I do?
Pay him the money? . . . Take a chance on firing him . . .
or what? I don't know.

**DUSSEL.** [*Frantic*] Don't fire him! Pay him what he asks . . .
keep him here where you can have your eye on him.

**MR. FRANK.** Is it so much that he's asking? What are they
paying nowadays?

**MR. KRALER.** He could get it in a war plant. But this isn't a

Vocabulary
**blackmail** (blak´ māl´)
*n.* the practice of
making someone do
what you want by
threatening to reveal
his or her secrets

Cause and Effect
How does Dussel's
reaction reflect his fear
about being caught
by the authorities?

---

2. **guilders** (gil´ dərz) *n.* monetary unit of the Netherlands.

war plant. Mind you, I don't know if he really knows . . . or if he doesn't know.

**MR. FRANK.** Offer him half. Then we'll soon find out if it's blackmail or not.

**DUSSEL.** And if it is? We've got to pay it, haven't we? Anything he asks we've got to pay!

**MR. FRANK.** Let's decide that when the time comes.

**MR. KRALER.** This may be all my imagination. You get to a point, these days, where you suspect everyone and everything. Again and again . . . on some simple look or word, I've found myself . . .

[*The telephone rings in the office below.*]

**MRS. VAN DAAN.** [*Hurrying to* MR. KRALER] There's the telephone! What does that mean, the telephone ringing on a holiday?

**MR. KRALER.** That's my wife. I told her I had to go over some papers in my office . . . to call me there when she got out of church. [*He starts out.*] I'll offer him half then. Goodbye . . . we'll hope for the best!

[*The group calls their good-byes halfheartedly.* MR. FRANK *follows* MR. KRALER *to bolt the door below. During the following scene,* MR. FRANK *comes back up and stands listening, disturbed.*]

**DUSSEL.** [*To* MR. VAN DAAN] You can thank your son for this . . . smashing the light! I tell you, it's just a question of time now.

[*He goes to the window at the back and stands looking out.*]

**MARGOT.** Sometimes I wish the end would come . . . whatever it is.

**MRS. FRANK.** [*Shocked*] Margot!

[ANNE *goes to* MARGOT, *sitting beside her on the couch with her arms around her.*]

**MARGOT.** Then at least we'd know where we were.

**MRS. FRANK.** You should be ashamed of yourself! Talking that way! Think how lucky we are! Think of the thousands dying in the war, every day. Think of the people in concentration camps.

**Cause and Effect**
Here, Kraler resists a cause-and-effect explanation for events that occurred in order. What else might explain the employee's demand?

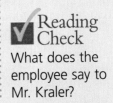

**Reading Check**
What does the employee say to Mr. Kraler?

**ANNE.** [*Interrupting*] What's the good of that? What's the good of thinking of misery when you're already miserable? That's stupid!

**MRS. FRANK.** Anne!

[*As ANNE goes on raging at her mother, MRS. FRANK tries to break in, in an effort to quiet her.*]

**ANNE.** We're young, Margot and Peter and I! You grownups have had your chance! But look at us . . . If we begin thinking of all the horror in the world, we're lost! We're trying to hold onto some kind of ideals . . . when everything . . . ideals, hopes . . . everything, are being destroyed! It isn't our fault that the world is in such a mess! We weren't around when all this started! So don't try to take it out on us! [*She rushes off to her room, slamming the door after her. She picks up a brush from the chest and hurls it to the floor. Then she sits on the settee, trying to control her anger.*]

**Cause and Effect**
How does Anne's speech reveal a gap between the adults' and the teenagers' perspectives on the outside world?

**MR. VAN DAAN.** She talks as if we started the war! Did we start the war?

[*He spots ANNE'S cake. As he starts to take it, PETER anticipates him.*]

**PETER.** She left her cake. [*He starts for ANNE'S room with the cake. There is silence in the main room. MRS. VAN DAAN goes up to her room, followed by VAN DAAN. DUSSEL stays looking out the window. MR. FRANK brings MRS. FRANK her cake. She eats it slowly, without relish. MR. FRANK takes his cake to MARGOT and sits quietly on the sofa beside her. PETER stands in the doorway of ANNE'S darkened room, looking at her, then makes a little movement to let her know he is there. ANNE sits up, quickly, trying to hide the signs of her tears. PETER holds out the cake to her.*] You left this.

**ANNE.** [*Dully*] Thanks.

[*PETER starts to go out, then comes back.*]

**PETER.** I thought you were fine just now. You know just how to talk to them. You know just how to say it. I'm no good . . . I never can think . . . especially when I'm mad . . . That Dussel . . . when he said that about Mouschi . . . someone eating him . . . all I could think is . . . I wanted to hit him. I wanted to give him such a . . . a . . . that he'd . . . That's what I used to do when there was an argument at school . . . That's the way I . . . but here . . . And an old man like that . . . it wouldn't be so good.

**Character's Motivation**
Why does Peter seek out Anne in her room?

**ANNE.** You're making a big mistake about me. I do it all wrong. I say too much. I go too far. I hurt people's feelings . . .

[*DUSSEL leaves the window, going to his room.*]

**PETER.** I think you're just fine . . . What I want to say . . . if it wasn't for you around here, I don't know. What I mean . . .

[*PETER is interrupted by DUSSEL'S turning on the light. DUSSEL stands in the doorway, startled to see PETER. PETER advances toward him forbiddingly. DUSSEL backs out of the room. PETER closes the door on him.*]

**ANNE.** Do you mean it, Peter? Do you really mean it?

**PETER.** I said it, didn't I?

**ANNE.** Thank you, Peter!

[*In the main room MR. and MRS. FRANK collect the dishes and take them to the sink, washing them. MARGOT lies down again on the couch. DUSSEL, lost, wanders into PETER'S room and takes up a book, starting to read.*]

Reading Check
Why does Peter admire Anne?

▶ **Critical Viewing**
This photograph shows a museum re-creation of a wall in Anne Frank's room. In what ways does her room resemble a typical teenager's room today? **[Relate]**

**PETER.** [*Looking at the photographs on the wall*] You've got quite a collection.

**ANNE.** Wouldn't you like some in your room? I could give you some. Heaven knows you spend enough time in there . . . doing heaven knows what . . .

**PETER.** It's easier. A fight starts, or an argument . . . I duck in there.

**ANNE.** You're lucky, having a room to go to. His lordship is always here . . . I hardly ever get a minute alone. When they start in on me, I can't duck away. I have to stand there and take it.

**PETER.** You gave some of it back just now.

**ANNE.** I get so mad. They've formed their opinions . . . about everything . . . but we . . . we're still trying to find out . . . We have problems here that no other people our age have ever had. And just as you think you've solved them, something comes along and bang! You have to start all over again.

**PETER.** At least you've got someone you can talk to.

**ANNE.** Not really. Mother . . . I never discuss anything serious with her. She doesn't understand. Father's all right. We can talk about everything . . . everything but one thing. Mother. He simply won't talk about her. I don't think you can be really intimate with anyone if he holds something back, do you?

**PETER.** I think your father's fine.

**ANNE.** Oh, he is, Peter! He is! He's the only one who's ever given me the feeling that I have any sense. But anyway, nothing can take the place of school and play and friends of your own age . . . or near your age . . . can it?

**PETER.** I suppose you miss your friends and all.

**ANNE.** It isn't just . . . [*She breaks off, staring up at him for a second.*] Isn't it funny, you and I? Here we've been seeing each other every minute for almost a year and a half, and this is the first time we've ever really talked. It helps a lot to have someone to talk to, don't you think? It helps you to let off steam.

**PETER.** [*Going to the door*] Well, any time you want to let off steam, you can come into my room.

**ANNE.** [*Following him*] I can get up an awful lot of steam. You'll have to be careful how you say that.

**PETER.** It's all right with me.

**ANNE.** Do you mean it?

**PETER.** I said it, didn't I?

[*He goes out. ANNE stands in her doorway looking after him. As PETER gets to his door he stands for a minute looking back at her. Then he goes into his room. DUSSEL rises as he comes in, and quickly passes him, going out. He starts across for his room. ANNE sees him coming, and pulls her door shut. DUSSEL turns back toward PETER'S room. PETER pulls his door shut. DUSSEL stands there, bewildered, forlorn.*

*The scene slowly dims out. The curtain falls on the scene. ANNE'S VOICE comes over in the darkness . . . faintly at first, and then with growing strength.*]

**Vocabulary**
**forlorn** (fôr lôrn´)
*adj.* sad and lonely

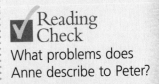

**Reading Check**

What problems does Anne describe to Peter?

**ANNE'S VOICE.** We've had bad news. The people from whom Miep got our ration books have been arrested. So we have had to cut down on our food. Our stomachs are so empty that they rumble and make strange noises, all in different keys. Mr. Van Daan's is deep and low, like a bass fiddle. Mine is high, whistling like a flute. As we all sit around waiting for supper, it's like an orchestra tuning up. It only needs Toscanini[3] to raise his baton and we'd be off in the Ride of the Valkyries.[4] Monday, the sixth of March, nineteen forty-four. Mr. Kraler is in the hospital. It seems he has ulcers. Pim says we are his ulcers. Miep has to run the business and us too. The Americans have landed on the southern tip of Italy. Father looks for a quick finish to the war. Mr. Dussel is waiting every day for the warehouse man to demand more money. Have I been skipping too much from one subject to another? I can't help it. I feel that spring is coming. I feel it in my whole body and soul. I feel utterly confused. I am longing . . . so longing . . . for everything . . . for friends . . . for someone to talk to . . . someone who understands . . . someone young, who feels as I do . . .

[*As these last lines are being said, the curtain rises on the scene. The lights dim on.* ANNE'S VOICE *fades out.*]

# Scene 2

[*It is evening, after supper. From outside we hear the sound of children playing. The "grownups," with the exception of* MR. VAN DAAN, *are all in the main room.* MRS. FRANK *is doing some mending,* MRS. VAN DAAN *is reading a fashion magazine.* MR. FRANK *is going over business accounts.* DUSSEL, *in his dentist's jacket, is pacing up and down, impatient to get into his bedroom.* MR. VAN DAAN *is upstairs working on a piece of embroidery in an embroidery frame.*

*In his room* PETER *is sitting before the mirror, smoothing his hair. As the scene goes on, he puts on his tie, brushes his coat and puts it on, preparing himself meticulously for a visit from* ANNE. *On his wall are now hung some of* ANNE'S *motion picture stars.*

*In her room* ANNE *too is getting dressed. She stands before*

---

3. **Toscanini** (täs´ kə nē´ nē) Arturo Toscanini, a famous Italian American orchestra conductor.
4. **Ride of the Valkyries** (val kir´ ēz) stirring selection from an opera by Richard Wagner, a German composer.

*the mirror in her slip, trying various ways of dressing her hair. MARGOT is seated on the sofa, hemming a skirt for ANNE to wear.*

*In the main room DUSSEL can stand it no longer. He comes over, rapping sharply on the door of his and ANNE'S bedroom.]*

**ANNE.** [*Calling to him*] No, no, Mr. Dussel! I am not dressed yet. [DUSSEL *walks away, furious, sitting down and burying his head in his hands.* ANNE *turns to* MARGOT.] How is that? How does that look?

**MARGOT.** [*Glancing at her briefly*] Fine.

**ANNE.** You didn't even look.

**MARGOT.** Of course I did. It's fine.

**ANNE.** Margot, tell me, am I terribly ugly?

**MARGOT.** Oh, stop fishing.

**ANNE.** No. No. Tell me.

**MARGOT.** Of course you're not. You've got nice eyes . . . and a lot of animation, and . . .

**ANNE.** A little vague, aren't you?

[*She reaches over and takes a brassiére out of Margot's sewing basket. She holds it up to herself, studying the effect in the mirror. Outside,* MRS. FRANK, *feeling sorry for* DUSSEL, *comes over, knocking at the girls' door.]*

**MRS. FRANK.** [*Outside*] May I come in?

**MARGOT.** Come in, Mother.

**MRS. FRANK.** [*Shutting the door behind her*] Mr. Dussel's impatient to get in here.

**ANNE.** [*Still with the brassière*] Heavens, he takes the room for himself the entire day.

**MRS. FRANK.** [*Gently*] Anne, dear, you're not going in again tonight to see Peter?

**ANNE.** [*Dignified*] That is my intention.

**MRS. FRANK.** But you've already spent a great deal of time in there today.

**ANNE.** I was in there exactly twice. Once to get the dictionary,

✓ Reading Check

How does Mrs. Frank feel about the time Anne spends with Peter?

**Vocabulary**
**intuition** (in´ tōō ish´ ən)
*n.* ability to sense immediately, without reasoning

and then three-quarters of an hour before supper.

**MRS. FRANK.** Aren't you afraid you're disturbing him?

**ANNE.** Mother, I have some intuition.

**MRS. FRANK.** Then may I ask you this much, Anne. Please don't shut the door when you go in.

**ANNE.** You sound like Mrs. Van Daan! [*She throws the brassière back in Margot's sewing basket and picks up her blouse, putting it on.*]

**Character's Motivation**
What prompts Mrs. Frank to make these requests of Anne?

**MRS. FRANK.** No. No. I don't mean to suggest anything wrong. I only wish that you wouldn't expose yourself to criticism . . . that you wouldn't give Mrs. Van Daan the opportunity to be unpleasant.

**ANNE.** Mrs. Van Daan doesn't need an opportunity to be unpleasant!

**MRS. FRANK.** Everyone's on edge, worried about Mr. Kraler. This is one more thing . . .

**ANNE.** I'm sorry, Mother. I'm going to Peter's room. I'm not going to let Petronella Van Daan spoil our friendship.

[MRS. FRANK *hesitates for a second, then goes out, closing the door after her. She gets a pack of playing cards and sits at the center table, playing solitaire. In* ANNE'S *room* MARGOT *hands the finished skirt to* ANNE. *As* ANNE *is putting it on,* MARGOT *takes off her high-heeled shoes and stuffs paper in the toes so that* ANNE *can wear them.*]

**MARGOT.** [*To* ANNE] Why don't you two talk in the main room? It'd save a lot of trouble. It's hard on Mother, having to listen to those remarks from Mrs. Van Daan and not say a word.

**ANNE.** Why doesn't she say a word? I think it's ridiculous to take it and take it.

**MARGOT.** You don't understand Mother at all, do you? She can't talk back. She's not like you. It's just not in her nature to fight back.

**ANNE.** Anyway . . . the only one I worry about is you. I feel awfully guilty about you. [*She sits on the stool near* MARGOT, *putting on* MARGOT'S *high-heeled shoes.*]

**MARGOT.** What about?

**ANNE.** I mean, every time I go into Peter's room, I have a feeling I may be hurting you. [MARGOT *shakes her head.*] I know if it were me, I'd be wild. I'd be desperately jealous, if it were me.

**MARGOT.** Well, I'm not.

**ANNE.** You don't feel badly? Really? Truly? You're not jealous?

**MARGOT.** Of course I'm jealous . . . jealous that you've got something to get up in the morning for . . . But jealous of you and Peter? No.

[ANNE *goes back to the mirror.*]

**ANNE.** Maybe there's nothing to be jealous of. Maybe he doesn't really like me. Maybe I'm just taking the place of his cat . . . [*She picks up a pair of short white gloves, putting them on.*] Wouldn't you like to come in with us?

**MARGOT.** I have a book.

[*The sound of the children playing outside fades out. In the main room DUSSEL can stand it no longer. He jumps up, going to the bedroom door and knocking sharply.*]

**DUSSEL.** Will you please let me in my room!

**ANNE.** Just a minute, dear, dear Mr. Dussel. [*She picks up her mother's pink stole and adjusts it elegantly over her shoulders, then gives a last look in the mirror.*] Well, here I go . . . to run the gauntlet.[5]

[*She starts out, followed by MARGOT.*]

**DUSSEL.** [*As she appears—sarcastic*] Thank you so much.

[DUSSEL *goes into his room.* ANNE *goes toward* PETER'S *room, passing* MRS. VAN DAAN *and her parents at the center table.*]

**MRS. VAN DAAN.** My God, look at her! [ANNE *pays no attention. She knocks at* PETER'S *door.*] I don't know what good it is to have a son. I never see him. He wouldn't care if I killed myself. [PETER *opens the door and stands aside for* ANNE *to come in.*] Just a minute, Anne. [*She goes to them at the door.*] I'd like to say a few words to my son. Do you mind? [PETER *and* ANNE *stand waiting.*] Peter, I don't want you

> Of course I'm jealous... jealous that you've got something to get up in the morning for...

Reading Check

Why does Anne fear she might be hurting Margot?

---

5. **run the gauntlet** (gônt´ lit) formerly, to pass between two rows of men who struck at the offender with clubs as he passed; here, a series of troubles or difficulties.

staying up till all hours tonight. You've got to have your sleep. You're a growing boy. You hear?

**MRS. FRANK.** Anne won't stay late. She's going to bed promptly at nine. Aren't you, Anne?

**ANNE.** Yes, Mother . . . [*To* MRS. VAN DAAN] May we go now?

**MRS. VAN DAAN.** Are you asking me? I didn't know I had anything to say about it.

**MRS. FRANK.** Listen for the chimes, Anne dear.

[*The two young people go off into* PETER's *room, shutting the door after them.*]

**MRS. VAN DAAN.** [*To* MRS. FRANK] In my day it was the boys who called on the girls. Not the girls on the boys.

**MRS. FRANK.** You know how young people like to feel that they have secrets. Peter's room is the only place where they can talk.

**MRS. VAN DAAN.** Talk! That's not what they called it when I was young.

[MRS. VAN DAAN *goes off to the bathroom.* MARGOT *settles down to read her book.* MR. FRANK *puts his papers away and brings a chess game to the center table. He and* MRS. FRANK *start to play. In* PETER'S *room,* ANNE *speaks to* PETER, *indignant, humiliated.*]

**ANNE.** Aren't they awful? Aren't they impossible? Treating us as if we were still in the nursery.

[*She sits on the cot.* PETER *gets a bottle of pop and two glasses.*]

**PETER.** Don't let it bother you. It doesn't bother me.

**ANNE.** I suppose you can't really blame them . . . they think back to what *they* were like at our age. They don't realize how much more advanced we are . . . When you think what wonderful discussions we've had! . . . Oh, I forgot. I was going to bring you some more pictures.

**PETER.** Oh, these are fine, thanks.

**ANNE.** Don't you want some more? Miep just brought me some new ones.

**PETER.** Maybe later. [*He gives her a glass of pop and, taking some for himself, sits down facing her.*]

**Cause and Effect**
How might Mrs. Van Daan's beliefs about what is socially acceptable reflect her own upbringing?

**ANNE.** [*Looking up at one of the photographs*] I remember when I got that . . . I won it. I bet Jopie that I could eat five ice-cream cones. We'd all been playing ping-pong . . . We used to have heavenly times . . . we'd finish up with ice cream at the Delphi, or the Oasis, where Jews were allowed . . . there'd always be a lot of boys . . . we'd laugh and joke . . . I'd like to go back to it for a few days or a week. But after that I know I'd be bored to death. I think more seriously about life now. I want to be a journalist . . . or something. I love to write. What do you want to do?

**PETER.** I thought I might go off some place . . . work on a farm or something . . . some job that doesn't take much brains.

**ANNE.** You shouldn't talk that way. You've got the most awful inferiority complex.

**PETER.** I know I'm not smart.

**ANNE.** That isn't true. You're much better than I am in dozens of things . . . arithmetic and algebra and . . . well, you're a million times better than I am in algebra. [*With sudden directness*] You like Margot, don't you? Right from the start you liked her, liked her much better than me.

**PETER.** [*Uncomfortably*] Oh, I don't know.

[*In the main room* MRS. VAN DAAN *comes from the bathroom and goes over to the sink, polishing a coffee pot.*]

▲ Bicycles were an easy way to get around the streets of Amsterdam, but Nazi regulations made them illegal for Jews.

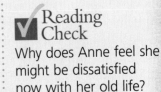
Reading
Check
Why does Anne feel she might be dissatisfied now with her old life?

**Character's Motivation**
What is Anne's possible motivation for asking Peter whether he likes Margot?

**ANNE.** It's all right. Everyone feels that way. Margot's so good. She's sweet and bright and beautiful and I'm not.

**PETER.** I wouldn't say that.

**ANNE.** Oh, no, I'm not. I know that. I know quite well that I'm not a beauty. I never have been and never shall be.

**PETER.** I don't agree at all. I think you're pretty.

**ANNE.** That's not true!

**PETER.** And another thing. You've changed . . . from at first, I mean.

**ANNE.** I have?

**PETER.** I used to think you were awful noisy.

**ANNE.** And what do you think now, Peter? How have I changed?

**PETER.** Well . . . er . . . you're . . . quieter.

[*In his room* DUSSEL *takes his pajamas and toilet articles and goes into the bathroom to change.*]

**ANNE.** I'm glad you don't just hate me.

**PETER.** I never said that.

**ANNE.** I bet when you get out of here you'll never think of me again.

**PETER.** That's crazy.

**ANNE.** When you get back with all of your friends, you're going to say . . . now what did I ever see in that Mrs. Quack Quack.

**PETER.** I haven't got any friends.

**ANNE.** Oh, Peter, of course you have. Everyone has friends.

**PETER.** Not me. I don't want any. I get along all right without them.

**ANNE.** Does that mean you can get along without me? I think of myself as your friend.

**PETER.** No. If they were all like you, it'd be different.

[*He takes the glasses and the bottle and puts them away. There is a second's silence and then* ANNE *speaks, hesitantly, shyly.*]

**ANNE.** Peter, did you ever kiss a girl?

**PETER.** Yes. Once.

**ANNE.** [*To cover her feelings*] That picture's crooked.

[PETER *GOES OVER, STRAIGHTENING THE PHOTOGRAPH.*]
  Was she pretty?

**PETER.** Huh?

**ANNE.** The girl that you kissed.

**PETER.** I don't know. I was blindfolded. [*He comes back and sits down again.*] It was at a party. One of those kissing games.

**ANNE.** [*Relieved*] Oh. I don't suppose that really counts, does it?

**PETER.** It didn't with me.

**ANNE.** I've been kissed twice. Once a man I'd never seen before kissed me on the cheek when he picked me up off the ice and I was crying. And the other was Mr. Koophuis, a friend of Father's who kissed my hand. You wouldn't say those counted, would you?

**PETER.** I wouldn't say so.

**ANNE.** I know almost for certain that Margot would never kiss anyone unless she was engaged to them. And I'm sure too that Mother never touched a man before Pim. But I don't know . . . things are so different now . . . What do you think? Do you think a girl shouldn't kiss anyone except if she's engaged or something? It's so hard to try to think what to do, when here we are with the whole world falling around our ears and you think . . . well . . . you don't know what's going to happen tomorrow and . . . What do you think?

**PETER.** I suppose it'd depend on the girl. Some girls, anything they do's wrong. But others . . . well . . . it wouldn't necessarily be wrong with them. [*The carillon starts to strike nine o'clock.*] I've always thought that when two people . . .

**ANNE.** Nine o'clock. I have to go.

**PETER.** That's right.

**ANNE.** [*Without moving*] Good night.

[*There is a second's pause, then* PETER *gets up and moves toward the door.*]

**Cause and Effect**
Based on Anne's comments, what effect is the war having on prewar attitudes?

Reading Check
How has Peter's view of Anne changed?

**PETER.** You won't let them stop you coming?

**ANNE.** No. [*She rises and starts for the door.*] Sometimes I might bring my diary. There are so many things in it that I want to talk over with you. There's a lot about you.

**PETER.** What kind of things?

**ANNE.** I wouldn't want you to see some of it. I thought you were a nothing, just the way you thought about me.

**PETER.** Did you change your mind, the way I changed my mind about you?

**ANNE.** Well . . . You'll see . . .

[*For a second* ANNE *stands looking up at* PETER, *longing for him to kiss her. As he makes no move she turns away. Then suddenly* PETER *grabs her awkwardly in his arms, kissing her on the cheek.* ANNE *walks out dazed. She stands for a minute, her back to the people in the main room. As she regains her poise she goes to her mother and father and* MARGOT, *silently kissing them. They murmur their good nights to her. As she is about to open her bedroom door, she catches sight of* MRS. VAN DAAN. *She goes quickly to her, taking her face in her hands and kissing her first on one cheek and then on the other. Then she hurries off into her room.* MRS. VAN DAAN *looks after her, and then looks over at* PETER'S *room. Her suspicions are confirmed.*]

**MRS. VAN DAAN.** [*She knows.*] Ah hah!

[*The lights dim out. The curtain falls on the scene. In the darkness* ANNE'S VOICE *comes faintly at first and then with growing strength.*]

**ANNE'S VOICE.** By this time we all know each other so well that if anyone starts to tell a story, the rest can finish it for him. We're having to cut down still further on our meals. What makes it worse, the rats have been at work again. They've carried off some of our precious food. Even Mr. Dussel wishes now that Mouschi was here. Thursday, the twentieth of April, nineteen forty-four. Invasion fever is mounting every day. Miep tells us that people outside talk of nothing else. For myself, life has become much more pleasant. I often go to Peter's room after supper. Oh, don't think I'm in love, because I'm not. But it does make life more bearable to have someone with whom you can

---

**Character's Motivation**
What causes Anne to want to share her diary with Peter?

exchange views. No more tonight. P.S. . . . I must be honest. I must confess that I actually live for the next meeting. Is there anything lovelier than to sit under the skylight and feel the sun on your cheeks and have a darling boy in your arms? I admit now that I'm glad the Van Daans had a son and not a daughter. I've outgrown another dress. That's the third. I'm having to wear Margot's clothes after all. I'm working hard on my French and am now reading *La Belle Nivernaise*.[6]

[*As she is saying the last lines—the curtain rises on the scene. The lights dim on, as* ANNE'S VOICE *fades out.*]

## Scene 3

[*It is night, a few weeks later. Everyone is in bed. There is complete quiet. In the* VAN DAANS' *room a match flares up for a moment and then is quickly put out.* MR. VAN DAAN, *in bare feet, dressed in underwear and trousers, is dimly seen coming stealthily down the stairs and into the main room, where* MR. *and* MRS. FRANK *and* MARGOT *are sleeping. He goes to the food safe and again lights a match. Then he cautiously opens the safe, taking out a half-loaf of bread. As he closes the safe, it creaks. He stands rigid.* MRS. FRANK *sits up in bed. She sees him.*]

**MRS. FRANK.** [*Screaming*] Otto! Otto! *Komme schnell!*[7]

[*The rest of the people wake, hurriedly getting up.*]

**MR. FRANK.** *Was ist los? Was ist passiert?*[8]

[DUSSEL, *followed by* ANNE, *comes from his room.*]

**MRS. FRANK.** [*As she rushes over to* MR. VAN DAAN] *Er stiehlt das Essen!*[9]

**DUSSEL.** [*Grabbing* MR. VAN DAAN] You! You! Give me that.

**MRS. VAN DAAN.** [*Coming down the stairs*] Putti . . . Putti . . . what is it?

**Character's Motivation**
Why is Mr. Van Daan being so cautious about making noise?

✓ Reading Check
Why does Mrs. Frank scream in the middle of the night?

---

6. *La Belle Nivernaise* story by Alphonse Daudet, a French author.
7. *Komme schnell!* (käm´ ə shnel) German for "Come quick!"
8. *Was ist los? Was ist passiert?* (väs ist los väs ist päs´ ērt) German for "What's the matter? What happened?"
9. *Er stiehlt das Essen!* (er stēlt däs es´ ən) German for "He steals food!"

**DUSSEL.** [*His hands on* VAN DAAN'S *neck*] You dirty thief . . . stealing food . . . you good-for-nothing . . .

**MR. FRANK.** Mr. Dussel! For God's sake! Help me, Peter!

[PETER *comes over, trying, with* MR. FRANK, *to separate the two struggling men.*]

**PETER.** Let him go! Let go!

[DUSSEL *drops* MR. VAN DAAN, *pushing him away. He shows them the end of a loaf of bread that he has taken from* VAN DAAN.]

**DUSSEL.** You greedy, selfish . . . !

[MARGOT *turns on the lights.*]

**MRS. VAN DAAN.** Putti . . . what is it?

[*All of* MRS. FRANK'S *gentleness, her self-control, is gone. She is outraged, in a frenzy of indignation.*]

**MRS. FRANK.** The bread! He was stealing the bread!

**DUSSEL.** It was you, and all the time we thought it was the rats!

**MR. FRANK.** Mr. Van Daan, how could you!

**MR. VAN DAAN.** I'm hungry.

**MRS. FRANK.** We're all of us hungry! I see the children getting thinner and thinner. Your own son Peter . . . I've heard him moan in his sleep, he's so hungry. And you come in the night and steal food that should go to them . . . to the children!

**MRS. VAN DAAN.** [*Going to* MR. VAN DAAN *protectively*] He needs more food than the rest of us. He's used to more. He's a big man.

[MR. VAN DAAN *breaks away, going over and sitting on the couch.*]

**Spiral Review**
**Conflict** What long-simmering resentments does Mr. Van Daan's action bring out into the open?

**MRS. FRANK.** [*Turning on* MRS. VAN DAAN] And you . . . you're worse than he is! You're a mother, and yet you sacrifice your child to this man . . . this . . . this . . .

**MR. FRANK.** Edith! Edith!

[MARGOT *picks up the pink woolen stole, putting it over her mother's shoulders.*]

**MRS. FRANK.** [*Paying no attention, going on to* MRS. VAN

DAAN] Don't think I haven't seen you! Always saving the choicest bits for him! I've watched you day after day and I've held my tongue. But not any longer! Not after this! Now I want him to go! I want him to get out of here!

[*Together*] {
    **MR. FRANK.** Edith!

    **MR. VAN DAAN.** Get out of here?

    **MRS. VAN DAAN.** What do you mean?

**MRS. FRANK.** Just that! Take your things and get out!

**MR. FRANK.** [*To* MRS. FRANK] You're speaking in anger. You cannot mean what you are saying.

**MRS. FRANK.** I mean exactly that!

[MRS. VAN DAAN *takes a cover from the* FRANKS' *bed, pulling it about her.*]

**MR. FRANK.** For two long years we have lived here, side by side. We have respected each other's rights . . . we have managed to live in peace. Are we now going to throw it all away? I know this will never happen again, will it, Mr. Van Daan?

**MR. VAN DAAN.** No. No.

**MRS. FRANK.** He steals once! He'll steal again!

[MR. VAN DAAN, *holding his stomach, starts for the bathroom.* ANNE *puts her arms around him, helping him up the step.*]

**MR. FRANK.** Edith, please. Let us be calm. We'll all go to our rooms . . . and afterwards we'll sit down quietly and talk this out . . . we'll find some way . . .

**MRS. FRANK.** No! No! No more talk! I want them to leave!

**MRS. VAN DAAN.** You'd put us out, on the streets?

**MRS. FRANK.** There are other hiding places.

**MRS. VAN DAAN.** A cellar . . . a closet. I know. And we have no money left even to pay for that.

**MRS. FRANK.** I'll give you money. Out of my own pocket I'll give it gladly. [*She gets her purse from a shelf and comes back with it.*]

**MRS. VAN DAAN.** Mr. Frank, you told Putti you'd never forget what he'd done for you when you came to Amsterdam. You said you could never repay him, that you . . .

**Cause and Effect**
What causes Mr. Van Daan to steal food, and what is the effect of his actions on the others?

The bread!
He was stealing the bread!

**Reading Check**
How does Mr. Frank react to his wife's demand that the Van Daans leave?

**MRS. FRANK.** [*Counting out money*] If my husband had any obligation to you, he's paid it, over and over.

**MR. FRANK.** Edith, I've never seen you like this before. I don't know you.

**MRS. FRANK.** I should have spoken out long ago.

**DUSSEL.** You can't be nice to some people.

**Character's Motivation**
What do Mr. Frank's lines show about his character and about what motivates him?

**MRS. VAN DAAN.** [*Turning on DUSSEL*] There would have been plenty for all of us, if *you* hadn't come in here!

**MR. FRANK.** We don't need the Nazis to destroy us. We're destroying ourselves.

[*He sits down, with his head in his hands. MRS. FRANK goes to MRS. VAN DAAN.*]

**MRS. FRANK.** [*Giving MRS. VAN DAAN some money*] Give this to Miep. She'll find you a place.

**ANNE.** Mother, you're not putting Peter out. Peter hasn't done anything.

**MRS. FRANK.** He'll stay, of course. When I say I must protect the children, I mean Peter too.

[*PETER rises from the steps where he has been sitting.*]

**PETER.** I'd have to go if Father goes.

[*MR. VAN DAAN comes from the bathroom. MRS. VAN DAAN hurries to him and takes him to the couch. Then she gets water from the sink to bathe his face.*]

**Character's Motivation**
What do Peter's words reveal about how he feels about leaving?

**MRS. FRANK.** [*While this is going on*] He's no father to you . . . that man! He doesn't know what it is to be a father!

**PETER.** [*Starting for his room*] I wouldn't feel right. I couldn't stay.

**MRS. FRANK.** Very well, then. I'm sorry.

**ANNE.** [*Rushing over to PETER*] No, Peter! No! [*PETER goes into his room, closing the door after him. ANNE turns back to her mother, crying.*] I don't care about the food. They can have mine! I don't want it! Only don't send them away. It'll be daylight soon. They'll be caught . . .

**MARGOT.** [*Putting her arms comfortingly around ANNE*] Please, Mother!

**MRS. FRANK.** They're not going now. They'll stay here until

Miep finds them a place. [*To* MRS. VAN DAAN] But one thing I insist on! He must never come down here again! He must never come to this room where the food is stored! We'll divide what we have . . . an equal share for each! [DUSSEL *hurries over to get a sack of potatoes from the food safe.* MRS. FRANK *goes on, to* MRS. VAN DAAN] You can cook it here and take it up to him.

[DUSSEL *brings the sack of potatoes back to the center table.*]

**MARGOT.** Oh, no. No. We haven't sunk so far that we're going to fight over a handful of rotten potatoes.

**DUSSEL.** [*Dividing the potatoes into piles*] Mrs. Frank, Mr. Frank, Margot, Anne, Peter, Mrs. Van Daan, Mr. Van Daan, myself . . . Mrs. Frank . . .

[*The buzzer sounds in* MIEP'S *signal.*]

**MR. FRANK.** It's Miep! [*He hurries over, getting his overcoat and putting it on.*]

**MARGOT.** At this hour?

**MRS. FRANK.** It is trouble.

**MR. FRANK.** [*As he starts down to unbolt the door*] I beg you, don't let her see a thing like this!

**MR. DUSSEL.** [*Counting without stopping*] . . . Anne, Peter, Mrs. Van Daan, Mr. Van Daan, myself . . .

**MARGOT.** [*To* DUSSEL] Stop it! Stop it!

**DUSSEL.** . . . Mr. Frank, Margot, Anne, Peter, Mrs. Van Daan, Mr. Van Daan, myself, Mrs. Frank . . .

**MRS. VAN DAAN.** You're keeping the big ones for yourself! All the big ones . . . Look at the size of that! . . . And that! . . .

[DUSSEL *continues on with his dividing.* PETER, *with his shirt and trousers on, comes from his room.*]

**MARGOT.** Stop it! Stop it!

[*We hear* MIEP'S *excited voice speaking to* MR. FRANK *below.*]

**MIEP.** Mr. Frank . . . the most wonderful news! . . . The invasion has begun!

**MR. FRANK.** Go on, tell them! Tell them!

[MIEP *comes running up the steps ahead of* MR. FRANK. *She has a man's raincoat on over her nightclothes and a bunch of orange-colored flowers in her hand.*]

**Cause and Effect**
What effect does Mr. Van Daan's action have on the tensions among the characters?

Reading Check

Why does Dussel bring the sack of potatoes to the table?

The Diary of Anne Frank, Act II **945**

**MIEP.** Did you hear that, everybody? Did you hear what I said? The invasion has begun! The invasion!

[*They all stare at* MIEP, *unable to grasp what she is telling them.* PETER *is the first to recover his wits.*]

**PETER.** Where?

**MRS. VAN DAAN.** When? When, Miep?

**MIEP.** It began early this morning . . .

[*As she talks on, the realization of what she has said begins to dawn on them. Everyone goes crazy. A wild demonstration takes place.* MRS. FRANK *hugs* MR. VAN DAAN.]

**MRS. FRANK.** Oh, Mr. Van Daan, did you hear that?

[DUSSEL *embraces* MRS. VAN DAAN. PETER *grabs a frying pan and parades around the room, beating on it, singing the Dutch National Anthem.* ANNE *and* MARGOT *follow him, singing, weaving in and out among the excited grown-ups.* MARGOT *breaks away to take the flowers from* MIEP *and distribute them to everyone. While this pandemonium is going on* MRS. FRANK *tries to make herself heard above the excitement.*]

**MRS. FRANK.** [*To* MIEP] How do you know?

**MIEP.** The radio . . . The B.B.C.![10] They said they landed on the coast of Normandy!

**PETER.** The British?

**MIEP.** British, Americans, French, Dutch, Poles, Norwegians . . . all of them! More than four thousand ships! Churchill spoke, and General Eisenhower! D-Day they call it!

**MR. FRANK.** Thank God, it's come!

**MRS. VAN DAAN.** At last!

**MIEP.** [*Starting out*] I'm going to tell Mr. Kraler. This'll be better than any blood transfusion.

**MR. FRANK.** [*Stopping her*] What part of Normandy did they land, did they say?

**MIEP.** Normandy . . . that's all I know now . . . I'll be up the minute I hear some more! [*She goes hurriedly out.*]

**MR. FRANK.** [*To* MRS. FRANK] What did I tell you? What did I tell you?

**Cause and Effect**
What is the effect of the news about D-Day on the people in the Annex?

---

10. **B.B.C.** British Broadcasting System.

[MRS. FRANK *indicates that he has forgotten to bolt the door after* MIEP. *He hurries down the steps.* MR. VAN DAAN, *sitting on the couch, suddenly breaks into a convulsive[11] sob. Everybody looks at him, bewildered.*]

**MRS. VAN DAAN.** [*Hurrying to him*] Putti! Putti! What is it? What happened?

**MR. VAN DAAN.** Please, I'm so ashamed.

[MR. FRANK *comes back up the steps.*]

**DUSSEL.** Oh, for God's sake!

**MRS. VAN DAAN.** Don't, Putti.

**MARGOT.** It doesn't matter now!

**MR. FRANK.** [*Going to* MR. VAN DAAN] Didn't you hear what Miep said? The invasion has come! We're going to

![check] **Reading Check**

What are the details of the news that Miep brings?

---

11. **convulsive** (kən vul′ siv) *adj.* having an uncontrolled muscular spasm; shuddering.

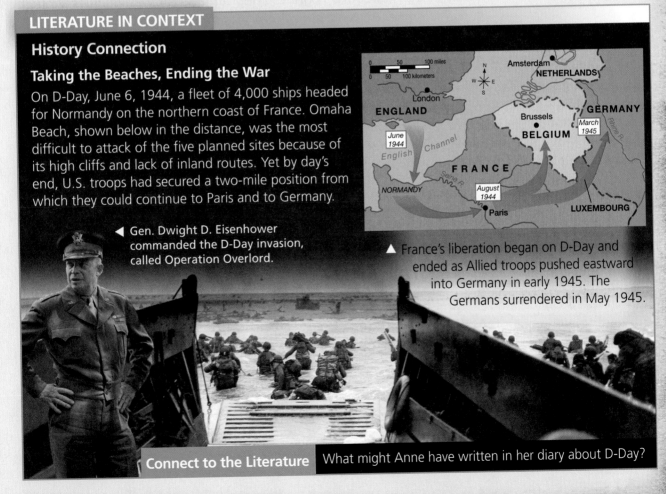

## LITERATURE IN CONTEXT

### History Connection

#### Taking the Beaches, Ending the War

On D-Day, June 6, 1944, a fleet of 4,000 ships headed for Normandy on the northern coast of France. Omaha Beach, shown below in the distance, was the most difficult to attack of the five planned sites because of its high cliffs and lack of inland routes. Yet by day's end, U.S. troops had secured a two-mile position from which they could continue to Paris and to Germany.

◄ Gen. Dwight D. Eisenhower commanded the D-Day invasion, called Operation Overlord.

▲ France's liberation began on D-Day and ended as Allied troops pushed eastward into Germany in early 1945. The Germans surrendered in May 1945.

**Connect to the Literature** What might Anne have written in her diary about D-Day?

The Diary of Anne Frank, Act II **947**

be liberated! This is a time to celebrate! [*He embraces* MRS. FRANK *and then hurries to the cupboard and gets the cognac and a glass.*]

**MR. VAN DAAN.** To steal bread from children!

**MRS. FRANK.** We've all done things that we're ashamed of.

**Character's Motivation**
What drives Anne to admit that she has treated her mother badly?

**ANNE.** Look at me, the way I've treated Mother . . . so mean and horrid to her.

**MRS. FRANK.** No, Anneke, no.

[ANNE *runs to her mother, putting her arms around her.*]

**ANNE.** Oh, Mother, I was. I was awful.

**MR. VAN DAAN.** Not like me. No one is as bad as me!

**DUSSEL.** [*To* MR. VAN DAAN] Stop it now! Let's be happy!

**MR. FRANK.** [*Giving* MR. VAN DAAN *a glass of cognac*] Here! Here! *Schnapps! L'chaim!*[12]

[VAN DAAN *takes the cognac. They all watch him. He gives them a feeble smile.* ANNE *puts up her fingers in a V-for-Victory sign. As* VAN DAAN *gives an answering V-sign, they are startled to hear a loud sob from behind them. It is* MRS. FRANK, *stricken with remorse. She is sitting on the other side of the room.*]

**MRS. FRANK.** [*Through her sobs*] When I think of the terrible things I said . . .

[MR. FRANK, ANNE *and* MARGOT *hurry to her, trying to comfort her.* MR. VAN DAAN *brings her his glass of cognac.*]

**MR. VAN DAAN.** No! No! You were right!

**MRS. FRANK.** That I should speak that way to you! . . . Our friends! . . . Our guests! [*She starts to cry again.*]

**DUSSEL.** Stop it, you're spoiling the whole invasion!

[*As they are comforting her, the lights dim out. The curtain falls.*]

**ANNE'S VOICE.** [*Faintly at first and then with growing strength*] We're all in much better spirits these days. There's still excellent news of the invasion. The best part about it is that I have a feeling that friends are coming. Who knows? Maybe I'll be back in school by fall. Ha, ha! The joke is on us! The warehouse man doesn't know a thing and we are

---

12. *Schnapps!* (shnäps) German for "a drink." *L'chaim!* (lə khä´ yim) Hebrew toast meaning "To life!"

paying him all that money! . . . Wednesday, the second of July, nineteen forty-four. The invasion seems temporarily to be bogged down. Mr. Kraler has to have an operation, which looks bad. The Gestapo have found the radio that was stolen. Mr. Dussel says they'll trace it back and back to the thief, and then, it's just a matter of time till they get to us. Everyone is low. Even poor Pim can't raise their spirits. I have often been downcast myself . . . but never in despair. I can shake off everything if I write. But . . . and that is the great question . . . will I ever be able to write well? I want to so much. I want to go on living even after my death. Another birthday has gone by, so now I am fifteen. Already I know what I want. I have a goal, an opinion.

[*As this is being said—the curtain rises on the scene, the lights dim on, and* ANNE'S VOICE *fades out.*]

> I have often been downcast myself... but never in despair.

## Scene 4

[*It is an afternoon a few weeks later . . . Everyone but* MARGOT *is in the main room. There is a sense of great tension.*

*Both* MRS. FRANK *and* MR. VAN DAAN *are nervously pacing back and forth,* DUSSEL *is standing at the window, looking down fixedly at the street below.* PETER *is at the center table, trying to do his lessons.* ANNE *sits opposite him, writing in her diary.* MRS. VAN DAAN *is seated on the couch, her eyes on* MR. FRANK *as he sits reading.*

*The sound of a telephone ringing comes from the office below. They all are rigid, listening tensely.* DUSSEL *rushes down to* MR. FRANK.]

**DUSSEL.** There it goes again, the telephone! Mr. Frank, do you hear?

**MR. FRANK.** [*Quietly*] Yes. I hear.

**DUSSEL.** [*Pleading, insistent*] But this is the third time, Mr. Frank! The third time in quick succession! It's a signal! I tell you it's Miep, trying to get us! For some reason she can't come to us and she's trying to warn us of something!

**MR. FRANK.** Please. Please.

**MR. VAN DAAN.** [*To* DUSSEL] You're wasting your breath.

**DUSSEL.** Something has happened, Mr. Frank. For three days

Reading Check

What new goal does Anne set for herself?

► **Critical Viewing**
What do you think the residents of the Annex fear most about being discovered and deported? **[Speculate]**

now Miep hasn't been to see us! And today not a man has come to work. There hasn't been a sound in the building!

**MRS. FRANK.** Perhaps it's Sunday. We may have lost track of the days.

**MR. VAN DAAN.** [*To* ANNE] You with the diary there. What day is it?

**DUSSEL.** [*Going to* MRS. FRANK] I don't lose track of the days! I know exactly what day it is! It's Friday, the fourth of August. Friday, and not a man at work. [*He rushes back to* MR. FRANK, *pleading with him, almost in tears.*] I tell you Mr. Kraler's dead. That's the only explanation. He's dead and they've closed down the building, and Miep's trying to tell us!

**MR. FRANK.** She'd never telephone us.

**DUSSEL.** [*Frantic*] Mr. Frank, answer that! I beg you, answer it!

**MR. FRANK.** No.

**Cause and Effect**
What is the effect of the ringing telephone?

**MR. VAN DAAN.** Just pick it up and listen. You don't have to speak. Just listen and see if it's Miep.

**DUSSEL.** [*Speaking at the same time*] For God's sake . . . I ask you.

**MR. FRANK.** No. I've told you, no. I'll do nothing that might let anyone know we're in the building.

**PETER.** Mr. Frank's right.

**MR. VAN DAAN.** There's no need to tell us what side you're on.

**MR. FRANK.** If we wait patiently, quietly, I believe that help will come.

[*There is silence for a minute as they all listen to the telephone ringing.*]

**DUSSEL.** I'm going down.
[*He rushes down the steps.* MR. FRANK *tries* ineffectually *to hold him.* DUSSEL *runs to the lower door, unbolting it. The telephone stops ringing.* DUSSEL *bolts the door and comes slowly back up the steps.*] Too late.

[MR. FRANK *goes to* MARGOT *in* ANNE'S *bedroom.*]

**MR. VAN DAAN.** So we just wait here until we die.

**MRS. VAN DAAN.** [*Hysterically*] I can't stand it! I'll kill myself! I'll kill myself!

**MR. VAN DAAN.** For God's sake, stop it!

**Vocabulary**
**ineffectually**
(in´ e fek´ chōō ə lē)
*adv.* without producing the desired results

[*In the distance, a German military band is heard playing a Viennese waltz.*]

**MRS. VAN DAAN.** I think you'd be glad if I did! I think you want me to die!

**MR. VAN DAAN.** Whose fault is it we're here?

[MRS. VAN DAAN *starts for her room. He follows, talking at her.*] We could've been safe somewhere . . . in America or Switzerland. But no! No! You wouldn't leave when I wanted to. You couldn't leave your things. You couldn't leave your precious furniture.

**MRS. VAN DAAN.** Don't touch me!

[*She hurries up the stairs, followed by* MR. VAN DAAN. PETER, *unable to bear it, goes to his room.* ANNE *looks after him, deeply concerned.* DUSSEL *returns to his post at the window.* MR. FRANK *comes back into the main room and takes a book, trying to read.* MRS. FRANK *sits near the sink, starting to peel some potatoes.* ANNE *quietly goes to* PETER'S *room, closing the door after her.* PETER *is lying face down on the cot.* ANNE *leans over him, holding him in her arms, trying to bring him out of his despair.*]

**ANNE.** Look, Peter, the sky. [*She looks up through the skylight.*] What a lovely, lovely day! Aren't the clouds beautiful? You know what I do when it seems as if I couldn't stand being cooped up for one more minute? I think myself out. I think myself on a walk in the park where I used to go with Pim. Where the jonquils and the crocus and the violets grow down the slopes. You know the most wonderful part about *thinking* yourself out? You can have it any way you like. You can have roses and violets and chrysanthemums all blooming at the same time . . . It's funny . . . I used to take it all for granted . . . and now I've gone crazy about everything to do with nature. Haven't you?

**Cause and Effect**
What effect has Mrs. Van Daan's love of expensive objects had on the family, according to Mr. Van Daan?

**Reading Check**

Why are the families upset?

**PETER.** I've just gone crazy. I think if something doesn't happen soon . . . if we don't get out of here . . . I can't stand much more of it!

**ANNE.** [*Softly*] I wish you had a religion, Peter.

**PETER.** No, thanks! Not me!

**ANNE.** Oh, I don't mean you have to be Orthodox[13] . . . or believe in heaven and hell and purgatory[14] and things . . . I just mean some religion . . . it doesn't matter what. Just to believe in something! When I think of all that's out there . . . the trees . . . and flowers . . . and seagulls . . . when I think of the dearness of you, Peter . . . and the goodness of the people we know . . . Mr. Kraler, Miep, Dirk, the vegetable man, all risking their lives for us every day . . . When I think of these good things, I'm not afraid any more . . . I find myself, and God, and I . . .

[PETER *interrupts, getting up and walking away.*]

**PETER.** That's fine! But when I begin to think, I get mad! Look at us, hiding out for two years. Not able to move! Caught here like . . . waiting for them to come and get us . . . and all for what?

**ANNE.** We're not the only people that've had to suffer. There've always been people that've had to . . . sometimes one race . . . sometimes another . . . and yet . . .

**PETER.** That doesn't make me feel any better!

**ANNE.** [*Going to him*] I know it's terrible, trying to have any faith . . . when people are doing such horrible . . . But you know what I sometimes think? I think the world may be going through a phase, the way I was with Mother. It'll pass, maybe not for hundreds of years, but some day . . . I still believe, in spite of everything, that people are really good at heart.

**PETER.** I want to see something now . . . Not a thousand years from now! [*He goes over, sitting down again on the cot.*]

---

13. **Orthodox** (ôr′ thə däks′) *adj.* strictly observing the rites and traditions of Judaism.
14. **purgatory** (pʉr′gə tôr′ ē) *n.* state or place of temporary punishment.

**Cause and Effect**
How do Anne's religious beliefs affect her ability to cope with a life in hiding?

▼ From the attic window, Anne and Peter could see the rooftops of Amsterdam and the neighboring Westertoren bell tower.

**ANNE.** But, Peter, if you'd only look at it as part of a great pattern . . . that we're just a little minute in the life . . . [*She breaks off.*] Listen to us, going at each other like a couple of stupid grownups! Look at the sky now. Isn't it lovely?

[*She holds out her hand to him. PETER takes it and rises, standing with her at the window looking out, his arms around her.*]

Some day, when we're outside again, I'm going to . . .

[*She breaks off as she hears the sound of a car, its brakes squealing as it comes to a sudden stop. The people in the other rooms also become aware of the sound. They listen tensely. Another car roars up to a screeching stop. ANNE and PETER come from PETER'S room. MR. and MRS. VAN DAAN creep down the stairs. DUSSEL comes out from his room. Everyone is listening, hardly breathing. A doorbell clangs again and again in the building below. MR. FRANK starts quietly down the steps to the door. DUSSEL and PETER follow him. The others stand rigid, waiting, terrified.*

*In a few seconds DUSSEL comes stumbling back up the steps. He shakes off PETER's help and goes to his room. MR. FRANK bolts the door below, and comes slowly back up the steps. Their eyes are all on him as he stands there for a minute. They realize that what they feared has happened. MRS. VAN DAAN starts to whimper. MR. VAN DAAN puts her gently in a chair, and then hurries off up the stairs to their room to collect their things. PETER goes to comfort his mother. There is a sound of violent pounding on a door below.*]

**MR. FRANK.** [*Quietly*] For the past two years we have lived in fear. Now we can live in hope.

[*The pounding below becomes more insistent. There are muffled sounds of voices, shouting commands.*]

**MEN'S VOICES.** *Auf machen! Da drinnen! Auf machen! Schnell! Schnell! Schnell!*[15] etc., etc.

[*The street door below is forced open. We hear the heavy tread of footsteps coming up. MR. FRANK gets two school bags from the shelves, and gives one to ANNE and the other to MARGOT. He goes to get a bag for MRS. FRANK. The sound of feet coming up grows louder. PETER comes to ANNE, kissing her good-*

---

**15. Auf machen! . . . Schnell!** German for "Open up, you in there, open up, quick, quick, quick."

**Character's Motivations**
What causes this sudden change in the characters' actions and mood?

Reading Check

How does Anne seek to comfort Peter?

▲ **Critical Viewing**
What does this museum re-creation of her writing space tell you about Anne Frank and her experience in hiding? **[Analyze]**

bye, then he goes to his room to collect his things. The buzzer of their door starts to ring. MR. FRANK *brings* MRS. FRANK *a bag. They stand together, waiting. We hear the thud of gun butts on the door, trying to break it down.*

ANNE *stands, holding her school satchel, looking over at her father and mother with a soft, reassuring smile. She is no longer a child, but a woman with courage to meet whatever lies ahead.*

*The lights dim out. The curtain falls on the scene. We hear a mighty crash as the door is shattered. After a second* ANNE'S VOICE *is heard.*]

**Character's Motivation**
Why does Anne leave her diary behind?

**ANNE'S VOICE.** And so it seems our stay here is over. They are waiting for us now. They've allowed us five minutes to get our things. We can each take a bag and whatever it will hold of clothing. Nothing else. So, dear Diary, that means I must leave you behind. Good-bye for a while. P.S. Please, please, Miep, or Mr. Kraler, or anyone else. If you should find this diary, will you please keep it safe for me, because some day I hope . . .

[*Her voice stops abruptly. There is silence. After a second the curtain rises.*]

## Scene 5

[*It is again the afternoon in November, 1945. The rooms are as we saw them in the first scene.* MR. KRALER *has joined* MIEP *and* MR. FRANK. *There are coffee cups on the table. We see a great change in* MR. FRANK. *He is calm now. His bitterness is gone. He slowly turns a few pages of the diary. They are blank.*]

**MR. FRANK.** No more. [*He closes the diary and puts it down on the couch beside him.*]

**MIEP.** I'd gone to the country to find food. When I got back the block was surrounded by police . . .

**MR. KRALER.** We made it our business to learn how they knew. It was the thief . . . the thief who told them.

[MIEP *goes up to the gas burner, bringing back a pot of coffee.*]

**MR. FRANK.** [*After a pause*] It seems strange to say this, that anyone could be happy in a concentration camp. But Anne was happy in the camp in Holland where they first took us. After two years of being shut up in these rooms, she could be out . . . out in the sunshine and the fresh air that she loved.

**MIEP.** [*Offering the coffee to* MR. FRANK] A little more?

**MR. FRANK.** [*Holding out his cup to her*] The news of the war was good. The British and Americans were sweeping through France. We felt sure that they would get to us in time. In September we were told that we were to be shipped to Poland . . . The men to one camp. The women to another. I was sent to Auschwitz.[16] They went to Belsen.[17] In January we were freed, the few of us who were left. The war wasn't yet over, so it took us a long time to get home. We'd be sent here and there behind the lines where we'd be safe. Each time our train would stop . . . at a siding, or a crossing . . . we'd all get out and go from group to group . . . Where were you? Were you at Belsen? At Buchenwald?[18] At Mauthausen? Is it possible that you knew my wife? Did you ever see my husband? My son? My daughter?

---

16. **Auschwitz** (oush′ vits′) Nazi concentration camp in Poland that was well known as a death camp.
17. **Belsen** (bel′ zən) village in Germany that, with the village of Bergen, was the site of Bergen-Belsen, a Nazi concentration camp.

▼ **Critical Viewing**
This is a 1979 German stamp. What changes after the war might make the German government decide to honor Anne? **[Infer]**

DEUTSCHE BUNDESPOST
60
ANNE FRANK · 12.6.1929 · 31.3.1945
1979

 **Reading Check**
Where were the families sent after they were picked up by the police?

That's how I found out about my wife's death . . . of Margot, the Van Daans . . . Dussel. But Anne . . . I still hoped . . . Yesterday I went to Rotterdam. I'd heard of a woman there . . . She'd been in Belsen with Anne . . . I know now.

[*He picks up the diary again, and turns the pages back to find a certain passage. As he finds it we hear* ANNE'S VOICE.]

**ANNE'S VOICE.** In spite of everything, I still believe that people are really good at heart. [MR. FRANK *slowly closes the diary.*]

**MR. FRANK.** She puts me to shame.

[*They are silent.*]

▲ Otto visits children in Dusseldorf where a new school, the Anne Frank School, would be built.

18. **Buchenwald** (bōō′ ken wôld′) Nazi concentration camp in central Germany.

## Critical Thinking

Cite textual evidence to support your responses.

© 1. **Key Ideas and Details** **(a)** What disturbing news does Mr. Kraler bring on New Year's Day? **(b) Connect:** What hint does this give about the ending of the play?

© 2. **Key Ideas and Details** **(a)** What is the time span of Act II? **(b) Interpret:** How have the characters changed since the end of Act I? **(c) Support:** How do you know that Anne has changed?

© 3. **Integration of Knowledge and Ideas** **(a)** How was Anne able to preserve her dignity despite her suffering? **(b)** From Anne's statements in Act II, do you think that she believed that differences—or similarities—matter most? Explain, using examples. **(c)** What does Mr. Frank mean when he says of Anne: "She puts me to shame"? [*Connect to the Big Question: Is it our differences or our similarities that matter most?*]

## Reading Skill: Cause and Effect

1. For each of these events, identify one **cause** and one **effect**: **(a)** Mr. Van Daan's decision to steal food. **(b)** Mrs. Frank's change of heart about wanting the Van Daans to leave.

2. What are some possible causes of Mrs. Van Daan's attitude toward Anne and Peter's relationship?

3. Living in close quarters has multiple effects on the people in the attic. List three effects that result from this single cause.

## Literary Skill: Character's Motivation

Ⓒ 4. **Key Ideas and Details** On a chart like the one shown, identify the possible **motivation** behind the actions listed.

| Character | Action | Motivation |
|---|---|---|
| Miep | Brings flowers and cake | |
| Mr. Van Daan | Breaks into tears | |
| Peter Van Daan | Offers to leave | |

Ⓒ 5. **Key Ideas and Details** What possible motivations might an informer have for telling the authorities about the families in hiding?

Ⓒ 6. **Craft and Structure** Give three examples of how the setting affects the characters and their actions.

## Vocabulary

Ⓒ **Acquisition and Use** Write a sentence for each item, using the words correctly.

1. inarticulate, candidate
2. apprehension, unknown
3. intuition, marry
4. ineffectually, weaker
5. blackmail, police
6. forlorn, rescue

**Word Study** Use the context of the sentences and what you know about the **Latin prefix in-** to explain your answer to each question.

1. What is one effect of an ear *infection*?
2. What happens to your lungs when you *inhale* deeply?

### Word Study

The **Latin prefix in-** can mean "into" or "within."

**Apply It** Explain how the prefix *in-* contributes to the meanings of these words. Consult a dictionary if necessary.

incision
inclusion
inherent

# Integrated Language Skills

## The Diary of Anne Frank, Act II

### Conventions: Clauses

A **clause** is a group of words with its own subject and verb.

There are two basic types of clauses:

- An **independent clause** has a subject and a verb, and it can stand by itself as a complete sentence.
- A **subordinate clause,** or **dependent clause,** has a subject and a verb but cannot stand by itself as a complete sentence. Subordinate clauses begin with subordinating conjunctions such as *although, if, when, while,* and *after.*

This chart shows both types of clauses. Subjects have a single underline; verbs have a double underline.

| Independent Clauses | Subordinate Clauses |
|---|---|
| She wore boots. | Because she wore boots |
| The cat shed its fur. | If the cat shed its fur |
| The thief heard noises upstairs. | When the thief heard noises upstairs |
| The war ended. | After the war ended |

**Practice A** Identify the independent clauses and subordinate clauses.

1. When Miep visited, she brought a cake.
2. As the scene continued, Anne and Peter prepared for their date.
3. Anne and Peter closed the door so they could have some privacy.
4. Mr. Frank hoped for liberation after the Allies landed.

© **Reading Application** In *The Diary of Anne Frank,* Act II, find two sentences that have an independent clause and a subordinate clause.

**Practice B** Identify each clause as independent or subordinate. For subordinate clauses, add independent clauses to make complete sentences.

1. Anne tried various hair styles
2. As Mrs. Van Daan objected
3. Mr. Van Daan was stealing the bread
4. When the car came to a stop

© **Writing Application** Use the following italicized words to write subordinate clauses about *The Diary of Anne Frank,* Act II: *although, after, when, since.* Then, add independent clauses to complete each sentence.

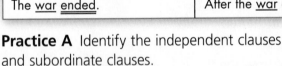

**PH WRITING COACH**   Further instruction and practice are available in *Prentice Hall Writing Coach.*

# Writing

 **Common Core State Standards**

L.8.1; RL.8.7; W.8.2, W.8.4, W.8.7; SL.8.1
[For the full wording of the standards, see page 916.]

**Informative Text** In preparation for writing a **film review,** watch a film version of *The Diary of Anne Frank.* As you view, use these questions to guide your note-taking:

- How do key scenes in the film compare to those in the written version? If scenes are changed or left out, how do these changes affect the film overall?

- Do the actors make good choices in their portrayals of characters, or do they not live up to your expectations? Why?

- What choices does the director make in sets, music, and camerawork? Do these choices enhance or distract from the mood of each scene?

After viewing, use your notes to draft your review. Be sure to highlight the differences between the filmed and the written versions, and explain which one you thought was more effective.

**Grammar Application** Your film review should be concise. Edit your writing to eliminate wordiness and repetition.

**Writing Workshop:** *Work in Progress*

**Prewriting for Exposition** Refer to the Questions List you generated earlier. Choose one question to develop. Write a *hypothesis*, or educated idea about the answer to this question, as a start to your research. Save this Research Hypothesis in your writing portfolio.

Use this prewriting activity to prepare for the **Writing Workshop** on page 982.

# Research and Technology

With a group, create a **bulletin board display** about the experiences of Jewish individuals or communities living under Nazi occupation during World War II. Follow these steps:

- As a group, decide the **audience and purpose** for the display. Use this information to focus your research.

- Begin by drafting a list of specific **research questions.** As you research, refine these questions and ask additional ones.

- Identify **primary sources,** such as photographs, diaries, documents, and letters; and **secondary sources,** such as encyclopedia articles, textbooks, books by historians, and Web pages. Plan to include **attribution** of your sources in captions in your display.

- **Draw conclusions** from the information you have gathered about the experience of living under occupation. Print these as **short summaries** to include in the display, along with **charts, quotations, maps, graphs, drawings, and photographs.**

**PHLit Online!**
www.PHLitOnline.com

- Interactive graphic organizers
- Grammar tutorial
- Interactive journals

# Test Practice: Reading

## Cause and Effect

### Fiction Selection

**Directions:** *Read the selection. Then, answer the questions.*

All over the news, reporters were covering the progress of a storm that was developing just to the east. Weather warnings are usual here, since we are so close to the ocean. Most of the times, they are just that, a warning. But when the reporters' tone grew serious, my parents began to worry. Rain, hail, and strong wind gusts were expected to arrive in only a few hours. The sky was already a dark gray. When the rain started to fall, we expected the winds to follow. Soon, the power went out as strong winds tore through trees. My favorite birch tree in the back yard fell with a deafening crack. The rain fell hard against the windows. Soon all you could hear was the storm and all I could do was try to sleep.

In the morning, when I woke up, I saw what the storm had caused. Our back yard was flooded. Luckily, our house suffered no damage and we were safe.

**1.** What caused the narrator's parents to worry?
   **A.** the power went out
   **B.** the serious tone of the reporters
   **C.** a tree fell
   **D.** the weather warning

**2.** What effect did the rain have?
   **A.** the yard flooded
   **B.** a car crashed
   **C.** heavy winds developed
   **D.** the warning sirens sounded

**3.** What caused the birch tree to fall down?
   **A.** the hail
   **B.** the strong winds
   **C.** the heavy rains
   **D.** the dark gray clouds

**4.** Which of the following actions is the family likely to take as a result of the storm?
   **A.** They will move to a new home.
   **B.** They will replace broken windows.
   **C.** They will remove the fallen tree.
   **D.** They will waterproof their house.

## Writing for Assessment

In a few sentences, explain the effects of the storm on the narrator. Use details from the passage to support each effect.

## Nonfiction Selection

**Directions:** *Read the selection. Then, answer the questions.*

The Great Hurricane of 1938 hit Long Island, New York, surprising the National Weather Service and residents. First rated as a Category 5 hurricane, the highest possible, the storm was supposed to taper off as it traveled north. A hurricane is propelled by warm water, and as soon as it hits land or cooler waters a hurricane should lose speed and strength. But before New England waters could cool the coming storm, the Great Hurricane of 1938 arrived, traveling at an extremely unusual 70 mph. The eye of the storm measured 50 miles across and the hurricane itself was 500 miles wide. The storm hit an unprepared Long Island, leaving in its wake unimaginable damage to homes, businesses, and lives. Surging water destroyed a barrier island, creating Shinnecock Inlet. The hurricane's force even moved large amounts of sand, bridging the gap between the former island of Cedar Point and the mainland.

1. According to the selection, what causes a hurricane to lose speed?
   A. when the eye of the storm decreases
   B. when the hurricane travels north
   C. when it has traveled so many miles
   D. when the storm hits cooler waters

2. What effect did the hurricane have on Cedar Point?
   A. Cedar Point became an island.
   B. Cedar Point became connected to Long Island.
   C. Cedar Point was completely destroyed.
   D. Cedar Point became submerged under water.

3. Why were so many people in Long Island unprepared for the storm?
   A. The storm was expected to slow down and lose strength before it arrived.
   B. In 1938, there was little knowledge of hurricanes, so there were no warnings.
   C. The storm was expected to move east.
   D. The National Weather Service was not tracking the storm.

4. According to the passage, what effect did surging waters have?
   A. Surging waters created an island.
   B. Surging waters caused the hurricane to speed up.
   C. Surging waters sank boats.
   D. Surging waters created an inlet.

## Writing for Assessment

**Connecting Across Texts**
In an essay, explain what effects the Great Hurricane of 1938 may have had on the people in Long Island. Use details from both passages to support your response.

- Online practice
- Instant feedback

# Reading for Information

## Analyzing Expository Texts

**Web Site**

**News Release**

**Common Core
State Standards**

**Reading Informational Text**
**5.** Analyze in detail the structure of a specific paragraph in a text, including the role of particular sentences in developing and refining a key concept.

**Language**
**4.** Determine or clarify the meaning of unknown and multiple-meaning words or phrases, choosing flexibly from a range of strategies.
**6.** Acquire and use accurately grade-appropriate general academic and domain-specific words and phrases; gather vocabulary knowledge when considering a word or phrase important to comprehension or expression.

## Reading Skill: Evaluate Unity and Coherence

When you **evaluate** a text for **unity and coherence,** you examine it for a **consistent** point of view and **logical** structure. Within paragraphs, sentences should build meaning in an organized and logical way. Paragraphs should then build coherent meaning in the work as a whole.

Begin to evaluate unity and coherence by examining details, noting how they are arranged and whether the arrangement makes sense. Next, determine if the details build logically on one another and support the main idea. After evaluating all of the details, consider the text as a whole and decide whether the writer has effectively used the details, sentences, and paragraphs to communicate a clear main idea.

---

**Checklist for Evaluating a Text**

- ❑ At every level of the text, do details all relate to the main idea?
- ❑ Do sentences, paragraphs, and graphic elements flow in a logical sequence?
- ❑ Is information clear, consistent, and logical?
- ❑ Does the author provide reliable facts, statistics, or quotations to support main points?

---

## Content-Area Vocabulary

These words appear in the selections that follow. You may also encounter them in other content-area texts.

- **exhibit** (eg zib´ it) *n.* display of art or other objects
- **archive** (är´ kīv) *n.* place where public records or historical documents are kept

Web Site

**Features:**

- information about an organization
- a home page with links to other pages
- illustrations or graphics
- content intended for a general or specific audience

**Florida Holocaust Museum**

EDUCATION   EVENTS   EXHIBITIONS   GET INVOLVED   PRESS ROOM   VISITOR INFORMATION

The home page provides an organized, logical list of topics covered by the Web site.

## VISITOR INFORMATION

The topic of the text is introduced under the first heading and carried throughout the text.

## About the Museum

### Mission

The Florida Holocaust Museum honors the memory of millions of innocent men, women, and children who suffered or died in the Holocaust. The Museum is dedicated to teaching members of all races and cultures to recognize the inherent worth and dignity of human life in order to prevent future genocides.

**Founders Walter and Edie Loebenberg**

### History

One of the largest Holocaust museums in the country, the Florida Holocaust Museum is the result of St. Petersburg businessman and philanthropist Walter P. Loebenberg's remarkable journey and vision. He escaped Nazi Germany in 1939 and served in the United States Army during WWII. Together, with a group of local businessmen and community leaders, the concept of a living memorial to those who suffered and perished was conceived. Among the participating individuals were survivors of the Holocaust and individuals who lost relatives, as well as those who had no personal investment, other than wanting to ensure that such atrocities could never again happen to any group of people.

To this end, the group enlisted the support of others in the community and were able to involve internationally renowned Holocaust scholars. Thomas Keneally, author of *Schindler's List*, joined the Board of Advisors and Elie Weisel was named Honorary Chairman of this Holocaust Center.

In 1992, the Museum rented a space it could afford, but would soon outgrow, on the grounds of the Jewish Community Center of Pinellas County in Madeira Beach, Florida, tucked away from the mainstream of Tampa Bay life. Starting with only one staff member and a small group of dedicated volunteers, it quickly surpassed all expectations.

Within the first month, over 24,000 visitors came to see *Anne Frank in the World*, the Center's inaugural **exhibit**. The Tampa Bay showing of this exhibition—which traces a young Jewish girl's journey from a complacent childhood in pre-World War II Holland, through her early teens hiding from the Nazis, to her death at Bergen-Belsen—poignantly touched all visitors.

**A painting from the exhibition *The Holocaust Through Czech Children's Eyes***

During the next five years, the new Holocaust Center greeted more than 125,000 visitors to view internationally acclaimed exhibits. Thousands more participated in lectures, seminars and commemorative events at the Center, which now reached directly into schools in an eight county area surrounding Tampa Bay with study guides, teacher training programs, and presentations by Center staff and Holocaust survivors.

The Center expanded to encompass a growing print and audio-visual library, a photographic **archive**, a repository for historic artifacts, and a research facility for educators and scholars—all of this crowded into a 4,000 square foot facility that was not designed for museum or educational purposes. . . .

FLORIDA
HOLOCAUST
MUSEUM

The main idea of
the text is presented
here.

# Local Holocaust Survivors And Liberators Attend Opening Event For Exhibition

**FOR IMMEDIATE RELEASE**
*July 12, 2006*
**Contact:** Andrea Moore,
PR Coordinator

The facts
presented in
the opening
paragraphs
are unified—
they answer
the questions
*Who?, What?,
Where?,* and
*When?*

**St. Petersburg, FL** The Florida
Holocaust Museum will honor
Holocaust survivors and liberators at the opening event for
the photography exhibitions
*Fragments: Portraits of Survivors*
by Jason Schwartz and
*Liberators: Unexpected Outcomes*
by Coe Arthur Younger. The reception will take place Thursday, July
13th at 5 pm and will be held at the Museum.

*Courtesy of the Florida Holocaust Museum*

Both exhibitions will run through October 22. Many of the survivors and liberators featured in the exhibitions, as well as Coe Arthur
Younger, photographer of the liberators exhibition, will be in atten-
dance at the event.

*Fragments: Portraits of Survivors* features one hundred-twelve (112)
16 x 20 black and white photographs of local Holocaust survivors.
Accompanying each portrait is a handwritten statement from the
survivor in the photo. "I survived . . . I beat Hitler" is just one statement of many that quietly communicates the importance of this

exhibition and its power to speak to all generations. The pictures and thoughts tell of the trials and triumphs of these extraordinary men and women survivors who bravely tell their stories as first-hand testimonies of a tragic time during the 20th century. Their memories give a voice to the voiceless.

*Courtesy of the Florida Holocaust Museum, copyright Coe Arthur Younger*

**A photograph from the exhibition *Liberators: Unexpected Outcomes***

The black and white photographs of the liberators tell a different story. *Liberators: Unexpected Outcomes* features 18 photographs of local U.S. troops who, as first responders and liberators at the end of WWII, witnessed the horrors behind camp gates. Without preparation or warning, these men happened upon unexpected and unimaginable scenes during regular military operations. Their stories are featured in photography by Coe Arthur Younger, as well as in an accompanying video that highlights the testimonies of several local liberators and survivors.

*The Florida Holocaust Museum honors the memory of millions of innocent men, women, and children who suffered or died in the Holocaust. The Museum is dedicated to teaching members of all races and cultures to recognize the inherent worth and dignity of human life in order to prevent future genocides.*

This paragraph gives details about the second of the two exhibits, *Liberators: Unexpected Outcomes*.

This paragraph sums up the organization's mission.

## Comparing Expository Texts

© **1. Craft and Structure** Compare and contrast the **coherence** of the Web site and news release. **(a)** How would you **evaluate** the **logic** and **consistency** of the texts? **(b)** Does one informational text have a better sense of **unity** than the other? Explain.

### Content-Area Vocabulary

**2. (a)** Review the definitions of *exhibit* and *archive*. **(b)** Then, use both words in a sentence about a school field trip to a museum.

## ⏱ Timed Writing

### Explanatory Text: Evaluation

**Format**
The prompt gives clues about what to write and suggests where to look for the information you need.

Write an essay that evaluates the coherence of the news release. Analyze whether details are presented in a logical, consistent order. Then, evaluate the success of the news release in communicating one main idea about the photography exhibits. Use examples from the text to support your evaluation. (45 minutes)

**Academic Vocabulary**
When you *analyze* a text, you closely examine its details and organization. When you *evaluate* a text, you judge its effectiveness.

### 5-Minute Planner

Complete these steps before you begin to write:

1. Read the prompt carefully. Look for key words, such as those that are highlighted, that will help you understand the assignment.

2. Reread the selection carefully. Pay attention to important details.

3. As you read, take notes about the photography exhibits.

4. Think about whether the details are in a logical order and whether the news release communicates its main idea successfully. Jot down notes about your ideas.

5. Refer to your notes as you write your evaluation.

# Comparing Literary Works

## Comparing Sources With a Dramatization

When Anne Frank's diary was published, it inspired Albert Hackett and Frances Goodrich to develop Anne's private thoughts into a play. To do this, they drew on these different types of sources:

- **Primary sources** are firsthand accounts that describe or document events that take place at the time of the writing. Primary sources often directly convey the author's point of view. Primary sources include letters, diaries, and legal documents.

- **Secondary sources** interpret information from primary sources. Secondary sources include biographies, magazine articles, journals, encyclopedias, and textbooks.

*The Diary of Anne Frank* is a **dramatization,** a play that has been adapted from another work. When playwrights dramatize a primary source, such as a diary, they may also draw on other sources to add information not known by the original author. In addition, they might choose to fictionalize aspects of certain events for dramatic effect.

As you read excerpts from Anne's diary and Miep Gies's memoir, *Anne Frank Remembered,* compare the information they contain with the type of information presented in the play. Look for details in the text that suggest the author's opinions and attitudes. Use a chart like this one to help you compare the two selections.

**Common Core State Standards**

**Reading Informational Text**
**6.** Determine an author's point of view or purpose in a text.

**Writing**
**9.** Draw evidence from literary or informational texts to support analysis, reflection, and research. *(Timed Writing)*

| Selections | Comparisons |
|---|---|
| *The Diary of Anne Frank* (the play) | |
| *Anne Frank: Diary of a Young Girl* (diary) | Reveals Anne's thoughts directly |
| *Anne Frank Remembered* (memoir) | |

**www.PHLitOnline.com**

- Vocabulary flashcards
- Interactive journals
- More about the authors
- Selection audio
- Interactive graphic organizers

# Is it our *differences* or our *similarities* that matter most?

## Writing About the Big Question

Both of these selections report the suffering that Anne Frank and her family endured because of their religious background. Use this sentence to develop your ideas about the Big Question:

> When authorities try to **discriminate** against others on the basis of race or religion, people can resist by _____.

# Meet the Authors

## Anne Frank (1929–1945)

### Author of *Anne Frank: The Diary of a Young Girl*

More than sixty years after her death, Anne Frank remains the world's best-known victim of the Holocaust. The tragedy of her death is made even more moving by the existence of her diary, a personal and revealing look into a life cut short.

**The Diary** At first, Anne's father Otto was reluctant to publish Anne's private thoughts, but eventually he overcame his doubts. The book quickly became a best-seller. Anne's diary enabled people to put a human face—the face of an ordinary teenage girl—on a tragedy that had been too enormous to grasp.

## Miep Gies (1909–2010)

### Author of *Anne Frank Remembered*

Miep Gies was born in Vienna, Austria. In 1922, she moved to Amsterdam and got a job working for Otto Frank. When the Franks were forced into hiding in 1942, Gies immediately offered her support. Despite her efforts, the Franks were discovered and sent to concentration camps after two years in hiding.

**An Unsung Hero** Miep Gies did not see herself as unusually brave. She said, "I am not a hero. I stand at the end of a long, long line of good Dutch people who did what I did or more—much more—during those dark and terrible times years ago . . ."

# From
# ANNE FRANK:
## The *Diary* of a
## *Young Girl*

# Saturday, 20 June, 1942

. . . There is a saying that "paper is more patient than man"; it came back to me on one of my slightly melancholy days, while I sat chin in hand, feeling too bored and limp even to make up my mind whether to go out or stay at home. Yes, there is no doubt that paper is patient and as I don't intend to show this cardboard-covered notebook, bearing the proud name of "diary," to anyone, unless I find a real friend, boy or girl, probably nobody cares. And now I come to the root of the matter, the reason for my starting a diary: it is that I have no such real friend.

Let me put it more clearly, since no one will believe that a girl of thirteen feels herself quite alone in the world, nor is it so. I have darling parents and a sister of sixteen. I know about thirty people whom one might call friends—I have strings of boy friends, anxious to catch a glimpse of me and who, failing that, peep at me through mirrors in class. I have relations, aunts and uncles, who are darlings too, a good home, no—I don't seem to lack anything. But it's the same with all my friends, just fun and joking, nothing more. I can never bring myself to talk of anything outside the common round. We don't seem to be able to get any closer, that is the root of the trouble. Perhaps I lack confidence, but anyway, there it is, a stubborn fact and I don't seem to be able to do anything about it.

Hence, this diary. In order to enhance in my mind's eye the picture of the friend for whom I have waited so long, I don't want to set down a series of bald facts in a diary like most people do, but I want this diary itself to be my friend, and I shall call my friend Kitty. No one will grasp what I'm talking about if I begin my letters to Kitty just out of the blue, so albeit[1] unwillingly, I will start by sketching in brief the story of my life.

My father was thirty-six when he married my mother, who was then twenty-five. My sister Margot was born in 1926 in Frankfort-on-Main, I followed on June 12, 1929, and, as we are Jewish, we emigrated to Holland in 1933, where my father was appointed Managing Director of Travies N.V. This firm is in close relationship with the firm of Kolen & Co. in the same building, of which my father is a partner.

---

**1. albeit** (ôl bē′ it) *conj.* although.

◀ **Critical Viewing**
What value do war-time diaries, such as Anne's, have for readers today? **[Analyze]**

**Sources**
What information in this paragraph would be hard to show in a dramatization?

**Vocabulary**
**enhance** (en hans′) *v.* make greater

**emigrated** (em′ i grāt′ əd) *v.* left one place to settle in another

✓ Reading Check
Who is Kitty?

▼ An Amsterdam street, labeled "Jewish Street" in German and Dutch, where Jews were permitted to shop.

**Sources**
Compare and contrast the presentation of this information with its presentation at the end of Act I Scene I in the play.

**Sources**
Why do you think the playwrights chose to omit this information about Anne's grandmother from the play?

The rest of our family, however, felt the full impact of Hitler's anti-Jewish laws, so life was filled with anxiety. In 1938 after the pogroms,[2] my two uncles (my mother's brothers) escaped to the U.S.A. My old grandmother came to us, she was then seventy-three. After May 1940 good times rapidly fled: first the war, then the capitulation,[3] followed by the arrival of the Germans, which is when the sufferings of us Jews really began. Anti-Jewish decrees followed each other in quick succession. Jews must wear a yellow star, Jews must hand in their bicycles, Jews are banned from trains and are forbidden to drive. Jews are only allowed to do their shopping between three and five o'clock and then only in shops which bear the placard "Jewish shop." Jews must be indoors by eight o'clock and cannot even sit in their own gardens after that hour. Jews are forbidden to visit theaters, cinemas, and other places of entertainment. Jews may not take part in public sports. Swimming baths, tennis courts, hockey fields, and other sports grounds are all prohibited to them. Jews may not visit Christians. Jews must go to Jewish schools, and many more restrictions of a similar kind.

So we could not do this and were forbidden to do that. But life went on in spite of it all. Jopie[4] used to say to me, "You're scared to do anything, because it may be forbidden." Our freedom was strictly limited. Yet things were still bearable.

Granny died in January 1942; no one will ever know how much she is present in my thoughts and how much I love her still.

In 1934 I went to school at the Montessori Kindergarten and continued there. It was at the end of the school year, I was in form 6B, when I had to say good-by to Mrs. K. We both wept, it was very sad. In 1941 I went, with my sister Margot, to the

---

2. **pogroms** (pō′ grəmz) *n.* organized killings and other persecution of Jews.
3. **capitulation** (kə pich′ yōō lā′ shən) *n.* act of surrendering.
4. **Jopie** (yō′ pē) Jacqueline van Maarsen, Anne's best friend.

Jewish Secondary School, she into the fourth form[5] and I into the first.

So far everything is all right with the four of us and here I come to the present day.

## Thursday, 19 November, 1942

Dear Kitty,

Dussel is a very nice man, just as we had all imagined. Of course he thought it was all right to share my little room.

Quite honestly I'm not so keen that a stranger should use my things, but one must be prepared to make some sacrifices for a good cause, so I shall make my little offering with a good will. "If we can save someone, then everything else is of secondary importance," says Daddy, and he's absolutely right.

The first day that Dussel was here, he immediately asked me all sorts of questions: When does the charwoman[6] come? When can one use the bathroom? When is one allowed to use the lavatory?[7] You may laugh, but these things are not so simple in a hiding place. During the day we mustn't make any noise that might be heard downstairs; and if there is some stranger—such as the charwoman for example—then we have to be extra careful. I explained all this carefully to Dussel. But one thing amazed me: he is very slow on the uptake. He asks everything twice over and still doesn't seem to remember. Perhaps that will wear off in time, and it's only that he's thoroughly upset by the sudden change.

Apart from that, all goes well. Dussel has told us a lot about the outside world, which we have missed for so long now. He had very sad news. Countless friends and acquaintances have gone to a terrible fate. Evening after evening the green and gray army lorries trundle past.[8] The Germans ring at every front door to inquire if there are any Jews living in the house. If there are, then the whole family has to go at once. If they don't find any, they go on to the next house. No one has a chance of evading them unless one goes into hiding. Often they go around with lists, and only ring when they know they can get a good haul. Sometimes they let them off for cash—so much per head. It seems like the slave hunts of olden times.

**Spiral Review**

**Conflict** Compare Anne's attitude toward Dussel in the diary with the feelings she expresses when she first meets him in the play.

Reading Check

What does Anne notice about Dussel?

---

5. **fourth form** fourth grade.
6. **charwoman** *n.* cleaning woman.
7. **lavatory** *n.* toilet.
8. **lorries trundle past** trucks move along.

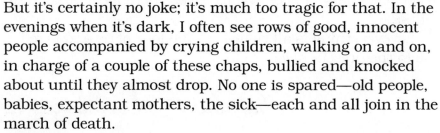

**Sources**
Compare this paragraph with the description on pages 888–889. How does the firsthand account differ from the play's version of similar events?

But it's certainly no joke; it's much too tragic for that. In the evenings when it's dark, I often see rows of good, innocent people accompanied by crying children, walking on and on, in charge of a couple of these chaps, bullied and knocked about until they almost drop. No one is spared—old people, babies, expectant mothers, the sick—each and all join in the march of death.

How fortunate we are here, so well cared for and undisturbed. We wouldn't have to worry about all this misery were it not that we are so anxious about all those dear to us whom we can no longer help.

I feel wicked sleeping in a warm bed, while my dearest friends have been knocked down or have fallen into a gutter somewhere out in the cold night. I get frightened when I think of close friends who have now been delivered into the hands of the cruelest brutes that walk the earth. And all because they are Jews!

Yours, Anne

## Critical Thinking

1. **Key Ideas and Details (a)** Why does Anne decide to write a diary? **(b) Analyze:** What other reasons might motivate her to write?

2. **Key Ideas and Details (a)** As Anne describes in the June 20 entry, how has life changed for Jews since May 1940? **(b) Infer:** What is the purpose of such restrictions?

3. **Key Ideas and Details (a) Contrast:** How is Anne's situation different from that of the Jews she sees outside? **(b) Evaluate:** Anne says she is "fortunate" to have a hiding place. Do you agree? Explain.

4. **Integration of Knowledge and Ideas (a)** Do the occupying Nazis succeed in creating distinctions between Dutch Jews and Dutch Christians? Explain. **(b)** Why are the Franks limited in their ability to resist the changes Anne describes? *[Connect to the Big Question: Is it our differences or our similarities that matter most?]*

*Cite textual evidence to support your responses.*

# From
# Anne Frank Remembered

## Miep Gies
### with Alison Leslie Gold

**Background** Miep Gies helped Anne Frank and her family hide in the attic of an office building during World War II. She was one of the thousands of Dutch citizens who bravely helped Jews hide from the Nazis. In this excerpt from her book, *Anne Frank Remembered*, Miep Gies describes welcoming back Otto Frank as a war refugee, learning of the fate of those who had hidden with him, and giving Anne's diary to him.

Henk flew home that day to tell me. It was June 3, 1945. He ran into the living room and grabbed me. "Miep, Otto Frank is coming back!"

My heart took flight. Deep down I'd always known that he would, that the others would, too.

Just then, my eye caught sight of a figure passing outside our window. My throat closed. I ran outside.

There was Mr. Frank himself, walking toward our door.

We looked at each other. There were no words. He was thin, but he'd always been thin. He carried a little bundle. My eyes swam. My heart melted. Suddenly,

**Vocabulary**
**liberated** (lib´ ər āt´ əd)
*v.* freed; released

▼ **Critical Viewing**
This photo shows
Auschwitz survivors
liberated by the Soviet
Army in January 1945.
The Nazi slogan above
the entrance reads
"Work makes freedom."
What details in the
photo give you insight
into the experiences
of concentration camp
survivors? **[Analyze]**

I was afraid to know more. I didn't want to know what had happened. I knew I would not ask.

We stood facing each other, speechless. Finally, Frank spoke.

"Miep," he said quietly. "Miep, Edith is not coming back."

My throat was pierced. I tried to hide my reaction to his thunderbolt. "Come inside," I insisted.

He went on. "But I have great hope for Margot and Anne."

"Yes. Great hope," I echoed encouragingly. "Come inside."

He still stood there. "Miep, I came here because you and Henk are the ones closest to me who are still here."

I grabbed his bundle from his hand. "Come, you stay right here with us. Now, some food. You have a room here with us for as long as you want."

He came inside. I made up a bedroom for him, and put everything we had into a fine meal for him. We ate. Mr. Frank told us he had ended up in Auschwitz. That was the last time he'd seen Edith, Margot, and Anne. The men had been separated from the women immediately. When the Russians liberated the camp in January, he had been taken on a very long trip to Odessa. Then from there to Marseille by ship, and at last, by train and truck to Holland.

He told us these few things in his soft voice. He spoke very little, but between us there was no need for words.

Mr. Frank settled in with Henk and me. Right away, he came back to the office and took his place again as the head of the business. I know he was relieved to have something to do each day. Meanwhile, he began exploring the network of information on Jews in the camps—the refugee agencies, the daily lists, the most crucial word-of-mouth information—trying everything to get news about Margot and Anne.

When Auschwitz was liberated, Otto Frank had gone right away to the women's camp to find out about his wife and children. In the chaos and desolation of the camps, he had learned that Edith had died shortly before the liberation.

He had also learned that in all likelihood, Margot and Anne had been transferred to another camp, along with Mrs. van Daan. The camp was called Bergen-Belsen, and was quite a distance from Auschwitz. That was as far as his trail had gone so far, though. Now he was trying to pick up the search.

As to the other men, Mr. Frank had lost track of Albert Dussel. He had no idea what had happened to him after the transit camp of Westerbork. He had seen with his own eyes Mr. van Daan on his way to be gassed. And Peter van Daan had come to visit Frank in the Auschwitz infirmary. Mr. Frank knew that right before the liberation of the camp, the Germans had taken groups of prisoners with them in their retreat. Peter had been in one of these groups.

Otto Frank had begged Peter to try to get into the infirmary himself, but Peter couldn't or wouldn't. He had last been seen going off with the retreating Germans into the snow-covered countryside. There was no further news about him.

Mr. Frank held high hopes for the girls, because Bergen-Belsen was not a death camp. There were no gassings there. It was a work camp—filled with hunger and disease, but with no apparatus for liquidation. Because Margot and Anne had been sent to the camp later than most other inmates they were relatively healthy. I too lived on hope for Margot and Anne. In some deep part of me, like a rock, I counted on their survival and their safe return to Amsterdam.

Mr. Frank had written for news to several Dutch people who he had learned had been in Bergen-Belsen. Through word of mouth people were being reunited every day. Daily, he waited for answers to his letters and for the new lists of survivors to be released and posted. Every time there was a knock at the door or footfalls on the steps, all our hearts would stand still.

**Reading Check**

How did Mr. Frank and Peter show concern for one another while they were imprisoned in Auschwitz?

Perhaps Margot and Anne had found their way back home, and we could see them with our own eyes at last. Anne's sixteenth birthday was coming on June 12. Perhaps, we hoped, . . . but then the birthday came and went, and still no news.

One morning, Mr. Frank and I were alone in the office, opening mail. He was standing beside me, and I was sitting at my desk. I was vaguely aware of the sound of a letter being slit open. Then, a moment of silence. Something made me look away from my mail. Then, Otto Frank's voice, toneless, totally crushed: "Miep."

My eyes looked up at him, seeking out his eyes.

"Miep." He gripped a sheet of paper in both his hands. "I've gotten a letter from the nurse in Rotterdam. Miep, Margot and Anne are not coming back."

We stayed there like that, both struck by lightning, burnt thoroughly through our hearts, our eyes fixed on each other's. Then Mr. Frank walked toward his office and said in that defeated voice, "I'll be in my office."

I heard him walk across the room and down the hall, and the door closed.

I sat at my desk utterly crushed. Everything that had happened before, I could somehow accept. Like it or not, I had to accept it. But this, I could not accept. It was the one thing I'd been sure would not happen.

I heard the others coming into the office. I heard a door opening and a voice chattering. Then, good-morning greetings and coffee cups. I reached into the drawer on the side of my desk and took out the papers that had been waiting there for Anne for nearly a year now. No one, including me, had

**Sources**
What do you learn here that only Miep would know?

touched them. Now Anne was not coming back for her diary.

I took out all the papers, placing the little red-orange checkered diary on top, and carried everything into Mr. Frank's office.

Frank was sitting at his desk, his eyes murky with shock. I held out the diary and the papers to him. I said, "Here is your daughter Anne's legacy to you."

I could tell that he recognized the diary. He had given it to her just over three years before, on her thirteenth birthday, right before going into hiding. He touched it with the tips of his fingers. I pressed everything into his hands; then I left his office, closing the door quietly.

Shortly afterward, the phone on my desk rang. It was Mr. Frank's voice. "Miep, please see to it that I'm not disturbed." he said.

"I've already done that," I replied.

The second printing of the diary sold out and another printing was planned. Mr. Frank was approached with the idea of permiting the diary to be translated and published abroad. He was against it at first, but then he succumbed to the pressure on him to allow the diary a more widespread audience.

Again and again, he'd say to me, "Miep, you must read Anne's writing. Who would have imagined what went on in her quick little mind?" Otto was never discouraged by my continuing refusal. He would always wait awhile and then ask me again.

Finally, I gave in to his insistence. I said, "All right, I will read the diary, but only when I'm totally alone."

The next time I was totally alone, on a warm day, I took the second printing of the diary, went to my room, and shut the door.

With awful fear in my heart, I opened the book and turned to the first page.

And so I began to read.

I read the whole diary without stopping. From the first word, I heard Anne's voice come back to speak to me from where she had gone. I lost track of time. Anne's voice tumbled out of the book, so full of life, moods, curiosity, feelings. She was no longer gone and destroyed. She was alive again in my mind.

**Spiral Review**

**Conflict** Why do you think Miep could not bring herself to read Anne's diary? What might have motivated her to change her mind?

Reading Check

How did Mr. Frank find out that his daughters were not coming back?

*from* Anne Frank Remembered **979**

**Sources**

How does Miep's description of her reaction to reading Anne's diary show you she knew Anne Frank well?

▲ The author, Miep Gies, with a picture of Anne and her published diary.

I read to the very end. I was surprised by how much had happened in hiding that I'd known nothing about. Immediately, I was thankful that I hadn't read the diary after the arrest, during the final nine months of the occupation, while it had stayed in my desk drawer right beside me every day. Had I read it, I would have had to burn the diary because it would have been too dangerous for people about whom Anne had written.

When I had read the last word, I didn't feel the pain I'd anticipated. I was glad I'd read it at last. The emptiness in my heart was eased. So much had been lost, but now Anne's voice would never be lost. My young friend had left a remarkable legacy to the world.

But always, every day of my life, I've wished that things had been different. That even had Anne's diary been lost to the world, Anne and the others might somehow have been saved.

Not a day goes by that I do not grieve for them.

## Critical Thinking

**1. Key Ideas and Details (a)** When Mr. Frank first returns to Amsterdam, what news does he bring of the other occupants of the Secret Annex? **(b) Infer:** Why is it so difficult for Miep and Otto Frank to find out about the rest of the Frank family?

**2. Key Ideas and Details (a) Analyze:** Why do you think Miep waited so long to read the diary? **(b) Interpret:** What does this selection add to your understanding of Anne Frank's life and legacy?

**3. Key Ideas and Details (a) Compare and Contrast:** How does Miep's attitude toward the diary change after she reads it? **(b) Make a Judgment:** Do you agree with Miep that it would have been better for Anne to have lived, even if her diary had been lost to the world? Explain.

**4. Integration of Knowledge and Ideas (a)** How do Miep and her husband Henk resist the Nazis' attempt to create differences between themselves and the Franks? **(b)** Is their method of resistance ultimately effective? Why or why not? *[Connect to the Big Question: Is it our differences or our similarities that matter most?]*

*Cite textual evidence to support your responses.*

## Comparing Sources With a Dramatization

**1. Integration of Knowledge and Ideas** Use the chart to compare the diary, the play, and the memoir.

|  | How Thoughts and Feelings Are Expressed | Whose Perspectives Are Shown | Accuracy of Retelling | How Time Is Represented |
|---|---|---|---|---|
| Diary |  |  |  |  |
| Play |  |  |  |  |
| Memoir |  |  |  |  |

**2. Integration of Knowledge and Ideas (a)** Do you think the playwrights create a fair and accurate portrait of Anne? Support your answer with evidence from the diary. **(b)** Identify two secondary sources you could consult to assess the accuracy of their portrayal.

**3. Integration of Knowledge and Ideas (a)** Identify the different purposes of the authors of these three works. **(b)** How do the characteristics of each form—play, diary, and memoir—help them meet their goals?

## ⏱ Timed Writing

### Explanatory Text: Essay

In an essay, make links across texts to compare the Anne revealed in the diary with the Anne of the later works. **(40 minutes)**

### 5-Minute Planner

**1.** Read the prompt carefully and completely.

**2.** Gather your ideas by jotting down answers to these questions:

- How might the passage of time affect the retelling of events?
- How well does the play capture Anne's thoughts and feelings?
- In the play, what is the effect of other characters on the way we view Anne? Do the other works change that view? Is the portrayal of the others in hiding different among the works?
- Is one of the three forms more powerful to you? Why?

**3.** Use the chart you created for question 1 to help you organize the categories in your essay and provide textual evidence.

**4.** Reread the prompt, and then draft your essay.

# Writing Workshop

## Write an Informative Text

### Exposition: Research Report

**Defining the Form** **Research writing** brings together information gathered from several sources in order to prove a central point, or thesis. You might use elements of a research report when writing informational articles, historical analyses, or business reports.

**Assignment** Write a research report based on information from a variety of sources. Your research report should feature the following:

✔ a specific focus, or *main idea,* expressed in a *thesis statement*

✔ supporting evidence collected from a variety of reliable *primary and secondary sources*, with *appropriate citations*

✔ a *clear organization* and *smooth transitions*

✔ a *bibliography* or "Works Cited" list that provides an accurate, complete citation of research sources

✔ error-free writing, including the *correct use of subordinate clauses*

To preview the criteria on which your research report may be judged, see the rubric on page 993.

 **Writing Workshop:** *Work in Progress*

Review the work you did on pages 915 and 959.

**WRITE GUY**
*Jeff Anderson, M.Ed.*

## What Do You Notice?

### Form and Structure

Read the following sentences from Robert MacNeil's "The Trouble with Television."

*It is difficult to escape the influence of television. If you fit the statistical averages, by the age of 20 you will have been exposed to at least 20,000 hours of television. You can add 10,000 hours for each decade you have lived after the age of 20. The only things Americans do more than watch television are work and sleep.*

With a partner, discuss what you notice about the passage. Then, look at the way MacNeil presents facts and statistics. Think of ways you might structure your own writing to present your ideas effectively.

**Writing**
**2.** Write informative/explanatory texts to examine a topic and convey ideas, concepts, and information through the selection, organization, and analysis of relevant content.
**2.a.** Introduce a topic clearly, previewing what is to follow; organize ideas, concepts, and information into broader categories; include formatting, graphics, tables, and multimedia when useful to aiding comprehension.
**7.** Conduct short research projects to answer a question, drawing on several sources and generating additional related, focused questions that allow for multiple avenues of exploration.

# Prewriting/Planning Strategies

Use the following prewriting strategies before you draft your report:

**Browse media.** To find topic ideas, flip through recently published magazines or newspapers. Tune in to television and radio broadcasts. Surf the Internet for ideas, creating and organizing bookmarks in your Internet browser to identify possible topics. In a chart like the one shown, list people, places, events, or current issues that you want to investigate.

**PHLit Online!**
www.PHLitOnline.com
- Author video: Writing Process
- Author video: Rewards of Writing

| People | Places | Events | Current Issues |
|--------|--------|--------|----------------|
| politicians | Washington, D.C. | mining accident | health care |
| entertainers | Los Angeles, CA | elections | worldwide hunger |
| scientists | the Middle East | soccer game | the economy |
| educators | South America | Hurricane Andrew | school funding |

**Develop a research plan.** Before you finalize your topic, conduct preliminary research to determine how much material is available. Using your general idea as a starting point, search through relevant books, Web sites, magazines, and indexes at a library. Jot down the names, ideas, and events that appear most often. Use this information to narrow a wide subject, such as educational toys, to a narrower one, such as electronic readers.

**Ask open-ended questions.** Thoughtful, interesting questions can help focus a research topic. To develop these questions, take the following steps:

- Draft a list of broad questions about your topic. These questions will be the starting points for your exploration of the topic and will guide your research.

- As you research, narrow your list by deleting unrelated questions and adding questions that are more specific to your focus.

**Use a variety of primary and secondary sources.** Use both *primary sources* (firsthand or original accounts, such as interview transcripts and newspaper articles) and *secondary sources* (accounts that are not original, such as encyclopedia entries) in your research. A secondary source often contains a bibliography or list of works cited. You can use these citations to find additional sources.

# Prewriting/Planning Strategies *(continued)*

**Common Core State Standards**

**Writing**

**8.** Gather relevant information from multiple print and digital sources, using search terms effectively; assess the credibility and accuracy of each source; and quote or paraphrase the data and conclusions of others while avoiding plagiarism and following a standard format for citation.

**Evaluate sources.** Just because something is in print or online does not mean it is true or unbiased. Often you will find articles written by unreliable authors, articles with a bias or agenda, or articles that lack factual evidence to support their claims. To ensure that you use the right sources, evaluate their reliability using these questions.

| | |
|---|---|
| Does the source go into enough depth to cover the subject? | ☐ yes ☐ no |
| Does the publisher have a good reputation? | ☐ yes ☐ no |
| Is the author an authority on the subject? | ☐ yes ☐ no |
| Do at least two other sources agree with this source? | ☐ yes ☐ no |

To ensure that your information is current, accurate, and balanced, follow these guidelines:

- Check publication dates to make sure the information is current.
- If you note discrepancies in the information given by two sources, check the facts in a third source. If three or more sources disagree, mention the disagreement in your paper.
- Consider the author's perspective. Examine the author's credentials—his or her background—before accepting a conclusion.

**Use source cards and note cards.** When you find information related to your topic, take detailed notes on index cards.

- Create a *source card* for each book, article, or Web site. For print sources, list the author, title, publisher, and place and date of publication. For each Internet source, list the sponsor, page name, date of last revision, date you accessed it, and address.
- As you take notes, write one idea on each card. When taking notes, be careful to avoid *plagiarism,* the unethical presentation of someone else's ideas as if they were your own. Clearly indicate if your note reflects an author's exact words or a paraphrase of an author's ideas.
- Use quotation marks whenever you copy words exactly. When using cursive, write legibly to avoid misquoting or misspelling.

Alternatively, you can use computer programs, such as database or word processing software, to keep track of source information.

**Note Card**

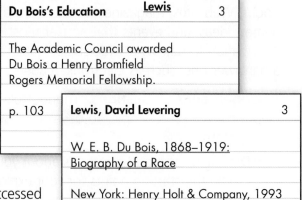

**Source Card**

# Drafting Strategies

**Define your thesis.** Sum up the main point you plan to address in your report in a single statement, called a **thesis statement.** Use your thesis statement to direct your writing and include it in the introduction to your report. The arguments and evidence that you present in the body of your report should connect logically to the thesis statement. If they do not connect, you should consider either modifying your original thesis or using other evidence.

**Make an outline.** Write a formal outline, such as the one shown, for your report before you begin to draft. Use Roman numerals for your most important points and capital letters for the details that support them. Make sure each point in your outline supports your thesis.

**Title of Your Report**

I. Introduction
   Thesis Statement
II. First main point
   A. Supporting detail #1
      1. Example
      2. Example
      3. Example
   B. Supporting detail #2
   C. Supporting detail #3
III. Second main point

**Balance research and original ideas.** As you write your draft, strive to achieve a balance between research-based information and your own original ideas. The highlighted portion in this example indicates the writer's original words, not research.

**Model:**

    The famous Underground Railroad, which operated from approximately 1780 to 1862 ("The Underground Railroad," PBS.org), was not underground, nor was it a railroad. Rather, it was a system operated by a secret network of courageous people who helped slaves escape from the American South and find their way to freedom. The first slaves had arrived in Jamestown, Virginia, in 1619, a year before the Pilgrims arrived at Plymouth Rock, Massachusetts (Buckmaster 11). By the early 1800s, there were about four million slaves in this country (Siebert 378). It was the Underground Railroad that saved many lives from the hardships of slavery in the American South.

**Prepare to credit sources.** Any material that is not an original idea should be credited, whether you paraphrase it or quote it directly. As you draft, circle all ideas and phrases that come directly from your research. At this stage, for each circled item, use parentheses to note the author's name and the page number of the source. Internet sources can be identified by Web addresses. You can create formal citations later.

# Drafting Strategies

**Make direct reference to sources.** You can use one of these methods to incorporate the information you have found.

- **Quote directly.** Support your thesis and conclusions with opinions from authorities. When using a source's exact words, enclose the entire statement in quotation marks. However, if the quotation is more than four lines, use a *block quote*. Introduce the quotation with a colon. Then begin on a new line, indenting the entire quotation and leaving out the quotation marks.

- **Paraphrase.** This technique involves restating a writer's specific ideas in your own words. Be sure to properly credit the source.

- **Summarize.** Where appropriate, summarize all major perspectives on the topic. This is especially important when you are describing controversial or complex ideas.

**Create visuals.** Use visual displays such as charts, graphs, and tables when you want to organize and display information in a way that illustrates your main point and is easy to grasp.

- Pie charts show parts of a whole, so they can be useful in showing any topic with data in percentages.

- Line graphs and bar graphs show information as it changes over time, so they can be useful in showing trends.

Three different ways of visualizing the same general topic—migration—are shown here. Note that important similarities or differences in tables and charts can be emphasized by using different colors and fonts.

Other types of visuals that can help you illustrate your points include photographs, diagrams, and maps. Always make sure the text in your visuals is readable. Add captions to photos so readers can understand what they show. Diagrams and maps should also be clearly labeled. A map requires a legend that tells what the symbols mean, a compass rose indicating where north is, and a scale showing distance.

**Create a "Works Cited" list.** When you finish drafting, provide full information about your sources in an alphabetical "Works Cited" list or "Bibliography" at the end of your report. Check the format required for your report and follow its style and punctuation guidelines. For more guidance on formats, see the Bibliography on page 992 and pages R34–R35.

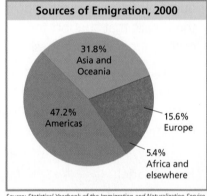

Sources of Emigration, 2000

Source: *Statistical Yearbook of the Immigration and Naturalization Service*

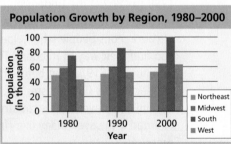

Population Growth by Region, 1980–2000

Source: U.S. Bureau of the Census, *The Statistical History of the U.S.* (1976) and 2000 Census of the U.S. www.census.gov

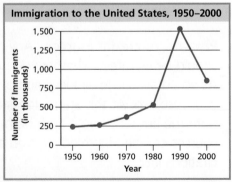

Immigration to the United States, 1950–2000

Source: *Yearbook of Immigration Statistics, 2003*

## Writers on Writing

# Cherie Bennett On Getting Facts and Words Right

Cherie Bennett is the author of *Anne Frank & Me* (p. 810).

*"We didn't want to get any facts wrong."*

— Cherie Bennett

I wrote the play *Anne Frank & Me* first, and then, with my husband, adapted it as a novel. The big difference between the two forms is that a novel gives you so much more freedom. You're not confined by what could go on a stage. But novels require even more research, since they contain so many details. The following selection is from the novel, and it covers part of the same scene as the excerpt from the play you just read.

---

**Professional Model:**

### from *Anne Frank and Me* (novel)

A sudden bump on the track jostled them; they reached to steady each other—Nicole felt as if jolts of electricity were coursing through her. "I remember . . . you thought your parents disapproved that you were kissing him."

Anne's voice became a whisper. "How is this possible?"

"I don't know—" Nicole began, then stopped. Because suddenly, she did know. "You kept a diary. I read it."

"But I left my diary in the Annex when the Gestapo came. You couldn't have read it."

"I did, though."

"How?"

"I don't know," Nicole admitted. "I wish I did."

Anne gave her an ~~dubious cock-eyed mischievous~~ **arched** look. "This is a very strange conversation."

The train lurched violently. People cried out in fear, but Nicole was oblivious, as a new thought surfaced, one so absurd that she was almost too embarrassed to say it. "Anne, I feel like it was—I know this will sound crazy—but I feel like it was in the future."

Research interviews with Holocaust survivors taught us about the rough track bed used by the transports. On stage, the actors synchronized unsteady movements with sound effects of a moving train.

In most plays, characters speak for themselves. But in a novel, you've got to pick a point of view. We wrote this story using a limited third-person point of view, revealing only Nicole's thoughts.

I remember my struggle for the right word to describe the look that Anne gives Nicole. I tried—and tossed out!— curious, cock-eyed, and dubious. Finally, I settled on arched. It conveys both how I imagine Anne raised her eyebrows and her mischievous tone.

# Revising Strategies

**Check for unity.** All the parts of your report should fit together in a complete, self-contained whole.

1. Check that every paragraph develops your thesis statement. Delete those that do not, or revise to show a connection.

2. Identify the main idea of each paragraph. Often, a topic sentence will directly state that main idea. If a paragraph does not contain a topic sentence, consider adding one.

3. In each paragraph, eliminate any sentences that do not support or explain the topic sentence or main idea.

4. Use transition words and phrases to smooth the flow between paragraphs and between ideas. Examples include *next, finally, although, as a result of, therefore, despite,* and *however.*

5. Check your conclusion to make sure it provides a sense of closure to the writing and that it reinforces your thesis.

**Common Core State Standards**

**Writing**

**2.c.** Use appropriate and varied transitions to create cohesion and clarify the relationships among ideas and concepts.

**2.f.** Provide a concluding statement or section that follows from and supports the information or explanation presented.

---

**Model: Revising for Unity**

The Underground Railroad had apparently been in existence toward the end of the 1700s, but it was not named as such until around 1831, when the steam railroads were emerging. Railroad terms were used to describe various aspects of the system. It had "stations" and "depots," the homes and businesses where the runaway slaves could rest and eat. The people who sheltered the fugitives in these stations were called "stationmasters." ~~They would hide people in barns, basements, and back rooms—anywhere they could.~~ People who contributed money or goods were called "stockholders." ~~The money was needed to buy decent clothing for the escaping slaves, for tattered clothing would send an unwanted message about the person's status.~~ The system also had "conductors," whose job was to move fugitives from one station to the next.

> The crossed-out sentences do not belong in a paragraph that deals with the terminology of the Underground Railroad.

---

**Check your citations.** You must cite an author's direct quotations as well as his or her ideas, even if you restate the information in your own words. An internal citation appears in parentheses and directly follows the information it references. It includes the author's last name and the page number on which the information appears.

**Example:** "The Duke of Lancaster, in 1888, controlled more than 163,000 acres of British countryside" (Pool 193).

## Peer Review

Ask a partner to read your draft, identifying details that wander too far from your thesis. Together, look for ways to link your information back to the main idea, or consider cutting the text.

# Revising to Combine Sentences Using Clauses

To eliminate choppiness and to show connections between ideas, use subordinate clauses to combine sentences.

**Identifying Subordinate Clauses** A clause is any group of words with a subject and a verb. A subordinate clause cannot stand alone.

**Subordinate clause:** <u>Although Rosa Parks said she was simply tired,</u> she became a symbol of strength.

**Combining Short Sentences** Writers often combine two short sentences by converting one into a subordinate clause that establishes a specific relationship between the two ideas.

**Time:** *After soccer practice,* we will eat pizza.
**Cause and effect:** *If the temperature drops,* winds may pick up.
**Contrast:** *Although the sun shone,* it was still raining.

**Combining Sentences Using Subordinate Clauses** To combine sentences by using subordinate clauses, follow these steps:

**1.** Identify two sentences whose ideas are connected.

**2.** Rewrite the less important idea as a subordinate clause.

**3.** Use punctuation and subordinating conjunctions to combine the two sentences:

- Use a comma after most introductory clauses. *When he arrived back in Missouri, he visited his family.*
  Do not use a comma if the subordinate clause follows the main clause. *He visited his family when he got to Missouri.*

- A list of subordinating conjunctions is shown here. Use these conjunctions to join the clause with the rest of the sentence.

| Frequently Used Subordinating Conjunctions | | | |
|---|---|---|---|
| after | as though | in order that | until |
| although | because | since | when |
| as long as | before | than | where |
| as soon as | even though | unless | while |

**Grammar in Your Writing**

Review the sentences in three paragraphs of your draft. Consider whether some of them could be improved by combining them. If so, combine them by using subordinate clauses.

---

**PH WRITING COACH**

Further instruction and practice are available in *Prentice Hall Writing Coach*.

# Student Model: James Barraclough, Los Alamos, NM

## Alexander the Great

Southeastern Europe and western Asia were continually plagued by wars and rebellions in the fourth century B.C. Out of all this strife rose a boy, Alexander III, a hero whose name would be remembered for thousands of years. Alexander became King of Macedonia at the young age of twenty and commenced to conquer the Persian Empire and part of modern-day India using brilliant battle strategy and a quickness to act that kept his enemies guessing. He earned his reputation as 'Alexander the Great' by carving an empire of approximately one million square miles out of a land filled with enemies who were often intent on overthrowing him (Walbank 248).

Alexander was born in July 356 B.C. to King Philip II of Macedonia and Olympias, daughter of the King of Epirus. Throughout his life, Alexander was very close to his mother, Olympias, from whom he learned to pray and to believe deeply in the gods. However, Alexander inherited his military genius and bravery from his father, who conquered all of the Greek city-states and then united them under his rule. Even as a child, Alexander had enough ambition for several men, as shown by his comment after his father had conquered a city: "My father will have everything, and I will have nothing left to conquer." (Wepman)

After uniting Greece, Philip began a campaign to conquer the Persian Empire, but his efforts were cut short when he was assassinated in 336 B.C. Alexander was only twenty years old, though he had been commanding troops with his father for four years. He was not guaranteed power after his father's death, so he quickly claimed the throne with the army's support (Wilcken 61). Picking up where his father left off, Alexander III, King of Macedonia, began a campaign that would change the world.

In the spring of 334 B.C., Alexander led a relatively small army of 30,000 infantry, comprised mostly of soldiers called *hoplites*, who carried 16-foot spears, and 5,000 cavalry, called the Companions, across the Hellespont, a narrow strait. There, he met a force of Persian cavalry and Greek mercenaries, sent by Darius III, King of the Persian Empire, which was intended to throw back the invaders. However, the Macedonians cut them to shreds by employing Alexander's innovative military strategy (Cartledge 28–29). After that battle, Alexander led his army down along the coast of Asia Minor, taking cities for Greece until he met Darius at Issus. There, Alexander's outnumbered soldiers again routed the Persians, but Darius escaped. As the ancient historian Arrian reports, Darius fled in such a panic, he abandoned his royal chariot. "He even left his bow in the chariot; and mounting a horse continued his flight." (Godolphin 450)

James introduces the overall focus— the impressive accomplishments of Alexander—in the first paragraph.

The paper's organization is chronological, following a clear path from Alexander's birth to his death.

James uses a variety of sources—both ancient and modern— for quotations and supporting evidence.

Choosing not to pursue Darius further, Alexander continued along the eastern Mediterranean coast into Egypt, liberating the Egyptians from their hated Persian overlords. In exchange for their liberation, the Egyptians named Alexander pharaoh of Egypt. After his victory, he planned a city called Alexandria to be built on the Mediterranean Sea. As Alexander pressed back into Asia he conquered many cities, but again Darius confronted him—this time better prepared for the man who was such a grave threat to the Persian Empire. However, Alexander employed a cunning ruse to distract the Persians during the battle and crashed back to the middle, crushing the unsuspecting Persians. When Darius fled, the empire was left to Alexander's control (Cartledge 32). At the age of twenty-five, Alexander had become ruler of the Persian Empire and the most powerful man in the world.

After some time in Babylon, the city he made his capital, Alexander decided to head towards India to conquer new land for his empire. Many of the Greek soldiers protested that they wished to go home after years of hard fighting. Even so, Alexander inspired such loyalty that the soldiers reluctantly followed him to India. After fighting their way through modern-day Afghanistan and Pakistan, Alexander crossed into India. Many of his men died when monsoon rains arrived and poisonous snakes, rats, and tropical diseases, such as malaria, became prevalent.

As the army moved deeper into India, King Porus, an Indian ruler, confronted Alexander's troops with approximately two hundred war elephants and an extensive cavalry. Even though the elephants made it difficult for Alexander's cavalry to fight, Alexander once again outsmarted his enemy and defeated the Indian army. Porus surrendered and agreed to be his ally. Following the restoration of Porus to his kingdom, Alexander's men, who were wearied by the intense heat and stricken with homesickness, refused to move on. Alexander sulked in his tent, until he finally relented and set out towards Babylon (Prevas 166–172).

Approximately one year after his return from India, Alexander developed a fever and stomach cramps. These may have been caused by heavy drinking, typhoid, malaria, or poison. The fatal illness kept him in bed until he died on June 11, 323 B.C. at the age of 32. Since Alexander did not appoint a successor to his throne, the mightiest empire of the time, perhaps of all time, fell into disorder and collapsed with his death (Prevas 202–207).

Smooth transitions give the paper a sense of flow.

James credits each source in parentheses—using only author's last name and page number— directly after the information taken from that source. Full citations appear at the end of the paper.

All in all, Alexander—who was just a boy in some people's eyes when he took the throne—rose to the occasion and conquered the world, forging an empire with his heart and sword. Alexander was a complex man who could be harsh, ruthless, and relentless in battle, but he could also be compassionate and sympathetic towards his wounded soldiers. These characteristics inspired loyalty and unity in thousands of soldiers. They followed Alexander wherever he led, even if they had a fierce desire to go home. The man known as Alexander the Great was a king, an emperor, a pharaoh, a conqueror, and most of all, a leader who could charge into battle, knowing his men would follow.

## Bibliography

Alexander, Caroline. "Alexander the Conqueror." *National Geographic,* March 2000: 42–75.

Cartledge, Paul. *Alexander the Great.* New York: Overlook Press, 2004.

Chrisp, Peter. *Alexander the Great The Legend of a Warrior King.* New York: Dorling Kindersley, 2000.

Godolphin, Francis R., ed. and Chinnock, Edward J., translator (Arrian). *The Greek Historians: The Complete and Unabridged Historical Works of Herodotus, Thucydides, Xenophon, Arrian.* New York: Random House, 1942.

Greenblatt, Miriam. *Alexander the Great and Ancient Greece.* New York: Benchmark Books, 2000.

Prevas, John. *Envy of the Gods.* Cambridge, MA: Da Capo Press, 2004.

Stark, Freya. *Alexander's Path.* New York: Harcourt, Brace and Company, 1958.

Walbank, Frank W. "Alexander the Great." *Encyclopedia Britannica.* 1990 ed.

Wepman, Dennis, *Alexander the Great,* book excerpt on <http://www.palmdigitalmedia.com/product/book/excerpt/11250> ( 14 April 2005).

Wilcken, Ulrich. *Alexander the Great.* New York: W.W. Norton, 1967.

Woodcock, George et al. *Ancient Empires.* New York: Newsweek Books, 1970.

All sources used are listed at the end of the paper in a Bibliography. To see the proper format for different sources, see *Citing Sources and Preparing Manuscript,* pages R34–R35.

You may use a List of Works Cited instead of a Bibliography. Find out which format your teacher prefers.

# Editing and Proofreading

Correct errors in grammar, spelling, and punctuation.

**Focus on citations.** Review your draft against your notes to be sure you have correctly quoted your sources. In addition, check that numbers, dates, and page references are correct.

**Focus on ellipses.** An ellipsis (...) is a punctuation mark that indicates text that is intentionally left out of a quote. Review your report for any long quotes with information that can be safely omitted without changing emphasis or meaning. Substitute an ellipsis for the omitted words to show where you have shortened the text.

# Publishing and Presenting

**Deliver an impromptu speech.** Now that you are knowledgeable about your topic, give an impromptu (unrehearsed) speech to your classmates. Describe your initial questions, your thesis, and what you found out as a result of your research. After you finish, answer questions from the audience.

# Reflecting on Your Writing

**Writer's Journal** Jot down your answers to these questions:

*What was the most surprising or interesting thing you learned about your topic? Why?*

# Rubric for Self-Assessment

FInd evidence in your writing to address each category. Then, use the rating scale to grade your work.

**Spiral Review**
Earlier in this unit, you learned about **dangling and misplaced modifiers** (p. 914) and **clauses** (p. 958). Check your report to make sure that you have used modifiers and clauses correctly.

| Criteria | Rating Scale |
| --- | --- |
| | not very → very |
| **Focus:** How clearly do you state your main idea? | 1  2  3  4  5 |
| **Organization:** How clear and logical is your organization? | 1  2  3  4  5 |
| **Support/Elaboration:** How well do you use evidence to support your statements? | 1  2  3  4  5 |
| **Style:** How clearly do you present the sources you used for research? | 1  2  3  4  5 |
| **Conventions:** According to an accepted format, how complete and accurate are your citations? Did you use subordinate clauses effectively? | 1  2  3  4  5 |

# Vocabulary Workshop

## Borrowed and Foreign Words

A number of English words have been taken directly from other languages. For example, words related to fruit or weather such as *tomato* and *hurricane* are borrowed from Native American languages. Many words borrowed from French relate to art or literature. For example, the word *critique* as a noun means "a critical essay or review." As a verb, *critique* means "to write a critical essay or review." The chart shows some borrowed and foreign words that have become part of the English language.

© **Common Core State Standards**

**Language**
**4.a.** Use context as a clue to the meaning of a word or phrase.
**4.d.** Verify the preliminary determination of the meaning of a word or phrase.

| Borrowed Word | Meaning | Example Sentence |
|---|---|---|
| café — French | coffee shop | Let's have dessert at a *café*. |
| balcony — Italian | a porch | The *balcony* overlooked the garden. |
| canyon — Spanish | a long, narrow valley | Our house has a view of the *canyon*. |

**Practice A** Use a dictionary to find the original language for each of these borrowed English words.

**1.** pretzel    **3.** bagel    **5.** waffle

**2.** burrito    **4.** curry    **6.** barbecue

Recall that context clues are the words and phrases surrounding a word that you may be unfamiliar with. Context clues can help you uncover the meaning of an unfamiliar word.

**Practice B** Use context clues to help you figure out the meaning of the italicized foreign words and phrases. Check a dictionary if you need help.

1. Darlene was impressed by the colorful *macaw* she saw sitting on the branches of a tree.

2. Bennie called out *"Ciao!"* as he left the party to go home.

3. While in Mexico, Jaime bought a *sombrero* to shade her from the sun's hot rays.

4. Duane told us all the boring details of his vacation, *ad nauseum.*

5. The students in the *anime* club like to illustate their favorite characters.

6. We like living on a street that is a *cul-de-sac* because there isn't much traffic.

7. Keisha had a strong sense of *dèjá vu* when she came to our town, although she had never been here before.

8. Just before parting with his friends at the Tokyo airport, James said, *"Sayonara."*

**Activity** Read each of the borrowed words related to music. Then, on a chart like the one shown, write each word next to the language from which it comes.

| suite | tempo | glockenspiel |
|-------|-------|--------------|
| ensemble | crescendo | piano |
| waltz | bassoon | violin |

| Language of Origin | Music Words |
|--------------------|-------------|
| Italian | |
| French | |
| German | |

**PHLit Online!**
www.PHLitOnline.com
- Illustrated vocabulary words
- Interactive vocabulary games
- Vocabulary flashcards

**Comprehension and Collaboration**

Some borrowed words come from the names of people or places. With two or three classmates, find the origin of each of these words: *frankfurter, argyle, cologne, manila paper, sandwich, denim, maverick, teddy bear, bloomers,* and *jersey.* Compare your findings with those of another group.

## Delivering a Narrative Presentation

In a **narrative presentation,** you organize and deliver information to tell a story that will inform or entertain your audience.

### Learn the Skills

**Consider your audience.** To increase the effectiveness of your presentation, take the time to analyze your audience. A profile like the one shown can help you identify the interests, concerns, and knowledge level of your listeners. Use your answers to help you choose the right words and details.

**Choose details wisely.** The events you choose for your narrative should be ones that help you tell a dramatic or informative story. Choose significant events that have a clear progression and that you can illustrate with specific action, description, and even dialogue.

**Practice beforehand.** Rehearsing will help you get comfortable with the words and find the right gestures, body movements, and voice modulations.

**Use appropriate sentences.** Speak in complete sentences, using correct grammar and the active voice. Save slang and sentence fragments for dialogue only. For added impact, vary your sentences by

- mixing short, powerful sentences with longer ones.
- using an interesting assortment of sentence openings.
- using correlatives—word pairs like *either/or*—and subordinate clauses, such as *As a result of the accident,* to indicate relationships between ideas (see pages 570 and 958).

**Focus on word choice.** Match your vocabulary to your audience and purpose. Use specific nouns and verbs as well as interesting, vivid adjectives. Choose words that help convey the mood of your story and bring it to life for your audience.

**Use audience feedback.** Gauge your audience's reactions in order to make adjustments to vocabulary level, organization, pacing, tone, and emphasis. If an audience seems confused by unfamiliar terms, define them using appositives (see page 785). If listeners appear bored, pick up the pace and skip unnecessary sections or details.

**Common Core
State Standards**

**Speaking and Listening**
**6.** Adapt speech to a variety of contexts and tasks, demonstrating command of formal English when indicated or appropriate.

**Audience Profile**
- What is the average age of my audience?
- What do they already know about my topic?
- What steps are necessary to understand this subject?
- What details will be most interesting to my audience?
- What background do I need to provide?

## Practice the Skills

© **Presentation of Knowledge and Ideas** Use what you've learned in this workshop to perform the following task.

> ### ACTIVITY: Prepare and Deliver a Narrative Presentation
>
> Prepare and deliver a brief narrative presentation about a time that you learned a valuable lesson. For example, you might discuss working hard to achieve a goal, discovering the value of teamwork, or overcoming a setback. In choosing your topic, consider how your audience might benefit from hearing the experience you are relating. To help you construct your presentation, answer the following questions.
>
> - Is my purpose in relating the narrative clear?
> - Have I described how others might benefit from hearing my narrative?
> - What background information will I need to provide for my presentation to be clear and easy to follow?
> - Do I present events in a logical sequence?
> - Are the events clearly related to each other and do they build toward the overall point I am trying to make?

As your classmates make their presentations, pay close attention and consider their narratives. Use the Presentation Checklist below to analyze their presentations.

> ### Presentation Checklist
>
> Does the presentation meet all of the requirements of the activity?
> Check all that apply.
>
> - ❏ The subject is appropriate for the audience.
> - ❏ The events of the narrative have a clear progression.
> - ❏ The speaker used action, description, and, if appropriate, dialogue.
>
> **Presentation Delivery**
> Did the speaker deliver the narrative well?
> Check all that apply.
>
> - ❏ The speaker used varied sentences and descriptive word choices.
> - ❏ The speaker used gestures and modulated his or her voice.
> - ❏ The speaker made adjustments as needed, according to audience feedback.

© **Comprehension and Collaboration** After you and your classmates have delivered your presentations, form small discussion groups. Group members should refer to their Presentation Checklists to provide feedback on each person's presentation, noting successes and areas for improvement.

# Cumulative Review

**Common Core**
**State Standards**

**RL.8.1, RL.8.3; W.8.2.b; L.8.4.a**
[For the full wording of the standards, see the standards chart in the front of your textbook.]

## I. Reading Literature

**Directions:** *Read the scene. Then, answer each question.*

*[The setting is a castle room in a mythical land. The* KING *sits in a big, plush chair. His 14-year-old daughter,* PRINCESS PRISCILLA, *enters.]*

**PRISCILLA.** Father, I am troubled. Troubled at heart.

**KING.** Why, Priscilla, what have you to be troubled with? You are young and care-free—are you burdened by your studies?

**PRISCILLA.** My studies? No, not at all.

**KING.** And you are too young to be in love.

**PRISCILLA.** I disagree with that, but I am not troubled by love.

**KING.** Then what? You know you can talk to me.

**PRISCILLA.** Well then, Father, I will come right to the point. [*Like a trial lawyer*] I have learned from the maids and cooks in our kitchen that you pay them one silver coin each month.

**KING.** That is true.

**PRISCILLA.** [*Passionately*] And yet you pay the *men* who work in the house and gardens one *gold* coin per month. The women keep house for us, cook, and serve us three meals each day. They work from before sunup to after sundown, inhale all our dust and only know if the sky is bright or cloudy by the light coming through the small windows into the castle. Surely, women deserve the same coin as the men who work outdoors and can breathe the crisp, fall air . . . [*Her voice trails off. Then, in a demanding tone.*] Why do you <u>discriminate</u> by giving the men gold and the women silver?
[*The KING takes a deep breath and gestures, but no words come out. He tries again. PRISCILLA taps her foot impatiently.*]

**PRISCILLA.** Well?

**KING.** [*Finally*] Because that is the way we have always done it?

**PRISCILLA.** Is that an answer or a question?

**KING.** [*Befuddled*] I do not know.

**PRISCILLA.** [*With patience and sympathy*] Father, I will leave you to your thoughts, but I would like to discuss this after my studies.

**KING.** [*Recovering, glad for a change of topic*] Yes, my dear, during lunch. And what are you studying this morning?

**PRISCILLA.** [*Brightly*] Economics!

**KING.** Ahhh, well, I'd better rest. [*He slouches and dozes off.*]

1. Which of the following is emphasized in the **stage directions** at the beginning of the play?
   A. The setting of the scene
   B. The reasons behind characters' speech and actions
   C. The development of the characters
   D. The characters' emotions

2. Based on their **dialogue**, which statement best describes the relationship between Priscilla and the King?
   A. He spoils her and she often takes advantage of him.
   B. He does not allow her to question his decisions.
   C. They are used to speaking openly with each other.
   D. He supervises her with a firm hand.

3. What conflict propels the **plot** of this scene?
   A. The King faces a revolt from his servants.
   B. The Princess struggles to gain independence.
   C. The King refuses to listen to the Princess's ideas.
   D. The Princess and her father have different views regarding servants.

4. What is Priscilla's likely **motivation** for challenging her father's payment practices?
   A. She believes the women work hard and should be paid the same as the men.
   B. She wants to have fun by upsetting her father with challenging questions.
   C. She wants to practice leadership skills to prepare herself to be queen.
   D. She wants to utilize what she is learning in economics.

5. Which description best fits this **stage direction** about the King: "[*Befuddled*]"?
   A. The King is tired and has lost his train of thought.
   B. The King is angry about Priscilla talking to the cooks and maids.
   C. The King is not sure whether to take Priscilla seriously.
   D. The King is surprised and confused by Priscilla's sudden challenge.

6. **Vocabulary** Which word or phrase is closest in meaning to the underlined word <u>discriminate</u>?
   A. make unfair choices
   B. decide
   C. justify
   D. make an excuse

7. Which statement *best* describes a **conclusion** that can be drawn about Priscilla, based on her dialogue and actions?
   A. She is afraid to confront her father.
   B. She stands up for what she believes in.
   C. She does not enjoy her studies.
   D. She wants only to please her father.

 Timed Writing

8. In an essay, describe Priscilla's **character traits. Support** your description with examples from the **dialogue** and **stage directions.**

 GO ON

## II. Reading Informational Text

**Directions:** *Read the passage. Then, answer the questions that follow.*

**Common Core State Standards**

RI.8.2, RI.8.5; L.8.3
[For the full wording of the standards, see the standards chart in the front of your textbook.]

### Smithtown Pool Rules

- All children under five must be accompanied by an adult.
- Diving is not permitted in the shallow end or from the pool's sides.
- No glass containers are allowed in the pool area.
- No running, hard shoving, or horseplay will be <u>tolerated</u>.
- Guests must be accompanied by members.
- Above all, keep in mind that the pool is here for everyone's enjoyment. Rowdy behavior ruins the experience for everyone.

### Application Process for Lifeguard Positions

1. Check our Web site for open positions, posted weekly.
2. Apply online for the position for which you are interested.
3. We will call you in for an interview, based on your qualifications.
4. Bring your lifeguard certification with you to the interview.
5. After the interview, we will perform a background check.
6. If your application is approved, you will need to complete the appropriate paperwork before your first day of work.

1. Which **generalization** could you make about the people who wrote the pool rules?
   - **A.** They want to keep children out.
   - **B.** They are interested in making money.
   - **C.** Safety is their primary concern.
   - **D.** Their goal is for guests to enjoy themselves.

2. How are the purposes of these materials different?
   - **A.** one is intended for a wider audience than the other
   - **B.** one is meant to inform; the other to entertain
   - **C.** one is meant for adults; the other for children
   - **D.** one is meant to persuade; the other to entertain

3. Which of the following *best* describes the structural patterns of these two materials?
   - **A.** The first is organized chronologically; the second is organized step-by-step.
   - **B.** The first is organized by order of importance; the second is organized chronologically.
   - **C.** The first is organized randomly; the second is organized step-by-step.
   - **D.** The first is organized step-by-step; the second is organized chronologically.

# III. Writing and Language Conventions

## Workplace Writing: Business Letter

**Directions:** *Read the passage. Then, answer the questions that follow.*

> You-Play-It Players
> 664 South Street
> Casaterra, CA  10000
>
> To Whom It May Concern:
>
> (1) I recently bought a faulty MP3 player from your company. (2) I press "play." (3) The unit makes an awful squeal.
>    (4) I have attempted to solve the problem. (5) I have called the number in the warranty several times. (6) My calls are never answered. (7) Please contact me so that we can arrange to fix the player by telephone. (8) Listening to music is my favorite hobby, so I hope we can take care of this without further delay. (9) You really need to tell your customer service representatives to wake up and do a better job.
>    (10) Sincerely,
>
>    Liz Alvarez

1. What **formatting** change would make this business letter conform to correct style?
   A. Move the inside address to the right.
   B. Eliminate indents.
   C. Combine paragraphs 1 and 2.
   D. Remove space after the salutation.

2. Which of the following is the best way to combine sentences 2 and 3, using a **subordinate clause?**
   A. I press "play"; the unit squeals.
   B. Whenever I press "play," the unit squeals.
   C. When I press "play"—the unit squeals.
   D. I press "play" and the unit squeals.

3. Which sentence in the letter should be revised to maintain a professional **tone?**
   A. Sentence 1
   B. Sentence 4
   C. Sentence 9
   D. Sentence 10

4. How could the writer *best* combine sentences 4 and 5?
   A. Attempting to solve the problem, I called the number in the warranty several times.
   B. I attempted to solve the problem and called the number in the warranty several times.
   C. I called the number in the warranty several times and tried to solve the problem.
   D. I called several times and no one answered.

STOP

# Performance Tasks

**Directions:** *Follow the instructions to complete the tasks below as required by your teacher.*

*As you work on each task, incorporate both general academic vocabulary and literary terms you learned in this unit.*

**Common Core
State Standards**

RL.8.1, RL.8.2, RL.8.3, RL.8.5; W.8.1, W.8.2; SL.8.1, SL.8.4, SL.8.6; L.8.1
[For the full wording of the standards, see the standards chart in the front of your textbook.]

## Writing

### Task 1: Literature [RL.8.2; W.8.1]
**Analyze the Development of Theme**

*Write an essay in which you focus on the impact of character on theme in one of the drama selections in this unit.*

- Identify the theme of your chosen play.
- Focus on one or more of the main characters in the play. Explain how each character's words or actions relate to or help develop the theme.
- Cite evidence from the drama, including dialogue and stage directions, that supports your claims.
- Check your writing for correct grammar and usage.

### Task 2: Literature [RL.8.3; W.8.2]
**Analyze Dialogue**

*Write an essay in which you analyze how particular lines of dialogue propel the action of a drama selection in this unit.*

- Choose a significant passage of dialogue from one of the plays in this unit.
- Explain how the passage moves the plot forward. Tell how the dialogue provided adds to the conflict, shapes the relationship between characters, or otherwise affects the action.
- Support your ideas with evidence from the text.
- Be sure to quote accurately from the text and to punctuate your quotations correctly.

### Task 3: Literature [RL.8.5; W.8.1]
**Analyze Text Structure**

*Analyze how the structures of literary works help to communicate meaning.*

- From this unit, select two works of different genres with distinctly different structures, such as a drama and a short story.
- Analyze the structure of each. Consider what is particular to each genre, such as stage directions in drama and a narrator in fiction.
- Compare the ways in which each text communicates information to the reader about character, plot, and theme.
- Draw logical, well-supported conclusions about the ways in which text structure contributes to the meaning of a work.
- Make sure you follow standard grammar conventions in your writing.

### Task 4: Literature [RL.8.3; W.8.2]
**Analyze Characterization**

*Analyze characterization in a play in this unit.*

- Select one of the plays in this unit with an interesting character. Tell what you found interesting about this character.
- Determine your character's function in the play—central character, antagonist, and so on.
- Cite specific plot events and dialogue that reveal aspects of your character. Explain.
- Review your completed essay for correct grammar, punctuation, and spelling.

# Speaking and Listening

## Task 5: Literature [RL.8.1; SL.8.4, SL.8.6]

### Analyze and Interpret a Speech

*Prepare an oral presentation in which you analyze a speech by a character in one of the plays in this unit. As part of your presentation, perform the speech in front of the class.*

- Select a significant speech from one of the plays in this unit. Reread it carefully, looking up any unfamiliar words in a dictionary.

- Analyze the message of the speech. It may contain arguments and specific claims. It may reveal something about the character or the plot. It may contribute to the overall theme of the play.

- Present your analysis to the class. Then, perform the speech in front of the class. Make decisions as to how the character should behave; if he or she is angry, upset, or confident, be sure your performance reflects this interpretation.

- Invite questions from the audience and respond with relevant evidence and ideas.

## Task 6: Literature [RL.8.1; SL.8.4]

### Critical Review

*Prepare and deliver a critical review of a play.*

- Select a play from this unit about which you have a definite opinion. The opinion may be either positive or negative.

- Cite your opinion and support it with logic and evidence. Include specific details from the text. Acknowledge both strong and weak points of the play.

- Write your points down on note cards. Put the cards in the most logical order and practice presenting them.

- Present your review to the class. Use appropriate eye contact, adequate volume, and clear pronunciation.

- Conclude your presentation with a question-and-answer period. When possible, make connections between your ideas and new ideas expressed by others.

## Task 7: Literature [RL.8.3; SL.8.1]

### Compare and Contrast Characters

*Lead a small group discussion in which you compare and contrast two characters in plays from this unit.*

- Choose two characters from different plays in this unit who share at least one key trait.

- Determine the similarities and differences of these characters and their effects on the action of the play.

- Come to the discussion prepared with your analysis of both characters. Prepare a list of questions to guide the discussion.

- Follow rules for collegial discussions. Keep the discussion balanced. Based on contributions from the group, pose further questions.

- Wrap up the discussion with a recap of the key points presented.

> **THE BIG ?**
>
> **Is it our differences or our similarities that matter most?**
>
> At the beginning of Unit 5, you participated in a discussion about the Big Question. Now that you have finished the unit, write a response to the question. Discuss how your views have developed—whether they have changed or been reinforced. Give specific examples from the plays, as well as from other subjects and your personal experiences, to support your ideas. Use Big Question vocabulary words (see p. 803) in your response.

# Featured Titles

In this unit, you have read a variety of dramatic works. Continue to read on your own. Select works that you enjoy, but challenge yourself to explore new playwrights and works of increasing depth and complexity. The titles suggested below will help you get started.

## Literature

### Eight Plays of U.S. History

Learn about important events in United States history in this collection of engaging **plays** that explores freedom, justice, culture, and social themes.

### Escape to Freedom: A Play About Young Frederick Douglass
by Ossie Davis

This **play** is an account of Douglass's early life. Douglass secretly taught himself to read in violation of state law, escaped from a brutal master, and became a forceful voice in the movement to abolish slavery.

### Nerdlandia
by Gary Soto

Martin and Ceci have crushes on each other. Martin tries to make himself cooler to appeal to Ceci, while Ceci tries to make herself nerdier to appeal to Martin. This unusual situation lays the groundwork for a funny **play** about the superficial differences between people.

### The Mousetrap and Other Plays
by Agatha Christie
NAL Trade, 2000

Full of plot twists and potential suspects, these eight **plays** by famed mystery writer Agatha Christie will delight murder-mystery buffs.

### Henry Wadsworth Longfellow: Poems and Other Writings
by Henry Wadsworth Longfellow

**EXEMPLAR TEXT** ©

When you enroll in college at age fifteen and become a professor at eighteen, clearly great things are expected of you. Longfellow did not disappoint, as he went on to write such beloved poems as "Paul Revere's Ride," included in this **anthology.**

### Anne Frank and Me
by Cherie Bennett and Jeff Gottesfeld

This **novel** presents the Holocaust through the eyes of a modern teenager. Nicole, a bored student, is suddenly jolted back in time. She meets Anne Frank in a cattle car filled with Jews bound for a concentration camp and experiences the horrors of the time firsthand.

## Informational Texts

### Narrative of the Life of Frederick Douglass
by Frederick Douglass
Signet, 1997

**EXEMPLAR TEXT** ©

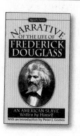

As someone who had personally felt the unimaginable cruelty of slavery, Douglass's was a unique voice for change. Through his powerful **autobiography,** Douglass gave the lie to the common notion that former slaves were incapable of intellectual achievement, and he inspired many readers to question slavery for the first time.

# Preparing to Read Complex Texts

**Attentive Reading** As you read on your own, ask yourself questions about the text. The questions shown below and others that you ask as you read will help you learn and enjoy literature even more.

 **Common Core State Standards**

**Reading Literature/Informational Text**
**10.** By the end of the year, read and comprehend literature, including stories, dramas, and poems, and literary nonfiction at the high end of grades 6–8 text complexity band independently and proficiently.

## When reading drama, ask yourself...

- Who is the main character? What struggles does this character face?
- What other characters are important? How do these characters relate to the main character?
- Where and when does the play take place? Do the time and place of the setting affect the characters? If so, how?
- Do the characters, settings, and events seem real? Why or why not?
- How does the play end? How does the ending make me feel?
- What theme or insight do I think the playwright is expressing? Do I find that theme to be important and true?

© **Key Ideas and Details**

- Does the play have a narrator? If so, what information does the narrator provide?
- Does the playwright include background information? If so, how does this help me understand what I am reading?
- How many acts are in this play? What happens in each act?
- Does the dialogue sound like real speech? Are there specific passages that seem especially real? Are there any that seem false?
- What do the stage directions tell me about the ways characters move, speak, and feel? In what other ways do I learn about the characters?
- At what point in the play do I feel the most suspense? Why?
- What speech or passage in the play do I like the most? Why?
- Does the playwright seem to have a positive or a negative point of view? How do I think the playwright's point of view affects the story?
- Do I agree with the playwright's point of view? Why or why not?

© **Craft and Structure**

- Does the play remind me of others I have read or seen? If so, how?
- In what ways is the play different from others I have read or seen?
- What new information or ideas have I gained from reading this play?
- What actors would I choose to play each role in this play?
- If I were to be in this play, what role would I want?
- Would I recommend this play to others? Why or why not?

© **Integration of Ideas**

# Are yesterday's *heroes* important today?

Unit

# 6

**PHLit**
# Online!
### www.PHLitOnline.com

### *Hear It!*
- Selection summary audio
- Selection audio
- BQ Tunes

### *See It!*
- Author videos
- Big Question video
- Get Connected videos
- Background videos
- More about the authors
- Illustrated vocabulary words
- Vocabulary flashcards

### *Do It!*
- Interactive journals
- Interactive graphic organizers
- Grammar tutorials
- Interactive vocabulary games
- Test practice

# Are yesterday's *heroes* important today?

Heroes are known for their bravery and their willingness to stand up for what they believe despite opposition. Some heroes become famous for their physical skills; others are admired for their kindness or intelligence. At times, stories about the challenges a hero overcomes are exaggerated to impress an audience.

Stories of all kinds of heroes come from folklore, literature, and real life, and they are passed down from generation to generation. Some heroes endure while others become outdated. Heroes who stand the test of time have the ability to inspire people of different historical periods and cultural backgrounds.

## Exploring the Big Question

**Collaboration: One-on-One Discussion** Start thinking about the Big Question by making a list of people you admire, whether from history, literature, contemporary life, or your personal experience. Make a list of examples of heroic deeds like these:

- rescuing someone from a dangerous situation
- taking an unpopular position to defend a principle
- sacrificing for others so that they might succeed
- preserving dignity despite forces that try to degrade or destroy
- helping people who are in need

    Share your examples with a partner. Talk about the aspects of the actions that make them heroic. Build on your partner's ideas, responding to each with related ideas of your own.

**Connecting to the Literature** Each reading in this unit will give you additional insight into the Big Question.

**PHLit Online!**
www.PHLitOnline.com
- Big Question video
- Illustrated vocabulary words
- Interactive vocabulary games
- BQ Tunes

# Learning Big Question Vocabulary

@ **Acquire and Use Academic Vocabulary** Academic vocabulary is the language you encounter in textbooks and on standardized tests. Review the definitions of these academic vocabulary words.

---

**aspects** (as´ pekts´) *n.* ways an idea or problem may be viewed or seen

**cultural** (kul´ chər əl) *adj.* relating to the customs and beliefs of a group

**emphasize** (em´ fə sīz´) *v.* stress; give one idea more importance than others

**exaggerate** (eg zaj´ ər āt´) *v.* speak of something as being

greater or more important than it is

**imitate** (im´ i tāt´) *v.* copy; follow the example of

**influence** (in´ floo əns) *v.* affect others' views, habits, plans, and so on

**symbolize** (sim´ bə līz´) *v.* stand for; take the place of and signify an idea

---

Use these words as you complete Big Question activities in this unit that involve reading, writing, speaking, and listening.

@ **Gather Vocabulary Knowledge** Additional Big Question words are listed below. Categorize the words by deciding whether you know each one well, know it a little bit, or do not know it at all.

---

| | | |
|---|---|---|
| accomplishments | courage | overcome |
| admirably | endure | suffering |
| bravery | outdated | |

---

Then, do the following:

1. Write the definitions of the words you know.

2. Consult a dictionary to confirm the definitions of the words you know. Revise your definitions if necessary.

3. Using a print or an online dictionary, look up the meanings of the words you do not know. Then, write the meanings.

4. Use all of the words in a brief paragraph about heroes.

@ **Common Core State Standards**

**Speaking and Listening**
**1.** Engage effectively in a range of collaborative discussions with diverse partners on *grade 8 topics, texts, and issues,* building on others' ideas and expressing their own clearly.

**Language**
**6.** Acquire and use accurately grade-appropriate general academic and domain-specific words and phrases; gather vocabulary knowledge when considering a word or phrase important to comprehension or expression.

# Elements of the American Folk Tradition

## The American folk tradition includes a rich collection of literature, which grew out of the oral tradition.

**Storytelling and the Oral Tradition**
People have always enjoyed telling and listening to stories. Long before reading and writing were invented, societies shared information with the next generation through storytelling. This was the origin of the **oral tradition,** in which stories were passed down over time by word of mouth. Eventually, these stories were collected and written down. American folk literature grew out of this same tradition. Told at festivals, around campfires, and at other gatherings, stories from the oral tradition reflect our culture's richness.

**Themes and Cultural Context** All good stories have a **theme**—a central message or insight about life. Stories in the oral tradition often express universal themes. **Universal themes** recur regularly in stories from many different cultures and time periods. Examples of universal themes include the power of love and the dangers of greed.

In the American folk tradition, universal themes are expressed from an American perspective, or **cultural context.** The stories are inspired by American history, geography, and beliefs. Set against the rugged landscape of America's past, they often celebrate American **heroes** and **heroines.** Some details in the stories are historically true. Others are based on truth but may be greatly exaggerated. This chart shows techniques that are common to the American folk tradition.

**Oral Tradition Storytelling Techniques**

| Technique | Definitions |
|---|---|
| **Hyperbole** | An exaggeration, used for comic effect or to express strong emotion |
| **Understatement** | A way of expressing something that treats it as smaller or less serious than it actually is, often used for comic effect |
| **Personification** | The technique of giving human characteristics to nonhuman subjects |
| **Dialect** | The language and grammar of a particular region or group; used to make dialogue sound realistic and to reflect the story's cultural background |
| **Idioms** | • Expressions that are not meant to be taken literally, such as "It's raining cats and dogs!" <br> • Developed and understood by people of a certain region or group |
| **Informal Speech** | Everyday, conversational language; often includes idioms, slang, and dialect |

## The American Folk Tradition

American folk stories can be divided into different types.

**Myths** explain the actions of gods or other supernatural forces and the heroes who interact with them. Ancient peoples often used mythology to explain natural phenomena.

**Fables** are brief stories that often feature animals that act like humans. The main purpose of a fable is to teach an important life lesson, or **moral.**

**Trickster tales** tell about tricks or pranks and the characters who play them. Trickster characters are typically clever and mischievous.

**Tall tales** rely on **hyperbole**—exaggeration for comic effect. The heroes of these tales perform impossible feats.

**Legends** often originate in fact. Through repeated tellings of a factual story, the real-life characters and events in the story become larger than life, and the story becomes a legend.

**Epics** are long narrative poems about heroes who engage in dangerous journeys, battles, or quests important to the history of a nation or culture.

### The American Folk Hero

American folk literature is a living tradition. Over time, new heroes and subjects appear that reflect the manners, customs, sayings, and stories of our changing culture. For example, American folk heroes of the nineteenth century included patriots, soldiers, farmers, and cowboys. A century later, American folk heroes included sports figures, aviators, civil rights leaders, and astronauts. In the American folk tradition, heroes can be real or fictional. However, they all display traits that Americans admire and strive to imitate.

Common Core State Standards

RL.8.2
[For the full wording of the standards, see the standards chart in the front of your textbook.]

| Common Traits of American Folk Heroes | | | | |
|---|---|---|---|---|
| adventurous determined | honest loyal | strong humble | courageous resourceful | intelligent creative |

| Fictional | Based to Some Degree on Fact | Real |
|---|---|---|
| Paul Bunyan, lumberjack | Johnny "Appleseed" Chapman, farmer | Sacajawea, Native American guide |
| Pecos Bill, cowboy | John Henry, African American steelworker | Rosa Parks, African American civil rights activist |
| Little Sal Fink, known for her powerful scream | Davy Crockett, frontiersman | Roberto Clemente, Hispanic baseball player |

# Determining Themes in American Stories

Themes in the American folk tradition have a distinctly American point of view.

**Common Core State Standards**

**Reading Literature 2.** Determine a theme or central idea of a text and analyze its development over the course of the text, including its relationship to the characters, setting, and plot; provide an objective summary of the text.

Themes in American folk stories express ideas about who we are as a people. These stories often present the American landscape as a challenge. Those who triumph over it are considered heroes and heroines.

**Social and Cultural Context** To recognize the themes in an American folk story, readers should consider the story's **social and cultural context—** the values and customs of the story's original tellers.

America has a rich multicultural heritage shaped by Native Americans, African Americans, Hispanics, Europeans, Asians, and others. All of these groups have contributed stories to the national folk literature. While the themes of these stories are distinctly American, they also reflect the cultures of their tellers.

Factors that can influence a storyteller's view of the world, or **social and cultural perspective,** include the historic events of an era. In America, events such as Westward Expansion, slavery, the Civil War, and the Great Depression deeply influenced those who lived through them. American folk stories often capture how Americans responded to the challenges of such events. The stories emphasize universal American themes such as resourcefulness.

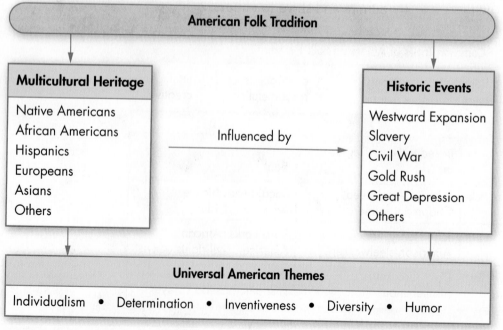

**American Folk Tradition**

| **Multicultural Heritage** | | **Historic Events** |
|---|---|---|
| Native Americans | | Westward Expansion |
| African Americans | Influenced by | Slavery |
| Hispanics | | Civil War |
| Europeans | | Gold Rush |
| Asians | | Great Depression |
| Others | | Others |

**Universal American Themes**

Individualism  •  Determination  •  Inventiveness  •  Diversity  •  Humor

# Analyzing the Development of Theme

As in other literary genres, themes in the American folk tradition are usually developed through details of character, setting, and plot. To determine the theme of a story, read carefully to analyze these details. Think about how the details relate to each other and what underlying message or insight about life they offer.

**Character** A character is a person, an animal, or an imaginary creature that takes part in the action of a story. In American folk stories, main characters often display remarkable confidence, physical strength, determination, and resourcefulness. These qualities allow them to overcome obstacles, no matter how challenging. The words and actions of these characters, as well as the lessons they learn, help to develop themes such as the value of determination.

> **Example: Character**
> Paul Bunyan is an incredibly large, strong, and inventive lumberjack. His deeds illustrate the theme that even the greatest challenge can be overcome through hard work and inventiveness.

**Setting** The setting is the time and place in which the action of a story occurs. American folk stories are often set in real locations. While the places may be real, the details that describe them are often exaggerated to create greater challenges for characters.

> **Example: Setting**
> Paul Bunyan's adventures are set in the logging camps of America's North Woods, in real locations such as Wisconsin and Minnesota.

**Plot and Conflict** Plot is the sequence of events in a story. The plots of many American folk stories, especially legends, are loosely based on real events.

In all stories, the plot is moved forward by the **conflicts,** or struggles that characters face. In American folk stories, the conflicts are often *external* —they take place between a character and an outside force. Characters may face problems posed by another character, the landscape, economics, or other external obstacles. In some cases, external conflicts may cause characters to deal with *internal* conflicts— struggles within themselves. However, most often the primary conflict in the story is external.

> **Example: Plot and Conflict**
> While tales about Paul Bunyan are fictional, the stories often feature activities that actually occurred in logging camps. Paul Bunyan's conflicts reflect the challenges that America's pioneers faced in moving west. These conflicts help to develop themes of determination.

# Close Read: Story Elements and Theme

**Whether traditional or modern, American folk stories consist of elements that reveal theme.**

All story elements work together to express the story's theme, or insight into life. To discover a story's theme, answer the questions in the following chart.

## Clues to Theme in American Folk Stories

### Setting
The setting in folk stories may or may not be specific. As you read, ask yourself

- Where and when does the story take place?
- Is this a real place or an imaginary place?
- If this is a real place, are any details changed or exaggerated?
- What effect does the setting have on the characters and the plot?

### Plot and Conflict
Plot is the sequence of events in a story that show how a conflict develops and is resolved. The main character's response to a conflict can be a key to the theme. As you read, ask yourself

- What conflict, or problem, do the characters face?
- How is the conflict resolved?
- How do the characters feel about the solution?

### Characters
Characters in American folk literature demonstrate traits that many Americans find admirable. The details that reveal these traits often relate to theme. As you read, ask yourself

- Is the main character a real person, a made-up person, or an animal?
- What does the main character say or do?
- How do the characters relate to each other?
- What do the characters learn, or how do the characters change?

### Statements and Observations
Characters or the narrator may make statements or observations that suggest a theme. As you read, ask yourself

- Does a character or the narrator sum up story events?
- Does a character or the narrator make an observation about how characters feel, how characters change, or what characters learn because of story events?

# Model

**About the Text** This excerpt is from the classic American novel *The Adventures of Tom Sawyer* by Mark Twain. The novel is set in the 1840s, in the small Mississippi River town of St. Petersburg, Missouri. In this excerpt, Tom's Aunt Polly sends him out on a Saturday morning to whitewash a fence as punishment for his mischievous behavior the day before.

## from *The Adventures of Tom Sawyer* by Mark Twain

. . . But Tom's energy did not last. He began to think of the fun he had planned for this day, and his sorrows multiplied. Soon the free boys would come tripping along on all sorts of delicious expeditions, and they would make a world of fun of him for having to work—the very thought of it burnt him like fire. He got out his worldly wealth and examined it—bits of toys, marbles, and trash; enough to buy an exchange of *work*, maybe, but not half enough to buy so much as half an hour of pure freedom. So he returned his straitened means to his pocket, and gave up the idea of trying to buy the boys. At this dark and hopeless moment an inspiration burst upon him! Nothing less than a great, magnificent inspiration.

He took up his brush and went tranquilly to work. Ben Rogers hove in sight presently—the very boy, of all boys, whose ridicule he had been dreading. Ben's gait was the hop-skip-and-jump—proof enough that his heart was light and his anticipations high. He was eating an apple, and giving a long, melodious whoop, at intervals, followed by a deep-toned ding-dong-dong, ding-dong-dong, for he was personating a steamboat. As he drew near, he slackened speed, took the middle of the street, leaned far over to star-board and rounded to ponderously and with laborious pomp and circumstance—for he was personating the Big Missouri, and considered himself to be drawing nine feet of water. He was boat and captain and engine-bells combined, so he had to imagine himself standing on his own hurricane-deck giving the orders and executing them:

"Stop her, sir! Ting-a-ling-ling!" The headway ran almost out, and he drew up slowly toward the sidewalk.

"Ship up to back! Ting-a-ling-ling!" His arms straightened and stiffened down his sides.

"Set her back on the stabboard! Ting-a-ling-ling! Chow! ch-chow-wow! Chow!" His right hand, meantime, describing stately circles—for it was representing a forty-foot wheel.

**Plot and Conflict** Tom's problem is that he has to work while all his friends play. His attempt to solve this problem sets the plot in motion.

**Characters** Although Tom is unhappy, he works "tranquilly" to trick Ben Rogers into believing he is having fun. Tom's trickery is a key to the story's theme.

ⓒ EXEMPLAR TEXT

## Model continued

"Let her go back on the labboard! Ting-a-ling-ling! Chow-ch-chow-chow!" The left hand began to describe circles.

"Stop the stabboard! Ting-a-ling-ling! Stop the labboard! Come ahead on the stabboard! Stop her! Let your outside turn over slow! Ting-a-ling-ling! Chow-ow-ow! Get out that head-line! *Lively* now! Come—out with your spring-line—what're you about there! Take a turn round that stump with the bight of it! Stand by that stage, now—let her go! Done with the engines, sir! Ting-a-ling-ling! *Sh't! s'h't! sh't!*" (trying the gauge-cocks).

Tom went on whitewashing—paid no attention to the steamboat. Ben stared a moment and then said: *"Hi-yi! You're* up a stump, ain't you!"

No answer. Tom surveyed his last touch with the eye of an artist, then he gave his brush another gentle sweep and surveyed the result, as before. Ben ranged up alongside of him. Tom's mouth watered for the apple, but he stuck to his work. Ben said:

"Hello, old chap, you got to work, hey?"

Tom wheeled suddenly and said:

"Why, it's you, Ben! I warn't noticing."

"Say—*I'm* going in a-swimming, *I* am. Don't you wish you could? But of course you'd druther *work*—wouldn't you? Course you would!"

Tom contemplated the boy a bit, and said:

"What do you call work?"

"Why, ain't *that* work?"

Tom resumed his whitewashing, and answered carelessly:

"Well, maybe it is, and maybe it ain't. All I know, is, it suits Tom Sawyer."

"Oh come, now, you don't mean to let on that you *like* it?"

The brush continued to move.

"Like it? Well, I don't see why I oughtn't to like it. Does a boy get a chance to whitewash a fence every day?"

That put the thing in a new light. Ben stopped nibbling his apple. Tom swept his brush daintily back and forth—stepped back to note the effect—added a touch here and there—criticised the effect again—Ben watching every move and getting more and more interested, more and more absorbed. Presently he said:

"Say, Tom, let *me* whitewash a little."

**Setting** The fact that it is a hot summer Saturday plays a key role in the conflict. Tom would rather go swimming than paint the fence.

Tom considered, was about to consent; but he altered his mind:

"No—no—I reckon it wouldn't hardly do, Ben. You see, Aunt Polly's awful particular about this fence—right here on the street, you know—but if it was the back fence I wouldn't mind and *she* wouldn't. Yes, she's awful particular about this fence; it's got to be done very careful; I reckon there ain't one boy in a thousand, maybe two thousand, that can do it the way it's got to be done."

"No—is that so? Oh come, now—lemme just try. Only just a little—I'd let *you*, if you was me, Tom."

"Ben, I'd like to, honest injun; but Aunt Polly—well, Jim wanted to do it, but she wouldn't let him; Sid wanted to do it, and she wouldn't let Sid. Now don't you see how I'm fixed? If you was to tackle this fence and anything was to happen to it—"

"Oh, shucks, I'll be just as careful. Now lemme try. Say—I'll give you the core of my apple."

"Well, here—No, Ben, now don't. I'm afeard —"

"I'll give you *all* of it!"

Tom gave up the brush with reluctance in his face, but alacrity in his heart. And while the late steamer Big Missouri worked and sweated in the sun, the retired artist sat on a barrel in the shade close by, dangled his legs, munched his apple, and planned the slaughter of more innocents. There was no lack of material; boys happened along every little while; they came to jeer, but remained to whitewash. By the time Ben was fagged out, Tom had traded the next chance to Billy Fisher for a kite, in good repair; and when *he* played out, Johnny Miller bought in for a dead rat and a string to swing it with—and so on, and so on, hour after hour. And when the middle of the afternoon came, from being a poor poverty-stricken boy in the morning, Tom was literally rolling in wealth. He had besides the things before mentioned, twelve marbles, part of a jews-harp, a piece of blue bottle-glass to look through, a spool cannon, a key that wouldn't unlock anything, a fragment of chalk, a glass stopper of a decanter, a tin soldier, a couple of tadpoles, six fire-crackers, a kitten with only one eye, a brass doorknob, a dog-collar—but no dog—the handle of a knife, four pieces of orange-peel, and a dilapidated old window sash.

He had had a nice, good, idle time all the while—plenty of company—and the fence had three coats of whitewash on it! If he hadn't run out of whitewash he would have bankrupted every boy in the village.

Tom said to himself that it was not such a hollow world, after all. He had discovered a great law of human action, without knowing it—namely, that in order to make a man or a boy covet a thing, it is only necessary to make the thing difficult to attain.

**Characters** By cleverly suggesting that Ben cannot do as good a job as he can, Tom makes Ben want to paint even more. This interaction relates to the theme.

**Theme** Tom tricks the other boys into doing his work for him. The theme might be stated like this: *A person can outwit a fool with cleverness.*

**Statements and Observations** The narrator states that Tom has discovered you can make people want something just by making it difficult to attain. This observation is closely related to the theme.

# Independent Practice

**About the Selection** Author Lan Samantha Chang grew up in Appleton, Wisconsin. There, she lived with her parents, sisters, and grandmother, Waipuo, who was born in Shanghai, China. This story was inspired by a story Waipuo told Chang and her sisters.

### "Water Names" by Lan Samantha Chang

Summertime at dusk we'd gather on the back porch, tired and sticky from another day of fierce encoded quarrels, nursing our mosquito bites and frail dignities, sisters in name only. At first we'd pinch and slap each other, fighting for the best—least ragged—folding chair. Then we'd argue over who would sit next to our grandmother. We were so close together on the tiny porch that we often pulled our own hair by mistake. Forbidden to bite, we planted silent toothmarks on each others' wrists. We ignored the bulk of house behind us, the yard, the fields, the darkening sky. We even forgot about our grandmother. Then suddenly we'd hear her old, dry voice, very close, almost on the backs of our necks.

"*Xiushila!* Shame on you. Fighting like a bunch of chickens."

And Ingrid, the oldest, would freeze with her thumb and forefinger right on the back of Lily's arm. I would slide my hand away from the end of Ingrid's braid. Ashamed, we would shuffle our feet while Waipuo calmly found her chair.

On some nights she sat with us in silence. But on some nights she told us stories, "just to keep up your Chinese," she said.

"In these prairie crickets I often hear the sound of rippling waters, of the Yangtze River," she said. "Granddaughters, you are descended on both sides from people of the water country, near the mouth of the great Chang Jiang, as it is called, where the river is so grand and broad that even on clear days you can scarcely see the other side.

"The Chang Jiang runs four thousand miles, originating in the Himalaya mountains where it crashes, flecked with gold dust, down steep cliffs so perilous and remote that few humans have ever seen them. In central China, the river squeezes through deep gorges, then widens in its last thousand miles to the sea. Our ancestors have lived near the mouth of this river, the ever-changing delta, near a city called Nanjing, for more than a thousand years."

**Characters** Why might Waipuo want her granddaughters to "keep up" their Chinese?

**Setting** How does Waipuo form a picture of the Yangtze delta in her granddaughters' minds? Why do you think she does this?

"A thousand years," murmured Lily, who was only ten. When she was younger she had sometimes burst into nervous crying at the thought of so many years. Her small insistent fingers grabbed my fingers in the dark.

"Through your mother and I you are descended from a line of great men and women. We have survived countless floods and seasons of ill-fortune because we have the spirit of the river in us. Unlike mountains, we cannot be powdered down or broken apart. Instead, we run together, like raindrops. Our strength and spirit wear down mountains into sand. But even our people must respect the water."

She paused. "When I was young, my own grandmother once told me the story of Wen Zhiqing's daughter. Twelve hundred years ago the civilized parts of China still lay to the north, and the Yangtze valley lay unspoiled. In those days lived an ancestor named Wen Zhiqing, a resourceful man, and proud. He had been fishing for many years with trained cormorants, which you girls of course have never seen. Cormorants are sleek, black birds with long, bending necks which the fishermen fitted with metal rings so the fish they caught could not be swallowed. The birds would perch on the side of the old wooden boat and dive into the river." We had only known blue swimming pools, but we tried to imagine the sudden shock of cold and the plunge, deep into water.

"Now, Wen Zhiqing had a favorite daughter who was very beautiful and loved the river. She would beg to go out on the boat with him. This daughter was a restless one, never contented with their catch, and often she insisted they stay out until it was almost dark. Even then, she was not satisfied. She had been spoiled by her father, kept protected from the river, so she could not see its danger. To this young woman, the river was as familiar as the sky. It was a bright, broad road stretching out to curious lands. She did not fully understand the river's depths.

"One clear spring evening, as she watched the last bird dive off into the blackening waters, she said, 'If only this catch would bring back something more than another fish!'

"She leaned over the side of the boat and looked at the water. The stars and moon reflected back at her. And it is said that the spirits living underneath the water looked up at her as well. And the spirit of a young man who had drowned in the river many years before saw her lovely face."

We had heard about the ghosts of the drowned, who wait forever in the water for a living person to pull down instead. A faint breeze moved through the mosquito screens and we shivered.

**Characters** How does Waipuo feel about the Yangtze River? How can you tell?

**Plot** The river is both familiar and unknown to the daughter. How might this detail influence the plot?

**Plot** What traditional folk element does this plot event include?

**Practice continued**

"The cormorant was gone for a very long time," Waipuo said, "so long that the fisherman grew puzzled. Then, suddenly, the bird emerged from the waters, almost invisible in the night. Wen Zhiqing grasped his catch, a very large fish, and guided the boat back to shore. And when Wen reached home, he gutted the fish and discovered, in its stomach, a valuable pearl ring."

"From the man?" said Lily.

"Sshh, she'll tell you."

Waipuo ignored us. "His daughter was delighted that her wish had been fulfilled. What most excited her was the idea of an entire world like this, a world where such a beautiful ring would be only a bauble![1] For part of her had always longed to see faraway things and places. The river had put a spell on her heart. In the evenings she began to sit on the bank, looking at her own reflection in the water. Sometimes she said she saw a handsome young man looking back at her. And her yearning for him filled her heart with sorrow and fear, for she knew that she would soon leave her beloved family.

"'It's just the moon,' said Wen Zhiqing, but his daughter shook her head. 'There's a kingdom under the water,' she said. 'The prince is asking me to marry him. He sent the ring as an offering to you.' 'Nonsense,' said her father, and he forbade her to sit by the water again.

"For a year things went as usual, but the next spring there came a terrible flood that swept away almost everything. In the middle of a torrential rain, the family noticed that the daughter was missing. She had taken advantage of the confusion to hurry to the river and visit her beloved. The family searched for days but they never found her."

Her smoky, rattling voice came to a stop.

"What happened to her?" Lily said.

"It's okay, stupid," I told her. "She was so beautiful that she went to join the kingdom of her beloved. Right?"

"Who knows?" Waipuo said. "They say she was seduced by a water ghost. Or perhaps she lost her mind to desiring."

"What do you mean?" asked Ingrid.

**Characters** What does the daughter's reaction to the ring reveal about her? What important idea do these details suggest?

**Statements and Observations** What does Waipuo say happened to the daughter? How might this relate to the story's theme?

---

1. **bauble** (bô´bəl) *n.* trinket.

"I'm going inside," Waipuo said, and got out of her chair with a creak. A moment later the light went on in her bedroom window. We knew she stood before the mirror, combing out her long, wavy silver-gray hair, and we imagined that in her youth she too had been beautiful.

We sat together without talking. We had gotten used to Waipuo's abruptness, her habit of creating a question and leaving without answering it, as if she were disappointed in the question itself. We tried to imagine Wen Zhiqing's daughter. What did she look like? How old was she? Why hadn't anyone remembered her name?

While we weren't watching, the stars had emerged. Their brilliant pinpoints mapped the heavens. They glittered over us, over Waipuo in her room, the house, and the small city we lived in, the great waves of grass that ran for miles around us, the ground beneath as dry and hard as bone.

## After You Read — Water Names

**1. Key Ideas and Details**
**(a) Summarize:** Write an **objective summary** of "Water Names." In your summary, include only central ideas and key details from the story. Do not include your own personal opinions or judgments. **(b) Interpret:** What do you think is the climax, or high point, of the story?

**2. Key Ideas and Details**
**(a) Speculate:** Why might the grandmother want to tell Chinese legends to her granddaughters?
**(b) Draw Conclusions:** Do you think these stories matter to the author and her sisters? Explain.

**3. Key Ideas and Details (a) Infer:** What is one **theme** in this story?
**(b) Analyze:** What story details combine to reveal that theme?

**4. Craft and Structure Identify:** Identify at least two examples of storytelling techniques or details in the story that are part of the **oral tradition.**

**5. Integration of Knowledge and Ideas (a)** In a chart like the one shown, use the second column to list possible explanations for two unusual events in the story. **(b)** Exchange charts with a partner, and use the third column to explain why you agree or disagree with each explanation.

| Event | Explanation | Why You Agree or Disagree |
|---|---|---|
| Face in the water | | |
| Ring in the fish | | |

**(c) Collaborate:** With your partner, choose the more persuasive explanation of each event to share with the class.

## ⓒ Leveled Texts

Build your skills and improve your comprehension of literature with texts of increasing complexity.

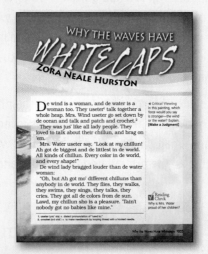

Read **"Coyote Steals the Sun and Moon"** to find out what happens when a wise eagle crosses paths with a mischief-making coyote.

Read **"Why the Waves Have Whitecaps"** to witness the results of an argument between Mrs. Wind and Mrs. Water over who has better children.

## ⓒ Common Core State Standards

Meet these standards with either **"Coyote Steals the Sun and Moon"** (p. 1026) or **"Why the Waves Have Whitecaps"** (p. 1032).

### Reading Literature
**2.** Determine a theme or central idea of a text and analyze its development over the course of the text, including its relationship to the characters, setting, and plot; provide an objective summary of the text. *(Reading Skill: Summarize; Literary Analysis: Mythology)*

### Writing
**3.** Write narratives to develop real or imagined experiences or events using effective technique, relevant descriptive details, and well-structured event sequences. **3.b.** Use narrative techniques, such as dialogue, pacing, description, and reflection, to develop experiences, events, and/or characters. **3.e.** Provide a conclusion that follows from and reflects on the narrated experiences or events. *(Writing: Myth)*

### Speaking and Listening
**5.** Integrate multimedia and visual displays into presentations to clarify information, strengthen claims and evidence, and add interest.

**6.** Adapt speech to a variety of contexts and tasks, demonstrating command of formal English when indicated or appropriate. *(Speaking and Listening: Oral Presentation)*

### Language
**1.** Demonstrate command of the conventions of standard English grammar and usage when writing or speaking. *(Conventions: Sentence Structure)*

**3.** Use knowledge of language and its conventions when writing, speaking, reading, or listening. *(Speaking and Listening: Oral Presentation)*

# Reading Skill: Summarize

A **summary** is a short statement that presents the key ideas and main points of a text. Summarizing helps you identify the most important information in a text. Follow these steps to summarize:

- **Reread to identify main events or ideas** in the passage or work. Then, jot them down.
- Organize your notes by putting main events or points in order and crossing off minor details that are not important for an overall understanding of the work.
- Finally, summarize by restating the major events or ideas in as few words as possible. Be sure your summary does not include your personal opinions.

# Literary Analysis: Mythology

A **myth** is a traditional tale that presents the beliefs or customs of a culture. Every culture has its own **mythology,** or collection of myths. Myths share the following characteristics:

- They explain events in nature or in a people's history.
- They often describe the actions of gods or other supernatural beings. Many myths also involve animal characters or natural forces that display human qualities.
- They convey *themes,* or insights, expressing the values of the culture that first told them.

To understand myths, it is helpful to understand the culture from which they come. As you read, think about how cultural beliefs might influence the characters and events in the text.

## Using the Strategy: Cultural Connection Chart

Record details on a **cultural connection chart** like this one.

| Detail | Cultural Connection |
| --- | --- |
| Prometheus steals fire from Zeus, king of the gods, and gives it to humans. | To ancient Greeks, fire was essential for cooking, forging weapons, and providing warmth. |

# Are yesterday's *heroes* important today?

## Writing About the Big Question

"Coyote Steals the Sun and Moon" explains a specific event in nature and features Coyote, a popular character in mythology. Use this sentence starter to develop your ideas about the Big Question.

Myths and their heroes have **endured** through the ages because they _____.

**While You Read** Look for interesting aspects of the myth that might help explain why it has endured for so many years.

## Vocabulary

Read each word and its definition. Decide whether you know the word well, know it a little bit, or do not know it at all. After you read, see how your knowledge of each word has increased.

- **sacred** (sā´ krəd) *adj.* considered holy; related to religious ceremonies (p. 1026) *The temple was a __sacred__ space for ancient Greeks.* *sacredly adv. sacredness n.*

- **pestering** (pes´ tər iŋ) *n.* constant bothering (p. 1027) *After ten minutes of __pestering__, Jan got permission to go to the movies.* *pester v. pestered adj.*

- **lagged** (lagd) *v.* moved slowly (p. 1028) *The turtle __lagged__ far behind the speedy rabbit.* *lag n.*

- **shriveled** (shriv´ əld) *v.* dried up; shrank and wrinkled (p. 1028) *The hot sun __shriveled__ the grass until it was dry and brown.* *shriveled adj.*

- **pursuit** (pər so͞ot´) *n.* chasing in order to catch (p. 1028) *The police sped off in __pursuit__ of the thief.* *pursue v.*

- **curiosity** (kyo͞or´ ē äs ə tē) *n.* the desire to obtain information (p. 1028) *Out of __curiosity__, she peeked behind the curtain.* *curious adj. curiously adv.*

### Word Study

The **Latin root -sacr-** means "holy."

In the myth "Coyote Steals the Sun and Moon," Eagle and Coyote watch the Kachina people perform their **sacred**, or holy, dances.

# "Coyote Steals the Sun and Moon"

A shared love of Native American culture brought together Richard Erdoes and Alfonso Ortiz—two men who grew up worlds apart. They worked together on several collections of Native American stories, some of which "were jotted down at powwows, around campfires, even inside a moving car."

## Richard Erdoes (1912–2008)

Richard Erdoes was born in Frankfurt, Germany, and educated in Vienna, Berlin, and Paris. As a young boy, he became fascinated by American Indian culture. In 1940, he moved to the United States to escape Nazi rule and became a well-known author, photographer, and illustrator. He wrote several books on Native Americans and the American West.

## Alfonso Ortiz (1939–1997)

Alfonso Ortiz was a Tewa Pueblo, born in New Mexico. He became a professor of anthropology at the University of New Mexico, and a leading expert on Pueblo culture.

## BACKGROUND FOR THE MYTH

### Zuñi Culture

"Coyote Steals the Moon" is a Zuñi myth. The Zuñi belong to a group of Native American peoples known as the Pueblos. According to Zuñi beliefs, the Great Spirit and other sacred beings guided the people to their homelands, showed them how to plant corn, and taught them to live in peace with each other. Zuñi myths often involve the sun and the moon, with daylight symbolizing life.

## DID YOU KNOW?

Coyote is a popular character in Zuñi myths. He is usually depicted as a mischief-maker whose curiosity often gets him into trouble.

# COYOTE STEALS the SUN and MOON

## RETOLD BY RICHARD ERDOES AND ALFONSO ORTIZ

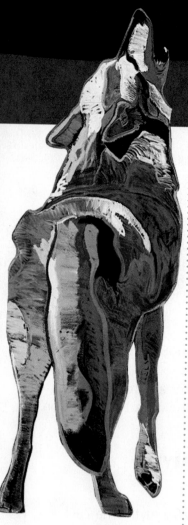

oyote is a bad hunter who never kills anything. Once he watched Eagle hunting rabbits, catching one after another—more rabbits than he could eat. Coyote thought, "I'll team up with Eagle so I can have enough meat." Coyote is always up to something.

"Friend," Coyote said to Eagle, "we should hunt together. Two can catch more than one."

"Why not?" Eagle said, and so they began to hunt in partnership. Eagle caught many rabbits, but all Coyote caught was some little bugs.

At this time the world was still dark; the sun and moon had not yet been put in the sky. "Friend," Coyote said to Eagle, "no wonder I can't catch anything; I can't see. Do you know where we can get some light?"

"You're right, friend, there should be some light," Eagle said. "I think there's a little toward the west. Let's try and find it."

And so they went looking for the sun and moon. They came to a big river, which Eagle flew over. Coyote swam, and swallowed so much water that he almost drowned. He crawled out with his fur full of mud, and Eagle asked, "Why don't you fly like me?"

"You have wings; I just have hair," Coyote said. "I can't fly without feathers."

At last they came to a pueblo,[1] where the Kachinas happened to be dancing. The people invited Eagle and Coyote to sit down and have something to eat while they watched the sacred dances. Seeing the power of the Kachinas, Eagle said,

**Vocabulary**
**sacred** (sā´ krəd) *adj.* considered holy; related to religious ceremonies

1. **pueblo** (pweb´ lō) Native American settlement in the southwestern United States.

"I believe these are the people who have light."

Coyote, who had been looking all around, pointed out two boxes, one large and one small, that the people opened whenever they wanted light. To produce a lot of light, they opened the lid of the big box, which contained the sun. For less light they opened the small box, which held the moon.

Coyote nudged Eagle. "Friend, did you see that? They have all the light we need in the big box. Let's steal it."

"You always want to steal and rob. I say we should just borrow it."

"They won't lend it to us."

"You may be right," said Eagle. "Let's wait till they finish dancing and then steal it."

After a while the Kachinas went home to sleep, and Eagle scooped up the large box and flew off. Coyote ran along trying to keep up, panting, his tongue hanging out. Soon he yelled up to Eagle, "Ho, friend, let me carry the box a little way."

"No, no," said Eagle, "you never do anything right."

He flew on, and Coyote ran after him. After a while Coyote shouted again: "Friend, you're my chief, and it's not right for you to carry the box; people will call me lazy. Let me have it."

"No, no, you always mess everything up." And Eagle flew on and Coyote ran along.

So it went for a stretch, and then Coyote started again. "Ho, friend, it isn't right for you to do this. What will people think of you and me?"

"I don't care what people think. I'm going to carry this box."

Again Eagle flew on and again Coyote ran after him. Finally Coyote begged for the fourth time: "Let me carry it. You're the chief, and I'm just Coyote. Let me carry it."

Eagle couldn't stand any more pestering. Also, Coyote had asked him four times, and if someone asks four times, you'd better give him what he wants. Eagle said, "Since you won't let up on me, go ahead and carry the box for a while. But promise not to open it."

"Oh, sure, oh yes, I promise." They went on as before, but now Coyote had the box. Soon Eagle was far ahead, and Coyote

## LITERATURE IN CONTEXT

### Culture Connection

#### Kachinas

The Zuñi and Hopi are Native American nations of the American Southwest. In both of these cultures, the Kachina dancers serve as links between the earthly world and the spirit world. Every year in colorful ceremonies, dancers perform, wearing masks representing various supernatural beings, or Kachinas.

The dancers play a central role in the religions of both cultures, where the blessings of the powerful spirits are sought every year for a good harvest and good fortune.

### Connect to the Literature

What details in the story show that the Kachinas are powerful beings?

**Vocabulary**
**pestering** (pes´ tər iŋ) *n.* constant bothering

Reading Check

What do Coyote and Eagle team up to do?

Coyote Steals the Sun and Moon **1027**

**Mythology**
What human trait does Coyote show here?


**Vocabulary**
**lagged** (lagd) *v.* moved slowly

**shriveled** (shriv´ əld) *v.* dried up; shrank and wrinkled

**pursuit** (pər soōt´) *n.* chasing in order to catch

**curiosity** (kyoōr´ ē äs ə tē) *n.* the desire to obtain information

**Spiral Review**
**Theme and Plot**
What lesson about the effects of bad behavior does the ending suggest?

**lagged** behind a hill where Eagle couldn't see him. "I wonder what the light looks like, inside there," he said to himself. "Why shouldn't I take a peek? Probably there's something extra in the box, something good that Eagle wants to keep to himself."

And Coyote opened the lid. Now, not only was the sun inside, but the moon also. Eagle had put them both together, thinking that it would be easier to carry one box than two.

As soon as Coyote opened the lid, the moon escaped, flying high into the sky. At once all the plants shriveled up and turned brown. Just as quickly, all the leaves fell off the trees, and it was winter. Trying to catch the moon and put it back in the box, Coyote ran in pursuit as it skipped away from him. Meanwhile the sun flew out and rose into the sky. It drifted far away, and the peaches, squashes, and melons shriveled up with cold.

Eagle turned and flew back to see what had delayed Coyote. "You fool! Look what you've done!" he said. "You let the sun and moon escape, and now it's cold." Indeed, it began to snow, and Coyote shivered. "Now your teeth are chattering," Eagle said, "and it's your fault that cold has come into the world."

It's true. If it weren't for Coyote's curiosity and mischief making, we wouldn't have winter; we could enjoy summer all the time.

## Critical Thinking

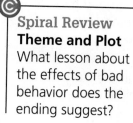
Cite textual evidence to support your responses.

**1. Key Ideas and Details (a)** Why does Coyote want to team up with Eagle? **(b) Compare and Contrast:** How do Coyote and Eagle differ in their abilities and attitudes? **(c) Connect:** How do each character's actions reflect his attitude?

**2. Key Ideas and Details (a)** Why do Eagle and Coyote want the Kachinas' box? **(b) Infer:** Why does Eagle agree to steal it?

**3. Key Ideas and Details (a)** How does Coyote finally get the box? **(b) Infer:** What does Coyote's behavior tell you about his character?

**4. Integration of Knowledge and Ideas (a)** What makes myths like this one still appealing in an age of scientific knowledge? **(b)** Could you find these same types of characters and attitudes in any of today's forms of popular entertainment? Explain. *[Connect to the Big Question: Are yesterday's heroes important today?]*

## Reading Skill: Summarize

**1.** The characters' actions in this myth can be divided into four "scenes," or sections. Use a graphic organizer like the one shown to **summarize** the important events in each section.

| Section | Summary |
|---|---|
| The Hunt | |
| At the Kachinas' Dance | |
| Running Away | |
| Coyote's Mistake | |

**2.** Using your chart, summarize the entire story in as few sentences as possible, leaving out minor details.

## Literary Analysis: Mythology

**3. Key Ideas and Details (a)** What element of nature does this **myth** explain? **(b)** In what ways do its animal characters resemble humans? **(c)** What theme, or message, regarding nature can you infer from the myth? Support your answer with story details.

**4. Key Ideas and Details** What does this myth reveal about Zuñi culture and beliefs?

## Vocabulary

**Acquisition and Use** Write a sentence to answer each question, using a word from the vocabulary list on page 1024.

**1.** How would you describe a sheriff chasing a fugitive?

**2.** What made the girl ask so many questions?

**3.** What happens to garden plants after the first frost?

**4.** How would you describe an annoying younger child?

**5.** Where did ancient Greeks worship their gods?

**6.** Why was the bicycle racer certain he would finish last?

**Word Study** Use context and what you know about the **Latin root -sacr-** to explain your answer to each question.

**1.** What might you *sacrifice* to do an extracurricular activity?

**2.** What would you avoid if you considered free time *sacrosanct*?

### Word Study

The **Latin root -sacr-** means "holy."

**Apply It** Explain how the root *-sacr-* contributes to the meanings of these words. Consult a dictionary if necessary.

sacrament
sacrilegious
consecrate

# Are yesterday's *heroes* important today?

## Writing About the Big Question

"Why the Waves Have Whitecaps" is a story whose characters act in ways that are humorous, but unheroic. Use this sentence starter to develop your ideas about the Big Question.

I think that story characters who (do / do not) behave **admirably** have more relevance today because _____.

**While You Read** Notice the main characters' unheroic behavior.

## Vocabulary

**Dialect** is the form of language spoken in a particular region or by a particular group of people.

- Dialects develop over time. They are usually based on ancestry, geographic location, regional isolation, and economic conditions. For example, people in coastal Georgia traditionally speak a slightly different dialect than people who live in the mountainous Appalachian region, even though they live in the same state. This is due to the historical role the mountains played in keeping people of these regions apart, as well as their different ancestry.

- Dialects of the same language may differ greatly in vocabulary, grammar, and pronunciation. It is not unusual to find that people who speak different dialects of the same language have a hard time understanding one another.

- Dialect is usually written *phonetically*, or the way it sounds when spoken. Letters and syllables may be dropped or altered at the beginning, middle, or end of words. For instance, residents of London's East End say *'ouse* instead of *house*.

When reading stories written in dialect, it helps to read the text aloud. Focus on the sounds of the letters in each word, and try to ignore the odd spellings. Your ear will probably pick out the word it most closely resembles in your own daily speech. If reading aloud does not help, think about the context of the word and what meaning would make the most sense in the sentence.

### Word Study

In this myth, the word *chillun* reflects a **dialect** spoken by African Americans in the South in the early nineteenth century. It is derived from the standard English word *children*.

# Meet
# Zora Neale Hurston
## (1891–1960)

## Author of
### WHY THE WAVES HAVE
### *WHITECAPS*

Zora Neale Hurston was one of the first writers to recognize the richness of African American folk tales. Hurston grew up in Eatonville, Florida. After moving north, she began writing with a group of authors in Harlem, New York, that included Langston Hughes.

**Belated Recognition** Hurston's talent was recognized by the founder of Barnard College, who arranged for her to study with the anthropologist Franz Boas. Part of Hurston's research involved traveling around the country and collecting folk tales. Without her research, many of these traditional stories might have been lost. Hurston was criticized during her lifetime for featuring local dialect so prominently in her writing style. Only later was her genius recognized and her books widely circulated once again.

## BACKGROUND FOR THE MYTH

**Waves**

"Why the Waves Have Whitecaps" is a myth that explains the natural phenomenon of whitecaps. There is, of course, a scientific explanation for the whitecaps on waves. Waves form when winds blow across the surface of water and transmit their energy to the water. As waves reach shallower water near the shore, the wave height increases until they topple over and break into water droplets. The droplets reflect light and appear as foamy whitecaps.

## DID YOU KNOW?

Hurston's most popular book is the novel *Their Eyes Were Watching God* (1937). She also wrote a play, *Mule Bone*, with Langston Hughes.

# Why the Waves Have

# WHITECAPS

## ZORA NEALE HURSTON

De wind is a woman, and de water is a woman too. They useter[1] talk together a whole heap. Mrs. Wind useter go set down by de ocean and talk and patch and crochet.[2]

They was jus' like all lady people. They loved to talk about their chillun, and brag on 'em.

Mrs. Water useter say, "Look at *my* chillun! Ah got de biggest and de littlest in de world. All kinds of chillun. Every color in de world, and every shape!"

De wind lady bragged louder than de water woman:

"Oh, but Ah got mo' different chilluns than anybody in de world. They flies, they walks, they swims, they sings, they talks, they cries. They got all de colors from de sun. Lawd, my chillun sho is a pleasure. 'Tain't nobody got no babies like mine."

---

1. **useter** (yoo´ stə) *v.* dialect pronunciation of "used to."
2. **crochet** (krō shā´) *v.* make needlework by looping thread with a hooked needle.

◀ **Critical Viewing**
In this painting, which force would you say is stronger—the wind or the water? Explain. **[Make a Judgment]**

**Spiral Review**
**Theme and Character** What theme might the characters' bragging suggest?

Reading Check
Why is Mrs. Water proud of her children?

Mrs. Water got tired of hearin' 'bout Mrs. Wind's chillun so she got so she hated 'em.

One day a whole passle of her chillun come to Mrs. Wind and says: "Mama, wese thirsty. Kin we go git us a cool drink of water?"

She says, "Yeah chillun. Run on over to Mrs. Water and hurry right back soon."

When them chillun went to squinch they thirst Mrs. Water grabbed 'em all and drowned 'em.

When her chillun didn't come home, de wind woman got worried. So she went on down to de water and ast for her babies.

"Good evenin' Mis' Water, you see my chillun today?"

De water woman tole her, "No-oo-oo."

Mrs. Wind knew her chillun had come down to Mrs. Water's house, so she passed over de ocean callin' her chillun, and every time she call de white feathers would come up on top of de water. And dat's how come we got white caps on waves. It's de feathers comin' up when de wind woman calls her lost babies.

When you see a storm on de water, it's de wind and de water fightin' over dem chillun.

## Critical Thinking

Cite textual evidence to support your responses.

1. **Key Ideas and Details** **(a)** What is Mrs. Wind's and Mrs. Water's relationship as the story begins? **(b) Infer:** What changes their relationship?

2. **Key Ideas and Details** **(a)** What qualities of their children do Mrs. Wind and Mrs. Water brag about? **(b) Connect:** How do these qualities relate to the behavior of wind and water in the natural world?

3. **Key Ideas and Details** **(a)** What happens to Mrs. Wind's children? **(b) Deduce:** What does this event reveal about Mrs. Water?

4. **Craft and Structure** **(a) Cause and Effect:** What are the results of the quarrel? **(b) Speculate:** Given the nature of the characters, could this story have ended differently?

5. **Integration of Knowledge and Ideas** **(a)** What qualities make Mrs. Water and Mrs. Wind unheroic? **(b)** Does a traditional story with antiheroes have as much relevance as a story featuring heroes? Explain. *[Connect to the Big Question: Are yesterday's heroes important today?]*

## Reading Skill: Summarize

1. The characters' actions in this myth can be divided into three "scenes," or sections. Use a graphic organizer like the one shown to **summarize** the important events of each section.

| Section | Summary |
|---|---|
| Mrs. Water and Mrs. Wind Compete | |
| Mrs. Water's Revenge | |
| Whitecaps and Storms | |

2. Using your chart, summarize the entire story in as few sentences as possible, leaving out minor details.

## Literary Analysis: Mythology

3. **Key Ideas and Details** How does this **myth** explain the phenomenon of whitecaps?

4. **Key Ideas and Details** **(a)** In what ways do the myth's characters act like humans? **(b)** How might the experiences of enslaved Africans have contributed to this myth? **(c)** What theme, or message, does the myth convey about human behavior?

## Vocabulary

**Acquisition and Use** Rewrite each sentence in Standard English.

1. Mrs. Wind <u>useter</u> go <u>set</u> down by <u>de</u> ocean.
2. <u>Ah</u> got <u>mo'</u> different <u>chilluns</u> than anybody in <u>de</u> world.
3. Mrs. Water got tired of <u>hearin'</u> <u>'bout</u> Mrs. Wind's <u>chilluns</u>.
4. When <u>them chillun</u> went to <u>squinch they</u> thirst Mrs. Water grabbed <u>'em</u> all.
5. When you see a storm on <u>de</u> water, it's <u>de</u> wind and <u>de</u> water <u>fightin'</u> over <u>dem chillun</u>.

**Word Study** An important part of Zora Neale Hurston's style is her use of authentic **dialect.** Would this myth have the same appeal if it were written in Standard English? Why or why not?

### Word Study

Keep in mind that **dialects** arise from the regional influences and isolation of a group of people.

**Apply It** What impact do you think television, radio, and other mass media have on the survival of specific regional dialects and on the rise of new dialects?

# Integrated Language Skills

## Coyote Steals the Sun and Moon • Why the Waves Have Whitecaps

### Conventions: Sentence Structure

The four basic **sentence structures** are shown below.

| Sentence Structures | Examples |
| --- | --- |
| **A simple sentence** has a single independent clause with at least one subject and verb. | **The cat sleeps on the chair.** |
| **A compound sentence** consists of two or more independent clauses usually joined by a comma and a conjunction. | **The cat sleeps on the chair,** and **the dog sleeps on the floor.** |
| **A complex sentence** consists of one independent clause and one or more subordinate clauses. | **Jack,** who is my cousin, **raises golden retrievers,** which he exhibits at dog shows. |
| **A compound-complex sentence** consists of two or more independent clauses and one or more subordinate clauses. | After she took her exam, **Sue remembered she had to pick up her sister,** but **she wanted to finish writing first.** |

**Practice A** Identify the structure of each of the following sentences.

1. When the world was still dark, Coyote and Eagle went in search of light.

2. Eagle could fly, but Coyote, who did not have feathers or wings, could not.

3. Eagle swooped and scooped up the box.

4. Although he promised not to, Coyote opened the box, and when he did, the sun and moon escaped.

© **Reading Application** In "Coyote . . .," find one example of each of the four basic sentence structures.

**Practice B** Change each of the following simple sentences into either a compound or a complex sentence. Then, identify its structure.

1. Mrs. Wind sat by the ocean and talked with Mrs. Water.

2. Mrs. Wind bragged about her children.

3. Mrs. Water developed a hatred for Mrs. Wind's children.

4. One day, Mrs. Wind's children didn't come home.

© **Writing Application** Write four sentences about either myth using each of the four sentence types.

**PH** **WRITING COACH** | Further instruction and practice are available in *Prentice Hall Writing Coach.*

# Writing

**Narrative Text** Create a **myth** to explain a natural phenomenon.

- First, choose a natural feature or event—for example, a rainbow, the seasons, or certain animal behaviors.
- Think of yourself as a storyteller. Entertain your audience with informal elements such as dialect, idioms, and humor.
- Develop the personalities of each character through their actions, expressions, physical description, and dialogue.
- Make sure your myth has a central problem that comes to a reasonable and satisfactory conclusion during the resolution of the plot. The resolution should be the basis for the myth.
- Edit to check that your resolution explains the natural event.

**Grammar Application** In your myth, use each of the four sentence structures at least once.

## Writing Workshop: *Work in Progress*

**Prewriting for Exposition** For a multimedia report you may develop, choose two subjects that you think will lend themselves to interesting visuals. Use the Internet to search for images. Then, print them out, along with source information. Save this Image Research in your writing portfolio.

# Speaking and Listening

**Comprehension and Collaboration** With a group, use the Internet and print sources to gather information for an **oral presentation** about the myth you read.

- If you read "Coyote . . .," look for ways in which history and traditional beliefs influence Zuñi life and culture today.
- If you read "Why the Waves . . .," look for ways in which the history and traditional folklore of African Americans have influenced modern culture.

Keep these tips in mind while completing the assignment:

- Display information with visuals—charts, maps, and graphs.
- Use appropriate digital tools to create your presentation. For example, you could use multimedia software to create a slide-show of images related to the culture, accompanied by music.
- As you present, choose language that shows sensitivity and respect when you discuss another culture's traditions.

**Common Core State Standards**

L.8.1, L.8.3; W.8.3; W.8.3.b, W.8.3.e; SL.8.5, SL.8.6
[For the full wording of the standards, see page 1022.]

Use this prewriting activity to prepare for the **Writing Workshop** on page 1084.

**www.PHLitOnline.com**
- Interactive graphic organizers
- Grammar tutorial
- Interactive journals

**Leveled Texts**

Build your skills and improve your comprehension of literature with texts of increasing complexity.

Read **"Brer Possum's Dilemma"** to see whether kindness is always repaid. Read **"John Henry"** to see the outcome when a man challenges a machine.

Read **"Chicoria"** for a lesson in good manners. Read the excerpt from ***The People, Yes*** to chuckle over absurd characters from American folklore.

## Common Core State Standards

Meet these standards with **"Brer Possum's Dilemma"** (p. 1042) and **"John Henry"** (p. 1045) or **"Chicoria"** (p. 1052) and the excerpt from ***The People, Yes*** (p. 1055).

### Reading Literature
**4.** Determine the meaning of words and phrases as they are used in a text, including figurative and connotative meanings; analyze the impact of specific word choices on meaning and tone, including analogies or allusions to other texts. *(Literary Analysis: Oral Tradition; Writing: Critical Analysis)*

**7.** Analyze the extent to which a filmed or live production of a story or drama stays faithful to or departs from the text or script, evaluating the choices made by the director or actors. *(Speaking and Listening: Storytelling Workshop)*

### Writing
**2.** Write informative/explanatory texts to examine a topic and convey ideas, concepts, and information through the selection, organization, and analysis of relevant content.

**9.** Draw evidence from literary or informational texts to support analysis, reflection, and research. *(Writing: Critical Analysis)*

### Speaking and Listening
**6.** Adapt speech to a variety of contexts and tasks, demonstrating command of formal English when indicated or appropriate. *(Speaking and Listening: Storytelling Workshop)*

### Language
**2.a.** Use punctuation to indicate a pause or break. *(Conventions: Commas)*

# Reading Skill: Summarize

A **summary** is a short restatement of the main points of a text or the main events of a plot. Summaries leave out minor details, providing a quick way to preview or review a longer work.

Before you summarize a work of literature, follow these steps:

- First, read the selection, and identify the main idea or main event. Consider details to determine whether each event or idea is important enough to be included in your summary.
- Then, **use graphics** to help organize the major events or ideas. For example, if you are summarizing an essay or a poem, you might use a cluster diagram with the main idea in the center and supporting details in attached circles.

# Literary Analysis: Oral Tradition

In the **oral tradition,** storytellers pass on legends, songs, folk tales, tall tales, and stories from generation to generation by word of mouth. Here are some key features of the oral tradition:

- As stories and songs are written down, they are often written in **dialect**—the language and grammar of a particular region.
- Stories and songs in the oral tradition frequently contain **idioms**—expressions that are not meant to be understood literally, such as "strictly for the birds" and "spoiling for a fight."

As you read, identify the tone, or attitude, created by the author's use of dialect and idioms.

## Using the Strategy: Oral Tradition Chart

Record story details on an **oral tradition chart** like this one.

| Oral Tradition | Story Detail |
|---|---|
| repetition and exaggeration (hyperbole) | |
| heroes who are brave, clever, or strong | |
| animal characters that act like humans | |
| dialect, idioms, and informal speech | |
| traditions of a culture | |

# Are yesterday's *heroes* important today?

## Writing About the Big Question

The human-like animals in "Brer Possum's Dilemma" and the larger-than-life hero "John Henry" are typical one-dimensional folk tale characters. Use this sentence starter to develop your ideas about the Big Question.

Although the **accomplishments** of folk heroes are **exaggerated,** these stories have value today because _____.

**While You Read** Look for story details that show qualities that we might admire or recognize in ourselves.

## Vocabulary

Read each word and its definition. Decide whether you know the word well, know it a little bit, or do not know it at all. After you read, see how your knowledge of each word has increased.

- **commenced** (kə menst´) *v.* began to happen (p. 1042) *The meeting commenced quietly, but then became noisy.* commencement *n.*

- **pitiful** (pit´ i fəl) *adj.* arousing sympathy (p. 1044) *The wet, lost puppy was a pitiful sight.* pitifully *adv.* pity *n.* or *v.*

- **coiled** (koild) *v.* twisted around and around (p. 1044) *The cat coiled up into a tight ball to take a nap on the sunny window ledge.* coil *n.* recoil *v.*

- **flagged** (flagd) *v.* gave a sign to stop, often with a flag or another object (p. 1047) *The stranded travelers flagged a passing motorist to ask for help.* flag *n.* flagging *adj.*

### Word Study

The **Old English suffix -ful** means "full of" or "having the qualities of." It can indicate a word is an adjective.

In "Brer Possum's Dilemma," one of the characters looks and acts in a way that is **pitiful,** or full of sadness and misfortune.

# Meet
# Jackie Torrence
## (1944–2004)

## Author of
# Brer Possum's Dilemma

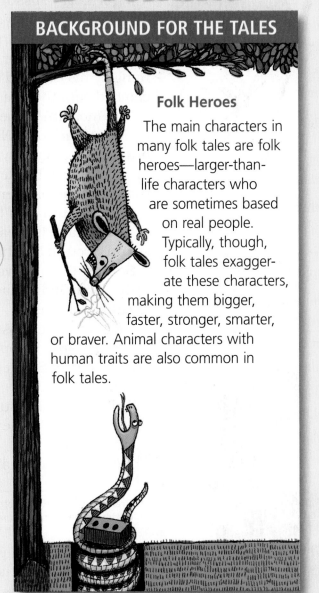

## BACKGROUND FOR THE TALES

### Folk Heroes

The main characters in many folk tales are folk heroes—larger-than-life characters who are sometimes based on real people. Typically, though, folk tales exaggerate these characters, making them bigger, faster, stronger, smarter, or braver. Animal characters with human traits are also common in folk tales.

Starting in the 1970s, Jackie Torrence became one of America's best-known and best-loved storytellers. Born in Chicago, she spent her childhood with her grandparents in a North Carolina farming settlement. From them, she learned the "Brer Rabbit" fables and other African American tales that had been passed along to the descendants of enslaved Africans in the South.

**A Lively Presenter** Torrence told classic ghost stories and her own tales, along with traditional folk tales. She animated her storytelling with humor, engaging language, hisses, shrieks, and facial expressions. Torrence collected stories in *The Accidental Angel, My Grandmother's Treasure*, and other books. She also recorded stories on compact discs, videos, and DVDs.

### DID YOU KNOW?

Jackie Torrence began telling stories in the public library, and soon large audiences were coming to hear "the Story Lady."

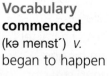

# Brer Possum's Dilemma

## Jackie Torrence

Back in the days when the animals could talk, there lived ol' Brer[1] Possum. He was a fine feller. Why, he never liked to see no critters[2] in trouble. He was always helpin' out, a-doin' somethin' for others.

Ever' night, ol' Brer Possum climbed into a persimmon tree, hung by his tail, and slept all night long. And each mornin', he climbed outa the tree and walked down the road to sun 'imself.

One mornin', as he walked, he come to a big hole in the middle of the road. Now, ol' Brer Possum was kind and gentle, but he was also nosy, so he went over to the hole and looked in. All at once, he stepped back, 'cause layin' in the bottom of that hole was ol' Brer Snake with a brick on his back.

Brer Possum said to 'imself, "I best git on outa here, 'cause ol' Brer Snake is mean and evil and lowdown, and if I git to stayin' around 'im, he jist might git to bitin' me."

So Brer Possum went on down the road.

But Brer Snake had seen Brer Possum, and he commenced to callin' for 'im.

"Help me, Brer Possum."

Brer Possum stopped and turned around. He said to 'imself, "That's ol' Brer Snake a-callin' me. What do you reckon he wants?"

Well, ol' Brer Possum was kindhearted, so he went back down the road to the hole, stood at the edge, and looked down at Brer Snake.

"Was that you a-callin' me? What do you want?"

**Vocabulary**
**commenced**
(kə menst´) *v.*
began to happen

---

1. **Brer** (brür) dialect for "brother," used before a name.
2. **critters** dialect for "creatures"; animals.

Brer Snake looked up and said, "I've been down here in this hole for a mighty long time with this brick on my back. Won't you help git it offa me?"

Brer Possum thought.

"Now listen here, Brer Snake. I knows you. You's mean and evil and lowdown, and if'n I was to git down in that hole and git to liftin' that brick offa your back, you wouldn't do nothin' but bite me."

Ol' Brer Snake just hissed.

"Maybe not. Maybe not. Maaaaaaaybe not."

Brer Possum said, "I ain't sure 'bout you at all. I jist don't know. You're a-goin' to have to let me think about it."

So ol' Brer Possum thought—he thought high, and he thought low—and jist as he was thinkin', he looked up into a tree and saw a dead limb a-hangin' down. He climbed into the tree, broke off the limb, and with that ol' stick, pushed that brick offa Brer Snake's back. Then he took off down the road.

Brer Possum thought he was away from ol' Brer Snake when all at once he heard somethin'.

"Help me, Brer Possum."

Brer Possum said, "Oh, no, that's him agin."

But bein' so kindhearted, Brer Possum turned around, went back to the hole, and stood at the edge.

"Brer Snake, was that you a-callin' me? What do you want now?"

Ol' Brer Snake looked up outa the hole and hissed.

"I've been down here for a mighty long time, and I've gotten a little weak, and the sides of this ol' hole are too slick for me to climb. Do you think you can lift me outa here?"

Brer Possum thought.

"Now, you jist wait a minute. If'n I was to git down into that hole and lift you outa there, you wouldn't do nothin' but bite me."

Brer Snake hissed.

"Maybe not. Maybe not. Maaaaaaaybe not."

Brer Possum said, "I jist don't know. You're a-goin' to have to give me time to think about this."

So ol' Brer Possum thought.

And as he thought, he jist happened to look down there in that hole and see that ol' dead limb. So he pushed the limb underneath ol' Brer Snake and he lifted 'im outa the hole, way up into the air, and throwed 'im into the high grass.

◀ **Critical Viewing**
What characteristics of Brer Possum and Brer Snake does this illustration show? **[Analyze]**

**Oral Tradition**
What examples of dialect here reflect the story's origins as an oral tale?

Reading Check

Why does Brer Snake first call for help?

**Oral Tradition**
What role does repetition play in building suspense in this story?

**Vocabulary**
**pitiful** (pit´ i fəl) *adj.* arousing sympathy

**coiled** (koild) *v.* twisted around and around

**Summarize**
What are the consequences of Brer Possum's kindness?

Brer Possum took off a-runnin' down the road.

Well, he thought he was away from ol' Brer Snake when all at once he heard somethin'.

"Help me, Brer Possum."

Brer Possum thought, "That's him agin."

But bein' so kindhearted, he turned around, went back to the hole, and stood there a-lookin' for Brer Snake. Brer Snake crawled outa the high grass just as slow as he could, stretched 'imself out across the road, rared up, and looked at ol' Brer Possum.

Then he hissed. "I've been down there in that ol' hole for a mighty long time, and I've gotten a little cold 'cause the sun didn't shine. Do you think you could put me in your pocket and git me warm?"

Brer Possum said, "Now you listen here, Brer Snake. I knows you. You's mean and evil and lowdown, and if'n I put you in my pocket you wouldn't do nothin' but bite me."

Brer Snake hissed.

"Maybe not. Maybe not. Maaaaaaaybe not."

"No sireee. Brer Snake. I knows you. I jist ain't a-goin' to do it."

But jist as Brer Possum was talkin' to Brer Snake, he happened to git a real good look at 'im. He was a-layin' there lookin' so pitiful, and Brer Possum's great big heart began to feel sorry for ol' Brer Snake.

"All right," said Brer Possum. "You must be cold. So jist this once I'm a-goin' to put you in my pocket."

So ol' Brer Snake coiled up jist as little as he could, and Brer Possum picked 'im up and put 'im in his pocket.

Brer Snake laid quiet and still—so quiet and still that Brer Possum even forgot that he was a-carryin' 'im around. But all of a sudden, Brer Snake commenced to crawlin' out, and he turned and faced Brer Possum and hissed.

"I'm a-goin' to bite you."

But Brer Possum said, "Now wait a minute. Why are you a-goin' to bite me? I done took that brick offa your back, I got you outa that hole, and I put you in my pocket to git you warm. Why are you a-goin' to bite me?"

Brer Snake hissed.

"You knowed I was a snake before you put me in you pocket."

And when you're mindin' your own business and you spot trouble, don't never trouble trouble 'til trouble troubles you.

*John Henry on the Right, Steam Drill on the Left,* 1944–47, Palmer C. Hayden, Museum of African American Art

# JOHN HENRY
## *Traditional*

▲ **Critical Viewing**
Based on this illustration, do you think John Henry can work faster than the man with the steam drill? Why or why not? **[Predict]**

John Henry was a lil baby,
Sittin' on his mama's knee,
Said: 'The Big Bend Tunnel on the C. & O. road[1]
Gonna cause the death of me,
5   Lawd, Lawd, gonna cause the death of me.'

---

**1. C. & O. road** Chesapeake and Ohio Railroad. The C & O's Big Bend railroad tunnel was built in the 1870s through a mountain in West Virginia.

Cap'n says to John Henry,
'Gonna bring me a steam drill 'round,
Gonna take that steam drill out on the job,
Gonna whop that steel on down,
10  Lawd, Lawd, gonna whop that steel on down.'

John Henry tol' his cap'n,
Lightnin' was in his eye:
'Cap'n, bet yo' las', red cent on me,
Fo' I'll beat it to the bottom or I'll die,
15  Lawd, Lawd, I'll beat it to the bottom or I'll die.'

Sun shine hot an' burnin',
Wer'n't no breeze a-tall,
Sweat ran down like water down a hill,
That day John Henry let his hammer fall,
20  Lawd, Lawd, that day John Henry let his hammer fall.

John Henry went to the tunnel,
An' they put him in the lead to drive,
The rock so tall an' John Henry so small,
That he lied down his hammer an' he cried,
25  Lawd, Lawd, that he lied down his hammer an' he cried.

John Henry started on the right hand,
The steam drill started on the lef'—
'Before I'd let this steam drill beat me down,
I'd hammer my fool self to death,
30  Lawd, Lawd, I'd hammer my fool self to death.'

John Henry had a lil woman,
Her name were Polly Ann,
John Henry took sick an' had to go to bed,
Polly Ann drove steel like a man,
35  Lawd, Lawd, Polly Ann drove steel like a man.

John Henry said to his shaker,[2]
'Shaker, why don' you sing?
I'm throwin' twelve poun's from my hips on down,
Jes' listen to the col' steel ring,
40  Lawd, Lawd, jes' listen to the col' steel ring.'

---

2. **shaker** (shā´ kər) *n.* person who sets the spikes and places the drills for a steel-
driver to hammer.

Oh, the captain said to John Henry,
'I b'lieve this mountain's sinkin' in.'
John Henry said to his captain, oh my!
'Ain' nothin' but my hammer suckin' win',
45  Lawd, Lawd, ain' nothin' but my hammer
        suckin' win'.'

John Henry tol' his shaker,
'Shaker, you better pray,
For, if I miss this six-foot steel,
Tomorrow'll be yo' buryin' day,
50  Lawd, Lawd, tomorrow'll be yo' buryin' day.'

John Henry tol' his captain,
'Look yonder what I see—
Yo' drill's done broke an' yo' hole's done choke,
An' you cain' drive steel like me,
55  Lawd, Lawd, an' you cain' drive steel like me.'

The man that invented the steam drill,
Thought he was mighty fine.
John Henry drove his fifteen feet,
An' the steam drill only made nine,
60  Lawd, Lawd, an' the steam drill only made
        nine.

The hammer that John Henry swung,
It weighed over nine pound;
He broke a rib in his lef'-han' side,
An' his intrels[3] fell on the groun',
65  Lawd, Lawd, an' his intrels fell on the
        groun'.

All the womens in the Wes',
When they heared of John Henry's death,
Stood in the rain, flagged the eas'-boun'
        train,
Goin' where John Henry fell dead,
70  Lawd, Lawd, goin' where John Henry fell
        dead.

***He Laid Down his Hammer and Cried,***
1944–1947, Palmer C. Hayden, Museum of
African American Art, Los Angeles, CA

**Oral Tradition**
Read the repeated lines
at the end of each
stanza. What is the
effect of this repetition?

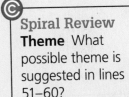

**Spiral Review**
**Theme** What
possible theme is
suggested in lines
51–60?

**Vocabulary**
**flagged** (flagd) *v.*
gave a sign to stop,
often with a flag or
another object

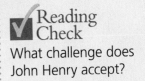

Reading
Check
What challenge does
John Henry accept?

---

**3. intrels** (en´ trālz) *n.* dialect for *entrails*—internal organs.

**Oral Tradition**
This ballad was meant to be sung. What makes a song more likely to be passed down than a story?

John Henry's lil mother,
She was all dressed in red,
She jumped in bed, covered up her head,
Said she didn' know her son was dead,
75 Lawd, Lawd, didn' know her son was dead.

Dey took John Henry to the graveyard,
An' they buried him in the san',
An' every locomotive come roarin' by,
Says, 'There lays a steel-drivin' man,
80 Lawd, Lawd, there lays a steel-drivin' man.'

## Critical Thinking

**Cite textual evidence to support your responses.**

1. **Key Ideas and Details (a)** What words does Torrence use to describe Brer Possum? **(b) Infer:** Is Brer Possum meant to look foolish or simply big-hearted? **(c) Compare and Contrast:** How are Brer Possum and Brer Snake different?

2. **Key Ideas and Details (a) Deduce:** Why might Brer Possum think it is safe to trust Brer Snake? **(b) Apply:** What is the lesson of this story?

3. **Key Ideas and Details (a)** Why does John Henry challenge the steam drill? **(b) Connect:** How do his actions contribute to his legend? **(c) Discuss:** Would the story of John Henry be remembered if he had beaten the machine but still survived? Share your answer with the class.

4. **Craft and Structure  Forms of Poetry:** A *ballad* is a song or poem that tells a story, often involving adventure or romance. Ballads are divided into short rhyming stanzas. They generally repeat certain lines, as in a refrain. How does the form of "John Henry" match the purpose and characteristics of a ballad?

5. **Integration of Knowledge and Ideas (a)** What common human qualities do John Henry and Brer Possum possess? **(b)** What might cause a folk hero like John Henry to transform over time from a local hero into a national folk hero? *[Connect to the Big Question: Are yesterday's heroes important today?]*

## Reading Skill: Summarize

**1. (a)** To help you **summarize** "John Henry," complete a timeline like the one shown. **(b)** Use your timeline to write a brief summary.

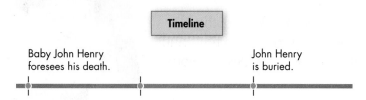

| Timeline |

Baby John Henry foresees his death.

John Henry is buried.

**2. (a)** What type of graphic organizer would be most helpful in writing a summary of "Brer Possum's Dilemma"? Explain. **(b)** Use that organizer and write a summary of the story.

## Literary Analysis: Oral Tradition

**© 3. Key Ideas and Details (a)** How is John Henry both typical and *not* typical of a hero of the **oral tradition**? **(b)** What story elements might explain why the story has endured?

**© 4. Craft and Structure (a)** Review the chart on page 1039. For each feature listed, give one example from "Brer Possum's Dilemma." Explain the effects of each. **(b)** Give the meaning of the example you list for "dialect, idioms, or informal speech." Explain the tone it helps to create.

## Vocabulary

**© Acquisition and Use** Use a word from page 1040 to form an **analogy** that matches the relationship of the other word pair given.

**1.** *Curl* is to _____ as *rod* is to *straight*.

**2.** *Opened* is to *closed* as *stopped* is to _____.

**3.** *Halted* is to _____ as *called* is to *shouted*.

**4.** *Champion* is to *strong* as *victim* is to _____.

**Word Study** Use context and what you know about the **Old English suffix -ful** to explain your answer to each question.

**1.** Would a ballerina want critics to describe her as *graceful*?

**2.** Is a well-written mystery likely to be *suspenseful*?

### Word Study

The **Old English suffix -ful** means "full of" or "having the qualities of."

**Apply It** Explain how the suffix *-ful* contributes to the meanings of these words. You may consult a dictionary, if necessary.

**meaningful**
**regretful**
**vengeful**

# Are yesterday's *heroes* important today?

## Writing About the Big Question

In both "Chicoria" and the excerpt from *The People, Yes*, the values and beliefs of a culture are passed on through the traits and qualities of its heroes. Use these sentence starters to develop your ideas about the Big Question.

In today's stories, qualities such as _____ may be considered **outdated** for a heroic character.

On the other hand, in movies and in books, characters with heroic qualities such as _____ are still relevant because _____.

**While You Read** Look for details that provide a window into the values a culture considers important.

## Vocabulary

Read each word and its definition. Decide whether you know the word well, know it a little bit, or do not know it at all. After you read, see how your knowledge of each word has increased.

- **self-confident** (self kän′ fə dənt) *adj.* certain of one's ability (p. 1054) *She is so self-confident that she does not worry about what others think.* self-confidently *adv.* self-confidence *n.*

- **cordially** (kôr′ jə lē) *adv.* warmly (p. 1054) *The gracious host welcomed his guests cordially.* cordiality *n.* cordial *adj.*

- **haughty** (hôt′ ē) *adj.* scornfully superior (p. 1054) *They thought the haughty prince was rude.* haughtily *adv.* haughtiness *n.*

- **straddling** (strad′ ′liŋ) *v.* standing or sitting with a leg on either side of something (p. 1056) *The cowboy sat high in the saddle, straddling his horse.* straddle *v.*

- **cyclone** (sī′ klōn′) *n.* violent, rotating windstorm; tornado (p. 1056) *The cyclone tore off the roofs.* cycle *n.* or *v.*

- **mutineers** (myo͞ot′ ′n irz′) *n.* rebels (p. 1056) *The mutineers plotted to take over the ship.* mutiny *n.* or *v.*

### Word Study

The **suffix -eer** means "one who does something." It is usually a noun ending.

In the excerpt from *The People, Yes,* the narrator describes a group of **mutineers**, or sailors who rebel against their ship's captain.

# José Griego y Maestas
(b. 1949)

# Rudolfo A. Anaya
(b. 1937)

### Authors of "Chicoria" (p. 1052)

José Griego y Maestas and Rudolfo A. Anaya share a common love of old New Mexican folktales, or *cuentos*. It is a true partnership. Griego y Maestas finds and collects the tales, and Anaya translates them into English.

**José Griego y Maestas** is an expert in bilingual education and is the dean of instruction at Northern New Mexico Community College. He also loves telling stories.

**Rudolfo Anaya,** author of novels, poetry, and stories, is a celebrated figure in Hispanic literature. His novel *Bless Me, Ultima* is a well-loved classic. Anaya says, "I am an oral storyteller, but now I do it on the printed page."

# Carl Sandburg
(1878–1967)

### Author of *The People, Yes* (p. 1055)

Carl Sandburg was a journalist and historian as well as a poet and folklorist. In the early 1900s, he was part of a writers' movement in Chicago, a city that inspired some of his best-known poems. Sandburg won the Pulitzer Prize twice—once in 1940 for a biography of Abraham Lincoln and again in 1951 for his *Complete Poems*.

## DID YOU KNOW?

As a young man, Sandburg worked as a truck driver and as a ranchhand. These jobs acquainted him with the rhythms of everyday speech.

▲ **Critical Viewing**
What features of this
painting indicate the
start of a festive occa-
sion, such as the feast
in the story? **[Analyze]**

# Chicoria

Retold in English
by Rudolfo A. Anaya

Adapted in Spanish by
José Griego y Maestas

There were once many big ranches in California, and many New Mexicans went to work there. One day one of the big ranch owners asked his workers if there were any poets in New Mexico.

Invitation to the Dance (el convite), Theodore Gentilz, courtesy of The Daughters of the Republic of Texas Library.

"Of course, we have many fine poets," they replied. "We have old Vilmas, Chicoria, Cinfuegos, to say nothing of the poets of Cebolleta and the Black Poet."

"Well, when you return next season, why don't you bring one of your poets to compete with Gracia—here none can compare with him!"

When the harvest was done the New Mexicans returned home. The following season when they returned to California they took with them the poet Chicoria, knowing well that in spinning a rhyme or in weaving wit there was no *Californio*[1] who could beat him.

As soon as the rancher found out that the workers had brought Chicoria with them, he sent his servants to invite his good neighbor and friend to come and hear the new poet. Meanwhile, the cooks set about preparing a big meal. When the maids began to dish up the plates of food, Chicoria turned to one of the servers and said, "Ah, my friends, it looks like they are going to feed us well tonight!"

The servant was surprised. "No, my friend," he explained, "the food is for *them*. We don't eat at the master's table. It is not permitted. We eat in the kitchen."

"Well, I'll bet I can sit down and eat with them," Chicoria boasted.

"If you beg or if you ask, perhaps, but if you don't ask they won't invite you," replied the servant.

"I never beg," the New Mexican answered. "The master will invite me of his own accord, and I'll bet you twenty dollars he will!"

**Oral Tradition**
What ability of Chicoria's could be considered admirable in his culture?

Reading Check
What request did the ranch owner make of the New Mexicans?

---

1. **Californio** (kä´ lē fôr´ nyō) term for the Spanish-speaking colonists who established ranches in California under Spanish and Mexican rule.

So they made a twenty-dollar bet and they instructed the serving maid to watch if this self-confident New Mexican had to ask the master for a place at the table. Then the maid took Chicoria into the dining room. Chicoria greeted the rancher cordially, but the rancher appeared haughty and did not invite Chicoria to sit with him and his guest at the table. Instead, he asked that a chair be brought and placed by the wall where Chicoria was to sit. The rich ranchers began to eat without inviting Chicoria.

So it is just as the servant predicted, Chicoria thought. The poor are not invited to share the rich man's food!

Then the master spoke: "Tell us about the country where you live. What are some of the customs of New Mexico?"

"Well, in New Mexico when a family sits down to eat each member uses one spoon for each biteful of food," Chicoria said with a twinkle in his eyes.

The ranchers were amazed that the New Mexicans ate in that manner, but what Chicoria hadn't told them was that each spoon was a piece of tortilla:[2] one fold and it became a spoon with which to scoop up the meal.

"Furthermore," he continued, "our goats are not like yours."

"How are they different?" the rancher asked.

"Here your nannies[3] give birth to two kids, in New Mexico they give birth to three!"

"What a strange thing!" the master said. "But tell us, how can the female nurse three kids?"

"Well, they do it exactly as you're doing it now: While two of them are eating the third one looks on."

The rancher then realized his lack of manners and took Chicoria's hint. He apologized and invited his New Mexico guest to dine at the table. After dinner, Chicoria sang and recited his poetry, putting Gracia to shame. And he won his bet as well.

---

**2. tortilla** (tôr tē´ yə) *n.* thin, round pancake of cornmeal or flour.
**3. nannies** (nan´ ēz) *n.* female goats.

# *from* The People, Yes

## Carl Sandburg

They have yarns[1]
Of a skyscraper so tall they had to put hinges
On the two top stories so to let the moon go by,
Of one corn crop in Missouri when the roots
5   Went so deep and drew off so much water

---

**1. yarns** (yärnz) *n.* tall tales that depend on humor and exaggeration.

▼ **Critical Viewing**
What type of mood does this illustration create? **[Analyze]**

**Vocabulary**
**straddling** (strad′ ′liŋ)
*v.* standing or sitting
with a leg on either
side of something

**cyclone** (sī′ klon′) *n.*
violent, rotating wind-
storm; tornado

**mutineers** (myo͞ot′
′n irz′) *n.* rebels

The Mississippi riverbed that year was dry,
Of pancakes so thin they had only one side,
Of "a fog so thick we shingled the barn and six feet out
    on the fog,"
Of Pecos Pete straddling a cyclone in Texas and riding it
    to the west coast where "it rained out under him,"
10  Of the man who drove a swarm of bees across the Rocky
    Mountains and the Desert "and didn't lose a bee,"
Of a mountain railroad curve where the engineer in his
    cab can touch the caboose and spit in the conductor's eye,
Of the boy who climbed a cornstalk growing so fast he
    would have starved to death if they hadn't shot
    biscuits up to him,
Of the old man's whiskers: "When the wind was with
    him his whiskers arrived a day before he did,"
Of the hen laying a square egg and cackling, "Ouch!"
    and of hens laying eggs with the dates printed on them,
15  Of the ship captain's shadow: it froze to the deck one
    cold winter night,
Of mutineers on that same ship put to chipping rust
    with rubber hammers,
Of the sheep counter who was fast and accurate: "I just
    count their feet and divide by four,"
Of the man so tall he must climb a ladder to shave
    himself,

**Oral Tradition**
Does Sandburg's use
of exaggeration and
repetition portray a
country at rest or on
the move? Explain.

Of the runt so teeny-weeny it takes two men and a boy to
   see him,
20  Of mosquitoes: one can kill a dog, two of them a man,
   Of a cyclone that sucked cookstoves out of the kitchen,
      up the chimney flue, and on to the next town,
   Of the same cyclone picking up wagontracks in Nebraska
      and dropping them over in the Dakotas,
   Of the hook-and-eye snake unlocking itself into forty
      pieces, each piece two inches long, then in nine seconds
      flat snapping itself together again,
   Of the watch swallowed by the cow—when they butchered
      her a year later the watch was running and had the
      correct time,
25  Of horned snakes, hoop snakes that roll themselves
      where they want to go, and rattlesnakes carrying bells
      instead of rattles on their tails,
   Of the herd of cattle in California getting lost in a giant
      redwood tree that had hollowed out,
   Of the man who killed a snake by putting its tail in its
      mouth so it swallowed itself,
   Of railroad trains whizzing along so fast they reach the
      station before the whistle,
   Of pigs so thin the farmer had to tie knots in their tails
      to keep them from crawling through the cracks in their
      pens,

**Summarize**
Would it be essential to list all of the characters and animals in a summary of this poem? Why or why not?

 Reading
Check

What tall tales from the poem do the illustrations on pages 1056 and 1057 show?

BM-17—Paul Bunyan and Babe, his Blue Ox, Bemidji, Minn.

**▶ Critical Viewing**
How do the figures shown here capture the spirit of this poem? **[Analyze]**

**Oral Tradition**
What characteristics are shared by the folk heroes mentioned at the end of the poem?

30  Of Paul Bunyan's big blue ox, Babe, measuring between the eyes forty-two ax-handles and a plug of Star tobacco exactly,
Of John Henry's hammer and the curve of its swing and his singing of it as "a rainbow round my shoulder."

## Critical Thinking

*Cite textual evidence to support your responses.*

© 1. **Key Ideas and Details** **(a)** In "Chicoria," how does the server respond when Chicoria says he expects to be fed well? **(b) Analyze:** Why does Chicoria assume that he will eat at the rancher's table?

© 2. **Key Ideas and Details** **Analyze:** Why does Chicoria tell the story about the goats?

© 3. **Key Ideas and Details** **(a)** Identify three people mentioned in the excerpt from *The People, Yes* who have amazing abilities or skills. **(b) Evaluate:** In what way does each character's ability contribute to survival in a wild, new country?

© 4. **Integration of Knowledge and Ideas** **(a) Interpret:** With a partner, interpret the meaning of the title *The People, Yes*. **(b) Discuss:** Are the heroes of these tales inspirational in today's world? Share your answers with the class.

© 5. **Integration of Knowledge and Ideas** **(a)** What traits do you think are valued by the cultures that developed these tales? **(b)** What aspects of these tales are most relevant to modern readers? *[Connect to the Big Question: Are yesterday's heroes important today?]*

## Reading Skill: Summarize

**1. (a)** To help you **summarize** "Chicoria," construct a timeline of events. **(b)** Use your timeline to write a brief summary.

**2. (a)** Fill in a cluster diagram like the one shown with images from *The People, Yes.* **(b)** Summarize the poem by stating the main idea behind the images.

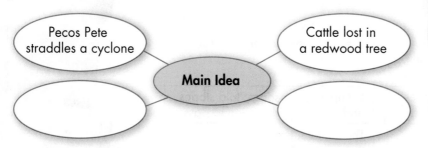

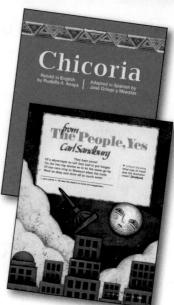

## Literary Analysis: Oral Tradition

©**3. Integration of Knowledge and Ideas** How is Chicoria both typical and *not* typical of a hero of the **oral tradition**?

©**4. Craft and Structure (a)** What features of the oral tradition are contained in lines 8–21 of Sandburg's poem? **(b)** Explain the meanings of *runt* and *teeny-weeny* (line 19) and the tone they create.

## Vocabulary

© **Acquisition and Use** Use a word from page 1050 to form an **analogy** that matches the relationship of the other word pair.

**1.** *Rain* is to *cloudburst* as *wind* is to _____.

**2.** *Rudely* is to *enemy* as _____ is to *friend*.

**3.** *Rebel* is to _____ as *hike* is to *mountaineers*.

**4.** *Arms* are to *hugging* as *legs* are to _____.

**5.** *Insecure* is to _____ as *talkative* is to *silent*.

**6.** *Gentle* is to *rough* as *humble* is to _____.

**Word Study** Use the context of the sentences and what you know about the **suffix -eer** to explain your answer to each question.

**1.** Does an *auctioneer* want responses from an audience?

**2.** Would it be helpful for a *balladeer* to have a pleasant voice?

### Word Study

The **suffix -eer** means "one who does."

**Apply It** Explain how the suffix -eer contributes to the meanings of these words. Consult a dictionary if necessary.

**mountaineer**
**profiteer**
**rocketeer**

# Integrated Language Skills

## Brer Possum's Dilemma • John Henry • Chicoria • from The People, Yes •

### Conventions: Commas

A **comma** is a punctuation mark that signals a brief pause.

| Use a Comma... | |
|---|---|
| 1) ...before a conjunction to separate two independent clauses in a compound sentence. | The wind howled, **and** the rain pelted the roof. |
| 2) ...between items in a series. | Campers sang **songs, told stories, and waited** for the storm to pass. |
| 3) ...between adjectives. | The **soaked, tired** hikers returned to the cabin. |
| 4) ...after introductory material. | **The next day,** the sun shined brightly. |
| 5) ...with parenthetical expressions. | Everyone was, **without a doubt,** eager to go outside. |
| 6) ...to set off appositives, participial phrases, or adjective clauses. | The water level at the lake, **where we swam every morning,** had risen slightly. |

**Practice A** Identify where commas are needed in each of the following sentences.

1. According to Sandburg's poem folk literature has preserved many tall tales.

2. The long thirsty roots of one corn crop in Missouri drained the Mississippi River dry.

3. The eggs of some hens were square and the eggs of others had dates on them.

4. A herd of cattle got lost inside the cavity of a redwood a giant tree.

© **Reading Application** In "Chicoria," find a sentence modeling each of the following uses of a comma listed in the chart above: Rules 1, 4, and 6.

**Practice B** Use the chart to explain where commas are needed in each sentence and why.

1. Brer Possum a kind critter never liked to see anyone in trouble.

2. One morning Brer Possum discovered Brer Snake at the bottom of a hole.

3. Brer Possum wanted to help but he didn't trust Brer Snake.

4. That mean evil lowdown snake was likely to bite him.

© **Writing Application** Include commas in three sentences you write about folk tales. Use a different comma rule from the chart above in each sentence.

**PH WRITING COACH** Further instruction and practice are available in *Prentice Hall Writing Coach.*

# Writing

**Common Core State Standards**

**L.8.2; RL.8.4; W.8.2, W.8.9; SL.8.1, SL.8.6**
[For the full wording of the standards, see page 1038.]

**Explanatory Text** Write a **critical analysis** to explain how language affects the tone, meaning, and mood in folk literature. Use these tips:

- Draw on specific examples from the stories and poems you read here, or find examples in other sources.
- Analyze the literal and figurative meanings of idioms, analogies, metaphors, and similes in the stories you choose. Then, explain how these word choices evoke an emotional response. For example, in "Chicoria," a goat analogy draws comparison and helps the reader appreciate Chicoria's cle ne The analogy also may entertain readers.
- Point out examples of comic techniques, su perbole (exaggeration) or understatement.

**Grammar Application** Check your draft to make ure u used commas correctly, particularly with introductory str

**Writing Workshop:** *Work in Progress*

**Prewriting for Exposition** To prepare for a multimedia r t review your Image Research. In a rough outline, write fac examples you could use to build a narrative with the visuals u identified. Save this Multimedia Outline in your writing portfolio.

 Use this prewriting activity to prepare for the **Writing Workshop** on page 1084.

# Speaking and Listening

**Comprehension and Collaboration** Working with a group, conduc a **storytelling workshop.**

- Choose a folk tale that the class has read, and discuss ways of presenting it.
- Each group member should then make his or her own determinations about the most effective way to interpret the story, including the use of voice and gestures to dramatize the action, the inclusion of props, and the addition of new descriptions using appropriate language.
- If there is dialect in the original, performers may choose to translate it for clarity or retain it for faithfulness to the original.
- In your group, take turns retelling the story for the class.
- Audience members should determine ways in which each retelling is faithful to or departs from the original. Then, they should evaluate the choices each performer has made, based on criteria such as dramatic impact, clarity of meaning, and consistency of approach.

**PHLit Online!**
www.PHLitOnline.com
- Interactive graphic organizers
- Grammar tutorial
- Interactive journals

# Test Practice: Reading

## Summarize

### Fiction Selection

**Directions:** *Read the selection. Then, answer the questions.*

Ms. Kline was fed up with kids riding through her driveway. Mrs. Kim was tired of dodging skateboarders in the supermarket parking lot while she tried to wheel her grocery cart out to her car. Mr. Perez was just worried that someone would get hurt. Members of the Elm Street Association wanted the situation to change.

So they met at City Hall to talk and create slogans addressing the problem with the skateboarders. Signs with slogans were posted on lawns and the local newspaper featured editorials and cartoons addressing the issue. The community was frustrated, and skateboarders were getting restless. Something had to be done. Finally, a proposal was written and a vote was scheduled. If approved, the new law would ban skating in all public spaces, including streets, sidewalks, and parking lots. However, the law also provides funding for a skate-park where kids could skateboard safely without bothering people.

**1.** Which detail is unnecessary in a summary of this selection?
   **A.** Mrs. Kim has trouble getting her shopping cart to her car.
   **B.** The new law would provide funding for a skate park.
   **C.** The neighbors want to protect their property.
   **D.** The association wanted to make a positive solution.

**2.** Which detail is *most* important in a summary of this selection?
   **A.** Kids are allowed to skate wherever they choose.
   **B.** The new law bans skating on public property.
   **C.** Kids are irresponsible on skateboards.
   **D.** Angry citizens punish kids for skateboarding.

**3.** What is the topic of this selection?
   **A.** Kids who skateboard cause trouble in the community.
   **B.** The town finds creative ways to advertise their problems.
   **C.** Citizens ban skateboarding in the community.
   **D.** Citizens meet to solve the problem of skateboarding in the community.

### Writing for Assessment

Summarize the selection in a few sentences. Include only the most important main ideas and key details.

# Nonfiction Selection

**Directions:** *Read the selection. Then, answer the questions.*

Political cartoons that often appear in print media present a particular point of view. These cartoons often focus on pressing and current issues that a community may be facing, such as banning skateboarding on public property. Political cartoonists emphasize an issue and try to persuade the reader to think a certain way. Cartoons usually focus on one image accompanied by a memorable and humorous slogan. Using exaggeration and humor, cartoonists make powerful statements.

Most political cartoons use symbols rather than a lot of words. A symbol is a concrete object that represents something else. Uncle Sam, for example, is often used to represent the United States. In analyzing a political cartoon, look at all the images and words. They are the keys to understanding the cartoonist's point of view.

1. Which of the following details could be left out of a summary of this passage?
   A. Political cartoons emphasize an issue.
   B. Political cartoons often appear in print media.
   C. Most political cartoons use symbols rather than a lot of words.
   D. A symbol is a concrete object that represents something else.

2. Which of the following forms would a summary of this selection *best* utilize?
   A. a timeline
   B. a chart
   C. an outline
   D. a Venn diagram

3. Which of the following statements is the *best* summary of this selection?
   A. A political cartoon uses humor to present a point of view and to influence readers.
   B. A political cartoon uses symbols to promote ideas, such as patriotism.
   C. To understand a political cartoon, you would need sufficient knowledge of the subject matter.
   D. Political cartoons make fun of society

## Writing for Assessment

**Connecting Across Texts**
In a paragraph, compare the signs with slogans discussed in the first selection with the political cartoons discussed in the second selection. What is similar and different about them?

**PHLit Online!**
www.PHLitOnline.com
- Online practice
- Instant feedback

# Reading for Information

## Analyzing Argumentative and Functional Texts

### Book Review

### Book Features

 **Common Core State Standards**

**Reading Informational Text**
**3.** Analyze how a text makes connections among and distinctions between individuals, ideas, or events (e.g., through comparisons, analogies, or categories).

**Language**
**4.** Determine or clarify the meaning of unknown and multiple-meaning words or phrases based on *grade 8 reading and content,* choosing flexibly from a range of strategies.

**6.** Acquire and use accurately grade-appropriate general academic and domain-specific words and phrases; gather vocabulary knowledge when considering a word or phrase important to comprehension or expression.

## Reading Skill: Evaluate Structural Patterns

**Structural patterns** in texts organize information. Articles, such as book reviews, and books typically include **text features** that reinforce the structural patterns of a text. The chart shows examples of features that keep text unified and coherent. As you examine the book review and the excerpt of features from a book, **evaluate** whether the author has successfully used structural patterns.

| Structural Features of Books | Structural Features of Book Reviews |
|---|---|
| • **table of contents:** an opening section that provides information to help the reader locate sections of a book<br>• **chapters:** sections that organize information by topic or by time period<br>• **index:** a listing of key words and phrases that helps readers to locate specific information in a book | • **heading:** large, bold text that identifies the book being reviewed<br>• **byline:** a line that shows who wrote the review<br>• **introduction:** an opening section that briefly describes the book being reviewed or provides information that is useful for context<br>• **conclusion:** a closing section that sums up the book's contents and the reviewer's opinion of it |

## Content-Area Vocabulary

These words appear in the selections that follow. You may also encounter them in other content-area texts.

- **annotated** (an´ ə tā´ id) *adj.* containing notes or comments
- **scholarship** (skäl´ ər ship) *n.* knowledge gained by study
- **acknowledgments** (ak näl´ ij mənts) *n.* a section of a book expressing gratitude or giving credit to those who have helped the author with the work

# A Life in Letters

## Book Review by Zakia Carter

**Zora Neale Hurston: A Life in Letters.**
Edited by Carla Kaplan
Doubleday; October 2002; 896 pages

Within days of having *Zora Neale Hurston: A Life in Letters* in my possession, I was inspired to devote the total of my lunch hour to selecting beautiful blank cards and stationery, a fine ink pen and a book of stamps. By the end of the day, I had penned six letters, the old-fashioned way, to friends and relatives—something I haven't done since summer camp. In our haste to save time, we check our inboxes with an eagerness that was once reserved for that moment before pushing a tiny silver key into a mailbox door. E-mail has replaced paper and pen, so much so that the U.S. Postal Service is losing business. But the truth of the matter is, folks will neither salvage nor cherish e-mail as they might a handwritten letter.

And so *A Life in Letters* is a gift. It includes more than 500 letters and postcards written by Zora Neale Hurston over four decades. The 800-plus-page collection reveals more about this brilliant and complex woman than perhaps the entire body of her published works combined, including her notoriously unrevealing autobiography, *Dust Tracks on the Road*. Amazingly, the urgency and immediacy (typos and all) we associate with e-mail can also be found in Zora's letters. She writes to a veritable who's who in American history and society, including Langston Hughes, Carl Van Vechten, Charlotte Osgood Mason, Franz Boas, Dorothy West and

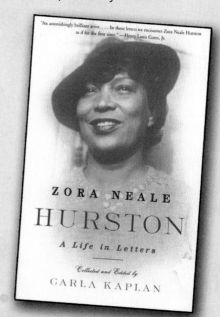

"An astonishingly brilliant artist. . . . In these letters we encounter Zora Neale Hurston as if for the first time." —Henry Louis Gates, Jr.

ZORA NEALE
HURSTON
A Life in Letters
Collected and Edited by
CARLA KAPLAN

# Book Review

The details provided here create coherence; the details give reasons that the book is worth reading.

A brief summary of the book's contents adds unity to a book review.

W.E.B. Du Bois among others, sometimes more than once or twice a day. In these, her most intimate writings, Zora comes to life.

While we are familiar with Zora the novelist, essayist, playwright and anthropologist, *A Life in Letters* introduces us to Zora the filmmaker; Zora the Barnard College undergrad and Columbia University student; Zora the two-time Guggenheim fellow; Zora the chicken specialist; Zora the thrice-married wife; and Zora the political pundit. Zora's letters are at times flip, ironic, heartbreaking and humorous. They are insightful, biting and candid as journal entries. One can only wish for responses to Zora's words, but the work is not incomplete without them.

A treasure trove of information, in addition to the **annotated** letters, a chronology of Zora's life, a glossary of the people, events, and institutions to which she refers in her letters, and a thorough bibliographical listing are generously included by editor Carla Kaplan. Each decade of writing is introduced by an essay on the social, political, and personal points of significance in Zora's life. Kaplan's is a fine, well edited and utterly revealing work of **scholarship** into the life of one of the greatest and often most misunderstood American writers. In many ways, *A Life in Letters* is, in fact, a long love letter for Zora. It is a reminder to salvage and cherish what should not be forgotten and an admonishment to write what you love on paper.

—Zakia Carter is an editor at Africana.com.

This structural feature provides information about the reviewer. Reviewers are often experts on the subjects of the books they review.

The table of contents gives an overview of the sections of the book.

# Book Features

**Features:**

- overview of the book's content
- structural patterns for parts of book
- nonfiction (usually)
- general or a specific audience

## ZORA NEALE HURSTON:
### *A Life in Letters*

## CONTENTS

The chapter titles reveal that the structural pattern of the book is chronological.

The listing of reference material helps readers evaluate the coherence and value of the information in the book.

# INDEX

The index provides an alphabetical listing of details provided in the book, along with page numbers that show where the information is located.

## Comparing Argumentative and Functional Texts

**1. Craft and Structure** **(a)** Explain how the book review distinguishes and connects different aspects of Zora Neale Hurston's life. **(b)** Compare the purpose of a book review to that of a table of contents and an index. **(c)** Explain how the **structural patterns** of each of these texts help you understand what a book is about.

## Content-Area Vocabulary

**2. (a)** Use a print or an online dictionary to identify and explain the meaning of the root *scholar* in the words *scholarship* and *scholarly.* **(b)** Then, use the words *scholar, scholarship,* and *scholarly* in a paragraph about students who achieve academic success.

## Timed Writing

### Explanatory Text: Explanation

> **Format**
> The prompt gives specific directions about the topic to discuss and the details to include in your writing.

> Examine the table of contents and index, noting the ways in which they present the information. Then, write an explanation of the purpose of those book features and give tips for using them as reference tools. Use examples from the text to make your points clear. (40 minutes)

> **Academic Vocabulary**
> When you *examine* something, you study the details in order to come to a conclusion.

### 5-Minute Planner

Complete these steps before you begin to write:

1. Read the prompt carefully, noting the key highlighted terms.
2. Examine the table of contents and index. Look for details that help explain their function and purpose.
3. List the types of information found in the two features.
4. Jot down two ways you would use each book feature.
5. Consult your notes as you draft your explanation.

## Comparing Heroic Characters

**Heroic characters** are men and women who show great courage and overcome difficult challenges. A hero in a literary work may be real, fictional, or even based in myth. Often, the hero in a tall tale or legend is a mixture of both—a real historical figure whose actions have become so exaggerated that he or she becomes a legend.

As these selections show, the **theme** of heroism runs across time periods and appears in different literary forms. Carl Sandburg and Stephen Vincent Benét wrote in the period between the world wars—a time when many Americans were looking back fondly at the heroes and values of the western frontier. In contrast, Davy Crockett wrote his own heroic story of the frontier as he lived it— except that he added a few creative touches to fuel his legend.

"Davy Crockett's Dream" and "Paul Bunyan of the North Woods" portray traditional heroes. The hero of "Invocation" is the American muse, who personifies the American spirit. As you read, look for instances in which the hero overcomes larger-than-life challenges. Identify the heroic traits, such as bravery and endurance, that help the hero to master each challenge. Then, fill in a character web like this one to compare the characters' heroic traits.

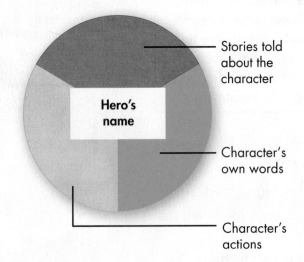

Stories told about the character

Hero's name

Character's own words

Character's actions

**Common Core State Standards**

**Reading Literature**

**3.** Analyze how a particular line of dialogue or incidents in a story propel the action, reveal aspects of a character, or provoke a decision.

**9.** Analyze how a modern work of fiction draws on themes, patterns of events, or character types from myths, traditional stories, or religious works such as the Bible, including describing how the material is rendered new. (*Literature in Context*)

**Writing**

**2.** Write informative/explanatory texts to examine a topic and convey ideas, concepts, and information through the selection, organization, and analysis of relevant content.

**9.** Draw evidence from literary or informational texts to support analysis, reflection, and research. (*Timed Writing*)

www.PHLitOnline.com

- Vocabulary flashcards
- Interactive journals
- More about the authors
- Selection audio
- Interactive graphic organizers

# Are yesterday's *heroes* important today?

## Writing About the Big Question

In different ways, these selections look back to the heroes of an earlier America. Use this sentence starter to develop your ideas.

To be a hero today, a person can win **admiration** through such actions as _____ and _____.

# Meet the Authors

## Davy Crockett (1786–1836)
### Author of "Davy Crockett's Dream"

Davy Crockett was a genuine frontiersman, but the colorful tall tales in his autobiography helped make him a legend. Crockett was also a politician, representing Tennessee in Congress. He joined the fight for Texas independence and was killed at the battle of the Alamo in 1836. The legends surrounding Crockett took on new form with the airing of the 1950's television show *Davy Crockett*. Millions tuned in, sparking a nationwide fad for Crockett-style coonskin caps.

## Carl Sandburg (1878–1967)
### Author of "Paul Bunyan of the North Woods"

Carl Sandburg had a lifelong interest in American history and folklore, especially the nation's myths and tall tales. These stories influenced much of his poetry in works such as *The People, Yes* (p. 1055). Sandburg was also a journalist and historian who wrote a widely admired biography of Abraham Lincoln that was six volumes long.

## Stephen Vincent Benét (1898–1943)
### Author of "Invocation" from *John Brown's Body*

A poet, novelist, and short-story writer, Stephen Vincent Benét often wrote about American history and its heroes. With his wife, Rosemary Carr, Benét wrote *A Book of Americans,* a collection of lively poems for young people about characters in American history. Benét's widely read Civil War epic, *John Brown's Body,* won him the Pulitzer Prize in 1929.

# Davy Crockett's Dream

## Davy Crockett

One day when it was so cold that I was afeard to open my mouth, lest I should freeze my tongue, I took my little dog named Grizzle and cut out for Salt River Bay to kill something for dinner. I got a good ways from home afore I knowed where I was, and as I had swetted some before I left the house my hat froze fast to my head, and I like to have put my neck out of joint in trying to pull it off. When I sneezed the icicles crackled all up and down the inside of my nose, like when you walk over a bog in winter time. The varmints was so scarce that I couldn't find one, and so when I come to an old log hut that had belonged to some squatter that had ben reformed out by the nabors, I stood my rifle up agin one of the door posts and went in. I kindled up a little fire and told Grizzle I was going to take a nap. I piled up a heap of chestnut burs for a pillow and straitened myself out on the ground, for I can curl closer than a rattlesnake and lay straiter than a log. I laid with the back of my head agin the hearth, and my eyes looking up chimney so that I could see when it was noon by the sun, for

Mrs. Crockett was always rantankerous[1] when I staid out over the time. I got to sleep before Grizzle had done warming the eend of his nose, and I had swallowed so much cold wind that it laid hard on my stomach, and as I laid gulping and belching the wind went out of me and roared up chimney like a young whirlwind. So I had a pesky dream, and kinder thought, till I waked up, that I was floating down the Massassippy in a holler tree, and I hadn't room to stir my legs and arms no more than they were withed together with young saplings. While I was there and want able to help myself a feller called Oak Wing that lived about twenty miles off, and that I had give a most almighty licking once, cum and looked in with his blind eye that I had gouged out five years before, and I saw him looking in one end of the hollow log, and he axed me if I wanted to get out. I telled him to tie a rope to one of my legs and draw me out as soon as God would let him and as

◀ **Critical Viewing**
Does Davy Crockett, pictured here, look like he might use "a heap of chestnut burs" for a pillow? Explain. **[Assess]**

Reading Check

Why does Crockett fall asleep looking up a chimney?

---

1. **rantankerous** (ran taŋ′ kər əs) *adj.* dialect for *cantankerous*, meaning "bad-tempered and quarrelsome."

much sooner as he was a mind to. But he said he wouldn't do it that way, he would ram me out with a pole. So he took a long pole and rammed it down agin my head as if he was ramming home the cattridge in a cannon. This didn't make me budge an inch, but it pounded my head down in between my shoulders till I look'd like a turcle with his head drawn in. This started my temper a trifle, and I ript and swore till the breath boiled out of the end of the log like the steam out of the funnel pipe of a steemboat. Jest then I woke up, and seed my wife pulling my leg, for it was enermost sundown and she had cum arter me. There was a long icicle hanging to her nose, and when she tried to kiss me, she run it right into my eye. I told her my dreem, and sed I would have revenge on Oak Wing for pounding my head. She said it was all a dreem and that Oak was not to blame; but I had a very diffrent idee of the matter. So I went and talked to him, and told him what he had done to me in a dreem, and it was settled that he should make me an apology in his next dreem, and that wood make us square,[2] for I don't like to be run upon when I'm asleep, any more than I do when I'm awake.

**Heroic Characters**
What examples of exaggeration and understatement can you find in this passage?

---

**2. square** even.

## Critical Thinking

© **1. Key Ideas and Details (a)** Why does Davy Crockett go out in the woods? **(b) Infer:** What can you infer about his home life?

© **2. Key Ideas and Details (a)** What happens in Davy Crockett's dream, and how does he react? **(b) Analyze Cause and Effect:** How does he actually settle the matter with Oak Wing? **(c) Analyze:** How does this outcome show that this narrative is a "tall tale"?

Cite textual evidence to support your responses.

© **3. Craft and Structure (a) Analyze:** How do the dialect, spelling, and grammar of the writing affect the tone of the tale? **(b) Infer:** From the way he tells this tale, how would you describe Davy Crockett?

© **4. Integration of Knowledge and Ideas (a)** Could an adventurer like Crockett become a hero today? Why or why not? **(b)** Do we expect today's heroes to have a sense of humor? Explain. *[Connect to the Big Question: Are yesterday's heroes important today?]*

# Paul Bunyan
## Of the North Woods

## Carl Sandburg

Who made Paul Bunyan, who gave him birth as a myth, who joked him into life as the Master Lumberjack, who fashioned him forth as an apparition[1] easing the hours of men amid axes and trees, saws and lumber? The people, the bookless people, they made Paul and had him alive long before he got into the books for those who read. He grew up in shanties, around the hot stoves of winter, among socks and mittens drying, in the smell of tobacco smoke and the roar of laughter mocking the outside weather. And some of Paul came overseas in wooden bunks below decks in sailing vessels. And some of Paul is old as the hills, young as the alphabet.

---

1. **apparition** (ap´ ə rish´ ən) *n.* sudden or unusual sight.

▶ Critical Viewing
What characteristics in this picture fit Paul Bunyan's role as a legendary hero? **[Analyze]**

Vocabulary
**shanties** (shan´ tēz)
*n.* roughly built cabins or shacks

32 USA

PAUL BUNYAN

**Vocabulary**
**commotion**
(kə mō′ shən) *n.* noisy movement

The Pacific Ocean froze over in the winter of the Blue Snow and Paul Bunyan had long teams of oxen hauling regular white snow over from China. This was the winter Paul gave a party to the Seven Axmen. Paul fixed a granite floor sunk two hundred feet deep for them to dance on. Still, it tipped and tilted as the dance went on. And because the Seven Axmen refused to take off their hobnailed boots, the sparks from the nails of their dancing feet lit up the place so that Paul didn't light the kerosene lamps. No women being on the Big Onion river at that time the Seven Axmen had to dance with each other, the one left over in each set taking Paul as a partner. The commotion of the dancing that night brought on an earthquake and the Big Onion river moved over three counties to the east.

One year when it rained from St. Patrick's Day till the Fourth of July, Paul Bunyan got disgusted because his celebration on the Fourth was spoiled. He dived into Lake Superior and swam to where a solid pillar of water was coming down. He dived under this pillar, swam up into it and climbed with powerful swimming strokes, was gone about an hour, came splashing down, and as the rain stopped, he explained, "I turned the darn thing off." This is told in the Big North Woods and on the Great Lakes, with many particulars.

Two mosquitoes lighted on one of Paul Bunyan's oxen, killed it, ate it, cleaned the bones, and sat on a grub shanty picking their teeth as Paul came along. Paul sent to Australia for two special bumblebees to kill these mosquitoes. But the bees and the mosquitoes intermarried; their children had stingers on both ends. And things kept getting worse till Paul brought a big boatload of sorghum[2] up from Louisiana and while all the bee-mosquitoes were eating at the sweet sorghum he floated them down to the Gulf of Mexico. They got so fat that it was easy to drown them all between New Orleans and Galveston.

---

**2. sorghum** (sôr′ gəm) *n.* tropical grasses bearing flowers and seeds, grown for use as grain or syrup.

Paul logged on the Little Gimlet in Oregon one winter. The cookstove at that camp covered an acre of ground. They fastened the side of a hog on each snowshoe and four men used to skate on the griddle while the cook flipped the pancakes. The eating table was three miles long; elevators carried the cakes to the ends of the table where boys on bicycles rode back and forth on a path down the center of the table dropping the cakes where called for.

Benny, the Little Blue Ox of Paul Bunyan, grew two feet every time Paul looked at him, when a youngster. The barn was gone one morning and they found it on Benny's back; he grew out of it in a night. One night he kept pawing and bellowing for more pancakes, till there were two hundred men at the cookshanty stove trying to keep him fed. About breakfast time Benny broke loose, tore down the cookshanty, ate all the pancakes piled up for the loggers' breakfast. And after that Benny made his mistake; he ate the red hot stove; and that finished him. This is only one of the hot-stove stories told in the North Woods.

## Critical Thinking

**1. Key Ideas and Details (a)** According to Sandburg, what is the origin of the Paul Bunyan stories? **(b) Interpret:** What does Sandburg mean by saying that "some of Paul is old as the hills, young as the alphabet"?

*Cite textual evidence to support your responses.*

**2. Key Ideas and Details (a) Classify:** Identify two actions that show that Paul Bunyan is clever as well as strong. **(b) Connect:** How do these qualities relate to the myth of the heroic character?

**3. Key Ideas and Details (a)** How does Paul Bunyan stop the rain? **(b) Generalize:** What do this anecdote and other details in the selection tell you about life in the Midwest in the early nineteenth century?

**4. Integration of Knowledge and Ideas (a) Speculate:** Do you think the Paul Bunyan stories might have been based on a real person? **(b) Hypothesize:** What type of person in today's world might inspire this kind of story?

**5. Integration of Knowledge and Ideas (a)** Why would a lumberjack have been a hero in frontier America? **(b)** What qualities does Paul Bunyan share with today's heroes? *[Connect to the Big Question: Are yesterday's heroes important today?]*

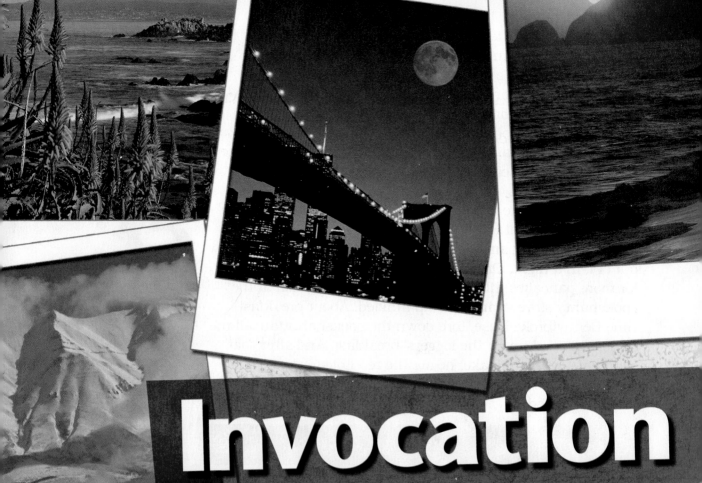

# Invocation

## from John Brown's Body

### STEPHEN VINCENT BENÉT

**Background** This invocation is the introduction to an **epic,** a long narrative poem about heroes. Traditionally, classical writers began an epic by appealing to the muse of poetry, a goddess who could provide inspiration. To begin his epic poem about the Civil War, Benét calls on a different muse—the spirit of America. He finds that this muse is hard to get to know because she—like the country she symbolizes—is so varied and ever-changing.

American *muse,* whose strong and diverse heart
So many men have tried to understand
But only made it smaller with their art,
Because you are as various as your land,

5    As mountainous-deep, as flowered with blue rivers,
Thirsty with deserts, buried under snows,
As native as the shape of Navajo quivers.
And native, too, as the sea-voyaged rose.

Swift runner, never captured or subdued,
10   Seven-branched elk[1] beside the mountain stream,
That half a hundred hunters have pursued
But never matched their bullets with the dream,

Where the great huntsmen failed, I set my sorry
And mortal snare for your immortal quarry.[2]

15   You are the buffalo-ghost, the broncho-ghost
With dollar-silver in your saddle-horn,
The cowboys riding in from Painted Post,
The Indian arrow in the Indian corn,

And you are the clipped velvet of the lawns
20   Where Shropshire grows from Massachusetts sods,
The grey Maine rocks—and the war-painted dawns
That break above the Garden of the Gods.

The prairie-schooners crawling toward the ore
And the cheap car, parked by the station-door.

25   Where the skyscrapers lift their foggy plumes
Of stranded smoke out of a stony mouth,
You are that high stone and its arrogant fumes,
And you are ruined gardens in the South

## LITERATURE IN CONTEXT

### Cultural Connection

**Allusions** This poem uses allusions, references to places and events, in order to capture the varied and changeable nature of the American spirit.

- **Navajo quivers** Cases for holding arrows used by Native Americans of the Southwest
- **buffalo-ghost, broncho-ghost** The buffalo and bronco (wild pony), symbols of the western frontier
- **Shropshire** English county known for its green countryside
- **prairie-schooners** Covered wagons used by pioneers moving westward
- **medicine-bag** Small leather bag containing herbs and other sacred objects used by Indian shamans, or healers
- **"Thames and all the rivers of the kings"** England's main river, and those of other Old World powers

**Vocabulary**
**subdued** (səb dood´)
*adj.* beaten; brought under control

**arrogant** (ar´ ə gənt)
*adj.* self-important

Reading Check

What is the speaker trying to understand?

_____

1. **seven-branched elk** *n.* large American deer with wide antlers that divide into several branches.
2. **mortal snare for your immortal quarry** The poet is only human and so cannot set a trap (snare) that can catch the muse, who is immortal.

And bleak New England farms, so winter-white
30 Even their roofs look lonely, and the deep,
The middle grainland where the wind of night
Is like all blind earth sighing in her sleep.

A friend, an enemy, a sacred hag³
With two tied oceans in her medicine-bag.

35 They tried to fit you with an English song
And clip your speech into the English tale.
But, even from the first, the words went wrong,
The catbird pecked away the nightingale.⁴

The homesick men begot high-cheekboned things
40 Whose wit was whittled with a different sound,
And Thames and all the rivers of the kings
Ran into Mississippi and were drowned . . .

. . . All these you are, and each is partly you,
And none is false, and none is wholly true.

45 So how to see you as you really are,
So how to suck the pure, distillate,⁵ stored
*Essence* of essence from the hidden star
And make it pierce like a riposting⁶ sword.

**Heroic Characters**
How does the imagery in lines 35–42 emphasize the young country's break with its past?

◄ **Critical Viewing**
How do you think this Colorado landscape came to be called the "Garden of the Gods"? **[Speculate]**

Reading Check
What does the speaker realize in lines 43–44?

---

**3. hag** (hag) *n.* a witch; also an ugly, old woman.
**4. catbird . . . nightingale** The catbird is an American bird; the nightingale a European one.
**5. distillate** (dis´ tə lāt´) *n.* a substance that has been reduced to its purest form, or essence.
**6. riposting** (ri pōst´ iŋ) *v.* in swordplay, thrusting to counter an opponent's blow.

For, as we hunt you down, you must escape
50 And we pursue a shadow of our own
That can be caught in a magician's cape
But has the flatness of a painted stone.

Never the running stag, the gull at wing,
The pure elixir[7], the American thing.

55 And yet, at moments when the mind was hot
With something fierier than joy or grief,
When each known spot was an eternal spot
And every leaf was an immortal leaf,

I think that I have seen you, not as one,
60 But clad in diverse *semblances* and powers,
Always the same, as light falls from the sun,
And always different, as the differing hours. . . .

---

**7. elixir** (i lik´ sər) *n.* a magic potion; or the essential quality of something.

## Critical Thinking

Cite textual evidence to support your responses.

1. **Key Ideas and Details (a)** To whom does Benét address this "Invocation"? **(b) Analyze:** What qualities does he first note about this subject? **(c) Connect:** How does this observation influence the rest of the poem?

2. **Craft and Structure (a) Forms of Poetry:** Review the Background note on page 1078. How does this poem fit the purpose and characteristics of an epic? **(b) Assess:** How does its subject suit an epic treatment?

3. **Integration of Knowledge and Ideas (a)** In what lines does Benét emphasize conflicts between England and America? **(b) Infer:** Why are those differences important to his vision of America? **(c) Assess:** Does Benét succeed in capturing the American spirit? Why or why not?

4. **Integration of Knowledge and Ideas (a)** What does Benét find heroic about the American muse? **(b)** Are the many "faces" of this muse still present today? **(c)** What places or figures would you add to Benét's list? *[Connect to the Big Question: Are yesterday's heroes important today?]*

## Comparing Heroic Characters

**1. Key Ideas and Details (a)** Identify examples of exaggeration in "Paul Bunyan of the North Woods." **(b)** Why would exaggeration be typical in stories about heroes?

**2. Key Ideas and Details** What heroic traits does Benét's American muse share with Paul Bunyan and Davy Crockett?

**3. Integration of Knowledge and Ideas (a)** Complete a chart like this one to compare heroic characters. **(b)** Choose two story incidents from your chart. Explain how each develops the heroism of the main character.

|  | Davy Crockett's Dream | Paul Bunyan of the North Woods |
|---|---|---|
| **Real or Legend?** | | |
| **Challenges** | | |
| **Heroic Actions** | | |
| **Exaggeration** | | |
| **Tone: Humorous or Serious?** | | |

## ⏱ Timed Writing

### Explanatory Text: Essay

Write an essay comparing how heroic characters are presented in these three works. Consider how each writer has explored the theme of American heroism. **(40 minutes)**

### 5-Minute Planner

**1.** Read the prompt carefully and completely.

**2.** Gather your ideas by jotting down answers to these questions:

- What do these American heroes have in common?
- How does each hero reflect the values of a time period?
- How important are humor and exaggeration in each work?

**3.** Use the chart you filled in above to help you compare Davy Crockett and Paul Bunyan. Since Benét's American muse is a special, unusual type of hero, consider that work separately.

**4.** Reread the prompt, and then draft your essay.

# Writing Workshop

## Write an Informative Text

### Research: Multimedia Report

**Defining the Form** A **multimedia report** presents information about a topic using a variety of delivery methods, such as audio and video. You might use elements of this form to produce documentaries, present scientific findings, or deliver news reports.

**Assignment** Write a report about a topic that interests you, using audio and visual media as support. Include these elements:

✔ a *focused topic* that you can cover adequately within the given time frame

✔ a *coherent thesis*, ending with a *well-supported conclusion*

✔ well-integrated and *appropriate audio* and *visual* materials from a variety of primary and secondary sources

✔ use of formatting and *presentation techniques* for *visual appeal*

✔ a presentation tailored to your specific *audience* and *purpose*

✔ *smooth transitions* between passages and ideas

✔ a *command of oral and written standard English conventions*

To preview the criteria on which your multimedia report may be judged, see the rubric on page 1089.

 **Writing Workshop:** *Work in Progress*

Review the work you did on pages 1037 and 1061.

## Prewriting/Planning Strategy

**Research your topic.** Choose a topic that interests you. To find creative ways of presenting the topic, conduct a multiple-step search using a variety of sources. While you collect basic information, also look for audio clips, video footage, photographs, charts, maps, and graphs. Take notes on what you find. Then, in a chart like the one below, list the media you plan to use.

|  | Interviews | Music | Art | Informational graphics |
|---|---|---|---|---|
| **Audio** |  |  |  |  |
| **Video/Photos/Visuals** |  |  |  |  |

**Reading Informational Text**
**7.** Evaluate the advantages and disadvantages of using different mediums to present a particular topic or idea.

**Writing**
**2.** Write informative/explanatory texts to examine a topic and convey ideas, concepts, and information through the selection, organization, and analysis of relevant content.
**6.** Use technology, including the Internet, to produce and publish writing and present the relationships between information and ideas efficiently as well as to interact and collaborate with others.
**7.** Conduct short research projects to answer a question, drawing on several sources and generating additional related, focused questions that allow for multiple avenues of exploration.

## Setting Off an Explosion of Ideas

**Ideas** are the starting points a writer uses to launch an interesting and effective presentation. When preparing an oral multimedia report, begin with creative ideas and a workable plan that fits your purpose, format, and audience. Ask yourself these questions:

- How will my audience react to the topic?
- What are the pros and cons of presenting my topic in a digital presentation rather than in a written work?
- What information, audio and visual aids, and digital tools should I use to keep the audience interested?

To address these questions, use a sunburst chart like this one.

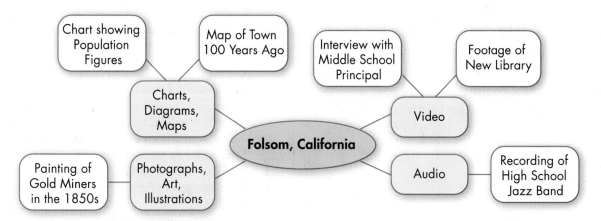

For further ways to generate ideas, consider these techniques:

**Borrowing from TV Shows or Movies** Think about television shows or movies that use media well. Evaluate the media techniques they use to see if those techniques would be appropriate and practical for your own audience and purpose.

**Using Computer Software** Various software programs can be used to pump up the excitement in your presentation. For instance, you might present a slideshow that combines a dramatic narrative with photographs, music, and sound effects.

**Creating a Web Site** Use web tools to create a Web site that provides information about your topic. Show your site to the class as part of your presentation.

# Drafting Strategies

**Sketch an outline.** Before you begin writing, develop an outline to shape the sequence of your presentation. Organize the outline to begin with an introduction that identifies your topic and *thesis*, or main idea. Next, in the body of the report, support and develop your main idea. Finally, in a conclusion, sum up your research and key points. Your outline will also help you to do the following:

- Decide how long to spend on each topic
- Maintain a balance between spoken, audio, and visual elements of your presentation
- Include information about how and when you will use media
- Create variety that will keep your audience engaged

The example outline shows how one writer plans to use multimedia in the introduction of her presentation.

**Respect copyright.** Remember that it is illegal and unethical to copy images and video from Internet sources without permission. If the owner of the site has indicated that the images are free for the public or can be used with source credit, you may use them. Otherwise, you must ask permission from the rights holder.

# Revising Strategy

**Revise to address your audience.** Consider the level of knowledge that your audience will bring to your topic.

- If the audience is well informed, delete facts that are too basic.
- If the group does not know a lot about your topic, add more background information and define any unfamiliar terms.

The chart shows how to help an audience that might be unfamiliar with a key term by using an *appositive phrase*.

 **Common Core**
**State Standards**

**Writing**

**2.a.** Introduce a topic clearly, previewing what is to follow; organize ideas, concepts, and information into broader categories; include formatting, graphics, and multimedia when useful to aiding comprehension.

**2.b.** Develop the topic with relevant, well-chosen facts, definitions, concrete details, quotations, or other information and examples.

**2.c.** Use appropriate and varied transitions to create cohesion and clarify the relationships among ideas and concepts.

**2.f.** Provide a concluding statement or section that follows from and supports the information or explanation presented.

I. Introduction
  A. Early years in Folsom
    Video: Slide on screen of a miner panning for gold in mid-1800s
    Audio: Taped interview with director of the Folsom History Museum
  B. The late 1800s in Folsom
    Still photograph: Folsom Powerhouse in 1896
    Map: Historic map of Folsom

| Original | Revised |
|---|---|
| City planners are thinking about removing the median from historic Sutter Street in Folsom. | City planners are thinking about removing the median, **the raised center divider,** from historic Sutter Street in Folsom. |

## Using Language to Maintain Interest

One way a multimedia presentation differs from a written one is that your audience cannot go back and review sections that are difficult to understand. For this reason, you must keep the audience actively engaged so that they can follow what you are saying.

**Engaging the Audience** Remember that the one key element in any presentation is variation. If you are overly repetitive, your audience will lose interest. Just as you should vary the media you show, work to vary the sentences you use to make your points.

- **Vary sentence length.** If you use one long sentence after another, your audience will have trouble following your speech. If you use one short sentence after another, your audience will start to feel jumpy. The key is to vary sentence length, alternating short sentences with long ones in a pleasing rhythm.

- **Vary sentence type.** Hearing the same type of sentence over and over can be boring. Add interest to your report by weaving together simple, compound, complex, and compound-complex sentences (see p. 1036) in an unpredictable pattern.

| **PH WRITING COACH** |
| --- |
| Further instruction and practice are available in *Prentice Hall Writing Coach*. |

| | |
| --- | --- |
| Compound | |
| Harlem in the 1920s was an exciting place to be, and the arts flourished. | |
| Simple | Complex |
| Creativity was everywhere. From the earthy folk tales of Zora Neale Hurston to the powerful poetry of Langston Hughes, artists and writers were shattering barriers. | |

**Using Transitions** To smooth sudden shifts in topic or changes in media, use transitions. The chart shows common transitions that indicate different types of relationships between ideas.

| Sequence | Comparison | Contrast | Examples | Summarizing |
| --- | --- | --- | --- | --- |
| again, also, and then, finally, further, last | in the same way, likewise, similarly, in like manner | although, and yet, but, despite, even so, however | an illustration of, for example, for instance | all in all, altogether, as has been said, in brief, in conclusion |

### Grammar in Your Writing

Read your draft. Revise it by adding variation in sentence structure and using appropriate transitions.

# Student Model: Jessica Leanore Adamson, Boise, ID

## The Attack on Pearl Harbor

**Slide 1**
**Visual:** Image of Pearl Harbor ca. 1940
**Sound:** Airplane/explosion
**Script:** Pearl Harbor was one of the principal naval bases of WWII. It is located approximately six miles west of Honolulu in Oahu, Hawaii. Early in the morning on December 7, 1941, Japanese submarines and carrier-based planes attacked the U.S. Pacific fleet at Pearl Harbor.

Jessica chose a title that reflects her topic.

The writer has chosen a topic that can be covered in the brief time allotted to her report.

**Slide 2**
**Visual:** Image of American battleship U.S.S. *Arizona.*
**Sound:** Bugle playing Taps
**Script:** Eight American battleships, including the U.S.S. *Arizona* shown here, and ten other navy vessels were sunk or badly damaged, almost 200 American aircraft were destroyed, and approximately 3,000 naval and military personnel were killed or wounded.

The sound effects and images are dramatic and appropriate to the topic, audience, and purpose.

**Slide 8**
**Visual:** Blank screen (black). Words "dereliction of duty" and "errors of judgment" appear letter by letter.
**Sound:** Typewriter
**Script:** Shortly after the attack, U.S. President Franklin D. Roosevelt appointed a commission to determine whether negligence had contributed to the raid. The commission found the naval and army commanders of the area guilty of "dereliction of duty" and "errors of judgment."

The writer uses bold-faced heads and other appropriate formatting to present the organization of the report clearly.

*This model represents the introductory and concluding slides of a multimedia report. Slides 3–7 are not shown. In the full report they present more information along with supporting audio and visual materials to develop the presentation's main idea.*

# Editing and Proofreading

**Focus on conventional English.** Look over the written version of your oral presentation, and correct all errors in grammar. Make sure your report demonstrates a command of standard English conventions. Eliminate any slang or incomplete sentences, unless you are quoting directly from your sources.

# Publishing and Presenting

Consider one of the following ways to share your writing:

**Deliver an oral presentation.** Give a practice performance and try to keep to a strict time limit. Do a final check of your equipment before presenting the report to your classmates.

**Post your presentation.** Using authoring software, post your presentation to a class Web site. If possible, link to related online sites and invite comments from classmates.

# Reflecting on Your Writing

**Writer's Journal** Jot down your answers to this question:

*If you had to create another multimedia report, what would you do differently?*

# Rubric for Self-Assessment

Find evidence in your writing to address each category. Then, use the rating scale to grade your work.

**Spiral Review**
Earlier in this unit, you learned about **sentence structure** (p. 1036) and **commas** (p. 1060). Check any written material you plan to present as part of your multimedia report for errors in comma usage and make sure that you vary your sentence structures.

| Criteria | Rating Scale |
| --- | --- |
| | not very          very |
| **Focus:** How clearly do you identify and cover your topic? | 1  2  3  4  5 |
| **Organization:** How well focused is your presentation, considering your specific audience? | 1  2  3  4  5 |
| **Support/Elaboration:** How well do you integrate audio and visual support for your topic? | 1  2  3  4  5 |
| **Style:** How well do you use formatting and presentation techniques for visual appeal? | 1  2  3  4  5 |
| **Conventions:** How well do you demonstrate a command of standard English conventions such as using transitions and varying sentence types? | 1  2  3  4  5 |

## © Leveled Texts

Build your skills and improve your comprehension of literature with texts of increasing complexity.

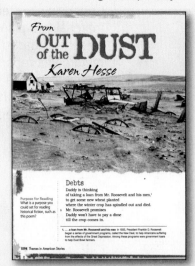

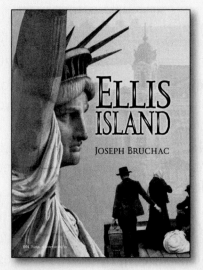

Read the excerpt from ***Out of the Dust*** to learn how a farm family coped with the drought and Great Depression of the 1930s.

Read **"Ellis Island"** to encounter a unique perspective on Ellis Island and what it means to be an American.

## © Common Core State Standards

Meet these standards with either the excerpt from ***Out of the Dust*** (p. 1094) or **"Ellis Island"** (p. 1104).

**Reading Literature**

**1.** Cite the textual evidence that most strongly supports an analysis of what the text says explicitly as well as inferences drawn from the text. *(Literary Analysis: Cultural Context)*

**Spiral Review: RL.8.2**

**Writing**

**3.** Write narratives to develop real or imagined experiences or events using effective technique, relevant descriptive details, and well-structured event sequences. **3.a.** Engage and orient the reader by establishing a context and point of view and introducing a narrator and/or characters; organize an event sequence that unfolds naturally and logically. **3.d.** Use precise words and phrases, relevant descriptive details, and sensory language to capture the action and convey experiences and events. *(Research and Technology: Letter)*

**7.** Conduct short research projects to answer a question (including a self-generated question), drawing on several sources. *(Writing: Research Proposal)*

**Language**

**2.** Demonstrate command of the conventions of standard English capitalization, punctuation, and spelling when writing. *(Conventions: Semicolons and Colons)*

**4.b.** Use common, grade-appropriate Greek or Latin affixes and roots as clues to the meaning of a word (e.g., *precede, recede, secede*). *(Vocabulary: Word Study)*

# Reading Skill: Purpose for Reading

Just as a writer might write for a variety of purposes, there are many reasons you might read. **Setting a purpose for reading** helps focus your attention. You might read for these purposes:

- To learn something new or seek out additional information
- To amuse or challenge yourself
- To seek out another person's point of view

When you read about people from a different time and place, a likely purpose is to learn about their views of the world and the problems they face. An effective way to achieve this purpose is to use a "K-W-L" chart to **ask questions** about the work.

## Using the Strategy: "K-W-L" Chart

Use this **"K-W-L" chart** to set a purpose for reading. Fill in the "K" and "W" columns before you read. If you can successfully fill in the "L" column after reading, you have achieved your purpose.

| K-W-L Chart | | |
|---|---|---|
| What I **K**now | What I **W**ant to Know | What I **L**earned |
| | | |

# Literary Analysis: Cultural Context

The **cultural context** of a literary work is the social and historical environment in which the characters live. Major historical events, such as bad economic times or the outbreak of war, can shape people's lives in important ways. Understanding the effects of such events can give you insight into characters' attitudes and actions.

To understand the cultural context of a literary work, prepare by reading information about the subject. Use the background before the story, an encyclopedia article, or a reliable Internet site to add to the knowledge you might already have from other classes. Then, as you read, look for and make inferences from textual evidence that shows how characters respond to the larger events that you researched.

# Are yesterday's *heroes* important today?

## Writing About the Big Question

In these three poems from *Out of the Dust*, Hesse explores how an ordinary farm family responds to the drought and economic depression that destroy their livelihood. Use this sentence starter to develop your ideas about the Big Question.

> Acts of **courage** can come from unexpected places. One person that others might not consider heroic, but I do, is _____ because _____.

**While You Read** Decide whether the characters in the poem are heroic. Consider how they respond to the series of negative events that confront them.

## Vocabulary

Read each word and its definition. Decide whether you know the word well, know it a little bit, or do not know it at all. After you read, see how your knowledge of each word has increased.

- **feuding** (fyo͞od´ iŋ) *v.* quarreling; fighting (p. 1095) *The two families were <u>feuding</u> over a piece of property.* feud *n.*

- **spindly** (spind´ lē) *adj.* long and thin (p. 1097) *The <u>spindly</u> legs of the table could not support much weight.* spindliness *n.* spindle *n.*

- **drought** (drout) *n.* lack of rain; long period of dry weather (p. 1098) *The plants dried out and died during the <u>drought</u>.* drought-stricken *adj.*

- **grateful** (grāt´ fəl) *adj.* thankful (p. 1098) *Sue was <u>grateful</u> her sister did not tell her parents about the broken lamp.* gratitude *n.* gratefully *adv.* gratify *v.* ungrateful *adj.*

- **sparse** (spärs) *adj.* thinly spread and small in amount (p. 1099) *The hair on the old man's head was <u>sparse</u>.* sparseness *n.* sparsely *adv.*

- **rickety** (rik´ it ē) *adj.* weak; likely to break (p. 1100) *The <u>rickety</u> old shed fell down during a storm.*

### Word Study

The **Latin root -*grat*-** means "thankful" or "pleased."

In *Out of the Dust*, characters are **grateful**, or thankful, when a change in the weather provides a break from destructive dust storms.

# Meet
# Karen Hesse

(b. 1952)

## Author of
# Out of the Dust

In her fiction, Karen Hesse shows a deep understanding of outsiders—characters who do not quite fit in—because that is how she felt as she was growing up in Baltimore, Maryland. A shy girl who lived in her imagination, Hesse loved curling up in an apple tree in her backyard and reading for hours at a time.

**Giving a Face to History** Hesse's imagination and powers of understanding enable her to create vivid characters who struggle to survive during difficult times in history. Characters in her historical novels include a Russian immigrant in 1919, a woman caught up in the drama of the Civil War, and a boy who stows away on an explorer's ship during the 1700s. "I love research, love dipping into another time and place, and asking questions," Hesse says.

## DID YOU KNOW?

Hesse spent weeks in her local library reading Depression-era newspapers on microfilm to prepare for writing *Out of the Dust*.

## BACKGROUND FOR THE POEMS

### The Dust Bowl

*Out of the Dust* is the story of a farm family's struggles during the 1930s. From 1931 to 1939, farmers in the southern Great Plains suffered from the worst drought in American history. Their crops dried up and died, and powerful dust storms blew away millions of tons of soil. By 1935, many farmers gave up and moved west to California. Meanwhile, the nation was also suffering from the effects of the Great Depression. Banks and other businesses failed, workers lost their jobs, and many Americans were left hungry and homeless.

# from
# OUT of the DUST
## Karen Hesse

**Purpose for Reading**
What is a purpose you could set for reading historical fiction, such as this poem?

## Debts

Daddy is thinking
of taking a loan from Mr. Roosevelt and his men,[1]
to get some new wheat planted
where the winter crop has spindled out and died.
5   Mr. Roosevelt promises
Daddy won't have to pay a dime
till the crop comes in.

---

1. **a loan from Mr. Roosevelt and his men**  In 1933, President Franklin D. Roosevelt began
   a series of government programs, called the New Deal, to help Americans suffering from
   the effects of the Great Depression. Among these programs were government loans to
   help Dust Bowl farmers.

Daddy says,
"I can turn the fields over,
10 start again.
It's sure to rain soon.
Wheat's sure to grow."

Ma says, "What if it doesn't?"

Daddy takes off his hat,
15 roughs up his hair,
puts the hat back on.
"Course it'll rain," he says.

Ma says, "Bay,
it hasn't rained enough to grow wheat in
20 three years."

Daddy looks like a fight brewing.

He takes that red face of his out to the barn,
to keep from feuding with my pregnant ma.

I ask Ma
25 how,
after all this time,
Daddy still believes in rain.

"Well, it rains enough," Ma says,
"now and again,
30 to keep a person hoping.
But even if it didn't
your daddy would have to believe.
It's coming on spring,
and he's a farmer."

*March 1934*

◄ **Critical Viewing**
Why does a dust storm like this one pose a danger to farms and farmers? **[Connect]**

**Cultural Context**
What does this conversation indicate about the effect of dry weather on farm families?

**Vocabulary**
**feuding** (fyo͞od´ iŋ) *v.* quarreling; fighting

**Purpose for Reading**
What can you learn from the poem about farmers' reactions to the lack of rainfall in 1934?

## Social Studies Connection

### The Great Depression

The stock market crashed October 29, 1929—"Black Tuesday"—ushering in the worst economic collapse the United States ever experienced. More than 15 million Americans lost their jobs. The Depression lasted through the early 1940s. Making matters worse, a drought spread through 75 percent of the country during the 1930s, causing devastating dust storms.

**BROOKLYN DAILY EAGLE**
And Complete Long Island News

89th YEAR—No. 295. ★ NEW YORK CITY, THURSDAY, OCTOBER 24, 1929. ★ 32 PAGES

LATE NEWS
WALL STREET
1:15 PRICES ★★
THREE CENTS

## WALL ST. IN PANIC AS STOCKS CRASH

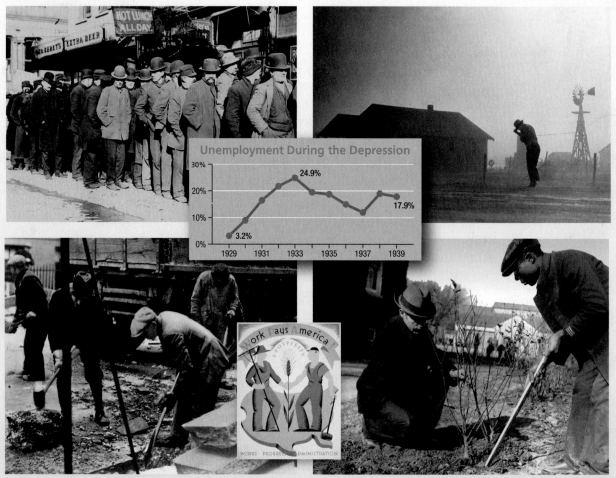

Bread lines were common city sights during ▼ the Depression.

President Franklin D. Roosevelt offered assistance to people in rural areas who were ▼ affected by the drought.

**Unemployment During the Depression**

3.2% (1929) ... 24.9% (1933) ... 17.9% (1939)

▲ In cities, the WPA (Works Progress Administration) put people to work repairing roads.

▲ Restoring drought-damaged land by planting new trees was another WPA goal.

**Connect to the Literature** How could government programs have helped Ma and Daddy?

# Fields of Flashing Light

I heard the wind rise,
and stumbled from my bed,
down the stairs,
out the front door,
5   into the yard.
The night sky kept flashing,
lightning danced down on its spindly legs.

I sensed it before I knew it was coming.
I heard it,
10  smelled it,
tasted it.
Dust.

While Ma and Daddy slept,
the dust came,
15  tearing up fields where the winter wheat,
set for harvest in June,
stood helpless.

**Purpose for Reading**
What would you want
to know after reading
this poem's title?

**Vocabulary**
**spindly** (spind′ lē)
*adj.* long and thin

Reading
Check
What noise wakes the
speaker from her bed?

Vocabulary
**drought** (drout) *n.*
lack of rain; long
period of dry weather

I watched the plants,
surviving after so much drought and so much wind,
20   I watched them fry,
or
flatten,
or blow away,
like bits of cast-off rags.
25   It wasn't until the dust turned toward the house,
like a fired locomotive,
and I fled,
barefoot and breathless, back inside,
it wasn't until the dust
30   hissed against the windows,
until it ratcheted the roof,
that Daddy woke.

He ran into the storm,
his overalls half-hooked over his union suit.[2]
35   "Daddy!" I called. "You can't stop dust."

Ma told me to
cover the beds,
push the scatter rugs against the doors,
dampen the rags around the windows.
40   Wiping dust out of everything,
she made coffee and biscuits,
waiting for Daddy to come in.

Sometime after four,
rubbing low on her back,
45   Ma sank down into a chair at the kitchen table
and covered her face.
Daddy didn't come back for hours,
not
until the temperature dropped so low,
50   it brought snow.

Ma and I sighed, grateful,
staring out at the dirty flakes,
but our relief didn't last.
The wind snatched that snow right off the fields,

Spiral Review
**Theme** What theme
might the sentence
"You can't stop dust"
suggest?

Cultural Context
What do the charac-
ters' reactions to the
dust storm tell you
about the emotional
effect of this natural
disaster?

2. **union suit** type of long underwear, common in the 1930s, that combines a shirt and leggings in one garment.

55 leaving behind a sea of dust,
waves and
waves and
waves of
dust,
60 rippling across our yard.

Daddy came in,
he sat across from Ma and blew his nose.
Mud streamed out.
He coughed and spit out
65 mud.
If he had cried,
his tears would have been mud too,
but he didn't cry.
And neither did Ma.

*March 1934*

# Migrants

We'll be back when the rain comes,
they say,
pulling away with all they own,
straining the springs of their motor cars.
5 Don't forget us.

And so they go,
fleeing the blowing dust,
fleeing the fields of brown-tipped wheat
barely ankle high,
10 and sparse as the hair on a dog's belly.

We'll be back, they say,
pulling away toward Texas,
Arkansas,
where they can rent a farm,
15 pull in enough cash,
maybe start again.

**Purpose for Reading**
What information does the poem provide about the Dust Bowl that you could not get from a history textbook?

**Cultural Context**
What economic forces drive away the migrants?

**Vocabulary**
**sparse** (spärs) *adj.*
thinly spread and small in amount

▶ **Critical Viewing** What details in this historic photograph indicate that this family is moving? **[Analyze]**

We'll be back when it rains,
they say,
setting out with their bedsprings and mattresses,
20  their cookstoves and dishes,
their kitchen tables,
and their milk goats
tied to their running boards[3]
in **rickety** cages,
25  setting out for
California,
where even though they say they'll come back,
they just might stay
if what they hear about that place is true.

30  Don't forget us, they say.
But there are so many leaving,
how can I remember them all?

*April 1935*



**Vocabulary**
**rickety** (rik´ it ē) *adj.*
weak; likely to break

---

3. **running boards** steps, or footboards, that ran along the lower part of each side of a car, as shown in the photograph (p. 1099). Running boards were common on cars of the 1930s.

## Critical Thinking

*Cite textual evidence to support your responses.*

1. **Key Ideas and Details (a)** In "Debts," what is the subject of the discussion between Ma and Daddy? **(b)** How does Ma explain Daddy's point of view? **(c) Infer:** What is Ma's point of view?

2. **Key Ideas and Details (a)** In "Fields of Flashing Light," what does the narrator do during the dust storm? **(b) Infer:** What is the purpose of these actions? **(c) Draw Conclusions:** How do you know that these actions are not very effective?

3. **Key Ideas and Details (a) Analyze Causes and Effects:** In "Migrants," why do the family's neighbors move? **(b) Speculate:** What effects might their decision have on the people who stay behind?

4. **Integration of Knowledge and Ideas (a)** Do the family members in these poems act in ways that you consider heroic? Why or why not? **(b)** What can we learn today from the struggles of Depression-era families like the one in *Out of the Dust*? **[Connect to the Big Question: Are yesterday's heroes important today?]**

## Reading Skill: Purpose for Reading

**1. (a)** What **purpose** did you set for reading the three poems?
**(b)** What questions did you ask to help you set a purpose?

**2. (a)** What details from the poems helped you answer your
questions? **(b)** Where could you look to find more information to answer your questions?

## Literary Analysis: Cultural Context

Ⓒ **3. Key Ideas and Details** Fill in the chart by explaining what
each detail from *Out of the Dust* reveals about the poem's
**cultural context**—the living conditions and attitudes of
farmers during the Dust Bowl.

| Detail | Cultural Conditions and Attitudes |
|---|---|
| Dust blew away and covered crops. | |
| Ma and Daddy do not cry when their wheat crop is destroyed. | |
| Daddy decides to plant again, but other families decide to move away. | |

## Vocabulary

Ⓒ **Acquisition and Use** Write a word from page 1092 that
matches the meaning of each pair of **synonyms.** Explain why
its meaning is similar.

**1.** weak, shaky, _____

**2.** long, thin, _____

**3.** quarreling, fighting, _____

**4.** scanty, scattered, _____

**5.** dryness, aridness, _____

**6.** thankful, appreciative, _____

**Word Study** Use context and what you know about the **Latin
root -*grat*-** to explain your answer to each question.

**1.** Why is *ingratitude* a poor reaction to receiving a gift?

**2.** Why might someone *congratulate* you?

### Word Study

The **Latin root -*grat*-**
means "thankful" or
"pleased."

**Apply It** Explain how
the root -*grat*- contributes to the meaning
of each word. Consult
a dictionary, if
necessary.

ingrate

gratitude

ingratiate

**Are yesterday's *heroes* important today?**

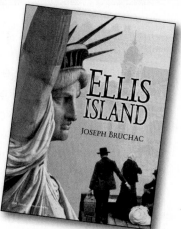

## Writing About the Big Question

In "Ellis Island," Joseph Bruchac writes of the conflicting feelings the famous immigrant processing station awakes in him. Use this sentence starter to develop your ideas about the Big Question:

Many people view the **accomplishments** of their immigrant ancestors with pride because _____.

**While You Read** Look for the ways that Bruchac describes the two branches of his ancestry.

## Vocabulary

Read each word and its definition. Decide whether you know the word well, know it a little bit, or do not know it at all. After you read, see how your knowledge of each word has increased.

- **quarantine** (kwôr´ ən tēn) *n.* period of separation from others to stop the spread of disease (p. 1105) *The passengers were kept in quarantine after one of them became sick.* *quarantine v.*

- **empires** (em´ pīrz´) *n.* powerful nations; countries ruled by emperors or empresses (p. 1105) *The Western Roman and the Byzantine Empires were governed by ancient Rome.* *emperor n. empress n.*

- **native** (nāt´ iv) *adj.* related to the place of one's birth (p. 1106) *He traveled far from his native land.* *native n. natively adv.*

- **invaded** (in vād´ əd) *adj.* forcibly entered in order to conquer (p. 1106) *In the science-fiction film, Earth is invaded by aliens from another galaxy.* *invasion n. invader n.*

### Word Study

The **Latin root -nat-** means "born."

The author of this poem speaks of **native** lands in America, referring to lands inhabited by people whose ancestors were the continent's first inhabitants.

Author of
# ELLIS ISLAND

"Ellis Island" describes Joseph Bruchac's heritage as the son of an Abenaki Indian mother and a Slovak father. Bruchac grew up in a small town in the Adirondack Mountains of New York State, where he still lives today.

**A Passion for Tradition and Diversity** When he became a father, Bruchac began telling traditional stories to his two young sons. Before long, he had established a career as a storyteller, sharing his stories with schoolchildren. He is also an award-winning author who has published more than three dozen books. Of his motivation to tell stories that bridge cultures, Bruchac says, "We learn about ourselves by understanding others."

## BACKGROUND FOR THE POEM

**Immigrants and Native Americans**

The speaker of "Ellis Island" pays tribute to his two sets of ancestors—European immigrants and Native Americans. These groups had very different experiences. From 1892 to 1924, about seventeen million European immigrants passed through government buildings on Ellis Island in New York Harbor. There, they received official permission to enter the United States. Meanwhile, from the 1600s through the 1800s, Native Americans had been pushed farther and farther west to make room for new settlers. By the 1890s, most Native American tribes had been moved onto reservations.

### DID YOU KNOW?

**Bruchac was chosen to write informational panels for the National Museum of the American Indian in Washington, D.C.**

# ELLIS ISLAND

## JOSEPH BRUCHAC

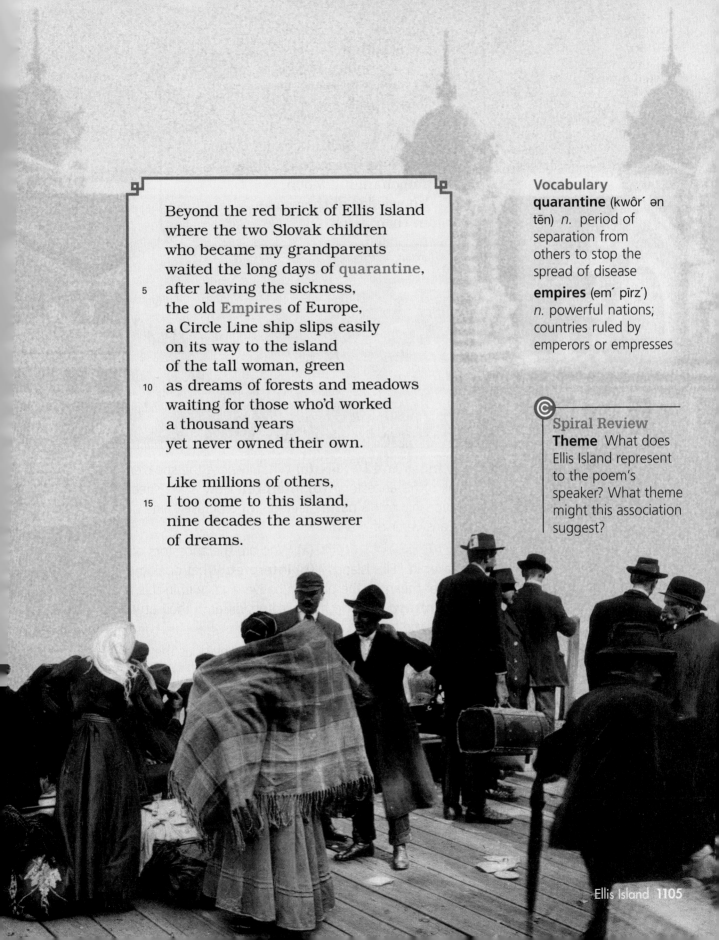

Beyond the red brick of Ellis Island
where the two Slovak children
who became my grandparents
waited the long days of quarantine,
5   after leaving the sickness,
the old Empires of Europe,
a Circle Line ship slips easily
on its way to the island
of the tall woman, green
10   as dreams of forests and meadows
waiting for those who'd worked
a thousand years
yet never owned their own.

Like millions of others,
15   I too come to this island,
nine decades the answerer
of dreams.

**Vocabulary**
**quarantine** (kwôr´ ən tēn) *n.* period of separation from others to stop the spread of disease

**empires** (em´ pīrz´) *n.* powerful nations; countries ruled by emperors or empresses

**Spiral Review**
**Theme** What does Ellis Island represent to the poem's speaker? What theme might this association suggest?

Yet only one part of my blood
  loves that memory.
Another voice speaks
20  of native lands
within this nation.
Lands invaded
when the earth became owned.
Lands of those who followed
25  the changing Moon,
knowledge of the seasons
in their veins.

## Critical Thinking

Cite textual
evidence to
support your
responses.

**1. Key Ideas and Details (a)** What inspires the speaker to think of his ancestors? **(b) Interpret:** How is the speaker's relationship to his past reflected in the phrase "nine decades the answerer of dreams"?

**2. Key Ideas and Details (a)** Who are the ancestors of the speaker in "Ellis Island"? **(b) Interpret:** What does the speaker mean by the phrase "native lands within this nation"? **(c) Contrast:** How do his ancestors differ in their attitudes toward the land?

**3. Key Ideas and Details (a) Apply:** Why does the speaker see the United States as "lands invaded"?

**4. Integration of Knowledge and Ideas (a)** How does the speaker's dual ancestry influence his feelings toward Ellis Island? **(b)** What people from the past might Bruchac consider to be heroes in his life? **(c)** Can the same people who are viewed as heroes by some be viewed as unheroic by others? Explain, using an example. *[Connect to the Big Question: Are yesterday's heroes important today?]*

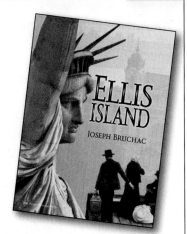

## Reading Skill: Purpose for Reading

1. **(a)** What **purpose** did you set for reading "Ellis Island"?
   **(b)** What questions did you ask to help you set a purpose?

2. **(a)** What details in "Ellis Island" helped you to answer your questions? **(b)** Where could you look for more information?

## Literary Analysis: Cultural Context

3. **Key Ideas and Details** Fill in the chart by explaining what each detail from "Ellis Island" reveals about the poem's **cultural context**—the living conditions and attitudes of immigrants and Native Americans in the late 1800s.

| Detail | Cultural Conditions and Attitudes |
|---|---|
| Immigrants were kept in quarantine. | |
| Immigrants dreamed of owning land. | |
| Native American lands were invaded. | |
| Native Americans had "knowledge of the seasons in their veins." | |

## Vocabulary

**Acquisition and Use** Write a word from page 1102 that matches the meaning of each pair of **synonyms**. Explain why its meaning is similar.

1. isolation, detention, _____
2. original, belonging, _____
3. kingdoms, realms, _____
4. assailed, infringed, _____

**Word Study** Use context and what you know about the **Latin word root -nat-** to explain your answer to each question.

1. Does a bird with an *innate* sense of direction get lost?
2. What might you expect to find in a hospital's *neonatal* room?

### Word Study

The **Latin word root -nat-** means "born."

**Apply It** Explain how the root -nat- contributes to the meanings of these words. Consult a dictionary, if necessary.

**nationality**
**denatured**
**natural**

# Integrated Language Skills

## *from* Out of the Dust • Ellis Island

## Conventions: Semicolons and Colons

A **semicolon (;)** joins independent clauses and takes the place of a comma or period. A **colon (:)** directs the reader's attention to the information that follows it.

- Use semicolons to join independent clauses that are not already joined by the conjunctions *and, but, or, nor, for, so,* or *yet.* Semicolons are also used to separate independent clauses that are joined by adverbs such as *however* and *therefore.*

- Use colons before lists of items that follow an independent clause.

| Incorrect | Correct |
|---|---|
| The car ran out of gas we had to call a tow truck. | The car ran out of gas; we had to call a tow truck. |
| We walked in the rain, however, our umbrellas kept us dry. | We walked in the rain; however, our umbrellas kept us dry. |
| Please bring the following supplies; a notebook, two pencils, and a pen. | Please bring the following supplies: a notebook, two pencils, and a pen. |

**Practice A** Rewrite each sentence, replacing the blank underline with the correct mark— a colon or a semicolon.

1. Two of Bruchac's grandparents were immigrants_ he was born in America.

2. Immigrants from many nations were processed at Ellis Island_ Ireland, England, Poland, Italy, Spain, France, and others.

3. Bruchac tells many stories from his Abenaki background_ however, he is in favor of learning from many cultures.

© **Reading Application** Write two sentences about the difficulties of farming. One should use a colon; the other, a semicolon.

**Practice B** Rewrite each sentence, adding a semicolon or a colon where it is needed.

1. Before the wind began, she sensed it in several ways hearing, smell, and taste.

2. Daddy decided they would stay on their farm however, many others had left.

3. The car was loaded with every sort of thing they even took their milk goats and kitchen tables.

© **Writing Application** Using each correct sentence in the chart as a model, write three more sentences about the immigrant experience.

---

**PH** **WRITING COACH** | Further instruction and practice are available in *Prentice Hall Writing Coach.*

# Writing

**Explanatory Text** Write a brief **research proposal** on how the Dust Bowl affected farmers in the 1930s or on immigrants' experiences as they passed through Ellis Island in the 1890s and early 1900s.

- First, generate three specific questions you would like to answer. In a chart, identify the type of source that might provide the information you need to answer each question.

- Find at least three sources, including both *primary sources* (first-hand accounts) and *secondary sources* (secondhand analyses). Use an approved format for a preliminary bibliography.

- In a paragraph, present and explain your thesis statement, the main idea that you would use to begin your research.

**Grammar Application** Check your research proposal to make sure you use semicolons and colons correctly.

**Writing Workshop:** *Work in Progress*

**Prewriting for Exposition** For a cause-and-effect essay you may write, list ideas from science or history that have causes and effects. For each cause, jot down possible effects. For each effect, jot down potential causes. Save this Causes-Effects List in your writing portfolio.

# Research and Technology

**Build and Present Knowledge** Write a **letter** that describes the experience of a migrant. If you read the poems from *Out of the Dust,* write a letter from California to a friend who stayed in the Midwest. If you read "Ellis Island," write a letter to a friend back in Europe. Use these steps:

- Research the experiences of Dust Bowl migrants to California or European immigrants who entered through Ellis Island. Use the Internet and a key word search to find and print a historic photograph related to your topic.

- Imagine that you are the person in the photograph you chose, and write a letter to your friend back in Europe or the Midwest.

- Establish context by giving details that indicate your situation. Using vivid sensory details, describe your thoughts, emotions, and experiences on the trip and then upon your arrival.

- Write your letter by hand, and use the proper format for a friendly letter. Be sure that your letter is neat and legible and has correct spelling and capitalization for place names.

**Common Core State Standards**

**L.8.2; W.8.3, W.8.3.a, W.8.3.d, W.8.7**
[For the full wording of the standards, see page 1090.]

Use this prewriting activity to prepare for the **Writing Workshop** on page 1156.

**PHLit Online!**
www.PHLitOnline.com
- Interactive graphic organizers
- Grammar tutorial
- Interactive journals

##  Leveled Texts

Build your skills and improve your comprehension of literature or literary nonfiction with texts of increasing complexity.

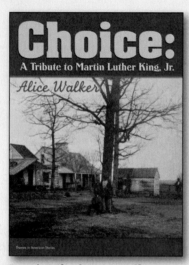

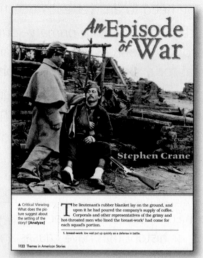

Read **"Choice: A Tribute to Martin Luther King, Jr."** to learn about the inspirational effect Dr. King had on a young African American woman.

Read **"An Episode of War"** to see how a wounded soldier—and those around him—respond to his plight.

##  Common Core State Standards

Meet these standards with either **"Choice: A Tribute to Martin Luther King, Jr."** (p. 1114) or **"An Episode of War"** (p. 1122).

**Reading Literature/Informational Text**
**1.** Cite the textual evidence that most strongly supports an analysis of what the text says explicitly as well as inferences drawn from the text. *(Literary Analysis: Author's Influences)*

**Spiral Review: RL.8.2**
**Writing**
**1.** Write arguments to support claims with clear reasons and relevant evidence. **1.a.** Introduce claim(s), acknowledge and distinguish the claim(s) from alternate or opposing claims, and organize the reasons and evidence logically. **1.d.** Establish and maintain a formal style. **1.e.** Provide a concluding statement or section that follows from and supports the argument presented. *(Writing: Persuasive Speech)*

**2.** Write informative/explanatory texts to examine a topic and convey ideas, concepts, and information through the selection, organization, and analysis of relevant content. *(Research and Technology: Newspaper Article)*

**Language**
**2.** Demonstrate command of the conventions of standard English capitalization. *(Conventions: Capitalization)*

**4.b.** Use common, grade-appropriate Greek or Latin affixes and roots as clues to the meaning of a word.

**6.** Acquire and use accurately grade-appropriate general academic and domain-specific words and phrases; gather vocabulary knowledge when considering a word or phrase important to comprehension or expression. *(Vocabulary: Word Study)*

# Reading Skill: Purpose for Reading

When you **set a purpose for reading,** you determine your focus before reading. Once you have set a purpose, you can **adjust your reading rate** to best meet that goal.

- For information: read *slowly* and *carefully.* After completing a difficult or important passage, take time to think about what you have read. If necessary, read it again.

- For entertainment: read more *quickly.* You may reread or linger over certain passages, but studying the text is less important.

Whatever your reading rate, check regularly to make sure you are meeting your purpose. If not, you may need to consult another source or work in order to better understand the first one.

## Using the Strategy: Reading Rate Chart

Complete a **reading rate chart** like the one shown to determine how to approach a specific source or literary work.

| Source | Purpose | Reading Rate |
| --- | --- | --- |
| Magazine article on rock star | Entertainment | Read quickly to find interesting details. |
| Biography of John F. Kennedy | Research | Read slowly, selecting facts for a report. |
|  |  |  |

# Literary Analysis: Author's Influences

An **author's influences** are the cultural and historical factors that affect his or her writing. Take these steps to connect a literary work with its author's heritage, attitudes, and beliefs:

- Read biographical information to learn about an author's important life experiences and cultural background.

- When reading, note any details in the work that show cultural values or attitudes. In addition, note references to historical events and figures or cultural influences that might have shaped the author's outlook and values. Make inferences from these references to determine the effect of culture and history on the author's views.

**Are yesterday's *heroes* important today?**

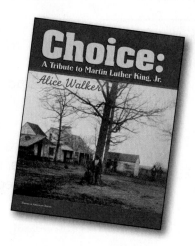

## Writing About the Big Question

In "Choice," Alice Walker recalls the tremendous influence of Martin Luther King, Jr., on herself and her community. Use the following sentence starters to develop your ideas about the Big Question.

> A figure from the past, besides King, who continues to **influence** people today is _____ because _____.

> People who have **overcome** difficult challenges, such as _____ can show us _____.

**While You Read** Look for the ways that King has influenced Walker's life — both while he was alive and after his death.

## Vocabulary

Read each word and its definition. Decide whether you know the word well, know it a little bit, or do not know it at all. After you read, see how your knowledge of each word has increased.

- **ancestral** (an ses´ trəl) *adj.* related to a family (p. 1115) *Since 1801, her relatives have lived on the ancestral estate.* *ancestor n. ancestry n.*

- **brutal** (broot´ 'l) *adj.* harsh; demanding (p. 1115) *The brutal cold destroyed the farmers' crops.* *brutally adv. brutality n. brute n.*

- **integrate** (in´ tə grāt´) *v.* make equally available to all members of society (p. 1116) *The Brown decision in 1954 ordered schools to racially integrate.* *integration n. integral adj.*

- **disinherit** (dis´ in her´ it) *v.* deprive a person or people of a right or privilege (p. 1116) *In his will, he chose to disinherit his son and left his money to charity.* *inherit v. inheritance n.*

- **revolutionary** (rev´ ə loo´ shə ner´ ē) *adj.* favoring or bringing about sweeping change (p. 1117) *Einstein's revolutionary ideas changed how people viewed the universe.* *revolution n. revolt v.*

### Word Study

The **Latin root -her-** means "heir" or "one who receives."

The author writes of King's concern for the **disinherited**, those who have been stripped of the rights they receive as citizens or members of a community.

# Alice Walker
### (b. 1944)

## Author of
# Choice:
## A Tribute to Martin Luther King, Jr.

Alice Walker's childhood in rural Georgia had a lasting impact on her writing. Walker's parents loved to tell her stories—so much so, that she later referred to her mother as "a walking history of our community."

**An Author's Influences** Walker's love of stories and learning inspired her to go to college, where she became involved in the civil rights movement. After meeting Martin Luther King, Jr., she participated in marches and registered African Americans to vote in Georgia, at a time when it was dangerous to do so. By the end of the 1960s, Walker had launched a writing career that included essays, novels, and poems.

## BACKGROUND FOR THE SPEECH
### The Great Migration

In "Choice . . . ," Alice Walker describes how her brothers and sisters wanted to leave the South. Beginning in the 1890s, millions of African Americans left the South and journeyed to northern cities. Economic need, racial violence, and inequality were all factors in what became known as "The Great Migration." In the 1970s, after the successes of the civil rights movement, this migration slowed and actually reversed course.

## DID YOU KNOW?

Walker's 1982 novel *The Color Purple* won the Pulitzer Prize and the National Book Award. It was adapted as a motion picture, directed by Steven Spielberg.

# Choice:

## A Tribute to Martin Luther King, Jr.

*Alice Walker*

**Background** This address was made in 1972 at a Jackson, Mississippi, restaurant that had refused to serve people of color until forced to do so by the civil rights movement a few years before.

▼ **Critical Viewing**
How do the faces of these former slaves reflect the same types of hardships that Walker's grandmother experienced? **[Connect]**

My great-great-great-grandmother walked as a slave from Virginia to Eatonton, Georgia—which passes for the Walker ancestral home—with two babies on her hips. She lived to be a hundred and twenty-five years old and my own father knew her as a boy. (It is in memory of this walk that I choose to keep and to embrace my "maiden" name, Walker.)

There is a cemetery near our family church where she is buried; but because her marker was made of wood and rotted years ago, it is impossible to tell exactly where her body lies. In the same cemetery are most of my mother's people, who have lived in Georgia for so long nobody even remembers when they came. And all of my great-aunts and -uncles are there, and my grandfather and grandmother, and, very recently, my own father.

If it is true that land does not belong to anyone until they have buried a body in it, then the land of my birthplace belongs to me, dozens of times over. Yet the history of my family, like that of all black Southerners, is a history of dispossession. We loved the land and worked the land, but we never owned it; and even if we bought land, as my great-grandfather did after the Civil War, it was always in danger of being taken away, as his was, during the period following Reconstruction.[1]

My father inherited nothing of material value from his father, and when I came of age in the early sixties I awoke to the bitter knowledge that in order just to continue to love the land of my birth, I was expected to leave it. For black people—including my parents—had learned a long time ago that to stay willingly in a beloved but brutal place is to risk losing the love and being forced to acknowledge only the brutality.

**Vocabulary**
**ancestral** (an ses´ trəl) *adj.* related to a family
**brutal** (brōot´l) *adj.* harsh; demanding

**Author's Influences**
What attachment does the author feel to her ancestors and their land?

✓ **Reading Check**
How does Alice Walker's last name honor her ancestors?

---

1. **Reconstruction** (1865–1877) period following the American Civil War when the South was rebuilt and reestablished as part of the Union.

▼ **Critical Viewing**
Why might Walker use
the word *fearless* to
describe King, shown
here in jail? **[Connect]**

It is a part of the black Southern sensibility that we
treasure memories; for such a long time, that is all of our
homeland those of us who at one time or another were forced
away from it have been allowed to have.

I watched my brothers, one by one, leave our home and
leave the South. I watched my sisters do the same. This
was not unusual; abandonment, except for memories, was
the common thing, except for those who "could not do any
better," or those whose strength or stubbornness was so
colossal they took the risk that others could not bear.

In 1960, my mother bought a television set, and each
day after school I watched Hamilton Holmes and Charlayne
Hunter[2] as they struggled to integrate—fair-skinned as
they were—the University of Georgia. And then, one day,
there appeared the face of Dr. Martin Luther King, Jr. What
a funny name, I thought. At the moment I first saw him,
he was being handcuffed and shoved into a police truck.
He had dared to claim his rights as a native son, and had
been arrested. He displayed no
fear, but seemed calm and serene,
unaware of his own extraordinary
courage. His whole body, like his
conscience, was at peace.

At the moment I saw his
resistance I knew I would never be
able to live in this country without
resisting everything that sought to
disinherit me, and I would never
be forced away from the land of
my birth without a fight.

He was The One, The Hero, The
One Fearless Person for whom we
had waited. I hadn't even realized
before that we *had* been waiting
for Martin Luther King, Jr., but we
had. And I knew it for sure when
my mother added his name to the
list of people she prayed for every
night.

---

2. **Hamilton Holmes and Charlayne Hunter** the
first two African American students to attend the
University of Georgia.

I sometimes think that it was literally the prayers of people like my mother and father, who had bowed down in the struggle for such a long time, that kept Dr. King alive until five years ago.[3] For years we went to bed praying for his life, and awoke with the question "Is the 'Lord' still here?"

The public acts of Dr. King you know. They are visible all around you. His voice you would recognize sooner than any other voice you have heard in this century—this in spite of the fact that certain municipal libraries, like the one in downtown Jackson, do not carry recordings of his speeches, and the librarians chuckle cruelly when asked why they do not.

You know, if you have read his books, that his is a complex and *revolutionary* philosophy that few people are capable of understanding fully or have the patience to embody in themselves. Which is our weakness, which is our loss.

And if you know anything about good Baptist preaching, you can imagine what you missed if you never had a chance to hear Martin Luther King, Jr., preach at Ebeneezer Baptist Church.

You know of the prizes and awards that he tended to think very little of. And you know of his concern for the think disinherited: the American Indian, the Mexican-American, and the poor American white—for whom he cared much.

You know that this very room, in this very restaurant, was closed to people of color not more than five years ago. And that we eat here together tonight largely through his efforts and his blood. We accept the common pleasures of life, assuredly, in his name.

But add to all of these things the one thing that seems to me second to none in importance: He gave us back our heritage. He gave us back our homeland; the bones and dust of our ancestors, who may now sleep within our caring *and* our hearing. He gave us the blueness of the Georgia sky in autumn as in summer; the colors of the Southern winter as

3. **until five years ago** Dr. Martin Luther King, Jr., was assassinated on April 4, 1968.

### History Connection

**Marching for Freedom**

In March 1965, Martin Luther King, Jr., organized a march from Selma to Montgomery, Alabama, to protest restrictions on African Americans' right to vote. The peaceful protest was turned back by police using tear gas and clubs.

After this incident, some people advised King to abandon nonviolence. King ignored these voices and tried again. He set out from Selma with 3,200 marchers. Four days and fifty miles later they arrived in Montgomery, 25,000-strong. Five months later, President Johnson signed the Voting Rights Act of 1965.

### Connect to the Literature

What qualities enabled King to become a voice for change?

**Vocabulary**
**revolutionary** (rev′ ə loo′ shə ner′ ē) *adj.* favoring or bringing about sweeping change

well as glimpses of the green of vacation-time spring. Those of our relatives we used to invite for a visit we now can ask to stay. . . . He gave us full-time use of our woods, and restored our memories to those of us who were forced to run away, as realities we might each day enjoy and leave for our children.

He gave us continuity of place, without which community is ephemeral.[4] He gave us home.                                     *1973*

---

4. **ephemeral** (e fem′ ər əl) *adj.* short-lived; fleeting.

## Critical Thinking

Cite textual evidence to support your responses.

© 1. **Key Ideas and Details** **(a)** Where is Walker making this speech? **(b) Connect:** What is significant about the location?

© 2. **Key Ideas and Details** **(a)** What impressed Walker when she first saw Martin Luther King, Jr.? **(b) Interpret:** What did she realize about King's significance for her own life?

© 3. **Integration of Knowledge and Ideas** **(a)** Before the civil rights movement, why did African Americans in the South feel left out of American society? **(b) Evaluate:** According to Walker, what was King's most important gift to African Americans?

© 4. **Integration of Knowledge and Ideas** **(a)** What aspects of Walker's life in Georgia prepared her to be so receptive to the actions of King? **(b)** Changes have occurred in the decades since Walker's speech. Do you think she would say that King continues to have an influence today? Why or why not? *[Connect to the Big Question: Are yesterday's heroes important today?]*

# Choice: A Tribute to Martin Luther King, Jr.

## Reading Skill: Purpose for Reading

**1. (a)** What **purpose** might you set for reading Walker's speech? **(b)** How does this purpose affect your reading rate?

**2.** If you were writing a research report on King's accomplishments as a civil rights leader, would this be an appropriate text to read for information? Why or why not?

## Literary Analysis: Author's Influences

**© 3. Integration of Knowledge and Ideas** Complete a chart like the one shown to evaluate the effect of the author's influences on her writing.

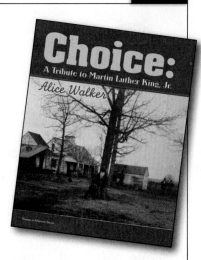

| | Influences | Effect on Her Portrayal of Dr. King |
|---|---|---|
| **Time and place of Walker's birth** | | |
| **Walker's cultural background** | | |
| **Major news events** | | |

**© 4. Integration of Knowledge and Ideas (a)** How did King's influence change Alice Walker's perspective toward Georgia? **(b)** How did the historic events in which King played a leading role influence her beliefs and values?

## Vocabulary

**© Acquisition and Use** Determine whether the following statements are true or false. Then, explain your answers.

**1.** If you *disinherit* someone, you will probably be thanked.

**2.** A *revolutionary* concept is one that is familiar to most people.

**3.** An *ancestral* background can be illustrated with a family tree.

**4.** If a race is *brutal*, it can be completed without much effort.

**5.** When schools *integrate*, no single group is excluded.

**Word Study** Use content and what you know about the **Latin root -her-** to explain your answer to each question.

**1.** Why might an *heirloom* have special meaning to a person?

**2.** Why might somone want to preserve his or her *heritage*?

### Word Study

The **Latin root -her-** means "heir" or "one who receives."

**Apply It** Explain how the root -her- contributes to the meanings of these words. You may consult a dictionary, if necessary.

**inheritance**
**hereditary**

# Are yesterday's *heroes* important today?

## Writing About the Big Question

"An Episode of War" explores various reactions to the wounding of a Civil War soldier, including those of the soldier himself. Use this sentence starter to develop your ideas about the Big Question.

The concept of heroism (is/is not) **outdated** in our times because _____.

**While You Read** Notice the behavior of the wounded soldier and those around him to decide if he acts heroically or not.

## Vocabulary

Read each word and its definition. Decide whether you know the word well, know it a little bit, or do not know it at all. After you read, see how your knowledge of each word has increased.

- **winced** (winst) *v.* shrank or drew back slightly, usually with a grimace, as in pain (p. 1123) *The boy winced when the doctor touched his injured arm.* wince *n.*

- **audible** (ô´ də bəl) *adj.* able to be heard (p. 1123) *The child spoke in a whisper that was barely audible.* audibly *adv.*

- **compelled** (kəm peld´) *v.* forced (p. 1123) *He felt compelled to defend himself against the unfair attack.* compelling *adj.* compulsive *adj.* compulsory *adj.*

- **tumultuous** (tōō mul´ chōō əs) *adj.* wild; chaotic (p. 1126) *The wind whipped the waves on the tumultuous sea.*

- **contempt** (kən tempt´) *n.* scorn; disrespect (p. 1127) *He felt only contempt for his enemy.* contemptuous *adj.* contemptuously *adv.*

- **disdainfully** (dis dān´ fə lē) *adv.* scornfully (p. 1127) *Convinced he was superior to his coworkers, he treated them disdainfully.* disdain *n.* disdainful *adj.*

### Word Study

The **Latin root -aud-** means "hear."

In this story, a soldier's silent breathing becomes **audible,** or able to be heard, when he is suddenly wounded during a peaceful moment in camp.

# Stephen Crane
## (1871–1900)

Author of
## *An Episode of War*

When Stephen Crane wrote *The Red Badge of Courage,* he set out to change the way people viewed war novels. As a journalist who was largely unknown outside of New York City, Crane created a novel about a young Civil War soldier. The book made him a household name.

**Stories of War** Although he was born years after the Civil War had ended, Crane was fascinated by the war. He interviewed Civil War veterans and pored over photographs, battlefield maps, and firsthand accounts of the fighting. All this research paid off in Crane's realistic portrait of Henry Fleming, the hero of *The Red Badge of Courage.*

## BACKGROUND FOR THE STORY

### Civil War Wounded

Like the lieutenant in "An Episode of War," soldiers who were wounded in the Civil War faced very long odds. Field hospitals were unsanitary and crowded with wounded soldiers. Medical practices of the time, such as not sterilizing surgical instruments, encouraged the spread of disease and infection. To save soldiers' lives from deadly infections, doctors were often forced to amputate limbs.

## DID YOU KNOW?

Crane was an influential writer despite his short life. He died of tuberculosis at age twenty-eight.

# An Episode of War

## Stephen Crane

▲ **Critical Viewing**
What does the picture suggest about the setting of the story? **[Analyze]**

The lieutenant's rubber blanket lay on the ground, and upon it he had poured the company's supply of coffee. Corporals and other representatives of the grimy and hot-throated men who lined the breast-work[1] had come for each squad's portion.

---

**1. breast-work** *n.* low wall put up quickly as a defense in battle.

The lieutenant was frowning and serious at this task of division. His lips pursed as he drew with his sword various crevices in the heap, until brown squares of coffee, astoundingly equal in size, appeared on the blanket. He was on the verge of a great triumph in mathematics, and the corporals were thronging forward, each to reap a little square, when suddenly the lieutenant cried out and looked quickly at a man near him as if he suspected it was a case of personal assault. The others cried out also when they saw blood upon the lieutenant's sleeve.

He had winced like a man stung, swayed dangerously, and then straightened. The sound of his hoarse breathing was plainly audible. He looked sadly, mystically, over the breast-work at the green face of a wood, where now were many little puffs of white smoke. During this moment the men about him gazed statuelike and silent, astonished and awed by this catastrophe which happened when catastrophes were not expected—when they had leisure to observe it.

As the lieutenant stared at the wood, they too swung their heads, so that for another instant all hands, still silent, contemplated the distant forest as if their minds were fixed upon the mystery of a bullet's journey.

The officer had, of course, been compelled to take his sword into his left hand. He did not hold it by the hilt. He gripped it at the middle of the blade, awkwardly. Turning his eyes from the hostile wood, he looked at the sword as he held it there, and seemed puzzled as to what to do with it, where to put it. In short, this weapon had of a sudden become a strange thing to him. He looked at it in a kind of stupefaction, as if he had been endowed with a trident, a sceptre, or a spade.[2]

Finally he tried to sheathe it. To sheathe a sword held by the left hand, at the middle of the blade, in a scabbard hung

Vocabulary
**winced** (winst) *v.* shrank or drew back slightly, usually with a grimace, as in pain
**audible** (ô´ də bəl) *adj.* able to be heard
**compelled** (kəm peld´) *v.* forced

Reading Check

What happens to the lieutenant while he is distributing coffee?

---

2. **a trident, a sceptre, or a spade** *n.* symbols of royal power.

at the left hip, is a feat worthy of a sawdust ring.[3] This wounded officer engaged in a desperate struggle with the sword and the wobbling scabbard, and during the time of it breathed like a wrestler.

But at this instant the men, the spectators, awoke from their stone-like poses and crowded forward sympathetically. The orderly-sergeant took the sword and tenderly placed it in the scabbard. At the time, he leaned nervously backward, and did not allow even his finger to brush the body of the lieutenant. A wound gives strange dignity to him who bears it. Well men shy from his new and terrible majesty. It is as if the wounded man's hand is upon the curtain which hangs before the revelations of all existence—the meaning of ants, potentates,[4] wars, cities, sunshine, snow, a feather dropped from a bird's wing; and the power of it sheds radiance upon a bloody form, and makes the other men understand sometimes that they are little. His comrades look at him with large eyes thoughtfully. Moreover, they fear vaguely that the weight of a finger upon him might send him headlong, precipitate the tragedy, hurl him at once into the dim, grey unknown. And so the orderly-sergeant, while sheathing the sword, leaned nervously backward.

There were others who proffered assistance. One timidly presented his shoulder and asked the lieutenant if he cared to lean upon it, but the latter waved him away mournfully. He wore the look of one who knows he is the victim of a terrible disease and understands his helplessness. He again stared over the breast-work at the forest, and then, turning, went slowly rearward. He held his right wrist tenderly in his left hand as if the wounded arm was made of very brittle glass.

And the men in silence stared at the wood, then at the departing lieutenant; then at the wood, then at the lieutenant.

As the wounded officer passed from the line of battle, he was enabled to see many things which as a participant

**Author's Influences**
What realistic details in this paragraph suggest the influence of first-hand accounts on the author's writing?

---

**3. sawdust ring** *n.* ring in which circus acts are performed.
**4. potentates** (pōt´ ən tāts´) *n.* rulers; powerful people.

in the fight were unknown to him. He saw a general on a black horse gazing over the lines of blue infantry at the green woods which veiled his problems. An aide galloped furiously, dragged his horse suddenly to a halt, saluted, and presented a paper. It was, for a wonder, precisely like a historical painting.

To the rear of the general and his staff a group, composed of a bugler, two or three orderlies, and the bearer of the corps standard,[5] all upon maniacal horses, were working like slaves to hold their ground, preserve their respectful interval, while the shells boomed in the air about them, and caused their chargers to make furious quivering leaps.

---

**5. corps** (kôr) **standard** *n.* flag or banner representing a military unit.

▲ **Critical Viewing**
How does this painting of a Civil War battle capture the confusion of the battlefield? **[Analyze]**

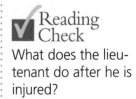
Reading Check
What does the lieutenant do after he is injured?

A battery, a **tumultuous** and shining mass, was swirling toward the right. The wild thud of hoofs, the cries of the riders shouting blame and praise, menace and encouragement, and, last, the roar of the wheels, the slant of the glistening guns, brought the lieutenant to an intent pause. The battery[6] swept in curves that stirred the heart; it made halts as dramatic as the crash of a wave on the rocks, and when it fled onward this aggregation of wheels, levers, motors had a beautiful unity, as if it were a missile. The sound of it was a war-chorus that reached into the depths of man's emotion.

The lieutenant, still holding his arm as if it were of glass, stood watching this battery until all detail of it was lost, save the figures of the riders, which rose and fell and waved lashes over the black mass.

Later, he turned his eyes toward the battle, where the shooting sometimes crackled like bush-fires, sometimes sputtered with exasperating irregularity, and sometimes reverberated like the thunder. He saw the smoke rolling upward and saw crowds of men who ran and cheered, or stood and blazed away at the inscrutable distance.

He came upon some stragglers, and they told him how to find the field hospital. They described its exact location. In fact, these men, no longer having part in the battle, knew more of it than others. They told the performance of every corps, every division, the opinion of every general. The lieutenant, carrying his wounded arm rearward, looked upon them with wonder.

At the roadside a brigade was making coffee and buzzing with talk like a girls' boarding-school. Several officers came

**Vocabulary**
**tumultuous** (tōō mul′ chōō əs) *adj.* wild; chaotic

**Purpose for Reading**
For what purpose might you read this story slowly?

▲ **Critical Viewing**
How do Crane's descriptions reflect the influence of Civil War photographs like the one shown here of an 1862 Virginia field hospital? **[Connect]**

---

6. **battery** (bat′ ər ē) *n.* military unit of men and cannons.

out to him and inquired concerning things of which he knew nothing. One, seeing his arm, began to scold. "Why, man, that's no way to do. You want to fix that thing." He appropriated the lieutenant and the lieutenant's wound. He cut the sleeve and laid bare the arm, every nerve of which softly fluttered under his touch. He bound his handkerchief over the wound, scolding away in the meantime. His tone allowed one to think that he was in the habit of being wounded every day. The lieutenant hung his head, feeling, in this presence, that he did not know how to be correctly wounded.  •

The low white tents of the hospital were grouped around an old schoolhouse. There was here a singular commotion. In the foreground two ambulances interlocked wheels in the deep mud. The drivers were tossing the blame of it back and forth, gesticulating and berating,[7] while from the ambulances, both crammed with wounded, there came an occasional groan. An interminable crowd of bandaged men were coming and going. Great numbers sat under the trees nursing heads or arms or legs. There was a dispute of some kind raging on the steps of the schoolhouse. Sitting with his back against a tree a man with a face as grey as a new army blanket was serenely smoking a corncob pipe. The lieutenant wished to rush forward and inform him that he was dying.

A busy surgeon was passing near the lieutenant. "Good-morning," he said, with a friendly smile. Then he caught sight of the lieutenant's arm, and his face at once changed. "Well, let's have a look at it." He seemed possessed suddenly of a great contempt for the lieutenant. This wound evidently placed the latter on a very low social plane. The doctor cried out impatiently, "What mutton-head had tied it up that way anyhow?" The lieutenant answered, "Oh, a man."

When the wound was disclosed the doctor fingered it disdainfully. "Humph," he said. "You come along with me and I'll 'tend to you." His voice contained the same scorn as if he were saying: "You will have to go to jail."

The lieutenant had been very meek, but now his face flushed, and he looked into the doctor's eyes. "I guess I won't have it amputated," he said.

"Nonsense, man! Nonsense! Nonsense!" cried the doctor.

**Spiral Review**
**Theme** Based on the descriptions of the wounded, what do you think a theme of this story might be?

**Vocabulary**
**contempt** (kən tempt´) *n.* scorn; disrespect
**disdainfully** (dis dān´ fə lē) *adv.* scornfully

Reading Check
How was the lieutenant made to feel by the first officer who bandaged his arm?

---

7. **gesticulating** (jes tik´ yōō lāt´ iŋ) **and berating** (bē rāt´ iŋ) *v.* waving arms about wildly and scolding.

▶ **Critical Viewing**
What do these sur-
geons' tools reveal
about the state of
medicine at the time of
the Civil War? **[Infer]**

**Purpose for Reading**
What insight does the
ending give you into
attitudes toward
wounded soldiers at
the time of this story?

"Come along, now. I won't amputate it.
Come along. Don't be a baby."

"Let go of me," said the lieutenant,
holding back wrathfully, his glance fixed
upon the door of the old schoolhouse, as
sinister to him as the portals of death.

And this is the story of how the
lieutenant lost his arm. When he
reached home, his sisters, his mother,
his wife, sobbed for a long time at the
sight of the flat sleeve. "Oh, well," he
said, standing shamefaced amid these
tears, "I don't suppose it matters so
much as all that."

## Critical Thinking

Cite textual
evidence to
support your
responses.

1. **Key Ideas and Details** **(a)** After he is hit, what does the
   lieutenant attempt to do with his sword? **(b) Infer:** Why
   does he feel the need to do this? **(c) Analyze:** How does
   his action expose the absurd nature of warfare?

2. **Key Ideas and Details** **(a)** How do the lieutenant's men
   behave toward him when he is wounded? **(b) Compare
   and Contrast:** How does this treatment compare with the
   way the lieutenant is treated after he leaves his men?
   **(c) Analyze:** In what ways does this interaction seem to
   strip him of his individuality?

3. **Key Ideas and Details** **Interpret:** Why do you think the
   lieutenant tells his family "I don't suppose it matters so
   much as all that"?

4. **Integration of Knowledge and Ideas** **(a)** Do the
   circumstances in which the lieutenant is wounded seem
   heroic to you? Why or why not? **(b)** Are his reactions to his
   wounds heroic? Explain. **(c)** Do you think the concept of
   heroism changes over time or that certain people and
   actions are always considered heroic? Support your answer
   with reasons. *[Connect to the Big Question: Are
   yesterday's heroes important today?]*

## Reading Skill: Purpose for Reading

1. **(a)** What **purpose** might you set for reading "An Episode of War"? **(b)** How would this purpose affect your reading rate?

2. Would this be an appropriate text to read for information for a research report on Civil War leadership? Why or why not?

## Literary Analysis: Author's Influences

3. **Integration of Knowledge and Ideas** Complete a chart like the one shown to evaluate the effect of the **author's influences** on his writing. Refer to the author's biography on page 1121 to help you.

|  | Influences | Effect on "An Episode of War" |
|---|---|---|
| **Crane's interests** |  |  |
| **Crane's research** |  |  |

4. **Integration of Knowledge and Ideas** Crane's writing was unique because it captured the effect of war on the individual soldier. What values are reflected in this approach to writing and in Crane's portrayal of the lieutenant?

## Vocabulary

**Acquisition and Use** Determine whether the following statements are true or false. Then, explain your answers.

1. A neat person would feel *compelled* to pick up litter.
2. Someone who gets seasick prefers a *tumultuous* ocean.
3. If a man *winced* while lifting a box, it was probably heavy.
4. If planes are *audible* from homes, residents often complain.
5. People who feel *contempt* for each other make great friends.
6. If I respect someone, I will respond to him or her *disdainfully*.

**Word Study** Use context and what you know about the **Latin root -aud-** to explain your answer to each question.

1. What should an *audience* expect to experience at a play?
2. If the music at a concert is *inaudible*, can you enjoy it?

### Word Study

The **Latin root -aud-** means "hear."

**Apply It** Explain how the root -aud- contributes to the meaning of each word. Consult a dictionary, if necessary.

auditorium
audio
audition

# Integrated Language Skills

## Choice: A Tribute to Martin Luther King, Jr. • An Episode of War

### Conventions: Capitalization

**Capital letters** are used at the beginnings of the first words of sentences and for the pronoun *I*. Proper nouns and proper adjectives are also capitalized.

The chart shows examples of how **capitalization** is used.

| Capitalize | Examples |
|---|---|
| the first word in a sentence | The blue jay is a very aggressive bird. Wait! Can you give me back my pen? |
| the first word in a quotation that is a complete sentence | Einstein said, "Anyone who has never made a mistake has never tried anything new." |
| the pronoun *I* | After swimming, I felt tired. |
| proper nouns, geographical names, and organizations | Elsa went sailing down the Hudson River with her Girl Scout troop. |
| titles of people | Mr. Donohue was not amused. |

**Practice A** Identify the capital letter or letters in each sentence. Then, give the reason for each use of capitalization.

1. The state of Georgia had been the Walker family's home for generations.

2. King is famous for saying, "Injustice anywhere is a threat to justice everywhere."

3. The American government now supports civil rights for all citizens.

4. When I go to the library, I will look for other books by Alice Walker.

© **Reading Application** In "Choice . . . ," find examples of three types of capitalization, and explain why each word is capitalized.

**Practice B** Rewrite each sentence to correct errors in capitalization. Substitute capital or lowercase letters where appropriate.

1. the Lieutenant approached and said, "captain, a Man has been wounded."

2. soldiers wounded in the civil war did not have the benefit of Modern Medicine.

3. life on the Battlefield was dangerous for soldiers from the north and the South.

4. When the War ended, my fellow soldiers and i felt great relief.

© **Writing Application** Write a paragraph about the American Civil War. In your writing, use each capitalization rule identified in the chart.

**PH** | **WRITING COACH** | Further instruction and practice are available in *Prentice Hall Writing Coach*.

# Writing

Common Core
State Standards

L.8.2; W.8.1, W.8.1.a,
W.8.1.d, W.8.1.e, W.8.2
[For the full wording of the
standards, see page 1110.]

**Argumentative Text** Write a **persuasive speech** in favor of building a memorial in honor of either Dr. King or Civil War soldiers.

- Reread the selection to find details about the goals your subject set and the sacrifices and emotions your subject experienced.
- Prepare a speech outline with an introduction, a body, and a conclusion. The introduction should provide a preview of your proposal. The body should offer reasons, and your conclusion should summarize these reasons.
- As you draft your speech, use a reasonable and appropriate tone to present evidence that supports your opinion.
- To make the speech more powerful when it is read aloud, add repetition, dramatic pauses, and vivid language.

**Grammar Application** Check your speech to make sure you capitalized place names and names of people.

**Writing Workshop:** *Work in Progress*

**Prewriting for Exposition** Use the Causes-Effects List from your writing portfolio to diagram a cause-effect chain. Each cause can lead to an effect, and each effect in turn can become a cause of other effects, and so on. Save your Cause-and-Effect Diagram in your writing portfolio.

Use this prewriting activity to prepare for the **Writing Workshop** on page 1156.

# Research and Technology

**Build and Present Knowledge** Write a **newspaper article** on one of the following topics:

- If you read "Choice . . . ," write an article for Martin Luther King Day that looks at King's career as a whole. Research his role in the civil rights movement and the hardships he faced.
- If you read "An Episode of War," write an article about the experience and cost of fighting in the Civil War. You can use information from modern sources, but write the article from the perspective of someone during, or shortly after, the war.

Follow these guidelines to complete the assignment.

- Start your article with an effective and attention-grabbing lead.
- Use quotations from individuals such as Alice Walker on civil rights, or Civil War soldiers on battle conditions, to provide first-hand accounts of the events you describe. Add comparisons to help readers understand your main idea.

**PHLit**
**Online!**
**www.PHLitOnline.com**

- Interactive graphic organizers
- Grammar tutorial
- Interactive journals

# Test Practice: Reading

## Purpose for Reading

### Fiction Selection

**Directions:** *Read the selection. Then, answer the questions.*

**Class Clown Strikes Again**

Our class had just finished a unit on famous African Americans, and Ms. Wilson had planned a field trip to the Tuskegee Institute National Historic Site. She was very excited about taking us to a "living history" museum to learn more about the people in the unit.

Pete Keegan had been the class clown since he moved to town in third grade. Pete decided to dress in honor of George Washington Carver who is remembered for such scientific achievements as inventing more than 300 uses for the peanut. When he arrived that morning of the trip, he was plastered with peanuts, from neck to ankles. We all burst out laughing. "You *said* "living" history, Ms. Wilson." Pete said with a big grin.

"Good thing we're going to a museum and not a zoo! You'd be elephant food!" someone called from the back of the room.

Ms. Wilson looked at Pete with a perfectly straight face and said, "Good morning, Peter. I see you brought snacks for the bus ride."

**1.** What is the most likely purpose for reading this story?
   **A.** to be entertained
   **B.** to find statistics
   **C.** to be persuaded
   **D.** to learn a new skill

**2.** What would be a good question to focus your reading purpose?
   **A.** What does Ms. Wilson want the students to learn?
   **B.** How does Pete reinforce his reputation as the class clown?
   **C.** What happens during the field trip?
   **D.** Who was George Washington Carver, and what made him famous?

**3.** What reading rate is most appropriate for this selection?
   **A.** quickly, to find facts
   **B.** quickly, to find out what happens
   **C.** slowly, to learn about history
   **D.** slowly, to critically analyze the text

## Writing for Assessment

What details in the story helped you determine your purpose for reading this selection? In a few sentences, explain how that determined your reading rate for the selection.

## Nonfiction Selection

**Directions:** *Read the selection. Then, answer the questions.*

**George Washington Carver: Plant Genius**

**Early Years** The son of African American slaves in Missouri, George Washington Carver grew up on a farm and began studying plants when he was only a child. By the time he was a teenager, his neighbors called on him as a "plant doctor" to help with their failing crops. He eventually became a national expert on breeding plants.

**An Aid to Farmers** As a professor in Alabama, Carver saw that farmers were destroying the soil by growing only plants that drain the ground of nitrogen—an important plant nutrient. He persuaded them to alternate their crops. One of those crops was the peanut, something that farmers could eat and sell. To persuade farmers to plant peanuts, Carver listed more than 300 of its uses, such as dyes, oils, and cooking.

1. What is the most likely purpose for reading this article?
   **A.** to be entertained
   **B.** to take action
   **C.** to get information
   **D.** to confirm predictions

2. What question is answered by this selection?
   **A.** What is a genius?
   **B.** How did Carver get involved with plants?
   **C.** How many types of plants are there?
   **D.** Why did Carver want to study plants?

3. How should you adjust your reading rate for this selection?
   **A.** Read quickly looking for details that entertain.
   **B.** Skim the selection focusing on the subheads.
   **C.** Scan the selection for difficult words.
   **D.** Read slowly to understand the facts.

4. Which of the following research questions would *not* be satisfied by reading this article?
   **A.** What obstacles did Carver face?
   **B.** What was Carver an expert on?
   **C.** How did Carver change agriculture?
   **D.** Where did Carver grow up?

## Writing for Assessment

**Connecting Across Texts**
Write a paragraph in which you compare the types of information provided in these selections. Then, explain how your purpose for reading differs for each.

www.PHLitOnline.com
- Online practice
- Instant feedback

# Reading for Information

## Analyzing Expository Texts

**Radio Transcript**

**Photo Essay**

**Political Cartoon**

**Common Core State Standards**

**Reading Informational Text**

**7.** Evaluate the advantages and disadvantages of using different mediums to present a particular topic or idea.

**Language**

**6.** Acquire and use accurately grade-appropriate general academic and domain-specific words and phrases; gather vocabulary knowledge when considering a word or phrase important to comprehension or expression.

## Reading Skill: Evaluate the Treatment, Scope, and Organization of Ideas

When doing research, always **evaluate the treatment, scope, and organization** of the ideas presented. *Treatment* refers to the manner in which a writer presents a topic. *Scope* is the range of information discussed. The *organization* of a text is its structure. When you evaluate these elements, you judge the quality, reliability, and appropriateness of the text you are considering. Use this checklist to evaluate the way a similar subject—readjustment to life after World War II—is presented in three different texts.

---

### Checklist for Evaluating Treatment, Scope, and Organization

❑ Has the author addressed the topic in a way that is neutral or biased?

❑ Does the author cover different sides of an issue or only one?

❑ Does the author present ideas in a logical sequence?

❑ Are details organized in a way that enhances the author's points?

---

## Content-Area Vocabulary

These words appear in the selections that follow. You may also encounter them in other content-area texts.

- **paraplegia** (par´ ə plē´ jē ə) *n.* paralysis of the legs and the lower part of the body

- **disabled** (dis ā´ bəld) *adj.* not able to perform certain actions that most people can perform

- **antibiotics** (an´ ti bī ät´ iks) *n.* substances produced by living things, especially bacteria or molds, that destroy or weaken germs

**Features:**
- speakers' exact words
- comments that are not interpreted
- text written for a general or a specific audience

# Morning Edition,

# NATIONAL PUBLIC RADIO

## November 11, 2003

PROFILE: World War II veterans who founded the Paralyzed Veterans of America.

BOB EDWARDS, host: This is MORNING EDITION from NPR News. I'm Bob Edwards.

In February of 1947, a small group of World War II veterans gathered at Hines VA Hospital near Chicago. The fact that they were there at all was considered extraordinary. The men were paralyzed, living at a time when **paraplegia** was still an unfamiliar word and most people with spinal cord injuries were told they would die within a few years. But these wounded veterans had other ideas, so they came from hospital wards across the country to start a national organization to represent veterans with spinal cord injuries. Today on Veterans Day, NPR's Joseph Shapiro tells their story.

> The reporter presents factual information in a neutral way, suggesting his reporting is unbiased.

JOSEPH SHAPIRO reporting: The logo of the Paralyzed Veterans of America looks a bit like the American flag, except that it's got 16 stars, one for each of the men who started the PVA when they gathered at that first convention nearly 57 years ago. Today only one of those 16 paralyzed veterans is still alive. His name is Ken Seaquist. He lives in a gated community in Florida. . . . It's there that Seaquist sits in his wheelchair and flips through some yellowed newspaper clippings . . .

PARALYZED VETERANS OF AMERICA — PVA

Mr. KEN SEAQUIST: Oh, here it is. OK.

SHAPIRO: . . . until he finds a photo. . . . The picture shows that convention. It was held in a veterans hospital just outside Chicago. A large room is filled with scores of young men in wheelchairs. Others are in their pajamas and hospital beds, propped up on white pillows.

Mr. SEAQUIST: There's Bill Dake. He came with us and then Mark Orr. Three of us came in the car from Memphis. Mark had one good leg, his right leg, and he was the driver of the car.

> Ken Seaquist, a PVA founder, is personally involved in the issue being discussed. That gives him a unique perspective.

SHAPIRO: Ken Seaquist was a tall, lanky 20-year-old in an Army mountain ski division when he was wounded in Italy. He was flown back to the United

States to a veterans hospital in Memphis. He came back to a society that was not ready for paraplegics.

**Mr. SEAQUIST:** Before the war, people in our condition were in the closet. They never went out hardly. They didn't take them out.

**SHAPIRO:** Few people had ever survived for more than a few years with a spinal cord injury. Infections were common and deadly. But that was about to change. David Gerber is a historian at the University at Buffalo. He's written about **disabled** veterans.

Comments are presented in chronological order, according to the order of the events being discussed.

**Mr. DAVID GERBER (University at Buffalo):** With the development of **antibiotics**, which came into general use in World War II, there were many healthy spinal cord-injured veterans who were able to survive and begin to aspire to have a normalized life.

**SHAPIRO:** Gerber says neither the wounded veterans, nor the world around them at that time knew what to make of men who were seen as having gone from manly warriors to dependent invalids.

**Mr. GERBER:** The society is emphatically not ready for them, and nor is the medical profession. To this extent, it was often the paralyzed veterans themselves who were pioneers in the development of a new way of life for themselves.

**SHAPIRO:** Seaquist and the others set out to overcome the fear and pity of others. After Seaquist was injured, he never heard from his girlfriend. His mother's hair turned white in a matter of months. People stared when he went out in public. It was a time when a president with polio felt he had to hide the fact that he used a wheelchair. Beyond attitudes, there was a physical world that had to change. When Seaquist arrived at the Memphis hospital, he could not get off the ward. There were steps in the way.

**Mr. SEAQUIST:** They had no idea of what they had to do for wheelchairs. So when we got there, they had to put in all these long ramps and this is what we were talking about. The ramping and just to get around the hospital and get out ourselves, you know; not having somebody help us all the time. We were an independent bunch.

**SHAPIRO:** There were about 2,500 soldiers with spinal cord injuries, most of them living in military hospitals around the country. Pat Grissom lived at Birmingham Hospital in California. He would become one of the first presidents of the PVA, but he was unable to travel from California to Chicago for that first convention. Grissom, too, had come back from war with little hope for his future.

Mr. PAT GRISSOM: I just suppose that we were going to live the rest of our lives either in the hospital or go to an old soldiers' home. We were just going to be there taking medicine and if you got sick, they would try to take care of you and you'd have your meals provided and your future was the hospital or the old soldiers' home.

SHAPIRO: At Birmingham Hospital, Grissom met a doctor who was about to become a pioneer in the new field of spinal cord medicine. Dr. Ernst Bors did a lot to improve the physical care of paraplegics. He also pushed the men at Birmingham to set goals for their lives, to go back to school, get jobs and marry. Bors and the veterans at Birmingham Hospital were the subject of a Hollywood film, *The Men*. The realistic and sympathetic portrayal helped the American public better understand paralyzed veterans. In the film, the kindly doctor in a lab coat is based on Bors. He urges on a wounded soldier in a white T-shirt, played by a young Marlon Brando.

(Soundbite of *The Men*)

Mr. MARLON BRANDO: Well, what am I going to do? Where am I going to go?

Unidentified Actor: Into the world.

Mr. BRANDO: I can't go out there anymore.

Unidentified Actor: You still can't accept it, can you?

Mr. BRANDO: No. What did I do? Why'd it have to be me?

Unidentified Actor: Is there an answer? I haven't got it. Somebody always gets hurt in the war.

Marlon Brando in *The Men*

SHAPIRO: For Grissom and the other paralyzed veterans, there was something else that helped them go out into the world, a new technology. The introduction of automatic transmission meant that a car could be modified with hand controls for the gas and brakes. Pat Grissom.

Mr. GRISSOM: Oldsmobile came up with the hydromatic drive and they put on hand controls and they sent people out to start giving driving lessons to us and we started having visions of saving up enough money to get a car and then things were looking better all the time.

Here, Pat Grissom is expressing the facts from his personal point of view.

SHAPIRO: Ken Seaquist says driving opened up all kinds of possibilities, from going out to a restaurant with a bunch of friends to romance.

Mr. SEAQUIST: In Memphis, we had—our favorite place was called the Silver Slipper and they welcomed us with open arms and we had maybe 10, 12 wheel-chairs going with our dates. Generally it was our nurses that we dated, 'cause, you know, we couldn't get out anywhere. We took the girls with us, you know. Eventually I married one of them.

SHAPIRO: Seaquist and his wife quickly had two daughters. And with a young family, he had to find work. He went to school and became a landscape archi-tect. Ken Seaquist stopped seeing himself as an invalid and became a man with a future. So in 1947, he and the other founders of the PVA met in Chicago to put together a collective voice to express their dreams and what they needed to accomplish them. They came up with a slogan to get others to join, "Awaken, gentle-men, lest we decay." Ken Seaquist explains what it meant.

Car modified with hand controls

Mr. SEAQUIST: If they forget us, we're going to decay. We're going to be left in the closet. We've got to get out there and speak out, getting things done so we can roll around this country and have access to the whole country.

SHAPIRO: The PVA quickly won some important legislative victories in Washington: money for paralyzed veterans to modify automobiles and houses, money for medical care. Later they would help push for laws that would make buildings and streets accessible to wheelchair users. The PVA has continued to advocate for veterans with spinal cord injuries through every war since World War II.

Joseph Shapiro, NPR News.

The reporter concludes by summing up the PVA's activities to date.

## Readjustment

### VETERANS AND EX-WARWORKERS HAVE DIFFICULTY IN PEACETIME LIFE

**Photo Essay**

**Features:**
- images that tell a story
- human-interest issue
- text for a general or specific audience

The boys were pouring home from the Army and Navy. Their presence gladdened homes all over the city—on the middle-class South Side, on swank Kessler Boulevard, in . . . homes along North Illinois Street. But the men were coming home to a community not altogether ready for them emotionally, or industrially. There were family tensions, misunderstandings between veterans and old civilian friends. Often the men could find no place to live. Sometimes they could not get jobs, not because there was no work in the city but because available jobs were low-paid or highly technical. Neither the veterans nor the warworkers, laid off from the Allison engine or Curtiss-Wright propeller plants, were willing enough in some cases or skilled enough in others to take them.

Together the veterans and the warworkers formed a restless, still-prosperous group of unemployed. Daily they journeyed to the Indianapolis office of the USES [United States Employment Service] . . . to shop for the work they wanted.

But the people worried little about the situation. Probably they were right in assuming that it would clear up as soon as reconversion, lagging badly, got under way in earnest. Meanwhile many a citizen of Indianapolis with a son or husband or friend in the service tried to get him out. They bombarded their congressmen with letters, telegrams, and personal calls. Said General Marshall, "Demobilization has become disintegration" because of a "widespread emotional crisis of the American people."

The scope of this photo essay is small, focusing on a specific place in Indianapolis.

These images and captions give the photo essay a sympathetic tone and make it more personal.

**THE RESTLESS UNEMPLOYED** appear at USES. Still prosperous, most of them are shopping for jobs, seeing what is available. From left to right: Cpl. Ralph Garbett, 38, who wants a job as a diesel mechanic; Carl A. Seherb, former worker at Allison, who wants precision-inspector work; Leah H. Blow, who wants a job as a pie baker.

**CLOSED TIGHT** is the Curtiss-Wright plant in Indianapolis. It made propellers during the war. Once 6,200 people worked there. A city of diversified industries, Indianapolis should be able to reconvert very successfully.

# *Life* Magazine Political Cartoon

**Features:**

- text and illustrations that comment on society
- familiar and easy-to-follow comic strip format
- text for a general or specific audience

Political cartoons treat serious subjects in a humorous way.

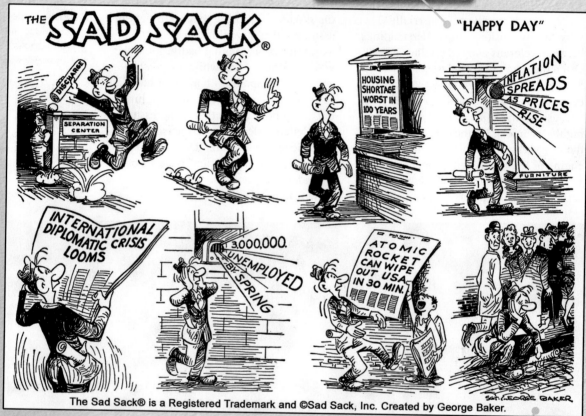

The Sad Sack® is a Registered Trademark and ©Sad Sack, Inc. Created by George Baker.

**Finally discharged** after 3½ years in the Army, Sad Sack meets his final disillusionment when he approaches the complexities of human reconversion.

This cartoon presents events chronologically, showing a day in the life of an army veteran.

## Comparing Expository Texts

**1. Craft and Structure (a)** Compare and contrast the **treatment, scope, and organization of ideas** in the three texts. **(b)** Suppose you are writing an informational report on challenges soldiers faced when rejoining civilian life after World War II. Evaluate the texts, explaining which would be the most appropriate source for such a report and why.

## Content-Area Vocabulary

**2. (a)** Explain the meaning of the prefixes *para-, dis-,* and *anti-,* as in *paraplegia, disabled,* and *antibiotics.* Consult a dictionary as needed. **(b)** Use each word in a sentence that shows its meaning.

## ⏱ Timed Writing

### Explanatory Text: Essay

**Format and Details**
The prompt gives specific directions about what to write and the types of details to include.

Write a brief essay that compares the effect produced by the photo essay with the impact of the political cartoon. Give examples to illustrate similarities and differences between your impressions of each. (30 minutes)

**Academic Vocabulary**
When you *illustrate* an idea, you give details and examples that help readers understand it.

### 5-Minute Planner

Complete these steps before you begin to write:

**1.** Read the prompt carefully and completely.

**2.** Review the text and images in the photo essay and the political cartoon. Jot down your impressions.

**3.** Compare your notes on the two texts, looking for similarities and differences. To help clarify your thoughts, take notes on the advantages and disadvantages of each type of media in addressing a topic as complex and emotional as readjustment.

**4.** Use your notes to make an outline before you begin writing.

## Comparing Works on a Similar Theme

The **theme** of a literary work is its central idea or underlying message. A **universal theme** is an insight or lesson that appears in literature across cultures and throughout different periods in history. Universal themes include the power of love and the desire for freedom.

These three selections represent very different forms—a poem, an open letter, and a personal essay. Each author comes from a different cultural background. However, all of the works focus on a similar universal theme: the need for self-expression.

Even when writers choose to focus on the same theme, they often produce contrasting results. This is because they have different purposes, or reasons for writing. One may write to reflect, another to entertain, and yet another to persuade or inform. In addition, writers may draw on different life experiences and cultural backgrounds, and they may explore different aspects of the same theme in their works.

Use a chart like this to analyze the way the theme is presented in these selections. Refer to page 1143 to find information about each author's cultural background.

| | Neruda | Mora | Nye |
|---|---|---|---|
| **Literary Form** | Poem | Open Letter | Essay |
| **Details About Culture** | | | |
| **Details That Reveal Theme** | | | |
| **Statement of Theme** | | | |

**Common Core State Standards**

**Reading Literature**

**2.** Determine a theme or central idea of a text and analyze its development over the course of the text, including its relationship to the characters, setting, and plot; provide an objective summary of the text.

**5.** Compare and contrast the structure of two or more texts and analyze how the differing structure of each text contributes to its meaning and style.

**Writing**

**9.** Draw evidence from literary or informational texts to support analysis, reflection, and research. *(Timed Writing)*

www.PHLitOnline.com

• Vocabulary flashcards
• Interactive journals
• More about the authors
• Selection audio
• Interactive graphic organizers

# Are yesterday's *heroes* important today?

## Writing About the Big Question

Many heroes are ordinary people who face challenges in their everyday lives. Use these sentence starters to develop your ideas.

Writing about one's feelings takes **courage** because _____.

Writers, past or present, could become personal heroes for me if they _____.

# Meet the Authors

## Pablo Neruda (1904–1973)
### Author of "Poetry" (La Poesía)

"Pablo Neruda" was the pen name taken by a young Chilean poet who was afraid his father would not approve of his writing. Eventually Neruda became one of the most popular poets writing in Spanish, and his pen name became his official name. In addition to his writing, Neruda also had a long political career as a diplomat.

## Pat Mora (b. 1942)
### Author of "My Own True Name"

In her work, Pat Mora explores cultural diversity and her own life experiences as a Mexican-American woman. Born in El Paso, Texas, she was raised partly by her grandmother and her Aunt "Lobo." Her writings include volumes of poetry and essays, children's books, and a memoir.

## Naomi Shihab Nye (b. 1952)
### Author of "Words to Sit in, Like Chairs"

Arab American writer Naomi Shihab Nye is widely admired for the keen observations and insights she brings to her poetry and short stories. Nye writes that "the primary source of poetry has always been local life, random characters met on the streets, our own ancestry sifting down to us through small essential daily tasks."

La

# Poesía

## Pablo Neruda

## Poetry

*translation by Alastair Reid*

| | |
|---|---|
| Y fue a esa edad...Llegó la poesía | And it was at the age...poetry |
| a buscarme. No sé, | arrived in search of me. I don't know, |
| no sé de dónde salió, | I don't know where it came from, from |
| de invierno o río. | winter or a river. |
| No sé cómo ni cuándo, | 5   I don't know how or when, |
| no, no eran voces, no eran | no, they were not voices, they were |
| palabras, ni silencio, | not words, not silence, |
| pero desde una calle me llamaba, | but from a street it called me, |
| desde las ramas de la noche, | from the branches of night, |
| de pronto entre los otros, | 10   abruptly from the others, |
| entre fuegos violentos | among raging fires |
| o regresando solo, | or returning alone, |
| allí estaba sin rostro | there it was, without a face, |
| y me tocaba. | and it touched me. |
| | |
| Yo no sabía qué decir, mi boca | 15   I didn't know what to say, my mouth |
| no sabía | had no way |
| nombrar, | with names, |
| mis ojos eran ciegos, | my eyes were blind. |
| y algo golpeaba en mi alma, | Something knocked in my soul, |
| fiebre o alas perdidas, | 20   fever or forgotten wings, |
| y me fui haciendo solo, | and I made my own way, |
| descifrando | deciphering |
| aquella quemadura, | that fire, |
| y escribí la primera línea vaga, | and I wrote the first, faint line, |
| vaga, sin cuerpo, pura | 25   faint, without substance, pure |
| tontería, | nonsense, |
| pura sabiduría | pure wisdom |
| del que no sabe nada, | of someone who knows nothing; |

y vi de pronto
el cielo
desgranado
y abierto,
planetas,
plantaciones palpitantes,
la sombra perforada,
acribillada
por flechas, fuego y flores,
la noche arrolladora, el universo.

Y yo, mínimo ser,
ebrio del gran vacío
constelado,
a semejanza, a imagen
del misterio,
me sentí parte pura
del abismo,
rodé con las estrellas,
mi corazón se desató en el viento.

and suddenly I saw
30 the heavens
unfastened
and open,
planets,
palpitating plantations,
35 the darkness perforated.
riddled
with arrows, fire, and flowers,
the overpowering night, the universe.

And I, tiny being,
40 drunk with the great starry
void,
likeness, image of
mystery,
felt myself a pure part
of the abyss.
45 I wheeled with the stars.
My heart broke loose with the wind.

**Theme**
What happens after the poem's speaker writes his first lines?

**Vocabulary**
**abyss** (ə bis´)
*n.* an immeasurable space

## Critical Thinking

© **1. Key Ideas and Details (a)** How does the writer's first experience with poetry occur? **(b) Support**: What lines or phrases describe this? **(c) Infer:** How difficult does he find writing, at first? Why?

© **2. Key Ideas and Details (a)** Identify at least two images that describe what happens once the poet begins to write. **(b) Connect:** What are his feelings about this experience? **(c) Speculate:** Do you think that this poem reflects Neruda's true experiences? Explain.

© **3. Integration of Knowledge and Ideas (a)** Are the obstacles Neruda overcomes real or imagined? **(b)** Do you think today's writers would see Neruda as a hero? Why or why not? *[Connect to the Big Question: Are yesterday's heroes important today?]*

Cite textual evidence to support your responses.

*from*
# My Own True Name

## Pat Mora

# Dear Fellow Writer,

A blank piece of paper can be exciting and intimidating. Probably every writer knows both reactions well. I know I do. I wanted to include a letter to you in this book because I wish I could talk to you individually. I'd say: Listen to your inside self, your private voice. Respect your thoughts and feelings and ideas. You—yes, you—play with sounds. With language(s), explore the wonder of being alive.

Living hurts, so sometimes we write about a miserable date, a friend who betrayed us, the death of a parent. Some days, though, we're so full of joy we feel like a kite. We can fly! Whether we write for ourselves or to share our words, we discover ourselves when we truly write: when we dive below the surface. It's never easy to really reveal ourselves in school, but remember that writing is practice. Without practice, you will never learn to hear and sing your own unique song.

I have always been a reader, which is the best preparation for becoming a writer. When I was in grade school in El Paso, Texas (where I was born), I read comic books and mysteries and magazines and library books. I was soaking up language.

I've always liked to write, too—but I was a mother before I began to create regular time for my writing. Was it that I didn't think that I had anything important to say? Was it that I didn't believe that I could say anything that well? Was it that when I was in school we never studied a writer who was like me—bilingual, a Mexican American—and so somehow I decided that "people like me" couldn't be writers?

I have a large poster of an American Indian storyteller right above my desk. Children are climbing all over her, just as my sisters and my brother and I climbed over *nuestra tía*, our aunt, Ignacia Delgado, the aunt we called Lobo. She was our storyteller. Who is yours? Would you like to be a storyteller? Would you like to write or paint or draw or sing your stories?

I became a writer because words give me so much pleasure that I have always wanted to sink my hands and heart into them, to see what I can create, what will rise up, what will appear on the page. I've learned that some writers are quiet and shy, others noisy, others just plain obnoxious. Some like

**Vocabulary**
**intimidating** (in tim´ ə dā´ tiŋ) *adj.* frightening

**Theme**
What two reasons does Mora give for writing?

**Vocabulary**
**bilingual** (bī liŋ´ gwəl) *adj.* able to speak two languages

☑ Reading Check
What helped Mora prepare to become a writer?

---

◀ **Critical Viewing** What feelings and ideas in the essay's first paragraph does this photograph best illustrate? Explain. **[Connect]**

enchiladas and others like sushi; some like rap and others like *rancheras*.[1] Some write quickly, and some are as slow as an elderly man struggling up a steep hill on a windy day. I'll tell you a few of our secrets.

The first is that we all read. Some of us like mysteries and some of us like memoirs, but writers are readers. We're curious to see what others are doing with words, but—what is more important—we like what happens to us when we open a book, how we journey into the pages.

Another secret is that we write often. We don't just talk about writing. We sit by ourselves inside or outside, writing at airports or on kitchen tables, even on napkins.

We're usually nosy and very good at eavesdropping. Just ask my three children! And writers are collectors. We collect facts and phrases and stories: the names of cacti,[2] the word for cheese in many languages.

In the last twenty years, I've spent more and more time writing my own books for children and adults. I have received many rejections and will probably receive many more, darn it. I just keep writing—and revising. Revising is now one of my favorite parts of being a writer, though I didn't always feel that way. I enjoy taking what I've written—a picture or a book or a poem—and trying to make the writing better, by changing words or rhythm. Sometimes by starting over!

Writing is my way of knowing myself better, of hearing myself, of discovering what is important to me and what makes me sad, what makes me different, what makes me me—of discovering my own true name. And writing makes me less lonely. I have all these words in English and Spanish whispering or sometimes shouting at me, just waiting for me to put them to work, to combine them so that they leap over mountains on small hooves or slip down to the sandy bottom of the silent sea.

And you? Maybe these poems—taken from my collections *Chants, Borders,* and *Communion,* along with some new poems written for this book, for you—will tempt you to write your

▲ **Critical Viewing**
Why might a writer keep an object such as this one in the place he or she writes? **[Connect]**

**Theme**
How does Mora use personification and imagery to explain her need to express herself?

---

**1.** *rancheras* (rän che′ räs) *n.* type of popular Latino music.
**2.** *cacti* (kak′ tī) *n.* plural form of cactus, a type of desert plant.

own poems about a special person or a special place, about a gray fear or a green hope. What are your blooms, your thorns, your roots?

Remember, my friend, never speak badly of your writing. Never make fun of it. Bring your inside voice out and let us hear you on the page. Come, join the serious and sassy family of writers.

◄ **Critical Viewing** Why might Pat Mora approve of this scene? **[Connect]**

## Critical Thinking

Cite textual evidence to support your responses.

©  1. **Key Ideas and Details** **(a)** Does Mora think it is easy or difficult for most students to reveal their thoughts and feelings in papers written as school assignments? **(b) Draw Conclusions:** Why does Mora address this issue?

©  2. **Key Ideas and Details** **(a)** According to Mora, what is the most important reason for writing? **(b) Evaluate:** Do you agree with her? Why or why not?

©  3. **Integration of Knowledge and Ideas** **(a)** What feelings or limitations did Mora have to challenge to start writing? **(b)** How does she use her experience to help other aspiring writers overcome their fears? *[Connect to the Big Question: Are yesterday's heroes important today?]*

# Words to Sit in, Like Chairs

## Naomi Shihab Nye

**▲ Critical Viewing**
What does their body language tell you about how well these students are listening? **[Evaluate]**

I was with teenagers at the wonderful Holland Hall School in Tulsa when the planes flew into the buildings on September 11, 2001. We were talking about words as ways to imagine one another's experience. A boy had just thanked me for a poem about Jerusalem that enabled him to consider the Palestinian[1] side of the story. He said he had never thought about that perspective before, so the poem was important to him.

The TV commentators were already saying the hijackers had been Arabs, which sent a deep chill into my Arab-American blood. I said to those beautiful students, "Please, I beg you, if Arabs are involved in this tragedy, remember there are millions of Arabs who would never do such a thing."

They nodded soberly. "Of course," they said. "We know that. This is Oklahoma." Their kindness overwhelmed me.

Then a boy said, "I hate to ask this so soon after it happened, but do you think you will write about it?"

---

**1. Palestinian** (pal´ əs tin´ē ən) *adj.* of the people of Palestine, a region bounded by Lebanon, Syria, Egypt, and Jordan. Many Arabs living in this area were displaced when the state of Israel was established by the United Nations in 1948.

"It would not be my choice of topic," I said, feeling sick, my head spinning, "but as writers, we are always exploring what happens, what comes next, turning it over, finding words to sit in like chairs, even in terrible scenery, so maybe I will have to write about it; maybe we all will. Because words shape the things that we live, whether beautiful or sorrowful, and help us connect to one another, this will be part of our history now."

Then a boy gave me a "Collapse-It" laundry basket that his parents had invented. Made of some kind of modern, waterproof, heavy-duty cardboard, it folded flat when not in use. He seemed mournful, handing it over.

"I brought this for you as a small gift," he said, "but after what happened today, it almost seems inappropriate."

Collapse-It. All Fall Down.

I clutched it to my chest and carried it with me on the long bus ride (since the planes were not flying) home to south Texas.

I have used the neat little white basket every time I've washed clothes since then. What came to me on a day of horror and tragedy and terrible mess, accompanied by kind words, continues as a helpful friend in daily life. Just the way words help us all not to be frozen in horror and fear.

USE WORDS. It is the most helpful thing I have learned in my life. We find words, we select and arrange them, to help shape our experiences of things. Whether we write them down for ourselves or send them into the air as connective lifelines between us, they help us live, and breathe, and see.

When I felt the worst after September 11, I called people. How is it for you? What are you thinking about? Have you heard anything helpful lately? Many of you probably did that, too. Sometimes it seemed good, and important, to call unexpected people—people who were not, in any way, expecting to hear from us right then. Hello, I'm thinking of you. Do you have any good news? If I had heard a useful quote or story recently myself, I shared it. Talking with friends felt like a connected chain. We passed things on down the wire.

It was very helpful for me to talk with Arab-American friends who automatically shared the doubled sense of sorrow. A poet friend of mine in New York City, just blocks from the disaster, said his wife saw him staring at a wall in their apartment one day, and said, "Don't withdraw! Speak!"

Sometimes we have to remind one another.

**Theme**
According to Nye, what is the value of words in our everyday lives?

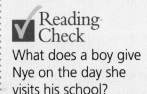
**Reading Check**
What does a boy give Nye on the day she visits his school?

Vocabulary
**turmoil** (tʉr´ moil´) *n.*
condition of great
confusion or agitation

I also wrote sentences and phrases down in small notebooks, as I have done almost every day of my life since I was six. It is the best clue I know for how to stay balanced as we live. Bits and pieces of lines started fitting together again, offering small scraps of sense, ways out of the turmoil-of-mind, shining as miniature beacons, from under heaps of leaves.

Very rarely did I hang up from speaking with anyone or close my notebook feeling worse. Usually, that simple sharing of feelings, whether with another person, or with a patient page, helped ease the enormous feeling that the sorrow was too big to get one's mind around.

War is too big to get one's mind around too.

I keep thinking—if people who are angry, or frustrated, could use words instead of violence, how would our world be different? Maybe if enough of us keep in practice using our own honest words, that basic human act can help balance bigger things in the world.

▲ **Critical Viewing**
Based on her essay, what advice might Nye offer this young woman? **[Speculate]**

## Critical Thinking

Cite textual evidence to support your responses.

@ 1. **Key Ideas and Details (a)** How did Nye deal with her emotions after the events of September 11, 2001? **(b) Evaluate:** Do you think this is an effective way to ease sorrow? Explain.

@ 2. **Key Ideas and Details (a)** What does Nye propose as a solution to the problem of violence in our world? **(b) Take a Position:** Do you think Nye's ideas could help change the world? Explain.

@ 3. **Integration of Knowledge and Ideas (a)** Did it take special courage for Nye to write about the events of September 11, 2001? Explain. **(b)** Do you think her words and the actions of other ordinary people on that day are still important today? Why or why not? *[Connect to the Big Question: Are yesterday's heroes important today?]*

## Comparing Works on a Similar Theme

**1. Key Ideas and Details** **(a)** What reasons does Mora give to discuss the value of expressing oneself in writing? **(b)** What reasons does Nye give?

**2. Integration of Knowledge and Ideas** **(a)** How does Neruda's description of his approach to writing differ from the other selections? **(b)** Are similar themes and ideas expressed differently in poetry than in prose? Explain.

**3. Integration of Knowledge and Ideas** How does the form each writer chose work to achieve a different purpose, despite their similarities in theme? Give specific examples of ways the structure of the works affect their meaning.

## ⏱ Timed Writing

### Explanatory Text: Essay

Write an essay to compare the three works. In your essay, discuss how each writer approaches the universal theme of self-expression. Provide details and quotations from the texts as support. **(40 minutes)**

### 5-Minute Planner

**1.** Read the prompt carefully and completely.

**2.** Gather your ideas by completing a chart like the one shown.

| Category | Poetry (La Poesía) | My Own True Name | Words to Sit In . . . |
|---|---|---|---|
| Topic/Situation | | | |
| Use of Personal Experience | | | |
| Influence of Form on Theme | | | |
| Influence of Cultural Background | | | |
| Tone/Style | | | |

**3.** Choose an organizational strategy. To use the block method, give your analysis of one work, then the next, focusing on the same categories each time. To use the point-by-point method, examine one category at a time, discussing all three works.

**4.** Reread the prompt, and then draft your essay.

# Writing Workshop

## Write an Explanatory Text

### Exposition: Cause-and-Effect Essay

**Defining the Form** Almost everything that happens involves causes and effects, from local events to those that impact people worldwide. When you write a **cause-and-effect essay,** you analyze the reasons an event occured or you consider its results.

**Assignment** Write a cause-and-effect essay about a question that interests you. Your essay should feature the following elements:

- ✔ a clear thesis that establishes a *controlling idea*
- ✔ a consistent and appropriate *organization*
- ✔ an explanation of how one or more events or situations results in another event or situation
- ✔ a thorough presentation of *facts*, *quotations*, and other *details* that *support* the explanation presented
- ✔ an *effective and well-supported conclusion*
- ✔ error-free grammar, including the avoidance of *run-on sentences and sentence fragments*

To preview the criteria on which your research report may be judged, see the rubric on page 1163.

 **Writing Workshop:** *Work in Progress*

Review the work you did on pages 1109 and 1131.

**WRITE GUY**
*Jeff Anderson, M.Ed.*

### What Do You Notice?

**Structural Elements**

Read the following sentences from Anaïs Nin's "Forest Fire."

*In Sierra Madre, following the fire, the January rains brought floods. People are sandbagging their homes. At four A.M. the streets are covered with mud. The bare, burnt, naked mountains cannot hold the rains and slide down bringing rocks and mud. One of the rangers must now take photographs and movies of the disaster.*

Discuss what you notice about the passage with a partner. Take note of how Nin presents cause-and-effect relationships, and think of ways you can do the same in your essay.

 **Common Core State Standards**

**Writing**

**2.** Write informative/explanatory texts to examine a topic and convey ideas, concepts, and information through the selection, organization, and analysis of relevant content.

**2.a.** Introduce a topic clearly, previewing what is to follow; organize ideas, concepts, and information into broader categories; include formatting, graphics, and multimedia when useful to aiding comprehension.

**2.b.** Develop the topic with relevant, well-chosen facts, definitions, concrete details, quotations, or other information and examples.

**Reading-Writing Connection**

To get the feel for a cause-and-effect essay, read "Why Leaves Turn Color in the Fall," by Diane Ackerman, on page 540.

# Prewriting/Planning Strategies

**Discuss with a classmate.** To determine topics that interest you, pair up with a classmate and take turns asking these questions:

- What are your favorite books? What natural or historical events are crucial to those books' subjects or plots?

- What is a science topic that you find interesting?

- Which political leader do you admire most? With which national or world events is he or she most closely associated?

- For what invention are you most grateful? Why?

Review your answers in order to choose a broad topic.

**PHLit Online!**
www.PHLitOnline.com
- Author video: Writing Process
- Author video: Rewards of Writing

**Narrow your topic.** Make sure you develop a topic narrow enough for you to cover in depth. First, take time to jot down subtopics of your broader topic. Continue this process until you pinpoint a well-defined subject for your writing. The chart shows how one topic is narrowed.

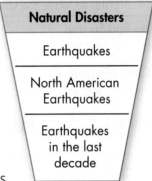

| Natural Disasters |
| :---: |
| Earthquakes |
| North American Earthquakes |
| Earthquakes in the last decade |

**Conduct research.** Gather the facts, statistics, examples, and other details you need to thoroughly illustrate cause-and-effect relationships. A K-W-L chart like the one shown is an excellent tool for planning and guiding your research.

## K-W-L Chart

| What I **K**now | What I **W**ant to Know | What I **L**earned |
| --- | --- | --- |
| • Air pollution is increasing and dangerous.<br>• Pollution smells bad.<br>• Cars and factories cause it.<br>• It hurts people and animals. | • How can it be reduced?<br>• What causes it besides cars and factories?<br>• Which countries or cities are the worst?<br>• How can we stop it?<br>• What does it do to people?<br>• To animals? | |

**Plan your support.** Now that have you gathered information, think through the cause-and-effect relationship you will explain. Determine which details are needed to clearly show a reader the connections between cause and effect. These supporting details can take the form of facts, expert opinions, or comparisons to similar cause-and-effect relationships.

# Drafting Strategies

**Common Core State Standards**

**Writing**
**2.a.** Introduce a topic clearly, previewing what is to follow; organize ideas, concepts, and information into broader categories; include formatting, graphics, and multimedia when useful to aiding comprehension.

**Focus and organize your ideas.** Review your research, and circle the main causes and effects. Identify which description below best fits your topic. Then, organize your essay accordingly.

- **Many Causes/Single Effect:** If your topic has several causes of a single event, develop a paragraph to discuss each cause.

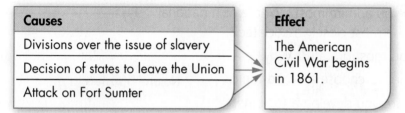

| Causes |
| --- |
| Divisions over the issue of slavery |
| Decision of states to leave the Union |
| Attack on Fort Sumter |

| Effect |
| --- |
| The American Civil War begins in 1861. |

- **Single Cause/Many Effects:** For one cause with several effects, devote a paragraph to each effect.

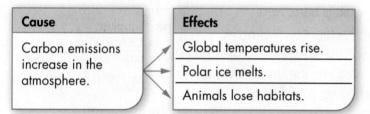

| Cause |
| --- |
| Carbon emissions increase in the atmosphere. |

| Effects |
| --- |
| Global temperatures rise. |
| Polar ice melts. |
| Animals lose habitats. |

- **Chain of Causes and Effects:** If you are presenting a chain of causes and effects, present them in chronological order with transitions to show the connections.

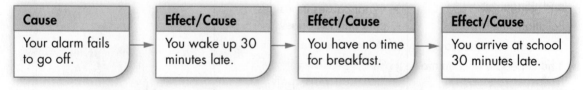

| Cause | Effect/Cause | Effect/Cause | Effect/Cause |
| --- | --- | --- | --- |
| Your alarm fails to go off. | You wake up 30 minutes late. | You have no time for breakfast. | You arrive at school 30 minutes late. |

**Prove the connection.** To convince your audience that the causes and effects you connect are not just coincidental, add details to elaborate on the link you are showing.

- **Weak connection:** The local hardware store is losing business because another hardware store opened.

- **Cause-and-effect connection:** The local hardware store is losing business because a larger hardware store *with a bigger inventory opened a few miles away.*

# Writers on Writing

## Lan Samantha Chang On Using Specific Details

Lan Samantha Chang is the author of "Water Names" (p. 1018).

At the heart of my story "San" is the idea that every child is a detective, searching for clues about her parents' mysterious past lives. In this passage, I tried to show the development of this obsession by describing the way that Caroline, the 13-year-old narrator, hunts through the closets in her own house. I tried to reveal this information through action and specific details, rather than summary.

*"I want to show, not tell . . ."*
—Lan Samantha Chang

### Professional Model:

### from "San"

At the back of the foyer closet, inside the faded red suitcase my mother had brought from China, I discovered a cache of little silk purses wrapped in a cotton shirt. When I heard her footsteps I instinctively closed the suitcase and pretended I was looking for a pair of mittens. Then I went to my room and shut the door, slightly dizzy with anticipation and guilt.

A few days later when my mother was out, I opened one purse. Inside was a swirling gold pin with pearl and coral flowers. I made many secret visits to the closet, a series of small sins. Each time I opened one more treasure. There were bright green, milky white, and ~~blood-red~~ *carmine* bracelets. Some of the bracelets were so small I could not fit them over my hand. There was a ring with a pearl as big as a marble. . . .

Here I tried to emphasize, through use of detail, that the mother had come from China and that it had happened years ago (the suitcase is "faded").

I don't use adverbs very often and when I *do* I want them to reveal character. In this case I wanted to reveal Caroline's instinctive need for secrecy, her desire to hide her private explorations from her mother.

I kept "blood-red" for many drafts because I liked the idea of blood (family) secrets being excavated. Later I crossed out the words, because they are a cliché.

# Revising Strategies

Common Core
State Standards

**Writing**
**2.c.** Use appropriate and varied transitions to create cohesion and clarify the relationships among ideas and concepts.
**2.d.** Use precise language and domain-specific vocabulary to inform about or explain the topic.
**5.** With some guidance and support from peers and adults, develop and strengthen writing as needed by planning, revising, editing, rewriting, or trying a new approach, focusing on how well purpose and audience have been addressed.

**Language**
**1.** Demonstrate command of the conventions of standard English grammar and usage when writing or speaking.

**Fill in gaps in support.** Read through your draft to determine if you clearly and persuasively connect causes with effects. One way to do this is to label your support (for example, "F" for fact). If it looks like you have too much of one type of support or there is no support at all for one of your main points, consider including additional information.

**Use transitions to show connections.** Your goal is to prove the link between cause and effect. Transition words can help you make sure the relationship between cause and effect is obvious to your readers. Use transitional words and phrases like the ones shown here to clarify connections.

| Cause-and-Effect Transitions | |
| --- | --- |
| **Introducing Causes** | since, if, because, as soon as, until |
| **Introducing Effects** | consequently, as a result, subsequently, then |

**Define key terms for your audience.** To make sure you have expressed your ideas clearly, follow these steps:

1. Reread your essay, circling any terms that your audience may not know.

2. Provide more background information or definitions where necessary. You may have to consult your research notes or other reference materials for this information. The example below uses an *appositive phrase* to provide the additional information.

| Original | Revision With Key Terms Defined |
| --- | --- |
| Henry's kitten had to get a shot to prevent feline leukemia. | Henry's kitten had to get a shot to prevent feline leukemia, an incurable disease in cats that is caused by a virus. |

## Peer Review

Ask a classmate to review your draft to help you identify places in your draft where adding transitions would improve the writing. Consider these suggestions while you are revising to clarify cause-and-effect relationships.

## Revising Run-on Sentences and Sentence Fragments

Sentence errors such as run-on sentences and sentence fragments can make writing difficult to understand.

**Identifying Sentence Errors** A **run-on sentence** is two or more complete sentences that are not properly joined or separated. This sentence error can be corrected by breaking the sentence into two, or by adding punctuation or words to clarify the meaning of a single sentence.

| Run-On | Revision Tips |
|---|---|
| Charles is an avid reader he also is a dedicated athlete. | **Separate sentences:** Charles is an avid reader. He also is a dedicated athlete. <br> *or* <br> **Add comma and coordinating conjunction:** Charles is an avid reader, but he also is a dedicated athlete. <br> *or* <br> **Use a semicolon:** Charles is an avid reader; he also is a dedicated athlete. |

A **sentence fragment** is a group of words that does not express a complete thought. To fix fragments, add more information to complete the idea.

**Fragment:** By the next day.

**Corrected:** By the next day, she felt better.

**Fixing Errors** Follow these steps to fix sentence errors.

**1.** To fix a run-on, rewrite it using one of these methods:

- Break the clauses into separate sentences.
- Join the clauses using a comma and a coordinating conjunction, such as *and, or, but, yet, so*.
- Join the clauses using a semicolon.

**2.** Fix a fragment by either adding it to a nearby sentence or adding the necessary words to turn it into a sentence.

### Grammar in Your Writing

Read through your draft to see if you have used run-on sentences or fragments. Correct them by adding the necessary words and punctuation.

> **PH** **WRITING COACH**
>
> Further instruction and practice are available in *Prentice Hall Writing Coach*.

## Student Model: Max Norowzi, Raleigh, NC

### Sleep—It's Healthy

Since the beginning of time, sleep has been an important factor in maintaining good health. While people sleep, they refuel their bodies and minds to help them through the next day. Many people do not get the proper amount of sleep, however, and this has a negative effect on their health.

During the day, our bodies and minds consume a great deal of energy. Sleep recharges our bodies and minds, giving our bodies and minds a chance to recover the energy that we have lost. We wake up feeling refreshed because, while we sleep, our brains do not need to focus and our muscles can relax.

Sleep deprivation occurs when someone receives fewer hours of sleep than his or her body needs. Many different things can cause sleep deprivation. A few of the main causes are drinking caffeine, living in a noisy environment, and working long hours. The effect on a person who does not get enough sleep can be devastating. Some effects of sleep deprivation are stress, anxiety, inability to concentrate, and loss of coping skills. Another effect is weight gain, which is very unhealthy for most people. Mood shifts, including depression, increased irritability, and loss of a sense of humor all result from not getting enough sleep.

I have observed some of these sleep deprivation effects in people I know. My friend Tim had to stay up late several nights in a row in order to finish a term paper on time. Here is how Tim describes how the loss of sleep affected him: "The first thing I noticed was that I couldn't concentrate in class. My attention would wander and I couldn't understand ideas that would ordinarily be very easy for me to grasp. My body was achy, my head was cloudy, and I was snapping at everyone about everything. The sleep that I did get wasn't very good because my dreams were bad ones about things like forgetting to turn my paper in."

People often dream when they have been thinking hard about something right before they go to sleep. Dreams can be good or bad for us. A good dream is relaxing and does not disturb the sleeper. A bad dream causes stress, anxiety, and restlessness. To avoid bad dreams, people should do something relaxing, like reading, before going to bed.

In conclusion, adequate sleep promotes good health and helps us feel better about ourselves. Sleep deprivation can seriously harm our minds and bodies. To counter these harmful effects, the answer is to simply get more sleep. Sleeping well can guarantee us better health and a better life.

Max clearly outlines the cause-and-effect relationship he will address.

This paragraph identifies the causes of sleep deprivation.

To support his explanation, Max offers detailed descriptions of sleep deprivation's effects.

Max concludes his essay effectively by summarizing the health benefits of sleep.

# Editing and Proofreading

Make corrections in grammar, usage, and mechanics to ensure that your final draft is error-free.

**Focus on prepositions.** Whenever possible, avoid ending sentences with a preposition.

> **Draft Sentence:** Which friend are you traveling **with**?

> **Revised Sentence: With** which friend are you traveling? Who is traveling with you?

# Publishing and Presenting

Consider one of the following ways to share your writing:

**Present a speech.** If your essay addresses a situation that others face, offer to speak to classes that can benefit from your work.

**Publish a feature article.** Submit your essay to your local or school newspaper. In a letter accompanying your essay, explain to the editor why the issue you address is important to readers.

# Reflecting on Your Writing

**Writer's Journal** Jot down your answer to this question:

*Did learning about the causes and effects of your topic motivate you to take any action?*

# Rubric for Self-Assessment

Find evidence in your writing to address each category. Then, use the rating scale to grade your work.

**Spiral Review**

Earlier in this unit, you learned about **colons and semicolons** (p. 1108) and **capitalization** (p. 1130). Check your essay to make sure that you have used semicolons and colons correctly and that you have correctly capitalized names of people, places, and things.

| Criteria | Rating Scale |
|---|---|
| | *not very*          *very* |
| **Focus:** How clearly do you explain the cause-and-effect relationship? | 1  2  3  4  5 |
| **Organization:** How clear and consistent is your organization? | 1  2  3  4  5 |
| **Support/Elaboration:** How convincing are the facts and statistics that support your explanations? | 1  2  3  4  5 |
| **Style:** How clearly does your language convey your conclusion? | 1  2  3  4  5 |
| **Conventions:** How correct is your grammar, especially your avoidance of fragments and run-on sentences? | 1  2  3  4  5 |

# Vocabulary Workshop

## Figurative Language

**Common Core State Standards**

**Language**
**5.** Demonstrate understanding of figurative language, word relationships, and nuances in word meanings.

**Figurative language** is writing that is imaginative and not meant to be taken literally. Writers use figurative language for its descriptive impact and to vividly convey emotions or ideas. The chart shows some examples of figurative language.

| Type of Figurative Language | Example |
|---|---|
| **Simile:** a comparison of two apparently unlike things using *like, as, than,* or *resembles.* | Her eyes are <u>like</u> diamonds. |
| **Metaphor:** a description of one thing as if it were another. | You <u>are</u> my sunshine. |
| **Analogy:** an extended comparison of relationships. An analogy shows how the relationship between one pair of things is like the relationship between another pair. | <u>Juggling</u> is like <u>riding a bicycle</u>. Once you learn how to do it, you never forget. |
| **Personification:** giving human characteristics to a nonhuman subject. | The <u>willow trees sang</u> a sad song as the wind blew through their branches. |
| **Hyperbole:** an intentional (and sometimes outrageous) overstatement, or exaggeration. | It is so hot outside that <u>you could fry an egg on the sidewalk</u>. |
| **Idiom:** an expression whose meaning differs from the meanings of its individual words. | Your description of the situation really <u>hit the nail on the head</u>. |

**Practice A** Identify the type of figurative language used in each of these sentences. Use the chart to help you.

1. This book weighs a ton.

2. Justine is as graceful as a swan when she dances.

3. My Aunt Nina's favorite photos are squirreled away in the attic.

4. His smile lights up the room.

5. The waves murmured their sleepy good-nights.

6. My brother is in the doghouse because he broke his curfew.

**Practice B** Identify the figurative language in each item as an example of simile, metaphor, personification, or hyperbole.

1. Jamie was as quiet as a mouse, hardly making a sound when she entered the room.

2. Moving quickly from one spot on the ground to another, the tumbleweed danced merrily over the prairie.

3. Jonah's little sister is as cute as a button when she giggles at her own made-up jokes.

4. Tyrone learned to swim like a fish at summer camp, perfectly mastering every stroke.

5. The school collected enough donations to sink a ship.

6. My mother is a whirlwind of activity; she never seems to rest.

7. The water cradled and rocked the young boy as he peacefully floated.

8. Her singing is so pleasant—a soft, sweet breeze that carries a lovely tune.

**Activity** Write a message that you might put in a postcard, describing an activity that you enjoy. Gather ideas for using figurative language in your message by completing a note card like the one shown. Use ideas from the note card to vividly convey your message with similes, metaphors, personification, or hyperbole.

| | |
|---|---|
| **Similes:** | |
| **Metaphors:** | |
| **Personification:** | |
| **Hyperbole:** | |

**Comprehension and Collaboration**

Working in a small group, create a poster for a school event. Do your best to use one example each of simile, metaphor, personification, and hyperbole in your poster. When the poster is completed, discuss what impact the use of figurative language has on the finished product.

# Communications Workshop

## Delivering a Persuasive Speech Using Multimedia

A persuasive multimedia presentation uses visuals, sound, speech, and text to persuade an audience.

### Learn the Skills

Use these strategies to complete the activity on p. 1167.

**Advocate a position.** Your presentation should flow from a sound, well-stated position, and every detail should relate to and advocate for this position. Write a statement, or *thesis*, to express your main idea.

**Use primary and secondary sources.** Support your ideas using firsthand accounts, as well as expert analysis or observation.

**Decide which media to use.** Choose media that emphasize your points. You might use a film with sound or even a still photo and silence.

**Choose an organization.** Use a structure suited to your purpose, such as point-by-point or block method (see p. 782).

**Make an outline.** Use an outline to organize your speech into sections, noting where you will use evidence and examples to support your arguments. Include an introduction, a body, and a conclusion.

**Be prepared.** If possible, practice the speech using the equipment. Have a backup plan in case a piece of equipment does not function.

**Be dramatic.** Use creative language, such as similes, idioms, and extended comparisons (analogies) to make your points. To add persuasive appeal, choose words for their emotional associations (connotations), as well as for their precise, literal meanings (denotations).

**Use verb voice and mood.** Be aware of the different ways you can use verb voice and mood to enhance your presentation.

**Active voice (emphasizes actor):** Sherman ordered his troops into battle.

**Passive voice (emphasizes action):** The proclamation was signed by Lincoln on January 1, 1863.

**Conditional/subjunctive (contrary to fact):** Were he to have run for another term, it's not certain he would have won.

**Be clear.** When presenting, use transitions, such as *because, next,* or *as a result,* to show connections between ideas. Also, be sure to clearly differentiate between facts and your own opinions.

**Common Core State Standards**

**Reading Informational Text**
**7.** Evaluate the advantages of using different mediums to present a particular topic or idea.

**Speaking and Listening**
**5.** Integrate multimedia and visual displays into presentations to clarify information, strengthen claims and evidence, and add interest.

**Language**
**3.a.** Use verbs in the active and passive voice and in the conditional and subjunctive mood to achieve particular effects.

## Practice the Skills

© **Presentation of Knowledge and Ideas** Use what you've learned in this workshop to perform the following task.

---

### ACTIVITY: Delivering a Persuasive Presentation

Prepare and deliver a persuasive presentation with multimedia.
Follow the steps below:

- Advocate a position on a school- or community-related issue.
- Include similes, idioms, analogies, and multimedia (text, graphics, images, and sound).
- Use speaking techniques to effectively deliver your presentation.
- Refer to the Model Outline to help you organize your presentation.

---

Construct an outline for your presentation similar to the model below. Draft your speech and rehearse with a partner, paying special attention to the smooth integration of media. In your presentation, remember to make eye contact, use natural gestures, vary your speaking rate and volume, and enunciate. Follow language conventions correctly to communicate your ideas effectively.

---

### Model Outline

**My Position**
  I. **Introduction:**
    A. Introduce the position for which I am advocating.
    B. Give background, accompanied by multimedia #1: slideshow.

  II. **Body of Presentation:**
    A. Discuss supporting example/evidence #1.
    B. Discuss supporting example/evidence #2.
       (include an analogy to help listeners understand)
    C. Discuss supporting example/evidence #3.
       i. Present multimedia #2: short video clip.
       ii. Explain implications of clip, using a simile.

  III. **Conclusion:**
    Use multimedia, along with a simile or an analogy, to create a strong ending to my persuasive message.

---

© **Comprehension and Collaboration** At the end of your presentation, discuss it with your audience, eliciting and responding to questions and comments. Ask your audience if you were successful in advocating for your position.

# Cumulative Review

**Common Core**
**State Standards**

**RL.8.2, RL.8.3; W.8.2.b; L.8.4.a**
[For the full wording of the standards, see the standards chart in the front of your textbook.]

## I. Reading Literature

**Directions:** *Read the story. Then, answer the questions that follow.*

The Ojibwa people have always lived in the northern United States and southern Canada, near Lake Superior. Winters here are long, cold, and snowy. Surviving the winter was hard, and the Ojibwa <u>eagerly</u> waited for warm weather, when they could plant crops and make maple sugar. But one year, spring and summer almost never came. Ojibwa elders told this story.

Once there was an evil giant who lived in the far south. When the summer birds flew south in the fall, the giant captured them. He locked them up in big cages—the robins and larks, the wrens and finches and warblers, and the cardinals and woodpeckers. He set two large, mean crows to guard them. (Crows have never gotten along with other birds!)

When it was time for winter to end, the summer birds could not fly north. Without them, spring could not arrive in the Ojibwa's lands. Rivers and lakes stayed frozen. Trees were bare of leaves. It was far too cold to hunt, and crops did not grow. People shivered and wondered what to do. Animals were cold and miserable, too.

In those days, animals and humans could talk to each other. So they all met together to think about what to do. They chattered and argued, but no one had a plan. Finally, one creature came forward with a plan. It was the kingfisher, a blue-gray and white bird with a tuft of feathers on his head.

Kingfisher flew south to look for the missing birds. He took only one weapon, a ball of wax. At last he spotted the cages full of birds, with the giant asleep nearby. Quickly he took the ball of wax and used it to seal the crows' bills shut so they could not wake the giant. Then he used his strong beak to break the locks on the cages.

"Quiet! Don't wake the giant," Kingfisher warned the birds. Silently, they stretched their wings and took to the air. As the summer birds flew north, the air got warmer. Ice and snow melted; leaves and blossoms grew on the trees. Spring returned to the Ojibwa.

1. What natural event does this **myth** explain?
   A. why spring returns
   B. why winters are cold
   C. why birds fly south
   D. why crows are mean

2. What is the **cultural context** of this story?
   A. a crowded city environment
   B. a society made up only of animals
   C. a culture of farming and hunting
   D. a culture of brave warriors

3. Which sentence is the *best* indicator that this story comes from the **oral tradition?**
   A. But one year spring and summer never came.
   B. In those days, animals and humans could talk to each other.
   C. Spring returned to the Ojibwa.
   D. Ojibwa elders told this story.

4. Which feature of the **oral tradition** does this story contain?
   A. An animal character is the hero.
   B. The story is told in dialect.
   C. The story ends with a moral, or lesson.
   D. The story is in the form of an epic poem.

5. What traits of a **heroic character** does Kingfisher show?
   A. He brags about his deeds.
   B. He is brave and clever.
   C. He can speak to human characters.
   D. He can fly.

6. What does the myth reveal about the **heritage,** or culture, of the Ojibwa people?
   A. They are not in touch with their natural environment.
   B. They celebrate the coming of spring so farming can begin.
   C. They prefer living in warmer climates.
   D. They dislike kingfishers and crows.

7. How does this story differ from a **legend?**
   A. It does not have a hero.
   B. It does not contain impossible or exaggerated incidents.
   C. It is not based on a real person or fact.
   D. It features both humans and animals.

8. **Vocabulary** Which word is closest in meaning to the underlined word <u>eagerly</u>?
   A. scarcely
   B. calmly
   C. willingly
   D. excitedly

## Timed Writing

9. In two paragraphs, **explain** how Kingfisher's trip to rescue the summer birds is like and unlike the quest of the hero of an **epic poem** to find or rescue something or someone. Use **details** from the story to **support** your answer.

GO ON

# II. Reading Informational Text

**Directions:** *Read these two examples of media types. Then, answer the questions that follow.*

**Common Core
State Standards**

RI.8.2, RI.8.5; L.8.1, L.8.2, L.8.4.a
[For the full wording of the standards, see the standards chart in the front of your textbook.]

**Interview**

***Reporter*** ("TV News at 5")**:** So, Coach Collins, how do you feel now that the soccer team has won its third state championship?

***Coach Collins:*** We've had a great season, and we can all be proud! I especially want to thank our team captain, Sofia. We're sorry to lose her, as she's graduating, but I'm happy to honor her as our MVP!

***Reporter:*** I didn't realize she was a senior. What's next for her?

***Coach Collins:*** She hasn't decided. But we are more focused on next year's young stars, for now.

**Movie Review**

His new comedy, *Morning Coffee*, may <u>astonish</u> fans of actor Ian Browne, who is best known for his roles in Shakespeare tragedies. In this clever film, however, Browne shows an unexpected skill for comedy as the host of a failing early-morning TV show. While some long-time fans may be disappointed, the film should win new fans for the actor. This reviewer gives it four stars.

1. What main **structural pattern** is evident in the interview?
   A. order of importance
   B. question and answer
   C. cause and effect organization
   D. chronological organization

2. What main **structural pattern** is evident in the movie review?
   A. increasing order of importance
   B. descending order of importance
   C. chronological organization
   D. cause and effect organization

3. In what way does the review show **unity?**
   A. the details all support its topic
   B. there is only one author
   C. the conclusion comes last
   D. two points of view are given

4. **Vocabulary** Which word is closest in meaning to the underlined word <u>astonish</u>?
   A. surprise
   B. scare
   C. horrify
   D. disappoint

# III. Writing and Language Conventions

**Directions:** *Read the sample multimedia report. Then, answer all the questions that follow.*

(1) In the 1800s, many nations dreamed of creating a channel through Central America. (2) The map shows how ships could then sail directly between the Atlantic and Pacific Oceans. (3) President Theodore Roosevelt was determined to make this dream real. (4) Roosevelt said "I took the Canal Zone and let Congress debate. (5) The canal cut across an isthmus in Panama. (6) Although the terrain was challenging, work moved quickly. (7) As this photograph shows, the first ship passed through the canal locks in 1914. (8) Now, instead of circumnavigating the southernmost promontory of South America to sail between oceans, ships could traverse the new Panama Canal.

**1.** How could the writer *best* **organize** the report so the multimedia prompts are easier to use and follow?
- **A.** Use more than one paragraph.
- **B.** List the details of the report on one page and the multimedia aids on another.
- **C.** Create an outline, noting when and how each multimedia aid is used.
- **D.** Use different symbols to show each multimedia aid.

**2.** An isthmus is a narrow strip of land. How could the writer use an **appositive** to clarify this term in sentence 5?
- **A.** The canal cut across an isthmus in Panama, a narrow strip of land.
- **B.** The canal cut across an isthmus which is a narrow strip of land in Panama.
- **C.** The canal cut across a narrow strip of land in Panama.
- **D.** The canal cut across an isthmus, a narrow strip of land, in Panama.

**3.** What is the correct way to **punctuate** the direct quotation in sentence 4?
- **A.** Roosevelt said, "I took the Canal Zone and let Congress debate."
- **B.** Roosevelt said I took the Canal Zone and let Congress debate.
- **C.** Roosevelt said "I took the Canal Zone, and let Congress debate.
- **D.** The quotation is punctuated correctly.

**4.** How should the writer revise sentence 8 to make it more suitable for an **audience** of classmates?
- **A.** Add more information.
- **B.** Choose different, less difficult words.
- **C.** Split the sentence in two and use a semicolon.
- **D.** Use a graph to explain meaning.

# Performance Tasks

**Common Core State Standards**

RL.8.1, RL.8.2, RL.8.3, RL.8.4, RL.8.9; W.8.2, W.8.9.a; SL.8.1, SL.8.4; L.8.1, L.8.2, L.8.5

[For the full wording of the standards, see the standards chart in the front of your textbook.]

**Directions:** *Follow the instructions to complete the tasks below as required by your teacher.*

*As you work on each task, incorporate both general academic vocabulary and literary terms you learned in this unit.*

## Writing

### Task 1: Literature [RL.8.1, RL.8.3; W.8.2]
**Analyze Characterization in a Story**
*Write an essay in which you analyze how the events in a story reveal aspects of character.*

- Choose a story from this unit that has clearly defined characters. Write a brief description of the character or characters you are analyzing.
- List several examples in which characters' reactions to a story event show something important about their personalities. The characters' responses may take the form of actions or dialogue.
- Analyze how these responses reveal key personality traits such as bravery, cleverness, or arrogance.
- Correct any run-on sentences or sentence fragments in your essay.

### Task 2: Literature [RL.8.2; W.8.9; L.8.2]
**Compare Themes in Two Works**
*Write an essay in which you analyze the themes in two works in this unit.*

- Select two stories in this unit that have identifiable themes.
- First, provide a summary of each story's plot. Explain how the story events you have summarized are connected to the theme, or message, of each story.

- Next, explain the theme's relationship to characters' attitudes and actions and the setting in each story.
- Finally, describe how the two themes are similar and note ways in which they differ. For example, you might explain how one or both stories have universal themes by showing how the same theme occurs in stories from other cultures or time periods.
- As you write, be sure to capitalize characters' names and place names correctly.

### Task 3: Literature [RL.8.4; W.8.2]
**Analyze Word Choice**
*Write an essay in which you analyze the use of figurative language in a story or poem.*

- Select a work in this unit that features figurative language, such as similes, metaphors, personification, or hyperbole.
- Give specific examples of figurative language in the text and explain the meaning of each example as well as its impact on the work's meaning and tone.
- Note the overall impact figurative language has on the story or poem. State whether or not you think the writer's use of figurative language is effective, and explain why.
- Choose language that expresses your ideas precisely, eliminating vague words.

# Speaking and Listening

**ⓒ Task 4: Literature** [RL.8.2; SL.8.4; L.8.1]

## Present a Speech on a Hero

*Present a speech about a hero from one of the texts in this unit.*

- Choose a heroic character from one of the texts in this unit.
- Describe the traits, qualities, and accomplishments that make this person a hero.
- Identify quotations and descriptions from the text that will help you characterize certain actions and behavior as heroic. Record these examples as evidence to present in your speech.
- Arrange your notes in logical order.
- Present your speech to the class, observing standard English grammar and usage.

**ⓒ Task 5: Literature** [RL.8.9; SL.8.1]

## Compare Legends and Retellings

*Moderate a group discussion in which you compare the heroes presented in the two Carl Sandburg pieces in this unit with the traditional legends from which they come.*

- As a group, list the heroes mentioned in the two Sandburg selections in this unit. Then, identify the original legends from which these heroes are drawn. (Obtain and read copies of the original stories as needed.)
- Ask participants to compare and contrast the way the heroes are represented in the traditional legends with the way that Sandburg represents them.
- Participants should base their responses on evidence from the texts, such as plot events, descriptions, and dialogue.

- Finally, ask participants to evaluate the effects that Sandburg's retellings produce and to judge whether his changes improve on or detract from the original tales.

**ⓒ Task 6: Literature** [RL.8.4; L.8.5]

## Analyze Word Choice

*Analyze how figurative language and idioms affect the tone, meaning, and mood of a work in this unit.*

- Identify a work in this unit that has strong examples of idioms and figurative language.
- Analyze the meaning of the idioms and figurative language in the text, and discuss the impact this language has on the tone, meaning, and mood of the work. For example, you could note when the use of idioms gives the work a humorous tone.
- Present your analysis and invite follow-up questions from the audience.

---

### Are yesterday's heroes important today?

At the beginning of Unit 6, you participated in a discussion about the Big Question. Now that you have finished the unit, write a response to the question. Discuss how and why the views you shared about the relevance of yesterday's heroes have either changed or been reinforced. Give examples from the stories, as well as from other subjects and your personal experiences, to support your ideas. Use Big Question vocabulary words (see p. 1009) in your response.

# Featured Titles

In this unit, you have read a variety of literary works that originated in the oral tradition. Continue to read on your own. Select works that you enjoy, but challenge yourself to explore new writers and works of increasing depth and complexity. The titles suggested below will help you get started.

## Literature

### The Adventures of Tom Sawyer

by Mark Twain                    EXEMPLAR TEXT

 Read about the escapades of mischievous Tom Sawyer and his best friend, Huck Finn, in this classic nineteenth-century American **novel.**

### Fast Sam, Cool Clyde, and Stuff

by Walter Dean Myers

 Stuff is new to Harlem when he meets Fast Sam, Cool Clyde, and Gloria. Watch Harlem come alive in this funny, sad, and realistic **novel** about city life in the 1970s.

### The American Songbag

Edited by Carl Sandburg
Mariner Books, 1990

 Carl Sandburg is best known as a poet, but he was also a collector of American **folk music.** This book includes 290 songs and their lyrics that give voice to many uniquely American experiences.

### Cut From the Same Cloth: American Women of Myth, Legend, and Tall Tale

by Robert San Souci

 San Souci explores larger-than-life adventures in these often humorous **folktales** featuring clever, brave, and strong women.

## Informational Texts

### John F. Kennedy

by Howard S. Kaplan

 Read about our thirty-fifth president, John F. Kennedy, in this **biography.** Kennedy was an inspirational leader whose promising term in office was cut short by his shocking assassination.

### Freedom Walkers

by Russell Freedman
Holiday House, 2006                    EXEMPLAR TEXT

 This **historical account** tells the story of the Montgomery Bus Boycott, which gave rise to the Civil Rights movement in the United States. Learn about famous figures such as Rosa Parks, as well as many other people who fought for justice and equality.

# Preparing to Read Complex Texts

**Attentive Reading** As you read on your own, ask yourself questions about the text. The questions shown below and others that you ask as you read will help you learn and enjoy literature even more.

**Common Core State Standards**

**Reading Literature/Informational Text**
**10.** By the end of the year, read and comprehend literature, including stories, dramas, and poems, and literary nonfiction at the high end of the grades 6–8 text complexity band independently and proficiently.

## When reading texts from the oral tradition, ask yourself...

- From what culture does this text come? What do I know about that culture?

- What type of text am I reading? For example, is it a myth, a legend, or a tall tale? What characters and events do I expect to find in this type of text?

- Does the text include the elements I expected? If not, how does it differ from what I expected?

- What elements of the culture do I see in the text? For example, do I notice beliefs, foods, or settings that have meaning for the people of this culture?

- Does the text teach a lesson or a moral? If so, is this a valuable lesson?

**Key Ideas and Details**

- Who is retelling or presenting this text? Do I think the author has changed the text from the original? If so, how?

- Does the text include characters and tell a story? If so, are the characters and plot interesting?

- What do I notice about the language used in the text? Which aspects seem similar to or different from the language used in modern texts?

- Does the text include symbols? If so, do they have a special meaning in the original culture of the text? Do they also have meaning in modern life?

**Craft and Structure**

- What does this text teach me about the culture from which it comes?

- What, if anything, does this text teach me about people in general?

- Does this text seem like others I have read or heard? Why or why not?

- Do I know of any modern versions of this text? How are they similar to or different from this one?

- If I were researching this culture for a report, would I include passages from this text? If so, what would those passages show?

- Do I enjoy reading this text and others like it? Why or why not?

**Integration of Ideas**

# Resources

# Glossary

Big Question vocabulary appears in **blue type**. High-utility Academic vocabulary is <u>underlined</u>.

## A

**abyss** (uh BIHS) *n.* immeasurable space, such as a bottomless gulf

**accomplishments** (uh KOM plihsh muhnts) *n.* things done successfully or completed

**account** (uh KOWNT) *n.* bill for work done

<u>**accumulate**</u> (uh KYOO myuh layt) *v.* collect or gather

**acquire** (uh KWYR) *v.* get; obtain

**admirably** (AD muhr uh blee) *adv.* in a manner deserving praise

**affectionate** (uh FEHK shuhn niht) *adj.* loving

**affluence** (AF loo uhns) *n.* wealth

**alibi** (AL uh by) *n.* believable reason why a suspect could not have been at the scene of a crime

**alienate** (AYL yuh nayt) *v.* make unfriendly

**alliance** (uh LY uhns) *n.* group united for a common goal

**ancestral** (an SEHS truhl) *adj.* related to a family

**anguish** (ANG gwihsh) *n.* distress

**anonymously** (uh NON uh muhs lee) *adv.* without a name or any identification

**antithesis** (an TIHTH uh sihs) *n.* direct opposite

**apprehension** (ap rih HEHN shuhn) *n.* fearful feeling about what will happen

<u>**argument**</u> (AHR gyuh muhnt) *n.* claim; persuasive reasoning

**aromas** (uh ROH muhz) *n.* smells

**arrogant** (AR uh guhnt) *adj.* feeling or showing proud self-importance and disregard for others

**ascent** (uh SEHNT) *n.* act of climbing or rising

<u>**aspects**</u> (AS pehkts) *n.* ways in which an idea or problem may be viewed

**aspirations** (as puh RAY shuhnz) *n.* strong desires or ambitions

**assail** (uh SAYL) *v.* attack with arguments, questions, doubts, etc.

**assumption** (uh SUHMP shuhn) *n.* act of taking for granted

**audacity** (aw DAS uh tee) *n.* bold courage; nerve

**audible** (AW duh buhl) *adj.* able to be heard

**authentic** (aw THEHN tihk) *adj.* genuine; real

**authorized** (AW thuh ryzd) *v.* approved

**avert** (uh VURT) *v.* avoid

**awed** (awd) *v.* filled with wonder

## B

**barren** (BAR uhn) *adj.* empty; bare

**beacons** (BEE kuhnz) *n.* signals meant to warn or guide, as a light or fire

**beckoning** (BEHK uhn ihng) *adj.* summoning

**bellow** (BEHL oh) *v.* make a deep, loud sound like a bull

<u>**benefit**</u> (BEHN uh fiht) *n.* advantage or positive result

**benign** (bih NYN) *adj.* kindly

**bewildered** (bih WIHL duhrd) *adj.* hopelessly confused

<u>**bias**</u> (BY uhs) *n.* tendency to see things from a slanted or prejudiced viewpoint

**bilingual** (by LIHNG gwuhl) *adj.* able to speak two languages

**blackmail** (BLAK mayl) *n.* forcing people to give you money by threatening to tell secrets about them

**bleak** (bleek) *adj.* bare and windswept; cold

**boulevard** (BUL uh vahrd) *n.* wide road

**bravery** (BRAY vuhr ee) *n.* courage or valor

**brutal** (BROO tuhl) *adj.* cruel

**burrow** (BUR oh) *n.* passage or hole for shelter

## C

**capricious** (kuh PRIHSH uhs) *adj.* tending to change abruptly, without apparent reason

**carelessness** (KAIR luhs nuhs) *n.* lack of responsibility

**cataclysm** (KAT uh klihz uhm) *n.* sudden, violent event that causes change

**ceaseless** (SEES lihs) *adj.* never stopping; continual

<u>**challenge**</u> (CHAL uhnj) *v.* calling into question; demanding of proof

**cicada** (suh KAY duh) *n.* large insect that resembles a fly; the male makes a loud high-pitched noise

<u>**class**</u> (klas) *n.* group of people or objects

**coiled** (koyld) *v.* twisted around and around

**commenced** (kuh MEHNST) *v.* began to happen

**common** (KOM uhn) *adj.* ordinary or expected

**commotion** (kuh MOH shuhn) *n.* noisy movement

**compassionate** (kuhm PASH uh niht) *adj.* deeply sympathetic

**compelled** (kuhm PEHLD) *v.* forced

**compensate** (KOM puhn sayt) *v.* pay

**compromise** (KOM pruh myz) *n.* settling of differences in a way that allows both sides to feel satisfied

**compulsory** (kuhm PUHL suhr ee) *adj.* required

**conceivable** (kuhn SEE vuh buhl) *adj.* able to be imagined

**conceivably** (kuhn SEE vuh blee) *adv.* in an imaginable or believable way

**confirm** (kuhn FURM) *v.* prove or establish as true

**confronted** (kuhn FRUHNT uhd) *v.* brought face to face

**connection** (kuh NEHK shuhn) *n.* joining or linking

**consoling** (kuhn SOH lihng) *adj.* comforting

**conspicuous** (kuhn SPIHK yoo uhs) *adj.* noticeable

**constructive** (kuhn STRUHK tihv) *adj.* leading to improvement

**contact** (KON takt) *n.* touching; communication

**contemplation** (KON tuhm PLAY shuhn) *n.* act of thinking about something

**contempt** (kuhn TEMPT) *n.* scorn; disrespect

**contemptuously** (kuhn TEHMP choo uhs lee) *adv.* scornfully

**contraction** (kuhn TRAK shuhn) *n.* act of becoming smaller

**contradict** (kon truh DIHKT) *v.* deny or go against a viewpoint

**conviction** (kuhn VIHK shuhn) *n.* strong belief; certainty

**cordially** (KAWR juhl lee) *adv.* warmly

**courage** (KUR ihj) *n.* valor or bravery

**credibility** (krehd uh BIHL uh tee) *n.* believability

**criteria** (kry TIHR ee uh) *n.* standards or tests by which something can be judged

**cultural** (KUHL chuhr uhl) *adj.* having to do with the collected customs and beliefs of a group or community

**cunningly** (KUHN ihng lee) *adv.* skillful in deception; crafty

**curiosity** (kyur ee OS uh tee) *n.* desire to get information

**cyclone** (SY klohn) *n.* violent, rotating windstorm; tornado

**cynically** (SIHN uh kuhl lee) *adv.* doubtfully; skeptically

## D

**debates** (dih BAYTS) *v.* tries to decide

**debris** (duh BREE) *n.* rough, broken bits of stone, concrete, or glass left after something is destroyed

**decadent** (dih KAY duhnt) *adj.* marked by decay or decline

**deceive** (dih SEEV) *v.* make someone believe what is not true; mislead

**deciphering** (dih SY fuhr ihng) *v.* working out the meaning of; decoding

**decision** (dih SIHZH uhn) *n.* choice; act of making up one's mind

**decrees** (dih KREEZ) *n.* orders with the force of law

**deductions** (dih DUHK shuhnz) *n.* judgments about something, based on available information

**deed** (deed) *n.* document which, when signed, transfers ownership of property

**deferred** (dih FURD) *adj.* delayed

**defiance** (dih FY uhns) *n.* refusal to obey authority

**deficiency** (dih FIHSH uhn see) *n.* lack of something that is necessary

**degrading** (dih GRAY dihng) *adj.* insulting; dishonorable

**deliberating** (dih LIHB uhr iht ihng) *v.* thinking carefully

**deprived** (dih PRYVD) *v.* not permitted to have

**derision** (dih RIHZH uhn) *n.* statements or actions that show you have no respect for someone or something

**derived** (dih RYVD) *v.* received or taken from a source

**descendants** (dih SEHN duhnts) *n.* children, grandchildren, and continuing generations

**descent** (dih SEHNT) *n.* act of climbing down

**desolate** (DEHS uh liht) *adj.* sad; lonely

**deterioration** (dih tihr ee uh RAY shuhn) *n.* the process of becoming worse

**development** (dih VEHL uhp muhnt) *n.* event or happening; outcome

**devoid** (dih VOYD) *adj.* completely without

**dew** (doo) *n.* tiny drops of moisture that condense on cooled objects at night

**diffused** (dih FYOOZD) *v.* spread out widely in different directions

**diplomatic** (dihp luh MAT ihk) *adj.* showing skill in dealing with people

**discharged** (dihs CHAHRJD) *v.* fired; released

**discreet** (dihs KREET) *adj.* careful with words or actions

**discrepancies** (dihs KREHP uhn seez) *n.* differences; inconsistencies

**discriminate** (dihs KRIHM uh nayt) *v.* see the difference between; tell apart

**discrimination** (dihs krihm uh NAY shuhn) *n.* ability to see differences between objects or ideas

**disdainfully** (dihs DAYN fuhl lee) *adv.* scornfully

**disinherit** (dihs ihn HEHR iht) *v.* deprive people of their rights as citizens

**dispel** (dihs PEHL) *v.* cause something to go away

**distinction** (dihs TIHNGK shuhn) *n.* difference

**distinguish** (dihs TIHNG gwihsh) *v.* mark as different; set apart

**diverged** (duh VURJD) *v.* branched off

**diverts** (duh VURTS) *v.* distracts; amuses

**divide** (duh VYD) *v.* separate

**dock** (dok) *v.* deduct part of one's salary or wages

**doubtful** (DOWT fuhl) *adj.* not likely; open to challenge

**drought** (drowt) *n.* lack of rain; long period of dry weather

## E

**eavesdropping** (EEVZ drop ihng) *n.* secretly listening to the private conversation of others

**eloquent** (EHL uh kwuhnt) *adj.* vividly expressive

**emancipated** (ih MAN suh payt uhd) *adj.* freed

**emigrated** (EHM uh grayt uhd) *v.* left one place to settle in another

**emphasize** (EHM fuh syz) *v.* stress; show the importance of

**empires** (EHM pyrz) *n.* powerful nations; countries ruled by emperors or empresses

**enchantment** (ehn CHANT muhnt) *n.* feeling of delight

**endure** (ehn DUR) *v.* hold up under; last

**enhance** (ehn HANS) *v.* make greater

**erosion** (ih ROH zhuhn) *n.* wearing away by action of wind or water

**evacuees** (ih VAK yoo eez) *n.* people who leave a dangerous area

**evaded** (ih VAYD uhd) *v.* avoided

**evidence** (EHV uh duhns) *n.* proof

**exaggerate** (ehg ZAJ uh rayt) *v.* magnify beyond fact

**exertion** (ehg ZUR shuhn) *n.* energetic activity; effort

**exiles** (EHG zylz) *n.* people who are forced to live in another country

**expansive** (ehk SPAN sihv) *adj.* characterized by a free and generous nature

**experience** (ehk SPIHR ee uhns) *n.* act of living through an event

**explanation** (ehks pluh NAY shuhn) *n.* act of giving meaning to an idea or concept

**exploitation** (ehks ploy TAY shuhn) *n.* act of using another person for selfish purposes

**exploration** (ehks pluh RAY shuhn) *n.* act of looking into closely or examining carefully

**express** (ehk SPREHS) *v.* put into words

**exquisite** (EHKS kwih ziht) *adj.* very beautiful

**extinction** (ehk STIHNGK shuhn) *n.* dying out of a species

**extinguished** (ehk STIHNG gwihsht) *v.* put out; ended

**exultantly** (ehg ZUHL tuhnt lee) *adv.* triumphantly

**exulting** (ehg ZUHLT ihng) *v.* rejoicing

# F

**factor** (FAK tuhr) *n.* any of the circumstances or conditions that lead to a result

**factual** (FAK choo uhl) *adj.* based on or limited to fact

**fantasy** (FAN tuh see) *n.* product of the imagination or make-believe

**fatalist** (FAY tuh lihst) *n.* one who believes that all events are determined by fate

**feedback** (FEED bak) *n.* response that sets a process in motion

**feuding** (fyood ihng) *v.* quarreling

**fiscal** (FIHS kuhl) *adj.* having to do with finances

**flagged** (flagd) *v.* gave a sign to stop, often with a flag or flag-like object

**flatterer** (FLAT uhr uhr) *n.* one who praises insincerely to win approval

**foreboding** (fawr BOH dihng) *n.* feeling that something bad will happen

**forlorn** (fawr LAWRN) *adj.* sad and lonely

**frail** (frayl) *adj.* slender and delicate

**fugitives** (FYOO juh tihvz) *n.* people fleeing from danger

# G

**generalization** (jehn uhr uh luh ZAY shuhn) *n.* statement that captures the broad idea

**gesture** (JEHS chuhr) *n.* something said or done merely as a formality

**global** (GLOH buhl) *adj.* complete, covering a large class of cases

**grateful** (GRAYT fuhl) *adj.* thankful

**guileless** (GYL lihs) *adj.* not trying to hide anything or trick people; innocent

# H

**haggard** (HAG uhrd) *adj.* having a wasted, worn look

**harmonious** (hahr MOH nee uhs) *adj.* combined in a pleasing arrangement

**haughty** (HAW tee) *adj.* scornfully superior

**horizon** (huh RY zuhn) *n.* imaginary line where the sky and earth appear to meet

**hostile** (HOS tuhl) *adj.* related to the enemy; unfriendly

**humiliating** (hyoo MIHL ee ayt ihng) *adj.* embarrassing

# I

**identify** (y DEHN tuh fy) *v.* recognize as being

**ignorance** (IHG nuhr uhns) *n.* lack of knowledge or awareness

**illogical** (ih LOJ uh kuhl) *adj.* contrary or opposed to fact

**imitate** (IHM uh tayt) *v.* copy or follow the example of

**immensely** (ih MEHNS lee) *adv.* greatly

**immensity** (ih MEHN suh tee) *n.* vastness; hugeness

**immortality** (ihm awr TAL uh tee) *n.* endless life

**immunities** (ih MYOO nuh teez) *n.* freedoms; protections

**impertinently** (ihm PUR tuh nuhnt lee) *adv.* disrespectfully

**imprint** (IHM prihnt) *v.* make a lasting mark

**inarticulate** (ihn ahr TIHK yuh liht) *adj.* unable to express oneself

**incentive** (ihn SEHN tihv) *n.* motivation

**indiscreetly** (ihn dihs KREET lee) *adv.* carelessly

**individuality** (ihn duh vihj oo AL uh tee) *n.* way in which a person or thing stands apart or is different

**ineffectually** (ihn uh FEHK chu uhl lee) *adv.* without producing the desired results

**inequality** (ihn ih KWOL uh tee) *n.* state of being unfair or not being treated equally

**inevitable** (ihn EHV uh tuh buhl) *adj.* certain to happen

**inexplicable** (ihn EHK spluh kuh buhl) *adj.* impossible to explain

**inexpressible** (ihn ihk SPREHS uh buhl) *adj.* not able to be described

**inferior** (ihn FIHR ee uhr) *adj.* lower in status or rank

**influence** (IHN floo uhns) *v.* sway or affect in some other way

**inform** (ihn fuhr MAY shuhn) *v.* tell; give information or knowledge

**ingratitude** (ihn GRAT uh tood) *n.* lack of appreciation

**injury** (IHN juhr ee) *n.* harm or damage to a person

**insecurity** (ihn sih KYUR uh tee) *n.* lack of confidence; self-doubt

**insolently** (IHN suh luhnt lee) *adv.* in an impolite manner

**insufferable** (ihn SUHF uhr uh buhl) *adj.* unbearable

**integrate** (IHN tuh grayt) *v.* make equally available to all members of society

**intellectual** (ihn tuh LEHK choo uhl) *adj.* relating to the ability to think intelligently

**interact** (ihn tuhr AKT) *v.* relate with others

**intimidating** (ihn TIHM uh dayt ihng) *adj.* frightening

**intolerant** (ihn TOL uhr uhnt) *adj.* not able or willing to accept

**introspective** (ihn truh SPEHK tihv) *adj.* inward looking; thoughtful

**intuition** (ihn too IHSH uhn) *n.* ability to sense immediately, without reasoning

**invaded** (ihn VAYD uhd) *v.* entered in order to conquer

**invaluable** (ihn VAL yu uh buhl) *adj.* extremely useful

**invariably** (ihn VAIR ee uh blee) *adv.* almost all the time

**investigate** (ihn VEHS tuh gayt) *v.* search; look for

**irritate** (IHR uh tayt) *v.* anger or annoy

## J

**jostling** (JOS uhl ihng) *n.* knocking into, often on purpose

**judge** (juhj) *v.* form an opinion about

**judicious** (joo DIHSH uhs) *adj.* showing sound judgment; wise

## K

**kindled** (KIHN duhld) *v.* built or lit

## L

**lagged** (lagd) *v.* moved slowly

**lax** (laks) *adj.* not strict or exact

**legacy** (LEHG uh see) *n.* something physical or spiritual handed down from an ancestor

**legitimately** (luh JIHT uh miht lee) *adv.* legally

**liable** (LY uh buhl) *adj.* likely

**liberated** (LIHB uh rayt uhd) *v.* freed; released from slavery, enemy occupation, etc.

**luminous** (LOO muh nuhs) *adj.* giving off light

## M

**malicious** (muh LIHSH uhs) *adj.* mean; spiteful

**maneuver** (muh NOO vuhr) *n.* series of planned steps

**meadows** (MEHD ohz) *n.* areas of grassy land

**meager** (MEE guhr) *adj.* small amount

**meaningful** (MEE nihng fuhl) *adj.* having significance or purpose

**media** (MEE dee uh) *n.* collected sources of information, including newspapers, television, and the Internet

**melancholy** (MEHL uhn kol ee) *adj.* sad; depressed

**mislead** (mihs LEED) *v.* give a wrong idea; deceive

**mistrusted** (mihs TRUHST uhd) *v.* be suspicious of or lack confidence in

**misunderstand** (mihs uhn duhr STAND) *v.* misinterpret; fail to understand

**mockery** (MOK uhr ee) *n.* false, insulting action or statement

**modes** (mohdz) *n.* ways of doing or behaving

**mutineers** (myoo tuh NIHRZ) *n.* rebels

**mutinous** (MYOO tuh nuhs) *adj.* rebellious

## N

**naïveté** (nah eev TAY) *n.* state of being simple or childlike

**native** (NAY tihv) *adj.* related to the place of one's birth

**negotiate** (nih GOH shee ayt) *v.* bargain or deal with another party to reach a settlement

**negotiation** (nih goh shee AY shuhn) *n.* bargaining; discussing; deal making

**ninny** (NIHN ee) *n.* simple or foolish person

## O

**objective** (uhb JEHK tihv) *adj.* open-minded; not influenced by personal feelings or prejudice

**obscure** (uhb SKYUR) *adj.* little known

**observation** (ob zuhr VAY shuhn) *n.* statement; point of view

**omens** (OH muhnz) *n.* sign of a bad or good event in the future

**opinion** (uh PIHN yuhn) *n.* personal view or attitude

**oppose** (uh POHZ) *v.* go against; stand in the way of

**oppressed** (uh PREHST) *v.* kept down

**option** (OP shuhn) *n.* choice

**outdated** (owt DAYT uhd) *adj.* behind the times; no longer popular

**overcome** (oh vuhr KUHM) *v.* conquer or get beyond a setback

**overwhelming** (oh vuhr HWEHL mihng) *adj.* emotionally overpowering

## P

**pageant** (PAJ uhnt) *n.* an elaborate play

**paradoxes** (PAR uh doks uhz) *n.* two things that seem directly at odds

**partition** (pahr TIHSH uhn) *n.* interior dividing wall

**passively** (PAS ihv lee) *adv.* without resistance

**perceived** (puhr SEEVD) *v.* grasped mentally; saw

**peril** (PEHR uhl) *n.* danger

**periscope** (PEHR uh skohp) *n.* tube on a submarine that raises and lowers to show objects on the water's surface

**perish** (PEHR ihsh) *v.* to be destroyed or wiped out

**persistent** (puhr SIHS tuhnt) *adj.* continuing to happen, especially for longer than is usual or desirable

**persuade** (puhr SWAYD) *v.* to convince; bring around to one's way of thinking

**pervading** (puhr VAYD ihng) *adj.* spreading throughout

**pestering** (PEHS tuhr ihng) *n.* constant bothering

**pitiful** (PIHT ih fuhl) *adj.* arousing sympathy

**pollen** (POL uhn) *n.* powdery grains on male plants

**ponderous** (PON duhr uhs) *adj.* very heavy

**possession** (puh ZEHSH uhn) *n.* ownership

**posterity** (pos TEHR uh tee) *n.* future generations

**predisposed** (pree dihs POHZD) *adj.* inclined

**predominantly** (prih DOM uh nuhnt lee) *adv.* mainly

**preliminary** (prih LIHM uh nehr ee) *adj.* introductory; preparatory

**presentable** (prih ZEHN tuh buhl) *adj.* neat enough to be seen by others

**pretext** (PREE tehkst) *n.* excuse; reason that hides one's real motives

**procession** (pruh SEHSH uhn) *n.* group moving forward, as in a parade

**prodigy** (PROD uh jee) *n.* an unusually talented person

**prove** (proov) *v.* show or demonstrate

**pursuit** (puhr SOOT) *n.* the act of chasing in order to catch

## Q

**quaint** (kwaynt) *adj.* unusual or old-fashioned in a pleasing way

**quality** (KWOL uh tee) *n.* characteristic or feature

**quantity** (KWON tuh tee) *n.* amount

**quarantine** (KWAWR uhn teen) *n.* period of separation from others to stop the spreading of a disease

## R

**radiation** (ray dee AY shuhn) *n.* the sending of waves of energy through space

**radical** (RAD uh kuhl) *adj.* favoring major change in the social structure

**rapture** (RAP chuhr) *n.* ecstasy

**ravaged** (RAV ihj) *v.* devastated

**reaction** (ree AK shuhn) *n.* response to an influence, action, or statement

**rebellion** (rih BEHL yuhn) *n.* open resistance to authority or dominance

**recede** (rih SEED) *v.* move away

**recoiled** (rih KOYLD) *v.* draw back in disgust

**reeds** (reedz) *n.* tall slender grasses that grow in wetland areas

**refugees** (rehf yuh JEEZ) *n.* people who flee from their homes in time of trouble

**refute** (rih FYOOT) *v.* give evidence to prove an argument or statement false

**rehabilitate** (ree huh BIHL uh tayt) *v.* restore the reputation of

**relentless** (rih LEHNT lihs) *adj.* persistent; unending

**relevant** (REHL uh vuhnt) *adj.* to the point; relating to the matter at hand

**reluctance** (ri LUK tuhns) *n.* hesitation; unwillingness

**remote** (rih MOHT) *adj.* aloof; cold; distant

**renounced** (rih NOWNST) *v.* gave up

**represent** (rehp rih ZEHNT) *v.* stand for or symbolize

**reputation** (rehp yuh TAY shuhn) *n.* widely held opinion about someone, whether good or bad

**resent** (rih ZEHNT) *v.* feel angry or upset out of a sense of unfairness

**resolute** (REHZ uh loot) *adj.* showing a firm purpose

**resolved** (rih ZOLVD) *v.* decided

**resounding** (rih ZOWND ihng) *adj.* sounding loudly

**respectively** (rih SPEHK tihv lee) *adv.* in the order previously named

**resurgence** (rih SUR juhns) *n.* reappearance; revival

**retribution** (reht ruh BYOO shuhn) *n.* punishment for wrongdoing

**reveal** (rih VEEL) *v.* make known; uncover

**revelation** (REHV uh LAY shuhn) *n.* something that suddenly becomes known

**revolutionary** (rehv uh LOO shuh nehr ee) *adj.* favoring sweeping change

**rickety** (RIHK uh tee) *adj.* weak; likely to break

**rituals** (RIHCH u uhlz) *n.* practices done at regular times

**roam** (rohm) *v.* go aimlessly; wander

**rotate** (ROH tayt) *v.* switch

**rut** (ruht) *n.* a groove in the ground made by a wheeled vehicle or natural causes

## S

**sacred** (SAY krihd) *adj.* considered holy; related to religious ceremonies

**sacrifices** (SAK rih fy sez) *n.* the act of deciding not to have or do something valuable or important in order to get something that is more important, often for someone else

**satisfactory** (sat ihs FAK tuhr ee) *adj.* adequate; sufficient to meet a requirement

**scampering** (SKAM puhr ihng) *v.* running quickly

**scarce** (skairs) *adj.* few in number; not common

**scheme** (skeem) *n.* organized way of doing something

**self-confident** (sehlf KON fuh duhnt) *adj.* assured of one's ability

**sensibility** (sehn suh BIHL uh tee) *n.* moral, artistic, or intellectual outlook

**sensory** (SEHN suhr ee) *adj.* having to do with the senses

**separate** (SEHP uh rayt) *v.* set apart

**serene** (suh REEN) *adj.* calm; undisturbed

**shackles** (SHAK uhlz) *n.* metal bonds used to restrain prisoners

**shanties** (SHAN teez) *n.* roughly built cabins or shacks

**shiftless** (SHIHFT lihs) *adj.* without ambition

**shriveled** (SHRIHV uhld) *v.* dried up; shrank; wrinkled

**sidling** (sy duh lihng) *v.* moving sideways in a sly manner

**significance** (sihg NIHF uh kuhns) *n.* importance

**simultaneously** (sy muhl TAY nee uhs lee) *adv.* at the same time

**singularity** (sihng gyuh LAR uh tee) *n.* unique or distinct feature

**sinister** (SIHN uh stuhr) *adj.* threatening harm or evil

**skeptically** (SKEHP tuh kuhl lee) *adv.* with doubt and distrust

**slung** (sluhng) *v.* hung loosely

**solution** (suh LOO shuhn) *n.* act of solving a problem or answering a question

**somber** (SOM buhr) *adj.* dark; gloomy

**sparse** (spahrs) *adj.* thinly spread and small in amount

**spindly** (SPIHN dlee) *adj.* long and thin

**spineless** (SPYN lihs) *adj.* lacking in courage or willpower

**spite** (spyt) *n.* nastiness

**squatter** (SKWOT uhr) *n.* someone who settles illegally on land or in a building

**stalemate** (STAYL mayt) *n.* standoff; outcome of a conflict where no one wins

**statistics** (stuh TIHS tihks) *n.* numerical facts or data

**stealthily** (stehlth uh lee) *adv.* in a secret or sly way

**straddling** (STRAD uhl ihng) *v.* standing or sitting with a leg on either side of something

**strife** (stryf) *n.* conflict

**studious** (STOO dee uhs) *adj.* devoted to learning

**subdued** (suhb DOOD) *adj.* beaten down; conquered

**succumbed** (suh KUHMD) *v.* gave way to; yielded

**suffering** (SUHF uhr ihng) *n.* undergoing of pain or injury

**superficial** (soo puhr FIHSH uhl) *adj.* limited to the surface; lacking depth

**supple** (SUHP uhl) *adj.* yielding; soft

**suppressed** (suh PREHST) *v.* yielding; soft

**surrogate** (SUR uh gayt) *n.* substitute

**sustain** (suh STAYN) *v.* keep up

**symbolize** (SIHM buh lyz) *v.* stand for

**sympathy** (SIHM puh thee) *n.* sameness of feeling; act of feeling for another person

# T

**tangible** (TAN juh buhl) *adj.* easy to see or notice, so there is no doubt

**tantalized** (TAN tuh lyzd) *v.* tormented by something just out of reach

**tedious** (TEE dee uhs) *adj.* boring; tiresome

**tenacious** (tih NAY shuhs) *adj.* holding on firmly; stubborn

**tension** (TEHN shuhn) *n.* nervous, worried, or excited state that makes relaxation impossible

**theory** (THEE uhr ee) *n.* idea based on gathered information or evidence

**thrives** (thryvz) *v.* does well; prospers

**timidly** (TIHM ihd lee) *adv.* in a shy or fearful manner

**tolerance** (TOL uhr uhns) *n.* freedom from prejudice; acceptance of the views of others

**tongue** (tuhng) *n.* language

**transfigured** (tranz FIHG yuhrd) *adj.* transformed in a glorious way

**trivial** (TRIHV ee uhl) *adj.* of little importance

**tumultuous** (too MUHL choo uhs) *adj.* wild; chaotic

**turbulent** (TUR byuh luhnt) *adj.* marked by wild, irregular motion

**turmoil** (TUR moyl) *n.* condition of great confusion or agitation

# U

**unanimous** (yoo NAN uh muhs) *adj.* in complete agreement

**undulation** (uhn juh LAY shuhn) *n.* curvy, wavy form

**uneasily** (uhn EE zuh lee) *adv.* restlessly

**unequivocal** (uhn ih KWIHV uh kuhl) *adj.* clear; plainly understood

**unify** (YOO nuh fy) *v.* bring together; to make united

**unobtrusively** (uhn uhb TROO sihv lee) *adv.* without calling attention to oneself

**unresponsive** (uhn rih SPON sihv) *adj.* not reacting

**unseemly** (uhn SEEM lee) *adj.* inappropriate

**urban** (UR buhn) *adj.* having to do with the city

# V

**valid** (VAL ihd) *adj.* backed by evidence

**valuable** (VAL yu uh buhl) *adj.* having worth or importance

**vertical** (VUR tuh kuhl) *adj.* straight up and down; upright

**vex** (vehks) *v.* annoy; distress

**victorious** (vihk TAWR ee uhs) *adj.* having won; triumphant

**viewpoint** (VYOO poynt) *n.* position regarding an idea or statement

**violation** (vy uh LAY shuhn) *n.* the breaking or ignoring of rules, laws, or rights

**violence** (VY uh luhns) *n.* result of the use of physical force, often causing injury

**virtue** (VUR choo) *n.* a quality that gives value

**vulnerable** (VUHL nuhr uh buhl) *adj.* likely to be hurt

# W

**wearisome** (WIHR ee suhm) *adj.* tiresome

**willingly** (WIHL ihng lee) *adv.* voluntarily; without needing to be forced

**winced** (wihnst) *v.* showed pain

# Y

**yearning** (YURN ihng) *v.* filled with the feeling of wanting something

# Spanish Glossary

El vocabulario de Gran Pregunta aparece en **azul**. El vocabulario acadēmico de alta utilidad está <u>subrayado</u>.

## A

**abyss / abismo** *s.* espacio que no se puede medir, como un golfo sin fondo

**accomplishments / logros** *s.* lo que se hace o completa con éxito

**account / cuenta** *s.* factura por servicios prestados

<u>**accumulate / acumular**</u> *v.* coleccionar; juntar

**acquire / adquirir** *v.* conseguir; obtener

**admirably / admirablemente** *adv.* de tal manera que se merece ser elogiado

**affectionate / afectuoso** *adj.* cariñoso

**affluence / opulencia** *s.* riqueza

**alibi / coartada** *s.* argumento que explica por qué un sospechoso no pudo estar presente en la escena de un crimen

**alienate / enajenar** *v.* alejarse de una relación de amistad

**alliance / alianza** *s.* grupo unido con una meta en común

**ancestral / ancestral** *adj.* relacionado a la familia

**anguish / angustia** *s.* intranquilidad, ansiedad

**anonymously / en anonimato** *adv.* sin nombre o identificación

**antithesis / antítesis** *s.* oposición o contrariedad

**apprehension / aprensión** *s.* sentimiento temeroso de lo que ocurrirá

<u>**argument / argumento**</u> *s.* debate; reclamación; perspectiva en un asunto controversial

**aromas / aromas** *s.* olores

**arrogant / arrogante** *adj.* persona engreída e indiferente a otros

**ascent / ascenso** *s.* acto de escalar o subir

<u>**aspects / aspectos**</u> *s.* maneras en que se ve o asimila una idea o problema

**aspirations / aspiraciones** *s.* deseos fuertes o ambiciones

**assail / asediar** *v.* atacar a alguien con argumentos, preguntas, dudas, etc.

<u>**assumption / suposición**</u> *s.* acto de asumir

**audacity / audacia** *s.* gran valor; osadía

**audible / audible** *adj.* que se puede oír

**authentic / auténtico** *adj.* genuino; real

**authorized / autorizó** *v.* aprobó

**avert / evitar** *v.* apartar algo

**awed / sobrecoger** *v.* asombrar

## B

**barren / baldío** *adj.* vacío; yermo

**beacons / faros** *s.* señales para advertir o guiar, como la luz o el fuego

**beckoning / convocar** *v.* llamar

**bellow / bramar** *v.* rugir profundamente, como el sonido que hace un toro

<u>**benefit / beneficio**</u> *s.* ventaja o resultado positivo

**benign / benigno** *adj.* bondadoso

**bewildered /desconcertado** *adj.* completamente confundido

<u>**bias / parcialidad**</u> *s.* tendencia a interpretar las cosas de manera sesgada o prejuiciosa

**blackmail / chantaje** *s.* amenaza de divulgar secretos de una persona, a cambio de dinero

**bleak / inhóspito** *adj.* desapacible y desértico; frío

**boulevard / bulevar** *s.* camino ancho

**bravery/ valentía** *s.* coraje; valor

**brutal / brutal** *adj.* cruel

**burrow / madriguera** *s.* espacio o hueco que sirve de refugio

## C

**capricious / caprichoso** *adj.* que tiende a cambiar abruptamente, sin razón aparente

**cataclysm / cataclismo** *s.* suceso súbito y violento que causa gran cambio

**ceaseless / incesante** *adj.* que no para; continuo

<u>**challenge / desafío**</u> *v.* cuestionar; exigencia de pruebas

**cicada / cigarra** *s.* insecto grande parecido a una mosca; el macho emite un sonido de tono alto

<u>**class /clase**</u> *s.* grupo de personas u objetos

**coiled / enroscarse** *v.* torcerse y ponerse en forma de espiral

**commenced / comenzó** *v.* empezó

**common / común** *adj.* ordinario; esperado

**commotion / conmoción** *s.* movimiento ruidoso y desordenado

**compassionate / compasivo** *adj.* de gran bondad

**compelled / obligó** *v.* forzó

**compensate / compensar** *v.* pagar

**compromise / solución** *s.* convenio satisfactorio entre dos partes

**compulsory / obligatorio** *adj.* requerido

**conceivable / concebible** *adj.* que se puede imaginar

**conceivably / posiblemente** *adv.* imaginable o creíble

**concise / conciso** *adj.* que incluye sólo los detalles necesarios; claro; breve

<u>**confirm / confirmar**</u> *v.* probar; establecer como cierto

**confronted / enfrentó** *v.* se puso frente a frente

<u>**connection / conección**</u> *s.* enlace o vínculo

**consoling / consolador** *adj.* confortador

**conspicuous / conspicuo** *adj.* notable

**constructive / constructivo** *adj.* que conduce al progreso

**contact / contacto** *s.* relación entre dos cosas; comunicación

**contemplation / contemplación** *s.* acto de pensar en algo o prestarle atencióna algo

**contemptuously / despectivamente** *adv.* con desprecio

**contraction / contracción** *s.* acto de hacerse mas pequeño

**contradict / contradecir** *v.* negar; oponerse a un punto de vista

**conviction / convicción** *s.* creencia fuertemente arraigada; certeza

**cordially / cordialmente** *adv.* calurosamente

**courage / coraje** *s.* valor; valentía

**credibility / credibilidad** *s.* característica de lo que es aceptable o creíble

**criteria / criterio** *s.* estándares o pruebas que se usan para juzgar algo

**cultural / cultural** *adj.* que es pertinente al conjunto de modos de vida y costumbres de un grupo o una comunidad

**cunningly / astutamente** *adv.* con facilidad para engañar; con ingenio

**curiosity / curiosidad** *s.* deseo de obtener información

**cyclone / ciclón** *s.* tormenta de viento rotativa y violenta; tornado

**cynically / cínicamente** *adv.* dudosamente; de modo escéptico

# D

**debates / debatir** *v.* tratar de decidir

**debris / escombro** *s.* desecho de piedra, concreto o vidrio que resulta de la destrucción de algo

**decadent / decadente** *adj.* marcado por descomposición o deterioro

**deceive / engañar** *v.* hacer a alguien creer lo que no es cierto; malinformar

**deciphering / decifrar** *v.* encontrar el significado de algo; decodificar

**decision / decisión** *s.* elección; el resultado de un juicio

**decrees / decretos** *s.* órdenes que se hacen cumplir, como la ley

**deductions / deducciones** *s.* juicios basados en información disponible

**deed / escritura** *s.* documento que al ser firmado transfiere posesión de propiedad

**deferred / diferido** *adj.* retrasado

**defiance / desafío** *s.* oposición a obedecer la autoridad

**deficiency / deficiencia** *s.* carencia, o falta, de algo necesario

**degrading / denigrante** *adj.* insultante; deshonroso; ofensivo

**deliberating / deliberar** *v.* pensar cuidadosamente

**deprived / privar** *v.* no permitirle a alguien tener algo

**derision / escarnio** *s.* declaraciones o acciones irrespetuosas

**derived / derivado** *v.* generado u obtenido de una fuente

**descendants / descendientes** *s.* hijos, nietos y las generaciones que siguen a una persona

**descent / descenso** *s.* acto de bajar de un lugar

**desolate / desolado** *adj.* triste; solitario

**deterioration / deterioro** *s.* proceso por el que algo se daña o empeora

**development / desarrollo** *s.* evento o suceso; resultado

**devoid / desprovisto** *adj.* que carece completamente

**dew / rocío** *s.* pequeñas gotas que se forman con el frío de la noche a raíz del vapor en el ambiente

**diffused / difuso** *v.* esparcido en diferentes direcciones

**diplomatic / diplomático** *adj.* que muestra elegancia y destreza al relacionarse con otras personas

**discharged / liberar** *v.* eximir a alguien de una obligación; poner en libertad

**discreet / discreto** *adj.* cuidadoso con sus palabras y acciones

**discrepancies / discrepancias** *s.* diferencias; inconsistencias

**discriminate / discriminante** *v.* notar la diferencia; distinguir

**discrimination / discriminación** *s.* trato injusto de una persona o grupo a causa de prejuicios

**disdainfully / desdeñoso** *adv.* con indiferencia

**disinherit / desheredar** *v.* privar a las personas de sus derechos como ciudadanos

**dispel / disipar** *v.* hacer que algo desaparezca

**distinction / distinción** *s.* diferencia

**distinguish / distinguir** *v.* tildar como diferente; considerar por separado

**diverged / divergir** *v.* separarse; tener diferencias

**diverts / desvía** *v.* distrae; entretiene

**divide / dividir** *v.* separar

**dock / descontar** *v.* quitar parte del sueldo de una persona

**doubtful / dudoso** *adj.* de baja probabilidad; dispuesto a ser desafiado

**drought / sequía** *s.* falta de lluvia; períodos largos de clima seco

# E

**eavesdropping / escuchar a escondidas** *v.* escuchar las conversaciones de otros de manera discreta

**eloquent / elocuente** *adj.* que se expresa de manera vívida

**emancipated / emancipado** *adj.* liberado

**emigrated / emigró** *v.* dejó un sitio para establecerse en otro

**emphasize / enfatizar** *v.* estresar; dar importancia a algo

**empires / imperios** *s.* naciones poderosas; países gobernados por emperadores o emperatrices

**enchantment / encanto** *s.* sentimiento de fascinación

**endure / aguantar** *v.* mantener guardado; que perdura

**enhance / mejorar** *v.* aumentar las cualidades buenas de algo; incrementar

**erosion / erosión** *s.* desgaste del terreno a causa del viento o del agua

**evacuees / evacuados** *s.* personas que se marchan de una zona peligrosa

**evaded / evadió** *v.* evitó

**evidence / evidencia** *s.* prueba

**exaggerate / exagerar** *v.* magnificar más allá de la realidad

**exertion / esfuerzo** *s.* ánimo, vigor

**exiles / exiliados** *s.* personas que se ven obligadas a vivir en otro país

**expansive / expansivo** *adj.* generoso; que se extiende y abarca gran espacio

**experience / experiencia** *s.* participación en una actividad que lleva a obtener conocimiento, sabiduría o destrezas

**explanation / explicación** *s.* dar a conocer razones, causas o motivos; aclaración

**exploitation / explotación** *s.* acto de usar a otra persona con intenciones egoístas

**exploration / exploración** *s.* acto de observar de cerca; examinar detenidamente

**express / expresar** *v.* poner en palabras

**exquisite / exquisito** *adj.* muy bello

**extinction / extinción** *n.* desaparición de una especie

**extinguished / extinguir** *v.* apagar; finalizar

**exultantly / de forma exultante** *adv.* con gran alegría y satisfacción

**exulting / exultar** *v.* mostrar gran alegría

## F

**factor / factor** *s.* circunstancias o condiciones que dan un resultado

**factual / basado en hechos** *adj.* basado en o limitado a lo real o que puede ser probado

**fantasy / fantasía** *s.* producto de la imaginación; ficción

**fatalist / fatalista** *s.* el que cree que todo lo que sucede lo determina el destino

**feedback / reacción** *s.* respuesta que provoca una sucesión de acontecimientos

**feuding / pelear** *v.* discutir

**fiscal / fiscal** *adj.* relacionado con las finanzas

**flagged / marcar** *v.* señalar para parar, usualmente con una bandera o un objeto semejante

**flatterer / adulador** *s.* el que prodiga alabanzas interesadas

**foreboding / premonición** *s.* presentimiento de que algo va a ocurrir

**forlorn / desolado** *adj.* triste y solitario

**frail / frágil** *adj.* débil y delicado

**fugitives / fugitivos** *s.* personas que huyen o se esconden

## G

**generalization / generalización** *s.* afirmación que refleja una idea amplia

**gesture / gesto** *s.* algo que se dice o hace como formalidad

**global / global** *adj.* completo; que cubre un tipo amplio de casos

**grateful / agradecido** *adj.* que siente gratitud

**guileless / sincero** *adj.* sin intención de ocultar o engañar a alguien; inocente

## H

**haggard / demacrado** *adj.* de mala apariencia

**harmonious / armonioso** *adj.* que combina de manera agradable

**haughty / arrogante** *adj.* altanero

**horizon / horizonte** *s.* línea imaginaria donde se unen el cielo y la tierra

**hostile / hostil** *adj.* relacionado con el enemigo

**humiliating / humillante** *adj.* embarazoso

## I

**identify / identificar** *v.* reconocer como existente

**ignorance / ignorancia** *s.* falta de conocimiento o conciencia

**illogical / ilógico** *adj.* contrario; que se opone a los hechos

**imitate / imitar** *v.* copiar; seguir el ejemplo de algo

**immensely / inmensamente** *adv.* de gran manera; en gran medida

**immensity / inmensidad** *s.* extensión grande; enormidad

**immortality / inmortalidad** *s.* vida eterna

**immunities / inmunidad** *s.* libertad; protección

**impaired / perjudicar** *v.* debilitar, hacer menos útil; dañar

**impertinently / de manera impertinente** *adv.* con irrespeto

**imprint / impresionar** *v.* dejar una marca

**inarticulate / inarticulado** *adj.* que se expresa con dificultad

**incentive / incentivo** *s.* motivación

**indiscreetly / indiscretamente** *adv.* sin cuidado

**individuality / individualidad** *s.* cualidad por la que una persona o cosa se da a conocer o se diferencia de otra

**ineffectually / ineficazmente** *adv.* sin producir el resultado deseado

**inequality / desigualdad** *s.* estado injusto o en el que no se da un tratamiento equitativo

**inevitable / inevitable** *adj.* que pasará con seguridad

**inexplicable / inexplicable** *adj.* que no se puede explicar o describir

**inexpressible / indescriptible** *adj.* que no se puede describir

**inferior / inferior** *adj.* de calidad, nivel o rango más bajos

**influence / influencia** *v.* poder o efecto sobre algo

**inform / informar** *v.* decir; dar información o conocimiento de algo

**ingratitude / ingratitud** *s.* falta de apreciación

**injury / lesión** *s.* daño o detrimento físico

**insecurity / inseguridad** *s.* falta de confianza en sí mismo

**insolently / insolentemente** *adv.* de manera descortés

**insufferable / insufrible** *adj.* insoportable

**integrate / integrar** v. hacer disponible de manera equitativa para todos los miembros de la sociedad

**intellectual / intelectual** adj. relativo a la habilidad de pensar de manera inteligente

**interact / interactuar** v. actuar junto con otros

**intimidating / intimidante** adj. atemorizante

**intolerant / intolerante** adj. que no puede o logra aceptar

**introspective / introspectivo** adj. que observa internamente; atento

**intuition / intuición** s. habilidad para sentir de inmediato, sin razonamiento

**invaded / invadió** v. entró con el propósito de conquistar

**invaluable / invaluable** adj. de gran valor

**invariably / invariablemente** adv. constante

**investigate / investigar** v. examinar detenidamente

**irritate / irritar** v. molestar; fastidiar

## J

**jostling / empujón** s. golpe, generalmente intencional

**judge / juzgar** v. formar una opinión o pronunciar juicio

**judicious / sensato** adj. que demuestra prudencia y honestidad

## K

**kindled / encender** v. prender

## L

**lagged / demorarse** v. moverse lentamente

**lax / laxo** adj. poco estricto o exacto, relajado

**legacy / herencia** s. algo físico o espiritual que se transmite de un ancestro

**legitimately / legítimamente** adv. legalmente

**liable / probable** s. factible, que puede ocurrir

**liberated / emancipó** v. liberó; libró de la esclavitud o de una ocupación

**luminous / luminoso** adj. que irradia luz

## M

**malicious / malicioso** adj. de malas intenciones

**maneuver / maniobra** s. serie de pasos planeados

**meadows / prados** s. áreas cubiertas de hierba

**meager / exiguo** adj. pequeña cantidad

**meaningful / significante** adj. que tiene importancia o propósito

**media / medios de comunicación** s. conjunto de fuentes de información incluyendo periódicos, televisión y la Internet

**melancholy / melancólico** adj. triste; deprimido

**mislead / despistar** v. inducir a creer lo que no es por medio de ideas fingidas; engañar

**mistrusted / desconfiar** v. sospechar de las acciones de alguien; no tener confianza en alguien

**misunderstand / malentender** v. malinterpretar; equivocación en el entendimiento de algo

**mockery / burla** s. farsa; acción o declaración ofensiva o falsa

**modes / modos** s. maneras de hacer cosas o de comportarse

**mutineers / amotinadores** s. rebeldes

**mutinous / amotinado** adj. rebelde

## N

**naïveté / ingenuidad** s. sencillez o carácter infantil

**native / nativo** adj. relacionado al lugar de nacimiento

**negotiate / negociar** v. decidir; llegar a un acuerdo

**negotiation / negociación** s. regateo; discusión; acuerdo

**ninny / tonto** s. persona que carece de razonamiento

## O

**objective / objetivo** adj. sin prejuicios; donde no influyen sentimientos personales o prejuicios

**obscure / críptico** adj. poco conocido

**observation / observación** s. aseveración; punto de vista

**omens / presagio** s. señal de algo bueno o malo en el porvenir

**opinion / opinión** s. visión personal o actitud

**oppose / oponer** v. ir en contra; ser un obstáculo

**oppressed / oprimido** v. comprimido o restringido

**option / opción** s. curso o decisión que se puede tomar

**outdated / anticuado** adj. propio de otra época; pasado de moda

**overcome / superar** v. vencer; salir adelante después de sufrir un cotratiempo

**overwhelming / abrumador** adj. emocionalemente fuerte

## P

**pageant / desfile** s. presentación o espectáculo elaborado

**paradoxes / paradoja** s. dos cosas que parecen completamente opuestas

**partition / mampara** s. pared que divide el interior de una edificación

**passively / pasivamente** adv. sin resistencia

**perceived / percibido** v. entendido; observado

**peril / riesgo** s. peligro

**periscope / periscopio** s. tubo de un submarino que se mueve para poder observar la superficie del agua

**perish / perecer** v. ser destruido o aniquilado

**persistent / persistente** adj. que continua, especialmente por más tiempo de lo usual o de lo debido

**persuade / persuadir** *v.* convencer; incitar a otro a pensar de la misma manera

**pervading / invasor** *adj.* que se extiende por todas partes

**pestering / molestia** *s.* fastidio constante

**pitiful / lastimoso** *adj.* que causa compasión

**pollen / polen** *s.* granos polvorosos de las plantas masculinas

**ponderous / ponderoso** *adj.* muy pesado

**possession / posesión** *s.* pertenencia

**posterity / posteridad** *s.* generaciones futuras

**predisposed / predispuesto** *adj.* de cierta tendencia

**predominantly / predominantemente** *adv.* principalmente

**preliminary / preliminar** *adj.* introductorio; preparatorio

**presentable / presentable** *adj.* lo suficientemente ordenado o limpio para que otros lo vean

**pretext / pretexto** *s.* excusa; razón que oculta los motivos reales

**procession / procesión** *s.* personas que se movilizan en grupo, como en un desfile

**prodigy / prodigio** *s.* persona con un talento extraordinario

**prove / probar** *v.* exponer; demostrar

**pursuit / persecución** *s.* seguimiento con la intención de capturar

## Q

**quaint / pintoresco** *adj.* curiosamente inusual o antiguo

**quality / calidad** *s.* característica o elemento

**quantity / cantidad** *s.* cuantía

**quarantine / cuarentena** *s.* período en que las personas permanecen separadas para detener la propagación de una enfermedad contagiosa

## R

**radiation / radiación** *s.* emisión de energía a través del espacio

**radical / radical** *adj.* que favorece un gran cambio de la estructura social

**rapture / embeleso** *s.* éxtasis

**ravaged / arruinó** *v.* devastó, destruyó

**reaction / reacción** *s.* respuesta a una influencia, acción o aseveración

**rebellion / rebelión** *s.* resistencia ante la autoridad o ante el dominio

**recede / alejarse** *v.* distanciarse

**recoiled / recular** *v.* retroceder con repugnancia

**reeds / caña** *s.* hierba de tallo alto que crece en pantanos

**refugees / refugiados** *s.* personas que han tenido que huir de su país en tiempos difíciles

**refute / refutar** *v.* evidencia que prueba la verosimilitud de un argumento

**rehabilitate / rehabilitar** *v.* restablecer la reputación de alguien o algo

**relentless / implacable** *adj.* persistente; sin fin

**relevant / relevante** *adj.* directo al punto; relativo al asunto del momento

**remote / remoto** *adj.* apartado; frío; distante

**renounced / renunció** *v.* abandonó; desistió

**represent / representar** *v.* figurar; simbolizar

**reputation / reputación** *s.* opinión, buena o mala, que comparte un grupo de personas sobre alguien

**resent / resentir** *v.* sentirse bravo o disgustado por una injusticia

**resolute / determinado** *adj.* que demuestra un propósito fijo

**resolved / resolvió** *v.* decidió

**resounding / resonante** *adj.* que suena muy duro

**respectively / respectivamente** *adv.* en el orden en que se nombró previamente

**resurgence / resurgimiento** *s.* reaparición; renacimiento

**retribution / sanción** *s.* castigo por haber cometido una falta

**reveal / revelar** *v.* exponer; descubrir

**revelation / revelación** *s.* algo que sale al descubierto

**revolutionary / revolucionario** *adj.* que favorece un cambio radical

**rickety / deteriorado** *adj.* débil; con aspecto frágil

**rituals / rituales** *s.* prácticas que se hacen en momentos específicos y con regularidad

**roam / vagar** *v.* andar sin rumbo fijo; merodear

**rotate / rotar** *v.* cambiar

**rut / surco** *s.* hendidura que se hace en la tierra con el arado

## S

**sacred / sagrado** *adj.* bendito; relacionado con ceremonias religiosas

**sacrifices / sacrificio** *s.* decisión de dejar de tener o hacer algo importante para obtener algo aún más importante, generalmente para otra persona

**satisfactory / satisfactorio** *adj.* adecuado; lo suficiente para cumplir con los requisitos

**scampering / corretear** *v.* correr apresuradamente

**scarce / escaso** *adj.* en poca cantidad; poco común

**scheme / esquema** *s.* manera organizada de hacer las cosas

**self-confident / seguro de sí mismo** *adj.* que confía en su propia habilidad

**sensibility / sensibilidad** *s.* actitud moral, artística, intelectual

**sensory / sensorial** *adj.* relativo a los sentidos de la vista, el oido, el gusto, el olfato y el tacto

**separate / separar** *v.* cosiderar aparte

**serene / sereno** *adj.* tranquilo

**shackles / grilletes** *s.* arco de hierro que se usa para restringir a prisioneros

**shanties / barracas** s. algergue o vivienda rústica construida toscamente

**shiftless / holgazán** adj. sin ambición

**shriveled / marchito** adj. seco; encogido, arrugado

**sidling / movimiento furtivo** v. moverse de manera astute, con cautela

**significance / significado** s. importancia

**simultaneously / simultáneamente** adv. al mismo tiempo

**singularity / singularidad** s. único o de rasgos distintos

**sinister / siniestro** adj. que amenaza con causar daño; malicioso

**skeptically / de modo escéptico** adv. con duda y desconfianza

**slung / colgar** v. suspender algo sin apretar

**solution / solución** s. acto de resolver un problema o responder a una pregunta

**somber / sombrio** adj. oscuro; lúgubre

**sparse / escaso** adj. en poca cantidad

**spindly / escuálido** adj. delgado, flaco

**spineless / débil** adj. que carece que corage y voluntad

**spite / rencor** s. resentimiento y hostilidad

**squatter / ocupante ilegal** s. alguien que se establece ilegalmente en un terreno o edificación

**stalemate / estancamiento** s. punto muerto; resultado de un conflicto en el que no hay ganador

**statistics / estadísticas** s. datos numéricos

**stealthily / a hurtadillas** adv. a escondidas o con disimulo

**straddling / horcajadas** adv. con las piernas a cada lado de un objeto

**strife / disputa** s. conflicto

**studious / estudioso** adj. devoto al aprendizaje

**subdued / dominado** adj. oprimido; conquistado

**succumbed / sucumbir** v. desistir; rendirse; ceder

**suffering / sufrimiento** s. padecer de dolor o de una lesión corporal

**superficial / superficial** adj. limitado a la superficie, que carece de profundidad

**supple / flexible** adj. que cede; suave

**suppressed / suprimido** v. reprimido

**surrogate / sustituto** s. de remplazo, suplente

**sustain / sostener** v. mantener

**symbolize / simbolizar** v. figurar

**sympathy / compasión** s. el acto de compartir un sentimiento o de sentir conmiseración por otra persona

# T

**tangible / tangible** adj. que se puede ver y notar con facilidad, sin duda alguna

**tantalized / tentar** v. atraer la atención intensamente con algo que está fuera del alcance

**tedious / tedioso** adj. aburrido; cansón

**tenacious / tenaz** adj. adherido firmemente, con fuerza; terco

**tension / tensión** s. estado nervioso, preocupado o exaltación que dificulta la relajación

**theory / teoría** s. idea basada en información recaudada o evidencia

**timidly / tímidamente** adv. de manera reservada o con inseguridad

**tolerance / tolerancia** s. libertad de prejuicios; aceptación de los puntos de vista de otros

**tongue / lengua** s. idioma

**transfigured / transfigurado** adj. que se transforma de manera gloriosa

**trivial / trivial** adj. de poca importancia

**tumultuous / tumultuoso** adj. salvaje; caótico

**turbulent / turbulento** adj. con movimientos irregulares y abruptos

**turmoil / confusión** s. condición de gran inquietud, desorden y falta de claridad

# U

**unanimous / unánime** adj. en acuerdo absoluto

**undulation / ondulación** s. curvatura

**uneasily / con intranquilidad** adv. con inquietud

**unequivocal / inequívoco** adj. claro; obvio

**unify / unificar** v. juntar; unir

**unobtrusively / discretamente** adv. sin llamar la atención

**unresponsive / indiferente** adj. que no reacciona; que no se ve afectado por algo

**unseemly / inecoroso** adj. inapropiado

**urban / urbano** adj. de la ciudad o relativo a ella

# V

**valid / válido** adj. convincente; contundente

**valid / válido** adj. que es apoyado por evidencia; digno

**valuable / valioso** adj. que tiene valor o importancia

**vertical / vertical** adj. que se extiende de arriba abajo en línea recta

**vex / irritar** v. molestar; disgustar

**victorious / victorioso** adj. que ha ganado; triumfador

**viewpoint / punto de vista** s. posición ante una idea o aseveración

**violation / violación** s. incumplimiento o ignorancia de la ley o los derechos

**violence / violencia** s. el resultado del uso de fuerza física, que con frecuencia es causante de lesión corporal

**virtue / virtud** s. cualidad que agrega valor

**vulnerable / vulnerable** adj. que puede ser herido

# W

**wearisome / pesado** adj. que fatiga, aburre o exhausta

**willingly / por voluntad propia** adv. con gusto; sin necesidad de ser forzado

**winced / estremecerse** v. demostrar dolor

# Y

**yearning / anhelar** v. desear o ansiar con vehemencia

# Literary Terms

**ALLITERATION** *Alliteration* is the repetition of initial consonant sounds. Writers use alliteration to draw attention to certain words or ideas, to imitate sounds, and to create musical effects.

**ALLUSION** An *allusion* is a reference to a well-known person, event, place, literary work, or work of art. Allusions connect literary works to a larger cultural heritage. They allow the writer to express complex ideas without spelling them out. Understanding what a literary work is saying often depends on recognizing its allusions and the meanings they suggest.

**ANALOGY** An *analogy* makes a comparison between two or more things that are similar in some ways but otherwise unalike.

**ANECDOTE** An *anecdote* is a brief story about an interesting, amusing, or strange event. Writers tell anecdotes to entertain or to make a point.

**ANTAGONIST** An *antagonist* is a character or a force in conflict with a main character, or protagonist.

See *Conflict* and *Protagonist.*

**ARGUMENT** See *Persuasion.*

**ATMOSPHERE** *Atmosphere,* or *mood,* is the feeling created in the reader by a literary work or passage.

**AUTHOR'S INFLUENCES** An *author's influences* include his or her heritage, culture, and personal beliefs.

**AUTHOR'S STYLE** *Style* is an author's typical way of writing. Many factors determine a writer's style, including diction; tone; use of characteristic elements such as figurative language, dialect, rhyme, meter, or rhythmic devices; typical grammatical structures and patterns, typical sentence length, and typical methods of organization. Style comprises every feature of a writer's use of language.

**AUTOBIOGRAPHY** An *autobiography* is the story of the writer's own life, told by the writer. Autobiographical writing may tell about the person's whole life or only a part of it.

Because autobiographies are about real people and events, they are a form of nonfiction. Most autobiographies are written in the first person.

See *Biography, Nonfiction,* and *Point of View.*

**BIOGRAPHY** A *biography* is a form of nonfiction in which a writer tells the life story of another person. Most biographies are written about famous or admirable people. Although biographies are nonfiction, the most effective ones share the qualities of good narrative writing.

See *Autobiography* and *Nonfiction.*

**CHARACTER** A *character* is a person or an animal that takes part in the action of a literary work. The main, or *major,* character is the most important character in a story, poem, or play. A *minor* character is one who takes part in the action but is not the focus of attention.

Characters are sometimes classified as flat or round. A *flat character* is one-sided and often stereotypical. A *round character,* on the other hand, is fully developed and exhibits many traits—often both faults and virtues. Characters can also be classified as dynamic or static. A *dynamic character* is one who changes or grows during the course of the work. A *static character* is one who does not change.

See *Characterization, Hero/Heroine,* and *Motive.*

**CHARACTERIZATION** *Characterization* is the act of creating and developing a character. Authors use two major methods of characterization—*direct* and *indirect.* When using *direct* characterization, a writer states the *character's traits,* or characteristics.

When describing a character *indirectly,* a writer depends on the reader to draw conclusions about the character's traits. Sometimes the writer tells what other participants in the story say and think about the character.

See *Character* and *Motive.*

**CHARACTER TRAITS** *Character traits* are the qualities, attitudes, and values that a character has or displays—such as dependability, intelligence, selfishness, or stubbornness.

**CLIMAX** The *climax,* also called the turning point, is the high point in the action of the plot. It is the moment of greatest tension, when the outcome of the plot hangs in the balance.

See *Plot.*

**COMEDY** A *comedy* is a literary work, especially a play, that is light, often humorous or satirical, and ends happily. Comedies frequently depict ordinary characters faced with temporary difficulties and conflicts. Types of comedy include *romantic comedy,* which involves problems between lovers, and the *comedy of manners,* which satirically challenges social customs of a society.

**CONCRETE POEM** A *concrete poem* is one with a shape that suggests its subject. The poet arranges the letters, punctuation, and lines to create an image, or picture, on the page.

**CONFLICT** A *conflict* is a struggle between opposing forces. Conflict is one of the most important elements of stories, novels, and plays because it causes the action. There are two kinds of conflict: external and internal. An *external conflict* is one in which a character struggles against some outside force, such as another person. Another kind of external conflict may occur between a character and some force in nature.

An *internal conflict* takes place within the mind of a character. The character struggles to make a decision, take an action, or overcome a feeling.

See *Plot.*

**CONNOTATIONS** The *connotation* of a word is the set of ideas associated with it in addition to its explicit meaning. The connotation of a word can be personal, based on individual experiences. More often, cultural connotations—those recognizable by most people in a group—determine a writer's word choices.

See also *Denotation.*

**DENOTATION** The *denotation* of a word is its dictionary meaning, independent of other associations that the word may have. The denotation of the word *lake,* for example, is "an inland body of water." "Vacation spot" and "place where the fishing is good" are connotations of the word *lake.*

See also *Connotation.*

**DESCRIPTION** A *description* is a portrait, in words, of a person, place, or object. Descriptive writing uses images that appeal to the five senses—sight, hearing, touch, taste, and smell.

See *Images.*

**DEVELOPMENT** See *Plot.*

**DIALECT** *Dialect* is the form of a language spoken by people in a particular region or group. Dialects differ in pronunciation, grammar, and word choice. The English language is divided into many dialects. British English differs from American English.

**DIALOGUE** A *dialogue* is a conversation between characters. In poems, novels, and short stories, dialogue is usually set off by quotation marks to indicate a speaker's exact words.

In a play, dialogue follows the names of the characters, and no quotation marks are used.

**DICTION** *Diction* is a writer's or speaker's word choice. Diction is part of a writer's style and may be described as formal or informal, plain or fancy, ordinary or technical, sophisticated or down-to-earth, old-fashioned or modern.

**DRAMA** A *drama* is a story written to be performed by actors. Although a drama is meant to be performed, one can also read the script, or written version, and imagine the action. The *script* of a drama is made up of dialogue and stage directions. The *dialogue* is the words spoken by the actors. The *stage directions,* usually printed in italics, tell how the actors should look, move, and speak. They also describe the setting, sound effects, and lighting.

Dramas are often divided into parts called *acts.*

The acts are often divided into smaller parts called *scenes.*

**DYNAMIC CHARACTER** See *Character.*

**ESSAY** An *essay* is a short nonfiction work about a particular subject. Most essays have a single major focus and a clear introduction, body, and conclusion.

There are many types of essays. An *informal essay* uses casual, conversational language. A *historical essay* gives facts, explanations, and insights about historical events. An *expository essay* explains an idea by breaking it down. A *narrative essay* tells a story about a real-life experience. An *informational essay* explains a process. A *persuasive essay* offers an opinion and supports it.
See *Exposition, Narration,* and *Persuasion.*

**EXPOSITION** In the plot of a story or a drama, the *exposition,* or introduction, is the part of the work that introduces the characters, setting, and basic situation.

See *Plot.*

**EXPOSITORY WRITING** *Expository writing* is writing that explains or informs.

**EXTENDED METAPHOR** In an *extended metaphor,* as in a regular metaphor, a subject is spoken or written of as though it were something else. However, extended metaphor differs from regular metaphor in that several connected comparisons are made.

See *Metaphor.*

**EXTERNAL CONFLICT** See *Conflict.*

**FABLE** A *fable* is a brief story or poem, usually with animal characters, that teaches a lesson, or moral. The moral is usually stated at the end of the fable.

See *Irony* and *Moral.*

**FANTASY** A *fantasy* is highly imaginative writing that contains elements not found in real life. Examples of fantasy include stories that involve supernatural elements, stories that resemble fairy tales, stories that deal with imaginary places and creatures, and science-fiction stories.

See *Science Fiction.*

**FICTION** *Fiction* is prose writing that tells about imaginary characters and events. Short stories and novels are works of fiction. Some writers base their fiction on actual events and people, adding invented characters, dialogue, settings, and plots. Other writers rely on imagination alone.

See *Narration, Nonfiction,* and *Prose.*

**FIGURATIVE LANGUAGE** *Figurative language* is writing or speech that is not meant to be taken literally. The many types of figurative language are known as *figures of speech.* Common figures of speech include metaphor, personification, and simile. Writers use figurative language to state ideas in vivid and imaginative ways.

See *Metaphor, Personification, Simile,* and *Symbol.*

**FIGURE OF SPEECH** See *Figurative Language.*

**FLASHBACK** A *flashback* is a scene within a story that interrupts the sequence of events to relate events that occurred in the past.

**FLAT CHARACTER** See *Character.*

**FOLK TALE** A *folk tale* is a story composed orally and then passed from person to person by word of mouth. Folk tales originated among people who could neither read nor write. These people entertained one another by telling stories aloud—often dealing with heroes, adventure, magic, or romance. Eventually, modern scholars collected these stories and wrote them down.

Folk tales reflect the cultural beliefs and environments from which they come.

See *Fable, Legend, Myth,* and *Oral Tradition.*

**FOOT** See *Meter.*

**FORESHADOWING** *Foreshadowing* is the author's use of clues to hint at what might happen later in the story. Writers use foreshadowing to build their readers' expectations and to create suspense.

**FREE VERSE** *Free verse* is poetry not written in a regular, rhythmical pattern, or meter. The poet is free to write lines of any length or with any number of stresses, or beats. Free verse is therefore less constraining than *metrical verse,* in which every line must have a certain length and a certain number of stresses.

See *Meter.*

**GENRE** A *genre* is a division or type of literature. Literature is commonly divided into three major genres: poetry, prose, and drama. Each major genre is, in turn, divided into lesser genres, as follows:

1. *Poetry:* lyric poetry, concrete poetry, dramatic poetry, narrative poetry, epic poetry

2. *Prose:* fiction (novels and short stories) and nonfiction (biography, autobiography, letters, essays, and reports)

3. *Drama:* serious drama and tragedy, comic drama, melodrama, and farce

See *Drama, Poetry,* and *Prose.*

**HAIKU** The *haiku* is a three-line Japanese verse form. The first and third lines of a haiku each have five syllables. The second line has seven syllables. A writer of haiku uses images to create a single, vivid picture, generally of a scene from nature.

**HERO/HEROINE** A *hero* or *heroine* is a character whose actions are inspiring, or noble. Often heroes and heroines struggle to overcome the obstacles and problems that stand in their way. Note that the term *hero* was originally used only for male characters, while heroic female characters were always called *heroines.* However, it is now acceptable to use *hero* to refer to females as well as to males.

**HISTORICAL FICTION** In *historical fiction,* real events, places, or people are incorporated into a fictional, or made-up, story.

**HUMOR** *Humor* is writing intended to evoke laughter. While most humorists are trying to entertain, humor can also be used to convey a serious theme.

**IMAGERY** See *Images.*

**IMAGES** *Images* are words or phrases that appeal to one or more of the five senses. Writers use images to describe how their subjects look, sound, feel, taste, and smell. Poets often paint images, or word pictures, that appeal to your senses. These pictures help you to experience the poem fully.

**INTERNAL CONFLICT** See *Conflict.*

**IRONY** *Irony* is a contradiction between what happens and what is expected. There are three main types of irony. *Situational irony* occurs when something happens that directly contradicts the expectations of the characters or the audience. *Verbal irony* is something contradictory that is said. In *dramatic irony,* the audience is aware of something that the character or speaker is not.

**JOURNAL** A *journal* is a daily, or periodic, account of events and the writer's thoughts and feelings about those events. Personal journals are not normally written for publication, but sometimes they do get published later with permission from the author or the author's family.

**LEGEND** A *legend* is a widely told story about the past—one that may or may not have a foundation in fact. Every culture has its own legends—its familiar, traditional stories.

See *Folk Tale, Myth,* and *Oral Tradition.*

**LETTERS** A *letter* is a written communication from one person to another. In personal letters, the writer shares information and his or her thoughts and feelings with one other person or group. Although letters are not normally written for publication, they sometimes do get published later with the permission of the author or the author's family.

**LIMERICK** A *limerick* is a humorous, rhyming, five-line poem with a specific meter and rhyme scheme. Most limericks have three strong stresses in lines 1, 2, and 5 and two strong stresses in lines 3 and 4. Most follow the rhyme scheme *aabba.*

**LYRIC POEM** A *lyric poem* is a highly musical verse that expresses the observations and feelings of a single speaker. It creates a single, unified impression.

**MAIN CHARACTER** See *Character.*

**MEDIA ACCOUNTS** *Media accounts* are reports, explanations, opinions, or descriptions written for television, radio, newspapers, and magazines. While some media accounts report only facts, others include the writer's thoughts and reflections.

**METAPHOR** A *metaphor* is a figure of speech in which something is described as though it were something else. A metaphor, like a simile, works by pointing out a similarity between two unlike things.

See *Extended Metaphor* and *Simile.*

**METER** The *meter* of a poem is its rhythmical pattern. This pattern is determined by the number of *stresses,* or beats, in each line. To describe the meter of a poem, read it while emphasizing the beats in each line. Then, mark the stressed and unstressed syllables, as follows:

M̆y fáth | ĕr wás | thĕ fírst | tŏ héar |

As you can see, each strong stress is marked with a slanted line (´) and each unstressed syllable with a horseshoe symbol (˘). The weak and strong stresses are then divided by vertical lines (|) into groups called feet.

**MINOR CHARACTER** See *Character.*

**MOOD** See *Atmosphere.*

**MORAL** A *moral* is a lesson taught by a literary work. A fable usually ends with a moral that is directly stated. A poem, novel, short story, or essay often suggests a moral that is not directly stated. The moral must be drawn by the reader, based on other elements in the work.

See *Fable.*

**MOTIVATION** See *Motive.*

**MOTIVE** A *motive* is a reason that explains or partially explains a character's thoughts, feelings, actions, or speech. Writers try to make their characters' motives, or motivations, as clear as possible. If the motives of a main character are not clear, then the character will not be well understood.

Characters are often motivated by needs, such as food and shelter. They are also motivated by feelings, such as fear, love, and pride. Motives may be obvious or hidden.

**MYTH** A *myth* is a fictional tale that explains the actions of gods or heroes or the origins of elements of nature. Myths are part of the oral tradition. They are composed orally and then passed from generation to generation by word of mouth. Every ancient culture has its own mythology, or collection of myths. Greek and Roman myths are known collectively as *classical mythology.*

See *Oral Tradition.*

**NARRATION** *Narration* is writing that tells a story. The act of telling a story is also called narration. A story told in fiction, nonfiction, poetry, or even in drama is called a *narrative.*

See *Narrative, Narrative Poem,* and *Narrator.*

**NARRATIVE** A *narrative* is a story. A narrative can be either fiction or nonfiction. Novels and short stories are types of fictional narratives. Biographies and autobiographies are nonfiction narratives. Poems that tell stories are also narratives.

See *Narration* and *Narrative Poem.*

**NARRATIVE POEM** A *narrative poem* is a story told in verse. Narrative poems often have all the elements of short stories, including characters, conflict, and plot.

**NARRATOR** A *narrator* is a speaker or a character who tells a story. The narrator's perspective is the way he or she sees things. A *third-person narrator* is one who stands outside the action and speaks about it. A *first-person narrator* is one who tells a story and participates in its action.

See *Point of View.*

**NONFICTION** *Nonfiction* is prose writing that presents and explains ideas or that tells about real people, places, objects, or events. Autobiographies, biographies, essays, reports, letters, memos, and newspaper articles are all types of nonfiction.

See *Fiction.*

**NOVEL** A *novel* is a long work of fiction. Novels contain such elements as characters, plot, conflict, and setting. The writer of novels, or novelist, develops these elements. In addition to its main plot, a novel may contain one or more subplots, or independent, related stories. A novel may also have several themes.

See *Fiction* and *Short Story.*

**NOVELLA** A *novella* is a fiction work that is longer than a short story but shorter than a novel.

**ONOMATOPOEIA** *Onomatopoeia* is the use of words that imitate sounds. *Crash, buzz, screech, hiss, neigh, jingle,* and *cluck* are examples of onomatopoeia. *Chickadee, towhee,* and *whippoorwill* are onomatopoeic names of birds.

Onomatopoeia can help put the reader in the action of a poem.

**ORAL TRADITION** *Oral tradition* is the passing of songs, stories, and poems from generation to generation by word of mouth. Folk songs, folk tales, legends, and myths all come from the oral tradition. No one knows who first created these stories and poems.

See *Folk Tale, Legend,* and *Myth.*

**OXYMORON** An *oxymoron* (pl. *oxymora*) is a figure of speech that links two opposite or contradictory words, to point out an idea or situation that seems contradictory or inconsistent but on closer inspection turns out to be somehow true.

**PERSONIFICATION** *Personification* is a type of figurative language in which a nonhuman subject is given human characteristics.

**PERSPECTIVE** See *Narrator* and *Point of View.*

**PERSUASION** *Persuasion* is used in writing or speech that attempts to convince the reader or listener to adopt a particular opinion or course of action. Newspaper editorials and letters to the editor use persuasion. So do advertisements and campaign speeches given by political candidates. An *argument* is a logical way of presenting a belief, conclusion, or stance. A good argument is supported with reasoning and evidence.

See *Essay.*

**PLAYWRIGHT** A *playwright* is a person who writes plays. William Shakespeare is regarded as the greatest playwright in English literature.

**PLOT** *Plot* is the sequence of events in a story. In most novels, dramas, short stories, and narrative poems, the plot involves both characters and a central conflict. The plot usually begins with an exposition that introduces the setting, the characters, and the basic situation. This is followed by the *inciting incident,* which introduces the central conflict. The conflict then increases during the *development* until it reaches a high point of interest or suspense, the *climax.* The climax is followed by the *falling action,* or end, of the central conflict. Any events that occur during the *falling action* make up the *resolution* or *denouement.*

Some plots do not have all of these parts. For example, some stories begin with the inciting incident and end with the resolution.

See *Conflict.*

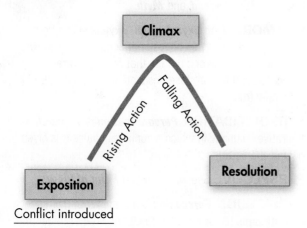

**POETRY** *Poetry* is one of the three major types of literature, the others being prose and drama. Most poems make use of highly concise, musical, and emotionally charged language. Many also make use of imagery, figurative language, and special devices of sound such as rhyme. Major types of poetry include *lyric poetry, narrative poetry,* and *concrete poetry.*

See *Concrete Poem, Genre, Lyric Poem,* and *Narrative Poem.*

**POINT OF VIEW** *Point of view* is the perspective, or vantage point, from which a story is told. It is either a narrator outside the story or a character in the story. *First-person point of view* is told by a character who uses the first-person pronoun "I."

The two kinds of *third-person point of view,* limited and omniscient, are called "third person" because the narrator uses third-person pronouns such as "he" and "she" to refer to the characters. There is no "I" telling the story.

In stories told from the *omniscient third-person point of view,* the narrator knows and tells about what each character feels and thinks.

In stories told from the *limited third-person point of view,* the narrator relates the inner thoughts and feelings of only one character, and everything is viewed from this character's perspective.

See *Narrator.*

**PROBLEM** See *Conflict.*

**PROSE** *Prose* is the ordinary form of written language. Most writing that is not poetry, drama, or song is considered prose. Prose is one of the major genres of literature and occurs in two forms—fiction and nonfiction.

See *Fiction, Genre,* and *Nonfiction.*

**PROTAGONIST** The *protagonist* is the main character in a literary work. Often, the protagonist is a person, but sometimes it can be an animal.

See *Antagonist* and *Character.*

**REFRAIN** A *refrain* is a regularly repeated line or group of lines in a poem or a song.

**REPETITION** *Repetition* is the use, more than once, of any element of language—a sound, word, phrase, clause, or sentence. Repetition is used in both prose and poetry.

See *Alliteration, Meter, Plot, Rhyme,* and *Rhyme Scheme.*

**RESOLUTION** The *resolution* is the outcome of the conflict in a plot.

See *Plot.*

**RHYME** *Rhyme* is the repetition of sounds at the ends of words. Poets use rhyme to lend a songlike quality to their verses and to emphasize certain words and ideas. Many traditional poems contain *end rhymes,* or rhyming words at the ends of lines.

Another common device is the use of *internal rhymes,* or rhyming words within lines. Internal rhyme also emphasizes the flowing nature of a poem.

See *Rhyme Scheme.*

**RHYME SCHEME** A *rhyme scheme* is a regular pattern of rhyming words in a poem. To indicate the rhyme scheme of a poem, one uses lowercase letters. Each rhyme is assigned a different letter, as follows in the first stanza of "Dust of Snow," by Robert Frost:

| | |
|---|---|
| The way a crow | *a* |
| Shook down on me | *b* |
| The dust of snow | *a* |
| From a hemlock tree | *b* |

Thus, this stanza has the rhyme scheme *abab.*

**RHYTHM** *Rhythm* is the pattern of stressed and unstressed syllables in spoken or written language.

See *Meter.*

**ROUND CHARACTER** See *Character.*

**SCENE** A *scene* is a section of uninterrupted action in the act of a drama.

See *Drama.*

**SCIENCE FICTION** *Science fiction* combines elements of fiction and fantasy with scientific fact. Many science-fiction stories are set in the future.

**SENSORY LANGUAGE** *Sensory language* is writing or speech that appeals to one or more of the five senses.

See *Images.*

**SETTING** The *setting* of a literary work is the time and place of the action. The setting includes all the details of a place and time—the year, the time of day, even the weather. The place may be a specific country, state, region, community, neighborhood, building, institution, or home. Details such as dialects, clothing, customs, and modes of transportation are often used to establish setting. In most stories, the setting serves as a backdrop—a context in which the characters interact. Setting can also help to create a feeling, or atmosphere.

See *Atmosphere.*

**SHORT STORY** A *short story* is a brief work of fiction. Like a novel, a short story presents a sequence of events, or plot. The plot usually deals with a central conflict faced by a main character, or protagonist. The events in a short story usually communicate a message about life or human nature. This message, or central idea, is the story's theme.

See *Conflict, Plot,* and *Theme.*

**SIMILE** A *simile* is a figure of speech that uses *like* or *as* to make a direct comparison between two unlike ideas. Everyday speech often contains similes, such as "pale as a ghost," "good as gold," "spread like wildfire," and "clever as a fox."

**SPEAKER** The *speaker* is the imaginary voice a poet uses when writing a poem. The speaker is the character who tells the poem. This character, or voice, often is not identified by name. There can be important differences between the poet and the poem's speaker.

See *Narrator.*

**STAGE DIRECTIONS** *Stage directions* are notes included in a drama to describe how the work is to be performed or staged. Stage directions are usually printed in italics and enclosed within parentheses or brackets. Some stage directions describe the movements, costumes, emotional states, and ways of speaking of the characters.

**STAGING** *Staging* includes the setting, lighting, costumes, special effects, music, dance, and so on that go into putting on a stage performance of a drama.

See *Drama.*

**STANZA** A *stanza* is a group of lines of poetry that are usually similar in length and pattern and are separated by spaces. A stanza is like a paragraph of poetry—it states and develops a single main idea.

**STATIC CHARACTER** See *Character.*

**SURPRISE ENDING** A *surprise ending* is a conclusion that is unexpected. The reader has certain expectations about the ending based on details in the story. Often, a surprise ending is *foreshadowed,* or subtly hinted at, in the course of the work.

See *Foreshadowing* and *Plot.*

**SUSPENSE** *Suspense* is a feeling of anxious uncertainty about the outcome of events in a literary work. Writers create suspense by raising questions in the minds of their readers.

**SYMBOL** A *symbol* is anything that stands for or represents something else. Symbols are common in everyday life. A dove with an olive branch in its beak is a symbol of peace. A blindfolded woman holding a balanced scale is a symbol of justice. A crown is a symbol of a king's status and authority.

**SYMBOLISM** *Symbolism* is the use of symbols. Symbolism plays an important role in many different types of literature. It can highlight certain elements the author wishes to emphasize and also add levels of meaning.

**THEME** The *theme* is a central message, concern, or purpose in a literary work. A theme can usually be expressed as a generalization, or a general statement, about human beings or about life. The theme of a work is not a summary of its plot. The theme is the writer's central idea.

Although a theme may be stated directly in the text, it is more often presented indirectly. When the theme is stated indirectly, or implied, the reader must figure out what the theme is by looking carefully at what the work reveals about people or about life.

**TONE** The *tone* of a literary work is the writer's attitude toward his or her audience and subject. The tone can often be described by a single adjective, such as *formal* or *informal, serious* or *playful, bitter,* or *ironic.* Factors that contribute to the tone are word choice, sentence structure, line length, rhyme, rhythm, and repetition.

**TRAGEDY** A *tragedy* is a work of literature, especially a play, that results in a catastrophe for the main character. In ancient Greek drama, the main character is always a significant person—a king or a hero—and the cause of the tragedy is a tragic flaw, or weakness, in his or her character. In modern drama, the main character can be an ordinary person, and the cause of the tragedy can be some evil in society itself. The purpose of tragedy is not only to arouse fear and pity in the audience, but also, in some cases, to convey a sense of the grandeur and nobility of the human spirit.

**TURNING POINT** See *Climax.*

**UNIVERSAL THEME** A *universal theme* is a message about life that is expressed regularly in many different cultures and time periods. Folk tales, epics, and romances often address universal themes like the importance of courage, the power of love, or the danger of greed.

**WORD CHOICE** An author's *word choice*—sometimes referred to as *diction*—is an important factor in creating the tone or mood of a literary work. Authors choose words based on the intended audience and the work's purpose.

# Tips for Literature Circles

As you read and study literature, discussions with other readers can help you understand and enjoy what you have read. Use the following tips.

- ## Understand the purpose of your discussion

  Your purpose when you discuss literature is to broaden your understanding of a work by testing your own ideas and hearing the ideas of others. Keep your comments focused on the literature you are discussing. Starting with one focus question will help to keep your discussion on track.

- ## Communicate effectively

  Effective communication requires thinking before speaking. Plan the points that you want to make and decide how you will express them. Organize these points in logical order and use details from the work to support your ideas. Jot down informal notes to help keep your ideas focused.

  Remember to speak clearly, pronouncing words slowly and carefully. Also, listen attentively when others are speaking, and avoid interrupting.

- ## Consider other ideas and interpretations

  A work of literature can generate a wide variety of responses in different readers. Be open to the idea that many interpretations can be valid. To support your own ideas, point to the events, descriptions, characters, or other literary elements in the work that led to your interpretation. To consider someone else's ideas, decide whether details in the work support the interpretation he or she presents. Be sure to convey your criticism of the ideas of others in a respectful and supportive manner.

- ## Ask questions

  Ask questions to clarify your understanding of another reader's ideas. You can also use questions to call attention to possible areas of confusion, to points that are open to debate, or to errors in the speaker's points. To move a discussion forward, summarize and evaluate conclusions reached by the group members.

  When you meet with a group to discuss literature, use a chart like the one shown to analyze the discussion.

| Work Being Discussed: | |
|---|---|
| Focus Question: | |
| Your Response: | Another Student's Response: |
| Supporting Evidence: | Supporting Evidence: |

# Tips for Improving Reading Fluency

When you were younger, you learned to read. Then, you read to expand your experiences or for pure enjoyment. Now, you are expected to read to learn. As you progress in school, you are given more and more material to read. The tips on these pages will help you improve your reading fluency, or your ability to read easily, smoothly, and expressively.

## Keeping Your Concentration

One common problem that readers face is the loss of concentration. When you are reading an assignment, you might find yourself rereading the same sentence several times without really understanding it. The first step in changing this behavior is to notice that you do it. Becoming an active, aware reader will help you get the most from your assignments. Practice using these strategies:

- Cover what you have already read with a note card as you go along. Then, you will not be able to reread without noticing that you are doing it.

- Set a purpose for reading beyond just completing the assignment. Then, read actively by pausing to ask yourself questions about the material as you read.

- Use the Reading Strategy instruction and notes that appear with each selection in this textbook.

- Stop reading after a specified period of time (for example, 5 minutes) and summarize what you have read. To help you with this strategy, use the Reading Check questions that appear with each selection in this textbook. Reread to find any answers you do not know.

## Reading Phrases

Fluent readers read phrases rather than individual words. Reading this way will speed up your reading and improve your comprehension. Here are some useful ideas:

- Experts recommend rereading as a strategy to increase fluency. Choose a passage of text that is neither too hard nor too easy. Read the same passage aloud several times until you can read it smoothly. When you can read the passage fluently, pick another passage and keep practicing.

- Read aloud into a tape recorder. Then, listen to the recording, noting your accuracy, pacing, and expression. You can also read aloud and share feedback with a partner.

- Use the *Prentice Hall Listening to Literature* audiotapes or CDs to hear the selections read aloud. Read along silently in your textbook, noticing how the reader uses his or her voice and emphasizes certain words and phrases.

## Understanding Key Vocabulary

If you do not understand some of the words in an assignment, you may miss out on important concepts. Therefore, it is helpful to keep a dictionary nearby when you are reading. Follow these steps:

- Before you begin reading, scan the text for unfamiliar words or terms. Find out what those words mean before you begin reading.

- Use context—the surrounding words, phrases, and sentences—to help you determine the meanings of unfamiliar words.

- If you are unable to understand the meaning through context, refer to the dictionary.

## Paying Attention to Punctuation

When you read, pay attention to punctuation. Commas, periods, exclamation points, semicolons, and colons tell you when to pause or stop. They also indicate relationships between groups of words. When you recognize these relationships you will read with greater understanding and expression. Look at the chart below.

| Punctuation Mark | Meaning |
| --- | --- |
| comma | brief pause |
| period | pause at the end of a thought |
| exclamation point | pause that indicates emphasis |
| semicolon | pause between related but distinct thoughts |
| colon | pause before giving explanation or examples |

## Using the Reading Fluency Checklist

Use the checklist below each time you read a selection in this textbook. In your Language Arts journal or notebook, note which skills you need to work on and chart your progress each week.

| Reading Fluency Checklist |
| --- |
| ☐ Preview the text to check for difficult or unfamiliar words. |
| ☐ Practice reading aloud. |
| ☐ Read according to punctuation. |
| ☐ Break down long sentences into the subject and its meaning. |
| ☐ Read groups of words for meaning rather than reading single words. |
| ☐ Read with expression (change your tone of voice to add meaning to the word). |

Reading is a skill that can be improved with practice. The key to improving your fluency is to read. The more you read, the better your reading will become.

# Types of Writing

Good writing can be a powerful tool used for many purposes. Writing can allow you to defend something you believe in or show how much you know about a subject. Writing can also help you share what you have experienced, imagined, thought, and felt. The three main types of writing are argument, informative/explanatory, and narrative.

## Argument

When you think of the word *argument,* you might think of a disagreement between two people, but an argument is more than that. An argument is a logical way of presenting a belief, conclusion, or stance. A good argument is supported with reasoning and evidence.

Argument writing can be used for many purposes, such as to change a reader's point of view or opinion or to bring about an action or a response from a reader.

There are three main purposes for writing a formal argument:

- to change the reader's mind
- to convince the reader to accept what is written
- to motivate the reader to take action, based on what is written

The following are some types of argument writing:

**Advertisements** An advertisement is a planned message meant to be seen, heard, or read. It attempts to persuade an audience to buy a product or service, accept an idea, or support a cause. Advertisements may appear in print, online, or in broadcast form.

Several common types of advertisements are public service announcements, billboards, merchandise ads, service ads, and political campaign literature.

**Persuasive Essay** A persuasive essay presents a position on an issue, urges readers to accept that position, and may encourage a specific action. An effective persuasive essay

- Explores an issue of importance to the writer
- Addresses an issue that is arguable
- Uses facts, examples, statistics, or personal experiences to support a position
- Tries to influence the audience through appeals to the readers' knowledge, experiences, or emotions
- Uses clear organization to present a logical argument

Forms of persuasion include editorials, position papers, persuasive speeches, grant proposals, advertisements, and debates.

## Informative/Explanatory

Informative/explanatory writing should rely on facts to inform or explain. Informative/explanatory writing serves some closely related purposes: to increase readers' knowledge of a subject, to help readers better understand a procedure or process, or to provide readers with an enhanced comprehension of a concept. It should also feature a clear introduction, body, and conclusion. The following are some examples of informative/explanatory writing:

**Cause-and-Effect Essay** A cause-and-effect essay examines the relationship between events, explaining how one event or situation causes another. A successful cause-and-effect essay includes

- A discussion of a cause, event, or condition that produces a specific result
- An explanation of an effect, outcome, or result
- Evidence and examples to support the relationship between cause and effect
- A logical organization that makes the explanation clear

**Comparison-and-Contrast Essay** A comparison-and-contrast essay analyzes the similarities and differences between or among two or more things. An effective comparison-and-contrast essay

- Identifies a purpose for comparison and contrast
- Identifies similarities and differences between or among two or more things, people, places, or ideas
- Gives factual details about the subjects
- Uses an organizational plan suited to the topic and purpose

**Descriptive Writing** Descriptive writing creates a vivid picture of a person, place, thing, or event. Most descriptive writing includes

- Sensory details—sights, sounds, smells, tastes, and physical sensations
- Vivid, precise language
- Figurative language or comparisons

- Adjectives and adverbs that paint a word picture

- An organization suited to the subject

Types of descriptive writing include descriptions of ideas, observations, travel brochures, physical descriptions, functional descriptions, remembrances, and character sketches.

**Problem-and-Solution Essay** A problem-and-solution essay describes a problem and offers one or more solutions to it. It describes a clear set of steps to achieve a result. An effective problem-and-solution essay includes

- A clear statement of the problem, with its causes and effects summarized for the reader

- The most important aspects of the problem

- A proposal for at least one realistic solution

- Facts, statistics, data, or expert testimony to support the solution

- A clear organization that makes the relationship between problem and solution obvious

**Research Writing** Research writing is based on information gathered from outside sources. A research paper—a focused study of a topic—helps writers explore and connect ideas, make discoveries, and share their findings with an audience. An effective research paper

- Focuses on a specific, narrow topic, which is usually summarized in a thesis statement

- Presents relevant information from a wide variety of sources

- Uses a clear organization that includes an introduction, body, and conclusion

- Includes a bibliography or works-cited list that identifies the sources from which the information was drawn

Other types of writing that depend on accurate and insightful research include multimedia presentations, statistical reports, annotated bibliographies, and experiment journals.

**Workplace Writing** Workplace writing is probably the format you will use most after you finish school. In general, workplace writing is fact-based and meant to communicate specific information in a structured format. Effective workplace writing

- Communicates information concisely

- Includes details that provide necessary information and anticipate potential questions

- Is error-free and neatly presented

Common types of workplace writing include business letters, memorandums, résumés, forms, and applications.

# Narrative

Narrative writing conveys experience, either real or imaginary, and uses time to provide structure. It can be used to inform, instruct, persuade, or entertain. Whenever writers tell a story, they are using narrative writing. Most types of narrative writing share certain elements, such as characters, a setting, a sequence of events, and, often, a theme. The following are some types of narration:

**Autobiographical Writing** Autobiographical writing tells a true story about an important period, experience, or relationship in the writer's life. Effective autobiographical writing includes

- A series of events that involve the writer as the main character

- Details, thoughts, feelings, and insights from the writer's perspective

- A conflict or an event that affects the writer

- A logical organization that tells the story clearly

- Insights that the writer gained from the experience

Types of autobiographical writing include personal narratives, autobiographical sketches, reflective essays, eyewitness accounts, and memoirs.

**Short Story** A short story is a brief, creative narrative. Most short stories include

- Details that establish the setting in time and place

- A main character who undergoes a change or learns something during the course of the story

- A conflict or a problem to be introduced, developed, and resolved

- A plot, the series of events that make up the action of the story

- A theme or message about life

Types of short stories include realistic stories, fantasies, historical narratives, mysteries, thrillers, science-fiction stories, and adventure stories.

# Writing Friendly Letters

## Writing Friendly Letters

A friendly letter is much less formal than a business letter. It is a letter to a friend, a family member, or anyone with whom the writer wants to communicate in a personal, friendly way. Most friendly letters are made up of five parts:

- ✔ the heading
- ✔ the salutation, or greeting
- ✔ the body
- ✔ the closing
- ✔ the signature

The purpose of a friendly letter is often one of the following:

- ✔ to share personal news and feelings
- ✔ to send or to answer an invitation
- ✔ to express thanks

## Model Friendly Letter

In this friendly letter, Betsy thanks her grandparents for a birthday present and gives them some news about her life.

---

11 Old Farm Road
Topsham, Maine 04011

April 14, 20—

Dear Grandma and Grandpa,

Thank you for the sweater you sent me for my birthday. It fits perfectly, and I love the color. I wore my new sweater to the carnival at school last weekend and got lots of compliments.

The weather here has been cool but sunny. Mom thinks that "real" spring will never come. I can't wait until it's warm enough to go swimming.

School is going fairly well. I really like my Social Studies class. We are learning about the U.S. Constitution, and I think it's very interesting. Maybe I will be a lawyer when I grow up.

When are you coming out to visit us? We haven't seen you since Thanksgiving. You can stay in my room when you come. I'll be happy to sleep on the couch. (The TV is in that room!!)

Well, thanks again and hope all is well with you.

Love,

Betsy

> The **heading** includes the writer's address and the date on which he or she wrote the letter.

> The **body** is the main part of the letter and contains the basic message.

> Some common **closings** for personal letters include "Best wishes," "Love," "Sincerely," and "Yours truly."

# Writing Business Letters

## Formatting Business Letters

Business letters follow one of several acceptable formats. In **block format,** each part of the letter begins at the left margin. A double space is used between paragraphs. In **modified block format,** some parts of the letter are indented to the center of the page. No matter which format is used, all letters in business format have a heading, an inside address, a salutation or greeting, a body, a closing, and a signature. These parts are shown and annotated on the model business letter below, formatted in modified block style.

## Model Business Letter

In this letter, Yolanda Dodson uses modified block format to request information.

Students for a Cleaner Planet
c/o Memorial High School
333 Veteran's Drive
Denver, CO 80211

January 25, 20—

Steven Wilson, Director
Resource Recovery Really Works
300 Oak Street
Denver, CO 80216

Dear Mr. Wilson:

Memorial High School would like to start a branch of your successful recycling program. We share your commitment to reclaiming as much reusable material as we can. Because your program has been successful in other neighborhoods, we're sure that it can work in our community. Our school includes grades 9–12 and has about 800 students.

Would you send us some information about your community recycling program? For example, we need to know what materials can be recycled and how we can implement the program.

At least fifty students have already expressed an interest in getting involved, so I know we'll have the people power to make the program work. Please help us get started.

Thank you in advance for your time and consideration.

Sincerely,

*Yolanda Dodson*

Yolanda Dodson

The **heading** shows the writer's address and organization (if any) and the date.

The **inside address** indicates where the letter will be sent.

A **salutation** is punctuated by a colon. When the specific addressee is not known, use a general greeting such as "To whom it may concern:"

The **body** of the letter states the writer's purpose. In this case, the writer requests information.

The **closing** "Sincerely" is common, but "Yours truly" or "Respectfully yours" are also acceptable. To end the letter, the writer types her name and provides a **signature**.

# 21st-Century Skills

New technology has created many new ways to communicate. Today, it is easy to contribute information to the Internet and send a variety of messages to friends far and near. You can also share your ideas through photos, illustrations, video, and sound recordings. *21st Century Skills* gives you an overview of some ways you can use today's technology to create, share, and find information. Here are the topics you will find in this section.

- ✔ Blogs
- ✔ Social Networking
- ✔ Widgets and Feeds
- ✔ Multimedia Elements
- ✔ Podcasts
- ✔ Wikis

## BLOGS

A **blog** is a common form of online writing. The word *blog* is a contraction of *Web log*. Most blogs include a series of entries known as *posts*. The posts appear in a single column and are displayed in reverse chronological order. That means that the most recent post is at the top of the page. As you scroll down, you will find earlier posts.

Blogs have become increasingly popular. Researchers estimate that 75,000 new blogs are launched every day. Blog authors are often called *bloggers*. They can use their personal sites to share ideas, songs, videos, photos, and other media. People who read blogs can often post their responses with a comments feature found in each new post.

Because blogs are designed so that they are easy to update, bloggers can post new messages as often as they like, often daily. For some people blogs become a public journal or diary, in which they share their thoughts about daily events.

### Types of Blogs

Not all blogs are the same. Many blogs have a single author, but others are group projects. These are some common types of blog:

- ✔ Personal blogs often have a general focus. Bloggers post their thoughts on any topic they find interesting in their daily lives.

- ✔ Topical blogs focus on a specific theme, such as movie reviews, political news, class assignments, or health-care opportunities.

---

### Web Safety

Always be aware that information you post on the Internet can be read by everyone with access to that page. Once you post a picture or text, it can be saved on someone else's computer, even if you later remove it.

Using the Internet safely means keeping personal information personal. Never include your address (e-mail or real), last name, or telephone numbers. Avoid mentioning places you can be frequently found. Never give out passwords you use to access other Web sites and do not respond to e-mails from people you do not know.

---

# Anatomy of a Blog

Here are some of the features you can include in a blog.

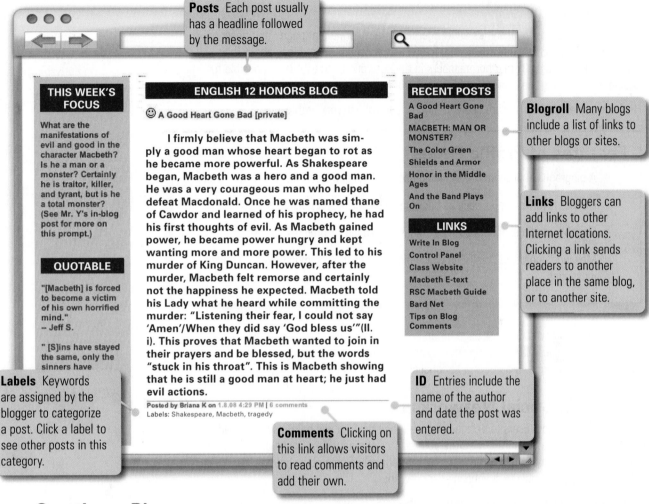

**Posts** Each post usually has a headline followed by the message.

**THIS WEEK'S FOCUS**

What are the manifestations of evil and good in the character Macbeth? Is he a man or a monster? Certainly he is traitor, killer, and tyrant, but is he a total monster? (See Mr. Y's in-blog post for more on this prompt.)

**QUOTABLE**

"[Macbeth] is forced to become a victim of his own horrified mind."
– Jeff S.

" [S]ins have stayed the same, only the sinners have

**ENGLISH 12 HONORS BLOG**

☺ A Good Heart Gone Bad [private]

I firmly believe that Macbeth was simply a good man whose heart began to rot as he became more powerful. As Shakespeare began, Macbeth was a hero and a good man. He was a very courageous man who helped defeat Macdonald. Once he was named thane of Cawdor and learned of his prophecy, he had his first thoughts of evil. As Macbeth gained power, he became power hungry and kept wanting more and more power. This led to his murder of King Duncan. However, after the murder, Macbeth felt remorse and certainly not the happiness he expected. Macbeth told his Lady what he heard while committing the murder: "Listening their fear, I could not say 'Amen'/When they did say 'God bless us'"(II. i). This proves that Macbeth wanted to join in their prayers and be blessed, but the words "stuck in his throat". This is Macbeth showing that he is still a good man at heart; he just had evil actions.

Posted by **Briana K** on 1.8.08 4:29 PM | 6 comments
Labels: Shakespeare, Macbeth, tragedy

**RECENT POSTS**

**A Good Heart Gone Bad**
**MACBETH: MAN OR MONSTER?**
**The Color Green**
**Shields and Armor**
**Honor in the Middle Ages**
**And the Band Plays On**

**LINKS**

Write In Blog
Control Panel
Class Website
Macbeth E-text
RSC Macbeth Guide
Bard Net
Tips on Blog Comments

**Blogroll** Many blogs include a list of links to other blogs or sites.

**Links** Bloggers can add links to other Internet locations. Clicking a link sends readers to another place in the same blog, or to another site.

**Labels** Keywords are assigned by the blogger to categorize a post. Click a label to see other posts in this category.

**ID** Entries include the name of the author and date the post was entered.

**Comments** Clicking on this link allows visitors to read comments and add their own.

# Creating a Blog

Keep these hints and strategies in mind to help you create an interesting and fair blog:

- ✔ Focus each blog entry on a single topic.

- ✔ Vary the length of your posts. Sometimes, all you need is a line or two to share a quick thought. Other posts will be much longer.

- ✔ Choose font colors and styles that can be read easily.

- ✔ Many people scan blogs rather than read them closely. You can make your main ideas pop out by using clear or clever headlines and boldfacing key terms.

- ✔ Give credit to other people's work and ideas. State the names of people whose ideas you are quoting or add a link to take readers to that person's blog or site.

- ✔ If you post comments, try to make them brief and polite.

# SOCIAL NETWORKING

Social networking means any interaction between members of an online community. People can exchange many different kinds of information, from text and voice messages to video images.

Many social network communities allow users to create permanent pages that describe themselves. Users create home pages to express themselves, share ideas about their lives, and post messages to other members in the network. Each user is responsible for adding and updating the content on his or her profile page.

Here are some features you are likely to find on a social network profile:

## Features of Profile Pages

- A biographical description, including photographs and artwork.

- Lists of favorite things, such as books, movies, music, and fashions.

- Playable media elements such as videos and sound recordings.

- Message boards, or "walls" in which members of the community can exchange messages.

You can create a social network page for an individual or a group, such as a school or special interest club. Many hosting sites do not charge to register, so you can also have fun by creating a page for a pet or a fictional character.

## Privacy in Social Networks

Social networks allow users to decide how open their profiles will be. Be sure to read introductory information carefully before you register at a new site. Once you have a personal profile page, monitor your privacy settings regularly. Remember that any information you post will be available to anyone in your network.

Users often post messages anonymously or using false names, or *pseudonyms*. People can also post using someone else's name. Judge all information on the net critically. Do not assume that you know who posted some information simply because you recognize the name of the post author. The rapid speed of communication on the Internet can make it easy to jump to conclusions—be careful to avoid this trap.

# Tips for Sending Effective Messages

Technology makes it easy to share ideas quickly, but writing for the Internet poses some special challenges as well. The writing style for blogs and social networks is often very conversational. In blog posts and comments, instant messages, and e-mails, writers often express themselves very quickly, using relaxed language, short sentences, and abbreviations. However, in a conversation, we get a lot of information from a speaker's tone of voice and body language. On the Internet, those clues are missing. As a result, Internet writers often use italics or bracketed labels to indicate emotions. Another alternative is using *emoticons*—strings of characters that give visual clues to indicate emotion:

| | | | | | |
|---|---|---|---|---|---|
| :-) | smile (happy) | :-( | frown (unhappy) | ;-) | wink (light sarcasm) |

Use these strategies to communicate effectively when using technology:

- ✔ Reread your messages. Before you click *Send,* read your message through and make sure that your tone will be clear to the reader.

- ✔ Do not jump to conclusions—ask for clarification first. Make sure you really understand what someone is saying before you respond.

- ✔ Use abbreviations your reader will understand.

## WIDGETS AND FEEDS

A **widget** is a small application that performs a specific task. You might find widgets that give weather predictions, offer dictionary definitions or translations, provide entertainment such as games, or present a daily word, photograph, or quotation.

A **feed** is a special kind of widget. It displays headlines taken from the latest content on a specific media source. Clicking on the headline will take you to the full article.

Many social network communities and other Web sites allow you to personalize your home page by adding widgets and feeds.

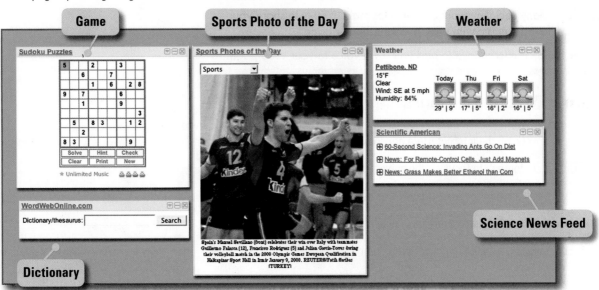

# MULTIMEDIA ELEMENTS

One of the great advantages of communicating on the Internet is that you are not limited to using text only. When you create a Web profile or blog, you can share your ideas using a wide variety of media. In addition to widgets and feeds (see page R31), these media elements can make your Internet communication more entertaining and useful.

## Graphics

| Graphics | |
|---|---|
| **Photographs** | You can post photos taken by digital cameras. |
| **Illustrations** | Artwork can be created using computer software. You can also use a scanner to post a digital image of a drawing or sketch. |
| **Charts, Graphs, and Maps** | Charts and graphs can make statistical information clear. Use spreadsheet software to create these elements. Use Internet sites to find maps of specific places. |

## Video

| Video | |
|---|---|
| **Live Action** | Digital video can be recorded by a camera or recorded from another media source. |
| **Animation** | Animated videos can also be created using software. |

## Sound

| Sound | |
|---|---|
| **Music** | Many social network communities make it easy to share your favorite music with people who visit your page. |
| **Voice** | Use a microphone to add your own voice to your Web page. |

## Editing Media Elements

You can use software to customize media elements. Open source software is free and available to anyone on the Internet. Here are some things you can do with software:

✔ Crop a photograph to focus on the subject or brighten an image that is too dark.

✔ Transform a drawing's appearance from flat to three-dimensional.

✔ Insert a "You Are Here" arrow on a map.

✔ Edit a video or sound file to shorten its running time.

✔ Add background music or sound effects to a video.

# PODCASTS

A **podcast** is a digital audio or video recording of a program that is made available on the Internet. Users can replay the podcast on a computer, or download it and replay it on a personal audio player. You might think of podcasts as radio or television programs that you create yourself. They can be embedded on a Web site or fed to a Web page through a podcast widget.

## Creating an Effective Podcast

To make a podcast, you will need a recording device, such as a microphone or digital video camera, as well as editing software. Open source editing software is widely available and free of charge. Most audio podcasts are converted into the MP3 format. Here are some tips for creating a podcast that is clear and entertaining:

- ✔ Listen to several podcasts by different authors to get a feeling for the medium. Make a list of features and styles you like and also those you want to avoid.

- ✔ Test your microphone to find the best recording distance. Stand close enough to the microphone so that your voice sounds full, but not so close that you create an echo.

- ✔ Create an outline that shows your estimated timing for each element.

- ✔ Be prepared before you record. Rehearse, but do not create a script. Podcasts are best when they have a natural, easy flow.

- ✔ Talk directly to your listeners. Slow down enough so they can understand you.

- ✔ Use software to edit your podcast before publishing it. You can edit out mistakes or add additional elements.

# WIKIS

A **wiki** is a collaborative Web site that lets visitors create, add, remove, and edit content. The term comes from the Hawaiian phrase *wiki wiki,* which means "quick." Web users at a wiki are both the readers and the writers of the site. Some wikis are open to contributions from anyone. Others require visitors to register before they can edit the content.

All of the text in these collaborative Web sites was written by people who use the site. Articles are constantly changing, as visitors find and correct errors and improve texts.

Wikis have both advantages and disadvantages as sources of information. They are valuable open forums for the exchange of ideas. The unique collaborative writing process allows entries to change over time. However, entries can also be modified incorrectly. Careless or malicious users can delete good content and add inappropriate or inaccurate information.

You can change the information on a wiki, but be sure your information is correct and clear before you add it. Wikis keep track of all changes, so your work will be recorded and can be evaluated by other users.

# Citing Sources and Preparing Manuscript

## Proofreading and Preparing Manuscript

Before preparing a final copy, proofread your manuscript. The chart shows the standard symbols for marking corrections to be made.

| Proofreading Symbols | |
|---|---|
| insert | ∧ |
| delete | ℰ |
| close space | ◯ |
| new paragraph | ¶ |
| add comma | ⋏ |
| add period | ⊙ |
| transpose (switch) | ∿ |
| change to cap | a̲̲ |
| change to lowercase | ✗ |

- Choose a standard, easy-to-read font.
- Type or print on one side of unlined 8 1/2" x 11" paper.
- Set the margins for the side, top, and bottom of your paper at approximately one inch. Most word-processing programs have a default setting that is appropriate.
- Double-space the document.
- Indent the first line of each paragraph.
- Number the pages in the upper right corner.

Follow your teacher's directions for formatting formal research papers. Most papers will have the following features:

- Title page
- Table of Contents or Outline
- Works-Cited List

## Avoiding Plagiarism

Whether you are presenting a formal research paper or an opinion paper on a current event, you must be careful to give credit for any ideas or opinions that are not your own. Presenting someone else's ideas, research, or opinion as your own—even if you have phrased it in different words—is *plagiarism*, the equivalent of academic stealing, or fraud.

Do not use the ideas or research of others in place of your own. Read from several sources to draw your own conclusions and form your own opinions. Incorporate the ideas and research of others to support your points. Credit the source of the following types of support:

- Statistics
- Direct quotations
- Indirectly quoted statements of opinions
- Conclusions presented by an expert
- Facts available in only one or two sources

## Crediting Sources

When you credit a source, you acknowledge where you found your information and you give your readers the details necessary for locating the source themselves. Within the body of the paper, you provide a short citation, a footnote number linked to a footnote, or an endnote number linked to an endnote reference. These brief references show the page numbers on which you found the information. Prepare a reference list at the end of the paper to provide full bibliographic information on your sources. These are two common types of reference lists:

- A bibliography provides a listing of all the resources you consulted during your research.
- A works-cited list indicates the works you have referenced in your paper.

The chart on the next page shows the Modern Language Association format for crediting sources. This is the most common format for papers written in the content areas in middle school and high school. Unless instructed otherwise by your teacher, use this format for crediting sources.

# MLA Style for Listing Sources

| | |
|---|---|
| **Book with one author** | Pyles, Thomas. *The Origins and Development of the English Language.* 2nd ed. New York: Harcourt, 1971. Print. |
| **Book with two or three authors** | McCrum, Robert, William Cran, and Robert MacNeil. *The Story of English.* New York: Penguin, 1987. Print. |
| **Book with an editor** | Truth, Sojourner. *Narrative of Sojourner Truth.* Ed. Margaret Washington. New York: Vintage, 1993. Print. |
| **Book with more than three authors or editors** | Donald, Robert B., et al. *Writing Clear Essays.* Upper Saddle River: Prentice, 1996. Print. |
| **Single work in an anthology** | Hawthorne, Nathaniel. "Young Goodman Brown." *Literature: An Introduction to Reading and Writing.* Ed. Edgar V. Roberts and H. E. Jacobs. Upper Saddle River: Prentice, 1998. 376–385. Print.<br>[Indicate pages for the entire selection.] |
| **Introduction to a work in a published edition** | Washington, Margaret. Introduction. *Narrative of Sojourner Truth.* By Sojourner Truth. Ed. Washington. New York: Vintage, 1993. v–xi. Print. |
| **Signed article from an encyclopedia** | Askeland, Donald R. "Welding." *World Book Encyclopedia.* 1991 ed. Print. |
| **Signed article in a weekly magazine** | Wallace, Charles. "A Vodacious Deal." *Time* 14 Feb. 2000: 63. Print. |
| **Signed article in a monthly magazine** | Gustaitis, Joseph. "The Sticky History of Chewing Gum." *American History* Oct. 1998: 30–38. Print. |
| **Newspaper** | Thurow, Roger. "South Africans Who Fought for Sanctions Now Scrap for Investors." *Wall Street Journal* 11 Feb. 2000: A1+. Print.<br>[For a multipage article that does not appear on consecutive pages, write only the first page number on which it appears, followed by the plus sign.] |
| **Unsigned editorial or story** | "Selective Silence." Editorial. *Wall Street Journal* 11 Feb. 2000: A14. Print.<br>[If the editorial or story is signed, begin with the author's name.] |
| **Signed pamphlet or brochure** | [Treat the pamphlet as though it were a book.] |
| **Work from a library subscription service** | Ertman, Earl L. "Nefertiti's Eyes." *Archaeology* Mar.–Apr. 2008: 28–32. *Kids Search.* EBSCO. New York Public Library. Web. 18 June 2008<br>[Indicate the date you accessed the information.] |
| **Filmstrips, slide programs, videocassettes, DVDs, and other audiovisual media** | *The Diary of Anne Frank.* Dir. George Stevens. Perf. Millie Perkins, Shelley Winters, Joseph Schildkraut, Lou Jacobi, and Richard Beymer. 1959. Twentieth Century Fox, 2004. DVD. |
| **CD-ROM (with multiple publishers)** | Simms, James, ed. *Romeo and Juliet.* By William Shakespeare. Oxford: Attica Cybernetics; London: BBC Education; London: Harper, 1995. CD-ROM. |
| **Radio or television program transcript** | "Washington's Crossing of the Delaware." *Weekend Edition Sunday.* Natl. Public Radio. WNYC, New York. 23 Dec. 2003. Television transcript. |
| **Internet Web page** | "Fun Facts About Gum." NACGM site. 1999. National Association of Chewing Gum Manufacturers. Web. 19 Dec. 1999<br>[Indicate the date you accessed the information.] |
| **Personal interview** | Smith, Jane. Personal interview. 10 Feb. 2000. |

All examples follow the style given in the *MLA Handbook for Writers of Research Papers,* seventh edition, by Joseph Gibaldi.

# Guide to Rubrics

## What is a rubric?

A rubric is a tool, often in the form of a chart or a grid, that helps you assess your work. Rubrics are particularly helpful for writing and speaking assignments.

To help you or others assess, or evaluate, your work, a rubric offers several specific criteria to be applied to your work. Then the rubric helps you or an evaluator indicate your range of success or failure according to those specific criteria. Rubrics are often used to evaluate writing for standardized tests.

Using a rubric will save you time, focus your learning, and improve the work you do. When you know what the rubric will be before you begin writing a persuasive essay, for example, as you write you will be aware of specific criteria that are important in that kind of an essay. As you evaluate the essay before giving it to your teacher, you will focus on the specific areas that your teacher wants you to master—or on areas that you know present challenges for you. Instead of searching through your work randomly for any way to improve it or correct its errors, you will have a clear and helpful focus on specific criteria.

## How are rubrics constructed?

Rubrics can be constructed in several different ways.

- Your teacher may assign a rubric for a specific assignment.
- Your teacher may direct you to a rubric in your textbook.
- Your teacher and your class may construct a rubric for a particular assignment together.
- You and your classmates may construct a rubric together.
- You may create your own rubric with criteria you want to evaluate in your work.

## How will a rubric help me?

A rubric will help you assess your work on a scale. Scales vary from rubric to rubric but usually range from 6 to 1, 5 to 1, or 4 to 1, with 6, 5, or 4 being the highest score and 1 being the lowest. If someone else is using the rubric to assess your work, the rubric will give your evaluator a clear range within which to place your work. If you are using the rubric yourself, it will help you make improvements to your work.

## What are the types of rubrics?

- A **holistic rubric** has general criteria that can apply to a variety of assignments. See p. R38 for an example of a holistic rubric.
- An **analytic rubric** is specific to a particular assignment. The criteria for evaluation address the specific issues important in that assignment. See p. R37 for examples of analytic rubrics.

# Sample Analytic Rubrics

## Rubric With a 4-point Scale

*The following analytic rubric is an example of a rubric to assess a persuasive essay. It will help you evaluate focus, organization, support/elaboration, and style/convention.*

| | Focus | Organization | Support/Elaboration | Style/Convention |
|---|---|---|---|---|
| 4 | Demonstrates highly effective word choice; clearly focused on task. | Uses clear, consistent organizational strategy. | Provides convincing, well-elaborated reasons to support the position. | Incorporates transitions; includes very few mechanical errors. |
| 3 | Demonstrates good word choice; stays focused on persuasive task. | Uses clear organizational strategy with occasional inconsistencies. | Provides two or more moderately elaborated reasons to support the position. | Incorporates some transitions; includes few mechanical errors. |
| 2 | Shows some good word choices; minimally stays focused on persuasive task. | Uses inconsistent organizational strategy; presentation is not logical. | Provides several reasons, but few are elaborated; only one elaborated reason. | Incorporates few transitions; includes many mechanical errors. |
| 1 | Shows lack of attention to persuasive task. | Demonstrates lack of organizational strategy. | Provides no specific reasons or does not elaborate. | Does not connect ideas; includes many mechanical errors. |

## Rubric With a 6-point Scale

*The following analytic rubric is an example of a rubric to assess a persuasive essay. It will help you evaluate presentation, position, evidence, and arguments.*

| | Presentation | Position | Evidence | Arguments |
|---|---|---|---|---|
| 6 | Essay clearly and effectively addresses an issue with more than one side. | Essay clearly states a supportable position on the issue. | All evidence is logically organized, well presented, and supports the position. | All reader concerns and counterarguments are effectively addressed. |
| 5 | Most of essay addresses an issue that has more than one side. | Essay clearly states a position on the issue. | Most evidence is logically organized, well presented, and supports the position. | Most reader concerns and counterarguments are effectively addressed. |
| 4 | Essay adequately addresses issue that has more than one side. | Essay adequately states a position on the issue. | Many parts of evidence support the position; some evidence is out of order. | Many reader concerns and counterarguments are adequately addressed. |
| 3 | Essay addresses issue with two sides but does not present second side clearly. | Essay states a position on the issue, but the position is difficult to support. | Some evidence supports the position, but some evidence is out of order. | Some reader concerns and counterarguments are addressed. |
| 2 | Essay addresses issue with two sides but does not present second side. | Essay states a position on the issue, but the position is not supportable. | Not much evidence supports the position, and what is included is out of order. | A few reader concerns and counterarguments are addressed. |
| 1 | Essay does not address issue with more than one side. | Essay does not state a position on the issue. | No evidence supports the position. | No reader concerns or counterarguments are addressed. |

# Sample Holistic Rubric

Holistic rubrics such as this one are sometimes used to assess writing assignments on standardized tests. Notice that the criteria for evaluation are focus, organization, support, and use of conventions.

| Points | Criteria |
|---|---|
| **6 Points** | • The writing is strongly focused and shows fresh insight into the writing task.<br>• The writing is marked by a sense of completeness and coherence and is organized with a logical progression of ideas.<br>• A main idea is fully developed, and support is specific and substantial.<br>• A mature command of the language is evident, and the writing may employ characteristic creative writing strategies.<br>• Sentence structure is varied, and writing is free of all but purposefully used fragments.<br>• Virtually no errors in writing conventions appear. |
| **5 Points** | • The writing is clearly focused on the task.<br>• The writing is well organized and has a logical progression of ideas, though there may be occasional lapses.<br>• A main idea is well developed and supported with relevant detail.<br>• Sentence structure is varied, and the writing is free of fragments, except when used purposefully.<br>• Writing conventions are followed correctly. |
| **4 Points** | • The writing is clearly focused on the task, but extraneous material may intrude at times.<br>• Clear organizational pattern is present, though lapses may occur.<br>• A main idea is adequately supported, but development may be uneven.<br>• Sentence structure is generally fragment free but shows little variation.<br>• Writing conventions are generally followed correctly. |
| **3 Points** | • Writing is generally focused on the task, but extraneous material may intrude at times.<br>• An organizational pattern is evident, but writing may lack a logical progression of ideas.<br>• Support for the main idea is generally present but is sometimes illogical.<br>• Sentence structure is generally free of fragments, but there is almost no variation.<br>• The work generally demonstrates a knowledge of writing conventions, with occasional misspellings. |
| **2 Points** | • The writing is related to the task but generally lacks focus.<br>• There is little evidence of organizational pattern, and there is little sense of cohesion.<br>• Support for the main idea is generally inadequate, illogical, or absent.<br>• Sentence structure is unvaried, and serious errors may occur.<br>• Errors in writing conventions and spellings are frequent. |
| **1 Point** | • The writing may have little connection to the task and is generally unfocused.<br>• There has been little attempt at organization or development.<br>• The paper seems fragmented, with no clear main idea.<br>• Sentence structure is unvaried, and serious errors appear.<br>• Poor word choice and poor command of the language obscure meaning.<br>• Errors in writing conventions and spelling are frequent. |
| **Unscorable** | The paper is considered unscorable if:<br>• The response is unrelated to the task or is simply a rewording of the prompt.<br>• The response has been copied from a published work.<br>• The student did not write a response.<br>• The response is illegible.<br>• The words in the response are arranged with no meaning.<br>• There is an insufficient amount of writing to score. |

# Student Model

## Persuasive Writing

This persuasive essay, which would receive a top score according to a persuasive rubric, is a response to the following writing prompt, or assignment:

**Most young people today spend more than 5 hours a day watching television. Many adults worry about the effects on youth of seeing too much television violence. Write a persuasive piece in which you argue against or defend the effects of television watching on young people. Be sure to include examples to support your views.**

Until the television was invented, families spent their time doing different activities. Now most families stay home and watch TV. Watching TV risks the family's health, reduces the children's study time, and is a bad influence on young minds. Watching television can be harmful.

> The writer clearly states a position in the first paragraph.

The most important reason why watching TV is bad is that the viewers get less exercise. For example, instead of watching their favorite show, people could get exercise for 30 minutes. If people spent less time watching TV and more time exercising, then they could have healthier bodies. My mother told me a story about a man who died of a heart attack because he was out of shape from watching television all the time. Obviously, watching TV put a person's health in danger.

> Each paragraph provides details that support the writer's main point.

Furthermore, watching television reduces childern's study time. For example, children would spend more time studying if they didn't watch television. If students spent more time studying at home, then they would make better grades at school. Last week I had a major test in science, but I didn't study because I started watching a movie. I was not prepared for the test and my grade reflected my lack of studying. Indeed, watching television is bad because it can hurt a student's grades.

Finally, watching TV can be a bad influence on children. For example, some TV shows have inappropriate language and too much violence. If children watch programs that use bad language and show violence, then they may start repeating these actions because they think the behavior is "cool." In fact, it has been proven that children copy what they see on TV. Clearly, watching TV is bad for children and its affects children's behavior.

In conclusion, watching television is a bad influence for these reasons: It reduces people's exercise time and students' study time and it shows children inappropriate behavior. Therefore, people should take control of their lives and stop allowing television to harm them.

> The conclusion restates the writer's position.

# Grammar, Usage, and Mechanics Handbook

## Parts of Speech

**Nouns**  A **noun** is the name of a person, place, or thing. A **common noun** names any one of a class of people, places, or things. A **proper noun** names a specific person, place, or thing.

A collective noun is a noun that names a group of individual people or things.

A compound noun is a noun made up of two or more words.

**Pronouns**  A **pronoun** is a word that stands for a noun or for a word that takes the place of a noun.

A **personal pronoun** refers to (1) the person speaking, (2) the person spoken to, or (3) the person, place, or thing spoken about.

|  | *Singular* | *Plural* |
|---|---|---|
| *First Person* | I, me, my, mine | we, us, our, ours |
| *Second Person* | you, your, yours | you, your, yours |
| *Third Person* | he, him, his, she, her, hers, it, its | they, them, their, theirs |

A **demonstrative pronoun** directs attention to a specific person, place, or thing.

> *These* are the juiciest pears I have ever tasted.

An **interrogative pronoun** is used to begin a question.

> *Who* is the author of "Jeremiah's Song"?

An **indefinite pronoun** refers to a person, place, or thing, often without specifying which one.

> *Everyone* bought something.

A relative pronoun begins a subordinate clause and connects it to another idea in the same sentence. There are five relative pronouns: *that, which, who, whom, whose*.

**Verbs**  A **verb** is a word that expresses time while showing an action, a condition, or the fact that something exists. An **action verb** indicates the action of someone or something. A **linking verb** connects the subject of a sentence with a noun or a pronoun that renames or describes the subject. A **helping verb** can be added to another verb to make a single verb phrase. An **action verb** is transitive if the receiver of the action is named in the sentence. The receiver of the action is called the object of the verb.

**Adjectives**  An **adjective** describes a noun or a pronoun or gives a noun or a pronoun a more specific meaning. Adjectives answer the questions *what kind, which one, how many,* or *how much.*

The articles *the, a,* and *an* are adjectives. *An* is used before a word beginning with a vowel sound.

A noun may sometimes be used as an adjective.

> *family* home              *science* fiction

**Adverbs**  An **adverb** modifies a verb, an adjective, or another adverb. Adverbs answer the questions *where, when, in what way,* or *to what extent.*

**Prepositions**  A **preposition** relates a noun or a pronoun following it to another word in the sentence.

**Conjunctions**  A **conjunction** connects other words or groups of words. A **coordinating conjunction** connects similar kinds or groups of words. **Correlative conjunctions** are used in pairs to connect similar words or groups of words.

> *both* Grandpa *and* Dad              *neither* they *nor* I

**Interjections**  An **interjection** is a word that expresses feeling or emotion and functions independently of a sentence.

## Phrases, Clauses, and Sentences

**Sentences**  A **sentence** is a group of words with two main parts: a complete subject and a complete predicate. Together, these parts express a complete thought.

A **fragment** is a group of words that does not express a complete thought.

**Subject**  The **subject** of a sentence is the word or group of words that tells whom or what the sentence is about. The **simple subject** is the essential noun, pronoun, or group of words acting as a noun that cannot be left out of the complete subject. A **complete subject** is the simple subject plus any modifiers.

A **compound subject** is two or more subjects that have the same verb and are joined by a conjunction.

> Neither the *horse nor the driver* looked tired.

**Predicate**  The **predicate** of a sentence is the verb or verb phrase that tells what the complete subject of the sentence does or is. The **simple predicate** is the essential verb or verb phrase that cannot be left out of the complete predicate. A **complete predicate** is the simple predicate plus any modifiers or complements.

A **compound predicate** is two or more verbs that have the same subject and are joined by a conjunction.

> She *sneezed and coughed* throughout the trip.

**Complement**  A **complement** is a word or group of words that completes the meaning of the predicate of a sentence. Five different kinds of complements can be found in English sentences: *direct objects, indirect objects, objective complements, predicate nominatives,* and *predicate adjectives.*

A **direct object** is a noun, pronoun, or group of words acting as a noun that receives the action of a transitive verb.

We watched the *liftoff.*

An **indirect object** is a noun, pronoun, or group of words that appears with a direct object and names the person or thing that something is given to or done for.

He sold the *family* a mirror.

An **objective complement** is an adjective or noun that appears with a direct object and describes or renames it.

I called Meg my *friend.*

A **subject complement** is a noun, pronoun, or adjective that appears with a linking verb and tells something about the subject. A subject complement may be a *predicate nominative* or a *predicate adjective.*

A **predicate nominative** is a noun or pronoun that appears with a linking verb and renames, identifies, or explains the subject.

Kiglo was the *leader.*

A **predicate adjective** is an adjective that appears with a linking verb and describes the subject of a sentence.

Roko became *tired.*

**Sentence Types** A **simple sentence** consists of a single independent clause.

A **compound sentence** consists of two or more independent clauses joined by a comma and a coordinating conjunction or by a semicolon.

A **complex sentence** consists of one independent clause and one or more subordinate clauses.

A **compound-complex sentence** consists of two or more independent clauses and one or more subordinate clauses.

A **declarative sentence** states an idea and ends with a period.

An **interrogative sentence** asks a question and ends with a question mark.

An **imperative sentence** gives an order or a direction and ends with either a period or an exclamation mark.

An **exclamatory sentence** conveys a strong emotion and ends with an exclamation mark.

**Phrases** A **phrase** is a group of words, without a subject and a verb, that functions in a sentence as one part of speech.

A **prepositional phrase** is a group of words that includes a preposition and a noun or a pronoun that is the object of the preposition.

An **adjective phrase** is a prepositional phrase that modifies a noun or a pronoun by telling *what kind* or *which one.*

An **adverb phrase** is a prepositional phrase that modifies a verb, an adjective, or an adverb by pointing out *where, when, in what manner,* or *to what extent.*

An **appositive phrase** is a noun or a pronoun with modifiers, placed next to a noun or a pronoun to add information and details.

A **participial phrase** is a participle modified by an adjective or an adverb phrase or accompanied by a complement. The entire phrase acts as an adjective.

*Running at top speed,* he soon caught up with them.

An **infinitive phrase** is an infinitive with modifiers, complements, or a subject, all acting together as a single part of speech.

At first I was too busy enjoying my food *to notice how the guests were doing.*

**Gerunds** A **gerund** is a noun formed from the present participle of a verb by adding *–ing.* Like other nouns, gerunds can be used as subjects, direct objects, predicate nouns, and objects of prepositions.

**Gerund Phrases** A **gerund phrase** is a gerund with modifiers or a complement, all acting together as a noun.

**Clauses** A **clause** is a group of words with its own subject and verb.

An **independent clause** can stand by itself as a complete sentence.

A **subordinate clause** has a subject and a verb but cannot stand by itself as a complete sentence; it can only be part of a sentence.

# Using Verbs, Pronouns, and Modifiers

**Principal Parts** A **verb** has four **principal parts:** the *present,* the *present participle,* the *past,* and the *past participle.* Regular verbs form the past and past participle by adding *-ed* to the present form.

Irregular verbs form the past and past participle by changing form rather than by adding *-ed.*

**Verb Tense** A **verb tense** tells whether the time of an action or condition is in the past, the present, or the future. Every verb has six tenses: *present, past, future, present perfect, past perfect,* and *future perfect.*

The **present tense** shows actions that happen in the present. The **past tense** shows actions that have already happened. The **future tense** shows actions that will happen. The **present perfect tense** shows actions that begin in the past and continue to the present. The **past perfect tense** shows a past action or condition that ended before another past action. The **future perfect tense** shows a future action or condition that will have ended before another begins.

**Pronoun Case** The **case** of a pronoun is the form it takes to show its use in a sentence. There are three pronoun cases: *nominative*, *objective*, and *possessive*.

The **nominative case** is used to name or rename the subject of the sentence. The nominative case pronouns are *I, you, he, she, it, we, you, they.*

The **objective case** is used as the direct object, indirect object, or object of a preposition. The objective case pronouns are *me, you, him, her, it, us, you, them.*

The **possessive case** is used to show ownership. The possessive pronouns are *my, your, his, her, its, our, their, mine, yours, his, hers, its, ours, theirs.*

**Subject-Verb Agreement** To make a subject and a verb agree, make sure that both are singular or both are plural. Two or more singular subjects joined by *or* or *nor* must have a singular verb. When singular and plural subjects are joined by *or* or *nor,* the verb must agree with the closest subject.

**Pronoun-Antecedent Agreement** Pronouns must agree with their antecedents in number and gender. Use singular pronouns with singular antecedents and plural pronouns with plural antecedents. Many errors in pronoun-antecedent agreement occur when a plural pronoun is used to refer to a singular antecedent for which the gender is not specified.

Incorrect: Everyone did their best.

Correct: Everyone did his or her best.

The following indefinite pronouns are singular: *anybody, anyone, each, either, everybody, everyone, neither, nobody, no one, one, somebody, someone.*

The following indefinite pronouns are plural: *both, few, many, several.*

The following indefinite pronouns may be either singular or plural: *all, any, most, none, some.*

**Modifiers** The **comparative** and **superlative** degrees of most adjectives and adverbs of one or two syllables can be formed in either of two ways: Use *–er* or *more* to form a comparative degree and *–est* or *most* to form the superlative degree of most one- and two-syllable modifiers. These endings are added to the *positive*, or base, form of the word.

*More* and *most* can also be used to form the comparative and superlative degrees of most one- and two-syllable modifiers. These words should not be used when the result sounds awkward, as in "A greyhound is *more fast* than a beagle."

# Glossary of Common Usage

**accept, except:** *Accept* is a verb that means "to receive" or "to agree to." *Except* is usually used as a preposition that means "other than" or "leaving out." Do not confuse these two words.

**affect, effect:** *Affect* is normally a verb meaning "to influence" or "to bring about a change in." *Effect* is usually a noun, meaning "result."

**among, between:** *Among* is usually used with three or more items. *Between* is generally used with only two items.

**bad, badly:** Use the predicate adjective *bad* after linking verbs such as *feel, look,* and *seem.* Use *badly* whenever an adverb is required.

**beside, besides:** *Beside* means "at the side of" or "close to." *Besides* means "in addition to."

**can, may:** The verb *can* generally refers to the ability to do something. The verb *may* generally refers to permission to do something.

**different from, different than:** *Different from* is generally preferred over *different than.*

**farther, further:** Use *farther* when you refer to distance. Use *further* when you mean "to a greater degree or extent" or "additional."

**fewer, less:** Use *fewer* for things that can be counted. Use *less* for amounts or quantities that cannot be counted.

**good, well:** Use the predicate adjective *good* after linking verbs such as *feel, look, smell, taste,* and *seem.* Use *well* whenever you need an adverb.

**its, it's:** The word *its* with no apostrophe is a possessive pronoun. The word *it's* is a contraction for *it is.* Do not confuse the possessive pronoun *its* with the contraction *it's,* standing for "it is" or "it has."

**lay, lie:** Do not confuse these verbs. *Lay* is a transitive verb meaning "to set or put something down." Its principal parts are *lay, laying, laid, laid. Lie* is an intransitive verb meaning "to recline." Its principal parts are *lie, lying, lay, lain.*

**like, as:** *Like* is a preposition that usually means "similar to" or "in the same way as." *Like* should always be followed by an object. Do not use *like* before a subject and a verb. Use *as* or *that* instead.

**of, have:** Do not use *of* in place of *have* after auxiliary verbs like *would, could, should, may, might,* or *must.*

**raise, rise:** *Raise* is a transitive verb that usually takes a direct object. *Rise* is intransitive and never takes a direct object.

**set, sit:** *Set* is a transitive verb meaning "to put (something) in a certain place." Its principal parts are *set, setting, set, set. Sit* is an intransitive verb meaning "to be seated." Its principal parts are *sit, sitting, sat, sat.*

**than, then:** The conjunction *than* is used to connect the two parts of a comparison. Do not confuse *than* with the adverb *then,* which usually refers to time.

**that, which, who:** Use the relative pronoun *that* to refer to things or people. Use *which* only for things and *who* only for people.

**when, where, why:** Do not use *when, where,* or *why* directly after a linking verb such as *is.* Reword the sentence.

*Faulty:* Suspense is *when* an author increases the reader's tension.

*Revised:* An author uses suspense to increase the reader's tension.

**who, whom:** In formal writing, remember to use *who* only as a subject in clauses and sentences and *whom* only as an object.

# Capitalization and Punctuation

## Capitalization

1. Capitalize the first word of a sentence.
2. Capitalize all proper nouns and adjectives.
3. Capitalize a person's title when it is followed by the person's name or when it is used in direct address.
4. Capitalize titles showing family relationships when they refer to a specific person, unless they are preceded by a possessive noun or pronoun.
5. Capitalize the first word and all other key words in the titles of books, periodicals, poems, stories, plays, paintings, and other works of art.
6. Capitalize the first word and all nouns in letter salutations and the first word in letter closings.

## Punctuation

### End Marks

1. Use a **period** to end a declarative sentence, an imperative sentence, and most abbreviations.
2. Use a **question mark** to end a direct question or an incomplete question in which the rest of the question is understood.
3. Use an **exclamation mark** after a statement showing strong emotion, an urgent imperative sentence, or an interjection expressing strong emotion.

### Commas

1. Use a comma before the conjunction to separate two independent clauses in a compound sentence.
2. Use commas to separate three or more words, phrases, or clauses in a series.
3. Use commas to separate adjectives of equal rank. Do not use commas to separate adjectives that must stay in a specific order.
4. Use a comma after an introductory word, phrase, or clause.
5. Use commas to set off parenthetical and nonessential expressions.

6. Use commas with places and dates made up of two or more parts.
7. Use commas after items in addresses, after the salutation in a personal letter, after the closing in all letters, and in numbers of more than three digits.

### Semicolons

1. Use a semicolon to join independent clauses that are not already joined by a conjunction.
2. Use a semicolon to join independent clauses or items in a series that already contain commas.

### Colons

1. Use a colon before a list of items following an independent clause.
2. Use a colon in numbers giving the time, in salutations in business letters, and in labels used to signal important ideas.

### Quotation Marks

1. A **direct quotation** represents a person's exact speech or thoughts and is enclosed in quotation marks.
2. An **indirect quotation** reports only the general meaning of what a person said or thought and does not require quotation marks.
3. Always place a comma or a period inside the final quotation mark of a direct quotation.
4. Place a question mark or an exclamation mark inside the final quotation mark if the end mark is part of the quotation; if it is not part of the quotation, place it outside the final quotation mark.

### Titles

1. Underline or italicize the titles of long written works, movies, television and radio shows, lengthy works of music, paintings, and sculptures.
2. Use quotation marks around the titles of short written works, episodes in a series, songs, and titles of works mentioned as parts of collections.

**Hyphens** Use a **hyphen** with certain numbers, after certain prefixes, with two or more words used as one word, and with a compound modifier that comes before a noun.

### Apostrophes

1. Add an **apostrophe** and *s* to show the possessive case of most singular nouns.
2. Add an apostrophe to show the possessive case of plural nouns ending in *s* and *es.*
3. Add an apostrophe and *s* to show the possessive case of plural nouns that do not end in *s* or *es.*
4. Use an apostrophe in a contraction to indicate the position of the missing letter or letters.

# Index of Skills

## Reading for Information

## Reading Skills

## Writing Strategies

# Index of Features

## Assessment Workshops

## Background

## Big Question, The

## Communications Workshop

## Comparing Literary Works

## Independent Reading

## Reading for Information

## Literary Analysis Workshops

# Index of Authors and Titles

**Notes:** Page numbers in *italics* refer to biographical information. Nonfiction appears in red.

Grateful acknowledgment is made to the following for copyrighted material:

*English—Language Arts Content Standards for California Public Schools* reproduced by permission, California Department of Education, CD Press, 1430 N Street, Suite 3207, Sacramento, CA 95814.

**Arte Publico Press** From *My Own True Name* by Pat Mora. Copyright © 2000 Arte Publico Press-University of Houston. Published by Arte Publico Press. "Baseball" by Lionel G. Garcia from *I Can Hear the Cowbells Ring* (Houston: Arte Publico Press - University of Houston, 1994). Used by permission.

**Ashabranner, Brent** "Always to Remember: The Vision of Maya Ying Lin" by Brent Ashabranner from *Always to Remember*. Copyright © 1988. Used by permission of Brent Ashabranner.

**The Bancroft Library, Administrative Offices** "Tears of Autumn" from *The Forbidden Stitch: An Asian American Women's Anthology* by Yoshiko Uchida. Copyright © 1989 by Yoshiko Uchida. Used by permission of the Bancroft Library, University of California, Berkeley.

**Bantam Doubleday Dell Publishing Group, Inc.** "A Wrinkle in Time" by Madeleine L'Engle Franklin from *Dell Publishing*. Copyright © 1962 by Madeleine L'Engle Franklin. All rights reserved.

**Berkley Books** From *A Small Enough Team to Do the Job* by Andrew Mishkin from *Sojourner*. Copyright © 2003 by Andrew Mishkin.

**Black Issues Book Review** "Zora Neale Hurston: A Life in Letters, Book Review" by Zakia Carter from *Black Issues Book Review, Nov-Dec 2002;* www.bibookreview.com. Used by permission.

**Brandt & Hochman Literary Agents, Inc.** "Invocation" from John Brown's Body by Stephen Vincent Benet Copyright © 1927, 1928 by Stephen Vincent Benet. Copyright renewed © 1955 by Rosemary Carr Benet. Any electronic copying or redistribution of the text is expressly forbidden. Used by permission of Brandt & Hochman Literary Agents, Inc.

**Curtis Brown London** "Who Can Replace a Man" by Brian Aldiss from *Masterpieces: The Best Science Fiction of the Century*. Copyright © 1966 by Brian Aldiss. Reproduced with permission of Curtis Brown Group Ltd, London on behalf of Brian Aldiss.

**Charlotte Observer** "The Season's Curmudgeon Sees the Light" by Mary C. Curtis *www.charlotte.com*. © Copyright 2004 Knight Ridder. All Rights Reserved. Used by permission.

**Child Health Association of Sewickley, Inc.** "Thumbprint Cookies" from *Three Rivers Cookbook*. Copyright © Child Health Association of Sewickley, Inc. Used by permission.

**Clarion Books, a division of Houghton Mifflin** Excerpt from "Emancipation" from *Lincoln: A Photobiography*. Copyright © 1987 by Russell Freedman. Reproduced by permission of Clarion Books, an imprint of Houghton Mifflin Company.

**Jonathan Clowes Ltd.** "The Adventure of the Speckled Band" from *The Adventure Of The Speckled Band*. Copyright © 1996 Sir Arthur Conan Doyle Copyright Holders. Used with kind permission of Jonathan Clowes Ltd., London, on behalf of Andrea Plunket, the Administrator of the Conan Doyle Copyrights.

**Ruth Cohen Literary Agency, Inc.** "Fox Hunt" by Lensey Namioka, copyright © 1993 from *Join In: Multi-Ethnic Short Stories by Outstanding Writers for Young Adults*, edited by Donald R. Gallo. Used by permission of Lensey Namioka. All rights are reserved by the Author.

**Don Congdon Associates, Inc.** "The Drummer Boy of Shiloh" by Ray Bradbury published in *Saturday Evening Post April 30, 1960*. Copyright © 1960 by the Curtis Publishing Company, renewed © 1988 by Ray Bradbury.

**Copper Canyon Press c/o The Permissions Company** "Snake on the Etowah" by David Bottoms from *Armored Hearts: Selected and New Poems*. Copyright © 1995 by David Bottoms. Used by the permission of Copper Canyon Press, www.copppercanyonpress.org. All rights reserved.

**Gary N. DaSilva for Neil Simon** "The Governess" from *The Good Doctor* © 1974 by Neil Simon. Copyright renewed © 2002 by Neil Simon. Used by permission. CAUTION: Professionals and amateurs are hereby warned that *The Good Doctor* is fully protected under the Berne Convention and the Universal Copyright Convention and is subject to royalty. All rights, including without limitation professional, amateur, motion picture, television, radio, recitation, lecturing, public reading and foreign translation rights, computer media rights and the right of reproduction, and electronic storage or retrieval, in whole or in part and in any form, are strictly reserved and none of these rights can be exercised or used without written permission from the copyright owner. Inquiries for stock and amateur performances should be addressed to Samuel French, Inc., 45 West 25th Street, New York, NY 10010. All other inquiries should be addressed to Gary N. DaSilva, 111 N. Sepulveda Blvd., Suite 250, Manhattan Beach, CA 90266-6850.

**Disney-Hyperion Books for Children** "Words We Live By: Your Annotated Guide to the Constitution" by Linda R. Monk from *The Stonesong Press*. Copyright © 2003 Linda R. Monk and The Stonesong Press, Inc. All rights reserved.

**Doubleday** "Table of Contents and Index Page" from *Zora Neale Hurston: A Life In Letters* Carla Kaplan. From *The Diary of a Young Girl: The Definitive Edition* by Anne Frank, edited by Otto H. Frank and Mirjam Pressler. Translated by Susan Massotty. Copyright © 1995 by Doubleday, a division of Random House, Inc. Used by permission of Doubleday, a division of Random House, Inc.

**Dramatic Publishing** From *Anne Frank & Me* by Cherie Bennett with Jeff Gottesfeld. Copyright © 1997 by Cherie Bennett. Printed in the United States of America. Used by permission. CAUTION: Professionals and amateurs are hereby warned that *Anne Frank & Me*, being fully protected under the copyright Laws of the United States of America, the British Empire, including the Dominion of Canada, and all other countries of the Universal Copyright and Berne Conventions, are subject to royalty. All rights, including professional, amateur, motion picture, recitation, lecturing, public reading, radio and television broadcasting, and the rights of translation into foreign languages, are strictly reserved. All inquiries regarding performance rights should be addressed to Dramatic Publishing, 311 Washington St., Woodstock, IL 60098. Phone: (815) 338-7170. All rights reserved. Used by permission.

**Farrar, Straus & Giroux, LLC** "Little Exercise" from *The Complete Poems 1927-1979* by Elizabeth Bishop. Copyright © 1979, 1983 by Alice Helen Methfessel. "Charles" by Shirley Jackson from *The Lottery*. Copyright © 1948, 1949 by Shirley Jackson and copyright renewed © 1976, 1977 by Laurence Hyman, Barry Hyman, Mrs. Sarah Webster and Mrs. Joanne Schnurer. "La Poesia" from *Isla Negra* by Pablo Neruda, translated by Alastair Reid. Translation copyright © 1981 by Alastair Reid. CAUTION: Users are warned that this work is protected under copyright laws and downloading is strictly prohibited. The right to reproduce or transfer the work via any medium must be secured with Farrar, Straus and Giroux, LLC. Used by permission of Farrar, Straus and Giroux, LLC.

**Florida Holocaust Museum** Florida Holocaust Museum Press Release from *www.flholocaustmuseum.org*. Copyright © Florida Holocaust Museum, 2001, 2005; All rights reserved. Used by permission.

**Florida Senate Office Building** "Senator Michael S. Bennett: Be a Sport: Professional Teams Should Pay Their Own Way and FL Senate Logo" from *http://www.flsenate.gov/cgi-bin/view_page*. Copyright © 2000-2006 State of Florida. Used by permission.

**Katherine Froman** "Easy Diver" by Robert Froman from *A Poke In The I*. Edited by Paul B. Janeczko. Used by permission of Katherine Froman on behalf of Robert Froman.

**Richard Garcia** "The City is So Big" by Richard Garcia from *The City Is So Big*.

**Maxine Groffsky Literary Agency** "The White Umbrella" by Gish Jen © 1984 by Gish Jen first published in *The Yale Review*. From the collection *Who's Irish?* by Gish Jen published in 1999 by Alfred A. Knopf. Used by permission of Maxine Groffsky Literary Agency, on behalf of the author.

**Gutenberg Website** Excerpt from "Narrative of the Life of Frederick Douglass: An American Slave" by Frederick Douglass. Copyright © 2011 *gutenberg.org*. All rights reserved.

**Harcourt, Inc.** "Choice: A Tribute to Martin Luther King, Jr." by Alice Walker from *In Search Of Our Mothers' Gardens: Womanist Prose*. Copyright © 1983 by Alice Walker. "For My Sister Molly Who in the Fifties" from *Revolutionary Petunias & Other Poems*, copyright © 1972 and renewed 2000 by Alice Walker. "Forest Fire" from *The Diary of Anais Nin 1947-1955, Volume V*. Copyright © 1974 by Anais Nin. Excerpt from *The People, Yes* by Carl Sandburg, copyright © 1936 by Harcourt, Inc. and renewed 1964 by Carl Sandburg. "Paul Bunyan of the North Woods" is excerpted from *The People, Yes* by Carl Sandburg, copyright © 1936 by Harcourt, Inc. and renewed 1964 by Carl Sandburg. This material may not be reproduced in any form or by any means without the prior written permission of the publisher. Used by permission of Harcourt, Inc.

**HarperCollins Publishers** "Brown vs. Board of Education" from *Now is Your Time: The African-American Struggle for Freedom* by Walter Dean Myers. Copyright © 1991 by Walter Dean Myers. From *An American Childhood* by Annie Dillard. Copyright © 1987 by Annie Dillard. "Why the Waves Have Whitecaps" from *Mules and Men* by Zora Neale Hurston. Copyright © 1935 by Zora Neale Hurston. Copyright renewed 1963 by John C. Hurston and Joel Hurston. Used by permission of HarperCollins Publishers. "A Poem for My Librarian, Mrs. Long" by Nikki Giovanni from Acolytes. Copyright © 2007 by Nikki Giovanni. All rights reserved.

**Hill and Wang, a division of Farrar, Straus & Giroux** "Thank You, M'am" from *Short Stories* by Langston Hughes. Copyright © 1996 by Ramona Bass and Arnold Rampersad. Used by permission of Hill and Wang, a division of Farrar, Straus and Giroux, LLC.

**Gelston Hinds, Jr. o/b/o Amy Ling** "Grandma Ling" by Amy Ling from *Bridge: An Asian American Perspective, Vol. 7, No. 3*. Copyright © 1980 by Amy Ling. Used by permission of the author's husband.

**Holiday House** "January" from *A Child's Calendar* by John Updike. Text copyright © 1965, 1999 by John Updike. All rights reserved. Used by permission of Holiday House, Inc.

**Georgia Douglas Johnson** "Your World" by Georgia Douglas Johnson from *American Negro Poetry*.

**The Estate of Dr. Martin Luther King, Jr. c/o Writer's House LLC** "The American Dream" by Dr. Martin Luther King, Jr. from *A Testament Of Hope: The Essential Writings Of Martin Luther King, Jr.* Copyright © 1961 Martin Luther King Jr.; Copyright © renewed 1989 Coretta Scott King. Used by arrangement with The Heirs to the Estate of Martin Luther King Jr., c/o Writers House as agent for the proprietor New York, N.Y.

**Alfred A. Knopf, Inc.** "Harlem Night Song" from *The Collected Poems of Langston Hughes* by Langston Hughes, edited by Arnold Rampersad with David Roessel, Associate Editor, copyright © 1994 by The Estate of Langston Hughes. From *Author's Note* by Patricia C. McKissack from *The Dark-Thirty*. Text copyright © 1992 by Patricia C. McKissack. "The Ninny" from *Image Of Chekhov* by Anton Chekhov, translated by Robert Payne, copyright © 1963 and renewed © 1991 by Alfred A. Knopf, Inc. "The 11:59" by Patricia C. McKissack from *The Dark Thirty* by Patricia McKissack illustrated by Brian Pinkney, copyright © 1992 by Patricia C. McKissack. Illustrations copyright © 1992 by Brian Pinkney. Used by permission of Alfred A. Knopf, a division of Random House, Inc.

**Barbara S. Kouts Literary Agency** "Ellis Island" by Joseph Bruchac from *The Remembered Earth*.

**Life Magazine** "Readjustment: A Life Photoessay" from *LIFE Magazine Vol. 19, No. 23 December 3, 1945*. Copyright © 1945 Life, Inc. Used by permission. All rights reserved.

**Little, Brown and Company, Inc.** "Ode to Enchanted Light" from *Odes to Opposites* by Pablo Neruda. Copyright © 1995 by Pablo Neruda and Fundacion Pablo Neruda (Odes in Spanish). Copyright © 1995 by Ken Krabbenhoft (Odes in English); Copyright © 1995 by Ferris Cook (Illustrations and Compliation). Used by permission of Little, Brown and Company. All rights reserved.

**Liveright Publishing Corporation** "your little voice/Over the wires came leaping" copyright © 1923, 1951, 1991 by the Trustees for the E. E. Cummings Trust. Copyright © 1976 by George James Firmage, from *Complete Poems: 1904-1962* by E. E. Cummings, edited by George J. Firmage. "Runagate Runagate" Copyright © 1966 by Robert Hayden, from *Collected Poems of Robert Hayden*, edited by Frederick Glaysher. This selection may not be reproduced, stored in a retrieval system, or transmitted in any form or by any means without prior written permission of the publisher. Used by permission of Liveright Publishing Corporation.

**Robert MacNeil** "The Trouble with Television" by Robert MacNeil condensed from a speech, *November 1984 at President Leadership Forum, SUNY*. Copyright © 1985 by Reader's Digest and Robert MacNeil. Used by permission of Robert MacNeil.

**Eve Merriam c/o Marian Reiner** "Thumbprint" from *A Sky Full of Poems* by Eve Merriam. Copyright © 1964, 1970, 1973, 1986 by Eve Merriam. Used by permission of Marian Reiner.

**The Miami Herald** Miami Herald Editorial: *Don't Refuse This Deal* from Miami Herald Online Tuesday, March 29, 2005 http://capefish. blogspot.com/2005/03/miami-herald-editorial-dont-refuse.html. Copyright © 2005 by McClatchy Interactive West. Used by permission of McClatchy Interactive West via Copyright Clearance Center.

**N. Scott Momaday** "New World" by N. Scott Momaday from *The Gourd Dancers*. Used with the permission of Navarre Scott Momaday.

**William Morris Agency** "Flowers for Algernon" (short story version edited for this edition) by Daniel Keyes. Copyright © 1959 & 1987 by Daniel Keyes. Expanded story published in paperback by Bantam Books. Used by permission of William Morris Agency, LLC on behalf of the author.

**William Morrow & Company, Inc., a division of HarperCollins** "The Drum (for Martin Luther King, Jr.)" from *Those Who Ride the Night Winds* by Nikki Giovanni. Copyright © 1983 by Nikki Giovanni. Used by permission of William Morrow & Company, Inc., a division of HarperCollins Publishers, Inc.

**Museum of New Mexico Press** "Chicoria" by Jose Griego Y Maestas y Rudolfo Anaya from *Cuentos: Tales from the Hispanic Southwest.* Reproduced by permission of Museum of New Mexico Press.

**National Public Radio** "Profile: World War II veterans who founded the Paralyzed Veterans of America" from *National Public Radio, November 11, 2003.* Copyright © 2005 National Public Radio. Used by permission. All rights reserved.

**New College of Florida** New College of Florida Work-Study Contract from *http://www.ncf.edu/index.html.* Copyright © 2001-2006 New College of Florida. Used by permission.

**Naomi Shihab Nye** "Words to Sit in, Like Chairs" by Naomi Shihab Nye from *911: The Book of Help.* "Hamadi" by Naomi Shihab Nye from *America Street.* Used by permission of the author, Naomi Shihab Nye.

**Harold Ober Associates, Inc.** "Cat!" by Eleanor Farjeon from *Poems For Children.* Copyright © 1938 by Eleanor Farjeon, renewed 1966 by Gervase Farjeon. Used by permission of Harold Ober Associates Incorporated. All rights reserved.

**Office of the Governor Arnold Schwarzenegger** "Transcript of Governor Arnold Schwarzenegger Signing Legislation Requiring Drivers to Use Hand Free Devices" from *http://gov.ca.gov/index.php?/speech/4116/.* Copyright © 2000-2007 State of California. Used by permission.

**Oxford University Press, Inc.** "Summary of The Tell-Tale Heart" by James D. Hart from *The Oxford Companion To American Literature.* Copyright © 1983. Used by permission of Oxford University Press, Inc. www.oup.co.uk.

**Pantheon Books, a division of Random House Inc.** "Coyote Steals the Sun and Moon" by Richard Erdoes and Alfonso Ortiz from *American Indian Myths and Legends,* copyright © 1984 by Richard Erdoes and Alfonso Ortiz. Used by permission of Pantheon Books, a division of Random House, Inc.

**Pearson Prentice Hall** "Series Circuits and Parallel Circuits" from *Prentice Hall Science Explorer Physical Science.* Copyright © 2005 by Pearson Education, Inc. or its affiliate(s). "The War in Vietnam" from *The American Nation* by Dr. James West Davidson and Dr. Michael B. Stoff. Copyright © 2003 by Pearson Education, Inc., publishing as Prentice Hall. Used by permission.

**Penguin Group (UK), Inc. & Curtis Brown** From "The History of the Peloponnesian War" by Thucydides, translated by Rex Warner, with an introduction and notes by M.I. Finley (Penguin Classics 1954, Revised edition 1972). Translation copyright © Rex Warner, 1954. Introduction and Appendices copyright © M.I. Finley, 1972.

**Penguin Group (USA), Inc.** "Kindertransport" by Diane Samuels from *Plume.* Copyright © Diane Samuels, 1995. All rights reserved.

**Perseus Books Group** "Vanishing Species" from *Sleeping At The Starlight Motel And Other Adventures On The Way Back Home* by Bailey White. Used by permission of Da Capo Press, a member of Perseus Books Group.

**Placer County Museums** Placer County Museum Job Description & Volunteer Application from *http://www.placer.ca.gov.* Copyright © 2006 County of Placer, CA. Used by permission.

**Puffin Books** From The One Who Watches by Judith Ortiz Cofer from *An Island Like You.* Copyright © Judith Ortiz Cofer 1995.

**G.P. Putnam's Sons** "Describe Somebody," and "Almost Summer Sky" from *Locomotion* by Jacqueline Woodson, copyright © 2003 by Jacqueline Woodson. Used by permission of G.P. Putnam's Sons, A Division of Penguin Young Readers Group, A Member of Penguin Group (USA) Inc., 345 Hudson Street, New York, NY 10014. All rights reserved. From *Hush* by Jacqueline Woodson. Copyright © 2002 by Jacqueline Woodson. From *Anne Frank and Me* by Cherie Bennett and Jeff Gottesfeld. Copyright © 2001 by Cherie Bennett and Jeff Gottesfeld.

**Moumin Manzoor Quazi** "Migrant Birds" by Moumin Manzoor Quazi from *Is This Forever, or What? Poems and Paintings from Texas.* Copyright © 2004 by Moumin Manzoor Quazi.

**Random House, Inc.** From *I Know Why the Caged Bird Sings* by Maya Angelou, copyright © 1969 and renewed © 1997 by Maya Angelou. "Raymond's Run" by Toni Cade Bambara from *Gorilla, My Love.* Copyright © 1971 by Toni Cade Bambara. "Why Leaves Turn Color in the Fall" from *A Natural History of the Senses* by Diane Ackerman. Copyright © 1990 by Diane Ackerman. *The Diary of Anne Frank* by Frances Goodrich and Albert Hackett. Copyright © 1956 by Albert Hackett, Frances Goodrich Hackett and Otto Frank. CAUTION: Professionals and amateurs are hereby warned that *The Diary of Anne Frank,* being fully protected under the copyright Laws of the United States of America, the British Empire, including the Dominion of Canada, and all other countries of the Universal Copyright and Berne Conventions, are subject to royalty. All rights, including professional, amateur, motion picture, recitation, lecturing, public reading, radio and television broadcasting, and the rights of translation into foreign languages, are strictly reserved. All inquiries should be addressed to Random House, Inc. Used by permission of Random House, Inc. "The Blue Stones" by Isak Dinesen from *Winter's Tales.* Copyright © 1942 by Random House, Inc. All rights reserved under International and Pan-American Copyright Conventions.

**Marian Reiner, Literary Agent** "Concrete Mixers" by Patricia Hubbell from *8 A.M. Shadows.* Copyright © 1965 Patricia Hubbell. Copyright renewed © 1993 Patricia Hubbell. Used by permission of Marian Reiner on behalf of the author.

**Reprint Management Services - A/R** "Hands-free Law Won't Solve the Problem" by Mike Langdon *Nov. 14, 2006* from *http://www.mercurynews.com/mld/mercurynews/business/column.* Copyright 2007 San Jose Mercury News. Used by permission. All rights reserved.

**Wendy Rose** "Drum Song" from *The Halfbreed Chronicles and Other Poems* by Wendy Rose. Copyright © 1985 by Wendy Rose, West End Press, Albuquerque, NM. Used by permission of the author.

**Russell & Volkening, Inc.** From *Harriet Tubman: Conductor on the Underground Railroad* by Ann Petry. Copyright © 1955 by Ann Petry, renewed in 1983 by Ann Petry. Used by permission of Russell & Volkening as agents for the author.

**Maria Teresa Sanchez** "Old Man" by Ricardo Sanchez from *Selected Poems.* Used by permission of Maria Teresa Sanchez for the Estate of Dr. Ricardo Sanchez.

**Sarasota School District** Sarasota School District Menu and Nutritional Analysis from *http://www.sarasota.k12.fl.us/fns/lunch.htm.* Copyright © 2007 Sarasota, FL School District. Used by permission.

**Savannah International Trade & Convention Center** Savannah Belles Ferry Schedule from *http://www.catchacat.org.* Copyright © 2007 Chatham Area Transit Authority. All Rights Reserved. Used by permission.

# Credits

## Photo Credits

**xlviii** Yaro/Shutterstock **Grade 8 Unit 1 11:** r. Hulton Archive/Getty Images Inc.; **11:** b. The Granger Collection, New York; **12:** b. Wolfgang Kaehler/CORBIS; **12:** t. Lake County Museum/CORBIS; **12:** b. AP/Wide World Photos; **15:** Swim Ink/CORBIS; **16:** Vintage Books; **18:** *The Ministries of Silence,* 2000 (oil on canvas) by Bob Lescaux (b.1928) Private Collection/The Bridgeman Art Library. French/in copyright; **20:** *The Ministries of Silence,* 2000 (oil on canvas) by Bob Lescaux (b.1928) Private Collection/The Bridgeman Art Library. French/in copyright; **22:** Courtesy of Diane Alimena; **22:** © David Fokos/CORBIS; **27:** Nikky Finney; **36:** Tony Freeman/PhotoEdit; **41:** Bettmann/CORBIS; **41:** b. Mary Evans Picture Library; **42:** Inset. New York State Historical Association, Cooperstown, New York; **46:** Images.com/CORBIS; **48:** l. Mary Evans Picture Library; **57:** t. Courtesy Raul Sedillo; **57:** b. "The Parker Family Collection, Fort Worth, TX"; **61:** "The Parker Family Collection, Fort Worth, TX"; **65:** t. Bettmann/CORBIS; **68:** Courtesy US Army Corp of Engineers; **69:** *The Champions of the Mississippi,* Currier & Ives, Scala/Art Resource, New York; **83:** © Charles E. Rotkin/CORBIS; **87:** b. Courtesy of the author. Photo by Don Perkins.; **87:** t. Jesse Stuart Foundation; **88:** M.P. Kahl/Photo Researchers, Inc.; **88-93:** border. istockphoto.com/; **90-91:** border. istockphoto.com/; **92:** National Geographic/Getty Images; **92-93:** border. istockphoto.com/; **99:** Portrait of a Mandarin, Chinese School, 19th century/The Bridgeman Art Library, London/New York; **113:** © Rosalie Thorne McKenna Foundation. Courtesy Center for Creative Photography, University of Arizona Foundation; **114:** Joe Squillante/Photonica; **117:** Edward Holub/Getty Images; **121:** Hulton Archive/Getty Images Inc.; **124:** from *The Complete Adventures of Sherlock Holmes,* illustration by Sidney Paget; **127:** from *The Complete Adventures of Sherlock Holmes,* illustration by Sidney Paget; **128:** from *The Complete Adventures of Sherlock Holmes,* illustration by Sidney Paget; **130:** from *The Complete Adventures of Sherlock Holmes,* illustration by Sidney Paget; **135:** from *The Complete Adventures of Sherlock Holmes,* illustration by Sidney Paget; **138:** from *The Complete Adventures of Sherlock Holmes,* illustration by Sidney Paget; **146:** t. Tek Image/Photo Researchers, Inc.; **146:** m. Getty Images; **146:** r. © Leonard Lessin/Peter Arnold, Inc.; **149:** from *The Complete Adventures of Sherlock Holmes,* illustration by Sidney Paget; **159:** t. Bettmann/CORBIS; **160:** Connie Ricca/CORBIS; **161-168:** border. Silver Burdett Ginn; **162:** Bettmann/CORBIS; **166-167:** b. Morey Milbradt/Brand X/CORBIS; **167:** t. Lake County Museum/CORBIS; **171:** t. Time Life Pictures/Getty Images; **171:** b. Reuters//Mannie Garcia/CORBIS; **172:** b. Flip Schulke/CORBIS; **172:** t. Corel Professional Photos CD-ROM™; **174:** t. Joseph Sohm/Visions of America/CORBIS; **174:** b. Michale Ventura/PhotoEdit; **175:** Martin Takigawa/Getty Images, Inc.; **181:** b. Thomas Victor; **183:** Charles Krebs/CORBIS; **184:** ©Daryl Benson/Masterfile; **186:** The Granger Collection, New York; **186:** Prentice Hall; **187:** Prentice Hall; **200:** *Drummer Boy,* Julian Scott, N.S. Mayer; **202:** Courtesy National Archives; **203:** Inset. Bettmann/CORBIS; **204:** David; **205:** Bkgrnd. Jackie DesJariais/istockphoto.com; **205:** The Granger Collection, New York; **206:** *Drummer Boy,* Julian Scott, N.S. Mayer; **208:** Index Stock Imagery, Inc.; **324:** ©2001 Mitchell, C.E./Stockphoto.com; **325: 326:** Steve Kraseman/DRK Photo

**Grade 8 Unit 2 191:** t. Courtesy of Ohio State Historical Society; **192:** © Skip Dickstein/NewSport/CORBIS; **193:** *Farm Boy,* 1941, Charles Alston, Courtesy of Clark Atlanta University; **196:** Alan D. Carey/Photo Researchers, Inc.; **198:** © Kevin R. Morris/CORBIS; **237:** Franco Vogt/CORBIS; **241:** Courtesy National Archives, photo no. (542390); **242:** Myrleen Ferguson Cate/PhotoEdit; **247:** t. Bassouls Sophie/CORBIS; **248:** Bkgrnd. Bruce Stoddard/Getty Images; **253:** Franco Brambilla/Airstudio; **256:** Dawid Michalczyk/Eon Works; **258:** Franco Brambilla/Airstudio; **263:** NO CREDIT NECESSARY; **267:** *Enoshima.* Island at left with cluster of buildings among trees. Fuji in distance at right, c. 1823. (detail), Katsusika Hokusai, The Newark Museum/Art Resource, NY; **271:** br. Brown Brothers; **271:** bl. Courtesy of State Museum Resource Center, California State Parks; **271:** tr. Michael Moran/© Dorling Kindersley; **271:** tl. Courtesy of the Library of Congress; **279:** ©1998 James McGoon; **282:** David Turnley/CORBIS; **283:** b. Bettmann/CORBIS; **283:** t. Major Keith Hamilton Maxwell/The Mariners' Museum/CORBIS; **284:** *Jubayl,* 1997 (oil on canvas) by Private Collection/The Bridgeman Art Library Nationality/copyright status: French/in copyright; **285:** Pearson Education; **286:** Image Source Black/Getty Images, Inc; **293:** t. Bettmann/CORBIS; **294:** © Thomas Paschke / istockphoto.com; **294:** Bkgrnd. © Ufuk Zivana / istockphoto.com; **294:** border. © Blackred / istockphoto.com; **294:** Inset. © Clint Spencer / istockphoto.com; **296:** Culver Pictures, Inc.; **297:** Culver Pictures, Inc.; **298:** Inset. © Duncan Walker / istockphoto.com; **298:** © Clint Spencer / istockphoto.com; **300:** © Zmajdoo / istockphoto.com; **301:** © Dylan Hewitt / istockphoto.com; **302:** © Janne Ahvo / istockphoto.com; **309:** Courtesy of the Library of Congress; **313:** t. Bettmann/CORBIS; **314:** © Bettmann/CORBIS; **315:** The Granger Collection, New York; **318:** Paul Nicklen/National Geographic Image Collection; **320:** Paul Nicklen/National Geographic Image Collection; **322:** Shutterstock, Inc.; **335:** t. AP/Wide World Photos; **345:** Miriam Berkley/Authorpix **347:** b. istockphoto.com/ GlobalP; **348-380:** istockphoto.com/Sharon Shimoni; **350:** m. © Dorling Kindersley; **350:** br. © Dorling Kindersley; **350:** tm. © Dorling Kindersley; **352:** t. Tim Flach/Getty Images; **354:** ©Cinerama/Archive Photos; **355:** Photofest; **358:** Photofest; **364:** Photofest; **371:** Will & Deni McIntyre/Getty Images; **373:** istockphoto.com/dra_schwartz; **378:** Photofest; **387:** t. New York Public Library, (Rare Book Division or Print Collection. Miriam and Ira D. Wallach Division of Art, Prints and Photographs); Astor, Lenox and Tilden Foundations; **387:** b. *Empire State,* Tom Christopher, Courtesy of the artist.; **388:** *Empire State,* Tom Christopher, Courtesy of the artist.; **391:** *Minnie,* 1930, William Johnson, National Museum of American Art, Washington, DC/Art Resource, NY; **395:** t. E.O. Hoppe/Stringer/Time Life Pictures/Getty Images; **395:** b. *Stirling Station,* 1887, William Kennedy, Collection of Andrew McIntosh Patrick, UK/The Bridgeman Art Library International Ltd., London/New York; **396:** *Stirling Station,* 1887, William Kennedy, Collection of Andrew McIntosh Patrick, UK/The Bridgeman Art Library International Ltd., London/New York; **399:** George Marks; **400:** *Pure Pleasure,* Pat Scott/The Bridgeman Art Library, London/New York; **401:** istockphoto.com; **410:** Courtesy of Amtrak; **411:** Jumpstart for Young Children, Inc.; **412:** © courtesy of City Harvest -http://www.cityharvest.org/; Photo by Timothy White; **415:** b. Courtesy of the author; **415:** AP/Wide World Photos; **416:** *Girl in Car Window,* Winson Trang, Courtesy of the artist; **420:** Will Faller; **422:** Arjan de Jager; **425:** Matt Wilson/istockphoto.com; **426:** Courtesy of Diane Alimena; **427:** LOOK Die Bildagentur der Fotografen mbH/Alamy; **428:** CORBIS; **430:** Pamela Moore/istockphoto.com; **431:** Werner Forman/Art Resource, NY; **433:** © Marilyn Angel Wynn/Nativestock.com; **434:** ©Tom Bean/CORBIS; **436:** Pamela Moore/istockphoto.com; **456:** (TR) James McGoon Photography

**Grade 8 Unit 3 467:** NASA Jet Propulsion Laboratory (NASA-JPL); **469:** Spots on the Spot; **470:** NASA; **472:** bl. NASA/JPL; **477:** t. ©HOUSTON CHRONICLE; **477:** b. Craig Barhorst; **478:** Craig Barhorst; **479:** Michael Newman/PhotoEdit; **481:** Cultura/CORBIS; **482:** Mike Ehrmann/Stringer/Getty Images, Inc.; **485:** t. AP/Wide World Photos; **490:** Tom Uhlman/Alamy; **492:** Bettmann/CORBIS; **503:** t. Courtesy Brent Ashabranner; **503:** b. Paul Conklin/PhotoEdit; **504:** Catherine Ursillo/Photo Researchers, Inc.; **506:** Paul Conklin/PhotoEdit; **508:** AP/Wide World Photos; **508:** Catherine Ursillo/Photo Researchers, Inc.; **510:** Richard Howard/Black Star; **513:** t. Getty Images; **515:** ©FPG International LLC; **520:** tr. ©2004 JupiterImages and its Licensors. All Rights Reserved.; **520:** br. Pearson Education/PH School Division; **520:** m. Pearson Education/PH School Division; **520:** bl. Pearson Education/PH School

## Staff Credits

## Additional Credits